JOYS OF
JEWISH FOLKLORE

JOYS OF JEWISH FOLKLORE

A Journey From New Amsterdam
to Beverly Hills and Beyond

DAVID MAX EICHHORN

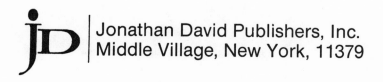

Jonathan David Publishers, Inc.
Middle Village, New York, 11379

JOYS OF
JEWISH FOLKLORE

Address all inquiries to:

JONATHAN DAVID PUBLISHERS, INC.
68-22 Eliot Avenue
Middle Village, New York 11379

Library of Congress Cataloging in Publication Data
Main entry under title:

Joys of Jewish folklore.

  1. Jews in the United States—History—Anecdotes,
facetiae, satire, etc. 2. United States—Ethnic
relations—Anecdotes, facetiae, satire, etc. I. Eichhorn, David Max.
E184.J5J86   973'.04924   80-13936

Printed in the United States of America

To Zelda, with love

Contents

Part Two

MIDDLE ATLANTIC STATES

"Give Me Your Huddled Masses"

Part Three

THE SOUTH

"Home of the Palm and the Pine"

Part Four

THE MIDWEST

"Lincoln Country"

Part Five

THE SOUTHWEST

"Arroyos, Coyotes, and Injuns"

Part Six

THE FAR WEST

"The Blessed Land of Room Enough"

Acknowledgments

I am deeply grateful to the many libraries, publishing houses, and writers who furnished needed data, rights of publication, and the fine articles, written without financial recompense, that helped immeasurably to make this book possible. Most of the names of these individuals and organizations are mentioned in connection with the particular articles that involved their participation. There are some, however, who are not mentioned in the body of the text. They are listed here in appreciation for their assistance in gathering material for this anthology:

Ms V. P. Allbert, Librarian, Kansas State Historical Society, Topeka, Kansas

Elias Cooper, late Editor, *The American Zionist*, New York, New York

Florida State Library, Tallahassee, Florida

Dr. Stephen B. Grove, Historian, U.S. Military Academy, West Point, New York

Hebrew Union College—Jewish Institute of Religion Libraries at Cincinnati (Herbert C. Zafren, Library Director) and New York (Philip E. Miller, Librarian)

Philip Hochstein, Editor, *The Jewish Week*, New York, New York

Samuel J. Jacobs, Secretary, Congregation Adath Israel, Massena, New York

Rabbi William Kramer, California State University, Northridge, California

Dr. Robert E. Levinson, San José State University, San José, California

Suzanne Nemiroff, Assistant Curator, Magnes Museum, Berkeley, California

New York Public Library, Jewish Division, New York, New York

Mark Preiser, Assistant Publisher, *The Jewish World*, Commack, New York

Robert Salz, Assistant Editor, *The Jewish Frontier*, New York, New York

Satellite Beach Public Library, Satellite Beach, Florida

Sheldon R. Shane, President, *Travel Magazine*, Floral Park, New York

Robert Sherman, President, Curtain Call Publications, Los Angeles, California

Dr. Norton B. Stern, Editor, *Western States Jewish Historical Quarterly*, Santa Monica, California

Asher Wolk, Editor, *Olam Hadash*, New York, New York

Ronald and Judith Zaid, Jericho, New York

FOREWORD

This is an anthology of American Jewish folklore. There will be common agreement on the meaning of the word "anthology," but there will be no general agreement about the term "American Jewish folklore," especially among Jews. The old cliché, "two Jews, three opinions," will most certainly apply.

So, in order to acquaint the reader with what one is likely to find in this book, I will try to define as precisely as possible what I mean by "American Jewish folklore," knowing full well that there are those who will disagree. Let us proceed, then, by considering each of these words, in the linguistic manner of our fathers, from right to left.

Folklore—In his book *New York City Folklore*, the late Benjamin A. Botkin, a Jew widely regarded as the most outstanding American folklore authority of our time, defines folklore as a people's "legends, tall tales, anecdotes, stories, sagas, heroes and characters, customs, traditions, and sayings." The reader is not likely to find any article in this book which does not fit into one of Mr. Botkin's categories.

Jewish—Mr. Botkin's criteria have been applied only to Jewish ethnic and religious personalities and themes, specifically those that are also American. Stories are included about the relationships of Jews to prominent American non-Jews, particularly American Presidents. There are a few tales about Americans who may or may not have been Jewish and a few told by non-Jewish Americans about Jews. No attempt has been made to present a glorified portrait of the American Jew. It has been painted just as it was and is, with all the warts and wrinkles.

American—That word covers a vast expanse, the whole Western Hemisphere from North Pole to South. In this book's scope, "American" refers only to the fifty states of the Union. No attempt has been made to include whatever Jewish folklore there may be in the outlying areas controlled by the United States. In addition, there is no material that could be labeled "imported from Europe." Much that has been presented to the general and Jewish publics as American Jewish folklore and humor is not that at all. It is pure European, predominantly East

European, translated from the Yiddish. This literature is a great literature and well worth reading and preserving, but it is not indigenously American. Some of the stories told herein begin in Europe and reach their culmination in America, but I have tried to avoid any and all that are essentially foreign transplants.

This collection of American Jewish folklore has 165 items of varying lengths—82 written by others, either entirely or in large part; 26 jokes, in the public domain and of unknown authorship; the remainder researched and written by me.

The purpose of this anthology is to entertain and enlighten. As my noted contemporary, Harry Golden, would *shrei*, "Enjoy!"—but it is hoped that somewhere along the way you will say to yourself, "I never would have believed it" or "Isn't that just great!" and, perhaps, occasionally, you might even have to brush back a tear. Finally, when you have finished reading this book, may it leave you with the feeling that the American Jewish community is no longer completely dependent on Europe either traditionally or culturally, but, after three and a quarter centuries, has attained ethnic maturity, the right to stand on its own two feet, and the ability to create its own folklore.

PART ONE

New England

"Where Witches Rode at Night"

Introduction

In terms of general American folklore, the outstanding areas of the country are New England, the South, the Southwest, and the Far West. Comparatively speaking, the Middle Atlantic and Midwest have made less significant contributions. But in the realm of American Jewish folklore the situation is quite different. Preeminent in Jewish folkloristic literature are the Middle Atlantic states. In a secondary position and fairly equal in importance are the South, Midwest, Southwest, and Far West. In last place, far behind the rest, is New England—Connecticut, Maine, Massachusetts, New Hampshire, Rhode Island, and Vermont.

Some might find this surprising. New England was not only the earliest producer of American folklore but also a very prolific source. In no other part of the country were there more witches, hobgoblins, angels, fairies, good spirits, evil spirits, and what not. The Puritans had somber living habits, but their imaginations ran riot, as did at times their reasoning powers. Nowhere else in the colonies was there as much bigotry, conservatism, and downright cantankerousness. This probably explains why the Jewish folklore in this region is so scarce. The only New England colony rich in Jewish folklore was the colony of Rhode Island, more specifically the town of Newport; and Rhode Island was the only New England province in the colonial period that had a tolerant, although far from liberal, attitude toward Jews. The Jews did not really settle in the rest of New England until comparatively recently.

Connecticut

The Dutch established a fur trading post in 1633 at what is now Hartford. Puritans from Plymouth came into central Connecticut, founded Wethersfield in 1634, Windsor in 1635, and, in 1636, drove away the Dutch and founded Hartford. In May 1637 the Massachusetts Puritans, aided by the Narragansett Indians, cleared the way for white occupation of eastern Connecticut by massacring the indigenous inhabitants, the

3

Pequot Indians. In 1639 the New Haven Colony was established in southern Connecticut. By 1641 a string of new towns extended from New Haven to Stamford. In 1662 King Charles II merged all the existing towns and colonies into one jurisdiction, the colony of Connecticut, and named Hartford its capital. The charter he granted stated that "the Christian faith is the only and principle end of this plantation."

Early on, Jewish peddlers from New Amsterdam, which became New York after 1664, traveled northeast to do business with the Connecticut Puritans and Indians. The Jewish presence was tolerated because of the need for their goods, but they were not allowed to settle permanently. In September 1661 the Hartford town council passed a special ordinance permitting "ye Jews which at present live in John Marsh his home liberty to sojourn in ye town for 7 months," which action indicates that this was an unusual privilege.

No Jews are known to have settled in Connecticut before the 1720s. The few who may have come a little later intermarried and disappeared. In 1760 Newport's Ezra Stiles noted in his diary that "there are no Jews in Connecticut." In 1763 the same source reported that "five Papists but no Jews live" in New Haven. On September 13, 1772, Dr. Stiles wrote:

"The summer past a family of Jews settled here, the first real Jews (except two Jew brothers Pinto who renounced Judaism and all religion) that settled in New Haven. They come from Venice, set down some time at Eustatia in West Indies, and lately removed there. They are three brothers (adults) with an aged mother, and a widow and her children, being in all about 10 or 8 souls, Jews, with 6 or 8 Negroes. Last Saturday they kept holy; Dr. Hubbard was sent for, then, to see one of them sick. He told me the family were worshipping by themselves in a room in which were lights and a suspended lamp. This is the first Jewish worship in New Haven. These Jews indeed worship in the Jewish manner; but they are not enough to constitute and become a synagogue for which there must be twelve men at least. So that if there should thereafter be a synagogue in New Haven, it must not be dated from this."

In 1818 a delegate to the state's constitutional convention was quoted in the *Hartford Courant* as declaring he was "willing that the legislature should tolerate Jews and Mohammedans; at the same time there had never been any in the state and probably never would be."

The first Connecticut Jewish congregation was established in New Haven in 1840, the present Temple Mishkan Israel; but the legal right to have such a congregation was not granted until 1843, when the constitution was amended to read that "Jews who may desire to unite and form religious societies shall have the same rights, powers and privileges as are given Christians of every denomination by the laws of the state." Temple Beth Israel of Hartford was granted the first charter under this new law. Not until 1876 did the Hartford congregation put up the state's first edifice built specifically as a synagogue. Until then the Connecticut congregations purchased or rented existing buildings to use as their houses of worship.

During the 1965 constitutional convention, it was discovered that the 1818 constitution stated that residence in Connecticut was limited to members of "every society or denomination of Christianity" and, technically, all Jews residing in Connecticut were doing so illegally. This law was, of course, never enforced. The 1965 convention changed the wording to include members of "every religious society and denomination."

There are now about 100,000 Jews in the state of Connecticut, 3.1 percent of the total population. The largest Jewish communities, in order of size, are Hartford, New Haven, Bridgeport, and Stamford.

Maine

The first permanent settlement in "the Province of Maine" was in 1625 at Pemaquid, now a tiny village on the Atlantic coast thirty-five miles northeast of Portland. Although in the beginning Maine had a separate royal charter, the area was gradually annexed by Massachusetts and did not regain its independence until 1819. It was admitted to the Union as the twenty-third state in 1820, with Portland as its capital.

As early as the Revolutionary War there were a few Jews living in Maine, but they assimilated and disappeared. The first Jewish congregation, Ahabat Achim of Bangor, was organized in the 1850s. Bangor was so hard hit by the panic of 1857 that the Jews moved away and Ahabat Achim disintegrated. About 1890 Bangor again had a congregation, Beth Israel, which erected Maine's first synagogue. The state's Jewish population has been and remains a tiny fraction of the general community. There are presently 8,000 Jews in Maine, 0.8 percent of the total population. More than half live in two cities, Portland and Bangor.

Maine's constitution, adopted in 1820, gave full civil and religious rights to all its citizens. Although no Maine Jew was elected to public office until 1902, the Jews have had complete political and religious freedom ever since Maine became a state.

Massachusetts

The Puritan Pilgrims who landed on Plymouth Rock in 1620 were members of a very peculiar sect. One of their most remarkable peculiarities was that they admired Judaism but disliked Jews. They loved to draw parallels between themselves and the Old Testament Israelites. As the Israelites had wandered across the Red Sea and the desert, so had the Puritans wandered to Holland and across the Atlantic. As the Israelites had reached their promised land of Palestine, so had they reached their

promised land of New England. As the Israelites had fought the Ca-
naanites, so did they fight the Indians whom, in their theological and
moral ambivalence, they believed to be the Ten Lost Tribes of Israel.
The God of Israel was their God, the Law of Moses their law, the
prophets of the Old Testament their prophets. In addition, of course,
they had what the Jews did not have and never wanted to have, a firm
belief in the god-man Jesus and the theology of St. Paul.

This plus made the big difference in the Puritan mind between
themselves and the despised Jews. The Puritans dubbed themselves
"Christian Israelites." They were the real Jews. Those others who called
themselves Jews were impostors. They had fallen from God's grace
when they refused to accept the divinity of Jesus. Just as all Catholics,
Anglicans, Muslims, Quakers, Chinese, Africans, idol worshipers and
non-Puritan Protestants were unbelievers and heretics, so, too, were the
Jews unbelievers and heretics.

When the Roundhead regime in England collapsed and Charles II
came to the throne in 1661, the harsh stance of the Puritans with regard to
all non-Puritans, including Jews, had to be toned down because of the
new ruler's tolerant attitude on religious matters. Some Jews may have
gone in and out of the Massachusetts colony as traveling merchants and
peddlers as early as 1649, perhaps even earlier, but none was allowed to
make the colony his permanent residence. The first Jewish person to set
up housekeeping in Boston was probably Rowland Gideon, who was
granted British citizenship in 1669, a privilege which gave him the right to
reside wherever he pleased within the Empire's domain. Gideon is listed
on the 1674 Boston tax roll as "ye Jew." In 1728 some Boston Jews bought
a piece of ground for a Jewish cemetery, but there is no evidence that it
was ever used for this purpose. The bodies of the few Massachusetts
Jews who remained faithful to their religion unto death were transported
for burial to the Jewish cemeteries in Newport, R.I., or New York City.
The first Jew to be naturalized in Massachusetts was Aaron Lopez of
Newport, R.I., in 1762.

The first Jewish congregation in Massachusetts, Boston's Ohabei
Shalom, was not organized until 1843. The first Jewish cemetery to be
used as such was acquired in Boston in 1844. The first synagogue
building, again in Boston, was not completed until 1852. As Massachusetts history goes, its organized Jewish community is comparatively new.
But this community has grown rapidly. It now numbers about 275,000,
4.7 percent of the state's population. Eighty percent of the Jews of
Massachusetts live in the Greater Boston area.

The high point of Puritan irrationalism was reached in the Salem
witch hunt of 1692. Nineteen women and one man were condemned to
death for witchcraft. The women were hanged and the man was pressed
to death with weights. The widespread revulsion engendered by this evil

deed was so strong that it effectively brought to an end all official religious intolerance in Massachusetts. From then on, an out-of-state Jew could spend some time in the colony without having to worry about being forced by the authorities to shorten his stay.

However, the Jew did not achieve full acceptance in the Commonwealth easily. In 1844 when the Jews asked the Boston city fathers for permission to establish a Jewish cemetery, their action triggered such a powerful anti-Jewish reaction that their request was denied. Three months later the town council reversed itself and granted the desired permission. Not until 1892 did the Massachusetts legislature pass an act authorizing rabbis to perform marriages within the state! While the Jews of Massachusetts have had full rights of citizenship for more than 125 years, they were rarely elected or appointed to state political positions until about fifty years ago.

New Hampshire

What is now New Hampshire was originally part of the Massachusetts Bay Colony. The first settlement was established in 1623 on the present site of Rye, five miles south of Portsmouth. Portsmouth dates from 1630. In 1679 New Hampshire was separated from Massachusetts and made a royal province with Portsmouth as its capital. From 1699 to 1741, Massachusetts and New Hampshire were ruled by the same royal governor.

New Hampshire was the first state to declare its independence from Great Britain and the last state to have laws on its statute books discriminating against Jews. Not until 1877 were Jews eligible to occupy all New Hampshire political offices.

The first bona fide Jew known to have settled in New Hampshire did not come there until after the American Revolution. He was Abraham Isaac, "the Jew of Portsmouth," who operated a store which he closed every Saturday. He was greatly respected in the community. When the Prussian-born Isaac died in 1803, the epitaph engraved on his tombstone in Portsmouth's North Burying Ground was written by J. M. Sewall, a well-known poet of the American Revolutionary period:

> Entombed where earthborn troubles cease,
> A son of faithful Abraham sleeps.
> In life's first bloom he left his native air,
> A sojourner as all his fathers were.
> Through various toils his active spirit ran,
> A faithful steward and an honest man.
> His soul, we trust, now freed from mortal woes,
> Finds in the Patriarch's bosom sweet repose.

The reluctance of Jews to settle in New Hampshire may be judged by the fact that the oldest existing congregation in New Hampshire, Beth Abraham in Nashua, was not organized until 1892. The state's Jewish population reached a peak of 5,200 in 1960. Since then it has been declining steadily. It is now estimated at about 4,000, 0.5 percent of the total population. Over 50 percent of New Hampshire's Jews live in Manchester and Portsmouth.

Rhode Island

In 1635 Roger Williams, a young Puritan minister, was banished from Salem, Massachusetts, for asserting that Massachusetts belonged to the Indians rather than the English and that every person has a God-given right to observe the Sabbath as his conscience dictates. In 1636 friendly Indians gave Williams and his followers a piece of land on which they settled and founded the city of Providence. Other members of Williams' company established the settlements of Portsmouth (1638), Newport (1639), and Warwick (1643). In 1644 these towns were united under the title of Providence Plantations and given a royal charter. The present state was formed in 1663, chartered by Charles II and named Rhode Island and the Providence Plantations.

Rhode Island was the only colonial province in which the inhabitants enjoyed religious freedom from the very beginning. In announcing the founding of Providence, Williams wrote: "I desire not that liberty to myself which I would not freely and impartially weigh out to all the consciences of the world besides; therefore I humbly conceive that it is the express and absolute duty of the civil powers to proclaim an absolute freedom of conscience in all the world." The law code governing the Providence Plantations stated, "[In our domain] all men may walk as their consciences persuade them, every one in the name of his God."

These declarations meant that the Jew was to have freedom of religious expression and worship and was to be tolerated civilly. He was not to have full rights of citizenship. Jews, Catholics, and non-believers were not granted civil equality. As late as 1762, Aaron Lopez, a prominent and respected Jew of Newport, was refused Rhode Island citizenship and obtained, instead, Massachusetts citizenship from that much less tolerant colony.

In 1764 Rhode Island passed a law that showed the clear distinction made between religious freedom and civil rights. The law gave the Jews permission to marry "within the degrees of affinity and consanguinity allowed by their religion." Thus it became possible, in Rhode Island, for a Jewish uncle to marry his Jewish niece, since this accords with Mosaic law. Rhode Island is the only state that now permits such a marriage.

Not until 1842 did the Jews of Rhode Island secure complete

political equality. Nevertheless, from the earliest days Rhode Island was, religiously, so much more liberal than the rest of New England that it was the only state in the region that attracted a sizeable group of Jewish immigrants. Fifteen Dutch families from the British island of Barbados migrated to Newport in 1658 and established a Jewish congregation there. For the next 150 years, the history of the Jews of Rhode Island is almost entirely a history of the Newport Jewish community. In the thirty-five years preceding the American Revolution, Newport and Phila-delphia were the most important Jewish communities in North America.

No Jews are known to have lived in Providence prior to 1781. The first Rhode Island synagogue besides that in Newport, Providence's Congregation of the Sons of Israel, did not come into being until 1855. The Newport community was moribund from about 1795 until the 1850s. In other words, the Jews avoided even Rhode Island, the most liberal of the New England states, for many years—until after it had granted the Jew the full rights of citizenship he desired and deserved.

Rhode Island now has about 25,000 Jews, 2.3 percent of the total population. The overwhelming majority is concentrated in the Greater Providence area.

Vermont

Until the middle of the eighteenth century, the territory that is now Vermont was a warring frontier, fought over continually by the French and the English. The French were finally driven out in 1758. Then New Hampshire and New York both claimed the right of possession. In 1764 the British crown ruled in favor of New York. The Green Mountain Boys, organized in 1771 and led by Ethan Allen, had as their main goals the eviction of all New Yorkers from their land and the establishment of an independent province. Their convention in April 1775 declared New York's claim to the area to be null and void.

When the Revolution broke out, Allen and his Boys immediately offered their services to the Continental Congress. Throughout the Revolution they waged what amounted to their own private war against the British and the Indians. In 1777 they proclaimed the establishment of "a free and independent state" to be known as New Connecticut. Soon thereafter they learned that this name was already in use in another part of the country. So they renamed their new state Vermont, which is a shortened form of the French words for "green mountain." This was intended to serve a dual purpose: to remind future generations that Vermont was originally settled by the French and that it had achieved its independence through being liberated from New York by the Green Mountain Boys.

In 1790 New York agreed to stop its opposition to the recognition of

Vermont as a separate state. Vermont then entered the Union in 1791 as its fourteenth state. The capital, named Montpelier (again note the French influence), was established by fiat in 1808 in the exact geographical center of Vermont.

Jews in Vermont have been conspicuous by their absence. The only Jew known to have lived in Vermont prior to the Civil War was Joshua Montefiore, uncle of famed Sir Moses Montefiore. Joshua came to Vermont at the age of seventy-three, lived for eight years in St. Albans, died there, and, not wishing to be interred in a Christian cemetery, was buried on his own farm.

In the early 1870s, a number of Jewish peddlers made their homes and headquarters in Poultney, a small town on the New York border, where they set up a small synagogue and a cemetery. The community lasted until about 1900. Most of Poultney's Jews moved to Burlington and Rutland, which had become and still are the major Jewish communities in the state. Burlington's first synagogue dates from 1885 and Rutland's from the early 1900s.

Vermont has consistently had fewer Jews than any other state east of the Mississippi. The impact of Jewish life upon it and its impact upon American Jewish life have been extremely light. One might say that Vermont and the Jews have mutually ignored each other almost completely.

The largest number of Vermont Jews ever reported was in 1917 (2,221). Since then the number has slowly declined. It is now estimated to be about 1,850, 0.4 percent of the total population. Burlington presently has about 1,200 Jews and Rutland 300.

—D.M.E.

THE NEWPORT CEMETERY
(1677)

Newport, Rhode Island, was founded in 1639 by colonists from Massachusetts. Its first Jews arrived in 1658, fifteen Dutch families from the British island of Barbados in the West Indies. These families organized Jeshuath Israel, the oldest Jewish congregation in the United States. At first they held their services in the home of Mordecai Campanell. There was no synagogue building until 1763, more than a century later. But, from very early times, Newport had a Jewish cemetery.

In 1677 Campanell and Moses Israel Pacheco, on behalf of Congregation Jeshuath Israel, purchased a plot of land, 30 by 50 feet, for use as a cemetery. Congregation Jeshuath Israel has three noteworthy distinctions in American Jewish history: first congregation, oldest inviolate cemetery, oldest existing synagogue.

The cemetery, later enlarged, is located on what was originally known as Jews Street. Then it was renamed Bellevue Avenue. The city map now places the cemetery at 2 Bellevue Avenue.

The deed conveying the property to the congregation contained a strange proviso, i.e., that if the Jews would again leave the community before any of their dead was buried in the cemetery, the property would revert to its original owners. The clear implication is that, sometime between 1658 and 1677, the Jews had left Newport and returned. Exactly what may have caused this is not known, but a guess may be hazarded. The Jews, having heard of the liberal views of Roger Williams, Rhode Island's pioneer leader, may have come to Newport expecting to receive full citizenship status. In 1663 the first provincial legislature decreed that only Christians could become citizens of Rhode Island. This may have prompted the Newport Jews to leave the colony. The royal charter received in 1665 inferred that men of all faiths would be permitted to apply for citizenship. This inference may have prompted the Jews to

---

This account, based on *The Story of the Jews of Newport* by Morris A. Gutstein, 1936, pp. 230-55, is used with the permission of Rabbi Gutstein.

11

return to Newport. If they came back with the expectation of being made citizens, their hope was in vain. Campanell received the privilege in 1685, but he was an inexplicable exception.

The Jeshuath Israel cemetery was maintained in worthy fashion as long as there was a viable Jewish community in Newport, i.e., until about 1795. After that it was neglected. Grass and weeds covered the tombstones. The wooden fence around the cemetery rotted and broke down.

In the summer of 1822, Abraham Touro, Boston merchant, son of Isaac Touro, Newport's first rabbi, spent a thousand dollars to clean up the cemetery and build a brick wall around it. In the middle of July, he wrote to the man in charge of the work, "I don't know but what I shall come to see it after you have finished." He never beheld with mortal eyes the end result of his goodness. On October 3, 1822, while viewing a military parade in Boston from his carriage, he was thrown from the carriage when his horse became frightened by the noise of the artillery firing. Abraham was injured fatally. He died on October 18 at the age of forty-eight.

The very first item in his will was, "I desire and direct that I may be buried in Newport, Rhode Island, in such manner as I have expressed to my friends." Further, "I give Ten thousand dollars to the Legislature of the State of Rhode Island, for the purpose of supporting the Jewish Synagogue in that State, in Special Trust to be appropriated to that object, in such manner as the said Legislature together with the Municipal Authority of the Town of Newport may from time to time direct and appoint. . . . I give to the Municipal Authority of the Town of Newport the Sum of Five thousand dollars, in Special Trust and confidence that they will appropriate the same in such manner they may judge best, for repairing and preserving the Street from the Burying Ground in said Town to the Main Street." In all, Abraham Touro bequeathed to charitable and religious institutions $80,000, a considerable sum in those days.

He was buried in the Jeshuath Israel cemetery on October 20 in a simple, dignified ceremony, typical of the manner in which this native son of Newport had conducted his life. The Town Council carried out the provisions of his bequests meticulously. The synagogue was painted, the grounds renovated and beautified. The street which began at the Jewish cemetery, passed by the synagogue and ended at the main street became the best paved street in town. Until then it had been known as Griffin Street. By action of the Town Council, it was known henceforth and to this day as Touro Street.

In the years that followed there were a number of burials in the cemetery of Jews born in Newport or their relatives. Only on these rare and somber occasions was the synagogue opened and used. By 1842 the cemetery was again in a sorry state. The brick wall had begun to crumble. The cemetery looked abandoned and forlorn. Abraham Touro had provided for the physical upkeep of the synagogue and the street that ran from the cemetery past the synagogue; but he had left no money for the maintenance and preservation of the cemetery.

The cemetery's deplorable condition was brought to the attention of Abraham's brother, Judah Touro, philanthropic New Orleans merchant. Judah commissioned a Boston architect to improve the cemetery. At a cost of $12,000, a beautiful new granite wall was constructed, the monuments were repaired and restored, and the grounds were again made attractive.

When the Town Council learned of Judah Touro's action, it decided to engage the same Boston architect to build a granite wall around the grounds of the synagogue. On July 9, 1842, the *Newport Mercury* reported:

"We understand that the Town Council, under authority given by the General Assembly, have contracted with Mr. Rogers of Boston to enclose the Synagogue lot with a substantial stone wall and Iron fence, similar to the one which he has just completed around the Hebrew Cemetery. The work will consist of an ornamental cast Iron fence with a basement of cut Quincy Granite on Touro and Barney Streets, and a substantial granite wall on the east and west sides of the lot. The Gateway will be on Touro Street and correspond with the Portico of the Synagogue."

The town of Newport spent $6,835 on this project, strong evidence of the great pride of the community in its historic synagogue and cemetery. In 1842 there were few, if any, Jews living in Newport.

Judah Touro died, at the age of seventy-nine, in New Orleans on January 18, 1854. The opening section of his will stated, "I desire that my mortal remains be buried in the Jewish Cemetery in Newport, Rhode Island, as soon as practical after my decease." Among his many bequests, totaling almost a half million dollars, was the following: "I give and bequeath ten thousand dollars for the purpose of paying the salary of a Reader or Minister to officiate in the Jewish Synagogue of Newport, Rhode Island, and to endow the Ministry of the same, as well as to keep in repair and embellish the Jewish Cemetery in Newport."

The Newport City Council [Newport was upgraded from "town" to "city" in 1853] accepted the Touro bequest on January 11, 1855. Up to $200 a year was to be used to take care of the cemetery. The rest was to be kept on reserve until such time as Newport would again have a rabbi. This came to pass in 1883. For many years after that, the income from the Touro Fund was used to help pay the rabbi's salary as well as to maintain the cemetery.

Judah Touro was buried in the Newport cemetery on June 6, 1854. Prominent rabbis and delegations of Jews and non-Jews were present from New Orleans, Boston, Hartford, New Haven, New York City, Buffalo, and Philadelphia. The local newspaper described the funeral:

"The procession was the longest which has been seen here for many years. The streets were crowded with people, the stores all closed, and the bells tolled. About 150 Jews were present from various parts of the country. The City Council assembled at City Hall and marched in procession to the Synagogue, the gallery of which was already densely crowded with ladies, and there were thousands on the street who could not gain admission.

"The coffin stood in front of the reading desk. Soon after the arrival of the city government, the Rabbis and other Jews came in procession, the former taking seats in the desk. As soon as the Synagogue was filled, the doors were closed, and thousands remained outside until the ceremonies were concluded."

After the service, those within and without the synagogue escorted the coffin to the cemetery. When the coffin was placed in the grave, a New York rabbi "deposited upon it a quantity of earth which was brought from Jerusalem for the purpose."

In 1858 Henry Wadsworth Longfellow visited Jeshuath Israel cemetery. Deeply moved by what he saw and felt, this gifted American wrote his famous poem, "The Jewish Cemetery in Newport":

> How strange it seems! These Hebrews in their graves,
>   Close by the street of this fair seaport town.
> Silent beside the never-silent waves,
>   At rest in all this moving up and down!
>
> The trees are white with dust, that o'er their sleep
>   Wave their broad curtains in the south-wind's breath,
> While underneath such leafy tents they keep
>   The long, mysterious Exodus of Death.
>
> And these sepulchral stones, so old and brown,
>   That pave with level flags their burial-place,
> Seem like the tablets of the Law, thrown down
>   And broken by Moses at the mountain's base.
>
> The very names recorded here are strange,
>   Of foreign accent, and of different climes:
> Alvares and Rivera interchange
>   With Abraham and Jacob of old times.
>
> "Blessed be God! for he created Death!"
>   The mourners said, "and Death is rest and peace";
> Then added, in the certainty of faith,
>   "And giveth Life that never more shall cease."

Closed are the portals of their Synagogue,
    No Psalms of David now the silence break,
No Rabbi reads the ancient Decalogue
    In the grand dialect the Prophets spake.

Gone are the living, but dead remain,
    And not neglected, for a hand unseen
Scattering its bounty, like a summer rain,
    Still keeps their graves and their remembrance green.

How came they here? What burst of Christian hate,
    What persecution, merciless and blind,
Drove o'er the sea—that desert desolate—
    These Ishmaels and Hagars of mankind?

They lived in narrow streets and lanes obscure,
    Ghetto and Judenstrass, in mirk and mire;
Taught in the school of patience to endure
    The life of anguish and the death of fire.

All their lives long, with the unleavened bread
    And bitter herbs of exile and its fears,
The wasting famine of the heart they fed,
    And slaked its thirst with marah of their tears.

Anathema marantha! was the cry
    That rang from town to town, from street to street;
At every gate the accursed Mordecai
    Was mocked and jeered, and spurned by Christian feet.

Pride and humiliation hand in hand
    Walked with them through the world where'er they went;
Trampled and beaten were they as the sand,
    And yet unshaken as the continent.

For in the background figures vague and vast
    Of patriarchs and of prophets rose sublime,
And all the great traditions of the Past
    They saw reflected in the coming time.

And thus for ever with reverted look
    The mystic volume of the world they read,
Spelling it backward, like a Hebrew book,
    Till life became a Legend of the Dead.

But ah! what once has been shall be no more!
    The groaning earth in travail and in pain
Brings forth its races, but does not restore,
    And the dead nations never rise again.

The Newport Synagogue
(1763)

As early as January 1754, the Newport congregation wanted to build a synagogue, but could not afford to do so. It appealed to the Bevis Marks Synagogue in London for financial assistance. In August the London congregation sent a reply, written in Spanish, stating that prevailing circumstances made it impossible for them to assist and expressing the devout hope that the Almighty would be of greater help than they: "May God be the One Who assists all, and of whose grace we would desire that He give to you as He is able, and may He prosper you in your pious plans!"

In the spring of 1759 another request for contributions was sent to a number of congregations. The result this time was much better. Especially generous was New York's Shearith Israel. Pledges were taken at its service on the seventh day of Passover. The money raised, amounting to 149 pounds sixpence, was turned over to the Newport congregation in July. This was no paltry sum. An apt comparison in contemporary terms: In 1769 a new Torah cost no more than 40 pounds. A new Torah now costs $2,000 or more. Using this as a yardstick, the New York contribution to the building of the Newport synagogue was the equivalent of more than $7,000.

Ground was broken on August 1, 1759. The synagogue proper and a small attached school building were to have a total of six corners and, accordingly, six cornerstones were laid. Peter Harrison, a pupil and associate of Sir Christopher Wren, was engaged as architect. The exterior of the building was designed in Colonial or Georgian style, often referred to as "classic colonial." The interior was patterned after the interior of the Spanish-Portuguese synagogue in Amsterdam. While the synagogue was being built, the congregation requested and was granted the loan of a Sefer Torah from the congregation in New York.

After two years construction was halted because of lack of funds. Once more Congregation Shearith Israel was asked to come to the aid of its sister congregation in Newport, and once more it did so. By July 1762 the exterior of the building was finished except for the portico, but the dedication did not take place until almost a year and a half later.

The dedication was held on December 2, 1763, the first day. of

---

The account of the building of the synagogue and the description of its exterior and interior are taken from *The Story of the Jews of Newport* by Morris A. Gutstein, pp. 91-110, and are used with the permission of Rabbi Gutstein.

Chanuka 5523, the same day on which the Holy Temple in Jerusalem had been rededicated by Judah the Maccabee 1928 years earlier.

While waiting for the ceremony to commence, the congregation sat in absolute silence. At the appointed time, three knocks were heard upon the closed door of the synagogue. Then the sound of the voice of Rabbi Touro came through the door chanting in Hebrew: "Lift up your heads, O ye gates, and be ye lifted up, ye everlasting doors, that the King of glory may come in." Those inside asked in Hebrew: "Who is the King of glory?" The voice on the outside responded: "The Lord of hosts, He is the King of glory. Open unto Me the gates of righteousness that I may enter."

The congregation rose. The doors opened. A procession, headed by the rabbi, entered. The rabbi and two of the congregation's officers carried three Scrolls of the Law. The perpetual lamp hanging above the Ark, a gift from Samuel Judah of New York City, was lit, while Chazzan Touro chanted the "Shehecheyanu": "Blessed art thou, O Lord our God, King of the universe, Who has given us life, sustained us and brought us to this memorable day."

The Scrolls were carried in procession around the synagogue seven times. Then the rabbi recited a "Prayer for the Royal Family," after which the congregation chanted, "The Lord shall reign forever, thy God, O Zion, unto all generations. Hallelujah!" and the Torahs were placed in the Ark.

Among those present was Dr. Ezra Stiles, minister of Newport's Second Congregational Church and later to be president of Yale University. He wrote in his diary:

"The Synagogue is about perhaps forty foot long and 30 wide, of Brick on a Foundation of Free Stone; it was begun about two years ago, and is now finished except the Porch and the Capitals of the Pillars. The Front Representation of the holy of holies, or its Partition Veil, consists only of wainscotted Breast Work on the East End in the lower part of which four long Doors cover an upright Square Closet the depth of which is about a foot or the thickness of the Wall, and in this Apartment (vulgarly called the Ark) were deposited three Copies and Rolls of the Pentateuch, written on Vellum or rather tanned Calf Skin: one of these Rolls I was told by Dr. Touro was presented from Amsterdam and is Two Hundred years old; the Letters have the Rabbinical Flourishes.

"A Gallery for the Women runs round the whole inside, except East End, supported by Columns of the Ionic order, over which are placed correspondent Columns of the Corinthian order supporting the Ceiling of the Roof. The Depth of the Corinthian Pedestal is the height of the Balustrade which runs round the Gallery. The Pulpit for Reading the Law is a raised Pew with an extended front table; this is placed about the center of the Synagogue or nearer the West End, being a Square balustrading Comporting with the Length of the indented Chancel before the end at the Foot of the Ark.

"On the middle of the North Side and affixed to the Wall is a raised Seat for the Parnas or Ruler, and for the Elders; the Breast and Back interlaid with Chinese Mosaic Work. A Wainscotted Seat runs round the Sides of the Synagogue below, and another in the Gallery. There are no other Seats or Pews.... The Synagogue has already cost Fifteen Hundred Pound Sterling."

The building plan called for five brass candelabra "pendant from a lofty Ceiling." These were subsequently installed.

Other features not mentioned by Stiles were: The synagogue was built at an acute angle from the street so that its Ark faced directly east. A small stairway led from back of the reading desk to a secret compartment in the basement. This was in the Marrano tradition of providing a hiding place in time of danger. In the school portion of the structure was an oven and a kneading trough for the baking of Passover matzot. In the courtyard was a cistern for the catching of rainwater for use in the mikveh [ritual bath]. Two brass candlesticks were on the railing before the Ark and four more on the railing in front of the altar.

There was a beautiful oil painting of the Tablets of the Law on the eastern wall directly above the Ark. The tablets were surmounted by three crowns, emblematic of the crowns of priesthood, royalty, and Torah. Also in the building was another painting of the Ten Commandments with a translation in Old Spanish under each Hebrew commandment and likenesses of Moses and Aaron on the two sides of the painting. Two mahogany receptacles, each bearing the inscription "Charity Box," were fixed to the columns in the rear of the synagogue. In the back was a clock, fastened to the balcony. The ceiling of the synagogue was painted blue and the rest of the interior white.

In time "the Porch and the Capitals of the Pillars" were completed and a heating unit was installed. When the building was finished inside and out and all its appurtenances added, it was estimated to have a value of 2,000 pounds sterling, which, in our time, would be the equivalent of about $100,000, no mean sum, and in those less affluent days regarded as a magnificent tribute worthy only of the King of kings. To try to duplicate the synagogue and its contents now would probably cost at least $300,000.

The eternal light and the lamps in the synagogue were originally kept lighted by means of whale oil. In 1882 electric bulbs replaced the oil and the oil wicks. The bulb which was placed in the Eternal Light at that time is still in use. The Jews of Congregation Jeshuath Israel look upon this as a modern American Chanuka miracle.

The present rabbi of Congregation Jeshuath Israel is Theodore Lewis, a Hibernian Ashkenazi from Dublin. On St. Patrick's Day he marches with the Irish in the Newport and Providence parades. The synagogue is now known as the Touro Synagogue. In 1946 it was designated a National Historic Site. It is administered jointly by the U. S. Department of the Interior, Congregation Shearith Israel of New York, and Congregation Jeshuath Israel. It is the most famous building in Newport.

A SOUTH CAROLINA JEW AIDS RHODE ISLAND COLLEGE (1770)

The first permanent English settlement in South Carolina was Charleston, founded in 1670 and, in honor of Charles II, named Charles Town, a name it kept for many years. Jews began to come to Charles Town before the end of the seventeenth century. By 1750 there were enough Jews in Charlestown (the two words by then had become one) to form a congregation, the fourth in the colonial period. The three earlier ones, in order of appearance, were Newport, New York, and Savannah.

The pre-Revolutionary Jews of Charlestown were mostly small traders. A few who became plantation owners, bankers, and manufacturers acquired a fair amount of wealth. These better circumstanced Jews became prominently identified with Charlestown's cultural and social life. Among those who achieved this distinction was Moses Lindo.

Lindo, born in London about 1712, was a well-to-do merchant before coming to South Carolina. He had a seat on the Royal Exchange and was an expert in grading indigo, an important blue vegetable dye used in the British textile industry to color cotton cloth. A cultured and intelligent man, he had attended a fine private school, wrote well, had a knowledge of chemistry and sought to develop new varieties of dyes through scientific experimentation.

Some planters in South Carolina had begun to grow indigo plants. Lindo became convinced that a better quality dye could be developed from these plants than from those grown elsewhere. He so testified before a committee of the House of Commons. Eager to aid in the maturation of the South Carolina indigo industry, he left England and took up residence in Charlestown in the fall of 1756.

The eminent American Jewish historian Jacob R. Marcus, in his definitive work *Early American Jewry,* describes vividly the man and his influence on the South Carolina indigo industry:

"Moses Lindo had a high respect for Moses Lindo's knowledge in all matters touching on indigo. For 25 years before coming to Charlestown he had worked at sorting and grading the plant. Once he modestly implied that he was one of the best judges of the product in America and in Europe, by which he meant to say that he had no peer anywhere. And, strangely enough, he was probably right. . . .

"Lindo was a one-man Chamber of Commerce, bent on promoting South Carolina indigo. He was so active in the trade that it was inevitable that his influence would evoke envy and slander. To combat those who were attacking him, he offered a reward of 500 pounds for substantial information about the people making malicious insinuations. But the best people appreciated his efforts; they accepted him socially and respected him as 'a noted Jew.'"

In 1762, at the suggestion of the indigo planters of the state, the governor created a special position, "Inspector General of Indigo, Drugs and Dyes," and appointed Lindo to the position. He held it for ten years and then voluntarily resigned, although he continued to use the title during the remaining two years of his life. In 1763 he wrote a paper titled "An account of a New Die from the Berries of a Weed in South Carolina," which was published in the prestigious British "Philosophical Transactions of the Royal Society."

Lindo died in 1774, when the South Carolina indigo business was at its peak. In later years people came to prefer the immaculate white of the natural cotton cloth to its being saturated with the royal blue of indigo. By the end of the nineteenth century a method had been perfected for making indigo dye from synthetic coal tar products, a dye which was much superior to that extracted from the genus indigofera. As a result the growing of indigo plants for commercial purposes has ceased almost entirely.

✻   ✻   ✻   ✻   ✻

In 1769 the Reverend Hezekiah Smith of New England visited Charlestown to solicit funds for the Rhode Island College in Providence, founded in 1765, now known as Brown University. Lindo heard with deep interest that the new college accepted students without inquiring into their religious antecedents. He recalled with bitterness that he had never been graduated officially from his boyhood school because he was a Jew. He had officially never even been a student, but was listed as an auditor.

Lindo joined a number of Charlestown Jews in making substantial donations to the school. He wrote the following letter to his New York representatives:

Charlestown, 17 April 1770.

Mess'rs Sampson & Solomon Simson, New York.

Gentlemen:
    You will be so kind as to order your correspondent in Rhode Island to pay unto the Trustees of the new college the sum of five pounds York currency on my account, and to transmit me th'ir receipt in my name.
    As the Rev'd Mr. Smith will inform th'm, the reason th't induces me to be a benefactor to this college is th'ir having no objection of admitting the youth of our nation without interfereing in principals of religion. If so, my donation shall exceed beyond the bounds of th'ir imagination.
    I presume this college is like Merchant Taylor's School in London where I went every day for three years, as well as two of my brothers, from 9:00 to 1:00 o'clock. There was at th't time about 800 boys, sons of the principal merchants and trading people in the city. I have lived to see two Lord Mayors and seven aldermen, and many toping [first class] merchants my school-fellows, which, I assure you, was no small service to me when I was a broker on the Royal Exchange. . . .
    I sincerely wish you well, and remain, with regard, gentlemen,

Your obliged humble serv't,

Moses Lindo.

When the Rev'd Mr. Smith reported the generosity of Moses Lindo and his fellow Charlestown Jews to the college trustees, they added to their charter, at the next annual meeting, the statement "that the children of Jews may be admitted into this institution and entirely enjoy the freedom of their own religion, without any constraint or imposition whatever."
    On January 1, 1771, the trustees informed Lindo that the following actions had been taken: Jewish students would not be required to attend the religious services which were compulsory for Christian students; and a Jewish tutor in the Jewish religion and Hebrew would be provided for the Jewish students if their numbers warranted.
    There is no record that Lindo contributed any more money to the Rhode Island College. Perhaps in a moment of extreme enthusiasm he had given in a single donation all he could afford to give.
    The Charlestown Jews were not the only Jews who helped get Rhode Island College on its way. Aaron Lopez and his father-in-law, Jacob Rodriguez Rivera, of Newport, gave the college 10,000 feet of lumber for its first building.
    During the years that the Jews of Charlestown and Newport were providing such generous assistance to Rhode Island College in appreciation for its "open door" policy, there were no Jews in Providence and no Jewish students at Rhode Island College.

An Early American Jewish Merchant Prince
(1782)

The epitaph on his tombstone in the Jewish cemetery at Newport, R.I., states:

"He was a Merchant of Eminence,
    of Polite and amiable manners.
Hospitality, Liberality and Benevolence
    were his true Characteristics.
An ornament and valuable Pillar
    in the Jewish Society
    of which he was a member.
His knowledge in Commerce was unbounded;
Thus he lived and Died,
Much regretted, esteemed and loved by all."

Aaron Lopez was born in 1731 in Lisbon, Portugal, as Duarte Lopez, a Marrano. He received a Catholic baptism and schooling. He married his cousin Anna in a Roman Catholic church. They had one child, a daughter, Elizabeth. Publicly the family was devoutly Catholic. Privately, to the maximum extent their situation permitted, they followed the laws and customs of Judaism. Aaron's oldest brother, suspected by the Inquisition of Judaizing, fled from Portugal to England. He came to Newport as Moses Lopez no later than 1746 and probably earlier. Another brother escaped to Jamaica and assumed the name of Abraham.

Duarte and yet another brother got out of Portugal with their families and joined Moses in Newport in October 1752. The other brother selected Gabriel as his Jewish name. Duarte and Anna were remarried in a traditional Jewish ceremony. He took the name of Aaron and she Abigail. Daughter Elizabeth became Sarah. Before his remarriage, Aaron, at age twenty-one, underwent circumcision.

Despite all such acts of resanctification, so deeply were Marrano habits imbedded in the mores of many of Newport's Sephardim that it was not uncommon to see a Jewish woman walking down the street counting off her Jewish daily prayers on a necklace of rosary beads.

In May 1762 Abigail passed away at age thirty-six, having borne Aaron seven children, all of whom died quite young. Less than sixteen months later Aaron married Sarah Rivera of the well-known Spanish Rivera family of Newport. From this second marriage ten children were born, two of whom were given the same name, Jacob. The first Jacob probably died soon after birth.

Even though the colony of Rhode Island tolerated people of all faiths, it did not grant equal rights to all. It refused to grant most foreign-born Jews the right of citizenship. So, when Aaron Lopez wanted to become a citizen, he had to go to Massachusetts and acquire citizenship in that colony, where he had property and did much business. To satisfy the residence requirement he moved temporarily to Swansea, Massachusetts, just across the eastern border of Rhode Island. He was naturalized on October 15, 1762, in the court at Taunton, Massachusetts, as a resident of Swansea and Newport. When he took the oath the usual words "on the true faith of a Christian" were omitted.

At first Lopez went into the whaling business, specializing in making candles from whale sperm oil, an industry created by the head of the Rivera family, Jacob Rodriguez Rivera, 1717-80. Then he began a coastal shipping enterprise, operating sailing vessels between the ports of Boston, Newport, New York, Philadelphia, and Charleston. Early in 1760 he started to send these cargo ships to England. They carried across the Atlantic rough timber, mahogany, sperm oil and other whaling industry products. They brought back dry goods, hardware, and other English manufactured items. This export-import exchange went so well that Lopez had to set up his own shipyard to provide enough bottoms to carry his merchandise. He also operated wholesale and retail stores and a building construction firm in Newport.

In those days Yankee shipowners engaged in a procedure, known euphemistically as the "West Indian Trade," considered quite respectable by a high percentage of New Englanders and the main source of the wealth of some of the best known New England families. The "West Indian Trade" worked like this: A ship made one round trip a year. In the case of Newport, the ship went from Newport to the west coast of Africa with a load of New England rum. In Africa the rum was exchanged for a cargo of slaves. The slaves were carried to the West Indies and exchanged for a cargo of sugar, which was then carried back to Newport, made into rum, traded for slaves, etc., etc., ad infinitum.

Lopez, having met with great success in his American coastal and English commercial ventures, wanted to get hold of a piece of this "West Indian" action, a desire in keeping with the accepted business practices of his place and time. For a reason or reasons which seem to have gone unrecorded, the attempt of Lopez to enter the slave trade was a complete failure and his financial loss therefrom considerable. To attribute this failure to either religious or ethical misgivings or business ineptness would be pure guesswork. The black cloud did have a silver lining. Until the outbreak of the Revolution Lopez's ships made profitable journeys to and from the West Indies, selling American rum and buying West Indian sugar.

A portrait of Lopez was painted by the famous American artist

Gilbert Stuart. It shows him dressed in clothes such as were worn by the wealthy British gentry of his day. Only his brilliant dark eyes and olive-colored skin indicate his Portuguese background.

Lopez's extensive commercial ventures helped to make Newport a boom town in the pre-Revolutionary years. It was a busier and better known seaport than New York. Jewishly, Lopez was the key figure in the building of the Newport synagogue, the oldest existing synagogue structure in the United States. On August 1, 1759, as parnas [president] of the Newport Jewish community, he was master of ceremonies at the cornerstone laying of the synagogue. He was a very observant Jew: his ships never left port on Saturday; his stores and offices were closed from sundown Friday until Monday morning; he contributed generously to Jewish and general community causes.

Early in the 1770s Newport's business began to decline because of the severe restrictions imposed by the British on American merchants and shipowners. Because of Lopez's widespread enterprises he was one of the worst hit. Shortly after the Revolution began his great fortune commenced to shrink. In 1775 he owned thirty ships. All were confiscated with their cargoes, either by the British or by American privateers who rationalized their greedy behavior by declaring that Lopez deserved such treatment because he, like practically every American businessman, had been trading with the enemy!

When a British fleet converged on Newport in 1777, Lopez and about seventy of his relatives went first to Philadelphia and then to Leicester, Massachusetts. While en route from Philadelphia to Leicester, Lopez and his family stopped in Worcester, Massachusetts, to rest and replenish their supplies. No one was willing to give shelter to the patriotic Jewish refugees except John Green, owner of Green Hill, a fine landed estate. Green took the Lopez family into his home. They were his guests for two nights.

In Leicester Lopez purchased a large plot of ground on which he built a splendid house. He set up and operated a general merchandise store. While his Leicester style of living did not match his style in Newport, he was far from poverty stricken and gave many a gay party and ball.

After Washington's victory at Yorktown in October 1781 brought an end to active hostilities, Lopez prepared to return to Newport. He began the homeward journey in May 1782. En route Lopez stopped again at Green Hill. In gratitude for the kindness shown him by John Green, he planted two sycamore trees in front of Green's house. These trees, which grew to giant size, were known in Worcester as the "Lopez trees." One of them had to be cut down many years ago when, in its old age, it was feared that the tree might fall and hit the front of the house. The remaining tree was blown down in the hurricane of 1938. Descendants of

John Green, including the late Senator Theodore Green of Rhode Island, have taken great pride in the good deed of their ancestor and through them the story of the "Lopez trees" has been preserved.

On May 28, 1782, near Smithfield, R.I., Lopez drove his gig into a pond to water his horse. The gig accidentally overturned and Lopez was drowned. His body was recovered almost immediately and his funeral was held in Newport two days later. The eulogy was delivered by a Christian minister, the president of Rhode Island College. In his will Lopez stipulated that the house and grounds in Leicester should be used to establish a boys' school. The property became Leicester Academy, a well-known secondary school which still exists and has had many famous Americans among its graduates.

Ezra Stiles, minister in Newport from 1755 to 1770 and president of Yale College from 1778 until his death in 1795, wrote in his diary upon learning that Lopez was dead:

"He was a Merchant of the first eminence, for Honor and Extent of Commerce probably surpassed by no Merchant in America. He did Business with the greatest ease and exactness—always carried about with him a sweetness of behaviour, a calm Urbanity, and agreeable and unaffected Politeness of manners. Without a single Enemy and the most universally beloved by an extensive acquaintance of any man I ever knew."

THE PITTSFIELD FIND

(1815)

Pittsfield, Massachusetts, beautifully located in the heart of the Berkshires, was originally a sparsely settled village of Mohegan Indians. In the early years of the eighteenth century, white settlers from Massachusetts cities and towns began to come to this region. In 1761 the town of Pittsfield was incorporated.

Captain Joseph Merrick settled in Pittsfield about 1800 and became the innkeeper of its chief hostelry. He owned a farm and garden a little out of the center of the village at the south end of Onata Lake on which was Indian Hill, more recently called Fort Hill.

While ploughing in the summer of 1815 on Indian Hill, Captain Merrick turned up with his plough what proved to be a phylactery.

From "The Phylactery Found in Pittsfield, Massachusetts" by Lee M. Friedman in *American Jewish Historical Society Publications* #2, 1917, pp. 81-85.

Elkanah Watson, one of Pittsfield's distinguished pioneers, gives the following contemporary account of the discovery:

Pittsfield, November 10, 1815

To Hugh Williamson

Dear Sir,
     In accordance with your request to ascertain all the facts in relation to the interesting discovery of the Jewish phylactery in this village, in June last, I reply. It was ploughed up in the yard of Mr. Joseph Merrick, a respectable inhabitant who resides on the border of the village, in the midst of rubbish, and lying some inches below the surface.
     Immediately on hearing the news of the discovery, I repaired to the home of Mr. Merrick, where I found six clergymen, whose curiosity was greatly excited by the strange incident and who believed with me that this article must have found its way into this recent wilderness by the agency of some of the descendents of Israel.
     ... Being impressed with the belief that the Indians of America were descended from the lost tribes of Israel and that they had been directed by the same Almighty hand which had brought them out of the land of Egypt to continue their journeying in a northeastern course, probably for many ages, and finally to reach this continent at Behring's Strait; yet retaining some knowledge of the arts and sciences, and always adhering to the rites of the Jewish religion. After reaching this continent and a lapse of many years and probably ages, some portions inclined to rest in the northern regions but most pursued a southern course, spreading in all directions, even to the southern extremity of South America, and north to the polar regions, and thus peopling the surface of both Americas, more or less densely, according to the varied climates. Those in the extreme north and south becoming the most savage, as in milder climates they have been found the most civilized and in possession of arts, etc., especially in the City of Mexico and Peru.
     ... This discovery forms another link of evidence by which our Indians are identified with the ancient Jews, who were scattered upon the face of the globe and to this day remain a living monument to verify and establish the eternal truth of Scripture.

Very respectfully,

E. Watson.

     Contemporary local tradition reported that this was a relic of early Jewish settlers in Pittsfield.
     Reverend Ethan Smith, pastor of the Congregational Church of Poultney, Vermont, in 1823 published his *View of the Hebrews* supporting the contention that the Indians were the Lost Ten Tribes. On the publication of this volume, President Griffin of Williams College called

his attention to the discovery of the phylactery in Pittsfield, and the reverend gentleman immediately undertook an investigation to use this find as further evidence to support his contention. He made a journey to Pittsfield. He interviewed different aged persons and convinced himself that "no Jew was ever known in Pittsfield." He got an account of the discovery from Captain Merrick himself. He tried to see the phylactery and found that it had been deposited with the American Antiquarian Society at Worcester, but had been misplaced as it could not be located. [The present librarian of this society has now informed me that the society does have the rolled scroll with Hebrew script that was inside the phylactery.—L.M.F.] Thereupon, being convinced that it was Indian in origin, he affirmed that this phylactery was convincing proof of the Hebraic origin of the Indians and inserted the story as an unanswerable argument to support his views in the second edition of his *Views of the Hebrews.*

I have made a diligent search to see if we could identify any of the early settlers of Pittsfield as Jews.

Situated on the Mohawk trail, the main colonial thoroughfare of western Massachusetts, not over two days' travel from Albany, and trading center of a prosperous, growing agricultural district, it would not be surprising to find enterprising Jewish traders visiting or settled there at an early date. We fail, however, to substantiate such a tradition from early records. . . .

But whether lost by an early settler or dropped by some pioneer traveller, the finding of the phylactery at Pittsfield affords another indication of the ubiquity of the Jew in early colonial America.

It is worthy of note that, when Christian missionaries began to work among the Cherokee Indians, they learned that the Cherokee word most often used for God was Ya Ho Wa, meaning "The Master of Life." This they took to be the word Jehovah and sure proof that the Indians were the Ten Lost Tribes. These missionaries did not know that Jehovah is not a Hebrew word. It is a word artificially fashioned by medieval Anglo-Saxons who had no knowledge of the correct pronunciations of the principal terms used for God in Biblical Hebrew.—D.M.E.

THE SAGA OF SIMMY FAIRCHILD
(1858)

Eleven times out of ten the peddler is a Jew.

But, after all, the peddler is not a beggar but a house-to-house merchant who runs about with his store on his back in order to dispose of it for good money. He has arrived today directly from Bremen or Havre, this honest Samuel or Aaron or Moses. During the long journey he was parsimonious; not only did he lose nothing, nay, he even made a little profit on the boat with his Palatinate cigars at six florins a thousand, which he sold at three cents, i.e., nine kreuzer a piece, to his fellow-passengers on the ship who had run out of tobacco. Now here he is in glorious New York, in the Promised Land. What now? Honest Samuel knows perfectly.

From his boarding-house he goes forthwith to a coreligionist. He does not have far to go, for "there are quite a lot" of his coreligionists in New York. The coreligionist is "Gut-ab" [well-off]. He has a nice store and in it a wife with a full, open neck and a graceful little niece, the sweet little Rebeksche with gazelle-eyes and delicate fingers which are so flexible that they nearly always produce four out of three yards;—and in addition, there is in the store a multitude of other things, such as neckties, underbodices, suspenders, ribbons, gloves, pocket-handkerchiefs, socks—a whole wardrobe.

"Regards from Aetti in Wankheim." "Ah, Sam! Sam! As I live! Sam Ferkelche from Wankheim in person."

Well, well, what jollification there is! Sam was still pretty small when his uncle "Gut-ab" left home; but the features cannot be disavowed. Sam takes after the family. Well, it is a great joy. Sam sits down.

"Well, what can we do for you, Sam?" says "Gut-ab." And so one word leads to another. Sam learns from "Gut-ab" how the latter had started and he puts it into his pipe and smokes it, and after two hours goes off to his lodging with a large bundle under his arm, and in the bundle there are drawers, undervests, socks, suspenders, neckties, collars, gloves, and a multitude of other things, all necessary in life, indispensable for daily needs. Uncle "Gut-ab" did not give it to him as a present, but he has done something over and above that; he solemnly swore that he was not making a kreuzer profit on his relative, and, therefore, he was giving

From Theodor Griesinger's *Lebende Bilder aus Amerika*, Stuttgart, 1858, pp. 20-25. Translated by Rudolf Glanz and published in his "Source Material on Jewish Immigration," in *Yivo Annual of Jewish Social Science*, Volume VI, 1951, Section 87. Reprinted by permission of Dr. Glanz and the editor of the *Yivo Annual of Jewish Social Science*.

it to him at "cost price," i.e., he didn't add on 50 but only 25 percent. "One must after all do something for a brother's own son," he said to his "ma" as they were going to bed that night to sleep the sleep of the righteous.

The next morning Sam is up early on his feet. He rents himself an obscure little garret room for two dollars a month. He purchases a peddler's chest, in order to arrange his merchandise neatly therein and off he goes! He goes from house to house, up the stairs, down the stairs; the merchandise is offered cheaply! From one saloon he runs to another, from one street to another—the merchandise is offered cheaply!

At first things are hard. Here he is turned away, and there he is chased out. But Sam lets nothing discourage him. If he has disposed of nothing in ten places, in the eleventh a sixpence bobs up after all! To be sure, it causes many a drop of perspiration, as it is quite hot in New York in the summer; to be sure, the feet get wet through and through, for in winter it is devilish getting through the mud of the streets; to be sure, it often means: "You Jewish swindler, get thee gone!"—to be sure, many a door is slammed in his face so that his coattail is almost left sticking in it; to be sure, on occasion, he has to depend on the speed of his legs, when it means: "Get him, Sultan; sick him, he is of the brood of Moses!"—but all this does not matter. In the evening when he comes to his little garret room, he counts up his money and he sees that after all he had made a couple of shillings. "Let yourself be banged, let yourself be buffeted," his old father, Issachar of the tribe of Levi, had told him. "As nobody examines you to see how many pokes in the ribs and raps on the nose and dog-kicks you got, once you have become a rich man," he said.

Sam goes on so for a week, perhaps even a fortnight. His food is dry bread, his drink is water. In two weeks he has spent no more than his Christian fellow-immigrant in the first twenty-four hours.

And he has also learned something. He has learned which days are the best for making sales and which streets are the most favorable; he has learned to speak with people and understands already "Yes" and "No" and above all "How much?" He has found out where the wholesale commercial houses are located from which Uncle "Gut-ab" himself buys, and Monsieur "Gut-ab" no longer makes 25 percent on it, in spite of "Ma" and "Rebeksche."

After three months Sam is an altogether different person. He is well off himself, at least for a peddler, and therefore, in addition to his dry bread, allows himself now and then a small piece of cheese, that is American, at nine kreuzer (three cents) a pound. His ready cash allows him to make a larger purchase and he makes up his mind to go into "the country." The country is big and there are still places through which railroads do not run, and where the people are so good-natured and so simple that they still allow themselves to be duped a bit. Sam finds these places and the farmers are happy to see the peddler, for then they need not make the long journey into the city. But Sam is still happier, since he sells at 200 percent profit and gets a night's lodging and evening meal free.

His business is no longer in drawers and handkerchiefs and socks and suspenders; he needs also buttons and needles and thread and yarn and lace and braids, and sponges and combs and steel penpoints and pencils, and thimbles and silk ribbon; he needs everything and he has everything. Sam knows how to help himself.

Most preferably Sam goes to the New England states, Connecticut, Massachusetts, Rhode Island and whatever their names are. Here there are few or altogether no Germans and Sam no longer likes to deal with Germans, since the "how much'ing," i.e., dealing with Americans, has become ever clearer to him. Sam's greatest affliction are the dogs on the farms and it is peculiar, but there is on American soil no dog that does not bark and bite whenever a Jewish peddler comes. Sam would therefore rather not be taken for a Jew, and he forbids his German countrymen to greet him as such. To the American farmer he poses as a Canadian Frenchman and the American acts as if he believes it. Only the accursed dogs do not believe it; it is not the odor of a Canadian Frenchman!

Sam travels only by day. "Night is no man's friend," says Sam, "and for heroic valor there are the soldiers!" After two years Sam no longer travels on foot. He does not particularly love exertion and a little wagon and horses are frequently obtainable cheaply. And in a fortnight the little wagon and horse have paid for themselves, as Sam now carries also cigars and goldware from Paris. God knows that this tobacco was not grown in Havana, but in the Palatinate, and Sam knows it, too, but the farmers and their farmhands don't know it. God knows that Sam's Parisian goldware, his watch chains, his brooches, his lockets, his watches, his earrings, have never seen Paris, but come from the famous city of Providence, where nothing but Gmund gold is wrought, with no more than six carats and no less than four carats. God knows it, and Sam knows it, too, but the farmer's wives don't know it and the young fellows, who are glad to leave "mementoes" to the girls, do not know it either. This ignorance brings in a lot of money to the peddler and one sees from this that ignorance, too, is good for something.

Thus it goes on for several years, but not for longer; for the peddler's business has one great unpleasantness. Sam dare not show himself twice in the same place. Such Parisian gold turns gray and smudgy all too soon, and not everybody wants to puff at his cigars, let alone suffer their odor. Sam is afraid of the cudgels; he knows their taste. Therefore Sam makes a quick decision. He gives up peddling, returns to New York after he has made a few hundred dollars, settles down and marries Rebeksche.

Sam is now a made man. He speaks nothing but English, because he

has completely unlearned German. His sign does not read "Sam Ferkelche," God forbid; it says "Simmy Fairchild." Sam has become Americanized.

Early Peddlers in Vermont
(1890)

Sixty years ago, i.e., about 1890, peddlers were frequently seen along
roads and farms of Wilmington and other towns in southern Vermont.
They seldom tried to sell their wares at homes in villages; but, on the
fringes to towns, they stopped at every farmhouse along the way.

The early peddlers were all pack peddlers, i.e., they carried their
stock of goods on their backs and traveled on foot. There were even
women peddlers in this part of the state. The women were dark skinned
and looked like gypsies. Some were Armenians. . . .

The peddlers' packs, strapped to their backs, sometimes weighed
nearly 100 pounds. They never stole from any farmer or molested
anyone. There was Louis Salkins from North Adams, Massachusetts,
who is believed to have been a Syrian Catholic. He weighed 250 pounds
and his pack weighed about 150 pounds. About 1900 he obtained a team
of chestnut horses and a peddler's cart to carry his goods. There was also
John Solomon, antecedents unknown, and two others who traveled with
horse and wagon, supposedly as dry goods peddlers, but their chief items
of stock were liquor and contraceptives.

Ben Schimelinski, a Jew from Bennington, started his selling career
as a pack peddler. He bought damaged or "irregular" goods from the
mills in Bennington. His wares, while not perfect, were of a quality which
would wear well. In a pair of socks, one might be blue while the other
was green. The fact that one sleeve of a wool undershirt or one leg of a
pair of drawers was two or three inches longer than its mate did not affect
its warmth or wearing ability. His sons worked with him when they were
grown. It is only within the last few years, after the old man died, that
their car and truck have stopped coming around the neighborhood.

There was a small blond tin peddler named Spitzer. Also a Muslim,
Mahmoud Wahba, who was either a Turk or an Arab. He was known as

---

About once a year the Green Mountain Folklore Society puts out a mimeographed
publication called *Green Mountain Whittlin's*. It consists largely of Vermont folktales and
of local residents' reminiscences of the happenings of their youth. These recollections about
early peddlers in Vermont are in Volume 2, c. 1950, pp. 55-58, and Volume 4, c. 1952, p. 30.

"Black Bob." At this writing, Black Bob is still alive and is believed to be about 100 years old. He does not know his exact birth date. He is living in Searsburg, Vermont. He lives in a tarpaper shack on Searsburg Mountain, alone, almost blind. He is the only one left of the old peddlers.

—Elizabeth Covey, Wilmington, Vermont

✿ ✿ ✿ ✿ ✿

"Old Zack" was a well-known peddler in the area around Montpelier, Vermont. He was a Russian Jew. He would never eat any meat, but loved cucumbers, of which he ate many when they were in season. He often stayed in my grandmother's house. He always drank tea. He started out with a horse and wagon and having his goods in two packs. He ended up traveling with only one pack. He was very much afraid of dogs.

—Daisy C. Young, Montpelier, Vermont

✿ ✿ ✿ ✿ ✿

Isaac Rosenberg, familiarly known as Old Flatnose, traveled through North Cambridge. He was always sure of a welcome. Peddlers brought a welcome breath of the outside world to these backwoods homes and all the thrills of a shopping trip in the city.

The Stern brothers carried packs through Pleasant Valley. Years later they opened a department store and mail order house in New York City.

—Henrietta Ellsworth, Cambridge, Vermont

A POSSIBLE EXPLANATION
(1892)

"You are a Jew, are you not?" asked the prejudiced man from New Hampshire of the elderly gentleman who was seated next to him on the train going to Boston.

"Yes," replied the elderly gentleman, "I am a Jew."

"Well, I'm not," the Yankee said proudly, "and I am happy to say that in the little village where I live there is not a single Jew."

To which the elderly gentleman quietly responded, "Perhaps that is why it is still a village."

A COOL CAT
(1902)

The new Hebrew teacher of Congregation Beth Israel on Chestnut Street in Springfield, Massachusetts, was very surprised when he came into his classroom for the first time and found only one boy present. When he inquired about the whereabouts of the other students, he was informed that they were out throwing cats into the Connecticut River. He was horrified.

A few minutes later, another boy arrived. "Why are you tardy?" the teacher asked angrily.

"I was throwin' cats in the river," the boy replied.

"How perfectly terrible! How could you do such a thing?"

One by one the students came into class, all with the same story. Finally, the last pupil, a very small boy, walked in. "Well, young man," said the teacher coldly, "what is your excuse? Were you throwing cats into the river, too?"

"No, sir. How could I?" the wet and sniffling youngster responded. "I'm Katz!"

FAITH DOETH MANY THINGS*
(1910)

Some American Orthodox synagogues still auction off ritualistic honors, especially on Jewish holy days.

One Yom Kippur Bostonian Samuel Gordon took his Irish neighbor to the synagogue so that he might witness the manner in which Jews observe this holiest of days. For several hours the visitor sat spellbound, listening to the cantor and the people's chanting of the prayers in the solemn ritual. Finally the praying stopped and the bidding for the ritual honors began.

"Who will pay twenty dollars for *Maftir Yonah* [the privilege of chanting in Hebrew the prophetic Book of Jonah]?" cried the shammus [the sexton].

The voice of Gordon was heard: "Thirty dollars."

"I bid sixty!" yelled the Irishman.

---

*Contributed by Rabbi Alfred J. Kolatch.

Gordon grabbed his friend's arm. "What are you doing?" he hissed. "Have you lost your mind?"

"Nothing of the sort," the Irishman replied. "I've known you a long time, Gordon. If you offer thirty dollars, whatever it is, it must be worth at least a hundred!"

A Great American Becomes a Great Zionist
(1912)

A son was born to Adolf and Frederica Dembitz Brandeis in Louisville, Kentucky, on November 13, 1856. He was named Louis David Brandeis.

Adolf had been forced to flee from Germany in 1848 after the failure of the revolution. Frederica came to Louisville from Zirke in the province of Posen, then in Prussia, now in Poland. Her brother, Lewis N. Dembitz, was an outstanding Jewish scholar and devoutly Orthodox; but Frederica and her husband were freethinkers. They acknowledged their Jewish origins but never identified in any way with Jewish religious life. They gave their children no formal religious training of any kind. In her *Reminiscences*, Frederica wrote that religion and ethics are synonymous, religious customs and practices unnecessary. "Love, virtue and truth are the foundations upon which the education of the child must be based." She had given her children "something that neither could be argued away nor would have to be given up as untenable, namely, a pure spirit and the highest ideals of morals and love. God has blessed my efforts."

Brandeis admired his uncle but was deeply influenced by his parents, especially his mother. When he reached maturity, he changed his middle name from David to Dembitz as a sign of his profound affection for his mother. He never was a member of a synagogue, either before or after his conversion to Zionism. Until he became a Zionist, Brandeis did not consider himself even ethnically Jewish. He did contribute, occasionally and modestly, to Jewish charities. In 1891 he married his second cousin, Alice Goldmark, niece of Austrian composer Karl Goldmark and daughter of New York chemist Joseph Goldmark. Louis and Alice were united in marriage by ex-rabbi Felix Adler, founder and leader of the Ethical Culture Society and also a son-in-law of Joseph Goldmark.

Brandeis was graduated from his Louisville high school at the head of his class at age fourteen. He was graduated from Harvard Law School at the head of his class at age twenty. He was admitted to the Massachusetts bar at age twenty-one. He practiced law in Boston from 1878 to 1916, when President Woodrow Wilson named him Associate Justice of the United States Supreme Court.

Louis' Uncle Lewis was an ardent Zionist. Louis may have acquired an intellectual interest in the movement from his uncle. After he read a magazine article about the first Zionist Congress in Basle, Switzerland, in 1897, he said to his wife, "Now there is a movement to which I could give myself." But the Zionists made no effort to enlist Brandeis' support nor did he contact them.

His interest in Jewish matters was aroused in a somewhat round-about fashion. In 1910, as a recognized authority on industrial law and champion of the underdog, Brandeis was asked to serve as chairman of the arbitration board set up to settle a New York City garment workers' strike. The union leaders involved, as well as the rank and file, were mostly Jewish. For the first time in his life Brandeis was in a situation where he came face to face for days on end with his fellow Jews. To Brandeis' surprise and delight, he found the experience exciting and rewarding. Although his Jewish background was predominantly West European and these Jewish workers were predominantly East European, Brandeis felt very much at ease with them. They were his kind of people; they measured up to his high standards of intelligence, integrity, and idealism. From this experience Brandeis became convinced that the Jews are a very special kind of people and came to understand that he was one of these people; he belonged to them and they belonged to him. Now he began to refer to the Jews as "my people." Before the New York experience ended he had become emotionally and intellectually Jewish, proud of his ethnic roots, aware of his ethnic obligations.

While he was in this mood he made the acquaintance of Jacob de Haas, editor of a Boston Jewish weekly. De Haas had been a good friend of Theodore Herzl and English secretary at the first Zionist Congress. A persuasive exponent of Herzl's vision, he won the heart and mind of Louis Brandeis. Brandeis joined the Federation of American Zionists in August 1912 and immediately offered his services as a recruiter of additional members. During the remainder of 1912 and all of 1913, Brandeis spoke all over the country on behalf of the Zionist cause. By the end of 1913 he was one of the acknowledged leaders of American Zionism and remained so for the rest of his life.

When World War I broke out, the center of international Zionist activity shifted from Europe to the United States. On August 30, 1914, the Provisional Executive Committee for General Zionist Affairs was formed in New York City. Brandeis was unanimously elected chairman. This meant that this johnny-come-lately was to be, at least for the duration of the war, the head of the world Zionist organization. By this time Brandeis had become an avid reader of everything he could find on "the Jewish question." Being the genius that he was, he not only became well informed on the subject but also developed his own set of ideas for resolving the "question."

Brandeis felt embarrassed about being placed in a position of such great responsibility after such a short Zionist apprenticeship. Following his election as chairman, he told the gathering:

> "I recognize that I am not fully qualified for this task. Through-
> out so many years of my professional life I have been, to a very
> considerable degree, separated from the Jewish people. I am very
> ignorant on the subject of Judaism. But recent professional experi-
> ences of mine have taught me that Jews and the Jewish people
> represent in themselves and have long represented those qualities
> which we are seeking to preserve in our 20th century struggle for
> justice and democracy. The Jew has a deep moral feeling; a deep
> sense of the brotherhood of man; and a high intelligence—all of
> these individually and together being the fruit of three thousand
> years of civilized effort."

Brandeis and those who worked with him on the Provisional Executive Committee made one serious miscalculation. They really did not
think that their committee was provisional. They thought they were
taking over the direction of the international Zionist movement permanently. They did not comprehend that the European Zionists were
permitting them to occupy a position of centrality in world Zionist affairs
only for the duration of World War I.

"Zionism and Patriotism," a speech by Brandeis, has become a
Zionist classic. Brandeis felt no conflict between his Zionism and his
Americanism. Every Jew, he maintained, has a free choice either to
become a pioneer in Palestine or, while continuing to be a loyal citizen of
his native or adopted country, to support the efforts of those Jews who
choose to live in Palestine. His stand on the relationship of Zionism to
Jewishness was clear-cut: A Jew who is not a Zionist is not a good Jew.
"To be good Americans, we must be better Jews, and to be better Jews,
we must become Zionists." At another time he said, "Assimilation is
national suicide. There must be a land where the Jew may lead a natural
life, where the Hebrew language is spoken and the spirit of the Jew
prevails."

Together with Woodrow Wilson and Stephen S. Wise, Brandeis
played a key role in the negotiations that led to the issuing of the Balfour
Declaration by the British government on November 2, 1917, a declaration generally interpreted as a promise that a Jewish state would be
established in Palestine at the end of the war. Brandeis threw himself
enthusiastically into the task of preparing for the creation of such a state.
In March 1919 the celebrated British Jewish novelist Israel Zangwill
proposed that Brandeis be elected the first President of Palestine.
William Jennings Bryan, noted orator and former American Secretary of
State, declared he would support with equal ardor the candidacy of
Justice Brandeis for the presidency of either Palestine or the United
States.

In the spring of 1919 Brandeis went to London and met Chaim Weizmann. The meeting was cordial but the two became aware almost immediately that each was determined to become the number one leader of international Zionism. Brandeis wrote his wife that, although Weizmann was neither as great nor as objective as many believed, he was, nevertheless, a very great man. Weizmann privately expressed his concern that Brandeis was possessed by a Messianic fervor. From London Brandeis went to Palestine. He was enthralled. It was everything he expected and more. He wrote home: "What I have seen of California and the Grand Canyon seems less beautiful than the view from the Mount of Olives upon the Dead Sea and the country below. . . . Our way is long, our path difficult; but the struggle is worthwhile. This is indeed a Holy Land."

Upon donning the robe of a Supreme Court justice in 1916, Brandeis had no intention of diminishing the intensity of his Zionist interests and activities. Zionism, he believed, was in the private sector of his life. It would not in the least influence his work or his decisions as a member of the highest American tribunal.

But by 1920 this had become for him a matter of utmost concern. The struggle for world Zionist leadership between Weizmann and himself became acute, particularly because each represented a Zionist philosophy that completely contradicted the position of the other. Weizmann favored continuous political action, continuous pressure on the world powers to have a Palestinian Jewish state established as quickly as possible. Brandeis wanted a strong economic Jewish buildup in Palestine before the beginning of an all-out effort to create a Jewish state. To Brandeis' dismay, the Zionists outside of America favored Weizmann's position, although the European Zionists agreed that efforts for economic development should proceed simultaneously with the political battle.

Brandeis finally realized that he must make a choice: He must either leave the United States Supreme Court and devote himself entirely to fighting for his point of view within the world Zionist organization, a step many of his supporters were urging him to take; or, if he wished to remain on the Supreme Court, he must give up his ambition to control the destiny of world Zionism. After a lengthy period of soul searching, he reluctantly decided to accept the latter alternative. He felt that the role America was destined to play in world affairs and the contribution he could make to our country's future as an American liberal and a Jewish idealist required that he remain on the Court. He agreed to be a behind-the-scenes advisor on Zionist affairs. This he felt was as far as he could go, and this was the part he would play in the development of Zionism during the next two decades.

In 1921 the ideological contest for supremacy between the economist and the politician reached a climax. That year the annual convention of the Zionist Organization of America supported Weizmann's position over that of Brandeis by a vote of about two to one. A number of prominent American Zionists, including Brandeis and Stephen S. Wise, promptly resigned from the World Zionist Organization. They retained their memberships in the Zionist Organization of America but for a few years refused to participate in the formal deliberations of that body.

Weizmann carried forward his political program by organizing what became the Jewish Agency for Palestine. Brandeis put his economic views into operation by helping to create the Palestine Economic Corporation, popularly known as the P.E.C., one of the chief instrumentalities in strengthening Jewish industries and agriculture in Palestine. The basic difference between these two Zionist geniuses was rooted in their differences in background and temperament. For East European-born Weizmann, Zionism was essentially an emotional drive designed to emancipate his East European brethren from their miserable ghettos. For West European-oriented Brandeis, Zionism was essentially an intellectual crusade, begun in late middle age and spurred on by the hope that a Palestinian Jewish state would be literally an *or lagoyim*, a beacon light of Jewish idealism that would radiate its influence over all the world. In his thinking and his vision, Brandeis reflected the thoughts and dreams of many other great Zionists, including Martin Buber, Felix Frankfurter, Asher Ginzberg (Achad Ha-Am), Judah Leon Magnes, Abba Hillel Silver, Henrietta Szold, and Stephen S. Wise.

After 1921 Brandeis occupied no official position in the Zionist Organization of America. Unofficially he was, to the end of his life, its mentor and guide. There was a private wire from the ZOA national office in New York to the judge's office in Washington. Every morning Brandeis received from the ZOA office a telephonic briefing on the business of the preceding day and a description of pending matters, concerning which he expressed his reactions and proffered his advice. The "old man," as he was affectionately known in the ZOA inner circle, was considered the most gifted and wisest mind in American Zionism. His counsel was valued and heeded. The existence of this private wire was for many years a well-kept secret, lest Mr. Justice Brandeis of the United States Supreme Court be accused by Jew-haters of being a disloyal American, a nefarious "Elder of Zion." Such an accusation would have been completely baselesss. Louis Dembitz Brandeis was a noble combination of environment and heredity—he was among the most loyal of Americans and the most faithful of Zionists.

On February 13, 1939, at age eighty-two, Brandeis resigned from the Supreme Court. On October 5, 1941, less than six weeks before his eighty-fifth birthday, Louis Brandeis died.

Stephen Wise who, more than any other person in American public life, knew the Brandeis character in all its brilliant facets—the intellectual genius, the people's advocate, the American dreamer, the dedicated Zionist—wrote in his autobiography:

"Since the days of Herzl, Brandeis was indisputably and incomparably our greatest Jew. I think not of his gifts as an economist, or even his genius as a statesman, least of all of his boundless personal generosity. Rather do I think of the spirit he brought to our [the Zionist] cause that I can best describe by using the Hebrew term *kedusha*, consecration, holiness."

TRADITION, TRADITION!
(1920)

In 1920 a Jewish family in Boston named Kabotshnick petitioned the court for permission to change its name to Cabot. Members of the famed Massachusetts socialite clan, "the" Cabots, were successful in persuading the judge to refuse the request on the basis that the surname Cabot is deeply imbedded in New England tradition and should be borne only by those who inherit the name from their parents. As a consequence of this legal decision, the following satirical lines were penned:

Here's to Massachusetts,
The land of the bean and the cod,
Where the Lodges can't speak to the Cabots
Because the Cabots speak Yiddish, by God!

DID THEY EVER FIND OUT WHO DID IT?
(1924)

The new young rabbi in the small Maine community made his first visit to one of the classes in his Hebrew School. Wishing to test the students' knowledge of the Bible, he asked one boy, "Who knocked down the walls of Jericho?"

"It warn't me, rabbi," the boy answered.

The teacher of the class said, "Rabbi, Jake's a good'un. If he says he didn't do it, I'll warrant he didn't do it."

Wishing to emphasize how greatly the religious schoolchildren needed improvement in their Biblical instruction, the rabbi reported the incident at the next meeting of the synagogue board. After a moment of silence, the president of the congregation said, "Wel-l-l, rabbi, there really ain't any point in makin' a big fuss over the matter. The shul will pay for the damage and jes' charge it off to childish foolishness. You know how kids are. Boys will be boys."

"HIYA, BABE!"
(1944)

First Lieutenant Frances Y. Slanger of Roxbury, Massachusetts, waded ashore on a Normandy beachhead on D-Day plus four [June 10, 1944]. She and three other nurses who were her tentmates set up a field hospital at St. Mare Eglise. There was heavy fighting all around and, in still wet uniforms, they were tending wounded within two hours after landing. It was four days before their barracks bags showed up, with a change of clothing. They slept, when they got the chance, on the ground. They stayed with the same medical platoon for five weeks and in that time cared for 3,000 men.

From Normandy Lieutenant Slanger went on with the advancing troops, deeper into France and then Belgium. She had been on frontline duty for more than four months when a shell struck her tent. Captain Isidore R. Schwartz of Far Rockaway, New York, found her there, still conscious but dying, and rushed her to a field hospital. She died half an hour later.

She was the first American nurse in World War II to die under the Nazi guns. That was on October 21, 1944. Seventeen days later, the GI newspaper *Stars and Stripes,* not yet knowing she had been killed, printed a letter to the editor which Nurse Slanger had written and mailed an hour or so before the German barrage in which she met her death.

She wrote it by the light of a flashlight, in a dark waterlogged tent during a driving rainstorm. The letter, which many a soldier clipped from his *Stars and Stripes* and long carried among his treasured possessions, was a fine, sensitive tribute to the American soldier, to the wounded who "do not cry." Unintentionally, too, it was a tribute to the good-humored and devoted nurse who wrote it—to the best in the wartime spirit of the Army Nurse Corps.

This is what Nurse Slanger wrote:

It is 0200 [2:00 A.M.] and I have been lying awake for an hour, listening to the steady, even breathing of the other three nurses in the

From *American Jews in World War II,* Volume I, pp. 147-51, by I. Kaufman, published by the National Jewish Welfare Board, New York, 1947.

tent, thinking about some of the things we had discussed during the day. The rain is beating down on the tent with torrential force. The wind is on a mad rampage and its main objective seems to be to lift the tent off its pole and fling it about our heads.

The fire is burning low and just a few live coals are on the bottom. With the slow feeding of wood and finally coal, a roaring fire is started. I couldn't help thinking how similar to a human being a fire is: If it is allowed to run down too low, and if there is a spark of life left in it, it can be nursed back. So can a human being. It is slow; it is gradual; it is done all the time in these field hospitals and other hospitals in the ETO [European Theatre of Operations].

We had read several articles in different magazines and papers sent in by a grateful GI praising the work of the nurses around the combat zones. Praising us—for what? I climb out of my cot. Lieutenant (Margaret M.) Bowler is the only one I waken. I whisper to her. Lieutenant (Christine) Cox and Lieutenant (Elizabeth F.) Powers slept on. Fine nurses and great girls to live with. Of course, like in all families, an occasional quarrel; but these are quickly forgotten.

I'm writing this by flashlight. In this light the place looks something like a "dive." In the center of the tent are two poles, one part chimney, the other a plain tentpole. Kindling wood lies in disorderly confusion on the damp ground. A French wine pitcher filled with water stands by. The GIs say we rough it. We in our little tent can't see it. True, we are set up in tents, sleep on cots and are subject to the temperament of the weather.

We wade ankle deep in mud—sometimes, when the guns go off, you have to lie in it. We are restricted to our immediate area, a cow pasture or a hayfield, but then who is not restricted? We have a stove and coal. We even have a laundry line in the tent. Our GI drawers are at this moment doing the dance of the pants what with the wind howling, the tent waving precariously, the rain beating down, the guns firing, and me with a flashlight, writing. It all adds up to a feeling of unrealness.

Sure we rough it, but, in comparison to the way you men are taking it, we can't complain, nor do we feel that bouquets are due us. But you, the men behind the guns, the men driving our tanks, flying our planes, sailing our ships, building bridges, and to the men who pave the way and to the men who are left behind—it is to you we doff our helmets. To every GI wearing the American uniform, for you we have the greatest admiration and respect.

Yes, this time we are handing out the bouquets—after taking care of some of your buddies, comforting them when they are brought in bloody, dirty with the earth, mud and grime, and most of them so tired. Somebody's brothers, somebody's fathers, somebody's sons, seeing them gradually brought back to life, to consciousness, and to see their lips separate into a grin when they first welcome you. Usually they kid, hurt as they are. It doesn't amaze us to hear one of them say, "Hiya, babe," or "Holy mackerel, an American woman!" or more indiscreetly, "Hey, how about a kiss?"

These soldiers stay with us but a short time, from ten days to possibly two weeks. We have learned a great deal about our American soldier and the stuff he is made of. The wounded do not cry. Their buddies come first.

The patience and determination they show, the courage and fortitude they have is sometimes awesome to behold. It is we who are proud to be here. Rough it? No, it is a privilege to be able to receive you and a great distinction to see you open your eyes and, with that swell American grin, say, "Hiya, babe!"

That's what she wrote.

They buried Lieutenant Slanger in a military cemetery on the Western front, with a wooden Star of David to mark her grave.

The Memorial Sermon at the Iwo Jima Cemetery
(1945)

The line between history and folklore is thin. Theoretically, the difference is that history consists of well-documented data and folklore of unauthenticated stories. In actual practice this neat differentiation does not hold up. There are unending complications and shadings in trying to make a distinction between the way it actually was and the way people say it was. In the reporting of any major event, ancient or recent, fact and fiction are inextricably and sometimes imperceptibly interwoven. Seldom does the full truth—in all its exactness and oftimes dullness—come to the surface. One of the basics of human nature is the attention-getting device known as exaggeration. How people love to exaggerate! The story created by the imagination is usually more exciting than the real one. Often folklore is history embellished and improved— also much of what is called history is really folklore—for example, who really won a particular struggle will depend primarily on which side of the conflict were the history writer or his ancestors.

The two most widely known stories involving Jewish chaplains during World War II were 1) the heroic death of Chaplain Alexander Goode and his three fellow chaplains on the USS *Dorchester* in February 1943 and 2) the sermon delivered by Chaplain Roland B. Gittelsohn at the dedication of a military cemetery on Iwo Jima in the spring of 1945.

No one has questioned the quintessence of the *Dorchester* story, i.e., four brave clergymen sacrificed their own lives so that others would have the opportunity to survive. But there have been some who have challenged the accuracy of a few details of the accepted account, particularly the description of the four chaplains standing together, linked arm to arm, in the stern of the boat as the *Dorchester* went down. Those who have endured one or more such torpedoings say that the confusion, the chaotic conditions that prevail aboard a vessel in such a catastrophic time, the comparatively brief period between the moment the boat is hit and its sinking, would have made it virtually impossible for the chaplains to have found each other before the ship sank to the bottom. Whether this conjoining did or did not occur would seem to be immaterial to the main thrust of the event; but there is no question that the picture it conveyed added a very dramatic quality to the grim facts surrounding the demise of four courageous young men. It is because of the attraction of such high drama that history is often transmuted into folklore and vice versa.

So it was with Gittelsohn's sermon at the Iwo Jima cemetery dedication. The picture that was drawn is a beautiful one: A Jewish chaplain in a time of deadly combat is chosen by his fellow chaplains to deliver the principal address at a joint service dedicating a battlefield cemetery, and he responds by preaching a brilliant memorial sermon which is an inspiring appeal for world peace and brotherhood, and a scathing denunciation of the immorality and futility of war. A-OK, as the soldiers were wont to say—except that that isn't the way it was. The sermon was a masterpiece, no doubt about that; but it was not delivered in an atmosphere of spiritual understanding and brotherly good will.

First a few facts about Gittelsohn and Iwo Jima.

Roland B. Gittelsohn is one of the most brilliant and respected rabbis of our day. He was rabbi of Central Synagogue of Nassau County, Rockville Centre, New York, from 1936 to 1953. After 1953 he was rabbi of Temple Israel of Boston, Massachusetts. He served as a chaplain in the U.S. Marines from 1943 to 1946.

The word for "island" in Japanese is *jima*. So Iwo Jima is the island of Iwo, a tiny atoll of rock, gravel, and sand less than eight square miles in size. It was and still is a minute part of the main island system of Japan. Iwo Jima was the first bit of territory invaded by Americans that had been an integral part of Japan before the military clique of that country embarked on its ill-fated campaign of conquest. On Iwo one of the bloodiest battles of the Pacific war was fought between the Japanese and three divisions of America's sea-soldiers, the United States Marines. The invasion began on February 19, 1945. The fighting ended on March 16. The American dead numbered 4,590. The Japanese dead were estimated to exceed 20,000.

The dedication of the Iwo Jima cemetery took place before the end of the battle. Chaplain Gittelsohn describes what happened:

It is commonly supposed throughout the country·that the sermon I delivered at the dedication of the Fifth Marine Division Cemetery on Iwo Jima was preached at a common, interdenominational Service of Dedication. It was not. And therein lies my saddest experience of brothers in arms.

Our Division Chaplain, Warren Cuthriell, had indeed originally planned such a joint service. First there was to be a secular dedication at which, of course, the address would be given by our Commanding General. Immediately thereafter all three faiths were to unite in a combined Religious Memorial Service, after which any group that so wished would be free to hold its own denominational service. As an eloquent expression of his own devotion to the teachings of Christianity and the high truths of democracy, Chaplain Cuthriell invited me, as spokesman for the smallest religious minority in the Division, to preach the memorial sermon.

I learned later that, immediately after the announcement of his plans, two of our Protestant chaplains visited Cuthriell to express their vigorous objection to the Jewish chaplain preaching over graves which were predominantly those of Christians. His answer was that the right of the Jewish chaplain to preach such a sermon was precisely one of the things for which we were fighting the war. Then the six Catholic padres with us on Iwo sent their senior representative to the Division Chaplain to speak for all of them. They were opposed in general to any joint Service of Memorial, and they were opposed in particular to a sermon preached by the Jewish chaplain! Furthermore, if the Division Chaplain insisted on carrying out his original intention, they would refuse to participate or even attend!

All this I discovered only later. Ten days had passed between the invitation to preach at the cemetery and the day when Chaplain Cuthriell called me in to explain his dilemma. The objection of the two Protestants he could withstand. The objection of an entire church, which would surely have made a *cause célèbre* out of the incident, was another matter. I had no right to expose my senior to that kind of embarrassment. I withdrew.

After a brief secular dedication, each faith went to its own specified corner to hold its own Service of Memorial. The sermon I had written for the combined service was actually delivered at our own little Jewish service. Perhaps it should be added here that not one word of the original manuscript was changed as a result of this incident. Whatever in the sermon may seem to reflect the background of its delivery had been written before any of the foregoing was even known to me.

I do not remember anything in my life that made me so painfully heartsick. We had just come through nearly five weeks of miserable hell. Some of us had tried to serve men of all faiths and of no faith, without making denomination or affiliation a prerequisite for help. Protestants, Catholics and Jews had lived together, fought together, died together, and now lay buried together. But we the living could not unite to pray together! My chief consolation at the moment was that another Jew besides myself would have been unacceptable as dedicator of the cemetery—even though these very men professed to teach in his name!

So the picture of wartime understanding is not nearly as lovely and unblemished as our professional back-patters would like to pretend. At the same time, however, it would be just as dangerous to assume that this kind of experience constitutes the whole picture as it would be to accept the other extreme of wishful thinking. Along with the heartache of open discrimination by fellow chaplains, I found also much that was enheartening. Paradoxically enough, the wide publicity given my Iwo sermon was a direct result of the prejudice which prevented its being preached as originally intended.

When the inside story of the cemetery dedication plans became known to the other chaplains in our Division, three of the Protestant ministers were so incensed that they boycotted their own religious service to attend mine as members of my congregation! It was one of these three who, after our Yizkor service, borrowed the only carbon of my sermon and, unknown to me, mimeographed several thousand copies which he distributed all over the island.

One other inspiring experience remains with me indelibly. It was our last night on Iwo before sailing away. Three chaplains were still on duty in the Division Cemetery. Since bodies were still being brought in for burial, we held off our final Service of Committal as long as possible to be sure all would be included. Finally, as we descended into the last grim trench of graves, darkness had already fallen. Off to the west the last suspicion of light was reluctant to leave the sky. Overhead there were stars. It was the first night since our arrival that no sounds of firing could be heard from the cemetery. All around there was peace—great, embracing, quiet peace. And three chaplains—a Baptist, a Methodist, a Jew—wearier than they had ever been before, climbed into the trench, stood there together before the last row of graves, and held the flashlight for each other as they prayed. It is just as impossible to forget the brotherhood and love of men like these as it would be to erase the jealous hatred of the others.

❈   ❈   ❈   ❈   ❈

Let us now turn to the sermon itself. In the opinion of many, it may be the greatest religious message to come out of World War II.

This is perhaps the grimmest and surely the holiest task we have faced since D-Day. Here before us lie the bodies of comrades and friends. Men who until yesterday or last week laughed with us, joked with us, trained with us. Men who were on the same ships with us, and went over the sides with us as we prepared to hit the beaches of this island. Men who fought with us and feared with us. Somewhere in this plot of ground there may lie the man who could have discovered the cure for cancer. Under one of these Christian crosses, or beneath a Jewish Star of David, there may rest now a man who was destined to be a great prophet, for all to live in plenty, with poverty and hardship for none. Now they lie here silently in this sacred soil, and we gather to consecrate this earth in their memory.

It is not easy to do so. Some of us have buried our closest friends here. We saw these men killed before our very eyes. Any one of us might have died in their places. Indeed, some of us are alive and breathing at this very moment only because men who lie here beneath us had the courage and strength to give their lives for ours. To speak in memory of such men as these is not easy. Of these, too, can it be said with utter truth: "The world will little note nor long remember what we say here. It can never forget what they did here."

No, our poor power of speech can add nothing to what these men and the other dead of our division who are not here have already done. All that we can even hope to do is follow their example. To show the same selfless courage in peace that they did in war. To swear that, by the grace of God and the stubborn strength and power of human will, their sons and ours shall never suffer these pains again. These men have done their job well. They have paid the ghastly price of freedom. If that freedom be once again lost, as it was after the last war, the unforgivable blame will be ours, not theirs. So it is we "the living" who are here to be dedicated and consecrated.

We dedicate ourselves, first, to live together in peace the way they fought and are buried in this war. Here lie men who loved America because their ancestors generations ago helped in her founding, and other men who loved her with equal passion because they themselves or their own fathers escaped from oppression to her blessed shores. Here lie officers and men, Negroes and whites, rich men and poor ... together. Here are Protestants, Catholics, and Jews ... together. Here no man prefers another because of his faith or despises him because of his color. Here there are no quotas of how many from each group are admitted or allowed. Among these men there is no discrimination. No prejudices. No hatred. Theirs is the highest and purest democracy.

Any man among us "the living" who fails to understand that will thereby betray those who lie here dead. Whoever of us lifts his hand in hate against a brother, or thinks himself superior to those who happen to be in the minority, makes of this ceremony and of the bloody sacrifices it commemorates, an empty, hollow mockery. To this, then, as our solemn, sacred duty, do we the living now dedicate ourselves: to the right of Protestants, Catholics, and Jews, of white men and Negroes alike, to enjoy the democracy for which all of them have here paid the price.

To one thing more do we consecrate ourselves in memory of those who sleep beneath these crosses and stars. We shall not foolishly suppose, as did the last generation of America's fighting men, that victory on the battlefield will automatically guarantee the triumph of democracy at home. This war, with all its frightful heartache and suffering, is but the beginning of our generation's struggle for democracy. When the last battle has been won, there will be those at home, as there were last time, who will want us to turn our backs in selfish isolation on the rest of organized humanity, and thus to sabotage the very peace for which we fight. We promise you who lie here: We will not do that! We will join hands with Britain, China, Russia—in peace, even as we have in war, to build the kind of world for which you died.

When the last shot has been fired, there will still be those whose eyes are turned backward, not forward, who will be satisfied with those wide extremes of poverty and wealth in which the seeds of another war can breed. We promise you, our departed comrades: This, too, we will not permit. This war has been fought for the common man; its fruits of peace must be enjoyed by the common man! We promise, by all that is sacred and holy, that your sons—the sons of miners and millers, the sons of farmers and workers—will inherit from your death the right to a living that is decent and secure.

When the final cross has been placed in the last cemetery, once again there will be those to whom profit is more important than peace, who will insist with the voice of sweet reasonableness and appeasement that it is better to trade with the enemies of mankind than, by crushing them, to lose their profit. To you who sleep here silently, we give our promise: We will not listen! We will not forget that some of you were burnt with oil that came from American wells, that many of you were killed by shells fashioned from American steel. We promise that when once again men seek profit at your expense, we shall remember how you looked when we placed you reverently, lovingly, in the ground.

Thus do we memorialize those who, having ceased living with us, now live within us. Thus do we consecrate ourselves, the living, to carry on the struggle they began. Too much blood has gone into this soil for us to let it lie barren. Too much pain and heartache have fertilized the earth on which we stand. We here solemnly swear: This shall not be in vain! Out of this, and from the suffering and sorrow of those who mourn, this will come—we promise—the birth of a new freedom for the sons of men everywhere.

Amen.

GOTT VEYS VUSS ER TUT

(1947)

An elderly woman, a survivor of the Nazi concentration camps, came to Worcester, Massachusetts, to live with her grandson. She was supremely happy, except for one thing: She could not speak English. This made going to the store quite a problem.

One day, while her grandson and his wife were at work, she went into a supermarket to buy a chicken. She stood in front of the butcher, flapped her arms wildly in the air and then, to make sure that the butcher understood, she gave out with a shrill cock-a-doodle-do, so loud that it was heard from one end of the establishment to the other.

The butcher grinned. "Grandma," he said in Yiddish, in a soft, kind voice, "just tell me what you want. With me, you don't have to wave your arms or make such noises."

"Bawruch ha-Shem! Praise the Lord!" cried the old lady, also in Yiddish. "You speak Yiddish!" Then she smiled. "So now I can stop talking to you in English!"

Now You Know
(1957)

Mrs. Rosenberg, whose features were as unmistakably Jewish as her accent, was stranded one evening in a very "exclusive" resort section of Cape Cod—"exclusive" meaning that Jews were excluded. She needed accommodations for the night. She entered the town's only good hotel, a posh establishment, and approached the desk.

"I vould like, please, a room for the night," said Mrs. Rosenberg.

The desk clerk made a quick appraisal of his visitor and shook his head. "Sorry," he said curtly.

"Vy you're sorry?"

"The hotel is full, madam."

"So vy the sign says 'rooms available?'"

The desk clerk hesitated and then confessed, "We don't admit Jews."

Mrs. Rosenberg drew herself up to her full height of five feet and addressed him heatedly: "From vere comes to you the idea that I am Jewish? From vere you get such a crazy idea? From vere? It so heppens that I'm a convoitable."

"You're what?"

"A convoitable. For a long time I'm vatching on the teewée this Fulton Shine and, finally, from listening to him, I'm convoited into a Kedillac."

"Ah, I see," the desk clerk said. "You're a Cadillac convertible."

"Execkly," responded Mrs. Rosenberg.

"Well, I happen to be a Catholic myself," said the innkeeper's vassal. "Do you mind if I test your knowledge of the religion?"

"Test! Test!"

"How was Jesus born?"

"From a voigin he was born. His mama's name was Mary and his papa's name was Yussel."

"Very good. Now tell me: Where was Jesus born?"

"He vas gevayn geborned in a menager."

"That's right. And why was he born in a manger?"

"Because," snapped Mrs. Rosenberg, "some paskudnyak [nauseating person, i.e., louse] like you vouldn't give to a respectable Jewish married lady a room for the night!"

JFK AND THE CHASSIDIC REBBE
(1963)

The Chassidic Rebbe, Rabbi Nachum Twersky, is eighty-three years old and came to Israel during the past year. Thirty-five years ago, fleeing from the persecutions of the anti-religious Soviet regime, he settled in Chelsea, a suburb of Boston.

The scion of a distinguished Chassidic dynasty, his influence in Orthodox Jewish circles of the Greater Boston area was considerable and was sought by both non-Jews and Jews, particularly in political matters. It was in this connection that he met Joseph Kennedy. A close friendship developed between the two.

At their second meeting, Joe Kennedy introduced him to his young son Jack, then twelve years old. He asked the Rebbe to give Jack his · blessing. After that the Rebbe met Jack many times. "He captured my heart," said the Rebbe. "He was a handsome lad, bright-eyed, alert, and brilliant."

"Many years later," the Rebbe continued, "Jack came to me with a request. He reminded me how I had blessed him when he was a lad. Now he again wants my blessing and my help. He intends to run for Congress. Would I help him win the support of Jewish voters? I knew he was capable and promised to do what I could. And I offered my blessing for his success. After that, whenever he ran for office, whether the House or the Senate, he came for a blessing and for support.

"He was a religious man," the Rebbe went on. "He had deep religious feelings and a deep affection for the Jewish people." Even after his election to the Presidency, he retained a friendly contact with the Rebbe. "When his father suffered a stroke, the President called me and asked me to pray for his well-being. When the State of Israel celebrated its tenth anniversary, I asked him for ten minutes of his time at a celebration in my synagogue and he gave me thirty."

Before leaving for Israel, the Rebbe visited the President at the White House. "I said to him, 'Mr. President, I am going to Israel, but I am a little worried about the enemies who surround the state.' 'Don't worry,' answered the President. 'You have nothing to fear, I assure you.'"

As the Rebbe was about to leave him, the President asked Rebbe

Based on an article that appeared in the Israeli weekly *Panim el Panim* shortly after the assassination of President Kennedy. It was translated and printed in his congregational bulletin of December 18, 1963, by Hayim Goren Perelmuter, Rabbi of Isaiah Israel Congregation of Chicago, in the condensed form given here. The condensation is reprinted with the permission of Rabbi Perelmuter.

Twersky to pray for him at the tomb of David in Jerusalem. He then gave him a walking stick with a carved knob as a personal gift. As he did so, the President said, "Moses turned a stick into a serpent. Here is another stick to remind you that your fears will be turned into a shrivelled twig."

PART TWO

Middle Atlantic States

"Give Me Your Huddled Masses"

Introduction

The Middle Atlantic section of the United States—Delaware, Maryland and the District of Columbia, New Jersey, New York, Pennsylvania, and West Virginia—is, collectively, the section richest in both Jewish history and folklore.

The principal centers of importance during the first 300 years of American Judaism have been the states of New York and Pennsylvania and the cities of New York and Philadelphia. New York City must be regarded as uniquely outstanding. While it did not become the chief Jewish city of America until the middle of the nineteenth century, it has maintained this dominance for over 125 years and appears destined to retain this position for many years to come.

Delaware

The area that is now Delaware was settled by the Swedes in 1638, annexed by the Dutch in 1655, and taken over by the English in 1664. It was given to William Penn in 1682 and owned by his family until 1776. Although after 1704 it had its own provincial legislature, adopted its own constitution in 1776, fought in the War of Independence as a separate political entity and was the first state to ratify the federal constitution, until about the end of the eighteenth century Delaware was popularly thought to be a small and insignificant appendage of the Commonwealth of Pennsylvania.

While Jewish traders traveled through the Delaware countryside in colonial times to barter with the settlers and the Indians, very few found it enough to their liking to remain there permanently. Delaware laws denying Jews full political rights were on the books until 1792.

The first synagogue in Delaware was a long time coming. It was founded in Wilmington in 1880. There are now about 9,000 Jews in the state, 1.6 percent of the total population. Ninety-six percent of these Jews live in Wilmington. Because of the small number of Jews involved and the brevity of its Jewish communal history, Delaware has little to offer in the way of Jewish folklore.

Maryland and the District of Columbia

Maryland was founded in 1632. The Toleration Act of 1649 granted freedom of religion to Protestants and Catholics but not to Jews. Maryland's constitution, adopted in 1776, continued to discriminate against Jews, denying them the right to hold public office, to practice law, and to serve in the state militia. This discriminatory legislation was not repealed until 1826. The remedial law was not entirely free from religious bias. It still required that holders of public office affirm their belief in a system of future rewards and punishments, thus, technically at least, excluding agnostics and atheists.

This unhappy inability to distinguish between matters of church and state had a decided influence upon the history of the Jews in Maryland. The first Jew known to have come to Maryland was Dr. Jacob Lumbrozo, who arrived in 1654 or 1655. In 1658 Dr. Lumbrozo, already a well-known and important member of the community, was accused by the city fathers of having denied the divinity of Jesus. He was ordered held for trial on the charge of blasphemy. The trial was never held. Ten days after the preliminary hearing, a general amnesty was proclaimed in honor of the accession of Richard Cromwell to the Lord Protectorship of England.

However, the Jews got the message and stayed out of Maryland for a long time. There is no record of any other Jew settling in the colony until more than a century later, the exact year being 1773. Even then the Jews came in very slowly and warily. It was not until after the "Jew Bill" of 1826 gave the Jews full citizenship rights that the Jewish population of Baltimore began to expand rapidly. The first synagogue, Baltimore Hebrew Congregation, was organized in December 1829. Its rabbi from 1840 to 1849, Abraham Reiss, was the first American-ordained rabbi.

Maryland now has about 230,000 Jews, 5.6 percent of the state's population. Only New Jersey and New York have a higher Jewish ratio. Ninety-four thousand Jews live in Baltimore. Sixty-five thousand live in Montgomery and Prince Georges counties, which are suburban appendages of the District of Columbia.

*   *   *   *   *

While the first Jewish settler in what is now the District of Columbia arrived in 1795, the District was not carved out of the state of Maryland by Act of Congress until 1800. A local ordinance that only Christian churches are exempt from payment of property taxes was abrogated when Congress granted a charter in 1855 to the District's first synagogue, Washington Hebrew Congregation.

Jews did not begin to make their homes in the District in substantial numbers until after the Civil War. Presently there are 33,000 Jews living in the District, about 4.4 percent of the population. As indicated in a preceding paragraph, the 65,000 Jews in adjacent Maryland counties are also primarily families of federal government employees who work in the District. While the District has a very active Jewish religious and communal program, it has not been able to develop a vibrant local historical tradition because the periodic changes in the political climate have created in many of the District's Jews the same kind of mood found among Jews in the military, a sense of impermanence, no deepening of roots, "here today and gone tomorrow." Although many of America's most prominent Jews have lived and served for a time in Washington, their names and deeds are associated with their communities of permanent residence. A number of Jewish inhabitants of the District have achieved national prominence. Three of them are included in this book: test pilot Arthur L. Welsh, singer Al Jolson, and Rabbi Alexander D. Goode, one of the heroic "Four Chaplains."

New Jersey

New Jersey, colonized in 1614, was originally part of Dutch New Netherland. When the British conquered New Netherland in 1664, the Duke of York (later to become England's King James II) split the colony of New Jersey in two and gave each half to a friend. In 1702 the halves were reunited as one province. New Jersey was one of four of the original thirteen colonies that had no established church. Full freedom of worship was permitted; but only Protestants were allowed to hold public office. Non-Protestants were not granted full political equality until 1844.

The first Jew to reside in New Jersey seems to have been Aaron Louzada, who came from New York City to Bound Brook in 1698. His home was known as "the Jew House." There were no sizeable Jewish groups in New Jersey until the 1840s. The first Jewish congregation in the state was Bnai Jeshurun in Paterson, organized in 1847. Large numbers of Jews began to come into New Jersey in the 1880s.

The state now has about 425,000 Jews, 5.7 percent of the total population. Only New York state has a higher percentage of Jews. Realistically as well as Jewishly speaking, northeastern New Jersey may be said to be a suburb of New York City and much of southwestern New Jersey a suburb of Philadelphia.

New York

In American Jewish history and folklore, the state of New York is number one in every major category—in age, in size, and in importance. The decisive element in this situation is the Jewish community of New York City. Were it not for New York City the state of Pennsylvania would rate highest in American Jewish historical and folkloristic annals.

Italian Giovanni de Verrazano, employed by the French, entered what is now New York harbor in 1524. After that, French vessels often sailed up what is now the Hudson River to trade with the Indians. In July 1609 Frenchman Samuel de Champlain entered the state from the north; and in September of the same year Englishman Henry Hudson, employed by the Dutch, went up the river—later named for him—as far as his ship could go.

The Dutch built a military post on the southern tip of Manhattan Island in 1615 and another in 1616 on Castle Island, now part of Albany. The province of New Netherland was formally proclaimed in 1623. In 1664 it was seized by the British and its name changed to New York. Under the British, their Anglican denomination was the established church.

Originally New York City consisted of only two boroughs, Manhattan and the Bronx. In 1898 the city was expanded into five boroughs in this way: Kings County became the borough of Brooklyn; Staten Island became the borough of Richmond; and the communities of Long Island City, Flushing, Newtown, and Jamaica, with the rural lands surrounding them, the borough of Queens.

Nowadays when one speaks of Greater New York or Metropolitan New York, he or she is speaking of an augmented megalopolis which includes not only the five boroughs but also Westchester, Nassau, and the western half of Suffolk counties in New York; Bergen, Hudson, Essex, and Union counties in New Jersey; and western Fairfield County in Connecticut. This megalopolis is the largest, richest, busiest, and most important commercial center in the world. It contains just about as many Jews as there are in the whole State of Israel. As Jerusalem is the spiritual capital of world Jewry, so Greater New York may be said to be the business capital of world Jewry.

The Jews came to New Amsterdam in 1654 and to what is now Albany in 1655. The first congregation in Manhattan, Sephardic Shearith Israel, was organized no later than 1695. For at least 130 years it was the only synagogue in the area now known as Greater New York. Not until 1825 did the second congregation, Ashkenazic Bnai Jeshurun, come into being.

Many New York Jews will be surprised to learn that there was not a single organized Jewish community in the state outside of New York City until twelve Jewish families left the city and founded the agricultural colony of Sholem in Ulster County in 1837. The oldest existing congregation outside New York City is Beth Emeth of Albany, founded in 1838. The dates of the first congregations in other Jewish communities in the state are: 1841, Syracuse; 1847, Buffalo; 1848, Oswego, Poughkeepsie, Rochester, Utica; 1851, Brooklyn; 1853, Troy; 1854, Kingston, Newburgh; 1856, Schenectady; 1862, Elmira, Plattsburgh; 1870, Yonkers (first in Westchester County); 1888, Staten Island; 1889, the Bronx; 1896, Flushing (first on Long Island); 1907, Ellenville (first in the "borsht belt.")

Although the official state religion was Anglicanism, freedom of religion for all New Yorkers was decreed in 1674 by the Duke of York, who had abandoned the Anglican communion in 1672 for Roman Catholicism. As a result of this change in religious allegiances, the duke almost lost his chance to become king of England. He did make it to the throne in 1685 but was ousted three years later. The reason for his desposition: He was accused of trying to make Roman Catholicism the official British religion.

In 1737 the New York provincial legislature took away from the Jews the right to vote. The right was restored in 1777.

New York State has 2,200,000 Jews, 11.8 percent of the total population. This is more than twice the percentage in any other American state. Only 100,000 of these Jews live north of Westchester County. About 1,300,000 live within the five-borough area. This is about 16 percent of the total population of New York City.

As one might expect, New York State provides more Jewish curiosa than any other state. Here are some examples, gleaned from that recently published gold mine of information, *American Jewish Landmarks*, by Bernard Postal and Lionel Koppman:

How did the Nevele Country Club at Ellenville get its name? The Slutsky family that started the resort had eleven children. Nevele is eleven spelled backwards. . . . The Lubavitcher chassidim operate a kosher pizza parlor on Washington Avenue in Albany. . . . The oldest Jewish gravestone in the Catskills is a solitary monument on the land of the Rockland Light and Power Company in Lumberland Township, Sullivan County. It marks the grave of a Bohemian immigrant, an itinerant peddler robbed and murdered in 1851 while traveling through this then thickly forested area. The inscription on the stone says: "He was an honest man." . . . Mark Twain and his Jewish son-in-law, Ossip Gabrilowitsch, famous pianist, are buried next to each other in Woodlawn Cemetery, Elmira. A common headstone contains sculptured likenesses of the two men. . . . Six miles north of Newburgh and 1½ miles south of Marlboro, on Millhouse Road, just off Route 9-W, stands the Gomez

House, oldest existing house in North America built and occupied by Jews. Constructed of stone, it was built in about 1717 as a combined Indian trading post, fortress, and residence by Lewis Gomez and his son Daniel. . . . The 1970 census reported that New York City has 600 blacks and 65 Puerto Ricans who listed Yiddish as their mother tongue. . . . Nearly 100,000 Israelis live in New York City, making it "Israel's fourth largest city." . . . New Square, near Spring Valley, a Chassidic community of 1,300 people, was founded in 1961 by the followers of the Ukrainian Skvirer rebbe, Rabbi David Twersky. The Chassidim went to the Ramapo Township clerk's office and requested that their town be named New Skvira. The person who typed out the required application, under the impression that the bearded gentlemen before him were mispronouncing the second word in the proposed name, wrote down "New Square"—and New Square it has remained.

Pennsylvania

The most influential American Jewish communities in the period preceding the Revolution were Philadelphia and Newport, Rhode Island. New York City was somewhat less prominent, along with Lancaster, Pennsylvania, Richmond, Savannah, and Charleston.

The first Jew known to have settled in Pennsylvania was Isaac Miranda who migrated from Italy between 1715 and 1720 and settled first in Lancaster County and then in Philadelphia. Sometime after arriving in this country, he converted to Christianity. He died in 1732.

The first honest-to-goodness Jew to become a Philadelphian seems to have been Nathan Levy, who moved in 1735 from New York City to Philadelphia, where he went into the import-export business. The first permanent Jewish citizen of Lancaster was Joseph Simon who arrived from somewhere in Central Europe about 1740 and remained in Lancaster until he died in 1804 at the age of ninety-two. He became a very well-to-do merchant and land speculator. He was closely associated both through business and marriages with the Gratz, Franks, and Levy families of Philadelphia, who were among the most prominent pre- and post-Revolutionary families of that city. The first Jews arrived in Reading in 1753, York, 1760, and Pittsburgh, 1768, although Fort Pitt served as the fur trading headquarters of Lancaster's Levy Andrews Levy as early as 1759.

The first Philadelphia congregation, Sephardic Mikveh Israel, was organized in 1771. Its first synagogue was built in 1782. High holy day services were held in Lancaster as early as 1776 but no congregation was established there until eighty years later. The first Ashkenazic congregation in the United States, Rodeph Shalom, was founded in Philadelphia in 1812.

Jews in Pennsylvania had full freedom of religion from the earliest days but they were not permitted to hold public office. This civil disability was removed in 1790.

Pennsylvania has about 500,000 Jews, 4 percent of the total population. The largest Jewish communities are Philadelphia, 350,000; Pittsburgh 45,000; Scranton-Wilkes-Barre, 10,000; and Harrisburg, 5,000. The other pioneer Jewish communities in the state have moderate-sized Jewish populations: Reading, 2,800; Lancaster, 1,700; York, 1,600.

West Virginia

West Virginia achieved statehood in 1863 when the western counties of Virginia split off from the rest of the state because Virginia had seceded from the Union, much to the disgust of its western mountaineers who remained fiercely loyal to the federal cause throughout the Civil War.

Before and after this area became a separate state, the rugged character of its terrain seems to have made it unattractive to prospective Jewish settlers. Widely scattered Jewish families appear in local annals beginning with the 1830s. The first congregation was organized in Wheeling in 1849.

Even though folklore in song and story is very much part of the tradition of the Mountain State (Who has not heard of the Hatfields and the McCoys?), none has been discovered that may be classified as being specifically Jewish. There were just not enough Jews around to create any folklore. Even now there are only about 4,000 Jews in the state, 0.2 percent of the population, and even this small number is gradually getting smaller. Many Jews born and reared in West Virginia seek fame and fortune elsewhere.

West Virginia Jews have never been subjected to any sort of civic disabilities for a number of reasons: a) West Virginia's laws were patterned after Virginia's liberal Bill of Rights; b) by the time West Virginia entered the Union, full citizenship for everyone was taken for granted; and c) a high regard and deep respect for the rights of every individual are part of the native tradition of these hardy mountain people.

—D.M.E.

The Jews Come to New Amsterdam
(1654)

Because the Dutch permitted Jews to serve in their armed forces from about the beginning of the seventeenth century, there may have been Jewish soldiers in the Dutch military garrison that occupied the southern extremity of Manhattan Island in 1615 and therafter. However, there is no proof that any Jews came to settle as permanent residents in what is now the United States prior to 1654. In the summer of that year a few Jews came to New Amsterdam from Holland. They had the permission of the Dutch West Indies Company to establish businesses in the company's American colony.

The first sizeable group of Jews arrived early in September 1654 aboard the French privateer *St. Charles*. There were twenty-three of them, four husbands, four wives, two widows, and thirteen children. Most, but not all, were Sephardic refugees from Recife, Brazil, people who had come to that city after the Dutch drove out the English in 1630 and who had to leave when the Portuguese drove out the Dutch in 1654. The rest, it seems, boarded the *St. Charles* when it stopped at the island of Jamaica. They, too, were Dutch citizens who had come to Jamaica and set up businesses; but their livelihoods were so greatly threatened by the English, Spanish, French, and Dutch men-of-war, privateers and pirates that infested the Caribbean waters that they decided to seek their fortunes in, hopefully, a more secure area of North America.

The newcomers landed with little more than the clothes on their backs and without having paid all their passage money to Jacques de la Motte, captain of the *St. Charles*. The captain had confiscated nearly all their personal possessions, which he proceeded to sell at auction to obtain part of the money due him. He also had the New Amsterdam authorities jail two of the husbands to make sure he would be paid the balance. It took a month of negotiating before Captain de la Motte agreed to wait for his money until the refugees received financial help from their relatives in Holland.

The few Jews already in the colony were not pleased by the arrival

60

of their needy coreligionists and refused to help them. The pastor of the local Dutch Reformed Church, the Reverend Johannes Megapolensis, came to the rescue with funds collected from his parishioners. The magnanimous dominie was not favorably impressed by the refusal of the better circumstanced Jews to aid their less fortunate brethren. Concerning these earlier arrivals, he wrote in March 1655 to the officials of the Dutch West Indies Company:

> As these people have no other goal but the unrighteous mammon, and no other aim than to gain possession of Christian property, and to ruin all other merchants by drawing all trade toward themselves, we request that these godless rascals who are of no benefit to this country, but look at everything for their profit, be sent away from here.

Governor Peter Stuyvesant did not want the newcomers to remain. On September 22 he wrote his Holland superiors that the *St. Charles* Jews were avaricious, deceitful, penniless "hateful enemies and blasphemers of Christ," who, if permitted to stay, would become a burden upon the community. In April 1655 Stuyvesant received a reply. His bosses' response did not please him. The expulsion of the Jews from the colony

> would be unreasonable and unfair, especially because of the considerable loss sustained by the Jews in the taking of Brazil, and also because of the large amount of capital which Jews have invested in the shares of this company.... These people may travel and trade to and in New Netherland, and live and remain there, provided that the poor among them shall be supported by their own nation.

The Company ordered Stuyvesant to permit the Jews to own their homes, trade with the Indians, and engage in the import-export business. They were not to be permitted to work at manual occupations or to operate retail stores. Stuyvesant added another prohibition: He would not allow the male Jews to serve in the colony's militia.

Such was the manner in which the first group of Jews to arrive in the United States was welcomed to the island which Peter Minuit had purchased from the Indians in May 1626 for the legendary price of twenty-four dollars.

FIRST SOLDIER AND FIRST CITIZEN
(1655)

One of the twenty-three who arrived in New Amsterdam in September 1654 was Asser Levy von Swellem. Asser, a tough, argumentative type of fellow, made his living from pursuits well adapted to his kind of personality: tavernkeeper, butcher, real estate broker. His aggressiveness soon earned him a position of leadership in the small Jewish community and of respect and influence in the general community.

In 1638 enterprising Peter Minuit, acting for the South Company of Sweden, purchased from the Indians a large area near the mouth of the Delaware River, encompassing portions of the present states of Delaware, New Jersey, and Pennsylvania. At first the acquisition was successfully and amicably colonized by both Swedes and Dutch. The Swedish company built its principal fortification and colony at Fort Christina, now Wilmington, Delaware. Other colonies were established near the present towns of Essington, Pennsylvania, and Salem, New Jersey. About ten years after the establishment of New Sweden, as it was named, the Dutch and Swedes began to quarrel over matters arising from barter trade with the neighboring Indians.

In 1651, to protect Dutch interests, Stuyvesant created a military post, Fort Casimir, near what is now New Castle, Delaware. In 1654 the Swedes drove the Dutch soldiers from Fort Casimir and occupied it. In 1655 Stuyvesant recruited seven hundred men, outfitted seven ships, invaded New Sweden, recaptured Fort Casimir, and conquered Fort Christina. The Dutch took over control of the area and New Sweden ceased to exist.

Among those who volunteered for the campaign against New Sweden were Asser Levy and several other Jews. Stuyvesant refused to allow them to join his expeditionary force. Instead the city council passed an ordinance in August 1655 that "owing to the disgust and unwillingness of the militia to be fellow soldiers with (the Jews), and to be on guard with same at the guardhouse in this center of commerce and industry, New Amsterdam," the Jews were not to be permitted to serve in the militia, local or expeditionary. Because of this exemption each male Jew was to pay a special monthly tax of 65 stivers, about $1.30.

Asser Levy refused to pay the tax. He petitioned the council on November 5, 1655, either to allow him to stand guard with the other burghers or to excuse him from the tax payment. His petition was denied. In its decision the council noted acidly that, if Levy was not satisfied with the manner in which New Amsterdam was being governed, he was free to seek his fortune elsewhere. Levy then went over the heads of the council and presented his case in writing to the Amsterdam headquarters of the West Indies Company. His appeal was successful. The city council was ordered to grant Asser Levy the right to serve in the local militia and did so.

Having won this important initial battle for civil rights, Levy then carried his campaign for civic recognition one step further. He produced a burgher's certificate from the city of Amsterdam and demanded of a city magistrate that he be given the same status in New Amsterdam. The court records show that, on April 9, 1657, "the Jew [Levy] claims that [burgher's rights] ought not be refused him, as he keeps watch and ward like other burghers." The magistrate turned down his request but suggested he carry his plea to the governor and council. Levy must have done so speedily and persuasively because, on April 21, 1657, the council issued an order that henceforth New Amsterdam Jews were to be given the same status as that enjoyed by the Jews of Amsterdam.

This was not yet full burghership. Like their Amsterdam coreligionists, the New Amsterdam Jews were still under certain restrictions. They could not intermarry with Christians or make adverse public comments about Christianity. They were not permitted to be teachers, lawyers, or government officials. But the 1657 order of the New Amsterdam governing body was a great step forward for the first Jewish community in what is now the United States and a giant victory for a Jew of great determination and courage, Asser Levy von Swellem.

THE "JEWS" OF SCHAEFFERSTOWN

(1720)

The time setting was approximately from 1720 to 1745. The place was a locality in that section of southeastern Pennsylvania where dwell that "wonderfully good" group of German origin known as the "Pennsylvania Dutch." Many are inclined to believe that all accounts of the happening are completely legendary. That all the facts are not known is clear; that some of the facts have been exaggerated by enthusiastic local historians is very possible; but that the story is completely or even largely without foundation is not very likely.

Early in the third decade of the eighteenth century some Welsh Seventh Day Baptists settled down alongside some German Baptists in what was then a part of Lancaster County. The Germans had named their township Heidelberg in honor of the beautiful German city on the Neckar River which was until 1720 capital of the Rhenish Palatinate. The American Heidelberg was located about twenty miles north of Lancaster at a spot now occupied by the village of Schaefferstown in Lebanon County. The Welsh newcomers persuaded their German coreligionists that it was unscriptural to eat pork and it was scriptural to observe Saturday as the Sabbath.

About this same time a number of Sephardic Jews, originally Portuguese Marranos, moved into the neighborhood to engage in trading with the Indians. These Jews had a profound religious influence on the Welsh and German Baptists. Whether or not any of the Baptists actually converted to Judaism in the fullest sense is a matter about which there is no firm evidence. However, a number of local historians are convinced that the following statements are accurate:

From about 1720 until about 1745 the Jewish traders and their "proselytes," as they are styled in the Pennsylvania Dutch historical narratives, formed a united religious community in the township of Heidelberg. They met on the Jewish Sabbath, observed the dietary laws and the rite of circumcision. They built a house of worship, known as "the Schul," out of rough logs "on the old Indian trail leading from the Conestoga to the Swatara creeks." Next to the Schul stood a log cabin, reputed to have been the home of the chazan or congregational leader. A cemetery, surrounded by a stone wall, was established about 1732. The cemetery, with tombstones and stone wall intact, still existed in 1885. Sometime between 1885 and 1901 it was destroyed and ploughed over. The log cabin in which the chazan is said to have lived was standing until 1926.

About 1743 a group of new German immigrants arrived to found the village of Schaefferstown. They were very hostile toward the Jews and their "proselytes." A. S. Brendle, in his history of Schaefferstown, written in 1901, states:

> The Jews remained here for some time after the arrival of the Europeans, but they gradually grew less in numbers and finally disappeared altogether. Their synagogue was in ruins long before the last of their race left the neighborhood and their graveyard here has also ceased to exist.

Jewish historian Jacob Rader Marcus has written:

> To be sure there were Jews in Heidelberg during the decade of the 1750s. Bernard Jacobs, for instance, lived in the neighborhood at a time when the Judaizers [self-converted Christians] were flourishing. Jacobs, moreover, functioned as a rabbi of sorts for the Jews throughout the area, but his circumcision book, which is still existent, makes no mention of the circumcision of a single proselyte. Some recollections of Jacobs probably linger on in the Schaefferstown story; late traditions have in all likelihood merged into one to make him out the rabbi of the Judaizing Sabbatarians and to recast

his home as the synagogue or shul. If there ever was a Jewish cemetery... it was probably a private burying ground for the two or three Jewish families who lived in the town and its immediate environs. The Schaefferstown Jewish community never existed outside the inventions of American folklore.

In a very literal sense, Dr. Marcus is, of course, completely correct. Heidelberg never had a congregation that would fit into the generally accepted concepts of what constitutes a synagogue or an organized Jewish community. But it may very well have had a small number of Marrano, i.e., "Christianized" Jewish families and a much larger number of "Judaized" Christian families who worshiped together amicably for twenty or more years.

Schaefferstown, Pennsylvania, no longer contains any discernible physical evidence of the existence of what one of its chroniclers calls "the first synagogue in the American desert." But there is in plain view easily discernible spiritual evidence. To this day there are in that neighborhood Pennsylvania Dutch or, more properly, Pennsylvania German families who observe Saturday as their Sabbath, eat no pork or shellfish, do not mix meat dishes with milk dishes, and whose males do not shave.

I was born and reared in Lancaster County. I remember being told by the handsome bearded Pennsylvania Dutchman who brought my mother our weekly supply of butter and eggs:

I am a more observant Jew than you. I keep your Sabbath strictly. I observe your dietary laws strictly. I do not shave. This has been the way my people has lived for the past two hundred years.

The Flames of Hell

(1753)

Within a few years after the first Jews arrived in New Amsterdam, Jewish itinerant peddlers were doing a thriving business with rural settlers in many sections of the northeastern part of the United States. If they could afford it, they traveled by horse and wagon. If they could not, they carried their heavy packs of all manner of household notions, utensils and piece goods upon their backs. Benjamin Franklin tells a story about one such peddler in his newspaper, *The Pennsylvania Gazette*, for March 13, 1753:

From Jacob R. Marcus' *American Jewry—Documents 18th Century*, 1958, p. 2.

New York, February 26.—We have an account from the country of the following comical affair which lately happened.

A Jew pedlar went into a house where he offered his goods for sale, but the good man being out, and all his family, except his wife, who told the pedlar that she could not buy any thing, for her husband had got the key of the money. The pedlar, then, finding that the woman was entirely alone, offered to make her a present of a piece of calicoe upon condition of her giving up her charms to him. The bait was very alluring, for the thoughts of sporting with a young man, and having a new gown in the bargain, made her readily yield to his desires.

He accordingly gave her the calicoe and, after taking a repast in the banquet of love, went about his business, but had not gone far before he met with her husband, and having some knowledge of him, said: "Sir, I have sold your wife a very cheap piece of calicoe, and on six months' credit." With that the poor man stood amazed and said: "I wonder at my wife's ill conduct in running me in debt, when she knows that I have a considerable sum of money to pay in a few months' time, and can't tell how to make it up." He then persuaded the pedlar to go back and take his piece of calicoe, which he readily consented to, and, when they came to the house, he ordered his wife to give the pedlar his calicoe again, which she did, after privately concealing a coal of fire in it.

The pedlar took the calicoe and put it up in his pack, which was a wallet slung across his shoulders, and so marched off, pleased with the thoughts of his success. But for his sweet meat he soon found sour sauce. He, not suspecting the cheat, jogged along till he met with a countryman, who, seeing his pack on fire and just ready to blaze, cryed: "Hey, friend, from whence came you?" *"From Hell,"* replied the pedlar. "So I perceive," says the countryman, "by the flames at your back." The pedlar then looked behind him, and to his great surprize found all his goods on fire, which made him stamp and rave like a mad man and curse his folly in cuckolding the poor man.

There Is No Escape

(1767)

Hayman Levy, 1721-89, was one of New York City's leading merchants. He had the largest fur trading business in all the colonies. One of his employees was John Jacob Astor, who became the most important fur trader in American history.

One evening, while Hayman was working late in his warehouse, his youngest and favorite son rushed in.

This legend has been handed down from generation to generation by the descendants of Hayman Levy.

"Father, I beg of you, let me have your carriage and your fastest team of horses," he cried out. "I must leave at once!"

"Why all the haste?" his father asked.

"Because," answered the youth, "only an hour ago, while I was in the garden at home, I saw the Malach ha-Mavet (the Angel of Death) standing there. When he caught sight of me, he stretched out his arms. There is no doubt that he was threatening to take me with him. I beg you, father, help me to escape!"

"Of course," said Hayman, thoroughly shaken. "Leave for Boston at once. Stay with your Uncle Nathaniel. He will be glad to shelter you. Take the carriage and the fastest horses in our stables. By traveling at top speed, you should be in Boston on Tuesday."

The father then hurried home and ran out into the garden. The Malach ha-Mavet was still there. Hayman sighed with relief. Then he went up to the angel and said, "How dare you make threatening gestures at my son!"

"Why, sir," responded the angel, clearly astonished. "I made no threatening gestures at your son. I only threw up my hands in surprise at finding him here in New York when I have a rendezvous with him in Boston on Tuesday!"

TOM PAINE WRITES A POEM
(1775)

The lot of the Jew in prerevolutionary America was not a particularly happy one. Only by comparing it with the manner in which the Jew was being treated in many other parts of the world, particularly in those countries still bedeviled by the Inquisition, ghettoization, ritual murder libels, and pogroms, may one correctly say that these colonial American Jews were relatively safe from overt oppression and physical abuse.

The average American in colonial times was convinced that most Jews were fit only to be petty tradesmen, that in matters of business Jews were shrewd, unworthy of trust, and that it was not wrong to cheat a Jew because in so doing one was merely beating the Devil at his own game. Perhaps these stereotyped notions were present in the minds of the better educated in somewhat less offensive form and measure, but not very much less. And the clergy continually endeavored to convince the small, scattered American remnants of the tribes of Israel and Judah that they were headed straight for Hell unless they accepted the unique revelation of religious truth possessed by believing Christians.

While the eighteenth-century attitude of most American non-Jews toward their Jewish neighbors was distorted and parochial, their political acumen was of a much better quality. They wanted a government free of clericalism, a way of life warmer and more humane that that of either rigorous, cold Puritanism or undemocratic Anglicanism. They were given these advanced political ideas by Methodists and Baptists, emancipated Episcopalians and Puritans, and by the Deists.

Deism was a naturalistic religious philosophy which grew out of the spirit of scientific realism generated by the Renaissance. The principal effects of Deistic thought upon American life were that it led to the schism within the Puritan church which split that denomination into Congregationalists and Unitarians; and it influenced the thinking and actions of many of those who inspired and guided the American Revolution, created the United States of America, and embodied in our constitution their ideals of freedom and justice. The best known of this enlightened group are John Adams, Benjamin Franklin, Thomas Jefferson, Thomas Paine, and George Washington. They initiated an all-too-brief period of political and intellectual sanity that may well have been "the golden age" of American liberalism. They had no interest whatever in downgrading Jews or converting them to Christianity.

Deist Tom Paine wrote what appears to be the only piece of its kind in the literature of prerevolutionary America, a satiric poem about the Jew and his Christian tormentors. Titled "A Bigot's Immersion," printed in 1775 in the *Pennsylvania Magazine* of Philadelphia, this poem, while not painting the Jew in the brightest of colors, certainly makes of him a finer person than his Christian detractors.

> An unbelieving Jew one day
> Was skating o'er the icy way,
> Which, being brittle, let him in
> Just deep enough to catch his chin,
> And in that woeful plight he hung,
> With only power to move his tongue.
>
> A brother skater near at hand,
> A Papist born in foreign land,
> With hasty steps directly flew
> To save poor Mordecai the Jew;
> "But first," quoth he, "I must enjoin
> That you renounce your faith for mine,
> There's no entreaties else will do,
> 'Tis heresy to help a Jew."
>
> "Forswear mine fait—no! Got forbit!
> Dat would be ferry base indeed;

Come, never mind such dings as deese,
Tink, tink, how ferry hart it freeze;
More coot you do, more coot you be,
Vat signifies your fait to me,
Come tink agen how cold and vet,
And help me out von little bet."

"By holy mass! 'tis hard, I own,
To see a man both hang and drown,
Yet can't relieve him from his plight,
Because he is an Israelite;
The church refuses all assistance,
Beyond a certain pale and distance,
So all the service I can lend
Is praying for your soul, my friend."

"Pray for mine soul! Ha, ha, you make me laugh;
You petter help me out py half.
Mine soul, I varrant, will take care
To pray for her own self, mine tear;
So tink a little now for me,
'Tis I am in the hole—not she.'"

"The church forbids it, friend, and saith
That all shall die who have no faith."

"Vell, if I must pelieve, I must,
But help me out vun little first."

"No, not an inch without amen,—
That seals the whole."

"Vell, hear me den:
I here renounce for coot and all,
De race of Jews both great and small;
'Tis de vurst trade peneath de sun;
Or vurst religion, dat's all vun.
Dey cheat and get deir living py it
And lie and swear de lie is right.
I'll go to mass as soon as ever
I get to toder side de river;
So help me out now, Christian friend,
Det I may do as I intend."

"Perhaps you do intend to cheat,
If once you get upon your feet."

"No, no; I do intend to be
A Christian—such a vun as dee."

For, thought the Jew, he is as much
A Christian man as I am such.
The bigot Papist, joyful hearted,
To hear the heretic converted,
Replied to the designing Jew—
"This was a happy fall for you;
You'd better die a Christian now,
For if you live you'll break your vow."
Then said no more, but in a trice
Popped Mordecai beneath the ice.

THE ORIGINAL "SAD SACK"
(1776)

Isaac Franks, 1759-1822, was the son of a prominent member of Congregation Shearith Israel of New York City. He enlisted in the Continental Army at the very outbreak of the Revolutionary War. In August 1776 he served under the direct command of General Washington before, during, and after the Battle of Long Island. He was captured by the British while on guard duty in New York City on September 15 and escaped three months later. Upon rejoining the Continentals he was placed in the supply section and was forage-master at West Point from 1777 to 1781.

After the Revolution Isaac lived in Philadelphia and became a real estate broker and notary public. In 1794 he was named a lieutenant-colonel in the Pennsylvania militia, in 1795 justice of the peace, and in 1819 prothonotary or chief clerk of the Pennsylvania Supreme Court. His portrait was painted by the famous artist Gilbert Stuart.

❋ ❋ ❋ ❋ ❋

Isaac Franks' chief claim to fame may be that he was the author of one of the most humorous military documents in the annals of the American armed forces. Shortly after the battle of Long Island and little more than a week before he was captured by the British, teen-aged Corporal Franks was ordered by General Washington to repair the roof of a building in which guns and ammo were being stored. The young soldier's misadventures in connection with this assignment are graph-

---

See *The Franks of Philadelphia* by Joseph Mendes, Baltimore, 1871.

ically described in the communication he subsequently sent to his commanding officer:

8 September 1776

Subject: Request for sick leave

To: General G. Washington

Respected Sir,
As per my orders to make repairs on the roof of Company Magazine B, I arrived at the building at seven o'clock in the morning, only to find that the storm of the previous night had torn loose some of the cross-beams from the eaves.

I therefore rigged up a beam with a pulley at the top of the building and hoisted up six heavy iron brackets and a hundred-weight kegge of nails.

Having effectuated the repairs I saw that I had brought up more brackets than I needed and I had used only a pound or two of the nails. So I hoisted up the empty kegge again and tied the rope at the bottom. Then I went up to the roof and filled the kegge with the iron brackets and nails. After that I returned to the ground to unfasten the rope.

Unhappily, the kegge of brackets and nails were heavier than my own weight, and ere I could say Jack Robinson, the kegge started down and jerked me into the atmosphere. I made a quick decision to hang onto the rope, but halfway up I met the kegge coming down and received a mighty blow on the head and shoulders. I then continued the rest of the way to the top, banging my head against the beam and getting my fingers caught in the pulley.

The kegge hit the ground with such force that the impact bursted the bottom, allowing those heavy brackets and the near-hundredweight of nails to spill out. I was now heavier than the broken kegge and so I started down again at an uncommonly fast rate of descent. Halfway down I met the kegge coming up and received several painful injuries to my legs.

When I hit the ground I landed on the spilled brackets and sharp nails which resulted in sustaining a number of grievous cuts from the sharp points. At that moment I fear I lost presence of mind because I released my hold on the rope. The kegge then came down again, giving me another blow on the head and putting me in the infirmary.

I respectfully request sick leave.

(signed) Cp. Isaac Franks

HAYM SALOMON, SON OF LIBERTY
(1778)

Much has been written of the invaluable contribution to the success of the American Revolution made by Philadelphia Jewish stockbroker and money lender Haym Salomon. The emphasis on Salomon's acumen and generosity as a financier has tended to obscure Salomon's role as revolutionary activist, a role which was directly responsible for Salomon's death at age forty-five and, according to his son, almost resulted in his dangling at the end of a British hangman's rope at age thirty-eight.

Salomon was born at Leszno [formerly known as Lissa] in the province of Posnan, Poland, in 1739 or 1740. He is reputed to be the first Polish-born Jew to become a permanent resident of North America. Leszno was only four miles from the Prussian frontier. Almost all its Jews were of German origin. It was an industrial community with close commercial ties to Prussia and Saxony, especially the annual Leipzig fairs.

In 1772 Poland was conquered by the combined armies of Austria, Prussia, and Russia and divided between the three countries. There is no clear-cut evidence that Salomon served in the armed forces of his doomed country during this war; but there is such a possibility. It appears that, during this conflict, he became acquainted with future American Revolutionary officers Tadeusz Kosciusko, military engineer, and Casimir Pulaski, expert cavalryman. After hostilities ceased, Salomon, like Kosciusko and Pulaski, left for western Europe and then migrated to the United States.

Settling in Manhattan, Salomon became a dealer in securities and bills of exchange. He soon acquired a reputation for personal integrity and sound business know-how. He also became active in the underground rebel group known as the Sons of Liberty.

After the British evacuated Boston in March 1776, George Washington went to New York City to organize the main American army that would eventually win the war. As the rebel units began to gather, most of the Tories or British sympathizers left town. Those who remained were badly treated. The Continental troops occupied the Tory homes and estates, pilfered their contents, and despoiled both the living quarters and the surrounding grounds.

In the third week of July an imposing fleet carrying thousands of well-trained British troops and Hessian mercenaries under the command of General Sir Henry Clinton sailed into New York harbor. On August 22 a series of battles began throughout what is now Greater New York that ended on September 15 with the defeat and retreat of the newly organized American army and the British capture of New York City. Before the city was abandoned it was set afire and almost a fourth of it destroyed.

The Tory refugees returned to what was left of their homes and exacted a heavy vengeance from their rebellious fellow townsmen. General Clinton appointed as provost marshal "a brutal, vicious clod of a man," William Cunningham, who had already earned a reputation as a cruel, unprincipled "law and order" bully during the British reign of terror in Boston after the battle of Bunker Hill. Thousands of New York City patriots and captured rebel prisoners were placed at the mercy and whimsy of this blackguard, who not only punished some of those in his custody with death if he so much as found their remarks offensive but also gathered in a tidy fortune by selling in the black market the British supplies given him to feed and clothe the imprisoned and the wounded. After the city jails had been filled to capacity and beyond, North Dutch Church and the French Church and the Old Sugar House on what is now Liberty Street and a number of worn-out, rotting, abandoned sailing vessels in New York harbor were turned into prisons and filled with beaten, ragged, sick, and starving civilians and Continentals.

Among those caught in the Cunningham dragnet was Haym Salomon. No formal charge seems to have been lodged against him. He was probably arrested because some Tory undercover agent reported he was a Son of Liberty. At first he was confined in the roofless Old Sugar House, where hygienic conditions were so bad that Salomon contracted the chronic fever from which he suffered the rest of his life. Because of his weakened physical condition he was transferred to the Provost Prison where the authorities used him as an interpreter for the German-speaking prisoners. After serving a short sentence he was released.

On January 2, 1777, Salomon married Rachel, fifteen-year-old daughter of a prominent New York German Jew, Moses B. Franks. Her seventeen-year-old brother Isaac, a soldier in Washington's army, had been captured when the British took the city. About two weeks before his sister's wedding, Isaac escaped and rejoined the Continentals. A little more than a year later, a month after Rachel had given birth to her first child, the British arrested Salomon again. This time he was charged with being a rebel spy.

There are two differing accounts of this episode. One was written by Salomon shortly after the event. The other was given by Salomon's son many years later.

In a statement submitted to the Continental Congress on August 25, 1778, Salomon says he was accused of being a spy; but he does not indicate whether or not the charge was true. Because of his knowledge of German he was placed in the custody of the Hessian commanding general to act as an interpreter for the German officers. While serving in this capacity he convinced a number of these officers of the unrighteousness of the cause for which they were fighting. In consequence they resigned their commissions. The British were greatly annoyed by this and demanded that the Hessians return Salomon to their military control. While memoranda with regard to this were going back and forth, Salomon escaped on August 11 and fled to Philadelphia. Salomon does not state how he escaped or who, if anyone, helped him. Afterward the Sons of Liberty claimed that they had engineered his deliverance. That it may have been an inside job, i.e., some of the Hessian officers did the engineering, seems a more plausible possibility and would explain why Salomon did not want to place his German friends in jeopardy by acknowledging their helpfulness in a statement made only two weeks after his escape.

According to Salomon's son, Salomon had received instructions from Washington's headquarters to set afire a number of warehouses containing British military supplies. He attempted to do so and was partially successful. He was apprehended, tried, and sentenced to be hanged. He managed to escape by paying a substantial bribe to a British prison guard.

In Philadelphia Salomon continued his efforts on behalf of Washington's forces. He became the broker through whom the Continentals' financial agent, Robert Morris, sold the rebel government's bonds. He lent money without interest, and often without repayment, to financially embarrassed members of the Continental Congress and Army. Among the many to whom he made such loans were Congressman Thomas Jefferson and James Madison and soldier James Monroe, the future third, fourth, and fifth presidents of these United States. At the time Madison wrote: "I have been a pensioner for some time on the favor of Haym Salomon, a Jew broker." He later wrote: "The kindness of our friend [i.e., Salomon] near the coffee house is a fund that will preserve me from extremities, but I never resort to it without great mortification, as he obstinately rejects all recompense."

To the cause of American freedom Haym Salomon literally contributed his life, his fortune, and his sacred honor. An ardent patriot, a devout and philanthropic Jew, Salomon died on January 6, 1785, a victim of the fever contracted during his first New York imprisonment. He left behind a noble name, a poverty stricken widow with three small children, and a paper "fortune" of more than $350,000 in national and state bonds and unpaid personal loans. The bonds were never redeemed and the loans were never repaid.

In 1976, as part of the American bicentennial observance, the United States acknowledged its indebtedness to Haym Salomon by having the Post Office Department issue a special ten-cent stamp honoring his memory.

THE AARONSBURG STORY
(1786)

Aaron Levy, 1742-1815, was born in Amsterdam. His family came originally from Russia or Poland. He migrated to America about 1760. The next twelve years he worked for relatives in Lancaster and Philadelphia.

One Saturday morning in 1767 or 1768 as Aaron was walking to synagogue, he passed the Philadelphia home of the wealthy Chew family and saw a pretty young girl crying bitterly as she scrubbed down the stone front steps of the mansion. "Why are you crying?" he asked. There was no answer. Acting on a sudden hunch he repeated the question in Yiddish. The girl stopped crying immediately. She was, as Aaron suspected, Jewish. Her name was Rachel Phillips. She had been indentured to the Chew family as a servant. She had to work seven days a week. She could not observe the religious way of life in which she had been reared. She was very unhappy.

It was love at first sight for both. Aaron solved all the pretty girl's immediate problems by borrowing money to pay off her indebtedness to the Chews. Three weeks later Aaron and Rachel were married.

In 1772 the Levys were among the pioneer founders of Sunbury in Northumberland County, a sparsely settled wilderness little more than 100 miles northwest of Philadelphia. They built a store where Levy sold supplies manufactured in Philadelphia or imported from Europe to the frontier soldiers and colonists. He also traded with the Indians and speculated in real estate. After the Revolutionary War broke out, the Iroquois Indians, allies of the British, began to harass the Northumberland pioneers. In 1778 these attacks became so frequent and violent that, fearing for their lives, the Levys moved to Lancaster.

In both Sunbury and Lancaster Levy served in the local militia. He loaned large sums of money to the Continental Congress and furnished greatly needed supplies to the fighting units. Like Haym Salomon, he was never repaid for much of this help.

In 1782 the Levys moved to Philadelphia and then, in 1786, back to Northumberland County. Levy soon became one of the area's leading real estate developers. The most ambitious and historically significant land project he promoted came to public attention on May 23, 1786, when he announced that "he hath laid out a town, called Aaronsburg, very pleasantly situated in that beautiful, healthy and fertile settlement called Penn's Valley," 35 miles west of Sunbury. Aaronsburg was the first town in the United States founded by, laid out by, and named for a Jew. The town plan was recorded in Sunbury on October 4. The main streets were to be known as Aaron's Square and Rachel's Way.

Aaronsburg is located at almost the exact geographic center of the state. Some historians maintain that the selection of this site was based on Levy's hope that Aaronsburg would become a natural choice to be the state's capital city. Others say he wanted his town to become the county seat of Center County, then being carved from the western portion of the Northumberland country. Neither of these hopes was realized. In 1812 Harrisburg was designated state capital; and Bellefonte, twenty miles west of Aaronsburg, became and remains the county seat.

The Levys never lived in Aaronsburg. From 1786 to 1790 they made their home in the town of Northumberland, a few miles north of Sunbury. In 1789 they gave Aaronsburg land on which to build a church and schoolhouse and to establish a cemetery. Both Aaron and Rachel signed the deed giving the land to the community. Rachel signed her name in Hebrew script. In 1799, when the building of Aaronsburg's Salem Lutheran Church was completed, the Levys presented to the church a pewter communion set, which is its most prized possession and is still being used. It was made in Philadelphia by Colonel William Will, well-known eighteenth-century pewterer, and bears a German inscription, "This gift to the German Congregations in Aaronsburg from Aaron Levy."

The Levys were not happy living in Northumberland. While their successful real estate dealings had brought them financial security, they had little opportunity for the kind of Jewish social and religious life they enjoyed. They had no children. They were lonely. They wished to be among their own kind. So in 1790 they returned to Philadelphia. In 1804 Levy transferred all his real estate interests in Center County to Rebecca Gratz's brother Simon, whom Aaron regarded as an adopted son.

❖   ❖   ❖   ❖   ❖

Reverend Mr. David A. Clement, present pastor of Aaronsburg's Salem Lutheran Church, has supplied the following information:

Aaronsburg now has a population of about 500. It has two churches, the Salem Lutheran and a United Church of Christ. Since the construction of State Highway 45, which passes by Aaronsburg between State College and Lewisburg, many who work at State College live in Aaronsburg. The town is still rural in character and is surrounded by farms. When the farmers retire, many buy a home in Aaronsburg. So the population is made up principally of elderly retired farmers and younger employees of Pennsylvania State College, 25 miles southwest.

Appearancewise the town has not changed much through the years. It is still laid out in the form of a rectangle, exactly as Aaron Levy planned it. Aaron's Square is now the main street and Rachel's Way is a side street. The homes are humble but well kept. The Reverend Mr. Clement and his family live on Rachel's Way. There are no Jews in Aaronsburg. As far as is known, no Jew has ever lived there.

On October 23, 1949, Salem Lutheran Church celebrated its 150th anniversary. An ecumenical pageant, "The Aaronsburg Story," was enacted before an audience of nearly 50,000 people. Famed clergy and laymen of many religious denominations gathered to honor the memory of Aaron Levy. Speeches were given and seminars on religious freedom and human rights were conducted by Rabbi Philip S. Bernstein of Rochester, N.Y., UN's Under Secretary General Ralph Bunche, World War II's General William J. Donovan, UN's Vice President Sir Muhammad Zafrulla Kahn of Pakistan, Supreme Court Justice Felix Frankfurter, the Reverend Daniel A. Poling, editor of the *Christian Herald* and father of "Four Chaplains" Clark Poling, NAACP's Channing H. Tobias, and many other nationally known leaders. Governor James H. Duff issued the following declaration: "I hereby proclaim that henceforth every October 23 will be Aaronsburg Brotherhood Day throughout the length and breadth of the Commonwealth of Pennsylvania!"

LIEUTENANT URIAH PHILLIPS LEVY, U.S.N.
(1817)

His defamers and belittlers called him "the damned Jew." Those who adopted a more moderate attitude toward him and his pugnacious disposition described him as unique and fiery. To his many Christian and Jewish admirers he was a superpatriot, a gifted naval officer and a devoted Jew. One might like or dislike Uriah Phillips Levy but, whatever the company or circumstances, he could not be ignored.

Uriah Phillips Levy was born in 1792 in Philadelphia, the third of fourteen children of merchant Michael and Rachel Levy. Rachel's father was Jonas Phillips, founding member and parnas of Mikveh Israel synagogue, to which Uriah's parents also belonged. There he received his early religious training. As a boy and throughout life, Uriah was handsome, quick-minded, self-assured, stubborn, and hot tempered.

Ten years and one week old, he ran away to sea. He signed up as cabin boy for a two-year voyage on a coaster, a sailing vessel that carried merchandise up and down the Atlantic between Boston and Savannah. He told the ship's captain he could not sign on for a longer period because he wanted to return home in time to prepare for Bar Mitsvah. Much to the good-natured amusement of the crew, he tried his very best, during his first cruise, to keep kosher.

When the two years ended the boy returned home, was forgiven by his parents, studied for his Bar Mitsvah, and celebrated it in fine style. But the sea was in his blood. He wanted to go back but his parents objected. In his time seafaring was not considered a proper calling for a Jewish boy. Much better to settle down and become a merchant. But Uriah could not be budged.

So, when Uriah was fourteen years and two months old, his parents reluctantly apprenticed him for four years as a common seaman to one of Philadelphia's leading shipowners. Except for about nine months in a local naval school studying navigation, Uriah spent his apprenticeship aboard ships journeying to Europe and the West Indies. Before the four years were up Uriah had been promoted to able-bodied seaman and then to second mate. He also had lived through a shipwreck and a month's impressment into the British Navy.

The latter incident was an indication of the shape of things to come: In 1809, while sitting in a tavern on the island of Tortola in the British West Indies, Uriah was approached by a British marine sergeant and his six-man squad. The sergeant demanded his identification papers. Levy gave the sea-soldier his certification as second mate of the American ship *Polly and Betsy*. As he handed back the paper the sergeant remarked, "You don't look like an American to me. You look like a Jew." If Levy had kept his mouth shut that probably would have been the end of it. But Levy was not one, in such a situation, to keep his mouth shut. "I am both an American and a Jew," he said. To which the sergeant replied, "If the Americans have Jew peddlers sailing their ships, it's no wonder they sail so badly." Uriah got up and punched the sergeant solidly on the jaw. As the surprised sergeant staggered backward, one of his squad hit Uriah on the head with the butt of his rifle and knocked him down and out. When the lad came to, he was on his way to the British ship *Vermyra*, on which he was forced to serve as a common seaman. After four weeks he was released by order of the Admiral of the British Atlantic fleet; but not before the captain of the *Vermyra*, impressed with Uriah's seamanship, paid him the compliment of trying to persuade him to accept a commission in His Britannic Majesty's naval forces. "Your country will be at war with ours before long. It would be well for you to be on the winning side," the captain said. "Thank you, sir, but I will serve the flag I was born under," young Levy replied.

In 1811 at age nineteen Levy became one-third owner and master of the schooner *George Washington*. On its first voyage, while in the port of the Isle of May, Cape Verde Islands, the ship, together with $2,500 in Spanish gold and a cargo of fourteen quarter-casks of Teneriffe wine, was stolen from Levy by his first mate and a number of members of his crew. The thieves' poor handling of the vessel caused it to founder five miles off the island of St. Lucia in the Windward Islands. The stranded shipmaster tracked down the culprits and had them brought to trial. They were convicted of piracy. The mate was hanged and the others received long prison terms.

When the War of 1812 erupted, Levy volunteered. Instead of applying for a naval commission in the lowest officers' rank, that of midshipman, which was the normal procedure, he applied for a warrant as a sailing master, a non-commissioned functionary. Levy felt that because of his ten years' seagoing experience he could best serve the war effort in this capacity. He received the warrant in October 1812.

In June 1813 he was given command of the brig *Argus* and the mission of carrying the American minister to France through the British blockade. Having accomplished this assignment, the *Argus* went on a successful capture-or-destroy search for British shipping along the English and Irish coasts. In August, while attempting to take a British ship loaded with sugar into the nearest French harbor, Levy and his prize were captured by an enemy frigate. He was locked up in the hell-on-earth Dartmoor Prison and spent sixteen miserable months there. Among the many ways in which he endeavored to spend these months as usefully as possible, he tried to organize a minyan but was able to find only four other American Jewish prisoners, including Levi Myers Harby, who had changed his name to and later became famous as sailor-soldier Levi Charles Harby. Levy was released in an officer prisoner exchange in December 1814. By the time he was returned to the United States the war had ended.

He remained in the U.S. Navy, reporting for duty to the Philadelphia Naval Yard in April 1815. At the Philadelphia Patriots Ball in June 1816 a drunken naval lieutenant deliberately bumped Levy and his dancing partner three times. The third time Levy slapped the lieutenant's face. "You damned Jew," roared the lieutenant. "I'll get you for this." The drunkard's companions apologized to Levy and led their inebriated friend from the ballroom. Levy thought this ended the matter; but it did not. The next morning the lieutenant challenged Levy to a pistol duel. Levy would have been considered a coward if he refused. He accepted out of necessity. On the dueling ground he announced that he would not fire at his opponent. The lieutenant fired first and failed to hit Levy. Levy then fired his pistol into the air. This should have ended the affair of honor; but the enraged lieutenant insisted on continuing the duel. Three times more he fired at Levy and missed; three times more Levy fired into the air. The lieutenant's fifth shot nicked Levy's left ear and again Levy fired into the air. When the lieutenant still insisted on continuing Levy's turning of the other cheek came to an end. On his sixth shot he took careful aim, hit his opponent in the chest and killed him. There were naval and civilian laws against dueling; so Levy had to stand trial for murder before both naval and civilian courts. He was acquitted twice.

Both courts agreed that Levy had killed in self-defense.

On March 5, 1817, Levy received a commission as Lieutenant and became the second Jew to be a U. S. naval officer. The first was Levi Charles Harby, commissioned four months earlier. Harby resigned from the Navy in 1827 and again in 1848, while Levy remained a naval officer continuously, either on active duty or in reserve, for the rest of his life. Therefore Uriah Phillips Levy was the first Jewish career officer in the history of the United States Navy.

Throughout his forty-five years as a naval officer Levy was hampered and maligned continuously for two reasons: He had begun his naval administrative career as a warrant officer instead of electing to apply for a midshipman's commission and he was a Jew. He endured a long series of almost incredible incidents of abuse, insult and calumny, much too numerous to be described here in detail. Between July 1816 and November 1827 he was court-martialed and found guilty five times on flimsy and petty charges. In every instance anti-Jewish prejudice was involved.

At the first court-martial Levy was reprimanded. At the second he was dismissed from the ship on which he was serving. President James Monroe, after studying the evidence, found the sentence too severe and set it aside. At the third Levy was ordered dismissed from the Navy. President Monroe again disagreed with the decision and nullified it. The charges at the fourth and fifth courts-martial were so minor that only reprimands were imposed.

After the fifth court-martial in November 1827 Levy was so discouraged that he asked to be relieved from active duty and given a six-month leave. The request was granted. From then until 1838 Levy used many kinds of excuses to have his leave time extended in three-month and six-month increments. During these years he began to speculate in Manhattan real estate. He did this so successfully that in four years he became a rich man. Bored with making money, Levy went to Paris in 1832 and stayed there until 1834.

During this Paris sojourn a number of noteworthy events occurred: 1) Levy fell in love with a French girl but would not marry her. "I am married to the sea," he told her. 2) Levy renewed his friendship with the aged Revolutionary hero, Marie Joseph Paul Ives Roch Gilbert de Motier, Marquis de La Fayette. 3) Levy arranged to have a French sculptor cast into bronze an heroic statue of Levy's political idol, Thomas Jefferson. 4) Levy became involved in another fracas.

La Fayette had invited Levy to accompany him to an 1833 Fourth of July banquet sponsored by a group of French and American businessmen. At the banquet the usual round of toasts was given. Toasts to George Washington and to French king Louis Philippe were followed by the traditional "Nine cheers and one more!" After President Andrew

Jackson's name was toasted, Levy sprang to his feet and shouted, "I propose nine cheers!" His proposal was hissed and booed. Jackson was extremely unpopular with the French and American businessmen. Levy became infuriated. Not only the person but the office of the American presidency had been insulted. He challenged two of the Frenchmen who had hissed to a duel. Terrified by this fuming American naval officer, they fled from the banquet. Next morning each sent Levy a written apology. Levy's action was reported and praised in the newspapers of Washington and Philadelphia.

After his return to the United States, Levy asked Congress to accept the statue of Jefferson as a gift to the people of the United States. This was done. The statue now stands to the right of the statue of Washington in Statuary Hall in the rotunda of our National Capitol. It is the only statue in this distinguished collection which was not paid for by the federal or a state government.

In 1836 Levy purchased the run-down former home of Thomas Jefferson in Monticello, Virginia, for $2,700. He restored and refurnished it and made it his second residence. He continued to use the fine house he already had on St. Mark's Place in New York City. In his will he left Monticello to "the People of the United States" to be used "as an Agricultural School for the purpose of educating as practical farmers" children of deceased naval warrant officers. Levy's relatives contested this clause in the will and broke it. Jefferson Levy, Uriah's nephew, sold the estate to the Thomas Jefferson Memorial Association in 1923 for a half million dollars. This non-profit organization now operates the Jefferson home as a national shrine.

Because of his courts-martial record Levy felt that his naval career was doomed. But early in 1837 a naval "miracle" happened. President Jackson promoted Levy from Lieutenant to Commander, probably as a reward for the Paris incident. Levy immediately applied for return to active duty. In 1839 he was recalled and given an assignment that some of the Navy brass must have dreamed up as a certain means of getting rid of this troublesome Jew once and for all.

He was given command of the war sloop *Vandalia*, berthed at Pensacola, Florida, a delapidated, worn-out ship with a crew that has been described as "a prize collection of drunkards, syphilitics, malingerers, incompetents, and insubordinates that commanders of other ships had been happy to transfer." In five months Levy had both the sloop and its crew in top shape and ready for sea duty. The *Vandalia* was sent on a nine-month tour of Mexican ports and then returned to Pensacola.

In 1817 Levy had witnessed his first flogging of a sailor who was being disciplined for breaching Navy regulations. Levy was so horrified by the sight that he determined to do everything within his power to have

Navy flogging outlawed. Year after year he attacked this practice verbally and in writing. During his fourteen months' command of the *Vandalia*, there was only one flogging, despite the unsavory backgrounds of many of his crew. But there was a related happening that got Levy into deep trouble.

A young cabin boy on the *Vandalia* had done something wrong. Instead of having him flogged, Levy determined to teach him a needed lesson in a less painful manner. He had the boy tied to a gun, bent over, his trousers taken down, and a bit of heated tar, no bigger than a half dollar, and a few feathers pasted to his posterior. The boy's dignity was ruffled a little; but he suffered no physical pain or damage. For this great crime Levy had to endure a sixth court-martial. He was found guilty and, for the second time, was ordered dismissed from the Navy. He was being punished for his opposition to flogging. The court held that the boy should have been flogged, that Levy's substitute punishment was more detrimental to the boy's welfare and more damaging to Navy discipline than flogging would have been. On review, President John Tyler did not agree with the court. He stated that Levy's punishment was much weightier than his offense. To placate the Navy judiciary he did not entirely exonerate Levy. He reduced the sentence to suspension without pay for a period of twelve months.

Levy was returned to reserve status. He resumed the operation of his real estate business and divided his time between his homes in New York and Monticello.

Two years later President Tyler showed his admiration for Levy by promoting him from Commander to Captain at age fifty-two. The average age at that time at which Navy Commanders were promoted to Captain was fifty-seven. But the Navy did not return Captain Levy to active duty. Sixteen times between 1844 and 1855 Levy asked for active duty. Sixteen times his request was either ignored or denied.

In 1853 at age sixty-one Levy finally married. He married his niece Virginia, eighteen years old, a beauty born in Kingston, Jamaica, daughter of Abraham Lopez and Uriah's sister Fanny. Such an uncle-niece marriage, permitted by traditional Jewish religious law, was legal in New York State until 1893.

In 1855 another Navy administrative bombshell exploded. Levy and 200 other Naval officers were informed that, under the provisions of a recent Act of Congress "to promote the efficiency of the Navy," their names had been stricken from the Navy rolls. Outraged, Levy demanded that a Naval Court of Inquiry be convened to determine whether his summary discharge from the Navy was justified. Such a Court was convened in 1857. The hearing lasted more than a month and was widely publicized. Many well-known naval officers and prominent civilians testified for and against Levy. The Court's decision was unanimous:

The said Levy is morally, mentally, physically and professionally fit for the Naval Service and the court respectfully reports that
he ought to be restored to the active list of the Navy.

Once more official Navydom was greatly embarrassed. There was
no way out except to restore Levy's name to the rolls and call him back to
active duty. In June 1858 he was given command of the sloop *Macedonian*, about to sail from Boston for duty in the Mediterranean.

Captain Levy of the *Macedonian* sent the Secretary of the Navy a
most unusual communication. Permission was requested to have his wife
travel with him on his ship because she is

an orphan and not a native of this country, without any protection
during my absence, and no friends to accompany her across the
Atlantic, or on the continent of Europe.

And, wonder of wonders, the request was granted. The Secretary
wrote:

It is not the rule to afford passage in ships of war to the wives of
officers, but you may take your wife from Boston to the first port in
Italy touched by the *Macedonian*.

On February 21, 1860, Captain Levy was named Flag Officer, i.e.,
Commanding Officer, of the Mediterranean Squadron, U.S.N., and
given the honorary title of Commodore, a rank equivalent to the Army's
Brigadier General. At this time the Navy had no actual rank higher than
Captain; but to have honorary Commodore status was a privilege
accorded all American naval fleet and subfleet commanders. The legal
ranks of Commodore and Admiral did not come into being in the U. S.
Navy until 1862.

Early in the summer of 1860 Commodore Levy was ordered to bring
part of his squadron home. Included in the homeward-bound *Macedonian's* cargo was a wagonload of earth from the Holy Land, secured by
Levy for his synagogue, Congregation Shearith Israel of New York City,
for use in connection with the burial of its dead. On July 14, 1860, Levy
was relieved from duty as CO of the Mediterranean Squadron. But his
active duty days were not yet over.

When the Civil War began in 1861, Levy made several unsuccessful
attempts to persuade the Secretary of the Navy to send him back to sea.
Finally he wrote directly to President Lincoln. In November he was
summoned into Lincoln's presence, or at least so the story goes. Uriah
wanted sea duty. The President told him he was "a mite old" for such
duty. "However, I seem to remember that you survived a few courts-
martial in your day." "Yes, sir. Six, plus a Court of Inquiry." "All that

experience ought not to go to waste, Commodore. I think you will be useful serving on the Court-Martial Board here in Washington."

Levy served on this Board from November 1861 to March 1862. Early in March he caught a severe cold which forced him to take a leave of absence and return to New York. Two weeks later pneumonia developed. On March 22 Levy died. He was buried from Shearith Israel synagogue with full military honors and interred in the congregation's Cypress Hills cemetery on Long Island. Over his grave stands a statue he designed and an epitaph he wrote:

> Uriah P. Levy, Captain in the United States Navy, Father of the law for the abolition of the barbarous practice of corporal punishment in the Navy of the United States.

Earlier Levy had admitted that this last statement was a bit of an exaggeration, but only a bit. Having Navy flogging outlawed was an honor Levy shared with Senator John P. Hale of New Hampshire. About his own efforts Levy wrote:

> I was one of the first to denounce the old system of punishment by the lash as barbarous in the extreme and inconsistent with the genius of our institutions and the best interests of the service. My humble share in this work of humanity and patriotism will ever be a spring of joy and consolation of which I cannot be deprived by persecution or injustice.

In World War II a destroyer escort was named the U.S.S. *Uriah P. Levy*. In 1959 the Jewish chapel at the Norfolk Naval Base was designated the Uriah Phillips Levy Chapel.

Levy's pride in being both a Jew and an American were nobly expressed in the following testimony he gave during his 1857 hearing:

> My parents were Israelites and I was nurtured in the faith of my ancestors. In deciding to adhere to it, I have but exercized a right, guaranteed to one by the constitution of my native state and of the United States—a right given to all men by their Maker—a right more precious to each of us than life itself. But, while claiming and exercising this freedom of conscience, I have never failed to acknowledge and respect the like freedom in others. I might safely defy the citation of a single act, in the whole course of my official career, injurious to the religious rights of any other person. Remembering always that the great mass of my fellow citizens were Christians; profoundly grateful to the Christian founders of our Republic for their justice and liberality to my long persecuted race; I have earnestly endeavored, in all places and circumstances, to act up to the wise and tolerant spirit of our political institutions.

Virginia, Levy's child bride, died in 1925 at the age of eighty-nine.

WAS REBECCA GRATZ SCOTT'S REBECCA?
(1819)

The Gratz family was Philadelphia's most famous Jewish family in the eighteenth and nineteenth centuries. Rebecca, born in 1781, was the daughter of Michael Gratz, 1740-1811, whose father-in-law was Joseph Simon, Lancaster, Pennsylvania's first permanent Jewish settler. During her entire adult life, Rebecca worked unceasingly for Jewish and non-sectarian philanthropic and educational organizations and causes.

In 1815 she helped start the Philadelphia Orphan Asylum and served as its secretary from 1819 to 1859. In 1819 she established and became secretary of the Female Hebrew Benevolent Society. In 1831 she was one of the founders of the first Jewish Sunday School in the United States and its president and superintendent until 1864. In 1855 she was elected the first president of the Jewish Foster Home and Orphan Asylum. Rebecca never married, yet, in her eighty-eight years, she acquired a large family of grateful beneficiaries of her rarely equaled goodness of heart.

As a young woman Rebecca fell in love with Robert Ewing, a non-Jew, but refused to marry him because of her fidelity to the Jewish religion. He appears to have been her one true love. After he married Rebecca maintained a warm and lifelong friendship with Ewing, his wife, and their family.

The first internationally prominent American writer, Washington Irving, began his professional career as a lawyer. While studying law in New York City in the office of Josiah Hoffman, he met and became enamored of Hoffman's teen-age daughter Matilda. The engagement of Mr. Irving and Miss Hoffman had been announced and a date for their wedding had been set when it was discovered that Matilda had tuberculosis and the wedding was postponed. Her condition grew steadily worse. In April 1809 she died at the age of eighteen. Irving and his fiancée had become close friends of the Gratz family and frequent visitors at their Philadelphia home. Rebecca was very fond of Matilda and, during the last months of her illness, nursed her devotedly.

Irving went to England in 1815 to live and to write. In 1817 he became well acquainted with the novelist Sir Walter Scott, then doing research for his next book, *Ivanhoe*. Irving described the character and deeds of Rebecca Gratz to Scott in such glowing terms that Scott decided to pattern the principal female character in *Ivanhoe* after her. When the book appeared in 1819, Scott is said to have written to Irving, "How does your Rebecca compare to mine?" Like Rebecca Gratz, *Ivanhoe's* Rebecca is a Jewish woman of great compassion and goodness. While nursing the novel's Christian hero, Wilfred of Ivanhoe, back to health, she falls in love with him but refuses to marry him because of the difference in their religious faiths. Rebecca Gratz was informed by Irving that Scott had her in mind when he wrote the book; but she was much too reserved to ever discuss this matter publicly.

The well-known Franks family of Philadelphia maintained that Scott modeled his Rebecca after their Rebecca, the beautiful and ardent Tory who was the adored "soldiers' sweetheart" of the British in the years they occupied Philadelphia during the American Revolution. When the British left, this Rebecca left with them, married a British colonel who later became a general, and lived for the rest of her life in Bath, a city often visited by Scott. However, Rebecca Franks Johnson in no way fitted the picture of the saintly Jewish woman portrayed in the novel. Mrs. Johnson was not a very admirable person; she was not a devout Jew; she did marry a Christian; she was fifty-nine years old when *Ivanhoe* appeared while Rebecca Gratz was then thirty-eight; and she was not as well acquainted with Washington Irving as was Rebecca Gratz.

There is not much doubt that the gentle and noble Rebecca Gratz of Philadelphia described to Scott by his and her good friend, Washington Irving, is the woman whose charm and spirituality are mirrored on the pages of *Ivanhoe*.

"BY THE GRACE OF GOD, GOVERNOR AND JUDGE OF ISRAEL!"
(1825)

Mordecai Manuel Noah, 1785-1851, the most prominent New York City Jew of his day, was ardent patriot, fervent Zionist, observant Jew, religious leader, successful dramatist, gifted orator, controversial journalist, diplomat, and politician—yes; utopian, self-glorifying, ostentatious showman—perhaps; deliberately dishonest—no.

He was a devoted member of the Sephardic Shearith Israel congregation of New York City. He delivered the principal address at the consecration of its enlarged Mill Street edifice in 1818 and at the dedication of its new Crosby Street building in 1834. He was very proud of his Sephardic ancestry. Actually only one grandmother was Sephardic and the rest of his grandparents were Ashenazim. Uriah Phillips Levy was his first cousin. George Washington is said to have been a guest at his parents' wedding.

Born in Philadelphia, Noah was orphaned at six and reared by his mother's parents. He began his career as a journalist at fifteen. At twenty-three he wrote his first play. Along the way he also was a newspaper editor and columnist and became a lawyer.

In 1813 Noah was appointed American consul at Tunis. There he negotiated the release of twelve American sailors from Algerian pirates by paying a ransom of some $20,000. Noah was instructed by his superiors to let the pirates think the ransom was being paid by the captives' families, when actually the money would come from the American government. After complying with this instruction, Noah was chagrined in 1816 to receive a message from the State Department in Washington that his payment of the ransom money had not been authorized. Then came a letter from the Secretary of State himself, James Monroe, containing an even bigger bombshell:

> At the time of your appointment as Consul at Tunis, it was not known that the religion you profess would form any obstacle to the exercise of your Consular functions. Recent information, however, on which entire reliance may be placed, proves that it would produce a very unfavorable effect. In consequence of which, the President [James Madison] has deemed it expedient to revoke your commission.

Why or how or which State Department bureaucrats brought about these inexcusable blunders is not known and probably never will be. At no time was Noah accused of lack of integrity. Madison and Monroe knew that Noah was a Jew when he was selected to go to Tunis. The Bey of Tunis, a Muslim, certainly harbored no more ill will toward a Jewish diplomat than toward a Christian. In addition, neither Madison nor Monroe was anti-Jewish. Both had benefited greatly from a Jew's generosity. Both had been loaned money without interest by Haym Salomon during the Revolution. In January 1817 the State Department admitted it had made a mistake. But Noah was not sent back to Tunis. As a matter of fact, he was never again employed by the federal government.

After returning to the United States in 1816, Noah became a permanent resident of New York City. He wrote plays, published and edited newspapers, practiced law, and was deeply involved in Jewish and Masonic affairs, communal organizations and politics. In 1822 he was appointed Sheriff of New York County. In 1827 he married a seventeen-year-old girl with whom he had seven children. In 1828 he was named Surveyor for the Port of New York. In 1842 he was elected president of the Hebrew Benevolent Society. Throughout the entire thirty-five years of his New York residency, Noah was one of that city's most highly respected citizens. His death in 1851 was deeply mourned by both the Jewish and general communities.

But none of these impressive facts explains the special place that Mordecai Manuel Noah occupies in American Jewish history and folklore. To bring into focus this facet of this unique and gifted man's career, the key word is Ararat.

Mordecai Manuel Noah was a devout traditional Jew. He prayed daily for the return of our people to the Holy Land and the restoration of the Jewish state. Noah had many strong beliefs; but not all were right or good. He believed strongly in the coming of a personal Messiah. He also believed strongly that the American Indians were the Ten Lost Tribes. He also believed strongly that America's enslavement of the pagan blacks was proper. He felt that the Jews should not leave entirely to God the task of getting them back to His Land. He felt that it would be very helpful if the Jews could assist God to fulfill this divinely ordained goal. He was America's first Zionist activist.

In his address, on April 17, 1818, at the consecration of the Mill Street synagogue, Noah stated that, in preparation for the return to Zion, the Jews, or at least a sizeable number of them, must take up farming as their major occupation. To make this theory a reality he petitioned the New York legislature at the beginning of 1820 to sell him a state-owned property, Grand Island in the Niagara River, near Buffalo and opposite Tonawanda, New York, for the purpose of establishing a Jewish agricultural settlement. Grand Island was a forested area of about 17,000 acres. Noah proposed to divide it into farming lots of 100 acres and to bring in 170 European Jewish families to develop it. This was obviously meant to be only the beginning of a much larger effort, since the Grand Island project would have provided for only about 1,000 Jews. Later Noah decided that, since Tonawanda was to be the western terminus of the Erie Canal, it would be advantageous to develop Grand Island into a mercantile as well as an agricultural center. At that time Buffalo had only about 2,500 inhabitants and no Jews. The prospect of having a large community of Jews on its borders who would be preparing themselves for ultimate migration to Palestine appealed greatly to the pious Christians of Buffalo.

The state legislature turned down Noah's request because the island had not yet been surveyed and there was no way to subdivide it into 100-acre lots. Such a survey was begun in 1824 and completed in 1825. Noah was then informed that he could purchase land on Grand Island.

Noah persuaded a Christian friend, Samuel Leggett of New York City, to purchase 1,020 acres on the northern end of the island for agricultural usage and 1,535 acres on the eastern shore opposite the Erie Canal terminus to serve as a marketing and distribution center for the products that would arrive on the Canal boats. The canal had just been completed. The boats were scheduled to begin their New York-Buffalo run in October 1825. Some unkind critics have suggested that Noah concocted this scheme for personal gain. If this was so it was not his primary motive. No American Jew of the time made such an accusation. Some European Jews, including Heinrich Heine, did; but none of these foreign detractors knew Noah personally, so their opinions were probably based entirely on their low estimates of such utopian schemes.

Noah announced that the name of his new community would be Ararat, "a city of refuge for the Jews." Just as the Biblical Noah had brought his boatload of humans and animals to safe rest on Mount Ararat and thus preserved human and animal life upon this planet, so would the modern Noah bring his boatloads of Jews to Ararat, the island refuge, and there begin the work of redemption that would eventually return the Jew to the land of his fathers and bring on the Messianic age. While the American Jewish community respected Noah's noble ambitions, it felt that the project had little chance for success; and so the effort had practically no Jewish support. The contemporary press had a field day. American newspapers ridiculed Ararat and said it was a bit of grandiose pageantry masterminded by a clever playwright. There may have been more than just a grain of truth in this allegation.

Noah arrived in Buffalo at the end of August 1825 to prepare for the dedication of Ararat's foundation stone. He brought with him for this purpose a block of sandstone. A Buffalo mason carved the Shema in Hebrew at the top of the stone, followed by these words:

ARARAT
A City of Refuge for the Jews
Founded by MORDECAI MANUEL NOAH in the Month Tizri 5586
Sept. 1825 & in the 50th year of American Independence.

September 2, 1825, was the great day. At dawn a gun salute was fired in front of the Buffalo courthouse. At 10:00 A.M an impressive parade of militia, Masons, civic officials, and clergy marched from the Masonic Lodge to the Episcopal church. Noah, "a man of large muscular frame, rotund person, benign of face," walked in the parade garbed in a judicial robe of black lined with ermine.

After a religious service based completely on the Old Testament, Noah made a speech and then read a proclamation:

I, Mordecai Manuel Noah, citizen of the United States of America, late Consul of said States to the City and Kingdom of Tunis, High Sheriff of New York, Counsellor at Law, and, by the grace of God, Governor and Judge of Israel, have issued this my Proclamation, announcing to Jews throughout the world, that an asylum is prepared and hereby offered to them, where they can enjoy that peace, comfort and happiness which has been. denied them through the intolerance and misgovernment of former ages, an asylum in a free and powerful country. . . .

It is my will that a census of the Jews throughout the world be taken. . . . Those of our people who . . . prefer remaining in their several parts of the world which they now respectively inhabit are permitted to do so . . . Those Jews who are in the military employment of the different sovereigns of Europe are enjoined to keep in their ranks until further orders . . . I command that a strict neutrality be observed in the pending wars between the Greeks and the Turks . . . The annual gifts which, for many centuries, have been offered to our pious brethren in our holy City of Jerusalem (to which may God speedily restore us) are to continue with unabated liberality . . . I abolish forever polygamy among the Jews . . . Prayers shall forever be said in the Hebrew language . . . Caraite and Samaritan Jews, together with the black Jews of India and Africa, and likewise those in Cochin China and the sect on the coast of Malabar, are entitled to equality of rights and religious privileges, as are all who may wish to partake of the great covenant and obey and respect the Mosaical laws . . . The Indians of the American continent . . . being, in all probability, descendants of the lost tribes of Israel, measures will be adopted to make them sensible of their condition and finally reunite them with their brethren, the chosen people . . . A capitation tax of three shekels in silver, per annum, or one Spanish dollar, is hereby levied upon each Jew throughout the world for the purpose of defraying the expenses of reorganizing the [Jewish] government. . . . I do appoint Rosh-hodesh Adar, February 7, 1826, to be observed with suitable demonstrations as a day of Thanksgiving to the Lord God of Israel, for manifold blessings. . . .

Given at Buffalo, in the State of New York, this second day of Tishri, in the year of the world 5586, corresponding with the fifteenth day of September, 1825, and in the fiftieth year of American independence.

By the Judge,

(signed) A. B. Seixas, Sec'y Pro tem.

As far as is known, Seixas and Noah were the only Jews present at the ceremony.

This is how Ararat began and this is where it ended. Noah returned to New York City and made no further effort to establish the colony. The foundation stone was removed from the church and put into the churchyard, leaning against the church's back wall. In 1834 it was carried to Grand Island and placed on exhibit. In 1866 it was given to the museum of the Buffalo Historical Society. In 1968 the foundation stone was returned to Grand Island. Since then it has been on display in the foyer of the Town Hall.

What is Grand Island like today? The late Rabbi Isaac Klein of Buffalo's Temple Shaarey Zedek furnished this description:

As one crosses the Grand Island bridge from Buffalo to Niagara Falls, it takes less than ten minutes to travel over the segment that passes through Grand Island. The island is six miles in width at its widest point and seven and a half miles in length. It contains one community, the Township of Grand Island, with a population of about 12,000. The island retains its rural atmosphere. There is still much farming of the truck garden variety. Mainly it is a resort area where people come for recreation and picnicking. The beaches, especially the one on the southern end called Beaver Island, are popular. Also popular are the state parks, the areas with boating and camping facilities. The island has no institutions of higher learning nor any major cultural institutions. For these it relies on Buffalo. Basically, it is a suburb of Buffalo. As the city expands, it is not likely that the island will retain its rural atmosphere much longer.

There are a few Jews on the island but not enough to form a congregation. Present-day Jewish interest in Grand Island is historical rather than practical, an interest symbolized by the stone of Ararat which rests in a large glass-covered frame in the lobby of Grand Island's Town Hall.

MARYLAND ENACTS THE "JEW BILL"
(1826)

In the State of Maryland, as early as 1649, the full rights of citizenship were denied to those not professing the Christian religion. The first movement looking for the enfranchisement of the Hebrews took place in 1797, and in 1818 the first persistent and organized effort was made in that direction. At that time, a citizen of Maryland, if of the Hebrew faith, though eligible to appointment to any office, under the Constitution of the United States, could not, under the government of Maryland, be appointed a Justice of the Peace, and though compelled to perform military duty, he could not rise even to the rank of ensign in the militia, nor plead as an attorney at the bar; in short, he was disqualified from holding any office under the State Government. The attempted removal of these disabilities by the House of Delegates in the year 1818 led to heated and protracted discussion. On December 9th of that year Mr. Kennedy of Washington County moved that a committee of three be appointed "to consider the justice and expediency of extending to persons professing the Jewish religion the same privileges that are enjoyed by Christians." Twelve days thereafter, Mr. Kennedy, who, with Messrs. Brackenridge and E. S. Thomas of Baltimore, had been appointed to such committee, made an exhaustive report recommending the passage of an act extending such rights and privileges. Numerous attempts were made to postpone consideration of the bill, and on the question being put, "Shall the Bill pass?" Mr. Kennedy opened the debate. In the course of his remarks, which cover thirty printed pages of the official report, and abound in eulogies of the Hebrew race, he said:

From Isaac Markens' *The Hebrews in America*, New York, 1888, pp. 97-100.

Poor, hapless, unfortunate children of Israel, how are ye fallen! once the peculiar people of God, and enjoying His favor, His protection and His immediate presence; blest with a land flowing with milk and honey, with a climate bland as the dew of heaven and a soil luxuriantly fertile; now scattered and dispersed, oppressed and persecuted, without a country and without a home! Ye have drank deep of adversity's bitter draught; ye have indeed emptied "the cup of trembling even unto the dregs"—yet scattered and dispersed as ye have been; amidst all your distresses and unparalleled sufferings—ye have still been faithful and true to the religion of your forefathers; ye have still worshipped the God of Abraham; and ye have lived to see your destroyers destroyed. But fear not, ye sons of Jacob—faint not, ye children of Israel; though cast down, ye shall never be destroyed; persecuted, ye shall never be utterly forsaken; the hour of your deliverance approaches; the day of your redemption draweth nigh; and he who led your fathers through the wilderness, he who has hitherto preserved you as a nation—as a peculiar people, will ere long restore you to the promised land.

I call upon you as legislators to whose hands are committed the destinies of a free and generous people, to do them justice. I call upon you, as Christians, to consider what you would expect, what you would ask, were you now in their situation, and to do them justice. I ask no more.

After a three-days' debate the bill was lost by a vote of twenty-four in the affirmative and fifty in the negative. A few days thereafter, a motion was made in the Senate for permission to bring in a bill to repeal such parts of the Constitution and Bill of Rights that establish a religious test as a qualification to office, which was also refused.

These exciting debates were the subject of discussion and formed the topic of newspaper comment in all parts of the country. The Natchez, Mississippi, *Independent Press* said:

As it was not required, when a soldier was enlisted in the armies of the Revolution, that he should give an account of his religious tenets before he could be permitted to shed his blood in defence of liberty; as it was not demanded of a citizen when he was called upon to give his property to support those heroes who were fighting the battles of his country, to what God he prayed to prosper her arms, before he was allowed to contribute to the achievement of her independence; little does it become us now, to say to one who has borne the heat or burthen of the combat, because he eats not of the same bread nor drinks from the same cup as we do—"Thou art not one of us."

The following verses appeared in the *Franklin Gazette* of Philadelphia after the rejection of the "Jew Bill":

What! still reject the fated race.
Thus long denied repose—

What! madly strive to efface
The RIGHTS that heaven bestows!

Say, flows not in each Jewish vein,
Unchecked, without control;
A tide as pure—as free from stain—
As warms the Christian's soul!

Do ye not yet the times discern,
That these shall cease to roam—
That SHILOH, pledged for their return,
Will bring his ransomed home!

Be error quick to darkness hurl'd!
No more with hate pursue—
For He who died to save a world,
IMMANUEL was a Jew.

After being voted down session after session, the bill was finally passed by both Houses of the Legislature in 1822. In accordance with the Constitution, its ratification was required by the next Legislature. This failed of accomplishment, but the friends of the measure were indefatigable and on Saturday, February 26, 1825, the last day of the session, the bill passed the Assembly [by one vote]. It was ratified at the succeeding session [in 1826] and thus became a law. According to Solomon Etting of Baltimore, the total Hebrew population of Maryland at that time did not exceed 125, whose combined wealth was estimated at $500,000, and at the same time he computed their total number in the United States at this period to be about 6,000, whose wealth was estimated at about ten million dollars. These facts were elicited in the course of an examination by a committee of the Legislature during the pendency of "The Jew Bill."

Sholem

(1837)

Among the hills in the extreme western part of Ulster County, in New York State, there is a rocky stretch of plateau land, sterile, lonely, unattractive, reached by mountain paths difficult, in places almost

Excerpted from "The Tragedy of Sholem," a paper by Gabriel Davidson, read before the annual meeting of the American Jewish Historical Society and reprinted in the New York weekly, *The Jewish Tribune*, June 16 and 23, 1922.

impossible, of access even in this day of modern modes of transportation. A bare half-score families, mainly old German residents or their descendants, most of them interrelated, constitute the sole population of this lonesome mountain fastness. The chance traveler will observe a few none-too-well preserved houses, ill-kept farm buildings, small cultivated fields, and large stretches of rough and stony land, unused and untillable. Farm animals are few and inferior. The wayfarer seldom meets anyone, and the few residents whom he happens to see are for the most part elderly people. He is struck by the almost entire absence of child life. Indeed, an atmosphere of brooding and desolation permeates the entire region. This place marks the scene of what was once the colony of Sholem, the [second] Jewish agricultural colony in the United States. [The first such Jewish farming community was established at Rising Sun, Indiana, about 1825.]

In 1837 a small group of New York Jews banded together for the purpose of founding a rural colony. They selected as the site for their settlement a tract of land in Ulster County, about six miles west of Wawarsing and four miles north of Lackawack. A site was set aside for a village named Sholem, which in Yiddish means "peace," and the land was subdivided into plots of about five acres each. This being before the day of the railroad, the colonists traveled by boat up the Hudson to Rondout and then by way of an old canal to Wawarsing, a journey that probably took three days or more.

The Ulster County Clerk's Office shows that a total of 484.54 acres and eleven lots in the Village of Sholem were conveyed in December 1837, to eleven Jewish families. The land was owned in parcels ranging in size from 20.7 to 70.5 acres. An average of $7.50 an acre was paid. Part was paid in cash and the rest in five-year mortgages bearing seven percent annual interest.

Contracts were awarded to build houses. The cost per house seems to have been around $300 or $400, which was ample for the erection of a very comfortable house in those early days. Indeed, the houses were out of the ordinary for that primitive time and in that primitive country, and the fact that the newcomers could afford the luxury of a frame house in place of the primitive log cabin commonly in use caused them to be regarded as men of means by their neighbors. A plot was set aside for a burial ground and a synagogue was erected. How hard it must have been to accomplish this latter object can be judged from the fact that a petition was sent to Shearith Israel Congregation in New York City in 1838 for financial help toward the erection of the synagogue.

The newcomers cleared their lands and fenced them; they dug wells; they built roads. They wisely did not depend upon farming alone, for they evidently realized the futility of trying to make a living from barren soil. They engaged in the manufacture of goose-quill pens and fur caps. They became cobblers, peddlers, and tailors. One conducted an inn and general store, and it is narrated that before he waited on his customers he took them into a room behind the store and served them with tea and cake. Another of their number served as Rabbi and Shochet.

The Jewish settlers were men of education and culture, people who for the most part had lived on a good, even though modest, standard in the city. This is indicated by the comparatively luxurious houses, and also by the character of the household furniture, their oil paintings, and the art objects which they brought with them. Thomas F. Benedict, an old, distinguished resident and the historian of Ulster County, maintains that they even had a small museum and art gallery.

For a time the newcomers were able to get along—how well it is doubtful—but by combining farming with their other occupations they managed somehow not only to eke out an existence but even to reduce their mortgages. But the odds were too heavy against them. Farming was impossible, especially for new recruits in that bare, cold, mountainous country where the soil was poor and the growing season short. For business the country was too sparsely settled. Removed from markets and from centers of population, the colonists soon found the road too thorny to travel. Their sufferings at times were intense, but they held on tenaciously as long as it was humanly possible. It is related that on one occasion their condition was so desperate that they slaughtered a day-old calf to assuage the hunger of their families, despite the fact that the Jewish law prohibits the use of an animal for food before its eighth day and although these people were conforming Jews.

The troubles of the Sholemites seem to have reached their climax with the temporary shutting down of the local tanning industry following the financial crisis of 1837. There were three tanning factories in the neighborhood. Some of the Sholemites were compelled to work there to stave off starvation. Deprived of even this meagre source of income, the condition of the colonists became so desperate that they were forced to give up. They could no longer meet the payments on their mortgages. Foreclosure suits were instituted. In 1842 nine of the twelve (a twelfth Jewish farmer arrived in 1840) were sold out. The other three managed to pay off their mortgages before the end of 1845. The last Jewish colonists seem to have returned to New York City before the end of 1850.

There is an atmosphere of mystery surrounding this colony. Why did this handful of immigrant Jews in that early day leave their homes in New York and select as their future abode a sterile, inaccessible, and forsaken country more than 100 miles from the metropolis? Surely there was better land closer to the city to be had for little, if anything, more than the price they paid in Sholem. They were people, if not of affluence, at least of comfortable circumstances. What was it that induced in them a desire for change? Men of culture and education, why did they select farming as the means of a livelihood? What was the common bond that brought these colonists together?

To seek the answers to these questions we took a trip to Sholem, interviewed old settlers, made search of official records at the County Seat, and traced descendants of five of the twelve Sholem founders. We heard many interesting human tales—some perhaps legendary—woven around these early settlers.

The spot where the colonists lived is now a wilderness covered with a second growth of timber. The stone foundations of houses, fences built out of the rocks gathered from the land, a lane, and abandoned wells are all that is left to mark this old habitation. We saw the place where the synagogue is supposed to have stood. It was moved from Sholem several decades later. We took a picture of a house near Wawarsing, part of which is purported to have been the synagogue. We saw the spot which is said to have been the burying ground, but found no evidence of graves or tombstones. It is said that there were at least three graves over which had been placed ordinary rectangular field stones without inscriptions. We saw an abandoned well, blocked up with stones, and met an old resident of Ellenville, formerly of Sholem, who told us that this well was formerly referred to as "Der Judenbrunnen." Two very old women remembered that the abandoned synagogue was used as a dance hall by the German young folks because it was the largest building in the neighborhood. From some of the old settlers we learned that several of the frame houses erected by the Jews were removed from Sholem about twenty years later and that one of them served as a schoolhouse.

Some of the colonists' furniture is still in existence, a number of pieces being in the possession of a Mrs. Leibolt of Napanoch. We saw an inlaid mahogany wall mirror, a folding table, a chair, and a rocking chair—all made of mahogany—and a piece of furniture which was a combination bureau and secretary. It seems that when misfortune overtook this colony it was found necessary to dispose of part of their belongings to make ends meet. The story is told that when the last of the colonists reached Lackawack on his way to New York, with his household furnishings loaded on a wagon, he was obliged to sell a fine mahogany bedstead so as to realize enough money to pay for his own food and for the feed of his horse until he reached New York City.

✿　✿　✿　✿　✿

The most recent word on Sholem is found in Postal and Koppman's *American Jewish Landmarks,* Volume I, page 280:

"Sholam Road" appears on a small marker on a blacktop road in the town of Warwarsing, along New York City's Rondout Reservoir, 11 miles from Ellenville. It is the only reminder of the [second] Jewish agricultural colony in the United States.

MICHAEL BOAZ ISRAEL, ZIONIST PIONEER
(1848)

Warder Cresson, Quaker, born Philadelphia, Pennsylvania, July 13, 1798.

Michael Boaz Israel, Jew, died Jerusalem, Palestine, tenth of Cheshvan, 5621 (November 6, 1860).

Same man.

His life is a strange and wondrous story.

His forebears were among the founders of New Haarlem, New York, now known as Harlem, in 1636. His great-grandfather moved to Philadelphia about 1700. His father, John Elliott Cresson, married his mother, Mary Warder, in 1795. His well-to-do Quaker parents gave their son as his name their surnames, Warder Cresson.

From early youth Warder Cresson was given to speculation about religious matters. In 1830 he wrote an anti-Catholic pamphlet deploring what he considered to be the evil tendencies and extravagances of that faith. Dissatisfied with the Society of Friends, he joined in succession a number of other Protestant denominations but failed to find in any of them the spiritual happiness he was seeking. In 1840 he met Isaac Leeser, rabbi of Philadelphia's oldest synagogue, Mikveh Israel, and editor of *The Occident* magazine. Under Leeser's influence Cresson became deeply interested in Judaism.

In May 1844 he persuaded the Department of State to name him American consul in Jerusalem, the first such in the Holy City. At that time he was successfully operating a farm in a Philadelphia suburb. He describes his departing for Jerusalem as follows:

> In the Spring of 1844 I left everything near and dear to me on earth. I left the wife of my youth and six lovely children (dearer to me than my natural life), and an excellent farm with everything comfortable around me. I left all these in pursuit of the Truth, and for the sake of the Truth alone.

It has been said that Cresson was urged to obtain the Jerusalem appointment by some missionary-minded Christians, who hoped that this fervently religious man would help bring the gospel message to the Jews of Palestine. Cresson studied Hebrew diligently until he was able not only to speak the language but also to read and comprehend difficult classical works such as the Talmud and Zohar. This led to a decision to convert to Judaism and to take up permanent residence in Eretz Yisrael. In March 1848, after having been given a hard time by the Sephardic chief rabbi and his Bet Din, Cresson was circumcised, taken to the Mikveh, given the name Michael Boaz and accepted as a full member of the Jewish community. Since settling permanently in Palestine meant subjugating oneself to Turkish sovereignty and Muslim law, Cresson gave up his position as American consul.

He returned to Philadelphia early in 1849 to try to persuade his family to sell the farm and join him in Palestine. His wife and all his children except one son refused to have anything to do with him. They believed him insane. In May 1849 they succeeded in having a judge declare he was unbalanced and, for a time, he was incarcerated in a mental institution. Cresson appealed to a higher court. His sanity trial in May 1851 lasted six days and was widely publicized. Prominent lawyers were engaged by both Cresson and his estranged family. Nearly one hundred witnesses gave testimony for and against him. The first judge's ruling was reversed. Cresson was declared to be completely sane. During his Philadelphia stay, Cresson attended services regularly at Mikveh Israel, observed the traditional Jewish laws and customs punctiliously, and contributed articles to *The Occident*. When the 1851 trial concluded, he divorced his wife.

Then he returned to Palestine where he attempted to establish an agricultural colony in the valley of Rephaim, south of Jerusalem on the way to Bethlehem. In March 1853 *The Occident* reproduced a circular, sent from Jerusalem by Michael Boaz Israel, asking American Jews to contribute to the support of his colony. It was to be the first of a number of such colonies intended to help reduce the widespread poverty of Palestinian Jewry and to enable oppressed Jews in all parts of the world to return to Zion. But Michael Boaz Israel did not receive enough financial backing to make his dream a reality. Yet he never abandoned the dream. Over the years *The Occident* published many communications from him about what he hoped to accomplish—but, alas, never did. Sir Moses Montefiore and Judah Touro were among those who contributed funds to this worthy but unsuccessful effort.

Michael Boaz was a prominent member of Jerusalem's Sephardic community. After 1851 he lived as a Sephardi, dressed in Oriental garb and married an Oriental Jewish woman. He was regarded as a "tsaddik," a mystic, a miracle worker. He was called upon frequently to intercede with God on behalf of the ill and the needy. When he died he was interred on the Mount of Olives with honors accorded only to the most pious. On the day of his funeral every Jewish place of business in Jerusalem closed in tribute to the passing of a saintly man.

Warder Cresson-Michael Boaz Israel was a "ger tsedek" par excellence and one of the first to understand that, in returning to Zion, the Jew must also return to the "dat avoda," the rustic way of life led by his Palestinian ancestors.

"THE RABBI DID IT!"
(1860)

On December 5, 1859, three days after John Brown was hanged at Charleston, Virginia (now West Virginia), for endeavoring to foment a slave insurrection, the 36th United States Congress held its opening session. It met in an atmosphere of hate and of fear. Those who were for and against slavery literally looked at each other with murder in their hearts. Whether black men and women would continue to be held in bondage in this "land of the free" was the burning issue of the day and was to lead, sixteen months later, to a long, bitter, and bloody fratricidal struggle.

In the 36th Congress were 114 Republicans, 92 regular Democrats, and 31 others, divided between Anti-Slavery Democrats and American (Know Nothing) Party representatives. The prevailing mood was so tense that, to quote a South Carolina senator, "every man in both houses went armed with a revolver—some with two —and a bowie knife." In addition, it is said that armed supporters of both factions often crowded the galleries.

In such a seething political cauldron the 36th Congress tried to organize itself and elect a Speaker. Since the Republicans were the majority party in the House (the Democrats controlled the Senate), Republican John Sherman of Ohio was nominated as Speaker. A long and stubborn deadlock ensued, lasting nearly two months, because Sherman had endorsed a book picturing the Southern slave states as backward and barbaric. Finally it was realized that Sherman could not win and would have to be replaced by a more conservative-minded Republican candidate.

It was at this point that the rabbi entered the legislative picture. For the first time in American history, a rabbi was asked to give the opening prayer at a session of Congress. The date was February 1, 1860, the same day which the House had set aside to make an all-out effort to solve its problem of finding an acceptable person to serve as presiding officer.

The rabbi upon whom this historic honor had been conferred was Morris Jacob Raphall of Orthodox Congregation Bnai Jeshurun of New York City, founded in 1825, second oldest and first Ashkenazic synagogue in the city.

Raphall, born in Stockholm in 1798, received his Hebrew education

The research materials for this story were supplied by Fannie Zelcer, Archivist, American Jewish Archives, Cincinnati, Ohio.

in Copenhagen. After earning a Ph.D. in Germany, he went to England, where he wrote many scholarly works and acted as honorary secretary to the Chief Rabbi. In 1841 he was appointed minister of the Birmingham Synagogue. Eight years later he was elected rabbi of Bnai Jeshurun. He served this congregation until 1866, greatly respected as orator and scholar. In 1861 he created a sensation in the northern American Jewish community by preaching a sermon in which he defended slavery as "a divinely ordained institution." He died in New York City in 1868.

✿   ✿   ✿   ✿   ✿

An eyewitness account of the Congressional happening was printed in *The Occident* on February 9, 1860. It was in the form of a letter to the editor and was signed by "An American Jew":

On a journey from the South to New York, business required that I should stay a day or two at Washington. I arrived there Tuesday afternoon, and repaired to my old quarters, Brown's Hotel, where I met several Southern members of Congress, old friends of mine. In the course of conversation, I was informed a Jewish minister from New York was to officiate as Chaplain to the House, and to open its proceedings with prayer. This intelligence surprised me. During all the years that Congress had held its sittings, no Jew had ever officiated, and I determined to witness an event so novel, and, at the same time, so interesting to me.

I went early and secured a seat that gave me a full view of the hall. By degrees, the galleries became densely crowded. The lobbies were full of people, and great excitement prevailed as the struggle for the election of a Speaker was drawing to a close. As the minute hand of the large clock opposite the Speaker's chair was approaching the hour of noon, a kind of impatient expectation seemed to prevail in the galleries which was interrupted by a buzzing sound, "There he is," and every eye was turned towards the Speaker's chair. Next to that chair, but one step lower, was seated an old man with a Tallith over his shoulders, and a velvet cap on his head. I at once recognized the Rev. Dr. Raphall, whose lectures on the Poetry of the Bible I had attended ten years ago, at Savannah. He appeared fatigued; and, as he looked languidly around him, I asked myself, How would I feel if, young and strong, and business-man as I am, I were about to address two hundred and fifty of the most talented and gifted men in the country, besides the immense crowd in the galleries, whose feelings, I have no reason to expect, are prejudiced in my favor? and, as I did not feel quite sure of my own moral courage, I began to doubt whether that pale old man would have enough nerve for the occasion. My doubts, however, were soon removed.

Before Dr. R. had been many minutes in the hall, the clock struck, down came the Clerk's hammer, and the next instant the "Rabbi" stood at the reading desk in the attitude of prayer. He had uttered but few words, when his eye kindled, his pale face became flushed, and, with a voice strong, clear and filling the entire hall, he offered his orisons to the "Lord God of Abraham, of Isaac, and of Jacob." The effect was wonderful; the members had all risen from their seats. At first their feeling seemed to be that of malicious curiosity; but as his melodious sentences, his correct elocution, and impressive intonation fell upon their ears, the change was most striking, both in the hall and in the galleries. Curiosity made room for attention, and that soon became devotion. Startling was the effect when he besought Him "that maketh peace in the high heavens" to direct the minds of the Representatives to elect a man to preside over them "without fear and without favor." In the whole assembly there was, as he spoke, "no ear so dull, no soul so cold that felt not fired at the tone." And when he pronounced the benediction, my heart leapt within me for joy, as I saw the proud Representatives of the United States submissively bow their heads to receive the blessing of "the ONE who liveth and reigneth forever." So proud, so happy, so delighted was I with the impression made by this beautiful prayer, delivered with the fluency and self-possession of a practiced orator, and with the fervent piety of the faithful servant of his God, that I intended to have the words engrossed on vellam, framed, and glazed, as an ornament to my home in the Sunny South.

In the evening, at the hotel, the exciting events of the day formed the topic of conversation. The merits of Mr. [William] Pennington, [a conservative Republican from New Jersey] the new Speaker, were canvassed, and one witty M.C. remarked, that after every Christian influence had failed during sixty days to make a Speaker, they had to go beyond the pale of Christianity. This called forth a general shout of "Yes, the Rabbi did it," which naturally directed the discourse to Dr. Raphall and his prayer.

As to the commanding talents and depth of religious sentiment in the man, and the beautiful simplicity and profound impressiveness of the prayer, there was but one opinion. Not so, however, with respect to his costume; some found fault with the Tallith, others called the cap in bad taste. I had no answer to make to these objections; for I confess when I first saw Dr. R. in the hall, I wished he had been less particular and wedded to ancient customs. One gentleman, an M.C. of great influence and talent, asked me if such was the regular costume of the Rabbi in the Synagogue? to which question having answered affirmatively, the M.C. remarked,

"Then the Rabbi did right in adhering to his costume; he came among us to pray according to his faith. For the moment, the Hall of Congress was his Synagogue. He had to maintain the perfect equality of his persuasion, and of its religious practices, with that of any other denomination. Had he departed from the regular practice of the Synagogue, had he yielded to our habits, so far as to come with his head uncovered, and without those vestments which a Jewish Rabbi wears at the time of solemn service, such concession to our views and feelings would also have been renouncing of that perfect equality which it was his duty as a Jew and a minister of religion to uphold."

To this reasoning, no answer was attempted, and though it did not quite satisfy me, I remained silent, as I could advance nothing to refute it; and, upon the whole, I think this view of the matter removes any little prejudice that, in the minds of some, might in any degree dim the glory of this most important and happy event.

* * * * *

The full text of Rabbi Raphall's prayer appeared in the same issue of *The Occident*. Both because of its significance as an historic "first" and because of the part it is said to have played in breaking the Congressional impasse over the choice of a House Speaker, it is reproduced here in full. The Hebrew transliterations, mistakes and all, are quoted exactly as they were printed in *The Occident*:

Almighty and most merciful God, we approach Thy presence this day to thank Thee for Thy past mercies, and humbly to beseech Thee to continue and extend the same to Thy servants, the Representatives of these United States in Congress assembled.

Lord, great and manifold have been Thy bounties to this highly favored land. Heartfelt and sincere are our thanks. While the vast despotisms of Asia are crumbling into dust, and the effete monarchies of the Old World can only sustain themselves by yielding to the pressure of the spirit of the age, it has been Thy gracious will that in this Western hemisphere there should be established a Commonwealth after the model of that which Thou, Thyself, didst bestow on the tribes of Israel, in their best and purest days. The Constitution and the institutions of this Republic prove to the world that men, created in Thy image and obedient to Thy behests, are not only capable, fully capable, of self-government, but that they know best how to combine civil liberty with ready obedience to the laws, religious liberty with warm zeal for religion, absolute general equality with sincere respect for individual rights. In acquiring and carrying out these most wise institutions, Thy protection, Lord, has been signally manifest. It was Thy right hand that defended the founders of this Commonwealth, during the long and perilous struggle of right against might. It was Thy wisdom that inspired them when they established this Congress, to be what Thy tabernacle, with the urim and thummin—right and equity—were intended to have been for the tribes of Israel—the heart of the entire nation, where the wants, the feelings, and wishes of all might become known, to be respected by all, so that union might create strength, and concord keep pace with prosperity.

Lord, the ordinary life-time of a man has barely elapsed since this Constitution came into force, and under its auspices our country, from being feeble and poor has become wealthy and powerful, ready to take rank with the mightiest, and Thou, O Lord, wilt realize unto it Thy gracious promise unto Thy chosen people: Vehosircha adonai letobeh—the Lord will distinguish thee for that which is good.

Supreme Ruler of the universe, many days and many weeks have gone by since thy servants, our Representatives, first met in this Congress, but not yet have they been able to organize their House. Thou who makest peace in Thy high Heavens, direct their minds this day that with one consent they may agree to choose the man who, without fear and without favor, is to preside over this assembly. To this intent, Father most gracious, do Thou endow them with Thy spirit; the spirit of wisdom and of understanding; the spirit of counsel and of amity; the spirit of knowledge and of fear of the Lord. Grant, Father, that amidst the din of conflicting interests and opinions, Thy grace may direct them so that each one of them and all of them may hold the even tenor of their way—the way of moderation and of equity; that they may speak and act and legislate for Thy glory and the happiness of our country; so that, from the North and from the South, from the East and from the West, one feeling of satisfaction may attend their labors; while the whole people of the land joyfully repeat the words of Thy Psalmist: "How good and how pleasant it is when brethren dwell together in unity."

Lord God of Abraham, of Isaac, and of Jacob, I, Thy servant, beseech Thee to bless these Representatives, even as Thou has directed Thy priests to bless Thy people:

Yebarekeka adonai Veyismireka.

Ya-air adonai panareleka wy-chaneneka.

Yissa adonai penar aleka veyasem Leka Shalom.

May the Lord bless ye and preserve ye.

May the Lord cause his countenance to shine upon ye and be gracious unto ye.

May the Lord raise his countenance unto ye and grant ye peace.

May this blessing of the one who liveth and who reigneth forever rest upon your counsels and yourselves this day, and evermore.

—Amen.

OUR FIRST COMBAT CHAPLAIN

(1863)

No rabbi served as a chaplain in the American Armed Forces prior to the Civil War. A law passed by Congress in July 1861 required that a regimental chaplain appointed by the regimental commander, "on the vote of the field officers and company commanders," be "a regularly ordained minister of some Christian denomination." Congressman Clement L. Valandingham of Ohio, later to become notorious as leader

---

Written by the late Chaplain (Rear Admiral) Bertram W. Korn, USN, ret. 1918-79. Chaplain Korn, noted American Jewish historian and rabbi of Congregation Keneseth Israel of Philadelphia, was the first rabbi to hold the rank of Admiral in the United States Navy. Indeed, he was the first rabbi to achieve two-star rank in the American military chaplaincy.

of the Copperheads, argued that this provision was unfair to the "large body of men in this country, and one growing continually, of the Hebrew faith, whose rabbis . . . are men of great learning and piety, and whose adherents are as good citizens and as true patriots as any in this country." His appeal was ignored, and the discrimination was inscribed on the statute books.

The same month that Congress passed this law about chaplains, the 65th Regiment of the 5th Pennsylvania Cavalry, probably unaware of the new law, elected as its chaplain a young Philadelphia Hebrew teacher, Michael Allen. The Commanding Officer and many of the officers and men of the 65th were Jewish. In September a YMCA worker visited the camp near Washington, D.C., where the unit was stationed and was horrified to discover that the 65th Regiment chaplain was neither a Christian nor an ordained minister. He raised such a fuss in the public press that, rather than suffer the disgrace of dismissal from the service, Allen resigned on September 23, 1861.

Within a few days, the regiment elected another Jew as its chaplain, but this time an ordained rabbi, Arnold Fischel of Shearith Israel Congregation of New York City. Fischel promptly applied to the War Department for a commission and the War Department just as promptly denied his application because he was a non-Christian.

The rejection of Rabbi Fischel's application caused a wave of protest throughout the North from both Jews and non-Jews. The issue was a broader one than that of discrimination against Jews. At stake was a basic principle of separation of church and state, the issue of whether Christianity was to be regarded by our government as the only legally valid religion or whether all religions, Christian and non-Christian, were to be accorded equal status before the law. Editors of Jewish periodicals wrote strong editorials on the subject and rabbis made frequent references to the matter in their sermons. Petitions to the Congress and President supporting the Jewish position came in from many Jewish communities, from 700 Baltimore Christians, from 38 members of the Maryland legislature, from 200 non-Jews in Bangor, Maine. A number of Protestant journals vehemently opposed the appointment of Jewish chaplains. One religious editor was appalled at the idea of granting the privilege of chaplaincy service to "Jewish rabbis, Mormon debauchees, Chinese priests, and Indian conjurers!"

Early in 1862 President Lincoln recommended to Congress that legislation be passed permitting non-Christian clergy to serve as military chaplains. After many committee meetings and much discussion, such a measure passed the Senate on March 12, 1862, the House on July 17, 1862, and was immediately signed by the President. The new regulation stated:

"No person shall be appointed a Chaplain in the United States

Army who is not a regularly ordained minister of some religious denomination, and who does not present testimonials of his good standing as such minister, with a recommendation for his appointment as an Army Chaplain, from some authorized ecclesiastical body of not less than five accredited ministers belonging to said denomination."

This law was of great historical importance. It gave rabbis and other non-Christian clergy the right to serve as chaplains in our Armed Forces; and it brought into being the denominational ecclesiastical endorsing agencies which, ever since, have been the means through which the government makes certain that its military chaplains are adequately trained and validly ordained clergymen. Because of the small number of chaplains involved, no national Jewish endorsing agency was established during the Civil War, although a Philadelphia Board of Rabbis was organized for that purpose. The first such Jewish national agency came into being in September 1917, five months after the beginning of the First World War.

The first Jewish chaplains to be commissioned were Jacob Frankel of Philadelphia, September 18, 1862, and Bernhard H. Gotthelf of Louisville, Kentucky, February 16, 1863. They were not assigned to combat units but served as hospital chaplains in the areas in which their congregations were located.

The honor of being the first American rabbi to serve with combat troops and to minister to men under fire belongs to Chaplain Ferdinand L. Sarner.

Ferdinand Leopold Sarner was born in 1820 in Lissa, Posen, which was also the birthplace of Haym Salomon. After attending a number of German universities and serving for a brief time as rabbi in Germany, he came to the United States in January 1859. Almost immediately he was elected rabbi of Congregation Berith Kodesh in Rochester, New York. There, apparently, he became embroiled in a conflict within the congregation between the Orthodox and Reform elements and he was compelled to leave after about two years.

Little is known about Rabbi Sarner's activities from the time he left Rochester until his election, on April 10, 1863, as Chaplain of the 54th New York Volunteer Regiment, also known as the "Schwarze Yaeger," i.e., "Black Riflemen." From an examination of the rolls of the regiment, it would appear that only three of the thirteen officers could possibly have been Jewish, and that Jews were a minority also among the enlisted men. It is quite possible that he was elected chaplain despite the fact that he was Jewish and because he was capable of ministering to the large number of German immigrants in the regiment. One of his letters of recommendation was from the Prussian ambassador in Washington, certifying his academic attainments.

Strangely enough, when Sarner was interviewed and approved by a committee of Army chaplains, they certified that he was "a regularly ordained minister of the Lutheran Church (!)." It must have been that Sarner spoke English so imperfectly that the chaplains did not understand that he was a rabbi, and presumed that a clergyman presenting certificates from German universities and the Prussian ambassador must be a Lutheran. That Sarner did not misrepresent himself is indicated by the correspondence he continued with the editors of Jewish weeklies of the time.

Chaplain Sarner's exposure to the hazards of war was not long in coming. May 2-4 found the 54th Infantry in action at Chancellorsville, Virginia, where the Union forces were defeated and the way paved for Lee's invasion of Pennsylvania and the epic battle of Gettysburg, July 1-4. Chaplain Sarner was severely wounded at Gettysburg. Seven months later a French Jewish magazine, the *Archives Israelites*, reported that Sarner's "horse was killed under him, and he himself received a dangerous wound, from which he subsequently recovered; this was the result of the very courageous manner in which he conducted himself during the terrible battle." Although Sarner returned to duty and participated in the invasion of South Carolina, he never fully recovered his health. He was hospitalized again in July 1864 and, after a time, was told he would be discharged for physical disability. After receiving this information, Sarner, probably no expert in military procedures, left the hospital without waiting for formal instructions to do so. The order of discharge was sent to the hospital by the War Department in October, but Sarner had already departed.

It took almost five years for Army red tape to catch up with him. By then, Rabbi Sarner had been preaching in various New York synagogues, editing a literary magazine, writing plays, and doing all sorts of things. On March 18, 1869, the Army Adjutant General solemnly announced, in Special Orders No. 63, that Special Orders No. 330, paragraph 36, dated October 3, 1864, which "honorably discharged Chaplain Ferdinand Sarner, 54th New York Volunteers, on account of physical disability, is hereby amended to discharge him for absence without leave." Thus Chaplain Sarner was the first American Jewish chaplain to become a battle casualty and the first American Jewish chaplain to go AWOL.

He was not the last in either category. In World War II two Jewish chaplains, Alexander D. Goode and Irving Tepper, died as the result of enemy action. Jewish chaplains were wounded in battle in World Wars I and II and Korea. Also, immediately following World War II, my Hebrew Union College classmate, Army Chaplain Abraham J. Klausner, who played an heroic role in helping to bring order out of chaos in the Jewish displaced persons camps in southern Germany, was listed for months on his unit's morning report as AWOL, because he was moving about so fast his CO did not know where he was or what he was doing!

Rabbi Sarner's service with the Union Army and the bad limp acquired from his war wound and his "less than honorable" military discharge did not deter Beth-El Emeth Congregation of Memphis, Tennessee, from calling him to its pulpit in 1872. He was its spiritual leader for six years. This soldier of God who had survived war and battle wound fell victim to yellow fever in the epidemic of 1878, an epidemic that also claimed the life of Civil War chaplain Bernhard Gotthelf.

THE GERMAN-JEWISH-AMERICAN WORD "BETZIMER"
(c. 1870)

The word *Betzimer* (pronounced "baytsimmer") for Irishman must have been coined by a jocose German Jew after his arrival in the U.S.A. It involves a double pun. "Irish" sounded to a German ear like "Eierish," "eier" being the German word for eggs. Our wit then substituted *betzim*, the Hebrew equivalent of "eier," and produced the locution *Betzimer*. The pun could only have been made in America, for in German the adjective "irisch" is pronounced "eerish." Nor could it have been made by a Yiddish speaking immigrant, for a) in Yiddish *betzim* is considered obscene, being used in the sense of "testicles"; and b) in most dialects of Yiddish the word "eier" is pronounced "ayer."

The word is familiar to most Jews of German descent, particularly those whose forebears came to this country at about the same time as the great Irish migration to the United States in the third quarter of the nineteenth century. It is not so well-known among those German Jews who came here during the Hitler period. The only instance I recall of its use in a literary context is in Elmer Rice's *Street Scene*, in which the Jewish schoolteacher objects to her young brother running around "with that Betzimer." Here, of course, the word is used wrongly. Elmer Rice (originally Reizenstein; his aunt, Miss Jennie Reizenstein, taught me in Sunday School) came from a Baltimore German Jewish family. He was not aware that the East Side Jews in his play would not have known the word. I have no idea whether the word appears in the printed version of the play or in the musical by Kurt Weill. I simply report my recollection of the original production many years ago.

Contributed by Rabbi Bernard J. Bamberger, New York City.

Name Calling

(1880)

Designating those whom one does not like by uncomplimentary names is a trait common to all groups in every period of recorded history. The Jews were no exception. From earliest times, in the Bible, Talmud, and Midrash, such names are found often.

The Hebrew word "goy" originally meant "nation," any nation. Then it came to mean only a non-Jewish nation and, finally, a non-Jew. At first it implied nothing uncomplimentary; but, as non-Jewish persecution of the Jew intensified during the Middle Ages, "goy" came to mean, particularly in Europe, not only a generic non-Jew but, more especially, one who thought and acted the way medieval Jews believed the average non-Jew thought and acted. It came to have a very disparaging meaning, denoting a person who was stupid or cruel or bigoted or a combination of any or all of these. To be called a goy by a fellow-Jew was a much resented insult. Probably the most frequently used form of this insult was for one Jew to say of another that he had a "goyishe kopf," i.e., he was as stupid as a non-Jew.

Another term of contempt for the non-Jewish male was "sheygetz" and, for the non-Jewish female, "shicksa." Both are Yiddish derivatives from the Hebrew word "sheketz," meaning "something loathsome, abhorred, despised," the lowest of the low. Strangely enough, most non-Jews, not knowing the linguistic origins of these words, were less offended by being called a "sheygetz" or a "shicksa" than if a Jew referred to them as a "goy." This may be because they heard one Jew speak of another Jew whom he did not like as a goy, while they rarely heard one Jew call another a sheygetz or shicksa.

Until comparatively recently, those Jewish regional groups that arrived on the American scene in its earlier stages looked down upon the Jewish regional groups that arrived later. The Sephardim felt superior to the West European Ashkenazim; the Sephardim and West European Ashkenazim felt superior to the East European Ashkenazim; and all three felt very much above the East European Chassidim. There are many Jewish individuals who still cling to these foolish biases.

What Hebrew, Spanish, Portuguese, or Ladino words the Sephardim may have used to indicate their contempt for the Ashkenazim I do not know; but some of the epithets West Europeans employed when they referred to their East European brethren are well-known. Later, these epithets were picked up by non-Jewish anti-Jews and were used to express their antipathy for every variety of Jew. I refer specifically to "kike," "mocky," and "sheeny." The anti-Jewish goyim added another, imported from Europe, i.e., "Yid." What is the derivation of each?

Many East European Jews had names ending in "ki." Accordingly, West Europeans began by calling East European Jews the "kikis." Subsequently, this was shortened to dub an individual East European Jew a "kike."

"Mocky" is derived from the Hebrew word "makka," meaning "a plague." "Mocky" was used in the sense of calling the person a nuisance, a troublemaker, an embarrassment. It carried the same connotation as the vulgar English phrase, "a pain in the ass."

The origin of "sheeny" is not known. It has been suggested that, just as the English word "sheen," meaning "beautiful," came into the language from the German "schoen," so the word "sheeny" may be an offshoot of the Yiddish "shayne," also meaning "beautiful." As a matter of fact, there is an Old English word "sheeny," meaning "shiny" or "lustrous." European Jews were accustomed to say of anything they liked or enjoyed that it was "schoen" (West European), "shayne" (East European), both pronounced exactly the same. "Sheeny" may have been a grudging compliment paid by the dignified West European to the much less inhibited East European, i.e., that he had a zest for living greater than that of the West European.

"Yid" is, of course, a diminutive of the German word for Jew, "Jude," pronounced "Yudeh."

Let it not be thought that those Jews who were called opprobrious names by their fellow-Jews failed to respond in kind. They most certainly did and in very colorful language. The one epithet that traveled the reverse circuit most frequently, said by the Chassid about the East European Ashkenazi who said it about the West European Ashkenazi who said it about the Sephardi, was the single word "goy," sometimes taking the more specific form of the word "Christ," pronounced "Krist" and meaning "Christian." The later arrivals believe themselves to be the only true-blue Jews. Their predecessors, they were convinced, were in various stages en route to assimilation and absorption.

THE AM OLAM TRIES FARMING

(1881)

The high point of the Haskalah or Enlightenment movement was reached among Russian Jewry in the reign of Czar Alexander II, 1855-81. Jewish students were permitted to attend universities in larger numbers than ever before. Many of these students, while retaining their ethnic feelings and loyalties, turned away from traditional Judaism, considering it parochial and outmoded. They were attracted to radical political philosophies and to what was termed the "Religion of Humanity," an ethical system without ceremonies or theology. This was exactly what Alexander II desired. He wanted the Jews to become secularists, to become Russified and disappear. He was assassinated by a bomb-throwing revolutionary on March 13, 1881.

Alexander II was succeeded by his son, Alexander III, 1881-94, a reactionary strongly under the influence of his former tutor, the monk Pobiedonostzev, a vicious enemy of the Jews. The new monarch appointed Pobiedonostzev head of the governing body of the Russian Orthodox Church. With the approval of the czar, this prelate devised a new program for getting rid of the Jews: a third to be converted, a third forced to migrate, a third killed. Well-organized pogroms soon broke out all over the southern part of the country—Elisavetsgrad, April 27-28; Kiev, May 8-9; Odessa, May 15-17. Jewish ghettos were invaded, houses looted and burned, Jews, male, female, old and young, brutally beaten and murdered. Panic seized the Jews of South Russia. Tens of thousands fled from the country, abandoning their property, glad to get away alive.

The most embittered and bewildered were the university students. Imbued with the Haskalah spirit, encouraged by the reforms of Alexander II, convinced that the way to solve "the Jewish problem" was to reject their ancestral religion and assimilate culturally, they witnessed, after the accession of Alexander III, the speedy collapse and destruction of their dream world. Like the Jewish villagers of Anitevke in *Fiddler on the Roof*, they realized they would have to await the coming of their Messianic Age somewhere else. They turned their gaze in two directions: some toward the ancient homeland, Palestine; many toward the land of freedom and plenty, the "goldene medina," the United States.

In Kharkov a group of students formed a society, named Bilu, for the purpose of establishing an agricultural colony in Palestine. Bilu was an abbreviation formed from the initial letters of the first four Hebrew words of Isaiah 2:5, "Bet Ya'akov, l'chu v'neylcha," "Come, O house of Jacob, let us go [to our land]." A few hundred joined Bilu, but only forty actually went to Palestine.

In Kiev a well-to-do printer and writer, Herman Rosenthal, 1843-1917, became the leader of a much larger group, the Am Olam, meaning "the eternal people," a group of mostly university students but also including a number of young, middle class Jewish families. The goal of Am Olam was to set up, in the United States, Jewish collective farms, operated under socialist or communist principles. The practice of the Jewish religion was not to be forbidden; but neither was it to be encouraged. Am Olam branches were organized in Odessa, Kharkov,

Kiev, Vilna, Elisavetsgrad and other cities to recruit and prepare young people for life in the New World as farmers.

These Russian Jews were helped to cross western Europe and the Atlantic by the Alliance Israelite Universelle, a relief organization born in Paris in 1860 in the wake of the 1858 Mortara kidnaping case. Even after the members of Am Olam reached the United States, the Alliance continued to assist them. A number of prominent American Jews strongly supported this back-to-the-farm effort, preeminently Judge Myer S. Isaacs, financier Jacob H. Schiff, and poet Emma Lazarus, all of New York City.

Rosenthal arrived in New York City with the first group of Am Olam pioneers in October 1881, 60 families plus some single men from Kiev and Elisavetsgrad, about 175 persons in all. They were sent to New Orleans, where they were well received by the Hebrew Foreign Missions Association, a local philanthropy created just for them. Then they journeyed to the site selected for the first colony, Sicily Island, Catahoula County, in the Mississippi Delta country about 160 miles northwest of New Orleans. This tract of 5,000 acres had been a cotton plantation before the Civil War. It was now overgrown with big trees. There were three abandoned houses on the property, as well as a few old shacks where slaves had lived. These were supposed to serve as the collective's living quarters until homes could be built. They were in such a deplorable condition that, in those parts of the rotted buildings that could be salvaged, ten or more persons had to live in a single room.

Even though the Jews of New Orleans tried mightily to help these amateur farmers and the newcomers attempted to laugh and sing and poetize and romanticize their way through their troubles, the project was doomed from the beginning. Cut off from their accustomed world, with rattlesnakes and mosquitoes as their constant companions, smitten by malaria, these idealistic Am Olamites were in an economically unrealistic and physically untenable situation. In the spring of 1882, the Mississippi overflowed and washed away Sicily Island's living quarters, cattle, equipment, and newly planted crops. That ended it. The farmers and their families departed, some to find their way back to New York City, some to try again in other colonies in Arkansas, the Dakotas, and Kansas. Many years later, one of these pioneers, asked to describe the Louisiana experience, said it left with him the following memories: "Work—mostly useless, hope, despair, love, song, poetry, happiness and misery—that was life as we young people lived it there on Sicily Island."

In July 1882 Rosenthal made another attempt to set up a collective enterprise, this time with twenty Russian families in southeastern South Dakota, Davison County, fourteen miles from the nearest railway station. The colony was called Cremieux, in honor of Isaac Adolph Cremieux, French minister of justice and, except for 1866-68, president of the

Alliance from 1863 until he died in 1880. The first year the colony grew oats, wheat, rye, barley, and flax with fair success. The second year bugs destroyed the crops and a prolonged drought killed many cattle. The third year brought hailstorms of such intensity that everything that had been planted was destroyed and the farms had to be mortgaged. By the end of 1885 Cremieux had ceased to exist.

Also in the summer of 1882 a colony known as New Odessa was established in southwestern Oregon near the California border by a group of mostly unmarried, young, socialist Russian Jews, who called themselves B'ney Chorin, "Free Men." Constant bickering over the respective merits of Anarchism, Socialism, Communism, Nihilism, and various other "isms" led to the demise of New Odessa in 1888.

Between 1882 and 1892 many other unsuccessful attempts were made by immigrant Russian Jews to form agricultural communes in the United States. There were practical reasons for the failure of these nobly motivated experiments: inexperienced leadership, poor selection of settlement sites, inadequate capital, lack of proper advance training. But the overriding difficulty was more ideological than practical. Too many of these youngsters were not prepared to carry out in actuality the anticapitalistic theories they mouthed so vehemently. They were not ready to subordinate their individual interests to the welfare of the entire community. It was much more difficult to be unselfish than they had anticipated.

Only in New Jersey and Connecticut did the Russian Jewish agricultural colonies succeed. There was only one experiment in collectivism. In the rest of the settlements the emphasis was on individual initiative and private gain. Living by the philosophy of the free enterprise system many farmers were successful. Some even became rich.

The one New Jersey colony that had a reputation for radicalism was Carmel, founded in 1882 by the Montefiore Agricultural Aid Society, whose moving spirit was Michael Heilprin, 1823-88. Heilprin came to the United States from Poland in 1856. After two years as a Hebrew teacher, he left the Jewish educational field and acquired an international reputation as a writer of encyclopaedia articles, book reviewer, and feature writer for *Nation* magazine. He was not a religious Jew and took no part in Jewish communal affairs until his concern for his fellow-Jews was aroused by the 1881 pogroms. From then on, Heilprin threw himself into the work of forming agricultural settlements with such zeal that his extraordinary efforts brought on a serious illness that hastened his death. Heilprin's society helped sponsor many of the short-lived collectives in Oregon, the Dakotas, and Kansas. Only the one in Carmel, New Jersey, outlived him.

In his 1971 book, *Immigrants to Freedom*, Joseph Brandes writes:

Among the rural tailors of Carmel, radicalism seemed to flourish more than in the other [New Jersey] colonies, perhaps because so few [in Carmel] succeeded as farmers. They developed a reputation as intellectuals imbued with ideas of Russian nihilism, atheism and even—some said—free love. Bold individuals among them tried to deliver inflammatory socialist lectures on the main street of Bridgeton, but they were chased off by the constabulary. . . . A consumers' cooperative, a farmers' cooperative for the purchase of seed and equipment, ephemeral producers' cooperatives—shirt and dress factories—in the 1890s, all were oddments of quasi-radicalism in a setting of individual enterprise.

The most successful and lasting settlements in New Jersey, in addition to Carmel, were Alliance, founded May 1882, Rosenhayn, 1883, and Woodbine, 1891. The latter three succeeded and endured because of three factors: the emphasis was on individual achievement; local factories were set up to supplement the income obtained through farming; and the Baron de Hirsch Fund, financed by French Maurice, second Baron de Hirsch, poured millions of dollars into the maintenance of these South Jersey settlements.

In 1894 the Baron de Hirsch Agricultural School was opened in Woodbine, the first such Jewish school in the United States. Because the interest in Jewish farming had greatly diminished, the school closed in 1917. The school building was turned over to the state and became New Jersey's Institution for Feeble-minded Males.

Woodbine had a weekly Jewish newspaper, the *Yiddishe Gazetten*, which had a strong bias against Reform Jews. Despite all the help they had gotten and were continuing to get from West European and American Reform Jews, Woodbine's East European Jews were offended by what they felt was often their benefactor's point of view, i.e., they were giving charity to Jews of an inferior kind. In May 1894 the *Yiddishe Gazetten*, states Brandes,

bitterly rejected the complaints of Rabbi Isaac Mayer Wise against those orthodox immigrants who refused to recognize Reform Jews as coreligionists. Why did he and others look down on the Russians as dirty, unrefined, and uncivilized? retorted the *Gazetten*. The Russian Jews in the agricultural colonies as well as the cities were tired of being charged with beggary or religious fanaticism; their children, the journal suspected, were shunted off into special training schools so that they would not shame their affluent cousins in the public schools.

Hurt pride brooked no compromise, it seemed, on a number of sensitive issues: "We leave it to the rabbis to decide if Reform Jews are our brothers in religion . . . but from a social point of view the Reform Jews themselves have declined us all brotherly feeling. . . . No wonder the Russian poor have come to regard help from the German Reform Jew as charity from a rich Goy."

As the years went on, less and less Jewish immigrants turned to farming and more and more of the immigrants' children went from the farms to the big cities to seek their fortunes. By 1943 Woodbine, with a population of over two thousand, had only fifty Jewish farmers, engaged mostly in truck farming and poultry raising. There was a brief resurgence of interest in Jewish agriculture in the late 1930s and early 1940s when European refugees from the terrors of Nazism established poultry, dairy and truck farms in eastern New Jersey and the New York Catskills area. But the idealistic socialistic dreams of the Am Olam had vanished long before that. Very few present-day Jews know that there ever was such a movement and, for the few who do, it is only a fascinating historical memory.

✿   ✿   ✿   ✿   ✿

Rabbi Seymour Atlas of Beth Judah Synagogue, Wildwood, New Jersey, has furnished the following interesting summation of the fate of the South Jersey Jewish agricultural settlements:

> Woodbine is the only one of these agricultural communities that has maintained its independent existence. Where once were Carmel, Rosenhayn and Alliance is now a part of the city of Vineland. Their Jewish cemeteries are all that remain. Occasionally I am called upon to officiate at the interment of some member of a pioneer family whose remains are brought to one of these cemeteries for burial.
>
> Woodbine, which once had two synagogues and one cemetery, now has one synagogue and two Jewish cemeteries. It has about fifteen Jewish families. None of them is in farming or poultry raising and only one is descended from a family that formerly was. The original Hebrew School building is now the city's post office. The original synagogue became, on May 29, 1977, Woodbine's City Hall. The remaining synagogue holds services only on the High Holydays.
>
> The Institution for Feeble-minded Males is now known as the Woodbine State School for the Mentally Retarded. Of its thousand patients, about eighty are Jewish. I have been their chaplain since 1970. If the present trend continues, it will not be many years before this ministry to our afflicted brethren will be the only Jewish activity that will remain in what was once heralded as "the first all-Jewish city in the United States."

"GIVE ME YOUR TIRED, YOUR POOR"

(1883)

In June 1871 French sculptor Frederic Auguste Bartholdi came to the United States in the hope of fulfilling a life dream. He wanted to build a towering statue in an American harbor as a gift from the people of France to the people of the United States, a gift to be presented in 1876 on the occasion of the centennial of American independence, to commemorate one hundred years of unbroken friendship between France and America. His statue would take the form of a beautiful woman holding a torch. It would symbolize "Liberty Enlightening the World." It would be named the Statue of Liberty.

Bartholdi enlisted the warm support of President Ulysses S. Grant, the poet Henry Wadsworth Longfellow and other prominent Americans. Before he left in the fall to return to his Paris studio, Bartholdi had selected the spot for the statue, Bedloe's Island at the entrance to New York harbor. The island is 12½ acres in size. It was known until 1670 as Love Island. The name was changed when British governor Francis Lovelace presented it to colonist Isaac Bedloe. In 1841 Fort Wood was built upon the island as part of New York's harbor defenses. By 1871 the fort had fallen into decay, but its thick walls remained intact. Bartholdi planned to put his statue inside these walls, which were in the form of an eleven-point star.

The statue would be 151 feet high, its pedestal 89 feet, its base 65 feet, or 305 feet high overall. The cost of the statue, $400,000, would be raised in France. The cost of the pedestal and base, originally estimated at $125,000 but eventually amounting to $225,000, would be raised in the United States.

It soon became obvious that the statue would not be completed in time for the 1876 Centennial. The money raising effort in France did not get underway until 1875. By 1879 less than $50,000 had been gathered. Then someone had a brilliant idea: "Let's get the money through a national lottery." That plus a few other little schemes and large contributions did it. In July 1881 the French committee informed its American counterpart that the French had the $400,000 needed for the statue. The Americans must now raise the money for the pedestal and base. Confident that the Americans would succeed, Bartholdi rented a very large workshop and began to fashion his statue. It was to be made of sheets of heavy copper hammered on to an iron frame. The engineering requirements were calculated by Alexandre Gustave Eiffel, who in 1889 would construct the Eiffel Tower.

In November 1881 the American committee held what was expected to be a big fund raising dinner. It was a dismal failure. There appeared to be little national interest in the project. In 1883 someone had a splendid idea: "Let's get part of the money by auctioning off original manuscripts of contemporary American literary figures." Among those who contributed a manuscript were Bret Harte, the Longfellow estate (the poet had died in 1882), Mark Twain, and Walt Whitman.

Some well-known writers were asked to donate an original composition. Among those asked was the eminent young American Jewish poet, Emma Lazarus. At first she declined, but not because of lack of interest. She was vitally interested. Ever since the Russian pogroms of 1881, she had turned away from her previous concentration on non-Jewish themes, had steeped herself in Judaism, had written and worked mightily on behalf of the oppressed Russian Jews and the newly arriving Jewish immigrants and the intense longing for human freedom and dignity that these fellow-Jews represented. Emma Lazarus declined because, a true artist, it was quite impossible for her to write on order. She had to be inspired. Then, almost miraculously, the inspiration came. Under its spell, she wrote a sonnet:

THE NEW COLOSSUS

Not like the brazen giant of Greek fame,
With conquering limbs astride from land to land;
Here at our sea-washed, sunset gates shall stand
A mighty woman with a torch, whose flame
Is the imprisoned lightning, and her name
Mother of Exiles. From her beacon-hand
Glows world-wide welcome; her mild eyes command
The air-bridged harbor that twin cities frame.
"Keep, ancient lands, your storied pomp!" cries she
With silent lips. "Give me your tired, your poor,
Your huddled masses yearning to be free,
The wretched refuse of your teeming shore.
Send these, the homeless, tempest-tost to me,
I lift my lamp beside the golden door!"

The committee got $1,500 for Emma Lazarus' sonnet.

Early in 1884 the statue was completed. At a Paris ceremony it was formally presented to the American people by the French on July 4, 1884. The poet James Russell Lowell, American ambassador to Great Britain, was present. Afterward he wrote to Miss Lazarus:

> I like your sonnet about the statue much better than the statue itself. Your sonnet gives its subject a raison d'être which it wanted before quite as much as it wanted a pedestal. You have set it on a noble one, saying admirably just the right word to be said, an achievement more arduous than that of the sculptor.

In the fall of 1884 the statue was dismantled and readied for shipment; but only $125,000 had been raised for its pedestal and base. Another $100,000 was needed. In March 1885 Hungarian-born, half-Jewish Joseph Pulitzer, publisher of the New York *World*, determined to obtain the money through appeals in his paper. In a few weeks he had the

$100,000, gathered in nickels, dimes, quarters, and dollars from tens of thousands of New Yorkers.

The statue, packed in 85 huge wooden cases, arrived at Bedloe's Island in May 1885. Within a year it was reassembled and erected. On October 28, 1886, President Grover Cleveland presided over the dedication ceremony. A poem was read, not Emma Lazarus' sonnet, but a less inspiring one by America's uncrowned poet laureate, John Greenleaf Whittier.

As the years moved on and the "woman with a torch" kept growing in spiritual stature, as she welcomed to America millions of immigrants from all over Europe, Whittier's poem faded away. In its stead Emma Lazarus' sonnet came to the fore. Schoolchildren all over the country memorized it. It became so meaningful to many that they could not think of the statue without thinking of the sonnet. It was as though, through the words of Emma Lazarus, the statue was speaking to them and to the world.

So it came to pass, as the story books say, that in 1903 a very appropriate event took place on Bedloe's Island. A plaque containing the sonnet was placed on the wall inside the base of the Statue of Liberty. Beneath the sonnet these words were inscribed:

> This tablet, with her sonnet to the Bartholdi Statue of Liberty engraved upon it, is placed upon these walls in loving memory of EMMA LAZARUS, born in New York City, July 22nd, 1849; died November 19th, 1887.

In 1924 Bedloe's Island was designated a national shrine. In 1933 it was put under the control of the National Park Service.

During the 1950s the government decided to build an American Museum of Immigration at the base of the Statue of Liberty to pay tribute to the immigrants for their splendid contributions to the history and development of our country. Among those who helped bring the project to completion were President John F. Kennedy, General U. S. Grant III, grandson of President Grant, Spyros Skouros, George Meany, and William Rosenwald. The museum was dedicated by the President of the United States on September 26, 1972.

The Ark and Torah which I, as an American military chaplain, used to conduct the first Jewish service in the Dachau concentration camp after its liberation from the Nazis in April 1945 occupies a position of honor in the Jewish section of the museum.

Bedloe's Island has been given a new name—Liberty Island.

How They Got Their Names
(1886)

In the Latvian village from which he came Jews had no last names. A Jew was known as So-and-so the son or daughter of Mr. So-and-so. His name was Jacob the son of Benjamin or, in Yiddish, Yainkele ben Reb Binyamin. When he was queried at the Castle Garden immigrant reception center about his name, he replied, "My name is Yainkele." "Say that very slowly," requested the immigration officer. "Yain-ke-leh," obligingly responded the immigrant. The officer, understanding no Yiddish, wrote down what his ears heard, which was "John Kelly." And thus did it come about that, for many years, there lived a Jewish tailor on the Lower East Side of New York City by the name of John Kelly.

❋   ❋   ❋   ❋   ❋

This Jewish immigrant had a long, hard-to-pronounce Polish name. The immigration official said to him, "In this country you would be much better off with a name that sounds more American." "What name do you suggest?" asked the immigrant. "How about Shapiro?" the official queried; "that's a good American Jewish name." Thus did it happen that another Shapiro was added to the already illustrious roster of American Jewish Shapiros.

❋   ❋   ❋   ❋   ❋

A Russian Jew made his way to Canada and later entered this country. The immigration inspector asked him his name. He thought he was being asked from what country he had just come—so he replied, "Kenneda." And so it was that a Jewish family named "Kennedy" came into being.

❋   ❋   ❋   ❋   ❋

An immigrant had been forced to adopt several pseudonyms because of his involvement in some Lithuanian revolutionary activities. When asked his name by the Castle Garden bureaucrat, he replied, "Shayne fergessen," meaning "I had to forget it a long time ago." The bureaucrat, hearing but not comprehending, wrote down "Shayne Ferguson"; and Shayne Ferguson it remained.

Contributed by Rabbi Samuel M. Silver, Delray Beach, Florida.

THE LOWER EAST SIDE ACQUIRES A CHIEF RABBI
(1888)

It is a universal trait of human nature that the person who got there first feels that he or she is superior to those who came later. Witness, for example, the Daughters of the American Revolution. Many of their earliest ancestors were vagabonds, slave traders, indentured servants, and other varieties of humanity not ranked very high on the social scale. Yet not so many years ago these ultrapatriotic colonial descendants denied a renowned singer the right to concertize in their auditorium in the National Capital because, although her character and professional skill were impeccable, her kin and skin were twentieth-century black.

A similar pattern of snobbery is found among Jewish migrants to America. The colonial Sephardim who came seeking their fortunes were generally of the merchant class, cultured, well educated, "poor but healthy," according to a contemporary clergyman. After nearly two centuries of American residence, the small number of descendants of these early Sephardim still affiliated with the Jewish community considered themselves very superior to the West European Jews, English, German, Austrian, and Hungarian, who started arriving in appreciable numbers in the first half of the nineteenth century.

These West Europeans came mostly from the lower and middle classes. They were primarily peasant farmers and urban artisans and shopkeepers. A high percentage of them made a living, in their first years in this country, by door-to-door or farm-to-farm peddling, selling dry goods or old clothes or pots and pans and other kinds of household knickknacks. After a half century of citizenship and considerable improvement in their economic status, they thought themselves incomparably better than the "Ost Juden," their poor country cousins from Eastern Europe who migrated to our shores in the 1880s and 1890s, also mostly peasant farmers or urban artisans and shopkeepers.

In New York City especially, a sharp social distinction developed between the predominantly German Reform "uptown" Jews and the predominantly Russian Orthodox "downtown" or Lower East Side Jews. Whenever they came in contact, which was not very often, the downtown Jew was made to feel that he was culturally and socially inferior and unacceptable. The uptown Jews believed they were fulfilling the

This article is based on the definitive study of this subject, "New York Chooses a Chief Rabbi," published in 1955 in Volume 44 of the Publications of the American Jewish Historical Society, and written by Dr. Abraham J. Karp, Bernstein Professor of Jewish Studies, Professor of History and Religious Studies, University of Rochester, Rochester, New York.

mitzvot of kindness and brotherhood in the fullest manner by feeding and clothing the East Side needy, protecting them from the Christian missionaries, and helping them become "Americanized."

For the East Side Jew this was a frustrating and demeaning situation. He sought to improve his position by devices of his own making. In 1852 the first Orthodox congregation had been organized on the East Side, Beth Hamidrash Hagadol. For four decades it was New York's leading East European synagogue. Its first rabbi, Abraham J. Ash, served intermittently from 1860 until his death in 1887.

Before the thirty-day mourning period for Rabbi Ash was ended, Beth Hamidrash Hagadol determined to take a giant step, to bring a Chief Rabbi to New York City who would be the spiritual head of all the Orthodox synagogues of the city and would regulate the kashrut situation, which at that time was [and, to some extent, still is] in a state of disrepute. The Chief Rabbi would be employed by the United Hebrew Orthodox Association, which had been organized in 1879.

In 1887 there were about 130 Orthodox congregations on the East Side; but only three or four had rabbis, rabbis who were largely ignored, officially and financially. Of unattached itinerant preachers and marriage performers there was an abundance. Congregations were more interested in having outstanding cantors who would enhance their synagogal prestige and income than in having learned rabbis. Only about twenty of these congregations were actively affiliated with the UHOA.

After a long search for the best available and qualified leader and after much discussion and negotiation, the Association selected Rabbi Jacob Joseph of Vilna, Lithuania, as Chief Rabbi of New York City for six years at an annual salary of $2,500 plus family living quarters. This was a huge salary when compared to the yearly income of the average East Sider. The late Rabbi Ash had never been paid more than $400 per annum.

Rabbi Jacob Joseph, forty years of age, was "communal preacher" and "religious judge" of Vilna, renowned center of East European Jewish scholarship and culture. He held the honorary appellation of "charif," "keen minded." He was a recognized rabbinic authority and a man of broad and liberal outlook. He was also heavily in debt. With his letter of acceptance of the position of Chief Rabbi, he requested a loan of 5,000 rubles, a little more than $2,500. The Association was able to raise only $1,000, which was sent to Rabbi Joseph.

The ship carrying the Chief Rabbi and his family arrived in the port of Hoboken, New Jersey, on Saturday morning, July 7, 1888. At the conclusion of the Sabbath, the rabbi was welcomed to his new home at Henry and Jefferson streets by a crowd of many thousands, who hoped this event marked the start of a spiritual revival for American Jewry and a new deal for the poorly regarded East European Jews.

From the beginning the Chief Rabbinate was sharply attacked by the Jewish secularists, the socialists, communists, and anarchists, who were to be found on the East Side in not inconsiderable numbers. The Chief Rabbi's authority was, of course, ignored by the Reform Jews. In addition, the few "uptown" Orthodox synagogues and many of the East Side congregations did not accept his spiritual leadership. In fact, in 1892, twenty East Side congregations, composed mostly of Galician Jews, set up a rival Chief Rabbi, Joshua Segal, the Sherpser Rav.

Just before Sukkot in 1888 Rabbi Joseph announced he was taking over the supervision of the slaughter of kosher chickens; every chicken so slaughtered would bear his plumbeh, i.e., lead seal of approval, and one cent per chicken would be charged for the affixing of the plumbeh. This action aroused the ire of the non-Association rabbis and the shochtim [ritual slaughterers] and the radicals. The word "karobka" became the anti-Association battle cry. Karobka was the name of the tax imposed by the Russian government on kosher meat. The Russians used this Jewish tax money for anti-Jewish purposes. The Jews in the "old country" who collected the karobka were considered traitors by their coreligionists. The Hebrew Poultry Butchers Association held a meeting on September 30 and enthusiastically voted not to put the plumbeh on their chickens. On October 11 the meat butchers met and voted less enthusiastically to allow their shops to be placed under the supervision of the Chief Rabbi, but only on condition that no tax be placed on their meat to pay for this supervision. They did agree to a Chief Rabbinical service charge of $4.00 a month per butcher.

In December Rabbi Joseph created a second kosher storm. He put a notice in the Yiddish press inviting wholesale flour merchants who sold flour for the baking of matzot to submit such flour to him for approval for a fee of $1.00 per barrel. The adverse reaction was immediate and devastating. It ended all hope that Rabbi Joseph could bring order out of chaos in Jewish religious life on the Lower East Side, raise the prestige of Orthodoxy and act as an effective instrument to halt the spread of Reform. The UOHA was threatened with extinction. A contract had to be arranged with a number of leading butchers that they would assume the responsibility of paying the Chief Rabbi's salary in return for his supervision of their kashrut. This arrangement gave the coup de grace to the "noble experiment." For all practical purposes, the Chief Rabbi and his staff of mashgichim [kashrut inspectors] were, from this point on, employees of the butchers whose products they were supposed to supervise. The UOHA continued to exist on paper and Rabbi Joseph continued to be Chief Rabbi—on paper.

In the spring of 1895 the butchers abrogated their agreement with Rabbi Joseph. For the remaining seven years of his life the story of Rabbi Joseph was one of abject poverty and physical torment. In 1897 he suffered a stroke, was paralyzed, and confined to bed. Throughout the long ordeal he uttered no public complaint, acted with utmost dignity and pious resignation. He died on July 28, 1902, at the age of fifty-nine.

When his death was announced the Jews of the East Side were seized by a deep sense of guilt because of the outrageous manner in which they had treated a learned and saintly rabbi. The Orthodox *Jewish Gazette* editorialized:

> In spite of all that was said against the Rabbi during his lifetime, we all loved him because of his estimable qualities and the blameless life he led. Against the man himself even his most bitter opponents never dared breathe a word, though it must be admitted, and with deep regret, that many of his unscrupulous opponents linked his name, unjustifiably and without the slightest reason, with the scandals that arose from time to time in the kosher meat affairs.

One hundred thousand Jews gathered for his funeral procession. It was the largest funeral the East Side had ever beheld and the mourning was genuine. And it seemed as though some evil tormentor was pursuing Jacob Joseph to the very brink of his grave. As the funeral cortège passed the building of R. H. Hoe and Company, manufacturers of printing presses, workmen bombarded the mourners with refuse, stones, and pieces of metal. A riot ensued in which more Jews than their assailants were bludgeoned by the police. Wide political repercussions followed. The report of an investigating committee appointed by Mayor Seth Low brought to an end the hitherto unchallenged anti-Jewish excesses of many East Side policemen.

Since then no segment of New York Jewry has ever attempted to obtain, appoint, or elect another Chief Rabbi. But this tragic incident was not altogether without benefit. It helped bring into being, in 1898, the Union of Orthodox Jewish Congregations of America; and it gave many an East Side Jew a feeling of dignity and pride that ultimately broke down the social and religious barriers separating the "downtown" Jews from the "uptown" Jews.

THE GHETTO POET LAUREATE

(1889)

Moishe Yankev Alter—that was the name by which he was known to hundreds of thousands of New York's East Side Jews for whom Yiddish was "mamalashon," their native tongue. Moishe Yankev Alter wrote deeply probing poems, "vundersheyn" articles for the *Arbeiter Tzeitung* and the famous Yiddish daily newspaper, the *Forward*. Moishe Yankev Alter was the voice par excellence of the sweatshop workers, the poet laureate of the New York ghetto.

For English speaking litterateurs Moishe Alter had another name, Morris Jacob Rosenfeld. But whether Moishe or Morris, Alter or Rosenfeld, this man was the finest of the many Yiddish writers and poets whose talents sprouted in the ghettos of eastern Europe and matured in the world's largest Jewish ghetto, New York City.

Moishe was born in Boksha in the province of Suwalki, Russian Poland, on the border of Lithuania, on December 28, 1862. His father was a fisherman. Moishe received a yeshiva training and was also taught German and Polish. His primary means of expression was Yiddish, the Litvakishe Yiddish spoken by the Jews of Lithuania. Moishe thought, talked, and wrote like a typical Litvak. In his very first poem, written at the age of fifteen, and throughout his entire career, Moishe's literary outpourings were marked by a sharpness, a cynicism, a shrewdness, a rationalism, an air of gloom and tragedy that were the inbred traits of Litvakishe Yidden.

Moishe married very young, before he was twenty. In 1882 he went to Amsterdam and attempted without success to learn the trade of diamond cutter. He returned to Poland, became a tailor, migrated to London in 1884 and to New York in 1886. During most of his life he was very poor. Even after he became internationally famous, he and his family lived very modestly.

From 1886 to 1894 Moishe worked in a New York sweatshop. What was a sweatshop?

New York City was the center of the ready-made garment industry. At first manufacturers cut their cloth into fixed sizes and then "farmed out" the sized piece goods to contractors who hired individuals living at home to make them into finished garments. The more garments one finished, the more he was paid. This was known as "piece work." A law, labeled the Tenement Law, was passed in New York State outlawing the "piece work" practice. So the contractors, and later the manufacturers themselves, installed rows of sewing machines and steam pressing irons in unventilated and unsanitary lofts, basements, and warehouses, and hired immigrants, mostly Jewish and Italian, to operate the machines and irons, which turned out neatly sewn and pressed ladies' and gentlemen's wearing apparel.

The operators worked long hours for little pay, sufficient only to allow them to live in crowded flats where they sweltered in summer and froze in winter and maintained their families at a bare subsistence level. The work in the sweatshops was enervating, without challenge, monotonous. The workers had no one to protect them, to plead their cause, to better their lot. They were exploited and degraded. Many of them, frustrated and bitter, put the blame for their plight on God, turned away from religion and became radical iconoclasts.

At a time when sweatshop slavery was at its worst, a voice arose from the very midst of the workers, a voice of protest, a voice of defiance, a voice of rebellion, the voice and pen of Moishe Yankev Alter, alias Morris Jacob Rosenfeld. Moishe's first book of poems, *Die Glocke*, *The Bells*, published in 1889, made him famous. He wrote many more poems, articles, and books. He read his poetry at many universities and colleges, including Harvard, Chicago, Wellesley, and Radcliffe, made a triumphal tour of Europe, was a delegate to the 4th Zionist Congress in London. His poems were translated into many languages, including Japanese. He became a writer for and an editor of a number of Yiddish magazines and newspapers. He was universally recognized as a dynamic realist and as the most gifted of American Yiddish poets. Moishe died in New York City in 1923, knowing he had been a key factor in the struggle that freed the sweatshop workers of New York City from serfdom.

In 1898 Leo Wiener, an instructor in Slavic languages at Harvard, brought Moishe's poems to the attention of the American literary public by producing a prose translation of some of Moishe's poems in a little book titled *Songs from the Ghetto, by Morris Rosenfeld*. Three of these poems, each having a different theme, now follow. In their prose translation some of the poetic rhythm and much of the poet's masterful use of the Yiddish idiom are lost, but enough vigor and strength remain to give the reader the sensation of being in the presence of an extraordinarily articulate and inspired weaver of words.

❖ ❖ ❖ ❖ ❖

In Schap (In the Sweatshop)

The machines in the shop roar so wildly that often I forget in the roar that I am; I am lost in the terrible tumult, my ego disappears, I am a machine. I work, and work, and work without end; I am busy, and busy, and busy at all times. For what? and for whom? I know not, I ask not! How should a machine ever come to think?

There are no feelings, no thoughts, no reason; the bitter, bloody work kills the noblest, the most beautiful and best, the richest, the deepest, the highest, which life possesses. The seconds, minutes and hours fly; the nights, like the days, pass as swiftly as sails;—I drive the machine just as if I wished to catch them; I chase without avail, I chase without end.

The clock in the workshop does not rest; it keeps on pointing, and ticking, and waking in succession. A man once told me the meaning of its pointing and waking,—that there was a reason in it; as if through a dream I remember it all: the clock awakens life and sense in me, and something else,—I forget what; ask me not! I know not, I know not, I am a machine!

And, at times, when I hear the clock, I understand quite

differently its pointing, its language;—it seems to me as if the Unrest [pendulum] egged me on that I should work more, more, much more. In its sound I hear only the angry words of the boss; in the two hands I see his gloomy look. The clock, I shudder,—it seems to me it drives me and calls me "Machine," and cries out to me, "Sew!"

Only when the wild tumult subsides, and the master is away for the midday hour, day begins to dawn in my head, and a pain passes through my heart; I feel my wound, and bitter tears, and boiling tears wet my meagre meal, my bread: it chokes me, I can eat no more, I cannot! O horrible toil! O bitter necessity!

The shop at the midday hour appears to me like a bloody battlefield where all are at rest: about me I see lying the dead, and the blood that has been spilled cries from the earth. . . . A minute later—the tocsin is sounded, the dead arise, the battle is renewed. The corpses fight for strangers, for strangers! and they battle, and fall, and disappear into night.

I look at the battlefield in bitter anger, in terror, with a feeling of revenge, with a hellish pain. The clock, now I hear it aright, it is calling: "An end to slavery, an end shall it be!" It vivifies my reason, my feelings, and shows how the hours fly; miserable I shall be as long as I am silent, lost—as long as I remain what I am. . . .

The man that sleeps in me begins to waken,—the slave that wakens in me is put to sleep. Now the right hour has come! An end to misery, an end let it be! . . . But suddenly—the whistle, the boss, an alarm! I lose my reason, forget where I am;—there is a tumult, they battle, oh, my ego is lost!—I know not, I care not, I am a machine! . . .

* * * * *

Der Mamser (The Bastard)

The school children do not want to play with me; the teacher pierces me with his look; there is no heart with human feelings for me,—and even the best would fain strangle me. . . .

The beadle drives me away, in wild anger, from the cup of benediction, from which all children sip. I am called "bastard," am not allowed to approach the Holy Ark, cursed are my "four cubits."

The Precentor carries around the Scroll before its reading, and everybody kisses it with ardor: I pout my lips to kiss it, they look at me in terror,—I turn away in pain and shame.

I think, and think, and cannot understand my transgression. What does it mean—"bastard"? Say, why do they plague me? And if I ask my mother, she weeps bitter tears, and kisses me fervently and will not answer me.

Other children have a father for their protector, and everybody takes the part of an orphan,—but I am forlorn, like a leaf carried by the wind,—excepting a weak woman no one loves me!

And what has become of my father! There is no answer to the outcast. Has he died? Has Heaven taken him? Why do I not say the Prayer for the Dead after my father?

I ask the wind. The world is mute to my sufferings; I hear no answer; I hear no one speaking—I only hear the truth deep in my heart: I am innocent, and suffer vain sufferings.

* * * * *

Maisse B'reyshis (Creation of Man)

When the Lord created our wonderful world, He asked nobody's advice, and did as He pleased,—

All after His own will, in accordance with His own plans: He worked at it long, and He did it well.

When He was about to create man, things did not go so well with Him, and He summoned His winged Senate:

"Listen to me, you my mighty ones, I have called you here that you may proffer me your advice how man is to be made.

"Help me, children, to create him, but take good counsel. He must resemble us, and he must be without faults and without blemish,

"For I shall crown him as a ruler, and I shall give him of My flame: he shall freely rule over air, and earth, and ocean.

"Before him shall fall the bird in the air, before his might shall fall the fish in the water and the wild lion in the chase."

The Senate became frightened: "If man, who is nothing but foam and smoke, were to rule the air, he would soon enter heaven."

And they answered God: "Make him in our image; give him reason, give him power, but give him no wings!

"No, he shall have no wings, for he will fly with his sword! Let him not enter heaven who rules upon that earth!"

"You are right," God answered, "your decision is good; but one exception I shall make, but one exception! Listen to Me!

"Let the poet be winged! He shall get My highest rank! I will open the heavens to the master of songs.

"And I shall choose an angel among you who shall be ready day and night to attach the wings to him whenever his holy song will rise!"

✻   ✻   ✻   ✻   ✻

Moishe Yankev Alter was obviously not one of those who thought that his God had forsaken him.

"THE IMPORTED BRIDEGROOM"

(1897)

[The way it began]

Asriel [who has been visiting his birthplace, Pravly, in Russia] kept Flora [his only daughter, a young lady of marriageable age] unadvised as

---

This is a portion of a short story written in 1897 by Abraham Cahan. Some explanatory notes have been added.

Abraham Cahan, 1860-1951, editor-in-chief of the New York Yiddish daily Forward, was a pioneer in Yiddish journalism in the United States. He was also an outstanding writer of stories. His 1917 novel The Rise of David Levinsky is considered an American classic.

to the name of the steamer or the date of its arrival [in New York City, where they lived]. Upon landing he did not go directly to his residence, but first took his importation into a large "clothing and gents' furnishing store" on Broadway, from which the illui [genius] emerged completely transformed. Instead of his uncouth cap and dragging coat which had hidden his top boots from view, he was now arrayed in the costliest "Prince Albert," the finest summer derby, and the most elegant button shoes the store contained.

Asriel snapped his fingers for delight. He thought him easily the handsomest and best dressed man on Broadway. "It is the Divine presence shining upon him!" he murmured. Barring the prodigy's side-locks, badges of divine learning and piety, which were tightly curled into two little cushions in front of his ears, he now thought him thoroughly Americanized. The prodigy, however, felt tied and fettered in the garb of Gentile civilization, and, as he trudged along by his convoy's side, he viewed his transformed self in the store windows, or started, rabbit-like, at the lumbering stage coaches and hurrying noblemen.

Asriel let himself and his charge in noiselessly with the latchkey, which accompanied him, together with a bunch of other keys, on his tour. They entered the hallway on tiptoe. Flora was alone in the house [playing the piano], and her unconscious welcome was all the sweeter to Asriel's soul for the grieving note which ran through it. His heart throbbed with violence. The heart of Shaya [the imported bridegroom] sank with awe. He had never heard a piano except through the window of some nobleman's house. "Hush! Do you hear?" the old man whispered. "That's your predestined bride." With that he led the way downstairs. There they paused to kiss the divine name on the Mezzuzah of the doorpost.

"Tamara!" Asriel called, under his breath, looking for his pious housekeeper in the dining room and in the kitchen. "She is not in. Must be out marketing or about her good deeds. A dear soul she! Oh, it's her fast day; she fasts Mondays and Thursdays." Then he stepped up in front of a tin box that was nailed to one of the kitchen doors and took out his pocketbook. It was one of the contribution boxes of "Meyer the Wonder-worker Fund," which is devoted to the support of pious old European Jews who go to end their days in the Land of Israel. Every orthodox Jew in the world keeps a similar box in his house and drops a coin into it whenever he escapes some danger. Asriel had safely crossed the wide ocean, and his offering was a handful of silver. "Well, you stay here, Shaya, and don't budge till you are called," he said; and, leaving the young man in his perplexity, he betook himself upstairs to surprise his daughter.

Flora burst into tears of joy, and hugged him again and again, while he stroked her black hair or stood scowling and grinning for admiration. "Ah, you dear, cranky papa," she burst out, for the fourth time, realizing that he was actually come back to her, and for the fourth time attacking him. At last he thought they had had enough. He was dying to protract the scene, but there was that troublesome job to get rid of, and Asriel was not the man to put such things off. Whenever he felt somewhat timid he would grow facetious. This was the case at the present juncture.

"Well, Flora, guess what sort of a present your papa has brought you," he said, reddening to his ears. "I'll bet you won't hit it if you keep on guessing until tomorrow. No girl has ever got such a present since America is America." Flora's eyes danced with joyous anticipation. Her mind was ablaze with diamonds, rubies, emeralds, sapphires, pearls.

"I have got a bridegroom for you—a fifteen thousand dollar one. Handsomest and smartest fellow on earth. He is an illui."

"A what?" she asked in amazement.

"Oh, a wonderful chap, you know, deep in the Talmud and the other holy books. He could knock all the rabbis in Europe to smithereens. The biggest bug in Pravly was after him, but I beat him clean out of his boots. Shaya! Come right up!" The girl gazed at her father in bewilderment. Was he joking or was he in dead, terrific earnest?

Shaya made his appearance, with his eyes on the floor and wringing the index finger of his right hand, as he was wont to do whenever he felt ill at ease, which was seldom, however. Flora's brain was in a whirl.

"This is your predestined bridegroom, my daughter. Fine present, is it not? Did you ever expect such a raisin of a sweetheart, hey? Well, children, I must go around to see about the luggage. Have a chat and get acquainted." With that he advanced to the door. "Papa! Papa!" Flora frantically called to him. But he never turned his head and went his way.

In despair she rushed to the young stranger, who was still wringing his finger, as he stood in the middle of the parlor, eyeing the carpet, and snapped out: "Mister, you had better go. If you think you are going to be my bridegroom, you are sadly mistaken." She spoke in Yiddish, but her pronunciation, particularly of the letter "r," was so decidedly American that to Shaya it sounded at once like his native tongue and the language of the Gentiles. However, it was Yiddish enough, and the fact of this imposing young lady speaking it gave him the feeling of being in the presence of a Jewish princess of Biblical times.

"Where shall I go? I don't know anybody here." He said it with an air of naive desperation which touched the girl's heart. "Where is my fault?" he asked pleadingly.

She gave him a close look, and, taking him by his clean-cut beardless chin, she opened her eyes wide at him and broke into a hearty laugh. "My father has really brought you over to marry me?" she questioned, for the first time awakening to the humorous side of the situation, and again she burst out laughing.

Shaya blushed and took hold of his finger, but he forthwith released it and also broke into a giggle. Her merriment set him at ease, and her labored Yiddish struck him as the prattle of a child.

Flora was amused and charmed as with a baby. Shaya felt as if he was playing with another boy.

Of all the immigrants who had married or were engaged to marry some of her girlfriends, none had, just after landing, been so presentable, so sweet faced, and so droll as this scholarly looking fellow. There would be nothing odd in her marrying him a year or two later, after he had picked up some broken English and some of the customs of the country. But then her mind was firmly made up, and she had boasted to her friends that she was bound to marry a doctor. This boy was not even going to be a businessman, but an orthodox rabbi or something of the sort. The word "rabbi" was associated in her mind with the image of an unkempt, long-skirted man who knew nothing of the world, took snuff, and made life a nuisance to himself and to others. Is she going to be a rebbitsin? No! No! No! Come what may, nothing but a refined American gentleman shall lead her under the nuptial canopy! And in her misery, she fled from the parlor, and went to nurse her misery in the dining room lounge.

Presently, as she lay with her hands clasped under her head, abandoned to her despair and fury and yet unable to realize that it was all in real earnest, a fretting sensation settled somewhere in her heart. At first it was only like a grain of sand, but it kept growing until it lay a heavy, unbearable lump. She could not stand the idea of that poor being, left alone and scared out of his wits. Still she would not stir. Let papa take him away or she will leave the house and go to work in a factory.

"Tamara!" she raised herself to say the moment the housekeeper came into the room. "There's a man upstairs. He must be hungry."

"Then why don't *you* give him something to eat?" Tamara responded tartly. "You know it is Monday and I am faint. But who is he and what is he doing upstairs? Let him come down."

"Go and see for yourself," snapped Flora. "You will find him one of your set—a Talmudical scholar, a pious soul," she added, with a venomous laugh. Tamara bent upon her a look of resentment as well as of devout reproach, and betook herself upstairs.

When Asriel came, he explained that Shaya was not going to be a rabbi nor dress other than as an American gentleman, but that he would lead a life of piety and spend his time studying the Talmud, partly at home and partly at some synagogue. "What, then, have I worked all my life for?" he pleaded. "I am only a boor, my daughter, and how long does a fellow live? Don't darken my days, Flora."

Tamara kept nodding pious assent. "In the old country a girl like you would be glad to marry a child of the Law," she expostulated with the girl. "It is only here that we are sinners and girls marry none but worldly men. May every daughter of Israel be blessed with such a worthy match!"

"Mind your own business," Flora exploded. She understood her father's explanation but vaguely, and it had the opposite of the desired effect upon her.

"Leave her alone. The storm will blown over," Asriel whispered.

*   *   *   *   *

[*The way it ended five or six months later*]

"It's all gone, Tamara! My candle is blown out," Asriel said, making his way from the dining room to the kitchen. "There is no Shaya any longer."

"A weeping, a darkness to me! Has an accident—mercy and peace! befallen the child?"

"Yes, he is 'dead and buried, and gone from the market place.' Worse than that: a convert Jew is worse than a dead one. It's all gone, Tamara!" he repeated gravely. "I have just seen him eating treife in a Gentile restaurant. America has robbed me of my glory."

"Woe is me!" the housekeeper gasped, clutching at her wig. "Treife! Does he not get enough to eat here?" She then burst out, "Don't I serve him the best food there is in the world? Any king would be glad to eat such dinners."

"Well, it seems treife tastes better," Asriel rejoined bitterly.

"A calamity upon his sinful head! We must have evil-eyed the child; we have devoured him with our admiring looks."

While Asriel was answering Tamara's volley of questions, Flora stealthily left the house. When Asriel missed her, he hurried off to Clinton Street [where Shaya has been living in a rooming house]. There he learned of the landlady that her lodger had left a short time before, in the company of his friend and a young lady, whom the two young men had found waiting in her parlor. In his despair Asriel betook himself to the Astor Library, to some of Flora's friends, and even to the Bowery restaurant [because he knew that these were the "sinful" places where Shaya had been spending much of his time].

When he reached home, exhausted with fatigue and rage, he found his daughter in her room. "Where have you been?" he demanded sternly.

"I'll tell you where, but don't aggravate yourself, papaly," she replied in beseeching, tearful accents.

"Where have you been?"

"I am going to tell you, but don't blame Shaya. He is awful fond of you. It's all my fault. He didn't want to go, but I couldn't help it, papaly. We've been to the city court and got married by a judge."

"You—married?"

"Yes, but don't be angry, papaly darlin'. We'll do everything to please you. If you don't want him to be a doctor, he won't."

"A doctor!" he resumed, still speaking like one in a daze. "Is that what you have been up to? I see—you have got the best of me after all. You married, Flora?" he repeated, unable to apply the meaning of the word to his daughter. "In court—without Chuppa and Kiddushin—like Goyim? What have you done, Flora?" He sank into a chair, gnashing his teeth and tearing at his sidelocks.

"Papaly, papaly, don't," she sobbed, hugging and kissing him. "You know I ain't to blame for it all."

It dawned upon him that no serious wrong had been committed after all, and that it could all be mended by a Jewish marriage ceremony; and so great was his relief at the thought that it took away all his anger, and he even felt as if he were grateful to his daughter for not being guilty of a graver transgression than she was.

"I know you are not to blame," he said, tragic in his calmness. "America has done it all. What is the use talking? It's gone, and I'm not going to take another sin upon my soul. I won't let you be his wife without Chuppa and Kiddushin. Let the Jewish wedding come off at once—this week—tomorrow. You have got the best of me and I don't kick, do I? It seems God does not want Asrielke the boor to have some joy in his old age, someone to say a Kaddish for his soul, when the worms will be feasting upon his silly bones—"

"Oh, don't say that, papa. It'll break my heart if you do. You know Shaya is as good as a son to you."

"An appikoros [heretic] my son? An appikoros my Kaddish? No," he rejoined, shaking his head pensively.

As he said it he felt as if Flora, too, were a stranger to him.

BOCHLOWITZ TO BUCKLEY TO BUCK
(1898)

The directory makers are experiencing less difficulty every year with the names of the Russian and Polish Jews on the East Side of New York. The names with which they are burdened when they come to this country are made pronounceable by the children or the teachers when the second generation goes to school, and, while in some instances the new names sound like the original, they are written differently, and in

From the New York *Tribune*, July 3, 1898.

most cases, bear no resemblance to the roots from which they were taken. This is true not only of family names but of the "front" names too.

A long-bearded pushcart man was asked in court recently, "What is your name?" "Yainkuf Rabinowski," he answered. The magistrate evidently thought that was the man's family name, and asked, "What's your Christian name?" The man became indignant at being suspected of having anything "Christian" about him, and "front name" has been the proper expression at that seat of justice ever since.

Yitschok, the Hebrew of Jacob, has been made Hitchcock, and an old man whose neighbors know him as Cheskel has assumed the more euphonious name of Elwell. There are many similar cases of evolution, but that there are more American, English, and even French names among the dwellers in the ghetto is the result of accident as much as anything else. Children are sent to school, and their names are placed on the records by the teacher, who does the best he can with the unpronounceable thing. After the children have been in school a short time they and their parents become known by the name given to them by the teacher.

An example of this kind was mentioned recently by a young woman who had been a teacher in a school where many Russian children were pupils. "A man came in one day," she said, "with two boys who could not say a word in English. Their names were impossible except for those who had acquired the East Side jargon. When the man was gone, I made one understand that his name would be John and the other that he would have to answer to the name William, and in some way or other their family name which was full of twists and turns, and ended with a 'witch,' became Holz. Within a few weeks John and William Holz made themselves understood in fair English, and within a year they were star pupils. One day the father called at the school to see me about his boys and introduced himself as Mr. Holz! He seemed to be as much at home with the name as though he had been born with it, and so there are hundreds in our district."

In many instances a sign bought at a bargain has caused men to assume a new name, and the changes are made without the least feeling in the matter. One East Side patriarch said, "We honor our fathers just as much, even if we drop their names. Nothing good ever came to us while we bore them; possibly we'll have more luck with the new names."

But there are cases where men changed their names because they wanted to obliterate their foreign origin. Thus a family came to New York with the name of Neuberger. Presently the name became Newburger; then it was changed to Newburg, and now the two remaining brothers are known, one as Mr. New and the other as Mr. Berg.

The merchant on the East Side who rejoices in the name Katzenellenbogen and his neighbor Leworosinski continue to do business despite the numerous syllables in their names, but not so Mr. Bochlowitz.

His son changed his name to Buckley, and even this was too long for the second son, who cut it down a peg and made it Buck. The father and son, it is said, are in business under the firm name of Bochlowitz and Buckley, and they send checks signed that way to the young Buck, who is still at school.

"It does some people good to change their names," said an East Side observer, "and I doubt whether Mr. Gladstone would ever have been the great man he was if his ancestors had not dropped the name Freudenstein for Gladstone or whether other German names would have been as well received as their Americanized substitutes." The man could not be convinced that Gladstone was not originally Freudenstein.

One group of names on the East Side is always recognized by the knowing ones as Bohemian. To that class belong the names Yelteles, Abeles, Karpeles, Kakeles, and a number of other names ending in "les." When the owners of some of these names outgrow the East Side and move uptown they drop one of the "e"s in their name and then blossom forth as Karpels, Kakels, etc. One Bohemian said that his countrymen were proud of the "les" names, because they show that Aristotles, Sophocles, Pericles, and Hercules were all Bohemians.

A DELI DILLY

(1899)

"A nickeleh a pickeleh" is an American Yiddish expression that became popular about the turn of the century. How did it originate?

Mrs. Klueg was in a Delancey Street delicatessen. She reached into the pickle barrel and pulled out a fat, juicy pickle. "How much costs this pickle?" she asked. "A nickel," replied the deli-keeper. "What! A nickel a pickle?" she cried with assumed outrage. "Too much!" She tossed back the pickle, plunged her arm deep into the brine and fished up a small pickle.

"Nu, and how much costs this little pickeleh?" she crooned.

"That pickeleh," crooned back the deli-keeper, "costs likewise a nickeleh."

In America Who Needs Shadchens?

(1900)

This has been a hard year for the Cupids of the Ghetto, as the matrimonial agents of the Jewish quarter might be called. To the Jews he is known as the shadchen, but unless the marriage business picks up, the broker is going to drop out of sight. Already he is branching out into other ways of making a living. He writes letters for the illiterate, acts as interpreter in business transactions, or does odd jobs around the synagogues. Marriage brokerage used to be one of the best paying businesses on the East Side, but that day has passed, and the shadchens think it will never return.

When the Jews began to come to this city in large numbers and to crowd the Germans out of the East Side district, they brought the marriage broker with them. They had always been accustomed to having a professional matchmaker arrange their marriages, and at that time they did not know how to get along without it. The young men were bashful and were more than willing to give up 10 percent of the girl's dowry if someone else would put the question. Besides, they made sure of getting a wife in this way. They would go to the broker or shadchen and outline their ideal of a wife, not forgetting to mention the amount of dowry they expected. The shadchan would take note of all of the young man's advantages—personal appearance, education, and money making ability. Then he would go among the young women of his extended acquaintance and speedily find someone who was willing to wed on the terms which the broker had to offer.

The shadchen's fee was paid as soon as the engagement was announced. It usually amounted to 10 percent of the dowry, but in some cases a stipulated fee was charged where the girl was very pretty and her people unable to give a large marriage portion. Sometimes the shadchen had trouble collecting his fee; in those cases he evened things up by breaking off the match. There were many ways of doing this. If the man was at fault, the shadchen would get the girl a more desirable match. As love had not entered into the first engagement, it was speedily broken, leaving the man sadder but wiser. If the shadchen discovered that the girl objected to paying the fee, he found a prettier girl for the man.

This was the way it used to be done. Let the oldest shadchen in the colony tell why it is that his services are no longer in great demand. He is to be found in Hester Street, and the sign outside his door asserts that he writes letters, makes translations, and teaches Hebrew or English.

From the New York *Tribune*, September 30, 1900.

"I would starve to death in a month if I depended on matchmaking for a living," he said bitterly. "Once I lived on the fat of the land, and most of the marriageable young men and women in the quarter depended on me to make them happy for life. Now they believe in love and all that rot. They are making their own marriages, and many of them will be unhappy. Several things combined to bring about the change. In the first place there are too many girls in the Jewish quarter. There are six or seven girls after every man. This makes the young fellows hard to deal with. They can marry into almost any family in the block just for the asking. Some of the women still come to me, but it is hard to find mates for them.

"They learned how to start their own love affairs from the Americans, and it is one of the worst things they have picked up. How can a Jewish couple expect to be happy in a marriage of their own making when it has been the custom of their fathers and mothers for ages not to see each other until after marriage? The love which they have learned to put so much faith in dribbles out in trips to Coney [an amusement park] and walks around the [public] parks before marriage. In a month they are figuring out ways of getting rid of each other. In the old way every month of married life made the young people more attached to each other. They may come back to the old way of doing things, and, for their own sake, I hope they do."

"MY SON-IN-LAW, THE DOCTOR"

(1901)

The choice of the son of the family may be poor and of inferior connections, and there will be nothing worse than disappointment, but should the daughter look beneath her, there are storms and entreaties and even curses. So great is the desire for sons-in-law above the rank of the family that extraordinary measures are taken to secure a desirable specimen. The son-in-law for whom the soul of every East Sider pines is a professional man—a doctor preferably. Now, there are not so many physicians to be had, and there is only a slight chance that one of the number will look kindly on any given girl; so the affair cannot be left to chance. An ambitious youth is "caught young," his fancy fired with pictures of social and professional glory; financial help is promised him, and then, like a pill in jelly, is tucked the condition "marry my daughter afterward." This practice is so common that there has arisen a saying, used when any girl marries a physician, "Her father bought a doctor for

From the New York *Tribune*, June 30, 1901.

her." The young men do not seem to object. Indeed, at the age of seventeen the prospect of marriage is little worthy of consideration to a boy. If repentance comes after, he manages to keep it to himself and to live up to the bargain.

The case of one young man, recently married, will serve to illustrate the practice. At the age of eighteen the father of a girl a year or two his senior made a contract with him, the one promising a medical education and the other side marriage and social elevation. The boy agreed, went through the medical school, and duly announced his engagement. The girl's father furnished his office and living rooms, paying the rent and promising support until the young man's practice should pay. They have put their daughter a rung higher up the social ladder; they shine with reflected glory. Henceforth, their conversation will be peppered and salted with "my son-in-law, Dr. So-and-so" and "my son-in-law—he's a doctor, you know." Should he be present when neighbors visit, his title will be hurled at their heads at least once a minute.

Still more extraordinary is the case of a girl doing the purchasing of a doctor quite without assistance. Some ambitious maidens, having no parents or having parents who lack social longings, have negotiated the whole affair alone. These cases are kept quiet, naturally, but the neighbors usually find out and spread the news that such a one "is buying a doctor." It amuses them. It excites them. Perhaps the game is worth the candle after all.

Haggling, the East Side's Favorite Sport
(1901)

It is generally conceded that to practice properly the art of shopping in any place at any time requires leisure and experience, and, if this is true of the great stores, it is infinitely more pithy in regard to many of the smaller establishments on the East Side. To decide on the style and quality one wants and on the price one is prepared to pay may be the only tasks of the well-to-do shopper, but in out-of-the-way parts of the city the element of bargaining enters into the transaction further to complicate the affair. The would-be purchaser must have not only a clear idea of what he wants, but also a knowledge of the value of the various prices of goods which are set before him. The price asked by the storekeeper is certainly not what he will be willing to accept under proper moral suasion, and it is necessary for the buyer to judge just how far it is safe to

From the New York *Tribune*, July 28, 1901.

push the seller without bringing on himself a torrent of abusive language and prematurely closing the deal. In many of the smaller East Side shops it is safe to assume that the seller will accept about one-half of the price he asks at first. To accomplish this, however, great tact and patience are required. The worm is likely to turn, and, after all, time, even on the East Side, has a certain value.

It is not uncommon to see two men in some small shop haggling for ten or fifteen minutes over the price of a suit of clothes, for instance. Eight dollars is the price demanded by the shopkeeper. The buyer laughs pleasantly and suggests that he means four dollars. With indignation in his honest eye the storekeeper states emphatically that he means what he said, that he sells his goods as cheaply as anybody, and that the clothes cost him $7.50, anyway. Automatically, the customer repeats, "Four dollars," and he gazes calmly while the man rages. This sort of thing will be kept up for ten minutes or so. Finally the situation is that the one has gone up to $4.50 and the other has come down to $6. About this time the customer will shake his head, apparently wondering at the depravity of traders in general, and will leave the place. Then the storekeeper rushes to the door and shouts, "Five an' a half!" The departing purchaser, whose walk has been suspiciously slow, will return and say, with an engaging smile, "Five," and the deal will be closed.

The whole transaction, irrespective of the choosing of the suit, has taken perhaps fifteen minutes. Neither grudges the time for the whole thing is sport to them—a case of finding foemen worthy of their steel— and they have enjoyed the combat. The "one-price" stores are tame in comparison; anybody can shop in them, even the women from uptown, who always hand over what is asked and have no spirit of sportiness discernible. Some good citizens of the East Side come, in time, to win a local reputation for their bargaining ability, and are sought after by their friends when there is any purchasing to be done.

A Non-Jew Describes the Yiddish Theater
(1902)

Audiences [in a New York Yiddish theater] vary from night to night rather more than in the uptown theater. On the evenings of the first four weekdays, the theater is let out to a guild or club, many hundreds of which exist among the working people of the East Side. Many are labor organizations representing different trades, many are purely social, and

From *The Spirit of the Ghetto* by Hutchins Hapgood, New York, 1902.

others are in the nature of secret societies. Some of these societies are formed on the basis of a common home in Russia. People, for example, who come from Vilnyus, a city in the old country, have organized the Vilnyus Club in the ghetto. Then, too, the anarchists have a society, there are many socialistic orders, the newspapers of the ghetto have their constituency, which sometimes hires a theater. Two or three hundred dollars are paid to the theater by the guild, which then sells tickets among the faithful for a good price. Every member of the society is forced to buy, whether he wants to see the play or not, and the money made over and above hiring the theater is for the benefit of the guild. These performances are therefore called benefits. The widespread existence of such a custom is a striking indication of the growing sense of corporate interests among the laboring classes of the Jewish East Side. It is an expression of the socialistic spirit which is marked everywhere in the ghetto.

On Friday, Saturday, and Sunday nights the theater is not let, for these are the Jewish holidays, and the house is always completely sold out, although the prices range from 25¢ to a $1.00. Friday night is, properly speaking, the gala occasion of the week. That is the legitimate Jewish holiday, the night before the Sabbath. [Editor's note: Hutchins Hapgood seems to have been better informed on the Yiddish theater than he was on the Jewish religion.] Orthodox Jews, as well as others, may then amuse themselves. Saturday, although the day of worship, is also of a holiday character in the ghetto. This is due to Christian influence, to which Jews are more and more sensitive. Through economic necessity, Jewish workingmen are compelled to work on Saturday, and, like other workingmen, look on Saturday night as a holiday in spite of the frown of the Orthodox. Into Sunday, too, they extend their freedom, and so in the ghetto there are three popularly recognized nights on which to go with all the world to the theater.

On these nights the theater presents a peculiarly picturesque sight. Poor workingmen and women with their babies of all ages fill the theater. Great enthusiasm is manifested, sincere laughter and tears accompany the sincere acting on the stage. Peddlers of soda water, candy, of fantastic gewgaws of many kinds, mix freely with the audience between acts. Conversation during the play is received with strenuous hisses, but the falling of the curtain is the signal for groups of friends to get together and gossip about the play or the affairs of the week. Introductions are not necessary and the Yiddish community can then be seen and approached with great freedom. On the stage curtain are advertisements of the wares of Hester Street stores and portraits of star actors.

The programs and circulars distributed to the audience are sometimes amusing announcements of coming attractions or lyric praise of the stars. Poetry is not infrequent; an example literally translated is:

Labor, ye stars, as ye will,
Ye cannot equal the artist.
  In the garden of art ye shall not flourish.
Ye can never achieve his fame.
Can you play Hamlet like him?
The Wild King? Or the Huguenots?
Are you gifted with feeling
  So much as to imitate him like a shadow?
Your fame rests on the pen;
On the showcards your flight is high;
But on the stage everyone can see
How your greatness turns to ashes.
Thomashevsky! Artist great!
  No praise is good enough for you,
  Everyone remains your ardent friend.
Of all the stars you remain the king.
You seek no tricks, no false quibbles.
One sees Truth itself playing.
Your appearance is godly to us,
Every movement is full of grace,
Pleasing is your every gesture,
Sugar sweet your every turn.
You remain the king of the stage;
Everything falls to your feet.

On the playboards outside the theater, containing usually a portrait of the star, are also lyric and enthusiastic announcements. Thus, on the return of the great [Jacob] Adler, who had been ill, it was announced on the boards that "the splendid eagle has spread his wings again."

Yiddish actors, as may be inferred from the verses quoted, take themselves with peculiar seriousness, justified by the enthusiasm, almost worship, with which they are regarded by the people. Many a poor Jew, man or girl, who makes no more than $10 a week in the sweatshop, will spend $5 of it on the theater, which is practically the only amusement of the ghetto Jew. He has not the loafing and sporting instincts of the poor Christian, and spends his money for the theater rather than for drink. It is not only to see the play that the poor Jew goes to the theater. It is to see his friends and the actors. With these latter he, and more frequently she, tries in every way to make acquaintance, but commonly is compelled to adore at a distance. They love the songs that are heard on the stage, and for these the demand is so great that a certain book shop on the East Side makes a speciality of publishing them.

The actor responds to this popular enthusiasm with a sovereign contempt. He struts about in the cafes on Canal and Grand streets, conscious of his greatness. He refers to the crowd as might Moses, with superior condescension or humorous vituperation. Like thieves, actors have a jargon of their own, which is esoteric and jealously guarded. Their pride gave rise a year or two ago to an amusing strike at the People's Theater.

The actors of the three Yiddish companies in New York are normally paid on the share rather than the salary system. In the case of the company now at the People's Theater, this system proved very profitable. The star actors, Jacob Adler and Boris Thomashevsky, and their wives, who are actresses (Mrs. Adler being the heavy realistic tragedienne and Mrs. Thomashevsky the star soubrette), have probably received on an average during that time of as much as $125 a week for each couple. But they, with Mr. Edelstein, the businessman, are lessees of the theater, run the risk, and pay the expenses, which are not small. . . . The subordinate actors, who risk nothing, since they do not share the expenses, have made amounts during this favorable period ranging from $14 a week on the average for the poorest actors to $75 a week for those just beneath the stars. But, in spite of what is exceedingly good pay in the Bowery, the actors of this theater formed a union, and struck for wages instead of shares. This, however, was only an incidental feature. The real cause was that the management of the theater, with the energetic Thomashevsky at the head, insisted that the actors should be prompt at rehearsals, and, if they were not, indulged in unseemly epithets. The actors' pride was aroused and the union was formed to insure their ease and dignity and to protect them from harsh words. . . . The actors easily triumphed . . . and the wage system was introduced. The triumphant actors now receive on an average probably $10 to $15 dollars a week less than under the old system. Mr. Conrad, who began the disaffection, receives a salary of $29 a week, fully $10 less than he received for months before the strike. But the dignity of the Yiddish actor is now placed beyond assault. As one of them recently said, "We shall no longer be spat upon or called dog."

A Horse Laugh

(1903)

Oscar Solomon Straus, scholar, statesman, philanthropist, friend of Presidents, Minister to Turkey, 1887-90, Secretary of Commerce and Labor, 1905-08, first Jew to serve in a Presidential Cabinet, Ambassador

---

Contributed by Rabbi Stanley R. Brav, St. Petersburg Beach, Florida.

to Turkey, 1909-10—this Oscar Straus, in the summer of 1903, engaged a suite in a fashionable Lake Placid resort hotel and went there with his horse. The management was trying to discourage Jews from coming to the hotel; but, fearful of the hue and cry that would be raised if such a prominent Jew was barred, said nothing to Straus about its anti-Jewish policy. However, to discourage him from ever coming again, when Straus left he was presented with a bill charging him double what he had expected to pay and also double for his horse. Straus, faced with this unanticipated discrimination, was righteously indignant. "Look," he protested to the desk clerk, "if I had known what kind of unmarried women's offspring run this place, I never would have come here. And I can understand why you are charging me double. But what have you got against my horse? He isn't Jewish."

JEWS COME IN VARIOUS DENOMINATIONS
(1904)

The feud between German Jews, especially German Reform Jews, and East European Jews, especially East European traditional Jews, has now [1979] faded. But seventy-five years ago the family quarrel was at its height.

❅   ❅   ❅   ❅   ❅

The disputes between German Jews and East European Jews led one "Yehud" (German Jew) to declare that Litvaks have "a tselem in kopf," a crucifix in their heads. Asked to prove it, he replied, "Break open his head and see for yourself."

❅   ❅   ❅   ❅   ❅

Reform Temples were dominated by German Jews for many years. Once a Litvak met a brother Litvak who had just been elected President of a Reform congregation. He said to him, "Chaver, you must be *very* rich!"

❅   ❅   ❅   ❅   ❅

The ridicule hurled by traditional Jews at Reform ones was illustrat-

Contributed by Rabbi Samuel M. Silver, Delray Beach, Florida.

ed when Dr. Solomon Schechter, president of the Conservative Jewish Theological Seminary, met the rabbi of Temple Emanuel, the Reform cathedral in New York, and offered him a cigar. The Reform rabbi said that he did not smoke. Responded Schechter, "So what do you do all day Saturday?"

✿   ✿   ✿   ✿   ✿

During his first week in New York, a greenhorn saw a man with a cigar in his mouth, sitting on Saturday on a park bench and reading a Yiddish newspaper. Cried out the greenie: "America is a goldene medina [a wonderful country]. In America ken afilu di goyim layenen Iddish" [In America even the Gentiles can read Yiddish].

✿   ✿   ✿   ✿   ✿

Asked about the difference between Orthodoxy, Conservatism, and Reform, a 1904 wag replied, "One's crazy, one's hazy, and one's lazy."

✿   ✿   ✿   ✿   ✿

An Orthodox rabbi and a Reform rabbi appeared on the same lecture platform to set forth their respective religious points of view. The Orthodox rabbi began his presentation by saying, "I really have nothing to debate with my Reform friend. He goes his way and I go God's way."

Stephen S. Wise Turns Down Temple Emanu-el
(1905)

The two greatest American Jews of the first three quarters of the twentieth century were Louis Dembitz Brandeis and Stephen Samuel Wise.

Rabbi Stephen S. Wise was born in Budapest, Hungary, on March 17 (St. Patrick's Day), 1874. Because of his natal day, Wise was, in later years, a renowned honorary member of the American Society of the Sons of St. Patrick. He was sixth in line in a family of distinguished rabbis. His father moved to the United States in 1875 and served as rabbi of Temple Rodeph Sholom in New York City until his death in 1896.

Stephen was educated privately for the rabbinate. After receiving his A.B. degree from Columbia University at the age of eighteen and ordination from his father at the age of nineteen, he served as rabbi of

New York's Madison Avenue Synagogue from 1893 to 1900 and of Temple Beth Israel of Portland, Oregon, from 1900 to 1906. In 1907 he founded the Free Synagogue of New York City and in 1922 the Jewish Institute of Relgion. He helped create the Zionist Organization of America in 1898, the American Jewish Congress in 1918, and the World Jewish Congress in 1936. From 1935 on, he edited the Jewish monthly *Opinion*.

He was active in politics on both the local and national levels as a leader in the Democratic Party, a courageous defender of human rights and attacker of political corruption, a staunch espouser of Zionism and an early enemy of Nazism. His personality and eloquence were overpowering. In his prime, he and William Jennings Bryan, 1860-1925, Secretary of State from 1912 to 1915 and ardent religious Fundamentalist, were considered America's most gifted orators. His brilliant wife, Louise, was best known as founder in 1916 and head of the Free Synagogue Child Adoption Service. Wise died on April 19, 1949.

* * * * *

Stephen Samuel Wise became a legend in his lifetime. The stories told about him by the members of his family, his friends, his students, his fellow rabbis, his coworkers in Zionist, political, and humanitarian causes, would fill several volumes. He was scintillating, dramatic, an intellectual giant, an organizing genius, intensely human and, beneath the veneer of a great religious showman, genuinely humble. He hated hypocrisy and pretense and he prized integrity.

In November 1905 he was offered and, on December 3, he declined the pulpit of New York City's prestigious Temple Emanu-El. Having declared he would accept only if accorded the right of full freedom of expression, he received a letter on December first from Louis Marshall, speaking for Temple Emanu-El and stating that its pulpit had always been and would continue to be "subject to and under the control of the board of trustees." Two days later Wise replied that no "self-respecting minister of religion could consider a call to a pulpit" governed by such a stipulation.

On January 5, 1906, Wise published an "Open Letter to the President and Members of Temple Emanu-El of New York City" which is a classic defense of freedom of the pulpit. It had such a profound effect that, ever since, lay attempts to censor American rabbinical pronouncements on or off the pulpit have been infrequent and, in almost all instances, unsuccessful. Wise wrote:

> The chief office of the minister, I take it, is not to represent the views of the congregation, but to proclaim the truth as he sees it. How can he serve a congregation as a teacher save as he quickens the minds of his hearers by the vitality and independence of his utter-

ances? But how can a man be vital and independent and helpful if he be tethered and muzzled? A free pulpit, worthily filled, must command respect and influence; a pulpit that is not free, howsoever filled, is sure to be without potency and honor. A free pulpit will sometimes stumble into error; a pulpit that is not free can never powerfully plead for truth and righteousness. . . . The minister is not to be the spokesman of the congregation, not the message-bearer of the congregation, but the bearer of a message to the congregation. What the contents of that message shall be must be left to the conscience and understanding and loyalty of him in whom a congregation places sufficient confidence to elect him to minister to it.

❖   ❖   ❖   ❖   ❖

Wise had a great love of humor and a great sense of humor. His wife's Child Adoption Service once received from a woman desiring to adopt a child a letter which read: "We have tried four times to have children of our own, but have always been unsuccessful." When Louise told Stephen about the letter, his response was: "What an impatient lady!"

❖   ❖   ❖   ❖   ❖

President Woodrow Wilson and Stephen Wise were close friends. The President sought Wise's advice on many occasions. In October 1917 the British government sent Wilson a copy of the proposed text of the Balfour Declaration for his private consideration. This could not be done through official channels because Palestine was a Turkish possession and the United States had not declared war against Turkey. Wilson asked Brandeis and Wise to appraise the document.

Wise was greatly disturbed because the suggested declaration announced Britain's intention to create "a national haven for Jews" in Palestine. He suggested that the phraseology be changed to "a national home for the Jewish people." Wise's suggestion was transmitted by Wilson to the British government, which approved his very significant change that in future years would be a decisive factor in the chain of events that led to the establishment of the State of Israel.

Woodrow Wilson, son of a Presbyterian minister and a deeply religious man, was an ardent Zionist. He believed sincerely that, among the many reasons prompting God to ordain that he should become President of the United States, was the role he would play in restoring the Jews to their own country. He said to Wise, "How proud I am that, because of the teachings instilled in me by my father, it has been my privilege to help restore the Holy Land to its rightful owners." When Wilson was told by Wise and Brandeis that a number of prominent

American Jews would probably write him letters of protest because of his support of the Balfour Declaration, Wilson replied, "My waste basket is big enough to take care of all such letters."

*   *   *   *   *

One of Wise's pet hates was machine politics which he combated vigorously: on the local New York scene through an unending feud with the leaders of Tammany Hall, on the national scene through struggles with other Democratic city bosses, and on the international scene through condemning the bureaucratic tendencies of some Zionist leaders. Among the New York Tammany-dominated Democratic mayors who smarted under Wise's public criticisms was John F. "Red Mike" Hylan, mayor from 1918 to 1925. On one occasion Wise and "Red Mike" were attending the same political function. Asked if he knew the famous rabbi, Hylan replied crossly, "He certainly has attacked me often enough for me to know him quite well." Wise heard of the reply soon after it was spoken. He walked up to "Red Mike" and said, "Mr. Mayor, I am sorry to inform you that the remark you made about me a few minutes ago was not entirely correct. It is true that I have criticized you often; but, in my humble opinion, I have not criticized you often enough."

*   *   *   *   *

I was among the many hundreds of rabbis who looked to Wise for counsel and leadership and was also privileged to be numbered among his friends. Very early in my rabbinate, in Springfield, Massachusetts, Wise and I spoke on the same program for the United Palestine Appeal. In his remarks Wise made some complimentary references to me; and then went on to say, "But there is one thing about Eichhorn I don't like. That mustache of his makes him look too much like Hitler." After the meeting, Wise said to me, "Eichhorn, I hope what I said will prompt you to shave off that damn thing." "No, Doctor," I responded, "what is good enough for Charlie Chaplin is good enough for me." A headline on the front page of next morning's Springfield newspaper read, "Stephen Wise compares local rabbi to Hitler."

*   *   *   *   *

Wise told the following story on himself: In the summer of 1933 he visited Siegmund Freud in Vienna. Over wine and cigars, the two celebrities amused themselves by trying to draw up a mutually agreeable list of the five most important Jews in the world. Wise said, "Of course, Dr. Freud, you are one, and, in addition, I would select Albert Einstein,

Chaim Weizmann, Justice Brandeis, and probably Henri Bergson."
Freud responded, "And why not also include Stephen Wise?" "Oh, no,
no, no, no," exclaimed Wise. Freud took his cigar out of his mouth and
said, smilingly, "My dear Dr. Wise, if you had answered 'no' only once, I
would believe you mean it; but when out come four 'no's,' I cannot
believe that you really meant it."

❊   ❊   ❊   ❊   ❊

In 1935, while on his third trip to Palestine, Wise decided during
Passover to go from Jerusalem to the Jordan River to dip his hands in the
water of the stream sacred to both Jew and Christian. He arrived at the
river at a time when a group of Russian peasant pilgrims was also there.
As Wise was about to put his hands into the water, an old peasant woman
shouted at him in Russian, "Zhid, how dare you put your Jewish hands in
our Christian river!" His guide told him the meaning of what the lady had
said. Wise instructed the guide to inform the elderly female that his
Jewish ancestors were already bathing in this river many hundreds of
years before her Russian ancestors had acquired the habit of taking a
bath.

❊   ❊   ❊   ❊   ❊

An exuberant lady once came up to Rabbi Wise after a religious
service and excitedly shook his hand.

"Doctor," she said animatedly, "after hearing you talk so often and
so enthusiastically about Palestine, I made it my business to see the
country for myself. I have just returned from Palestine and I tell you it's a
wonderful place. I was particularly impressed by Lake Tiberias and the
Sea of Galilee. They are simply gorgeous."

"Madam," answered Dr. Wise, suppressing a smile, "those two
bodies of water happen to be synonymous."

"That may be, that may be," replied the lady, nothing daunted, "but
to me it seemed that the Sea of Galilee is much more synonymous than
Lake Tiberias."

A BINTEL BRIEF (A BUNDLE OF LETTERS)
(1906)

The following advice-seeking letters to the editor, and the advice
given in response, appeared in the Yiddish daily newspaper the *Forward*

in New York City during 1906. They are excerpted from the volume *A Bintel Brief: Sixty Years of Letters from the Lower East Side to The Jewish Daily Forward*, compiled and edited by Isaac Metzker in 1971 and published by Doubleday and Company. They are reprinted here with the permission of Mr. Metzker.

❀ ❀ ❀ ❀ ❀

Worthy Editor,
    We are a small family who recently came to the "Golden Land." My husband, my boy and I are together, and our daughter lives in another city.
    I had opened a grocery store here, but soon lost all my money. In Europe we were in business; we had people working for us and paid them well. In short, there we made a good living but here we are badly off.
    My husband became a peddler. The "pleasure" of knocking on doors and ringing bells cannot be known by anyone but a peddler. If anybody does buy anything "on time," a lot of the money is lost, because there are some people who never intend to pay. In addition, my husband has trouble because he has a beard, and because of the beard he gets beaten up by the hoodlums.
    Also we have problems with our boy, who throws money around. He works every day till late at night at a grocery for three dollars a week. I watch over him and give him the best because I'm sorry that he has to work so hard. But he costs me plenty and he borrows money from everybody. He has many friends and owes them all money. I get more and more worried as he takes here and borrows there. All my talking doesn't help. I am afraid to chase him away from home because he might get worse among strangers. I want to point out that he is well versed in Russian and Hebrew and he is not a child any more, but his behavior is not that of an intelligent adult.
    I don't know what to do. My husband argues that he doesn't want to continue peddling. He doesn't want to shave off his beard, and it's not fitting for such a man to do so. The boy wants to go to his sister, but that's a twenty-five dollar fare. What can I do? I beg you for a suggestion.

Your constant reader,

F.L.

Answer: Since her husband doesn't earn a living anyway, it would be advisable for all three of them to move to the city where the daughter is living. As for the beard, we feel that if the man is religious and the beard is dear to him because the Jewish law does not allow him to shave it off, it's up to him to decide. But if he is not religious, and the beard interferes with his earnings, it should be sacrificed.

❀ ❀ ❀ ❀ ❀

Honorable Editor,

I have a grievous wound in my heart and maybe through the "Bintel Brief" I will find relief.

I am a young woman. I was happily married, but a year ago death suddenly took my husband. He was handsome and I am considered attractive. When we used to walk together we often heard the comment, "What a good-looking couple." We were in love and faithful to each other in the full sense of the word.

When he died and left me with our only daughter, fifteen years of age, my world collapsed. I was in despair but not for financial reasons. My husband left a generous policy, quite a bit of money, and I run a successful business.

I cried till my eyes were swollen, and when they laid my dear husband in the coffin and took it out of the house, I fainted four times. In the carriage on the way to the cemetery I sat in a daze. My daughter and a young man, my husband's best friend, were with me.

When they covered my husband's coffin I became hysterical, screamed and tried to stop them. Finally they dragged me away from the grave and calmed me down.

My husband's friend didn't leave my side. They had been comrades since they came to America, prepared to face any dangers for each other. The friend had been like a member of the family in our house and my daughter was very attached to him. The friend was not as handsome, well built or attractive as my husband and he had never shown the least interest in me as a woman. Nor had I ever thought of him as anything but a friend. Suddenly this changed.

I don't know how it happened that during the drive home from the cemetery I was alone in the carriage with my husband's friend. He told me later that it was pure chance. Seated in the carriage, I began to cry again, and the friend comforted me, patted my hands and begged me not to endanger my health. As if in a dream, a thought came to me: Isn't this more than friendly sympathy, isn't this perhaps the interest of a man in a woman? In my sorrow and confusion I didn't know what was happening to me. As he comforted me, the friend began to kiss my hands and I looked at him in amazement. Instead of drawing back, though, he began to stroke my hair and swore that he felt toward his dead friend's wife as toward an unhappy sister. He spoke with tears in his eyes, drew me to him and kissed me passionately. Those were passionate kisses from a man to a woman, but they were mingled with his tears for the death of his dear friend and for my fate.

I had no will to protest and he held me and kissed me again and again. And then I heard words of love from him. I felt like a sinner. When I got home I was afraid to look my daughter in the eyes. I imagined I heard my husband calling me a hypocrite and saying my tears were false.

The next morning my husband's friend came to my house. He cried bitterly and told me he felt like a traitor, but he loved me so much that he would waste away if I didn't become his. He begged me in his friend's name to marry him and then he could show his faithfulness to his friend's family.

Dear Editor, I swear to you that in my heart there was only one love, for my husband, but I am a weak woman and I couldn't fight against the passionate pleas and kisses. I was helpless and I gave him my word when my husband was barely two weeks in the grave. I told him I would marry him a year after my husband's death. But I feel guilty toward my husband. My daughter realized everything. With tears in her eyes, she blurted out that her father's grave was not an hour old when I already had taken a new bridegroom. Her words hurt me, and I had no answer. But in time she accepted him.

My close friends advise me to marry my husband's friend, and I will do so because I know that he will be good to my daughter and to me. But before the wedding I would like your opinion on all that has happened to me.

Sincerely,

B.V.

Answer: The woman's excuse that she was unable to protest against the passionate advances of her husband's friend is a weak one. Better if she had opened the carriage door and asked him to get out. There is no excuse for the disgusting behavior of the young man. He should not have acted so shamefully after his friend's death. It is possible the widow is making a mistake in deciding to marry him, because it is doubtful whether she can be happy with such a man.

❊ ❊ ❊ ❊ ❊

Dear Editor,

I am a girl from Galicia and in the shop where I work I sit near a Russian Jew with whom I was always on good terms. Why should one worker resent another?

But once, in a short debate, he stated that all Galicians were no good. When I asked him to repeat it, he answered that he wouldn't retract a word, and that he wished all Galician Jews dead.

I was naturally not silent in the face of such a nasty expression. He maintained that only Russian Jews are fine and intelligent. According to him, the Galitzianer are inhuman savages, and he had the right to speak of them so badly.

Dear Editor, does he really have a right to say this? Have the Galician Jews not sent enough money for the unfortunate sufferers of the pogroms in Russia? When a Gentile speaks badly of Jews, it's immediately printed in the newspapers and discussed hotly everywhere. But that a Jew should express himself so about his own brothers is nothing? Does he have a right? Are Galicians really so bad? And does he, the Russian, remain fine and intelligent in spite of such expressions?

As a reader of your worthy newspaper, I hope you will print my letter and give me your opinion.

With thanks in advance,

B.M.

Answer: The Galician Jews are just as good and bad as people from other lands. If the Galicians must be ashamed of the foolish and evil ones among them, then the Russians, too, must hide their heads in shame because among them there is such an idiot as the acquaintance of our letter writer.

FIRST AMERICAN JEWISH AVIATOR
(1910)

Leibel Wellcher was born in Mehileff, a small town near Kiev, Russia, on August 14, 1881. His parents migrated to the United States in 1890 and settled in Philadelphia. Leibel was sent to cheder to receive the traditional Jewish training leading to Bar Mitsvah. His father died in 1894. His mother then married Frank Silverman. The Silvermans moved to Washington, D.C., in 1898.

In April 1901 Leibel enlisted in the Navy as Arthur L. Welsh, presumably to avoid discrimination because of his original name. For the rest of his life he was known as Arthur L. Welsh. His friends called him Al. He was honorably discharged at the end of his four-year enlistment, went to business school and then got a job as a bookkeeper. But his real interest was mechanics.

His stepfather was an active member of Orthodox (now Conservative) Congregation Adas Israel. Al belonged to the Young Zionist Union, one of the synagogue's youth clubs. Here he met and fell in love with Anna Harmel, daughter of Latvia-born Zionist Paul Harmel. Al and Anna were married at Adas Israel by Rabbi George Silverstone on October 10, 1907.

Al soon became interested in the development of aeronautics. He was a spectator on July 30, 1909, at Fort Myer, Virginia, when Orville Wright made his first "cross country" flight from Fort Myer to Shuter's Hill and back, a distance of ten miles, in 14 minutes, 40 seconds.

Welsh went to Dayton, Ohio, to apply for admittance to the newly opened Wright Flying School. At first he was rejected because of his lack of skill in repairing engines. He persisted and was finally accepted. In March 1910 he became a member of the Wright flying class at Montgomery, Alabama. He was an apt student. In May Orville Wright persuaded Al to remain with him as a flight instructor and took him to Dayton to teach in the larger school there. Welsh was sent around the

Based on article "Al Welsh, Pioneer of American Aviation" by Samuel H. Holland in the May 1969 *The Record*, published by the Jewish Historical Society of Greater Washington, Washington, D.C.

country to make demonstration flights. On December 24, 1910, he took his sister, Mrs. Sidney A. Wiseman, for a plane ride. She was undoubtedly the first American Jewish female aeroplane passenger. Among Al's students was Army Lieutenant Henry "Hap" Arnold, destined to become a five-star general and Chief of the Army Air Force during World War II. On July 22, 1911, Al set a new American two-man altitude record by carrying a passenger to a height of 2,648 feet.

In 1912 he became chief test pilot for one of the earliest military planes, the CM-1 Wright Military Scout. The government contract required that this aeroplane, powered by a six-cylinder engine, have the capability of climbing two thousand feet with a 450-pound load in ten minutes, with enough fuel for four hours of flight and at a minimum speed of 45 miles an hour. In February the War Department ordered ten such planes. The first of them was completed on May first.

On May 18 Welsh began to make test flights in the plane. At the end of three weeks all requirements had been met except the loaded climb of 2,000 feet in ten minutes. Even under ideal conditions this would be a very difficult requirement to fulfill. On June 11, at six P.M., Welsh took off for this final test with Lieutenant J. W. Hazelhurst, Jr., as his passenger. He climbed to about two hundred feet, then dove down at a very steep angle to gain momentum to assist the start of his maximum ascent. Nearing the ground, as he attempted to change direction, the center section of the plane collapsed under the great stress, the wings folded and the craft crashed to the ground, killing both men instantly.

Al's funeral was held on the afternoon of June 13 at the home of his father-in-law. An account in a New York Yiddish newspaper said in part:

> There were present many prominent Jews and several representatives of the Army and Navy in full uniform. The deceased was draped in a silken Talis. His head was in bandages, so as to cover the broken head, but his face was uncovered. Rev. Joseph Glushak, Cantor of the Orthodox Adas Israel Congregation, delivered a very appropriate eulogy. All present were in tears, including Mr. Orville Wright and his sister, who were doing all they could to console the mother and wife of the deceased. Even though Mr. Welsh professionally covered up his Jewish identity, he was frequently in attendance at Jewish meetings and participated in Jewish activities.

The Washington *Herald* of June 12 editorialized:

> Al Welsh was one of the five original pupils of Orville and Wilbur Wright and was adjudged by his tutors to be the most skillful instructor in the art of flying in aviation circles. Only recently Wilbur Wright declared him the peer of any man in the world as a pilot. He was intrepid but cautious. He never "played to the grandstand" and time and again condemned men who jeopardized their lives by attempting "circus stunts."

The Washington *Times* of the same date said:

> Both [Welsh] and Lieutenant Hazelhurst enjoyed a large meas-
> ure of popular esteem. The grief occasioned by their deaths is far-
> reaching and sincere. The one consolation in a tragedy like this is that
> the victims shall not have died in vain. It is only by building up
> experimental results and by avoiding weaknesses in structure or
> principle that the science of aviation, yet comparatively in its
> infancy, can be brought to perfection. These courageous pioneers
> will be entitled to remembrance as martyrs to a worthy cause. It was
> in no foolhardy flight that they lost their lives, but in an effort to
> further the development of a science which, like every step in the
> world's great pathway of progress, has demanded its victims.

Al is buried in the family plot in Adas Israel's Alabama Street
Cemetery. His grave is marked by a footstone bearing the simple
inscription, "Arthur L. Welsh, Father." (At the time of his death Al had a
two-year-old daughter.) A few miles away, the trophies Leibel Wellcher
won as an aviation pioneer are on permanent exhibit in the National
Aeronautical Collections of the Smithsonian Institution.

"You Ain't Heard Nuthin' Yet!"
(1911)

By strictly conventional standards Al Jolson was not much of a Jew.
Reared in rigidly Orthodox fashion by a stern father, he rebelled at an
early age. Throughout his life he rarely went to synagogue. None of his
four wives was Jewish.

But Al Jolson's Jewishness was literally written all over his face. He
was proud of it. He boasted about it. Yiddish was his second language.
He gave generously of both time and money to the United Jewish Appeal
and to Israel. Even when he entertained in black face, as he did for most
of his stage years, to his adoring audiences of every nationality and
religion he was a Jew who was the greatest American musical comedy
star of his time. However one regards Jolson's credits and debits, and he
had plenty of both, he is and will remain a super-attraction in the
twentieth century's Jewish theatrical Hall of Fame.

"Listen," Jolson would have said, "you ain't heard nuthin' yet."—
One night in the early 1920s Al went with some friends to a New York
nightclub where Ben Bernie the "old maestro" and "all the lads" were
playing. The crowd asked Al to sing for them. He consented. He said,
"Today happens to be my sainted mother's birthday. I am going to sing
one of the songs she loved. I am going to sing it in her language. And

because many of you do not know Yiddish, I'll have to explain the song to you first. It's called 'Ein Chazan auf Shabbas,' which means 'A Cantor sings on the Sabbath.'" He told the audience the meaning of the text of this famous Jewish folksong. He told them about the ways in which the tailor and the shoemaker and the wagon driver reacted to the singing of the cantor. A newspaper reporter who was there described what happened:

> Jolson made his audience live with him momentarily in that faraway ghetto in a tiny Russian village. Having told them what the song meant, he sang it. Bernie, who knew the song, accompanied him on the fiddle. There stood Jolson, no bigger than five feet six inches, slender, puckish, singing in a foreign tongue of a foreign place. Did I say Jolson sang it? It was more than singing. He wept it. He laughed it. It played in his heart and the hearts of all responded to it. Not an eye was wholly dry.

*   *   *   *   *

Asa Yoelson was born in Lithuania in 1886. The exact date is not known. Later in life, wanting a birthday, he picked May 26 and celebrated it annually as his birthday. He was the youngest son of Cantor Moses Yoelson and his wife Naomi. The Yoelsons had been cantors for five generations.

Moses Yoelson came to the United States in 1890 and worked as a common laborer for four years to save enough money to bring his family over. In 1894 he became cantor of a small synagogue in Washington, D.C. He spent the rest of his life in Washington and died there in 1945 at the age of ninety.

The Yoelsons had four children, Rose, Etta, Hirsch, and Asa. A year and a half after arriving in Washington, Naomi died. Some time later the cantor married Naomi's cousin Hessi, who Americanized her name to Ida. From this second union another daughter, Gertrude, was born. At first the boys resented their kind, good stepmother. After they got to know her they loved her very much. When Hirsch was fifteen he decided to change his name to Harry. Asa followed his brother's lead and at twelve changed to Al. Both Anglicized Yoelson to Jolson.

Very early in life the boys determined to be singers and actors. They sang duets on the street. People threw coins to them. Papa was horrified. "Bums," he called them, "No-goods." He was not entirely wrong. They ran with street gangs, got into fights. But they were not all bad. They also earned money by selling newspapers and peddling watermelons. The stage urge was so insistent that Harry and Al ran away from home, individually and collectively, a number of times. Whenever their money and luck ran out they returned home.

Shortly after Asa became Al, the twelve-year-old skipped town and joined a traveling circus, which folded some weeks later in York, Pennsylvania. He then got a job as a singing waiter in a Baltimore saloon. Picked up as a wayward minor by the Baltimore police, he was placed in St. Mary's Industrial School for Boys, a Catholic institution. In St. Mary's at this same time were two other juvenile delinquents who also made quite a name for themselves in later years, baseball's Herman "Babe" Ruth and dancer Bill "Bojangles" Robinson. Cantor Yoelson came to St. Mary's and took his boy back to Washington.

Then Harry and Al became a singing duo on a Chesapeake Bay excursion boat. On this boat Al learned to roll dice. For the rest of his life gambling was a major addiction. When he became rich and famous he added betting on horses to his mania for crap shooting. In 1899 Harry got a job selling peanuts and candy in the Bijou, Washington's burlesque house. From that he went on to become a burlesque actor. After a while Al joined him. For a few years they did a two-man act with fair success but then had a bitter quarrel and split up.

Al went into business for himself as a blackface singer and comedian. In 1906 he married his first wife. The marriage lasted officially for thirteen years but actually it was over long before that. Until he married his fourth wife when he was nearly sixty years old, Al was not a one-woman man. He played the field. He was able to have his fun without undue worry because his semen contained no viable sperm. Despite this inability to become a natural father, Al loved children. He adopted several and was a generous and kind foster parent.

When Cantor Yoelson learned that Al had married a non-Jew, he sat shiva [the seven-day period of mourning for the dead] for his son. Despite Al's constant efforts to convince his father that he really was not such a bad guy, father and son did not become even partially reconciled until about 1925. A relationship of genuine affection and understanding never developed.

Fame came to Al almost overnight. In March 1911 he opened at Shubert's Winter Garden in New York in the musical *La Belle Paree*. The first two nights the show laid a great big egg. On the third night Jolson was given the star billing and rescued the musical from oblivion. On Broadway he was hailed as a miracle man, "the king." He signed an exclusive contract with the Shubert organization at $1,500 a week and a percentage of the take of every production in which he would appear.

One night in 1913, while singing and dancing in *Honeymoon Express*, Al felt a sharp pain caused by an ingrown toenail. Loyal to the stage tradition that "the show must go on," Al stopped dancing, dropped to one knee to ease his pain, instinctively spread out his arms, and kept on singing the pathetic lament he had been warbling while dancing, "You made me love ya; I diden' wanna do it; I diden' wanna do it." The audience ate it up. The impromptu pose brought down the house. From that moment on, singing on one knee with outstretched arms became Jolson's trademark.

Al had many eccentricities. He was very volatile, highly emotional. Only toward the end of his life did he become more mellow and easygoing. He was a hypochondriac, always thinking he was sick, always taking pills, obsessed with thoughts about illness and death. He was a devoted sun worshiper, believing that a deep suntan is a certain sign of good health. He was arrogant; he was self-centered; he was, many times, downright obnoxious; but he had an appealing singing voice and a great natural talent. And when Jollie, as he liked to call himself, was out there on the stage entertaining "my public," his mannerisms were not phony. He was being himself, doing what he felt he had been born to do.

In 1927 Warner Brothers revolutionized the motion picture industry by making the first talking picture, *The Jazz Singer*, about a cantor's son who became a musical comedy star. The lead role was offered first to George Jessel, who had the lead in the stage play, then to Eddie Cantor, and then to Jolson. All refused. But by this time Al's long day in the Broadway spotlight was beginning to darken, so after much hesitation he finally consented to do the picture in the hope it might help improve his fading image. He got no money for acting in the film, only Warner Brothers stock. The movie was an extraordinary success. Its high point was Jolson's beautiful chanting of Kol Nidre. This was one time that his father was very proud of him. In his wildest dreams Al did not imagine the fame and fortune that were to come to him through the picture. It not only made him an international celebrity but a wealthy one as well.

In 1935 Al became the permanent host on the popular NBC Radio series, Kraft Music Hall. He served in this capacity, on and off, for the rest of his life. But also about 1935 Al's long reign as "King of Broadway," as the greatest stage attraction in America, came to an end. Younger stars captured the place in the hearts of the theatergoing public where Jolson had once reigned alone. The Jolson ego was badly bruised. Al could not take it. He became melancholy, bitter, resentful, jealous. His third wife, young Ruby Keeler, was one of the successful rising stars. Al had married Ruby in 1928 when he was forty-two and she nineteen. At first the marriage was a happy one. As the years went on, Al began to belittle Ruby privately and publicly. Disgusted, she left him in 1939 and divorced him in 1940. After Ruby walked out on Al he became more morose than before. For a few years he went into almost total seclusion.

World War II brought Al out of these doldrums. Entertaining American troops became his new obsession. He began making overseas tours for USO early in 1942 and continued to do so until the termination of the war.

One World War II incident involving Al is a lulu. In 1943, toward the end of the North African campaign, he went to Morocco and Algiers to sing for General Eisenhower's troops. He carried with him a letter to Ike from Ike's wife Mamie. Invited to dine with the general, Al handed him the sealed envelope. Ike opened it, read it, roared with laughter, and handed it to Al to read. It stated that when Al met Ike he was to give him two tokens of Mamie's affection, a. a kiss; b. a swift kick in the behind for not writing her more often. Al read the instructions and turned red. He was nonplused. Show biz is show biz but this? Here? In front of these big-shot military dinner guests? To the Commander-in-Chief of all U. S. forces in Africa?

Ike solved Al's dilemma. He turned his back to Al and bent over. "Jolson," he said, "please carry out the order of my Commanding General." Al shrugged his shoulders and obeyed. When Ike unbent and turned around, there stood Al, with lips puckered, ready to carry out Mamie's other command. "Oh, no," said Eisenhower, laughing, "not that. You can give that one back to my wife when you return to the States."

In 1942, in the Pacific, Al got malaria. In 1943, while touring Europe and Africa, he got pneumonia. He almost died. His left lung had to be removed. In 1945 he married twenty-one-year-old Erle Galbraith, a lab technician he met while undergoing tests and also giving a concert at the Army hospital in Hot Springs, Arkansas. His five years with Erle were the happiest married years of his life.

The supersuccessful movie, *The Jolson Story*, made in 1946, in which Al sang the songs through the lips of his impersonator Larry Parks, is not a true story of Al's life. Ruby Keeler refused to let her name be used in the picture and so a fictional wife was substituted. Al's father is depicted as an easygoing, understanding individual who has no serious objection to his son's marrying a non-Jew! Al's stage career begins when a vaudeville actor hears him singing in the Catholic choir at St. Mary's School!

There is one story about the movie that is absolutely true. While it was being made, Jolson became seriously ill. Harry Cohn, head of Columbia Pictures and producer of *The Jolson Story*, visited Al in the hospital. Fearing that the large investment his firm had made in the picture was in jeopardy, Cohn asked Jolson how he felt. Jolson replied that he felt fine. Cohn then took his big cigar from his mouth, waved it at Jolson and said, "If anything more happens to you and you die before the picture is finished, so help me, I'll kill ya!"

When the Korean War broke out in June 1950 Al volunteered immediately to go to the Pacific. He went within weeks and spent several months entertaining our military men and women in Japan and Korea. While in the Far East he developed a severe bronchial infection in his remaining lung, but he tried manfully to keep on going.

The effort did him in. The show was over. Al died in San Francisco on October 23, 1950. When word reached New York City, the mayor ordered the street lights on broadway dimmed. The funeral service was held in Temple Israel in Hollywood. Jack Benny and George Jessel spoke. Jack said, "In our time, Al Jolson was the greatest showman in America." Jessel said, "The king is dead; but we cannot shout, 'Long live the new king,' for there is no one to pick up his sceptre."

Upstairs
(1912)

An old rabbi lived over a grocery store on New York's Lower East Side. In front of the grocery store was a sign: RABBI RABINOWITZ IS UPSTAIRS. When the old rabbi died, after a long life dedicated to study rather than trying to make a living, he left no money and no relatives to pay for his burial. So his little congregation raised enough dollars to give him a dignified funeral and a resting place in a Jewish cemetery. When the time came to put a tombstone on his grave, his congregants could not afford to purchase such a stone. One of them had a brilliant idea. They would take the sign that had been in front of the grocery and they would set it up over their rabbi's grave. So now everyone who passes by that grave is impressed by the appropriateness and the spirituality of the holy man's epitaph: RABBI RABINOWITZ IS UPSTAIRS

All Was Not Lost
(1913)

In November 1910 a group of Jewish garment workers organized, at 63 Hester Street, "The East Side Sick Benefit and Fraternal Society, Lodge Number One." At the peak of its popularity, in 1913, Lodge Number One (the Society never progressed as far as Lodge Number Two) welcomed to its fraternal bosom Chaver Eliezer Cherkis. There was an impressive initiation ceremony with hailing signs, secret hand-clasps, ritual, and all the rest of it. The new chaver entered with enthusiasm into the mysteries of the society.

A few days later Cherkis received a postcard announcing that the Lodge had moved to the Union Square Building, a three-story structure where a number of other clubs and associations also maintained meeting halls. On the meeting night of Lodge Number One, Cherkis went to the new address, sought out the meeting room and rapped three times on the locked door.

Fifteen minutes after that, the said Cherkis, looking very disconsolate, encountered one of the officers of his lodge a few blocks from the building. "What's the big idea you wouldn't let me in tonight?" Cherkis demanded heatedly. The other looked at him, mystified. "Eliezer, whatever are you talking about?" "Well, it was like so," replied Eliezer. "At seven o'clock I climbed up the stairs and I'm knocking on the door. A little slot opens up in the door like from a mailbox and somebody inside sticks his eye to the hole and hollers at me, 'What d'ye want?' So I made the Grand Hailing Sign and I say to him like I'm supposed to, 'L'shana habaa biYerushalayim [Next year in Jerusalem].' And he says, 'Who gives a damn?' and slams shut the peepee hole."

"Idiot! Shlemiel!" yelled the lodge officer. "Don't you know that our meeting doesn't start til nine o'clock?"

"No, I didn't know that. So who is meeting there earlier?"

"The Knights of Columbus, that's who. And you have given those Catholics our secret passwords."

"Oy vey!" gasped the penitent blunderer. For a moment the enormity of his error stunned him. Then he brightened.

"Listen, it could be worse."

"Worse? How could it be worse?"

"Well, look at it like this. I gave them our passwords; but you will have to admit—I got from them their countersign!"

"A Study in American Strength"

(1917)

During World War I, the following item appeared in the daily press:

Three American airmen, Edward Mallory Vogel from Tennessee; Izzie Goldberg from the Bronx, N.Y.; and Edwin J. Sipowski from Waukegan, Illinois, killed in a takeoff in San Juan harbor, Puerto Rico, were buried today side by side, with a Protestant chaplain, a Roman Catholic priest and a rabbi officiating. The flag under which they had served together now flies over their graves.

Greatly moved by this story, H. I. Phillips of the New York *Sun* wrote the following poem, titled "A Study in American Strength":

A chaplain, a priest and a rabbi—
Protestant—Catholic—Jew
Three Yanks in three simple caskets—
Three colors—red, white and blue.

A hush on a tropical island
    As notes from a bugle fall—
Three rituals slowly chanted—
    Three faiths in a common call!

A lad from the Bronx, another
    Who joined up in Tennessee;
A third one from far Waukegan—
    A typical bunch, those three.
A crash in a naval aircraft . . .
    A rush to its crumpled side . . .
And nearby Old Glory marking
    The reason the trio died.

They answered a call to duty
    From church and from synagogue—
From hills and from teeming city—
    Three names in a naval log.
Each raised in his separate concepts—
    Each having his form to pray—
But all for a faith triumphant
    When rituals fade away!

A prayer in Latin phrases—
    And one with more ancient lore;
A Protestant simple service—
    Three paths to just one door.
"Qui tollis peccata mundi,"
    And "Enter ye into rest,"
A blessing from ancient Moses
    For three who had met the test.

This is the story mighty
    Making our sinews strong;
Boys from many altars
    Warring on one great wrong.
This is the nation's power,
    This is its suit of mail;
Land where each narrow bigot
    Knows that he can't prevail!

THE JEWISH LEGION
(1917)

In London in the spring of 1917 a group of ardent Zionists, including Chaim Weizmann, Vladimir Jabotinsky, and Lord Rothschild, met with officials of the British War Office to urge the formation of a Jewish Legion to liberate Palestine from the Turks. Hard pressed by the war, the British were receptive to the idea of voluntary military help.

Jabotinsky became the active organizer of the Jewish Legion. He was helped greatly by Joseph Trumpeldor, a hero of the Russo-Japanese War, who lost his arm at the siege of Port Arthur, Manchuria. For his bravery under fire Trumpeldor had been awarded the Order of St. George, the highest Russian decoration. Jabotinsky and Trumpeldor persuaded the British that a specific insignia, the Magen David, would be attached to the soldier's uniform; that Jewish holidays would be observed; that kosher food would be served; and that the Jewish soldiers would be sent only to Palestine. On August 23 the London *Gazette* announced the official formation of the Jewish Regiment, designated the 38th Battalion of Royal Fusiliers, under the command of an Irishman, Lieutenant Colonel John Henry Patterson. Jabotinsky received the rank of lieutenant, but Trumpeldor was rejected because of his handicap, though he had been second in command in the preliminary Jewish Force attached to the British Army—the Zion Mule Corps, which took part in the difficult Gallipoli campaign in 1915.

The early recruits were largely Yiddish-speaking Polish and Russian immigrants from London's teeming Whitechapel district, who worked as tailors. For them exchanging the needle for a heavy rifle called for a major transformation in mind and body. There were times when the regular Army men were nonplused by the approach of these recruits to military routines. In his book *Soldiers in Judea*, Roman Fruelich relates a typical incident during target practice at the firing range. The sergeant shouted, "Cease fire." Everyone obeyed except one ex-tailor who kept shooting away. In Yiddish "sheess" means "shoot." Being a Litvak, this particular soldier pronounced "sheess" as "seess." He stoutly maintained that he was only following orders. Fortunately the private in charge of targets got away with only an arm wound.

At their military camp near Plymouth, the rigorous training helped transform this pale-faced, sedentary group into a hardened fighting unit.

From "The Historic March of the Jewish Legion" in the *American Zionist*, June 1978, pp. 25-28, by Maurice Bleifeld. Reprinted with the permission of Mr. Bleifeld and the *American Zionist*.

Colonel Patterson declared himself proud of his tailors. The men demolished the concept of passive ghetto mentality and became psychologically set to fight for the realization of their age-old dream. One of the most ardent recruits was Private Jacob Epstein, who was later to become the noted sculptor, Sir Jacob Epstein.

The movement for a Jewish Legion spread to the United States and Canada later in 1917. The American government granted permission for the recruitment of men who were not subject to the draft. Recruitment stations were opened in all the large cities, seeking Jewish immigrants between the ages of eighteen and forty-five. Men between twenty-one and thirty-one who had taken out first citizenship papers were also considered eligible, with the permission of their draft boards.

In New York City soap-box orators appeared in the garment district at lunchtime, when thousands of shop workers spilled out into the streets, and appealed to their listeners to enlist and free Palestine from the Turks. The chief recruiting office was located at 220 West 42nd Street. Before long, another was opened on Delancey Street on the East Side.

The volunteers came from various walks of life. They were shop workers, storekeepers, students, teachers, writers, and, in some cases, just adventurers. Quite a few were underage. Regardless of background they shared a common bond of idealism, a determination to return Eretz Yisrael to the Jewish people. The recruits were given two weeks to get ready. The first drill was held on the Williamsburgh Bridge.

On February 28, 1918, the first contingent of 140 men left New York City. The night before they had been feted at an emotional farewell dinner held in the Hotel Imperial. They were given an enthusiastic send-off in a parade on Fifth Avenue, marching behind the blue and white colors of the Jewish flag, the American and British flags. Then they loaded on the train that would take them to the Canadian training camp at Windsor, Nova Scotia. Every three weeks additional contingents of volunteers followed the same route.

The American and Canadian volunteers became the nucleus of the 39th Battalion Royal Fusiliers and were eventually placed under the command of Lieutenant Colonel Eliezer Margolin. Margolin was born in Russia and had been brought to Palestine as a young boy. He served in the Australian Army as a lieutenant and was wounded. At the urging of Jabotinsky he joined the Legion. Two other Jewish battalions were formed, the 40th and 42nd, the latter organized too late for overseas duty. All told, the Jewish Legion consisted of 10,000 men, most of whom were volunteers from the United States. The others came from England, Ireland, Canada, Argentina, Russia, Poland, Palestine, and Roumania.

Groups of volunteers came from various American cities. David Gruen of New York City, later to be known as David ben Gurion, was among the first to sign up. In Baltimore seventeen-year-old William

Braiterman was prevented from joining by his mother. William took matters into his own hands, went to Philadelphia, and there enlisted as William Cohen. Another Baltimorean to join was an Irishman named O'Brien, a former captain in the American Army. He signed up as a private and was quickly promoted to sergeant. He was a source of curiosity and pride to the contingent and explained his action by saying, "I believe in the ideal for which the Jewish Battalion is going to fight. The Jews are entitled to their home in Palestine. This is their historic home, the inheritance of their forefathers." One of the young ardent Zionists from Milwaukee who tried to enlist and was rejected was Golda Mabovitch, later to become famous as Golda Meir. In her autobiography she relates that she felt "crushed" when she was turned away because girls were not being accepted.

After training in Canada, the new soldiers boarded camouflaged troop transports and crossed the ocean in convoy. The initial American Jewish contingent reached England on April 6, 1918. They were warmly greeted by Chief Rabbi Joseph H. Hertz and a large assemblage of Jews. After receiving additional training in England, they were ferried across the Channel, sent in "40 and 8" cattle cars to Italy, and then shipped by boat to Alexandria, Egypt. In Alexandria they were passionately welcomed by the Grand Rabbi of Egypt. Their route took them to Kantara on the Suez Canal and finally to the military camp of Sarafand, in the desert near Rishon Lezion.

The Americans were greatly irked by the fact that their training had been so prolonged that they did not arrive in Palestine until after the Turks had signed an armistice. The British contingent of the Legion did get to participate in the last drive of General Allenby from Jerusalem to Damascus. The Legion was assigned the task of guarding the Turkish military prisoners. Among them were Turkish and Palestinian Jews who had been inducted into the Turkish military service. Many of them offered to join the Legion and were accepted. Colonel Margolin became military governor of the Es-Salt district.

After the Turkish signing of the Armistice, life on the hot sands of the camp in Sarafand and the other bases of the Legion at Helmieh, Kantara, Tel-el-Kebir, and Bir Salim crawled at a slow pace. It was during this time that David ben Gurion's tent became the center of much activity. Visitors streamed in and out from other Jewish camps to plan future Zionist activities. After being demobilized, Ben Gurion did not return to America. He stayed on in Palestine and became active in the Palestinian Jewish labor movement. In 1935 he was named chairman of the Jewish Agency Executive. When the State of Israel was established in 1948, he became its Prime Minister. Jabotinsky, founder of the Legion, died in 1940.

Over 400 American and Canadian veterans of the Jewish Legion chose to remain in Palestine after their discharge. Most of them worked the land. All devoted themselves to the cause of a Jewish state. In 1921 a number settled on desert land allocated them by the British in the northeastern Negev near Tel Arad. This pioneering effort came to naught when no water could be found in the area. In 1932 sixty from the United States, Canada, and Argentina founded the settlement of Avi Chayil on a stretch of sand dune north of Natanya. This prospered. In 1961 the veterans opened the Jewish Legion Cultural Center, Bet Hagdudim, and the museum there, sponsored by the Israel Defense Ministry.

Other Legionnaires left their mark as leaders of Israel. Ben Gurion's companion in arms, Yitschak ben Zvi, also recruited in America, was elected the second president of the country in 1952. Levi Eshkol, originally Levi Shkolnick, became Prime Minister after Ben Gurion's retirement. Yaakov Dori, who, as Jacob Dostrowsky, was a sergeant in the Legion, served as Chief of Staff of the Haganah and led the small, heroic Jewish forces in 1948 that repulsed the invading Arab armies. A Philadelphia recruit who went to New York to sign up in the Legion, Gershon Agronsky, founded the *Jerusalem Post* and became the mayor of Jerusalem as Gershon Agron. Private Eliezer Sukenik became professor of archeology at the Hebrew University and translated the famed Dead Sea Scrolls. The recent Prime Minister, Yitschak Rabin, is the son of Nechemiah Rabinowitz, who joined the Legion in Chicago. Motke Gur, recent Chief of Staff of the Israel Defense Forces, is also the son of a Jewish Legion volunteer.

At the end of the victorious Palestine campaign the British War Office changed the name of the Royal Fusiliers to the Judean Regiment. A new insignia was provided for the uniform, a menorah with the Hebrew word "kadimah," meaning "Forward!" Inwardly each veteran carried with him the knowledge that he had helped pave the way for the creation of the State of Israel.

Jabotinsky expressed this feeling when he said farewell to the soldiers at the Rishon camp in 1919:

> Far away, in your home, you will one day read glorious news of a free Jewish life in a free Jewish country—of factories and universities, of farms and theaters. Then you will lose yourself in thought and the newspaper will slip from your fingers; and there will come to your mind a picture of the Jordan Valley, of the desert at Rafa, of the hills of Ephraim and of Abou Ein. Then you will stand up, walk to the mirror, and look yourself proudly in the face. Jump to "attention" and salute yourself—for it is you who have made it.

THE JEWISH COURT OF ARBITRATION
(1920)

The Jewish way to settle a dispute between two individuals is not through the use of a judge and a jury. The Jewish way is to set up a Bet Din, a court of three judges, preferably judges learned in Jewish law but not necessarily so. These judges need not be ordained rabbis, although the presence of a rabbi on a Bet Din, where this is possible, is considered advantageous.

The Jewish aim in disputes between persons is not so much to adjudge guilt or to inflict punishment as it is to arrive at a mutually agreeable solution and, hopefully, a reconciliation. The modern term for this is arbitration. The Jews have been practicing arbitration for a very long time. Mishna Sanhedrin, written down about 200 c.e., provides that, in private disputes, each litigant shall choose one arbiter and the two arbiters shall choose a third, who will preside over the ensuing proceedings. The litigants agree in advance to accept the decision of the Bet Din, no matter what it may be.

Zechariah 8:16 says, "This is the way of life you are to follow: Speak truthfully to each other; resolve your differences in a spirit of truth and of 'mishpat shalom,' peaceful settlement." "Mishpat shalom"—what a beautiful and meaningful Hebrew phrase! Ever since the Jews began to colonize modern Palestine, under Turkish, English, and Israeli rule, the "peace court," the Bet Mishpat Ha-shalom, the court of arbitration, has been used to settle many disputes between persons and organizations rather than have these quarrels go to the more formal and technical state tribunals or the religious rabbinic courts.

Influenced by this Palestinian development, the first American Bet Mishpat Ha-shalom, known as the Jewish Court of Arbitration, was organized in 1920 in New York City by lawyer Louis Richman and Rabbi Samuel Buckler. The first session was held in February in the Grand Jury Room of New York's Criminal Court Building. Now the sessions are usually held at Central Synagogue's Community Building on East 55th Street.

In December 1930 the Bet Mishpat Ha-shalom was incorporated as the Jewish Conciliation Court of America. Some years ago it became an agency of the Jewish Family Service of New York's Federation of Jewish Philanthropies and, at that time, the name was changed to the Jewish Conciliation Board of America.

The case histories in this article were furnished by the late Sidney Wallach, who was, for a number of years, executive director of the Jewish Conciliation Board of America.

From 1920 until today the modus operandi of the JCB, as it is now known, has remained essentially the same. A volunteer panel of judges, consisting of a rabbi, a lawyer, and a businessman, are assisted in their deliberations by a staff psychiatrist. The proceedings are extremely informal. Sessions are held about once a month. As many as ten cases may be considered at a single session. The deliberations begin late in the afternoon, because many of those involved are working people, and continue until about nine P.M. Since the late 1940s Isaac Metzker of the Yiddish *Jewish Daily Forward* has been attending every session and reporting its proceedings in his newspaper.

There is no charge to the litigants. The court was founded to help keep quarrels between Jews out of the non-Jewish courts and to spare poor Jews, especially recent immigrants, the heavy cost of having their cases adjudicated through the regular legal channels. Down through the years most of the litigants have been poor, elderly, Yiddish speaking residents of the lower East Side. As the Jews have moved out of this section and spread all over Greater New York, Jews from all parts of the metropolis and of all ages now come to the JCB for advice and relief from some family or organizational burden. The Board gets about 600 complaints annually. Three-fourths are settled by a consultation between the person involved and a JCB staff member or by referral to an appropriate communal agency. The remaining approximately 150 cases are handled by the Board's panel of judges.

During the 60 years of its existence, over 20,000 cases have been adjudicated, some grave, some trivial, some tragic, some very funny. All have one common element: Someone has a problem-situation that he or she considers serious and wants to have changed.

Here are a few of these situations and the manner in which the rabbi, the lawyer, the businessman, and the psychiatrist helped solve them.

*   *   *   *   *

His hands were trembling as he sat down to tell his story. What had shaken him had occurred after the sudden death of his wife to whom he had been married for over 40 years. In a low voice he told of the blow his wife's death had been to him. He spoke of her with eloquent tenderness and described their life together with pride. Then he revealed what seemed to him a desecration of the earthly remains of this woman he loved.

She had died at the beginning of winter. The funeral was on Friday afternoon. The sun would set and the Sabbath would begin very early. There were unforeseen delays at the chapel funeral service. The hearse lost its way and arrived late at the cemetery. The undertaker's men, working quickly and with frozen fingers, had let the coffin slip out of their control so that a part of it struck the ground.

There was no indication of damage either to the coffin or its precious. contents. But the injury was not of a simple, material kind. It was the culminating blow to a man already torn apart inside by the unexpected loss he had suffered.

The man could not be comforted by being told that the accident was not serious enough to warrant such inner agony. The conciliation board never minimizes anyone's feeling of hurt. Its essential aim is to heal and not to be merely logical.

The director of the funeral home testified that the man's story was essentially correct and that he was ready to make whatever amends the board considered appropriate.

The board's decision: A charitable gift is to be made by the funeral home to the synagogue where the couple had been members. It is to arrange to have Kaddish recited for the deceased for a year and to have her name included on the memorial list read annually on Yom Kippur.

A great load was lifted from the widower's heart. A healing process was set in motion. The undertaker was freed from his sense of guilt that he had not properly served a human being who had turned to him for help in one of life's darkest moments.

*   *   *   *   *

An elderly Orthodox couple appealed to the panel for advice. Their son, a professor of physics at a leading midwestern university, had no interest in Judaism. He had been married to a Jewish woman who was an avowed atheist. They had three children—two daughters and then a son. There was no religious observance in their home.

The son's wife died shortly after the birth of the third child. Some years later the son married a non-Jew. To the surprise of the parents, the second wife was more willing to accommodate the religious wishes of her in-laws than the Jewish mother had been. She made special arrangements to provide them with kosher food when they came to visit and she encouraged them to return each Passover to conduct a traditional Seder for the family.

A crisis had arisen. The boy was almost thirteen. No arrangements had been made for his Bar Mitzvah. The grandfather's entreaties were of no avail. Neither his son nor his grandson wanted the ceremony to be held.

The grandfather had reached a painful decision. He would never again visit his son or grandson. The grandmother, a woman of great intelligence and dignity, felt otherwise. She was emotionally upset by the prospect of separation from her son and grandson. She persuaded her husband to come before the panel to decide what the elderly couple should do.

The board's decision: It is in the best interest of all concerned for the couple to maintain the warmest possible relationship with their son and his family. There must be no break because of the Bar Mitzvah matter. It is possible that, if the proper relationship is maintained, the young man may, at some future time, decide to have a Bar Mitzvah ceremony and in other ways return to his Jewish origins. They were to visit their son's family on Passover and the grandfather should conduct the Seder, as he has been doing.

The couple happily accepted the decision. After their Passover visit, they reported that there had been such a hospitable and loving atmosphere within their son's home that they were very much encouraged to hope that their grandchildren would maintain a proper Jewish identity.

✻ ✻ ✻ ✻ ✻

This complaint was brought to the JCB by a member of a "landsmanschaft," one of the self-help societies set up by East European Jews during the decades of their heavy migration into the United States. These societies, made up of immigrants from the same towns or areas, performed many services for their members, including making loans at little or no interest and establishing their own sections in Jewish cemeteries. As Jewish integration into American life progressed, there was less need for the landsmanschaften. Most of them disappeared when all the old members died. A few, however, have survived. This story concerns one that shows remarkable vigor after over 80 years. The children and grandchildren of the founders have joined and have brought in new points of view.

It is these new points of view that were disturbing to an elderly, long-time member. His first complaint was that the society was permitting women to be full voting members. His second complaint involved the "reserved" gravesites in the cemetery. Their cost had been raised from $50 to several times that amount. He was a recent widower. He wanted to be buried next to his wife. However, he was afraid that when he died there would not be enough money in his estate for this wish to be fulfilled.

The society's officers, a high-spirited group of young and middle-aged Jews, testified that they were determined to carry on the work of the landsmanschaft but they wanted to do this in terms of the circumstances and outlooks of contemporary life.

The board's decision: The society was confirmed in its right to let women be full voting members. Furthermore, it was congratulated for maintaining a Jewish institution with such a fine record of service. However, it was requested to modify its ruling on reserved gravesites, so that those who were above the age of sixty when the new rates were set up would be permitted to pay in accordance with the previous more modest rate.

The society officers agreed with the decision. The elderly member grumbled about the women having the right to vote; but he was mollified and comforted by the gravesite cost decision. Now he knew he would be able to rest beside his wife. And that is what was most important to him.

I Remember Jewish Harlem
(1921)

For first-hand recollections of Jewish Harlem one has to go back more than half a century. Most Jews, pressed by Hispanics and blacks, left the area before the great depression of the 1930s. Thereafter, Harlem's heyday as an important center of Jewish life was over. The scene I recall best stems chiefly from the decade following the First World War; but Harlem was probably not very much different ten years earlier or five years later. My *medinah* ran from 100th to 125th streets and from Morningside Park to Second Avenue. The area I knew best, however, was more limited—110th to 120th between Lenox and Lexington.

No Great Wall marked off this province; still, Jewish kids hesitated to go beyond these lines without adult protection because of the hazards involved. An excursion too far east brought one into Italian territory, living space not altogether safe for a Jewish boy alone and even less so for a group of us. On some streets the hostiles were not Italian; they were Irish. So who needed it?

Some people will declare these boundaries ridiculously arbitrary. "I lived between First and Second," they'll say, "and it was very much Jewish Harlem." Or: "Since when was 98th not Harlem?" They have a point, and I'm not one to haggle. Anywhere down to East 86th, which everyone knows is Yorkville, can be called Harlem if one insists.

I don't really know how many Jews lived in Harlem during the years of its greatest popularity, and I doubt that anyone else does. But, if in the 1920s Jews in the United States numbered three million, which should not be too wide of the mark, and if half lived in the New York metropolitan

---

A memoir written by an ex-Harlemite, Rabbi A. Elihu Michelson of Flushing, New York.

area, then it is likely that at any one time Harlem was home to as many as 400,000. Taking into consideration those who came and went in a ten-year period, we would probably have to double that number. Like many other neighborhoods in the city, Harlem was a way-station. In those years most of New York's Jews stopped there.

Economically we were distributed on a bell-curve from the sadly impoverished to the wealthy. The overwhelming majority was very low middle class. Housing consisted chiefly of four-story tenement buildings with two railroad flats to a floor. A railroad flat was a unit of four to six rooms running along the length of a narrow brick structure. Normally, air-shafts provided air and daylight for the middle rooms. Most tenants could count on hot water, but central steam heat was a feature only in the better houses.

Bedding was aired on the windowsill, weather permitting. Clothes-lines were attached from a rear window or fire escape to a tall wooden pole set in concrete in the backyard. The entire process of washing and ironing was difficult; in most households it was done at home on a weekly basis. Apartments without central heating had a kitchen coal-stove that kept part of the place warm in the winter. Gas radiators and, later, electric heaters helped make the other rooms tolerable in very cold weather.

In the early years we used gas-tips for illumination. Later we had Welsbach mantles made of a woven material that made the gas burn with a bright luminous glow. In my home we used mantles for a few years; then we switched to electricity. In winter the gas supply was uncertain. On the coldest days the gas, channeled through outdoor pipes, some-times froze. In that kind of a blackout we made do with candles and cold food. At such times people with kitchen coal-stoves counted themselves lucky.

When our apartment was wired for electric lights we used bare bulbs at first and then very simple fixtures. The wealthy, even in earlier years, had Tiffany lamps above their dining-room tables. Not all living places in Harlem were tenements. On select side streets there were long rows of private houses, brownstones. Such homes, generally three stories high, had ground-floor layouts to accommodate much of the family's living. Upper floors were for bedrooms and bath. In addition to these private houses, Harlem had some tall elevator apartment houses with elegant names, like Gainsborough Apartments, not just street numbers. There were relatively few such buildings and generally they faced a park or a tree-planted avenue. My father called them, in Yiddish, "the tall windows." Depending on his inflection, that term could convey either the respect due wealth and status or distaste for obvious pretense and social climbing. Clearly Jewish Harlem had an upper crust—cultured, well educated, Americanized—with substantial incomes. Additionally, there was a small aristocracy of real wealth.

Few Harlem Jews owned cars. By and large, they did not have telephones. One way an enterprising youngster could earn some money was by hanging around the nearest candy store or the corner drugstore where there were public phone booths. The would-be errand-boy answered incoming calls and agreed to inform someone living nearby that he or she was wanted. Such calls frequently involved dating or a job. The errand was worth a nickel or even a dime and the system was firmly established.

There were other ways for kids to earn money. Toward evening, on any civic holiday or on an ordinary Sunday in summer, one could carry baggage from the subway station. Women returning alone from a weekend or a vacation were eager to have a heavy valise carried by a youthful porter. If you arranged the price in advance the job could yield as much as a quarter.

Before Passover boys could get work delivering matzahs or sacramental wine or an order of special holiday foods. A once-a-year source of income was burning chametz, leaven. On the day before the Passover festival, Jewish householders, having performed a ritual search for leavened bread and cracker and cake crumbs and having gathered the crumbs into a wooden spoon and wrapped spoon and crumbs in a cloth, were obliged to have this little bundle burned outdoors by midmorning. Adults, women particularly, were reluctant to go down to the street and start a fire at the curb. A Jewish boy who could be trusted to undertake this chore on Erev Pesach, when the housewife was busy preparing for the Seder, had it made—if the price was right.

Few Jewish homes were without a musical instrument, even if it was no more than a phonograph. Many had pianos or violins. Telephones, no! Pianos, yes! A piano, albeit an upright, was a badge of gentility, of refinement, of upward social mobility. Before radio and television, phonographs provided home entertainment. For Jews, there were cantorial recordings and a profusion of Yiddish songs. Later, when Harlem was becoming Spanish, Jewish music had to compete with Latin American jazz at the open windows of the courtyards.

Although in some neighborhoods as many as 80 percent of the pupils were Jewish, in all Harlem public schools Christmas was observed with trees, classroom decorations, assembly programs, carols, plays, and class parties. Red and white peppermint canes were a constant at the parties. Children brought gifts for their teacher. Even Orthodox Jewish parents made no fuss about Christmas in the school or about Halloween on the street. These observances were part of the American way of life and, in many ways, Jewish Harlem was part of the American mainstream.

There was a Turk (or maybe he was a Sephardic Jew) who for many years arrived on our block several times a week, except in winter, carrying a tray of candy. There were two kinds, specialties of the house, one a diamond of sesame seed and honey, the other, more exotic, a hard fruit-and-nut bar. Both of them were delicious; to look at them made your mouth water. It's more than 50 years since I last saw the Turk in his red fez, but the memory of his goodies is still sharp. Nor have I forgotten the outdoor vendor of coconut cuts which floated in a bowl of milky water. The vendor dipped his hand into the bowl for a piece sized according to the price you were ready to pay and no one worried about hygiene.

Central Park was really part of the world outside but it was important to the Jews of Harlem. It had a ritual use. On the first day of Rosh Hashana (or on the second day if the first was a Sabbath), traditional Jews gather near a body of water, a lake, a pond, a stream, to read a short prayer and symbolically discard their sins by shaking them into the water. For Harlemites the most available body of water was the lake in Central Park near 110th Street. Given fair weather, by midafternoon on the proper New Year day a myriad of Jews were at the lake, strolling through the park or seated on the benches watching the parade. Adolescents in all their holiday finery were on hand in the hope of a pickup or just to flirt. Small fry, too, were drawn by the excitement.

One might have thought that the many synagogues in Harlem were sufficient to meet the religious needs of the community. They were during most of the year; but for the High Holidays additional accommodations were needed to provide for all who wanted to worship. For Rosh Hashana and Yom Kippur, movie houses and other establishments were converted into "mushroom synagogues." Entrepreneurs or philanthropic organizations would engage an auditorium for the services. An ark, a pulpit, a Torah scroll, an "eternal light," and a few decorative chairs were furnishings enough for a temporary shul. The essential personnel were a cantor and choir and someone to read the Torah and blow the shofar. To judge by the big signs hung up outside, all the cantors on the inside were "world famous." They were accompanied by makeshift choirs, young and old, amateurs and semiprofessionals, sometimes their own children. Like the year-around synagogues, the "mushrooms" sold tickets of admission but at cut-rate prices. In the temporary shul there was seldom a preacher, but no one regretted that. The chanting of important prayers, the cantors' traditional show-pieces, was what was important. People waited eagerly for the familiar Hebrew melodies, sung, hopefully, with superb vocal virtuosity and faultless falsetto.

Kosher catering halls were sometimes pressed into service as temporary High Holiday shuls. In those days synagogues were not yet in the catering business; but, for the holidays, caterers were likely to be in the shul business.

As far as I know, no present-day catering establishment owns a pair of pigeons which fly over the assembled guests at the conclusion of a wedding ceremony. In Harlem no self-respecting kosher caterer would have thought of running a wedding hall without a pair of turtle doves to symbolize the loving couple's eternal affection for each other. Harlem Jews were very sentimental.

Between 1925 and 1935 the bulk of Harlem's Jewish population cleared out. Their institutions were transferred elsewhere or closed their doors. The Harlem Jews moved to the East Bronx, the West Bronx; to the West Side of Manhattan, to Washington Heights; to Flatbush, Brighton; to Astoria, Jamaica, Jackson Heights, Flushing, the Rockaways, the Five Towns, all over western Long Island.

Just as our parents brought something of the European shtetl to America and later transferred much of the life-style of the Lower East Side to Harlem, so those who migrated from Harlem took along a bit of the scene we knew and loved. To us, these memories are important because they involve a feeling, shared by all authentic Jewish ex-Harlemites, of Jewish identity, continuity, commitment. They involve core values, hopes and dreams. It was a good life. We hope we have been able to transmit to our children the wholesome spiritual virtues generated by this enriching experience.

ABBOT CHAO KUNG AND PRINCE MICHAEL ROMANOFF
(1922)

The two "gentlemen" whose names stand at the head of this article were born as Jews. They did not live as Jews and they did not conduct themselves in a manner designed to reflect honor upon the Jewish people. They share two dubious distinctions: Both were adventurous rogues and both gave the American Immigration and Naturalization Service a very large amount of trouble. As a matter of fact, they occupy the #1 and #2 spots on the all-time American deportation list. Ignatz Trebitsch, the one above denominated "Abbot Chao Kung," was deported from the United States via Ellis Island more times than any other individual before him or since. And Harry Gerguson, "Prince Michael Romanoff," ran second to Trebitsch in the Ellis Island deportation marathon. This does not entitle them to a place in a volume devoted to distinguished American Jews; but it certainly makes them worthy of being included in a work dealing with American Jewish folklore. In the annals of American Jewish eccentricity they rate very high.

❋   ❋   ❋   ❋   ❋

Ignatz Trebitsch was born in Budapest in 1879. The son of a Jewish grain merchant, he received a good religious and secular education. In 1898 he was converted to Christianity in Hamburg, Germany, by a Presbyterian missionary and was placed in a seminary to study for the ministry. Charged with immorality, he was expelled therefrom in 1900.

He was then sent to Montreal, Canada, where he acted as assistant to the Presbyterian missionary to the Jews of that city. In 1902 Trebitsch entered the employ of the Montreal branch of the London Jews Society, an Anglican organization, was ordained a priest by the Anglican Archbishop and was dubbed the Reverend Father Ignatius Timothy Trebitsch-Lincoln. In 1903 ill health forced him to leave Canada and go to England, where he became rector of a small rural parish. Several years later the Archbishop of Canterbury unfrocked Father Trebitsch-Lincoln for filching parish funds.

The ex-priest embarked on a new career as secretary to B. Seebohm Rountree, English cocoa magnate. Persuaded by Rountree, Trebitsch-Lincoln became a Quaker. With the help of his employer he was elected in 1910 to the House of Commons as M.P. from Darlington. At this time he assumed temporarily the name of Ignatius T. Lincoln.

When World War I broke out Lincoln was given a position in the post office as a censor of foreign mail. Soon thereafter he was accused of forgery and fled to the United States. He supported himself in this country by giving public lectures on his activities on the Continent and in England as a German spy, lurid, blood-curdling tales that were completely fictitious. In 1916, at the request of the British government, he was returned to England, convicted of forgery, and sentenced to three years in jail. After finishing this jail term he was deported to Hungary.

In Hungary he became involved in political intrigue. He attempted to organize a rightist revolt against the Allies, but the Hungarian extremists distrusted him because of his Jewish origin. Failing in Hungary, he went to Germany and joined the militarist group of Wolfgang Kapp, who in March 1920 staged a dramatic putsch that gained control of the German government for a few days. During this farcical rebellion Trebitsch-Lincoln served as press chief for the rebels.

After the collapse of the Kapp revolt Trebitsch-Lincoln again fled to the United States. During the next two years he was in and out of the hands of American immigration officials so often that he became a legendary figure in the annals of Ellis Island.

In 1922 he went to China and became one of the advisors of Marshal Wu Pei-Fu, anti-Japanese warlord. In 1925 the British gave him permission to return to England long enough to bid farewell to his son, John Lincoln, sentenced to hang for murdering a bartender. The return journey took too long. Upon reaching Marseilles Trebitsch-Lincoln learned that his son had been hanged the day before. Overcome with grief the father returned to China and entered a Buddhist friary.

In 1927 the former Trebitsch-Lincoln came to the United States for the last time. He now announced himself as Chao Kung [Chinese for "light of the universe"], abbot of a Tibetan Buddhist monastery. He had come to make known his intention of converting the Western world to Buddhism. Unimpressed, the Immigration Service ordered him to leave the country. For the next seven or eight years Chao Kung traveled about Europe on his evangelistic mission. Wherever he went he left behind unpaid hotel bills, disillusioned white "Buddhists," and foiled police.

Returning to the Orient about 1935, he became ardently pro-Japanese and was used by the Japanese as a propagandist among the Chinese. At the end of 1939 he again came to international notice by advocating a fantastic peace plan which called for the immediate resignation of the warring British, French, Italian, and German governments.

Abbot Chao Kung died in a Shanghai hospital on October 7, 1943.

*　*　*　*　*

Harry Gerguson was born in Russia about 1890. His parents brought him to New York City when he was about ten. They died a few years later. Harry drifted around the city selling newspapers, sleeping in bars and pool rooms, living for a time in an orphan home, finding shelter with sympathetic ladies of the night who one and all soon tired of his mannerisms, eccentricities, and foolish escapades and bade him seek shelter elsewhere.

In some unrecorded way he went to Germany either shortly before or during World War I. During the winter of 1922 he arrived at Ellis Island on a vessel carrying a large number of World War I veterans and their French and German war brides. He told a dramatic story of having spent ten years in a German dungeon for killing a youth in a duel. Even though he had no proof of American citizenship and no American passport, the immigration authorities took pity on him and allowed him to post bond and land.

In 1923 he pulled the great hoax which gained him lifelong fame. Posing as Prince Demitry Michael Alexandrovitch Obolenski, whose mother was a Romanoff, he fooled many wealthy American socialites for almost a year. He was paid large sums to give lectures on Russia. He spent several weeks in a Kansas City department store as a special attraction, drawing in customers who would be able to say that they had shaken hands with a genuine Russian prince. Late in the year he was invited to Harvard to lecture to a group of students. While there he borrowed much money from the students and, when he departed, left behind many unpaid mercantile bills. That did it. The disenchanted students and shopkeepers hunted him down and had him arrested. His bond was forfeited and he was detained at Ellis Island to await deportation. The records do not indicate that he was actually deported. The prince claimed he escaped from Ellis Island by swimming to Battery Place at the foot of the island of Manhattan.

From that time on, Prince Romanoff cut a royal figure in the kingdom of Broadway with his handsome physique, regal manner, dashing clothes, walking stick, and Dunhill pipe. He was extremely charming, had a fine talent for inventing the weirdest stories and for ignoring reality. Whenever he got into trouble with the New York police, which was very often, he was taken to Ellis Island and deported to Europe on the next available ship. That never daunted Prince Mike. In a month or so he would be back, having bribed some steward to let him occupy an empty first-class cabin on some luxury liner, where he proceeded to dazzle and to plunder one or more naive persons of wealth through his special kind of royal magic.

His frequent voyages across the Atlantic gained him much notoriety. He became a featured act on the vaudeville circuit and was used in bit parts in movies. Even the normally unimpressible officers of the Immigration Service came to admire and respect him. Whenever he "came aboard" at Ellis Island, he made their day brighter. He was such a genuine pixie, such a 100 percent faker. Edward Corsi, long-time U. S. Commissioner of Immigration, wrote of him:

> Prince Mike will never be just a memory in the minds of the Ellis Island officials who dealt with him through the years. For them he is a twentieth-century legendary hero—or villain, if you will. He is one of our popular scalawags. He represents the bravado of the big cities, which has replaced that of the vanished frontier.

Sometime during the early 1950s Prince Mike tired of Ellis Island and Broadway. He followed Horace Greeley's advice. He went West, west to the glittering delights of Hollywood. There fascinating Prince Mike found his "big rock candy mountain," a place where he could exploit his charm and twirl his stick and tell his stories without being hounded by the police. He got a job in Hollywood as maître d'hotel in a fancy nightclub— and lived happily ever after.

GOT TWO TWENTY-FIVES FOR A FIFTY?

(1923)

For about forty years, from the mid-1880s to the mid-1920s, there flourished on New York's upper and lower East Side a unique itinerant dealer in alteh shmattehs (old rags) and used clothing. His cry, "I-kesh-cloze," as he weaved his way through the tenemented streets, was a familiar sound in those years. The bargaining was done in Yiddish. Few of the wandering businessmen knew that the words "I-kesh-cloze" meant "I give cash for clothes."

The merchandise which was bought for resale to larger dealers was carried on the left arm, always the left arm. When the load grew too heavy to carry, the burden was lightened by wearing the clothing, one jacket or coat upon the other, sometimes in 100-degree weather. Old hats, bought for a few pennies, were often worn one atop the other, adding to the ludicrous appearance,

A popular story in the early 1920s was that an alteh shmatteh man knocked on the door of a likely looking prospect. As usual, when the door was opened, he said, "I-kesh-cloze." "Not today," said the man who had answered the knock. The ragman persisted, in Yiddish of course, "Don't you have anything at all that is old and worn out that you would like to get rid of?" "I certainly do," sighed the man, "but right now she is out shopping."

Only the Good Lord Knows

(1925)

Alfred E. "Al" Smith, popular Governor of the State of New York, 1919-21 and 1923-29, and first Roman Catholic to be nominated for the Presidency (1928) by a major American political party, had many close Jewish friends. He also had a cabin in the mountains. Whenever he wanted to get away from it all, summer or winter, he would invite a number of his cronies to spend a weekend with him in his mountain cabin. There they would hunt or fish or play cards or swim or just sit around and swap stories.

One weekend Al and his friends were up at the cabin in the dead of winter. Came Sunday morning and, good Catholics that they were, Al and the Catholics in his party got up at the break of dawn to walk a mile into the nearest village to attend early mass. As they were getting dressed in the unheated cabin, shivering and wishing they had not stayed up so late the night before, Al looked at the bunks in which his Jewish guests were snoozing on, unconcernedly, soundly and comfortably. "Gee, fellows," Al whispered to his fellow-dressers, "wouldn't it be just too bad, now, if they are right and we are wrong!"

THE MASSENA BLOOD LIBEL INCIDENT
(1928)

For those who naively believe that "it couldn't happen here," the tale about to be told may serve a salutary purpose.

On September 22, 1928, the day before Erev Yom Kippur, little Barbara Griffith, age four, of Massena, New York, was sent by her mother into a nearby woods to find her older brother and tell him to come home. She did not locate her brother. He returned home but she did not. Many people went through the woods trying to find her. The search was unsuccessful. She had disappeared.

When this became known in the community, a Massena restaurant owner repeated a story told him in his childhood by his maternal European grandmother. The story: When she was a little girl, all the Jews of the area came to her village the night before Easter and murdered the small son of the village baker. Then they went to the synagogue, pierced the victim's body in many places, poured his blood into a shofar, drank it and then went mad, uttering incoherent sounds in an unknown language. They buried the boy's body at the edge of a local forest. A voice was heard crying from the grave, "Oh, Mother of God! Rescue me, a poor, murdered child!" The villagers dug up the body and reburied it in their cemetery. Then they confiscated the clothing and jewels of the Jews and drove them from the area.

Massena is a small community in the uppermost part of New York State, on Highway 37 and the Raquette River, a few miles from the St. Lawrence River and the Canadian border. In 1928 its population was about 10,000, about equally divided between Protestants and Catholics. It was a thriving middle class town with factories that made aluminum, mica products and silk, and retail establishments doing an annual business of about five and a half million dollars. Nearly all its small congregation of Jews were retail merchants. It was surrounded by a fertile countryside filled with farms and dairies. In almost every respect one might say that it was "a typical American town."

The story of the restaurateur, updated and embellished, spread through Massena like wildfire. A Jewish tailor had been seen carrying a large pair of shears through the streets. A Jewish doctor had purchased a large quantity of ether from a druggist. A local expressman had delivered a packing case, big enough to hold a coffin, to a Massena Jewish store. Little Barbara had been murdered by the Jews so that they might drink her blood in the synagogue as part of their Yom Kippur ritual! The tale grew ever bigger and wilder. Two children's bodies had been found—

some said three! Perhaps the Jews were out to murder every non-Jew in Massena!

A large crowd in an ugly mood gathered around the City Hall. The Jews of Massena were sought out, insulted, and threatened. Vainly did they deny all knowledge of the missing Barbara. Indignantly did they assert that the shedding of human blood, except in self-defense or in defense of one's country, is forbidden by the Jewish religion. The Jews feared for their lives.

Massena's tiny police force did not know how to cope with the situation. Mayor Hawes decided to appeal to the State Police for help. After a conference at the nearest State Police headquarters, Corporal McCann of Troop B was dispatched to the home of Rabbi Berel Brenglass of Massena's Congregation Adath Israel to bring him in for questioning. The trooper's manner was crude and menacing. The rabbi felt demeaned and insulted. He told the mayor and the police that Judaism forbids the use of all blood, both human and animal. Jews never drink blood even symbolically, as Christians do when they use wine in their communion service. The mayor restored a measure of calm to the tense situation by assuring the mob outside his office there would be no let up in the search for Barbara until the mystery of her disappearance was solved.

The next day, a few hours before Kol Nidre, Barbara was found alive and well. After she had failed to locate her brother, she had wandered farther and farther away from home, not realizing she would not know her way back. Finally, tired and hungry, she sat down and fell asleep. The next morning she tried to walk in the direction of home but, completely confused, only succeeded in increasing the distance between herself and her dear ones. When her rescuers found her she was frightened and somewhat hysterical but otherwise unharmed. The terrible accusation leveled against Massena's Jews was completely false.

National Jewish and non-Jewish organizations demanded that New York's Governor Alfred E. Smith and the Commandant of its State Police seek out and punish the individuals responsible for what could have resulted in a massacre of the innocent. Mayor Hawes publicly apologized to the Jews: "I was just doing my duty. I never for a moment suspected that the charge was true. Some of my best friends are Jews." Corporal McCann was reprimanded by his superiors and transferred.

Throughout this unpleasant episode Massena's Roman Catholics, mostly of French Canadian derivation, maintained utmost calm and declared they would not participate in any kind of anti-Jewish action unless and until there was proof positive that the Jews had committed the horrible crime of which they were accused. But at this time the Ku Klux Klan had a strong organization in Massena which exercised a large measure of influence over many in the Protestant community. It was the

KKK and its supporters who were loudest in their demand that Jewish blood be shed in revenge for the murder they alleged the Jews had done. It was this element in the local population that made up the crowd that gathered around the City Hall. Even after the truth was established and little Barbara was restored to her family safe and unharmed, these pogrom-minded zealots continued their nefarious propaganda. For more than a year the Jewish merchants of Massena were boycotted by many local residents who still believed the false assertions of the Klan. Ultimately these hoodwinked Protestants became very much ashamed of themselves. They broke up the Massena Klan klavern and were again what they had been before Yom Kippur 1928—good friends and good customers of Massena's Jewish merchants.

The earliest reference to the charge that Jews sacrifice non-Jews on their altars as part of their worship is found in the first century C.E. essay "Contra Appion" of the Jewish historian Josephus. The earliest recorded instance of Jews being accused of killing a Christian and using his blood for the Passover observance occurred in England in 1144. After that the blood libel folktale spread throughout Europe. Accusations of ritual murder have continued to be made against European Jews ever since, especially among the illiterate peasantry of eastern Europe.

The Massena case is the only known instance of its kind in the entire history of the United States.

FROM GARMENT LOFT TO CHICKEN FARM
(1928)

The early part of 1928 I took my first trip out of New York City. My father was told by his doctor that it was urgent that he leave New York for his health and settle somewhere in the quiet of the country. This meant leaving the "luxury" surroundings of the Bronx and the Manhattan garment loft on Seventh Avenue.

The guiding arm for Jews wishing to settle in the country was the Jewish Agricultural Society. They pointed us toward Toms River, New Jersey, where Pop and I went to survey possible sites for a chicken farm. I was seven years old and remember the trip from the Bronx. It was an expedition of subways, ferry, and trains. We were met in Toms River and shown around. Our dream farm was chosen on Long Swamp Road, later

By Philip Horowitz in *History of Pioneers: Reminiscences and Personal Histories of the Jews of Toms River*, pp. 28-30, Toms River, N.J., 1976, edited by Jeanne Littman and Mildred Robinson and sent to the editor by Rabbi Richard Hammerman of Congregation B'nai Israel of Toms River.

changed to Brookside Drive which developers thought sounded more fashionable.

Now the time came to move. Shortly before Thanksgiving we packed and journeyed to faraway Toms River, Mom, Pop, and five children. We arrived early and awaited the truckers. I remember the day well. It was cold and dreary. The chill was not helped by the coal furnace in the basement, with only one heating outlet in the center of the dining room floor. The truckers arrived about eight hours late due to their finding some wine Mom had made for Thanksgiving. That day we stood gazing out the window at a barn and a strange shack called a coop. I kept asking where the candy store is, forgetting this wasn't the Bronx.

Things have a way of falling into place and shaping up. We started school and made friends with our non-Jewish neighbors who were happy to see that we looked human. We soon received cute little baby chicks which grew up to be very stupid. They were raised in quaint little huts called brooder houses. This part was fun for about three days. Then I found myself pushing a wheelbarrow around for hours—feeding, watering, and lugging pails of coal to each brooder house to keep the stoves going for heat. We had no water at first in the fields, so we would carry two pails at a time from the house about a half-mile away. I developed muscles you can't get in the Bronx. Later on we had the luxury of having a hand-operated water pump installed in the fields.

Time passed. Soon these cute chicks were laying eggs; and the fruits of our labor were seen. Now we had to prepare new quarters for these chickens called laying houses. You prepared like it was a festival—spreading litter on the floor—hanging up nests—arranging feed hoppers and eggshell boxes. We went out at night and took the pullets, as they were called, and carefully stuffed them in crates. Since we could not afford any other kind of transportation, I learned to stack up these crates on a wheelbarrow and push them like a donkey to their new quarters. I don't know if this showed that I was strong or just stupid.

Well, we were now in full swing—the eggs were bringing in real money. I started to learn new words like—go pack the eggs—candling—wet mash—go clean the dropping board. Soon we progressed to a horse and some cows. Again a new expression—go clean the barn—it seemed all you did on a farm was clean something. The horse relieved me somewhat of having to make like a donkey. I remember riding to Lakewood with a horse and wagon and chickens to be killed. I went with Pop to the shochet (kosher chicken killer) there. It was a ten-hour round trip. In the spring we planted large gardens, did canning and prepared for another season, somewhat wiser and more adept at raising chickens.

I became an expert at culling chickens, at catching a chicken on the run with a hook, at milking cows, at brushing on black leaf forty (not a job for city people). All these chores disciplined me for later life, when I opened a dress shop. Every year we knew the summer was over when all the relatives went back to the city after telling us they would be back to visit us on Thanksgiving. By now we had learned how to cope with coccidiosis—production drops—molting birds—broken water pipes— high feed costs—low egg prices—and a hundred other things. We looked forward to meetings and socials at the Jewish Community Center, where we discussed everything and discovered our problems were not unique. Work was hard; but somehow we gradually added to our farm, improved our standard of living, bought a car, all the while developing a wonderful family closeness.

As the years passed each of the children went his separate way. Now we are all doing well and have the fine conveniences of modern living. I don't push wheelbarrows anymore. I haven't cleaned a dropping board in years. But, as I look back, I often daydream of sitting in the warm brooder house with the chirping and lovely aroma of small baby chicks all around me—and, somehow, it seems like something which happened to me a different world ago.

THE SCHNORRER

(1930)

One type of beggar keeps strictly within the limits of Jewish communities in the city [of New York]. He is the schnorrer, a bearded mendicant, who begs at the doors of the synagogues, at the gates of Jewish cemeteries, and wherever a Jewish wedding is being held. On the East Side a good many storekeepers leave outside the door a handful of pennies in a small container, the pushke, from which the schnorrer takes his mite—a single cent. This type of beggar has tradition behind him; he survives chiefly because of the ancient Oriental belief that the giver is blessed for his generosity and by it stores up heavenly credit. Shopkeepers know the beggars operating in their neighborhoods and are rarely imposed upon by outsiders. The newer generation of Jews tends to ignore the schnorrer, but up to five years or so ago his take was fairly high. One bank in Grand Street even used to have a separate counter for schnorrers where they could make up their coppers, nickels, and dimes in rolls for deposit without delaying the lines at the regular tellers' windows. There were a great many women schnorrers among the Jews in the old

From *The Eight Million, Journal of a New York Correspondent,* by Meyer Berger, p. 310. Copyright, 1942, by Meyer Berger. New York: Simon and Shuster. Reprinted with permission of the publisher.

days. Some of them would hire a neighbor's child and take it with them to increase their appeal, particularly in the shopping and market districts. The usual rental for a baby was twenty-five cents a day. Another trick was showing a landlord's dispossess notice, generally faked, to entice larger contributions.

THE ROOF
(1935)

Hot nights in New York before air conditioners were invented were often spent on rooftops. My family and I lived in the East Bronx where July and August was a welcome sign to roaches and bedbugs. The suffocating heat on one side and the crawling insects on the other drove us for respite up on the rooftop with a blanket and pillow to stretch out on the tar surface and look up at the stars. Sometimes we would actually fall asleep when the honking of car horns would quiet down. Other times some of us would roll up the blankets and go back to the apartment as the first cool breeze would fan the rolling sweat off our faces. Some stayed on the roof until morning.

I remember one particular summer evening when there was no breeze even on the roof. It was getting close to midnight. The more tired tenants began to doze off, while others chatted quietly in little groups as they sat on their blankets. People talked about their jobs, unions, politics. The younger tenants tried to find new dating possibilities. Occasionally a few men would stare down into an open window across the street or look at the parade of ever moving traffic below.

Suddenly out of the darkness came a beautiful voice—a woman's voice. She was singing in a clear, strong voice an aria from *Carmen*. I have never heard it sung more beautifully. I was then a senior in high school. My brother, sitting next to me on the same blanket, was fifteen. We sat upright like the others, listening intently to the singer. Then, when she finished amidst thunderous applause, she proceeded to sing some popular songs. The dozers awakened one by one and sat up as if transfixed. There was no sound except her magnificent voice coming through the humid air of the night.

I remember, too, a bright moon, casting enough light to illuminate the face of the singer. She was a stranger. She had come from Boston, I learned, to visit her relatives who lived in our apartment house. Dis-

---

Written by Ruth Z. (Mrs. Joseph) Cooper, Chevy Chase, Maryland.

turbed by the heat like the rest of us, she, too, had decided to come up to the roof for a breath of air. She was a music student and gave promise of a great singing career, her aunt later told us. She was more beautiful to me than any other woman I had ever seen off the screen. And her figure—she was like a flawless statue, slender, tall, and graceful. She was about twenty-five. Amidst the squalor of the East Bronx, with its noise, its crowding, its honking of cars, its crying of babies, this beautiful girl and her superb voice transported me into an unreal world. I felt further and further removed from the drabness of my surroundings with each note that came from her throat. The crowd began to applaud for encores. The applause became wilder and wilder—and she responded generously with more songs. She sang Italian popular songs with as much skill as she sang the arias, it seemed to me.

One middle-aged man who was seated on a blanket near me seemed particularly affected. His mouth hung wide open and tears streamed down his eyes as she went into her Italian repertoire. He was Harry Klein, short, bald, with a heavy Yiddish accent. He lived on the third floor with two teen-age daughters and a short, heavy-bottomed, heavy-legged wife who ruled the household with an iron hand. Her commands could frequently be heard through the open windows as she issued commands to the members of her family with a loud nasal intonation. Her vituperations were a mixture of Yiddish, Polish, and broken English.

Mr. Klein was taking a respite from his long and tiring day at the brassiere factory by cooling off on the roof. This served also as an escape from his wife's beratings. He often sat on the roof on these hot nights, smoking, discussing politics, or talking about his unfulfilled dream of being an actor on the Jewish stage. He spoke of his contacts with Maurice Schwartz, the idol of the Yiddish theater. This particular night he just listened to the songs of the girl. He listened and he wept. Then, without a word, he left. Ten minutes later he reappeared with a neatly wrapped package under his arm. By then the singer was tired. She sat down on a folding chair brought for her by one of the admiring males. She rested there quietly, until a new round of applause began and the requests for encores resumed. She obliged. When she stopped Mr. Klein waited for the applause to subside. Then, with a frenzied plunge in her direction, he grabbed her hand and said, "You are beautiful! Your voice is beautiful! I shall never forget you or this night. Take this present as a token of my appreciation." He handed her a package, apparently oblivious to anyone's overhearing him.

"Open it, open it," my brother shouted; and this spread like an epidemic. "Open it, open it," we all shouted.

The girl, with the moonlight streaming down her blonde hair, opened the package gently, methodically loosening the scotch tape on the brown paper. When she had it unwrapped, out came two white brassieres—the by-product of Klein's labors at the factory. The girl thanked him graciously, as the audience on the roof flew into an outburst of laughter and whistles.

My younger brother, seeing an opportunity for mischief or sensing the possible beginning of a marital betrayal, promptly got up and, without explanation, disappeared.

Five minutes thereafter, Mrs. Klein, followed by my brother, appeared on the roof. "Get the hell down to the apartment!" she said to Mr. Klein. "I'll fix you! You are a bum, a bum! I'll teach you to give gifts to girls, and gifts like that! And giving gifts to shiksas [non-Jewish girls]—a man your age!" She ran over to the girl, grabbed the brassieres from her and fled down to her apartment, dragging the red-faced Mr. Klein after her. I assured my brother he would get a beating for being an informer.

That night Mrs. Klein screamed louder than usual. Her multilingual profanities pierced my head like stilettos as I tried to fall asleep next to my open window. Then I heard the loud slam of a door. Fully awakened, I went out onto the fire escape to enjoy the faint breeze. There I sat looking at the occasional nightwalkers, strolling by in pairs or leading a dog on a leash. Suddenly I saw Mr. Klein walking along, carrying a big valise. His gait was brisk and young. There was a new energy, a new dignity in his bearing as he walked further and further away toward the subway station. A moment later I saw the dumpy figure of Mrs. Klein running, running and screaming, "Come back, you bastard! Come back, you no-good bum!"

But Mr. Klein was no longer to be seen. The darkness of the night was his ally now.

ONE OF THE "FOUR CHAPLAINS" WAS A RABBI

(1943)

Alexander David Goode was born on Myrtle Avenue in Brooklyn, New York, on May 10, 1911. He was the oldest son of Orthodox Rabbi Hyman S. Goodkowitz. He was named after his grandfather, who had lived for many years in High Point, North Carolina. When Alex was about eight years old his father became rabbi of a synagogue in Washington, D.C.

An exceptional student and good athlete, Alex was the fastest runner and best boxer in his neighborhood. In his high school French class he met and fell in love with auburn-haired, winsome Theresa Flax. He was very shy. Theresa did much to help him feel more at ease in the company of others. She taught him to dance. In turn he improved her athletic prowess by teaching her to play tennis.

When Alex finished high school he was persuaded to study for the rabbinate by Rabbis Abram Simon and William F. Rosenblum of the Washington Hebrew Congregation and Rabbi Simon's energetic wife, Carrie, one of the founders of the National Federation of Temple Sisterhoods.

Alex attended Cincinnati's Hebrew Union College during the depression years. While he did well in his studies, he was constantly in financial difficulty. When after six years he finally attained a modest measure of economic security through a biweekly weekend pastorate, he speedily persuaded his long-time sweetheart to marry him. The wedding ceremony was performed by Cantor Moses Yoelson, Theresa's grandfather and also father of Theresa's Uncle Al, better known as Al Jolson.

Upon being ordained in 1937, Alex became rabbi of Temple Beth Israel in York, Pennsylvania, which was close enough to Baltimore to enable him to do post-graduate work at Johns Hopkins University. At twenty-eight he was awarded the degree of Doctor of Philosophy by that famous school.

In January 1941 Alex applied for but was denied a commission as a Navy chaplain because at that time the Navy Jewish chaplaincy quota was filled. Shortly after Pearl Harbor he became an Army chaplain. He was assigned to the Army air base at Goldsboro, North Carolina. By sheer coincidence this was about 125 miles from High Point, where his grandfather had lived, and about 150 miles from Winston Salem, where his father was now rabbi.

Even though Alex dearly loved his parents and wife and new little daughter Rosalie, he was anxious to be where the action was. So he asked to be assigned to an overseas combat area. His request was quickly granted, or so Alex thought. In November 1942 he was sent to Camp Miles Standish in Massachusetts to be processed for overseas duty. At Standish he met and became a good friend of Roman Catholic Chaplain James M. Liston, who also had just come to the overseas processing center after serving with me in the same chapel at Camp Croft, Spartanburg, South Carolina.

In December Alex and Jimmy were transferred to the Boston Port of Embarkation to await shipment to their foreign destinations. Early that same month I was sent to the five weeks' training course at the Army Chaplain School at Harvard University in Cambridge. At rabbinical school Alex and I had been pinochle pals and Jimmy Liston shared our love for this intriguing card game. So one night late in December Alex and Jimmy traveled from the POE to my Harvard room for a night of fellowship and pinochle. We had dinner together and then spent several enjoyable hours at our favorite pastime.

It was not an entirely happy evening. Alex now knew he was scheduled to go to Greenland and Jimmy knew he was bound for Iceland. Alex felt that, in a way, he had been betrayed. He wanted to go to a European or Asiatic battle front. He did not want to go to a quiet foreign zone like Greenland. For that he might just as well have remained at the North Carolina air base and had the comforting presence of his wife and baby. But he was told by the higher ups to whom he protested that a Jewish chaplain was greatly needed at the Greenland air bases. It would be tough, lonely, arduous duty. Later on, perhaps, he could be sent to Europe or Asia.

Another shadow hung over our friendly get-together. Both Alex and Jimmy had strong premonitions that their Arctic sea voyage would end in disaster. The North Atlantic submarine war was at its height. As many as 100 ships were being sunk every month in the Battle of the Atlantic. Jimmy had contributed $50 to a church in Boston to have masses said for the repose of his soul in case he did not make it.

The last week of January a convoy of ships left Boston harbor for Greenland and Iceland. On the slow, old, rusty freighter *Dorchester* bound for Greenland were four chaplains, George L. Fox and Clark V. Poling, Protestants, John P. Washington, Roman Catholic, and Alexander D. Goode, Jew. On another equally wornout tub headed for Iceland was Chaplain James M. Liston.

On February 2 the convoy reached the harbor of St. Johns, Newfoundland. Fresh supplies were taken aboard and letters mailed. At eight o'clock that evening the convoy left the protection of St. Johns and reentered "the strange white darkness of the Arctic night." At one A.M. the *Dorchester*'s bell sounded the hour for the last time. A moment later a torpedo from a German submarine hit her amidships below the water line. At approximately the same time another torpedo smashed into the vessel carrying Jimmy Liston. Both transports were doomed.

When Navy LTJG John H. Mahoney of the *Dorchester* was rescued after drifting in the frigid waters for twelve hours, he said that when the order came to abandon ship he grabbed his parka and life preserver and went topside. Then he remembered that he had left behind his heavy duty gloves. As he started back to his cabin he met Chaplain Goode and told him his problem. "You can take these," said Alex, pulling off his own gloves, "I have another pair." Mahoney learned later that Alex did not have "another pair" and that he had already given away his life preserver to an enlisted man who did not have one. So had Chaplains Fox, Poling, and Washington. Before rescue came, 38 of the 40 men in Mahoney's lifeboat died from exposure. Alex's gloves helped keep Mahoney's hands from freezing and helped save Mahoney's life.

As the *Dorchester* began the list that presaged its final plunge into the ocean's depths, some who were in the lifeboats and rafts nearby later affirmed that, in the dim gray-white light of that tragic Arctic night, they believed they saw the four chaplains standing together linked arm to arm united in life and in death by a shared conviction that "greater love hath no man than this, that he lay down his life for another."

Jimmy Liston also went down with his ship. In humble tribute to a group of supremely dedicated clergymen and two very dear friends, I place this fact on the record: On February 3, 1943, not four but five chaplains died for God and country in the stormy, icy waters of the North Atlantic.

❂   ❂   ❂   ❂   ❂

In an article written by Chaplain Goode, shortly before he went on board the *Dorchester* he wrote:

> We are fighting for the new age of brotherhood that will usher in the world democracy that we all want. . . . Justice and righteousness as dreamed by the prophets will cover the earth. People the world over will have enough to eat, clothes to wear, opportunity for education and full employment. . . . What has seemed like civilization up to this point is but a crude effort compared to the era that lies just before us. The new world will be the goal of the cavalcade of democracy through the ages. Toward the new world the cavalcade of democracy marches on, heralding the century of humanity.

Alex's dream has not yet come true; but he gave his life with the hope, nay, with the firm belief that some day his dream will become a reality.

On Shevuoth the Sky Opens
(1944)

A moving example of the kind of Jewish folklore brought to this country by the East European immigrant and fused into the American scene is found in the following childhood reminiscence, written by Rabbi Reeve Robert Brenner of Brooklyn, New York, and author of a recently published book, *The Faith and Doubt of Holocaust Survivors*.

❂   ❂   ❂   ❂   ❂

I was eight years old at the time, growing up in Boro Park, Brooklyn, attending Yeshiva Ets Haim, walking by Public School 103 each morning and afternoon. The series of fist fights with Walter Kaslowsky next door, invariably on Sunday after he would return from church, was going on with great regularity and intensity. Call them a draw, perhaps; thus far at least. Andy down the street, a ten-year-old, had jumped me for the first time several days before Shevuoth, his jacket yanked up over his head menacingly. His first reaction was surprise when the yarmulke-boy fought back. Hard. But he refused to go limp, the unspoken signal for capitulation. His back arched, his legs thrashing, he was pinned like a folded cardboard box, half on the sidewalk, shoulders up against an old green Pontiac parked on the street. But he soon broke free. Much, much later we became friends, thank God; he grew to be twice my size. But he fought on angrily then.

My birthday would be in a few days, eight days before Shevuoth. My bris had been on the Yontiff itself, much to the joy of my mother's family, especially grandpa, who arranged for the Kiddush at his shul. I was learning to chant Akdamos, although it wasn't until fifteen years later at my aufruf that I was finally called upon to chant it at the Young Israel in Boro Park, with my fiancée beaming at me from behind the mechitza in the women's section. By then it was called Akdamut.

Now I was eight and the Aramaic was hardly tripping lightly from my tongue, even with papa's silver dollars smoothing its way, a healing balm for its proper articulation.

Do I think I could stay up until midnight this Shevuoth? my papa asked. Certainly, I answered. I am a big boy now, I could stay up all night if I had to. Why? Papa explained: To catch the sky open for a fraction of an instant; and, if I am alert, any wish or prayer I would make would be fulfilled, because, on the eve of the Festival of Revelation, the sky opens annually in a symbolic reenactment of that singular event at Sinai. Yes, really, he said. His heavy figure seemed to rock on its heels to set his lips in motion, his voice so deep my own throat ached clearing it for him. He waved toward the sky with his cigar—its paper ring already around my thumb—pointing to where the sky was to split for me like the Red Sea had for Moses.

I wanted to believe. I did believe. It was so easy to believe. When I returned with my father from shul, we ate dinner, dairy, of course, for Shevuoth. The Jews after Sinai had no meat prepared which conformed with the new laws of kashruth. They ate only permitted dairy foods. My father would return to the synagogue and spend the night there in study. I would take a nap. My father promised to come back to wake me at 11:30, so that I might rehearse my wish and prayer, which I had already been practicing saying in half a breath, and then wait for midnight and the yearly miracle.

I am not sure if I had slept or not when my father gently placed his hand on mine and I bolted upright. Presently I was leaning from my bed over the radiator onto the windowsill, a pillow placed snug beneath my chin; and I was staring over Kaslowsky's rooftop into the Shevuoth sky.

It was a perfectly clear night, brilliant and luminous, a lustrous purple blackness. No haze, no smog, no thickness. Stars were fixed in their places; the few cotton candy clouds, spinning around like twisted paper, pulled this way and that, passed across a prominent, growing piece of the moon. The moon appeared like a chalk drawing I had made earlier that morning on the sidewalk along the stoop of our front porch. My erudite older sister had called me Reeve the screeve. I was fascinated with the phrase and its sound and what she had told me it meant until my constant repetition turned it into a little Hassidic niggin I chanted to myself all that morning: Reeve the screeve, Reeve the screeve. The chant now returned to my lips as I stared at the purple midnight sky. When would it happen?

A minute to go and less and less and less; the second hand came around, the clouds parted and the moon rolled aside like a wheel revolves to open a door. And there it was. My timing was impeccable. I didn't freeze. "Let me be smarter and stronger than they are, God." He knew who "they" were. No need to elaborate to him. And I got it all in just before the skies closed up again.

I remember having trouble falling back to sleep; but I had no further trouble taking on Walter Kaslowsky or Andy.

FACE TO FACE WITH GABRIEL

(1947)

It was the kind of snowy, windy night when movie houses are half empty, dates are called off, and most people settle down in their easy chairs after dinner, happy to be warm and comfortable and at home.

But at the McKinley Avenue Temple in Canton, Ohio, the pews were filled to overflowing this night of January 6, 1950. The entire congregation as well as many who were not regular worshipers—Jews and Christians alike—braved the blustery weather to attend the service. For it was the first time in 35 months that George Lieberman, beloved rabbi of the temple, was to ascend the pulpit.

It was a tense, agonizing moment for every man and woman in that synagogue. Rabbi Lieberman moved slowly down the aisle, every step filled with pain. The congregation followed each faltering step breathlessly, aware that they were witnessing a great personal struggle. What flood of memories must have raced through George Lieberman's mind as he made the effort to resume his work—a comeback no one had dared hope for. . . .

The first section of this article was written by Rabbi Morris N. Kertzer for *Guideposts* magazine. It is reprinted with the permission of that publication; copyrighted 1953 by Guideposts Associates, Inc., Carmel, New York 10512. Rabbi Kertzer, nationally known lecturer and author, resides in Scottsdale, Arizona.

One February night, three years before, George and Sylvia Lieberman had caught the crack Red Arrow Express, bound for New York. They were fast asleep in their berths when suddenly, without warning, the train shuddered violently, left the track and plunged into a deep ravine. Half a dozen passenger cars were scattered over the hillside like a toy train tossed in all directions by a youngster at play.

Rabbi Lieberman was in the upper berth of a Pullman car. When the train jumped the track his berth snapped shut, trapping Lieberman with his legs inside the jammed compartment and his body hanging, head down, in the aisle.

The pain and the shock brought immediate unconsciousness. When he came to, there were moans and shrieks—and utter darkness. He shouted his wife's name, but there was no answer. The car had buckled and Sylvia Lieberman had been hurled to the other half of the Pullman car, badly bruised but safe.

He groped for some way to change position, tried to raise his head. After much fumbling his fingers came upon the little net hammock found in all berths to hold the traveler's personal effects. Painfully he shifted his body so that his head rested in the hammock. Realizing that the damage to his spine would be aggravated without some support for his back, Rabbi Lieberman also managed, with the aid of a fellow passenger, to pull some suitcases and bedding under him, so that he achieved some small measure of relief while waiting for the rescue squads.

Someone called for a match. George Lieberman felt pillow feathers on his face and around his head, and his reaction was immediate: "Don't light a match or we'll all burn! Spread the word around—Don't light a match!"

Through the car, and then through the other coaches, the warning echoed: "Don't light a match!" The rabbi's presence of mind saved the wreckage from becoming a flaming deathtrap for all his fellow passengers.

Others among the injured and dying heard there was a rabbi in their car and called on this man of God to pray. Over the sound of the moaning and the tears the calm voice of the rabbi was heard, repeating the familiar words of the psalm: "Yea, though I walk through the valley of the shadow of death, I will fear no evil; for Thou art with me."

A Catholic who lay dying asked the rabbi to help him make his peace with God. A Protestant, petrified with fear for his loved ones, took new courage from the measured phrases of a rabbi's prayers. Lieberman, in such severe pain that he blacked out for minutes at a time, resolutely forced his weary voice to continue to bring solace to those around him.

Slowly the work of finding and removing the dead and the injured got underway. There were 25 dead, 100 injured. Some six hours after the derailment the railway's salvagers reached the rabbi's berth. "There are six dead and one living here," a man called out. "One living!" George Lieberman caught the phrase. "They mean me, I guess."

The rescue men set to work on the locked berth. The tedious work of prying the rabbi loose took almost half an hour. For a while it was thought that his legs would have to be amputated to release him.

As his closest rescuer labored with his tools, George Lieberman tried to remove some of the tension under which he was working. "What is your name, my friend?" he asked. "Gabriel," was the reply. "Gabriel!" the rabbi whispered, half in jest, half in delirium. "Are you from here or from up there?"

The six hour ordeal in that locked Pullman berth left the rabbi's legs paralyzed. Some of his doctors held out little hope that he would ever leave a wheelchair. Without the wonders of modern science he would never have survived.

But medical science alone did not work this miracle. Equally effective was Lieberman's indomitable courage and spirit—a spirit kept buoyant during weeks and months of pain, uncertainty, and disappointment by the unfailing love and devotion of all who took care of him.

In Altoona, Pennsylvania's Mercy Hospital, where Rabbi Lieberman spent the first frightening, agonizing weeks after the wreck, there was the warmth and kindness of the nursing sisters. "A challenge has been placed in our hands by Jesus to keep the rabbi alive," they said . . . and it was a challenge they spared no effort to meet.

Later, as weeks became months and months years, when even as strong a spirit as that of George Lieberman was tempted to give way to despair, there was the faith of his congregation to sustain him. They waited patiently, making no effort to replace him, certain that one day he would return.

From the very first day of the accident his congregation of well-wishers had mushroomed to include the entire community of Canton. Gifts and letters came to Lieberman's bedside from Jews and non-Jews to wish him well and to assure him that he was not alone.

During these years Rabbi Lieberman ministered to his fellow sufferers, giving solace and hope to other patients. He wrote to a friend: "Even when submerged in a whirlpool of hot water, in a cast, in a wheelchair or on crutches, undergoing physical therapy or lying in my room, I carry on my ministry."

Lieberman determined to find his rescuer, Gabriel. With only his first name to go on, Gabriel's employer, the Pennsylvania Railroad, traced the man to a Cleveland hospital, where he lay seriously ill. Rabbi Lieberman made the painful trip to visit and comfort his rescuer, grateful for the opportunity to once again meet Gabriel face to face.

Finally, on that cold January night in 1950, Rabbi Lieberman returned to his pulpit. A steel brace supported his back, another brace lent strength to his legs, as he inched his way to the center of the lectern and eased himself into a specially constructed device which made him appear to be standing, although he was sitting down. In one of the front pews his wife gave him a smile of loving encouragement.

In his sermon Rabbi Lieberman asked, "What are life's most precious possessions?" He spoke of simple things, homely happenings we take as much for granted as the air we breathe. He concluded: "Whatever the circumstance, the crisis, the pain, or the failure, whatever 'the bludgeonings of chance,' do not give up. Hold on! Live on! Pray on! Amen."

As the congregation left the sanctuary, they filed past the rabbi and his wife. "Good Sabbath, Rabbi. Good Sabbath, Mrs. Lieberman. Welcome back."

George Lieberman had come home.

❖   ❖   ❖   ❖   ❖

Four years later Rabbi Lieberman was called to the pulpit of Central Synagogue of Nassau County, Rockville Centre, New York, one of the largest Reform temples on Long Island.

In 1959 Rabbi Lieberman wrote:

> Pain is a cruel master. But can it not also be a teacher? Yes. The first lesson it teaches is faith, religious faith. Of course there are moments of rebellion when it seems easier to reject, to denounce— and to shake the fist against heaven. But in the midst of despair and helplessness, the feeling that we can still lift our voices to a Power beyond ourselves, that we can still communicate our torment and our triumph to the Unseen Friend and retain a light however dim— that is faith.
>
> My training and philosophy helped me cling to my faith. Even during the most desolate and devastating moments of my experience, I never recall doubting the existence of God or changing my views on the spiritual meaning of life. On the contrary, the companionship of pain brought to me the steady and steadfast companionship of God.
>
> I associated pain with what I like to call the cycle of human eternity: Where there is life, there is pain, for there can be no life without pain. Where there is pain, there is love. Where there is love, there is healing. Where there is healing, there is hope; and, where there is hope, there is life. Life—pain—love—healing—hope—life— a never ending, divinely devised circle.

In the course of the years Rabbi Lieberman combined his ministry with scholarly pursuits, including a period in England where he was the Senior Associate and Visiting Scholar at St. Antony's College, Oxford University. In May 1977 Roman Catholic Molloy College conferred on him a doctorate of Humane Letters. The citation read on that occasion spells out some of the ways in which Rabbi Lieberman has sought to repay his Maker and his fellow human beings for the lessons learned through years of suffering:

Scholar, professor, orator and leading authority on Eastern European history and literature, Rabbi Lieberman has accomplished much by weaving these activities into a living reality. The quest for truth and unity are essential parts of Rabbi Lieberman's studies; but an equally important aspect of his work is to demonstrate their relationship to God. On one of his visits to Russia Rabbi Lieberman discovered in the libraries of Moscow and Leningrad ancient Hebrew manuscripts and rare books which were thought to have been lost during the revolution and World War II. . . . As rabbi of Central Synagogue of Nassau County, Adjunct Professor of Religious Studies at Molloy College, Professor of Eastern European History and Literature at the Hebrew Union College—Jewish Institute of Religion, Rabbi Lieberman has made manifest his many talents. His teaching, kindness and concern, so familiar to Molloy students, have earned for Rabbi Lieberman respect, admiration and love.

Now It Can Be Told
(1947)

It was November 1947. The member states of the United Nations would soon be called upon to vote for or against the creation of the State of Israel.

Samuel Simpson was one of the principal partners in the sightseeing business that daily took busloads of visitors on tours of New York's Chinatown. Sam was a key figure in Chinatown's commercial life. The tourists he bussed downtown from Times Square brought many millions of dollars annually into Chinatown coffers and were the mainstay of Chinatown's economy.

Through friends who were intimately acquainted with the members of the U.N. delegation of Chiang Kai-shek's Republic of China, Sam learned that the attitude of the delegation toward the creation of the State of Israel was lukewarm and that the delegation might cast a negative vote on the issue. Sam was incensed. The Jews of Palestine were among the staunchest adherents to democracy in the Mideast and were staunchly

---

Written by Mr. Jack Garrell of Spartanburg, South Carolina, formerly an attorney in New York City and Washington, D.C.

opposed to Communist penetration into the area. Sam felt that the Taiwan Chinese should be made aware of this and should be made to understand that a strong and independent Israel would benefit them in their own struggle with Communism.

He conveyed these feelings to my brother Louis and to me. We strongly shared his sentiments. At that time Lou was the attorney for Sam's firm and I was an Assistant Attorney General of New York State. It was agreed that Sam would arrange a luncheon at a Chinatown restaurant with a number of the prominent Chinese businessmen of the community in order to place this important matter before them. Such a luncheon was arranged. In addition to the businessmen, Sam, Lou and I were present.

Lou and Sam addressed the meeting. Lou gave the background information and pointed out that the establishment of the State of Israel was definitely in the best interest of the Chinese people. After that, Sam really laid it on the line. He said he was strongly committed to the principle of Jewish survival and it was his firm opinion that, if a Jewish state was not brought into being, the Jewish people would go down the drain. He was determined to do what he could to help bring about a favorable vote on the resolution before the U.N.

Therefore he strongly urged the Chinatown community to bring all its influence to bear on the U.N. delegation of the Republic of China to vote for the Israel resolution. He warned the merchants that, if the Taiwan delegation voted against the resolution, the American Jewish community would be justifiably angered and that this could have a detrimental effect on American Jewish-Chinese commercial relationships. He said that it might even lead to a suspension of the sightseeing tours to Chinatown. That some of the principal operators of these tours were Jewish was no secret to the Chinese. They also knew that the loss of these tours would deal a crippling blow to their economy.

The cogent words of Sam and Lou had the desired effect. The community leaders of Chinatown carried the message to the Chinese U.N. delegation. The delegation, which to this point had treated the Israel resolution with indifference, gave it considerable thought and attention and decided that it was, indeed, in the Republic of China's self-interest to vote for the resolution and did so.

Samuel Simpson's courageous action, his willingness to take a great personal financial gamble to be of service to the Jewish people, may well have played a decisive role in China's affirmative vote for the creation of the State of Israel. My brother Louis and Sam, of blessed memory, were among the many unsung heroes who contributed gallantly to the dramatic behind-the-scenes struggle and won a memorable victory when the United Nations voted for the establishment of the State of Israel on November 29, 1947.

Mickey the American
(1948)

As one walks into the cemetery at the U. S. Military Academy, West Point, New York, the first grave seen bears the epitaph "A SOLDIER FOR ALL HUMANITY. " It is the grave of the only West Pointer buried in this American Valhalla who died while in the service of a foreign country. It is the grave of Colonel David Marcus, Class of 1924, USMA. Thus is this hero's name recorded on the Academy's proud roster. But in the annals of the State of Israel the hero will be remembered as Mickey the American.

❋   ❋   ❋   ❋   ❋

David Marcus was born in 1901 in the Brownsville section of Brooklyn to Roumanian immigrant parents who were observant Orthodox Jews. His father died when he was nine. Early on, his older brother Mike taught him to box. He became one of the best scrappers in the neighborhood. As a result of his being trained by brother Mike, David was known to his friends as "little Mickey" which eventually was shortened to just Mickey, the nickname by which David Marcus was known throughout his life.

He became a West Point plebe in 1920. While at the Academy he won the intercollegiate welterweight boxing championship. He was graduated in 1924 and assigned to Fort Hamilton, New York. Second Lieutenant Marcus had a high pitched voice. Once during close order drill, as Mickey gave the required commands, they came out of his mouth in sounds that resembled the squeaking of a mouse more than the roaring of a lion. Some of the soldiers laughed out loud. Marcus, who was not very tall but was very strong, very courageous and very sensitive, took off his officer's bars, picked out the biggest man who had laughed, challenged him to a fight and knocked him out in less than one minute. That was the first and last time anyone at Fort Hamilton scoffed publicly at Lieutenant Marcus' high pitched voice.

Mickey quit the Regular Army in 1926 to study law. That same year he married Emma Chaison, a schoolteacher, who had been his steady lady since 1921. He got a degree from Brooklyn Law School in 1928 and rapidly achieved a reputation as a hard working and capable lawyer. The high point of his civilian career was reached in 1940 when Mayor Fiorello LaGuardia appointed him New York City's Commissioner of Corrections. His tenure of office was brief.

In the summer of 1941 Mickey was recalled to active duty as a captain in the JAG section of the 27th Infantry Division. He was speedily

promoted to lieutenant colonel. Because of his ability to solve complicated legal problems, Lieutenant Colonel Marcus was transferred to
Washington to serve under the Chief of Staff, General George Marshall,
in the section working on post-war policies in occupied territories. He
achieved such outstanding expertise in this field that in 1945 he accompanied President Roosevelt to the Yalta conference as a consultant and
the same year went to Potsdam with President Truman.

While hostilities were in progress Mickey made a number of trips to
the war fronts to attend planning sessions on G-5 (military occupation)
matters. He happened to be at such a meeting at SHAEF headquarters in
London the first week in June 1944 as the long awaited European invasion
was about to begin. He learned that the first troops to reach the Continent
would be the 101st Airborne Division, commanded by his West Point
classmate, General Maxwell Taylor. Being both impulsive and daring,
Mickey went AWOL from his G-5 assignment in order to parachute into
France with his friend Max. He had had no paratrooper training. He had
never jumped from a plane before; but jump he did. When properly
constituted military authority caught up with this errant daredevil in the
thick of the Normandy fighting and directed him to resume his assigned
duties, Mickey had just wiped out a six-man German machine gun crew
with his automatic rifle. Obediently, Mickey put aside his weapon and
combat boots and returned to his decidedly less exciting desk job in
Washington.

When V-E Day was imminent, Mickey, now a colonel, was sent to
Germany to serve in the post-war military government. To this point in
his life Mickey had been a Jew in name only. The Orthodoxy of his
childhood had turned him off. To him it was foreign, out of date, almost
un-American. He never joined a synagogue or attended religious services. He thought of himself as an American who happened to be a Jew.

Then in early May 1945 Mickey visited Dachau. What he saw and
heard there made his blood boil. That visit did not change Mickey's
views on organized religion; but it did convert him into an ardent Zionist,
prepared to do what he could to help his people reestablish themselves in
the land of his and their fathers.

Mickey remained in Germany until March 1946. During this period
he was of great help to the members of the Hagana who were organizing
the Palestinian aliyah in the displaced persons camps and begging,
borrowing, and stealing large amounts of American military weapons,
ammunition, and supplies in the many military posts where sympathetic
American officers and soldiers were making these items available. From
April to June 1946 Mickey was with General MacArthur's headquarters in
the Pacific. Then he returned once more to Washington to work with
G-5's War Crimes branch.

Mickey was about to be promoted to brigadier general but he

wanted out of the Army. He wanted to get back to civilian life where he could support the cause of Zionism without being compromised by the holding of an American military commission. He resigned from the Army. His commission was terminated on April 5, 1947. The West Point graduate was now at liberty to work for the creation of a Jewish state without violating any American legal or military statutes.

He opened a law office on Fifth Avenue in New York. For a few months he tried to adjust to a civilian routine. On November 29, 1947, the United Nations voted to partition Palestine into two states, one Arab, the other Jewish. On December 7 David ben Gurion sent Major Shamir of the Hagana to New York to recruit David Marcus as chief instructor of the Jewish army that was about to come into being. On December 9 Major Shamir was in Marcus' new law office. Mickey said "Yes" immediately. Major Shamir asked, "Why are you so willing to leave your office and your profession and your wife and your home to help a new little country to which you owe no allegiance?" Marcus replied, "Have you been to Dachau, Major? Have you ever seen and heard a group of Jewish skeletons singing 'Hatikva'? Have you ever stood and cried as I was crying then and as I am crying now, shedding tears which were and are at one and the same time tears of anger, tears of pride and tears of joy?"

Shortly thereafter Marcus came to Palestine under the pseudonym "Michael Stone." After appraising the Hagana situation, he reported to the Jewish Agency leaders that they had a fine contingent of brave guerrilla fighters; but they did not have an army, units trained to contend with disciplined combat forces in a conventional war. In a few months Marcus alias Stone helped build such a Jewish army from scratch. He worked night and day having American military manuals translated into Hebrew. He established officer training schools. He traveled the length and breadth of Palestine, becoming acquainted with the terrain of mountain and plain, planning stratagems for the inevitable war with the Arabs. By April 1948, three months after "Michael Stone"'s arrival, the Hagana had been welded into a disciplined, combat-ready military force. Those who worked with "Stone" referred to him as "Mickey" or "the American" or, on semiformal occasions, "Mickey the American." The officers and men of the Hagana regarded their miracle worker with an admiration and awe such as soldiers seldom confer on their leaders.

Soon after Mickey's arrival in Palestine, he and Ben Gurion were on their way to an important meeting when they were stopped by a British patrol. A British officer asked Mickey, "What is your name?". "Michael Stone." "Occupation?" "Foundry worker." Mickey could easily pass for one. His broad nose, flattened by his opponents in his more youthful boxing days, gave him the look of a real tough guy. He produced well-worn identification papers and showed them to the Britisher, who then allowed the two men to proceed. The officer, fortunately, paid no attention to the gold ring the "foundry worker" was wearing on the third finger of his left hand. Once safely away, Mickey hastily removed the ring and never again wore it in Palestine. "It's my West Point ring," he explained to B.G., "with my real name engraved inside."

Feeling he had done as much as he could prior to the actual outbreak of the war, Mickey returned to Emma and his law office near the end of April. But not for long.

The State of Israel was born at noon on May 14, 1948, the fifth of Iyar, 5708. A few hours later it was attacked by the combined armies of Egypt, Iraq, Jordan, Lebanon, Saudi Arabia, and Syria. The next day "Mickey the American" was on his way back to Israel—technically to serve as a military advisor—actually to be not only Israel's chief tactician but also its most outstanding military leader. He left a note for Emma on the kitchen table, which she found after his unannounced departure: "Dearest Snippy, I promise you I'll be back in June—Mickey." He kept his promise. He came back to Emma on the last day of June—in a plain wooden box covered by the American flag.

Ben Gurion pleaded with Mickey not to expose himself to the hazards of front-line fighting. Dead tacticians, he said, do not win military victories. Mickey smiled and quoted Kohelet 5:4 "It is better not to promise than to promise and not keep one's word." Ben Gurion, also a non-synagogue-goer but deeply learned in the Bible, looked at him with amazement. "I had been told you are not religious," B.G. said. Mickey answered, "I am not religious in any formal sense, but I know and I revere our people's ethical and spiritual teachings."

Mickey commanded the Israeli forces in the Jerusalem sector. Where the action was, Mickey was. He was completely fearless. He planned and he led and he fought. He seemed to be under the special protection of the Almighty. Through almost two months of continuous combat, he stayed alive and well.

By the end of the first week in June the Arab forces had suffered total defeat and asked for a cease fire. The cease fire was arranged. It was to take effect at 10:00 A.M. on June 10.

On the night of June 9 Mickey was in Abu Ghosh, an Arab village a few miles west of Jerusalem, the village where the Palmach had its central front HQ. He had a lengthy conference with the Palmach commander, Yigal Allon, who many years later would be Israel's foreign minister.

Mickey was restless, tense, tied up in knots. The victory for which he had worked so hard, for which he had risked his life, was about to become a reality. He could not sleep. At 2:15 A.M. he went out alone for a walk in the darkness. At 3:50 A.M., as he was returning to his quarters, he was challenged by a sentry who did not understand English. Mickey did not speak Hebrew. Most Israelis understood English. Mickey tried to tell the sentry in English who he was. The sentry thought that Mickey must be one of the British officers who were with Jordan's Arab Legion. The sentry fired a single shot. Mickey fell dead, six hours and ten minutes before the cease fire. He may have been the last Israeli casualty of the 1948 war.

Ben Gurion cabled Emma: "His name will live forever in the annals of the Jewish people. We feel confident that American Jewry will be proud of this great and gallant man who has given his life for the liberation of Israel." The Israelis wanted to bury "Mickey the American" among their own heroic dead. Emma said "No." Mickey had told her he wanted to lie in the cemetery at his beloved West Point.

The funeral was held on July 1, 1948, at Union Temple in Brooklyn. Among the thousands of mourners were the Governor of the State of New York, the Mayor of New York City, General Maxwell Taylor, and Moshe Dayan. From the synagogue the cortège moved on to New York's City Hall, where further homage was paid. Then it proceeded up the Hudson Valley to the cemetery at West Point. There the body of Colonel David Marcus, USMA '24, "a soldier for all humanity," was laid to rest.

A KOREAN YOM KIPPUR MIRACLE
(1950)

In one of the Marine Corps regiments which slugged their way into Inchon harbor in the early months of the Korean War there was a corporal named Abraham Geller who had been brought up a nickel phone call from Delancey Street. Even at the front where sleep is the most important thing in the world, he never failed to wake a half hour before his buddies and go through the morning prayers.

On September 20 Abe's regiment crossed the Han and cut the Seoul-Kaesong road and, what with snipers in every rice paddy, by dusk the men were glad to dig in and catch a few hours of clammy sleep—especially since they knew that the drive for the Korean capital itself was scheduled for sunup.

An hour before dawn, aside from the sentries, only two men in the company were awake: Corporal Geller, bent over his prayerbook, and Captain George O'Conner, surveying the terrain and figuring out how best to deploy his troops in the coming action.

When Abe was finished the captain said, "Go back to the chow truck

---

From Billy Rose's column, "Pitching Horseshoes," as reprinted in the *Jewish Digest*, November 1966.

and get yourself a cup of coffee." "Thanks, Captain," said Geller, "but today is Yom Kippur, and I'm supposed to fast until sundown." "You mean to say you are not going to eat the day we bust into Seoul?" The East Sider grinned. "I figure I've got enough calories packed away for twenty-four hours," he said.

The marines ran into plenty of trouble the first day of the drive. Along about sundown, Captain O'Conner's men were inching their way across a field littered with dead North Koreans. One of the Commies, though badly wounded, was only playing dead and, as the officer came within range, he rolled over on his side and aimed his pistol. Abe, who was only a few feet from his commanding officer, saw the body move and made a dive for the enemy soldier; but, in finishing him off, he got three bullets which had been intended for Captain O'Conner.

The operation lasted over an hour. When the surgeon finally came out, Captain O'Conner was waiting for him. "How does it look?" he asked.

"The bullets went through his abdomen and several loops of intestine," answered the surgeon. "Wounds like that are generally fatal if penicillin isn't administered pretty fast. The spillage almost always causes peritonitis."

"I don't get all the words," said the captain, "but his pulling through seems like something of a miracle."

"In a manner of speaking it is," said the surgeon. "Geller owes his life to the fact that when he was shot there was hardly any food in his stomach."

Always Ask Someone Who Knows
(1963)

Stage director and choreographer Jerome Robbins was helping get the musical *Fiddler on the Roof* in shape. He needed to do some research. One of the scenes called for the staging of an Orthodox Jewish wedding. Jerome had sort of wandered away from Jewish traditional ways and how Orthodox Jews get married was a subject on which he no longer considered himself to be an expert. So he phoned his father Harry. "Hey, pa," he asked, "what's the best place to go to see an Orthodox Jewish wedding?" "An Orthodox Jewish wedding? A Jewish catering establishment, of course."

From Leonard Lyon's column "The Lyons' Den" in the *New York Post*.

Robbins was not satisfied with his father's reply. He had heard that weddings at Jewish caterers are shmaltzy but not authentic. He wanted to attend a "real" Orthodox wedding. So he went to the authorities. He called the American Jewish Historical Society and asked them to find out for him when and where he could witness such a wedding. Ten minutes later his phone rang. The scholar had the information. On such-and-such a day, at such-and-such a time, he was to go to such-and-such an address and he would witness an authentic Orthodox wedding. "What's the name of the synagogue?" "Synagogue?" came the reply, "You're not going to a synagogue. You're going to a catering place on the Lower East Side."

THE CATSKILLS: LAND OF MILK AND MONEY
(1964)

Any account of the Catskill Mountains must begin with Grossinger's. On either side of the highway out of New York and into Sullivan County, a two-hour drive north, one is assaulted by billboards. DO A JERRY LEWIS—COME TO BROWN'S. CHANGE TO THE FLAGLER. I FOUND A HUSBAND AT THE WALDEMERE. THE RALEIGH IS ICIER, NICIER, AND SPICIER. All the Borscht Belt billboards are crisscrossed with lists of attractions, each hotel—and there are some 300 of them competing for an annual three million visitors—claiming the ultimate in golf courses, the latest indoor and outdoor pools, and the most tantalizing parade of stars. The countryside between the signs is ordinary, without charm. Bush land and small hills. And then finally one comes to the Grossinger billboard. All it says, *sotto voce*, is GROSSINGER'S HAS EVERYTHING.

"On a day in August, 1914, that was to take its place among the red-letter days of all history," begins a booklet published to commemorate Grossinger's fiftieth anniversary, "a war broke out in Europe. Its fires seared the world. . . . On a Summer day of that same year, a small boardinghouse was opened in the Town of Liberty." The farmhouse was opened by Selig and Malka Grossinger to take in guests at $9.00 a week. Today Grossinger's, spread over 1,200 acres, can accommodate 1,400 guests. It represents an investment of ten million dollars.

Grossinger's, on first sight, looks like the consummate kibbutz. Even in the absence of Arabs there is a security guard at the gate. It has its own

Condensed from the article of the same title by Mordecai Richler in *Holiday* magazine, July 1965, Volume 38, pp. 56ff. Reprinted with the permission of Travel Magazine, Inc., Floral Park, N.Y., which now owns the rights to all *Holiday* magazine assets.

water supply, a main building—Sullivan County Tudor with picture windows—and a spill of outlying lodges named after immortals of the first Catskill aliyah, such as Eddie Cantor and Milton Berle.

I checked in on a Friday afternoon. There was to be a get-together for singles in the evening, but the prospects did not look dazzling. A truculent man sitting beside me in the bar said, "I dunno. I swim this morning. I swim this afternoon—indoors, outdoors, my God, what a collection! When are all the beauties checking in?"

I decided to take a stroll before dinner. The five lobbies at Grossinger's are nicely paneled in pine, but the effect is somewhat undermined by the presence of plastic plants everywhere. There is plastic sweet corn for sale in the shop beside the Olympic-sized outdoor pool and plastic grapes in the Mon Ami Gift and Sundry Shop in the main building. Among those whose pictures hang on the Wall of Fame are Cardinal Spellman and Yogi Berra, Irving Berlin, Governors Harriman and Rockefeller, Ralph Bunche, Zero Mostel, and Herman Wouk. The indoor pool, stunningly simple in design, smelled so strongly of disinfectants that I was reminded of the modest "Y" pool of my boyhood. I fled. Grossinger's has its own post office and is able to stamp all mail, "Grossinger's, N.Y." There is also Grossinger Lake, "for your tranquil togetherness"; an eighteen-hole golf course; stables; an outdoor artificial ice rink; a ski trail and toboggan run; a His'n'Hers health club; and, of course, a landing strip adjoining the hotel, the Jennie Grossinger Field, for your private aircraft—and Grossinger's.

The ladies had transformed themselves for dinner. Gone were the curlers; out came the minks. "Jewish security blankets," a guest watching the parade with me called them, but fondly, with that sense of self-ridicule that redeems the establishment.

I suppose it would be easiest, and not unjustified, to present the Catskills as a cartoon. A Disneyland with knishes. After all, everywhere you turn the detail is bizarre. A long hall of picture windows overlooks a parking lot. There are rooms that come with two adjoining bathrooms. ("It's a gimmick. People like it. They talk about it.") All leading hotels now have indoor ice-skating rinks because, as the lady who runs the Laurels told me, "Our guests find it too cold to skate outside." Every new convenience conspires to protect the guests from the countryside.

The archetypal Grossinger's guest belongs to the most frequently fired-at class of American Jews. Here they are, sitting ducks for satire. Manna for sociologists. Here they are, breathless, but at play, so to speak, suffering sour stomach and cancer scares, one Israeli bond drive after another, and unmarried daughters and sons gone off to Mississippi to help the Negroes overcome. Grossinger's is their dream of plenty realized. If you find it funny, larger than life, so do the regulars. In fact, there is no deflating remark I could make about minks or matchmaking that has not already been made by visiting comedians or guests. Indeed, for an innocent goy to even think some of the things said at Grossinger's would be to invite the wrath of the B'nai B'rith Anti-Defamation League.

At Grossinger's guests are offered the traditional foods, but in superabundance. Here, too, are the big TV comedians, only this is their real audience and they appreciate it. They reveal the ethnic joke behind the bland story they had to tell on TV because Yiddish punch lines do not make for happy Nielsen ratings.

The food at Grossinger's, the best I ate in the Catskills, is delicious as long as you like traditional kosher cooking. But entering the vast dining room, which seats some 1,500 persons, makes for an agonizing moment for singles. "The older men want young girls," the head waiter told me, "and the girls want presentable men. They want to line up a date for New York, where they sit alone all week. They've only got two days, you know, so they've got to make it fast. After each meal they're always wanting to switch tables. The standard complaint from the men runs, 'While a girl is talking to me, she's looking over my shoulder at the dentist at the next table. Why should I ask her for a date, such an eye-roamer?'"

I picked up a copy of the daily "Tattler" at my table and saw how, given one bewitching trip through the hotel duplicating machine, the painfully shy old maid and the flat chested girl were transformed into "sparkling, captivating Barbara" and "Ida, the fun-loving frolicker." Students from all over the United States compete for jobs at the hotel. They can clear as much as $150 a week. My companions at the table included two forlorn bachelors, a teenager with a flirtatious aunt, and a bejeweled and wizened widow in her sixties. The loudspeaker crackled. The get-together for singles was announced. The teenager turned to her aunt. "Are you going to dance with Ray again?" "Why not? He's fun." "Sure, sure. Only he's a faigele (a homosexual). And did you see that girl in the Mexican squaw blanket? She told her mother, 'If I don't come back to the room tonight after the single's party, you'll know I'm engaged.' What an optimist!"

The singles get-together was thinly attended. A disaster. Bachelors looked in, muttered, pulled faces, and departed. The ladies in their finery were abandoned to the flatteries of staff members, twisting in turn with the hair dresser and the dance teacher, both of whom may have had an eye for tomorrow's trade. My truculent friend of the afternoon had resumed his station at the bar. "Hey," he said, turning to a "G-man" (staff member), "where'd you get all those dogs? You got a contract maybe with New York City they should send you all the losers?" Later another G-man walked over to my truculent friend. "Look here," he said, "you can't sit down at a table and say to a lady you've just met that she's well stacked. It's not refined." "You'll have to change your table again," he was told. "O.K., O.K. I like women. So that makes me a louse."

Grossinger's has everything—plus a myth. The myth of Jennie [daughter-in-law of the original owners]. There are photographs of Jennie with celebrities everywhere in the hotel. A romantic but mediocre oil painting of her hangs in the main lobby. She has appeared on TV's "This is Your Life," an occasion so thrilling that as a special treat on rainy days guests are sometimes allowed to watch a rerun of the tape. Jennie, now in her seventies, can no longer personally bless all the honeymoon couples who come to the hotel. Neither can she "drift serenely" through the vast dining room as she used to. So a younger lady, Mrs. Sylvia Jacobs, picked by Jennie to succeed her as hostess, now fills many of Jennie's former functions. Mrs. Jacobs, in charge of Guest Relations, is seldom caught without a smile. "Jennie," she told me, "loves all human beings, regardless of race, color, or creed. Nobody else has her vision and charm. She personifies the grace and dignity of a great lady."

If Jennie Grossinger is the Dr. Schweitzer of the Catskills, then Arthur Winarick must be counted its Dr. Strangelove. Winarick, once a barber, made his fortune with Jeris Hair Tonic, acquired the Concord Hotel for $10,000 in 1935, and is still its guiding genius. He is seventy-five years old. On first meeting him I was foolish enough to ask if he had ever been to any of Europe's luxury resorts. "Garages with drapes," he said. "Warehouses."

To drive from the G to the Concord is to leap a Jewish generation; it is to quit a haimeshe (homey) place, however schmaltzy, for chrome and concrete. The sweet but professional people-lovers of one hotel yield to the computerlike efficiency of the other.

The Concord is the largest and most opulent of the Catskill resorts. It is a fantastic place. A luxury liner permanently in dry dock. Nine stories high, the Concord can cope with 2,800 guests who consume, I'm assured, 9,000 latkas and ten tons of meat a day. The largest of the three nightclubs, the Imperial Room, seats 2,300 people. It is dangerous to attempt a physical description of the hotel. Even as I checked in, the main dining room was making way for a still larger one. It is just possible that, since my departure, the five interconnecting convention halls have been opened up and converted into an indoor spring training camp for the New York Mets.

Mac Kinsbrunner, the genial resident manager, took me on a tour. "We've got five million bucks' worth of stuff under construction here right now. People don't come to the mountains for a rest anymore. They want tummel." Tummel means noise in Yiddish and the old-time non-stop Catskill comics were known as tummlers or noise-makers. "In the old days, you know, we used to go in for calisthenics, but no more. People are older. Golf, O.K., but—well, I'll tell you something—in these hotels we cater to what I call food-oholics."

The Concord—indeed, most of the Catskill resorts—now does a considerable out-of-season convention business. While I was staying at the hotel a group of insurance agents and their wives, coming from just about every state in the Union, were whooping it up. The theme-sign read: ALL THAT GLITTERS IS NOT GOLD, EXCEPT ANNUITIES. Groups representing different areas got into gay costumes to march into the dining room for dinner. The men wore cardboard mustaches and Panama hats at rakish angles and their wives wiggled shyly in hula skirts. Once inside the dining room they all rose to sing a punchy sales song to the tune of "Mac the Knife." It began, "We're behind you, Old Jack Regan, to make Mutual number one." Then they bowed their heads in prayer for the company and held up lit sparklers for the singing of the national anthem.

Other large hotels, not as celebrated as Grossinger's or the Concord, tend to specialize. The Raleigh, for instance, has five bands and goes in for young couples. Their ads proclaim LIVE "LA DOLCE VITA" AT THE RALEIGH. "We get the young swingers here," the proprietor told me. Brown's, another opulent place, is more of a family hotel. Jerry Lewis was once on its social staff and he still figures in most of its advertisements. Bernie Miller, tummler-in-residence, took me to see the hotel's pride, The Jerry Lewis Theater Club. "Lots of big stars were embryos here," he said.

In addition to the big places, numerous kochaleins [places where you do your own cooking] and bungalow colonies operate in Sullivan County—such as Itzik's Rooms, the Bon-Repos, and Altman's Cottages. Altman's is run by Ephraim Weisse, a most engaging man, a refugee who survived four concentration camps. "The air is the only thing that's good in the Catskills," Ephraim said. "Business? It's murder. I need this bungalow colony like I need a hole in the head." He shrugged, grinning. "I survived Hitler. I'll outlast the Catskills."

Of all the hotels I visited, only the Laurels does not serve kosher food and is actually built on a lake, Sackett Lake. Oddly enough, neither the dining room nor the most expensive bedrooms overlook the lake. As at the other leading resorts, there are pools inside and out, a skating rink, a health club, and a nightclub or two. "People won't make their own fun anymore," said the lady who runs the hotel with her husband. "Years ago, the young people here used to go in for midnight swims. Now they're afraid it might ruin their hairdo. Today nobody lives here like it's the mountains."

A GIFT TO AMERICA
(1967)

America is great because its immigrants have made it great. The Jewish people, along with many other nationalities of varying colors and creeds, has played an important role in this accomplishment. One of the Jew's gifts to the United States has been in the area of linguistics. Many Yiddish words have been taken into American English.

People who look over the shoulders of card players are no longer second-guessing; they are kibbitzing. If you drag something slowly, you are shlepping; and, if you lag behind unduly, you are a shlepper. Cheap looking clothes are now shmattes. Actors don't perform their parts anymore; they do their shtick. One is no longer audacious; he now has chutzpa—and everyone knows the classical example of chutzpa—the man who murders his parents and then throws himself on the mercy of the court because he is an orphan.

And for the sad sack we now have the shlemiel. One defines a shlemiel by comparing him to a shlimazal, one who has no luck. If you are a waiter and spill the soup, you are a shlemiel. If you are the one on whom the soup is spilled, you are the shlimazal. And he who has to clean up the mess is a zhlob, i.e., low man on the totem pole. Or a shlemiel is the one who buys a two-pants suit—and burns the coat.

When a genius of the likes of William Buckley refers to a complex situation as a shmeer, then those who are interested in making Yiddish Americana an influence to be reckoned with in the creation of an indigenous American English may, indeed, begin to feel that they are working their way into the rarified atmosphere of the most distinguished literati.

ROCHESTER HAS A VERY FUNNY RABBI
(1970)

Rabbi Philip S. Bernstein is the beloved rabbi emeritus of Temple Brith Kodesh of Rochester, New York. He is also a superb storyteller. On the evening of June 30, 1970, a thousand of his friends sat in the courtyard of his synagogue and listened to a hilarious lecture by Rabbi Bernstein on

---

Contributed by Rabbi Samuel M. Silver.

"Why Jews Laugh." Mitch Miller, one of the rabbi's fond admirers, produced and distributed a recording of the lecture. Here is one of the stories Rabbi Bernstein told that evening.

✶   ✶   ✶   ✶   ✶

It was Ne'ila time on Yom Kippur. The day of fasting and prayer was almost over. As the Va-anachnu was being recited, the prayer during which the rabbi and the cantor traditionally fall on their knees before the holy ark and then go forward full-length on their faces to demonstrate the sincerity of their penitence and humility, the rabbi went to his knees and then stretched out full-length shouting in Yiddish, "Ich bin a gur nit; Ich bin a gur nit! I am a nothing; I am a nothing!"

The cantor likewise assumed the traditional position, shouting also, "Ich bin a gur nit; Ich bin a gur nit!"

The executive secretary of the synagogue, who was sitting in his customary chair on the other side of the pulpit, overcome by the emotional impact of the moment, got up and he, too, went flat on his face, shouting, "Ich bin a gur nit; Ich bin a gur nit!"

This unexpected happening was too much for the cantor. His face still to the floor, he crawled over to the rabbi and whispered, "Look who's having the chutzpa to say that he, too, is a gur nit!"

MORE MODERN AMERICAN JEWISH FOLK HUMOR
(1976)

It was the slow season in heaven, so the Admitting Angel was having a friendly little game of pinochle with Father Abraham, the Recording Angel. Suddenly there sounded a loud rapping on the Heavenly Portal and, when they opened the gates, in walked arrogant Harry Sperling, the most notorious miser in all New York City.

"All right, let's get the preliminaries over with!" ordered Harry. "Sign me up and then assign me to an exclusive neighborhood up here. I don't want to mix with the yentas."

"Abe, look up this guy's history," said the Admitting Angel to the Recording Angel. The latter found Harry's dossier and handed it over.

"Ah, yes, you died an hour ago," said the Admitting Angel. "Tell me, what kind of work did you do?"

Harry assumed a hurt attitude. "Whaddyamean, work!! I'll have you know I was the biggest dress goods manufacturer in the business. I had two thousand employees working for me."

The Recording Angel checked the record and nodded. "That's correct," he said.

"Now then, what good deeds have you done to merit a place in heaven?" asked the Admitting Angel.

"We-l-l, let me see. Hmmmm! Oh yes, Once I gave fifteen cents to a starving widow and her children. I'd have given more, y'understand, but it doesn't pay to spoil these people."

"Any other magnificent works of charity?" asked the Admitting Angel sarcastically.

"Yeah, so long as you are asking. I don't wanna brag but once I found a dog lying in the street. It was terribly skinny and near death from hunger. Know what I did? I put a nickel along side of it, figuring that somebody would come along sooner or later and buy it something to eat."

The Admitting Angel turned to the Recording Angel. "Abe," he asked, "what should we do with this character?"

"Do?" replied Father Abraham. "Give him back his twenty cents and tell him to go to hell!"

✿   ✿   ✿   ✿   ✿

Manny, who still has the first penny he ever earned, went into the Last National Bank of New York and asked for a one year loan of a dollar.

"Do you have any collateral?" queried the assistant vice president.

"Yeah," answered Manny, producing a bulky envelope, "stocks and bonds worth $50,000."

"That's fine," said the assistant vice president. "At the end of the year you will owe us 12 percent interest on your dollar loan, and your security will be returned to you."

The bank president, sitting at his desk a few yards away, heard the discussion and could not contain his curiosity. As Manny was leaving, the president stopped him. "Mister," he asked, "why should anybody with $50,000 in stocks and bonds want to borrow a dollar from a bank?"

"Why?" answered Manny. "Because I don't know a better way to get a safe deposit box for only twelve cents a year!"

✿   ✿   ✿   ✿   ✿

A UJA "inside" joke: During the Israel-Arab 1967 war, a group of Syrians broke into the Bank of Tel Aviv. They escaped with over a million dollars—in pledges.

✿   ✿   ✿   ✿   ✿

A rabbi was invited to conduct a service at a Long Island VA mental hospital. Before the service started he was told by one of the doctors to disregard any remarks that the patients might make during his sermon.

After the rabbi had preached for about a half hour, a patient stood up and in a loud voice declared, "Good Lord, this is awful! Never in my whole life have I heard a lousier sermon."

The rabbi ignored the interruption, as he had been told to do. After the service the doctor came up to him and shook his hand warmly: "Rabbi, you have no idea how much you have helped that poor man. What he said was the first rational statement he has uttered in more than three years!"

* * * * *

A gorilla walked into Goldman's delicatessen and ordered a pastrami sandwich on pumpernickel with a piece of pickle on the side—to go.

When Goldman handed the gorilla the sandwich, he said, "That will be three dollars, please; and I must say that I never expected to see a gorilla in my store."

"And if you keep on charging three dollars for a pastrami sandwich," snapped the gorilla, "you never will again."

* * * * *

For six months business was so hectic at Barney Klein's shop that he invariably came home late for dinner. Every morning Barney promised faithfully he would be home early, but something always came up to keep him at the shop after hours. Finally Mrs. Klein could stand it no longer.

"Barney, for more than six months I've been slaving over a hot stove so you should have a hot, nourishing meal when you get home. But are you ever here on time? No. For the last time, Barney, I'm telling you— either you are here at six o'clock sharp every night and not a minute later, or no more cooking. You can eat in a restaurant."

Barney was worried. He loved his wife and realized that her resentment was justified. "From tomorrow night on, I'm turning over a new leaf," he promised her solemnly. "From tomorrow night on, six o'clock sharp!"

The next evening he closed up shop earlier than usual and was on his way home when, walking against a traffic light, he was struck down by a car. An ambulance rushed him to the hospital where fortunately his injuries were found to be minor. Several hours later he was able to continue his interrupted journey. It was after eight when he appeared at the door of his apartment.

"What kind of an hour is this to come home?" Mrs. Klein wailed. "The dinner is ruined—and after all your promises."

"But, honey, I have an explanation," he told her. "I left the shop early; but I'm two hours late because I was run over by a car."

"So what?" she responded. "It takes more than two hours to get run over by a car?"

❋   ❋   ❋   ❋   ❋

For twenty years the same customer had eaten his lunch at the same Jewish restaurant. And for twenty years he had always ordered the same dish—borsht. In all that time he never complained about the food or service. He was a model customer.

One noon, when the waiter had served him his customary dish, the customer called the waiter back to the table.

"Waiter, taste this borsht."

"Why, what's the matter with it?"

"Just taste it."

"Listen. It's too cold; it doesn't taste right—whatever it is, I'll take it back and bring you another serving."

"Taste the borsht."

"Why should I taste? You don't want it? O.K., you don't want it. So I'll change it without charge. Why should I argue with such a good customer?"

The customer, his face dark with fury, stood up. "For the last time," he screamed, "TASTE THE BORSHT!"

What could the poor waiter do? Intimidated, he sat down at the table. "O.K., if you insist, I'll taste it." He looked around. "Where is the spoon?" "Ah-HAH," the customer beamed. "Now you know!"

❋   ❋   ❋   ❋   ❋

Soon after Henry Kissinger was appointed Secretary of State, he wrote to Golda Meir, Prime Minister of Israel:

As you know, I have been appointed Secretary of State. I very much hope that we shall be able to work well together for the benefit of both our countries. In order that there may be complete understanding between us, I trust that you will always be aware of my priorities, which are in this order: I am an American citizen, Secretary of State, and a Jew.

To which Golda replied:

> Your letter makes me very happy. Now I am sure that we shall at all times be in complete accord.
> P.S. I am sure that you are aware that in Israel we read from right to left.

❀   ❀   ❀   ❀   ❀

During a visit to the United States, Golda was received officially at the White House by President Nixon and Secretary of State Kissinger.

During their conversation, President Nixon commented to Mrs. Meir, "Madame Prime Minister, it must be a source of great satisfaction to you to observe that in the United States Jews are so well regarded and are given the political equality that they so well deserve that in my administration a Jew serves as my Secretary of State or, to use the nomenclature employed in your country, my Foreign Minister."

Golda smiled and said, "This certainly is one of the many indications that the United States is truly a genuine democracy." Then she added facetiously, "I am sure that you will be delighted to know, Mr. President, that our Foreign Minister is also a Jew who differs in one respect from your Foreign Minister. Our Foreign Minister [Abba Eban] speaks English without an accent."

Both the President and Mr. Kissinger laughed heartily at Mrs. Meir's good-natured sally.

A BISSEL YIDDISH
(1977)

"Mama, I'm home!"

"I'm on the phone, Joshua."

"Mama, today in school we learned long division and tomorrow we're going to start playing gym so I have to get sneakers or the teacher says I can't play and so you have to—"

"I'm on the phone! Hock mir nisht keyn tchynik!"

Joshua immediately stops talking and waits impatiently for his mother to get off the phone. When she hangs up, Joshua continues: "Mama, I need sneakers by tomorrow so I can play gym so can we go and

---

Written by Michael Tyler in *Jewish World*, Commack, New York, October 28, 1977, p. 7. Reprinted with the permission of the publisher of *Jewish World*.

buy them today now so I can have them tomorrow? Huh? Can we, Mama?"

"Oy, stop nudjering me, Joshua. We'll go, we'll go."

And mama and Joshua go shopping for his sneakers and Joshua is quiet the entire time. His strategy has paid off. Joshua's strategy, whether he knew it or not, was to obtain his mother's attention. But he goes too far and mama is forced to quiet him. The two Yiddish phrases she uses to do this, "Hock mir nisht keyn tchynik" and "Stop nudgering me" are prime examples of what the Ashkenazic Jew of yore would say when faced with a similar situation.

"Hock mir nisht keyn tchynik" literally means "Stop banging on my tea kettle." This, like so many other Yiddish sayings, originated in the old, poor European shtetl, where there never was more than what was necessary to survive. Children had no toys, so instead they often improvised. One explanation of the origin of the phrase is that children used to bang on tea kettles and pretend they were playing drums. The constant clamor coming from the kettle irritated many a parent. As a result, many a child was told to stop hocking his mother's tchynik.

Another explanation is that tea kettles were used to boil water for more than just tea. Water was boiling so often that the rattle of tea kettles was a normal, if annoying, noise. Since today the phrase is used almost exclusively to halt a persistent bother, especially talking, this explanation is somewhat more plausible.

To "nudjer," i.e., pester, someone has a slightly different meaning. Like the English "nudge," the Yiddish "nudj," pest, "nudjers" people. However, the English "nudge" does so gently and privately. The Yiddish "nudj" is constantly pestering someone to an extreme degree. "Nudnik" is the worst thing a nudj can be called. The nudnik is so persistently pestering, boring, talkative, obnoxious, indomitable, and annoying that the word has no legitimate translation into any other language. It is for this reason that in America anyone who fits the qualifications of a Yiddish nudnik is peerless among human pests.

The etymologies of "Hock mir nisht keyn tchynik," nudj," and "nudnik" are known, but the origin of the English "nudge" is not. "Hock mir nisht keyn tchynik" is derived from the Slavic, with pure Yiddish intonation. "Nudj" comes from the Russian word for "fretting" or "aching dully." "Nudnik" is a direct descendant of "nudj." There has been speculation that the English "nudge" comes from the Yiddish "nudj" but this has not been proven. [Another theory is that it may be of Scandinavian origin, because the Icelanders have a similar word, "nugga," meaning to push. But who knows? Perhaps some Ashkenazic Jew wandered into Iceland and nudged them into putting the word into their language.]

In America meanwhile, when Joshua starts nudjering mama and mama tells him to stop hocking her tchynik, the nudnik stops his nudjering after mama goes out and buys his sneakers.

Are There Authentic Black American Jews?
(1978)

Avraham R. Coleman lives in a converted three-family house in the Crown Heights section of Brooklyn with his wife Rose and their eight children. A portrait of Menachem Schneerson, the Lubavitcher Rebbe, dominates one living room wall. On top of a Talmud-filled bookcase are photographs of the Satmar Rebbe and other great ones. The chanting of students filters upstairs from the yeshiva in the basement.

The Coleman residence might appear to be a typical home in the heavily Chassidic neighborhood. But Avraham R. Coleman is not typical. He is a black man, a former Baptist minister who converted to Judaism and is now an ordained Orthodox rabbi.

When Coleman converted to Judaism fifteen years ago, he did not intend to become a rabbi. What compelled him to seek ordination, he says, was the publicity and aid given to groups of blacks who call themselves Jews but who, in Coleman's estimation, are not legitimate Jews.

These groups, known by such names as the Commandment Keepers and Black Israelites and located in New York, Chicago, Boston, and elsewhere, are illegitimate according to Coleman because

> they have not converted according to halacha [Jewish religious law], are largely ignorant of Jewish customs, and many use rhetoric that is racist if not downright anti-Semitic. For instance, some groups say the blacks are the true Jews. Non-black Jews are considered Edomites or impostors. Many Jewish organizations are unknowingly giving these groups status because of the notion that "they call themselves Jews; therefore they must be Jews," without examining their practices. In the process, halachically converted blacks are neglected.

Coleman estimates the number of illegitimate black Jews at 35,000 and of the legitimate ones, 1,500.

Rabbi Coleman says he became the spokesman "by default" for legitimate black Jews in 1970 when he was named Director of the Social Justice Section of the Synagogue Council of America. He realized that in order to be more effective as well as to be a role model for black Jewish youngsters he would have to become a full-fledged rabbi. He received

Written by Andy Edelstein in *The Jewish Week*, December 25, 1977, p. 16. Reprinted with permission of *The Jewish Week*.

ordination in 1972. In September 1975 he started the congregation which he named Kolel Zichron Rabbi Eliezer Meskin, in honor of the late Bronx rabbi who converted the Colemans as well as other blacks. Coleman explains:

> My synagogue is designed specifically to address the needs of the isolated minority segments of the Jewish community, the black and Spanish-speaking Jews. I believe strongly in the concept of a unified Jewish community, but to have a synagogue with which blacks could identify was essential to their development as Jews. Right now it's located in this junky old basement.

The "junky old basement" has three hard wooden benches. There are tables covered with Hebrew books. On the benches and around the tables sit twelve day and sixteen night students who learn Chumash, Mishnah, Gemarra, and Shulchan Aruch. Twenty black Jewish families from Crown Heights and East Flatbush worship here. The congregation is Orthodox but not Chassidic, even though it is located in a Chassidic neighborhood. Coleman says he has great admiration for the Chasidic rebbes, but that he is guided by the teachings of the noted Orthodox scholar, Rabbi Moshe Feinstein.

Coleman says he has had little trouble integrating into the Jewish community. Rarely does he find surprise or prejudice among the Orthodox. "But there are many blacks, unfortunately, who are anti-Semitic and have spewed their venom at me." When he speaks in suburban synagogues he encounters what he considers "implied racism" in such questions as "Whom will your children marry?" His reply is, "A Jewish person should marry a Jewish person. Halachic criteria have nothing to do with the color of one's skin."

Coleman's eight children, ranging in age from five to sixteen, attend various Brooklyn yeshivas. "The first thing to tell Jewish youngsters is that we are all descendants of Abraham whether we have just converted or are direct descendants with a long lineage. In the sight of God, the Jewish people and the Halacha, we are all equal."

Rabbi Coleman's concluding remark was, "The Torah is color-blind."

PART THREE

The South

"Home of the Palm and the Pine"

Introduction

In the Southern states—Alabama, Florida, Georgia, Kentucky, Mississippi, North Carolina, South Carolina, Tennessee, and Virginia—their great wealth of both joyous and sad folklore attests to the proud and resilient nature of the spirit of the blacks who were brought to the Southern plantations as slaves in the holds of horror-ships, many owned and operated by pious New Englanders. In body, the Southern white controlled the black; in spirit, the Southern black conquered the white. An obvious example: The most original contribution that America has made to the world of music, the gospel song from which evolved jazz from which eructed rock-and-roll, came from the Southern black. Distinctly Southern literature is either a direct narration or imitation of the colorful creations of black dreamworlds or is an attempt on the part of white writers to avoid black romanticism and to depict the less attractive world of white reality.

The Jew of the South was affected by this non-violent spiritual takeover in the same manner as were the rest of the Southern whites. The Jew was no better than his white neighbor and no worse. His attitude toward the black was, at best, paternalistic and, at worst, racist. Like their non-Jewish middle-class contemporaries, Southern Jews were normally easygoing, inclined to be gentlemanly and ladylike in a superficial kind of way, parochial in interest and outlook, quick to take offense, generous in victory, undaunted in defeat. Also, as was the case with the Southern patrician, the average Southern Jew felt quite superior in intellect and manners not only to the black but also to his own coreligionists in other parts of the world, especially those in the North.

Just as Newport was the most prominent Jewish community in colonial New England and Philadelphia in the colonial Middle Atlantic states, so Charleston, South Carolina, was the outstanding Jewish community in the colonial South. Although there were religious fanatics and bigots in the South, as there were and are all over the world, the Southern Jew was spared some of the indignities suffered by Jews in more northern states, mainly because of the ubiquitous presence of a convenient scapegoat, the black. I remember hearing a Southern policeman say, not more than 40 years ago, "Man, I feel so good today I could go out and beat me up a nigger." In colder climes that kind of mental giant would have proclaimed his willingness to go out and beat himself up a Jew. In the South the blacks endured for many years the torments that, in like times and other places, would have been heaped upon the Jew.

Alabama

The French established a settlement in 1702 on the Mobile River, a few miles north of Mobile Bay. In 1711 the city of Mobile was founded. Until 1722 it was the capital of the French colony of Louisiana. In these early years a few Jews came to live in or near Mobile. They were not allowed to remain very long. In 1724, by command of the French Regency, Governor Bienville issued a Code Noir, Black Code, which ordered the Jews to leave the colony and proclaimed that none but Roman Catholics would be welcome.

In 1763 France ceded what is now Alabama to Great Britain. The British permitted a number of Jewish merchants to settle in Mobile. In 1783 the British withdrew and the Spanish came in. Once again the Jews had to leave the area.

In 1789 Abraham Mordecai, "Old Mordecai," moved from Georgia to live with the Creek Indian nation near the present site of Montgomery. His story is told in this section.

In the War of 1812 the Creeks were allies of the British. In 1813 these Indians attacked Fort Mims, a stockade 35 miles north of Mobile, and massacred 538 men, women and children. That same year American General Wilkinson wrested Mobile from the Spaniards. In March 1814 General Andrew Jackson and his Tennessee militia defeated the Creeks at Horseshoe Bend on the Tallapoosa River in eastern Alabama and broke the power of the Creek confederacy, which surrendered most of its land to the whites.

What is now Alabama became the eastern part of the Mississippi Territory. In 1817 it was split off and named the Alabama Territory. In 1819 Alabama was admitted to the Union as the twenty-second state. From 1826 to 1846 the capital was Tuscaloosa. Since then it has been Montgomery.

By 1824 Jews had settled in Mobile for the third time; and this time they remained permanently. The city's Congregation Shaarai Shomayim was organized in 1840. The next oldest congregation is in Montgomery. Kahal Montgomery, now known as Temple Beth Or, dates from 1849.

There are presently 10,000 Jews in Alabama, three-tenths of one percent of the total population. The largest Jewish communities are Birmingham, 4,000; Montgomery, 1,800; Mobile, 1,000.

Florida

In the first half of the sixteenth century bands of Spanish marauders landed on the east coast of Florida in search of slaves and jewels. Most of these plundering expeditions came to a disastrous end. Florida's Seminole Indians were hardy and brave and resisted stubbornly the efforts of the conquistadores to enslave, rob, and kill them. Two centuries later the United States had to fight two bitter wars before overpowering the courageous Seminoles.

In 1564 a group of French Huguenot soldiers built a military post, Fort Carolina, at the mouth of the St. John's River, near the present site of the Jacksonville Naval Air Station. Claiming that, by virtue of the earlier invasions of its freebooters, it had a rightful claim to Florida, in 1565 Spain sent an expedition headed by Pedro Mendenez de Aviles to destroy Fort Caroline. Mendenez carried out his mission ruthlessly, killing almost everyone in the fort. Then he set up a Spanish military post further down the coast, naming it St. Augustine, thus bringing into existence the oldest permanent settlement in the United States. St. Augustine tourists are told the fictional story as they smell or, what is even worse, taste the sulphuric waters of the Fountain of Youth that this fountain was discovered in 1513 by Ponce de Leon.

In 1696 the Spanish colonized West Florida by founding Pensacola. In 1763 Spain ceded Florida to England in exchange for Cuba and the Philippines. At the close of the American Revolutionary War England gave Florida back to Spain. In 1812 West Florida rebelled against Spain and became part of the United States. A section of West Florida was added to Louisiana and the rest to the Mississippi Territory.

In 1819 the United States purchased Florida from Spain and took possession in 1821. At this time there were a few Jews living in Florida. The most prominent was Moses Elias Levy, whose story is told in this section. Florida was admitted to the Union as the 27th state in March 1845. It came in as a slave state paired with the free state of Iowa.

There were not many Jews in Florida until the twentieth century. The first congregation, Beth El in Pensacola, was orgaized in 1864. The first Jew arrived in Miami in 1896. The first synagogue in Miami, Bnai Zion, now known as Beth David, was founded in 1912.

In 1900 there were about 3,000 Jews in Florida. By 1940 the number had increased to about 25,000. There are now well over 400,000 Jews in the state, five percent of the total population. Over 80 percent live in the southern third, i.e., south of North Palm Beach. The heaviest Jewish concentrations are: Miami-Miami Beach, 310,000; Palm Beach-West Palm Beach, 27,000; Tampa-St. Petersburg-Sarasota, 27,000; Fort Lauderdale, 25,000; Jacksonville, 8,000; Orlando, 7,000.

Georgia

The colony of Georgia was created in 1732 by George II of Great Britain by splitting off the southern end of the colony of the Carolinas. Originally Georgia also included most of Alabama and Mississippi. Its present contour was fixed in 1782. The first and for more than a century the only major settlement in Georgia was Savannah, founded February 13, 1733. Savannah's first Jews arrived on July 11, 1733.

From the very beginning Georgia's Jews had the right to vote; but they were not permitted to hold public office. The Church of England was the official church. Public officials were sworn in "upon the faith of a Christian." In 1777 a state constitution was adopted which disestablished the Church of England and replaced it with generic Protestantism as the state religion. Catholics and Jews were still barred from positions of authority. In 1789 Jews were given the privilege of occupying public offices, although Protestantism continued to be the official religion. Not until 1798 was the provision for a state religion removed from the constitution.

In 1795 the state capital was moved from Savannah to Louisville; in 1807 to Milledgeville; in 1868 to Atlanta, where it has been ever since.

The state's Jewish population grew slowly. The first Jew came to live in Augusta in 1825; to Atlanta, then known as Marthasville, population about 100, in 1846. Congregation Children of Israel, Augusta, was organized in 1850; Beth Israel, Columbus, 1857; Beth Israel, Macon, 1859; Hebrew Benevolent Congregation, Atlanta, 1867. Georgia now has 30,000 Jews, six-tenths of one percent of the total population. The principal Jewish communities are Atlanta, 18,000; Savannah, 3,000; Augusta, 1,200; Columbus, 1,000.

Kentucky

Harrodsburg, founded by James Harrod in 1774, was the first permanent settlement in what is now Kentucky. Boonesborough, founded by Colonel Daniel Boone, and Lexington, both dating from 1775, were the next two. Louisville, 1780, was the fourth. Until the end of the Revolutionary War these settlements and the entire area were considered part of Virginia. After the war Kentucky broke away from the rest of Virginia. In 1792 it was admitted to the Union as the 15th state. For the first six months Lexington was the capital; after that, Frankfurt.

No Jews lived in Kentucky before the nineteenth century. However, as early as 1781, Colonel Boone was buying Kentucky land for Jewish land speculators based in Richmond, Virginia. The first Jew came to settle in Louisville in 1802; to Harrodsburg in 1808; and to Lexington in 1816. The first Jewish cemetery was set up in Louisville in 1836. Congregation Adas Israel of Louisville was organized in 1843; Adath Israel, Owensboro, and Temple Israel, Paducah, 1865; and the first Lexington congregation, 1878.

By 1900 there were about 12,000 Jews in Kentucky. The state's Jewish population, three-tenths of one percent of the total, has remained static ever since. Louisville has 9,200 Jews and Lexington 1,200.

Mississippi

In 1716 the French founded Mississippi's first permanent settlement, Fort Rosalie, now known as Natchez. Control of the area passed to the English in 1763 and, in 1781, to Spain. In 1798 the United States gained control and created the Mississippi Territory which, in 1817, was admitted to the Union as the 20th state. Jackson became the capital in 1822.

A few Sephardic Jews lived in or near Natchez from the time the English took over. They traded with the Indians and the white settlers. One of the commodities in which they dealt was black slaves. In the 1840s German Jewish immigrants began to come into the state as pack peddlers and operators of small stores. Until then there was no organized Jewish life in the state. From then on, wherever a minyan or more of German Jews came to live, they set up a congregation and/or a cemetery. These early Jewish communities include:

	Congregation	Cemetery
Bnai Israel, Natchez	1840	
Anshe Chesed, Vicksburg	1843	
Bnai Israel, Columbus	1845	1850
Beth Israel, Jackson	1857	1854
Gemiluth Chassed, Port Gibson	1859	1871
Beth Israel, Meridian	1869	1868
Ohavey Scholem, Summit	1870	
Bnai Israel, Canton	1870	1877

There are now about 4,500 Jews in Mississippi, two tenths of one percent of the total population. They are widely scattered. The largest concentrations are Greenville, 700; Jackson, 420; Meridian, 385; Clarksdale 320.

North Carolina

In 1585 Sir Walter Raleigh settled 108 colonists on Roanoke Island, off the northeast coast of North Carolina between the mainland and the

Cape Hatteras archipelago. Between 1587 and 1591 the settlement vanished, its fate an unresolved mystery. The first permanent settlement was in 1660 at Albemarle, in the southwestern part of the state near the present city of Charlotte.

Early on, a few Jews came into the Albemarle area, probably from Barbados. The first legislature in 1665 established the Church of England as the official church but, influenced by the liberal spirit of Charles II, enfranchised all citizens regardless of faith. At first no boundary line separated North and South Carolina. They were referred to simply as "the Carolinas." The task of fixing an official boundary was begun in 1732. There were so many difficulties and disputes that a final determination was not achieved until 1815. Raleigh became North Carolina's capital in 1792.

In time the province came under the control of Protestant Dissenters. The first state constitution, adopted at the end of 1776, made Protestantism the state religion and denied non-Christians the right to hold public office. Because, prior to the Civil War, the state's commerce was not well developed, the government inefficient, the population narrowminded, the crime rate high, North Carolina was not a good state in which to live, especially for Jews. So until the 1870s North Carolina numbered its Jews only in the hundreds.

The first Jewish congregation, Temple of Israel in Wilmington, was founded in 1867. In 1868 the state constitution was revised and all civic disabilities based on religious differences were abolished. After that Jews began to come into North Carolina in larger, but never in really large, numbers. A Jewish cemetery was set up in Raleigh in 1870 and a congregation in 1885. Congregations were established in the boom towns of Tarboro, 1875, and Statesville, 1883. When the boom collapsed the congregations vanished. Congregation Oheb Sholom of Goldsboro dates from 1883. All other North Carolina congregations date from the 1890s or later. North Carolina now has about 11,000 Jews, two tenths of one percent of the total population. The largest Jewish concentrations are: Winston Salem-Greensboro-High Point, 2,700; Charlotte, 2,600; Asheville, 750; Wilmington, 500.

South Carolina

There were short-lived Spanish settlements on the east coast of South Carolina in 1526 and 1566, a vain French effort in 1562 and an English failure in 1670. The first colony which endured was the 1680 English settlement of Charles Town, later spelled Charlestown and now known as Charleston.

After 1710 North and South Carolina were considered separate entities because their respective populated areas were separated by many miles of land and sea.

South Carolina established its own government in April 1776. Charlestown was the capital until 1790; after that, Columbia. Initially the importation of black slaves into the area was strongly opposed; but, as cotton growing gradually became the chief industry, the opposition gradually vanished.

From its beginning South Carolina was proudly parochial and fiercely independent. It threatened to secede from the Union in 1833. It was the first state to actually do so on December 10, 1860. The siege and capture of Fort Sumter in Charleston harbor, April 12-14, 1861, marked the beginning of the Civil War.

The "Fundamental Constitution" of the Carolinas, written by philosopher John Locke and presented to the colony in 1669 by Charles II, granted religious toleration to all inhabitants, "including Heathens, Jues and other disenters." The first Jew to take advantage of this liberal spirit came to Charles Town in 1694. The spirit was tarnished somewhat in 1698 when the Church of England was declared the official church. It became even more discolored in 1704 when it was decided that Jews could continue to vote but could not hold public office. This legal provision was ignored in the early stages of the Revolution when Francis Salvador was twice elected to the State Assembly. South Carolina did not grant unrestricted political equality to its Jews until 1790.

Charlestown's Sephardim founded Congregation Beth Elohim in 1749. It is the fifth oldest congregation in the United States. Its four predecessors were Jeshuath Israel, Newport, Rhode Island, 1658; Shearith Israel, New York City, 1695; Mickve Israel, Savannah, Georgia, 1735; and Mikveh Israel, Philadelphia, Pennsylvania, 1745. From about 1795 to 1825 Charleston was the largest and wealthiest Jewish community in North America and probably the most cultured. American Reform Judaism was born in Charleston in 1824 when 44 members seceded from Congregation Beth Elohim and founded the Reformed Society of Israelites.

There are now 8,000 Jews in South Carolina, three tenths of one percent of the total population. Three thousand or about four percent of Charleston's present inhabitants are Jews. Other sizable Jewish communities are Columbia, 2,000, and Greenville, 600.

Tennessee

The area occupied by Tennessee was originally part of North Carolina. Dissatisfied with the inadequate protection given them by the North Carolina militia and the failure of the state legislature to comprehend their needs, the western frontiersmen seceded from North Carolina in August 1784 and asked Congress to recognize their area as a separate state. In December they named their new state Franklin, in honor of Benjamin Franklin. The first session of Franklin's legislature was held at Jonesborough in March 1785. In November of that year a constitution was adopted. There were severe internal problems and dissensions. By the end of 1788 the state of Franklin had ceased to exist. The area embracing Tennessee was ceded to the United States by North Carolina in February 1790 and given the designation "Territory south of the River Ohio." Knoxville became the capital of the territory in 1792. Tennessee was admitted to the Union on June 1, 1796, as the 16th state. Nashville became the state capital in 1843.

In American prerevolutionary history the area now Tennessee played little part. It contained practically no white inhabitants until 1757, when the English built Fort Loudon in its eastern section. A few years later the entire garrison of the fort was massacred by the Cherokee, a proud and highly intelligent Indian nation that wanted no palefaces encroaching on its land. The principal cities of Tennessee all date from the postrevolutionary years: Nashville, 1784; Knoxville, 1791; Memphis, 1819; Chattanooga, 1851.

Some Jewish traders are said to have set up posts on the Holston River in Hawkins County in the northeast corner of what is now Tennessee as early as 1778; but Jews did not come into the state in appreciable numbers until the 1840s. A Jewish cemetery was set up in Memphis in 1847. Congregation Children of Israel of Memphis was founded in 1853. That same year an Orthodox congregation, Mogen David, was established in Nashville. In 1862 there was a congregational split and Reform Congregation Bnai Jeshurun of Nashville came into being. In 1868 the congregations reunited to form the Vine Street Temple. Mizpah Congregation, Chattanooga, dates from 1866 and Temple Beth El, Knoxville, from 1868.

Tennessee now has 20,000 Jews, four tenths of one percent of the total population. The largest Jewish communities are Memphis, 9,000; Nashville, 4,000; Chattanooga, 2,500; and Knoxville, 1,000.

Virginia

On May 14, 1607, an expedition sponsored by the Virginia Company of London, chartered by James I, founded Jamestown, first permanent English settlement in North America. It was agrarian in character as were almost all the early Virginia settlements. Hampton, established in 1609, was an exception. It was intended primarily as a trading post. From the beginning the Church of England was the official church.

The first session of the House of Burgesses, America's pioneer representative assembly, met in 1619. In dramatic contrast to this experiment in democracy, the first shipment of black slaves arrived in Virginia the same year. A constitution was adopted in 1621. The next year brought the first Indian wars, highlighted by the March 22 massacre of 350 colonists. In 1641 the first British governor arrived. This marked the beginning of a lengthy period of friction between a long line of British governors and the American governed. In 1676, a century before the War of Independence, Nathaniel Bacon and his frontiersmen rebelled, for a few months successfully, against His Majesty's government. When the rebellion was quelled 23 of its leaders were executed.

After the Revolution began, a new constitution was adopted in 1776, eliminating the state church. Richmond became the capital in 1779. Richmond also served as the national capital of the Confederacy during most of the Civil War.

Elias Legardo, who arrived on the *Abigail* in 1621, may have been Virginia's first Jew. The first about whom there is no doubt was Moses Nehemiah, already in the colony in 1658. There was only a handful of Jews in Virginia prior to 1750, partly because of the primacy of the agrarian culture, dominated by large plantations and slave labor, with few towns and limited commercial possibilities, and partly because of the religious and political disabilities to which Jews were subjected. As late as 1753 Jews were not permitted to employ Christian servants.

In the 1750s Jews began to come into Virginia in somewhat larger numbers, although there was no organized Jewish life until after the Revolutionary War. A few Jews were in the Virginia militia under the command of Colonel George Washington who fought the French and Indians at Fort Duquesne in 1755.

The Jews were finally granted full religious and political equality in 1786. The first congregation was Beth Shalome of Richmond, organized in 1789, sixth oldest Jewish congregation in the United States. Congregations were formed in Norfolk, 1836; Petersburg, 1857; Alexandria, 1859; and Harrisonburg, 1867.

There are now 65,000 Jews in Virginia, one and three tenths percent of the state's population. The largest Jewish concentrations are: Alexandria, 16,000; Norfolk-Newport News-Portsmouth, 16,000; Richmond-Petersburg, 12,000.

—D.M.E.

"THE JEWS HAVE NO SYNAGOGUE— WHICH IS THEIR OWN FAULT"

(1739)

The impression received from history books studied a long time ago in my elementary and high school days was that the colony of Georgia was settled by a motley array of ne'er-do-wells and cutthroats. The inmates of debtors' jails and hardened imprisoned criminals were given their release from penal confinement on condition that they settle in the buffer state about to be created between the English colonies and the hostile Spanish settlements in Florida.

This picture had in it a certain amount of truth; but, in its totality, the truth was not nearly as foreboding as painted in those textbooks. There were some unruly rascals among the early Georgia colonists. They did get into an above average number of fights and they committed an above average number of crimes; but they were not typical of the early Georgia colonists. Most of Georgia's pioneers were sober, hard working, law abiding men and women.

The creator of the colony of Georgia, James Edward Oglethorpe, 1696-1785, arrived in Charlestown harbor late in 1732 with a group of 116 persons representing many nationalities. After friendly negotiations with the indigenous Creek Indians, he founded the community of Savannah on February 12, 1733. An additional boatload of immigrants, which reached Savannah on July 11, brought, among others, 42 Jews—21 adult males, 8 adult females, 13 children. Six adults and two children were German Ashkenazim. The rest were Sephardim of Spanish, Portuguese, and Italian Marrano extraction. Some had paid for their own passage. Most had had their passage money paid by the London Jewish community.

These Jews came to the New World without the permission of Georgia's London trustees. The trustees wanted no Jews or Catholics in

---

The letters cited in this article are in Rabbi Malcolm H. Stern's "New Light on the Jewish Settlement of Savannah" in Volume 52 (1963) of the quarterly publication of the American Jewish Historical Society. Valuable information was also provided by Rabbi Saul J. Rubin of Savannah's Congregation Mikve Israel.

the colony of Georgia, only good, God fearing Protestants. However, the Georgia charter specifically excluded only "papists." Since the charter made no reference to Jews, Oglethorpe informed the trustees that he would allow the uninvited Jews to remain. The trustees' response made no strong objection but directed Oglethorpe not to permit any Jew to acquire land in the colony.

In August Oglethorpe wrote the trustees that there had been a plague in the colony which had caused twenty deaths and that a Jewish physician, Dr. Samuel Nunez, one of the July arrivals, had "entirely put a stop to" the plague "so that not one died afterwards." This placated the trustees somewhat:

> The Trustees are very much pleased with the Behaviour of the Jewish Physician and the Service he has been to the Sick: As they have no doubt you have given him some Gratuity for it, they hope you have taken any other Method of rewarding him than in granting of Lands.

The hope of the trustees was in vain. Oglethorpe empowered the Jews to buy land just like everyone else. The land in and around the town was carved into lots of 50 acres each. Everyone was allowed to acquire as many lots as he could afford. Dr. Nunez bought six. Sixteen other Jews bought lots in varying numbers. David Cohn Delmonte bought 30.

Before the end of 1738 12 more Jewish families, totaling about 40 persons, arrived, some from other American colonies, most directly from Europe. Three of these families were Sephardim, the rest German Ashkenazim. So by 1739 Savannah had about 80 Jews, about equally divided between Sephardim and Ashkenazim.

The first group of Sephardim brought with them a Sefer Torah. In July 1735 they formed a congregation and named it K. K. Mickve Israel. A house was rented for use as a synagogue. In 1737 another congregation which had been organized by the Ashkenazim received from a London benefactor a Torah, a Chanuka lamp, and a supply of prayerbooks.

A letter written in 1738 by a Savannah German Lutheran pastor to a colleague in Germany contains a vivid description of the contemporary state of the religious life of Savannah's Jews:

> Some Jews in Savannah complained to me the other day that the Spanish and Portuguese Jews persecute the German Jews in a way no Christian would persecute another Christian. He asked me to use my influence with the authorities on behalf of the German Jews. . . . The Jew . . . promised to tell me sometime the reason why there is so much bitterness among themselves. They want to build a Synagogue, but the Spanish and German Jews cannot come to terms. I do not know the special reason for this.
> The Spanish and Portuguese Jews are not so strict insofar as

eating is concerned as the others are. They eat, for instance, the beef that comes from the warehouse or that is sold anywhere else. The German Jews, on the other hand, would rather starve than eat meat they do not slaughter themselves.

. . . The [German] Jews use at their service, which they are holding in an old and miserable hut, men and women separated, the same ceremonies which I have seen in Berlin. A boy speaking several languages and especially good in Hebrew is their reader and he is paid for his services. There are not more than two families who can speak Jewish-German [i.e., Yiddish-Deitsch]. They do not know if they will ever get permission from the Trustees to build a synagogue. It will be quite some time; as I mentioned before, the Spanish and Portuguese Jews are against the German Jews and they are going to protest the petition by the German Jews to build a synagogue. The German Jews would like to be on good terms with us [German Lutherans], and they have done us small favors time and again. But as far as their religion is concerned, they have been obstinate and there is very little that we can do about it.

Earlier, in 1735, a Savannah Anglican clergyman, writing to his mission's headquarters in England, made these comments:

You desire in one of your letters to know whether the Jews amongst us seem inclined to embrace Christianity. We have here two sorts of Jews, Portuguese and Germans. The first, having professed Christianity in Portugal or the Brazils, are more lax in their way, and dispense with a great many of their Jewish Rites, and two young men, the Sons of a Jew Doctor [Dr. Samuel Nunez], Sometimes come to Church, and for these reasons are thought by some people to be Christians but I cannot find that they really are So, only that their education in these Countries where they were obliged to appear Christians makes them less rigid and stiff in their ways. The German Jews, who are thought the better sort of them, are a great deal more strict in their ways and rigid observers of their Law. . . . They all in general behave themselves very well, and are industrious in their business.

Throughout these early pioneer years the Sephardic and Ashkenazic groups in Savannah led completely separate existences. In July 1739 another letter written by the aforementioned Lutheran minister says:

The Jews have no synagogue, which is their own fault; the one element hindering the other in this regard. The German Jews believe themselves entitled to build a Synagogue and are willing to allow the Spanish Jews to use it with them in common; the latter, however, reject any such arrangement and demand the preference for themselves.

The Sephardim continued to worship in their rented house and the Ashkenazim in their "old and miserable hut" until 1740, when the Savannah settlement entered upon a temporary period of almost complete collapse.

When the trustees formulated the regulations for the conduct of the Georgia colony, they decreed that trade in rum and slaves was prohibited. The other American colonies derived much financial and physical strength from these means of trade. The nobly motivated decree of the trustees deprived Georgia of much income and much cheap labor. The trustees encouraged the colonists to concentrate on the growing and marketing of grapes, silk, hemp, indigo, and medicinal herbs. The colonists tried and failed.

By 1740 most of Savannah's debt-ridden population, including its Jews, had left the colony and settled elsewhere. This exodus was triggered not only by bad economic conditions but even more by rumors of an impending Spanish invasion from Florida. The majority of the Jews reestablished themselves in Charlestown, South Carolina, or New York City. K. K. Mickve Israel disbanded. At the beginning of 1742 only about 200 persons remained in Savannah. The German Sheftall and Minis families, and possibly one or two other Jewish families, did not leave. In 1743 Oglethorpe, disgusted and worn out, returned to England.

By 1749 the trustees realized they had made a basic business blunder and they consented to permit Georgians to traffic in rum and slaves. After slave labor was introduced into the Georgia economy, the farmers shifted from their cultivating of unprofitable crops to the successful and lucrative growing of cotton and tobacco. On the backs of their black serfs those who had been humble dirt farmers rose to be lordly plantation owners. Georgia rapidly became one of the busiest and most affluent of the American colonies.

This gave Savannah a new lease on life. Its population, including its Jewish population, again began to grow. By the time of the Revolution there was a sizable number of Jews in Savannah, Jews fiercely loyal to the cause of independence. In 1773 a Jewish cemetery was established. In 1786 K. K. Mickve Israel was reborn and was granted a permanent charter in 1790. By then the feud between the Sephardim and the Ashkenazim was past history. All the Jewish families, regardless of ancestry, belonged to the one congregation.

Mickve Israel still has in its membership families who stem from the original Jewish settlers of Savannah. The present-day Sheftalls and Minises are interwoven descendants of Ashkenazim and Sephardim who, unmoved by the petty discords of the 1730s, fell in love, married, and helped to develop a strongly united Jewish community.

THE FIRST JEW TO DIE FOR INDEPENDENCE
(1776)

The Jews of the South during the American Revolution proved conclusively not only that Jews were staunch patriots but also that they were willing to shed their blood as well as risk their fortunes in their country's cause. In South Carolina and in Georgia, the majority of the Jews entered the ranks and served well on the field of battle. The names of several of these patriots have been handed down to posterity, and yet the one who was perhaps the most prominent of all has been comparatively neglected.

He was reared in luxury. He placed his fortune at the disposal of his adopted country; he fought for that country on the field of battle, and besides this took rank with the leaders of the Revolution in South Carolina as the colleague of Rutledge, of Pinckney, and of Drayton. His career was unfortunately brief, yet it was as brilliant as it was brief. The name of the Jewish patriot to whom I refer is Francis Salvador.

His forebears came to England from Holland, bringing with them considerable wealth. Their name was originally Jessurum Rodriguez and the date of their arrival is uncertain. By the middle of the eighteenth century the Salvadors were numbered among the merchant princes of England.

[Francis Salvador, born in 1747, was the son of Jacob Salvador, who died when Francis was two years old. Upon reaching maturity Francis received an inheritance of 60,000 pounds. He married his first cousin Sarah, daughter of his father's brother Joseph. Sarah brought with her a bridal dowry of 13,000 pounds. Her father also gave Francis a large tract of land he owned in the northwestern corner of South Carolina.]

Wealth is exceedingly unstable; misfortune will come when least expected. Two events, equally sudden, swallowed up the vast fortune of these merchant princes. One was the [1755] earthquake in Lisbon where their interests were considerable; and the other, but far the more important, was the failure of the Dutch East India Company. [It was not the failure of the Dutch East India Company but the suspension of trade between England and Holland in 1772-73, when the two countries were at war with each other, that brought financial disaster to the London

---

Excerpted from article by Leon Huehner, "Francis Salvador: A Prominent Patriot of the Revolutionary War," in Volume 9 (1901) of American Jewish Historical Society Publications. The bracketed insertions are additional comments supplied by the editor of this anthology.

Sephardic merchants.] Finally all that remained of the immense wealth, outside of a slender fortune, was the tract of land in America. In 1773 Francis Salvador undertook a voyage to the New World in order to retrieve the family fortunes. We are told that in due time letters came advising of his safe arrival and announcing his intention of seeking his property. He left his wife and four children in England, meaning to send for them as soon as possible. At the time of his arrival he was certainly no more than thirty-five or forty years of age. [He was actually only twenty-six years old.]

At this period all of the colonies were more or less agitated by the attitude of Great Britain. The revolutionary spirit was ripening. In South Carolina lines had long since been drawn between Whig and Tory— between the advocates of representative government and the blind adherents of the Crown. Nowhere, perhaps, did factional feeling run higher. A man of Salvador's temperament and education naturally took sides at once. The principles involved in the approaching struggle must have appealed to him with great force: the idea of liberty as against despotism and the idea of civil and religious emancipation, must have had especial charms for him as a Jew [particularly because, in 1753, England had denied its Jews full citizenship rights]. Without a moment's hesitation, he threw himself heart and soul into the patriotic cause. He became the intimate of the great leaders of the colony. With him these patriots advised on some of the most important questions, as their correspondence abundantly shows.

Such was the esteem in which he was held that when he had been but a year in the colony he was elected a member of the General Assembly of South Carolina. [He thus became the first Jew to serve as a member of an American legislative body. Joseph Ottolengui served in the Assembly of Georgia from 1761 to 1765, but Ottolengui had converted to Christianity before coming to America.] This dignity Salvador retained up to his untimely death which occurred about two years later.

The Congress assembled at Charlestown on January 11, 1775. As the subject of this sketch is repeatedly mentioned as belonging to the Jewish nation, it is of interest to discover whether he had to violate any religious scruple before taking his seat in the Provincial Congress. No such obstacle existed. Under the first state constitution members were simply required to take the oath to support the constitution of South Carolina; only the President being required to swear, in addition, to support the Protestant religion.

The Congress prepared an address to the royal Governor setting forth the grievances of the Assembly. The Governor replied that he did not recognize the Provincial Congress and that body thereupon at once recommended that the inhabitants learn the use of arms. The 17th of February was set apart "as a day of fasting, humiliation and prayer before Almighty God devoutly to petition him to inspire the King with true wisdom, to defend the people of North America in their just title to freedom and to avert the impending calamities of civil war." The members who took part in this Congress certainly ran grave chances of arrest for treason and confiscation of property.

The battle of Lexington in 1775 inflamed the South no less than the North. Open hostilities began in Carolina and Salvador was among the first to take the field. Tories were plentiful in the northern part of the colony and William Henry Drayton, the patriot Chief Justice, at once pitched his camp ready for hostilities. The Tories thereupon sent representatives to the camp and an agreement was drawn up that the Tories might live in peace but must not aid the British. Any offense against the compact was to be severely punished. The document concludes: "Done in Camp, near Ninety Six, this 16th day of September, 1775." It is signed by six Tories, by Drayton for the Committee of Safety, and for the patriots it is witnessed by Francis Salvador. [Salvador's 6,000-acre plantation, tended by 30 slaves, was at Coronaca Creek, 15 miles northwest of Ninety Six.]

The second Provincial Congress of South Carolina was held at Charlestown in November 1775. From the records of that historic assembly, we can plainly see the great confidence reposed by Salvador's colleagues in his ability, his judgment, and his fidelity. Salvador was appointed to a committee "with all possible dispatch to stamp and any three of them to sign, and when stamped, signed and numbered, from time to time to deliver to the Colony Treasurers, bills amounting to 120,000 pounds for paying the army."

On February 6, 1776, our patriot was appointed by the Congress along with four others "to inquire into the state of the interior parts of the colony—to consider what means are proper to be pursued to preserve the peace and secure the safety, and to prevent future commotions therein, and also to consider the cases of the State prisoners." Salvador appears to have presented this committee's report to the Congress on February 21.

The British, afraid of the aggressive patriots, soon adopted a despicable means of subjugation. In order to divert the attention of the patriots from British operations, they stirred up and assisted the Indians to make inroads and massacre the colonists. Throughout this period Salvador kept in close touch with the leading statesmen and commanders. Chief Justice Drayton appears to have stayed at Salvador's plantation for some time previous to June 28. The letters directed to Salvador by military men are remarkable in the abundance of intricate information regarding military affairs which they contain.

Many efforts were made by the patriots to conciliate the Cherokees, but John Stuart, the British superintendent, won them over, and an attack against the frontier was prepared as a diversion in favor of British operations on the seacoast. Being informed that the British fleet had arrived off Charlestown, the Indians on July 1, 1776, poured down on the frontier of South Carolina, "massacring without distinction of age or sex all persons who fell into their power."

Salvador was informed by a refugee of the savage attack, and the annalist tells us "that Mr. Salvador forthwith mounted his horse and galloped to Major Williamson residing 28 miles away and gave the alarm." The people were helpless, destitute of arms and ammunition. On July 18 Salvador wrote to Drayton, giving a detailed description of what had happened:

> The whole country was flying, some to make forts, others as low as Orangeburg. Williamson was employed night and day sending expresses to raise the militia, but the panic was so great that on Wednesday the major and myself marched to the late Captain Smith's with only forty men. We have been gradually increasing ever since, though all the men in the county were loth to turn out till they had secured some kind of fancied security for their families. However, we had last night five hundred men.

[During the entire month of July Salvador served without military rank as Major Williamson's second-in-command. In the month's final two weeks, the regiment of militia headed by Williamson and Salvador fought a number of successful engagements against the Tories and Indians.]

It is doubtful that Salvador ever knew that the Declaration of Independence had been adopted. News of the event does not seem to have reached South Carolina until about July 25. On July 24 Drayton wrote to Salvador: "No news yet from Philadelphia; every ear is turned that way anxiously waiting for the word 'Independence.' I say, 'God speed the passage of it.' 'Amen,' say you."

On the subject of Williamson and Salvador's expedition, Drayton wrote:

> It is expected that you will make smooth work as you go, that you will cut up every Indian cornfield and burn every Indian town. For my part, I shall never give my voice to a peace with the Cherokee nation upon other terms than their removal beyond the [Appalachian] mountains. That victory will conduct your march is the expectation of, dear Sir, your most humble and obedient servant, William Henry Drayton.

It was while on this expedition that our patriot perished. On his way he received news of the American victory over the British fleet. Near Esseneka [Seneca, about 35 miles southwest of Greenville], at two o'clock in the morning on August 1, 1776, the Tories and Indians opened fire. Salvador was shot and, falling among the bushes, was discovered by the Indians and scalped. The account of his death as described by the contemporary historian is exceedingly pathetic, but too lengthy to be given here. It states that Salvador died in 45 minutes, without being sensible that the savage act had been performed upon him.

Major Williamson at once sent a report of the death to John Rutledge, President of South Carolina. After giving considerable detail, the report concludes:

> When I came up to him after dislodging the enemy and speaking to him, he asked whether I had beaten the enemy. I told him "Yes." He said he was glad of it, and shook me by the hand and bade me farewell and said he would die in a few minutes.

Drayton, in his memoirs, after mentioning Salvador's services in the assembly of South Carolina, speaks of him as having had a warm heart toward those in distress and adds:

> His fate excited universal regret. . . . His manners were those of a polished gentleman and as such he was intimately known and esteemed by the first Revolutionary characters of South Carolina. He also possessed their confidence in a great degree as his literary correspondence with them sufficiently proves. . . . At the side of his friend, Major Williamson, he received those wounds which sacrificed his life in the service of his adopted country.

[A plaque in City Hall Park, Charleston, dedicated to the memory of Francis Salvador, reads:

Born an aristocrat, he became a democrat.
An Englishman, he cast his lot with America.
True to his ancient faith, he gave his life
For new hopes of liberty and understanding.]

OLD MORDECAI

(1789)

His parents named him Abram Mordecai. But for about the last 50 of the almost 100 years that he lived, he was known affectionately to the frontiersmen of central Alabama as "Old Mordecai."

The claim that Old Mordecai was the founder of the city of Montgomery is not true. However, he seems to have been the first native born white man to settle in what is now Montgomery County, Alabama.

Abram Mordecai was born in Pennsylvania on October 24, 1755. His parents were German immigrants. His father was Jewish. His mother was not. Mordecai seems to have received a Jewish religious training and to have considered himself a Jew. He served in the American Revolutionary army for three years. At the end of the war, restless and with a roving disposition, he headed south.

In 1783 he settled among the Koasati Indians, a branch of the Creek nation, at Buzzard Roost on the Flint River in the southwest corner of Georgia, somewhere between where Albany and Bainbridge are now located. He established a trading post, exchanging white men's goods for Indian medicinal herbs, hickory nut oil, and many kinds of fur pelts. He carried the items acquired from the Indians to Augusta and Pensacola by packhorse and to Mobile and New Orleans by boat; and he brought back white men's merchandise by the same means. He was considered completely honest by both redskin and paleface and was often the go-between in negotiations of various departments of the government with the Indian tribes.

Mordecai believed that the Indians had originally been Jews. He stated that, in their Green Corn dances, in which they gave thanks to the Great Spirit for having blessed them with an abundant harvest, the word they kept repeating as they were dancing was "Yavoyaha! Yavoyaha!" which he felt was their inherited pronounciation of a Hebrew phrase meaning "O God, continue to come to us." As further evidence of his belief that the Indians were fellow Semites, he married an Indian woman whose skin, according to Colonel Pickett, "was considerably darkened

---

The principal source of information on this interesting man is an article in Volume 13 of the American Jewish Historical Society Publications, written in 1905 by Rabbi Abraham J. Messing of Temple Beth Or, Montgomery, Alabama, and titled "Old Mordecai: The Founder of the City of Montgomery." Most of Rabbi Messing's facts were gathered from *The History of Alabama*, published in Birminham in 1900 but written by Colonel Albert Jones Pickett many years before. Pickett interviewed Old Mordecai in his "Indian hut" at Dudleyville, Tallapoosa County, Alabama, on September 30, 1847, less than a month before Mordecai's ninety-second birthday.

with the blood of Ham," i.e., she was part Indian and part black, and looked more black than Indian. Pickett pictured her as a loving and faithful spouse.

Pickett describes Mordecai as "a queer fellow," "a dark eyed Jew of amorous disposition," one who enjoyed living among border ruffians and had a long record of romances with Indian squaws, unmarried and married. Pickett says that the almost ninety-two-year-old Mordecai was short, round, compactly built; hair white, forehead well formed, mouth large and expressive; mind unimpaired, physically active.

In 1789 Mordecai moved into central Alabama. He opened a trading post among the Curvalla Indians at Weathersford, about 18 miles from what is now the city of Montgomery. In addition to English he spoke Spanish and a number of Indian dialects.

Eli Whitney of Connecticut invented the cotton gin in 1794. Mordecai set up the first gin in Alabama ten years later. The gin was built for him by two Jews from Georgia, named Lyons and Barnett, who brought in their working tools on the backs of horses. Mordecai bought cotton grown by the Indians, ginned it and then sold it in Augusta. His cotton ginning business lasted only one year. It ended disastrously when Mordecai incurred the fierce anger of an Indian chief.

According to the story that Mordecai told Pickett, two of his horses strayed into an Indian corn patch and ate some ears of young corn. Mordecai offered to pay for the damage but the Indians' chief refused his offer. The chief did not like having a white man so near his tribe and determined to use the incident as an excuse to get rid of Mordecai. Sixteen of his braves invaded Mordecai's property and beat him into unconsciousness. Thinking him dead, they cut off his left ear. They burned down his gin, destroyed his cotton and chopped to pieces a fine boat he had purchased in New Orleans for $400. After several months of painful suffering, he regained his health through the tender care of his devoted wife.

A different version of this happening was furnished Pickett by another white who lived nearby. This neighbor said that the Indian chief became enraged when he discovered that Mordecai was having an affair with a pretty married squaw. Since at this time Mordecai had been living peacefully with the Indians of Georgia and Alabama for more than 20 years and since he was reputed to be a woman-chaser, it is much more likely to have been Mordecai's indiscreet eating of forbidden fruit rather than the hunger of his horses that cost him his gin, his cotton, his boat, and his left ear.

Financially ruined, Mordecai returned to southwestern Georgia and labored there for a number of years. At the outbreak of the War of 1812 he joined the Georgia militia. After Andrew Jackson crushed the Creek rebellion in 1814, Mordecai left the Army and brought his family back to

Alabama. He settled once more among the Creeks in Tallapoosa County, northeast of Montgomery County. He remained in Tallapoosa County for the rest of his life.

In 1834 Congress decided to move the Creek nation from the southeastern part of the United States to what was then called the Indian Territory and is now part of the State of Oklahoma. The Creeks moved in 1836 but Mordecai did not accompany them. He went to the nearby town of Dudleyville. There he stayed until he passed away about 18 years later, having lived to see almost 1200 new moons.

THE PRESIDENT WRITES TO ALL SIX CONGREGATIONS
(1790)

When George Washington was born in 1732 he had everything going for him except one thing. His ancestors were English nobility. His family was fourth generation wealthy Virginian. He belonged to the Anglican Episcopalians, most aristocratic of the non-Roman churches. The one thing he did not have was the right of primogeniture, the privilege of inheritance and of power that belonged to the first-born son. But God or Nature or whoever or whatever takes care of such things took care of that. His father died in 1743. His elder brother, master of the estate at Mount Vernon in Virginia, took George in to live with him in 1748. And then in 1751 his elder brother became seriously ill and in 1752 he died; and George at the age of twenty became the new lord of Mount Vernon with its 5,000 acres and 49 slaves.

So George was born with a silver demitasse spoon in his mouth which, at age twenty, changed into a silver teaspoon. When he was twenty-six he wooed and won a wealthy widow who had 15,000 acres and 300 slaves and $100,000 in cash and the teaspoon changed into a silver tablespoon.

But George on his own went farther than that. At nineteen he was a major, at twenty-one a colonel, at twenty-six a state legislator, at forty-three a general and commander-in chief, and at fifty-seven a President. He could have gone even further. Had he so desired, at age fifty-seven he could have become a king, King George the First, first king of the United States of America. But George did not so desire. And after he had served as President for two terms of four years each, George, had he so wished, could have been nominated and elected for a third term. But George did not so wish. He felt that eight years as American President was enough for one man. And his modesty was respected and preserved by his Presidential successors for the next 143 years.

George Washington was a superhuman being. Most Americans take him for granted, glibly call him the "Father of our country," laughingly remark, "Some father—never had any kids," not knowing that the reason Washington had no offspring was probably because at age nineteen he was stricken with smallpox while accompanying his elder brother on a sea voyage in a vain attempt to help restore his brother's failing health.

A born leader, iron willed, a man of absolute integrity, Washington had a God-given knack for appraising human beings correctly and making use of their special talents. Despite his austere appearance he was no puritan. He enjoyed dancing, drinking, hunting, and the theater. Technically he was an Episcopalian. He tried to set a proper example for those who looked to him for guidance by going to church regularly and praying sincerely and often. This was no pose. He was genuinely devout; but, ideologically, he was no run-of-the-mill churchman. Ideologically he was a Deist, one of that select company of religious thinkers which included many other Revolutionary leaders, Benjamin Franklin, Thomas Jefferson, Thomas Paine, James Madison, and a host of lesser lights. These Deists were men who despised parochialism, who spoke, philosophically and theologically, in universal terms.

Like all Deists Washington felt at ease with Masons and Jews because they spoke his kind of intellectual language. Washington was an active Mason and enjoyed being in the company of Jews. He did not have the latter pleasure very often because in his day only about one American in every thousand was Jewish. His confidential aide-de-camp throughout the Revolutionary War was a Philadelphia Jew, Colonel Isaac Franks.

Together with almost every American of the last quarter of the eighteenth century, American Jews revered Washington. To them he represented the best of what America was and what it was destined to become. He was for them, in the most genuine sense, "Mr. America."

✿   ✿   ✿   ✿   ✿

In 1755 Colonel Washington visited Newport, Rhode Island, for the first time, en route from Mount Vernon to Boston to confer with Massachusetts Governor Shirley, commander-in-chief of all American colonial military forces. There is no evidence that he came in contact with the Newport Jewish community during this visit.

In 1781 he came to Newport again, this time as General Washington. The local welcoming committee was headed by a prominent Jew, Moses Isaacks, in whose home the general was entertained. The meeting to plan the welcome for Washington was held in the Newport synagogue. The local Masonic lodge played a leading role in feting their renowned fellow-Mason. On this occasion the Worshipful Grand Master, the Senior

Warden, and a large proportion of the brethren of Newport's King David Lodge were Jews.

Early in 1790 Mr. Jackson, a member of Congress, presented to President Washington a message of congratulation upon his election from the "Hebrew Congregation of the City of Savannah, Georgia." It read, in part:

Sir:

Your unexampled liberality and extensive philanthropy have dispelled that cloud of bigotry and superstition which has long as a vail shaded religion—unrivetted the fetters of enthusiasm—enfranchised us with all the privileges and immunities of free citizens, and initiated us into the grand mass of legislative mechanism. By example you have taught us to endure the ravages of war with manly fortitude, and to enjoy the blessings of peace with reverence to the Deity and benignity and love to our fellow-creatures. . . .

Levi Sheftal, President

Washington replied, in part, as follows:

Gentlemen:

I rejoice that a spirit of liberality and philanthropy is much more prevalent than it formerly was among the enlightened nations of the earth, and that your brethren will benefit thereby in proportion as it shall become still more extensive; happily the people of the United States have in many instances exhibited examples worthy of imitation, the salutary influence of which will doubtless extend much farther if, gratefully enjoying those blessings of peace which (under the favor of heaven) have been attained by fortitude in war, they shall conduct themselves with reverence to the Deity and charity toward their fellow-creatures.

May the same wonder-working Deity, who long since delivered the Hebrews from their Egyptian oppressors, planted them in a promised land, and whose providential agency has lately been conspicuous in establishing these United States as an independent nation, still continue to water them with the dews of heaven and make the inhabitants of every denomination participate in the temporal and spiritual blessings of that people whose God is Jehovah.

On August 17-18, 1790, President Washington, in the course of a nationwide inspection tour, made his third visit to Newport. Among those who greeted him with appropriate formal remarks was a representative of Congregation Jeshuat Israel. Later Washington sent a letter of thanks to the Newport congregation, using words and phrases much quoted ever since:

Gentlemen:

. . . The citizens of the United States of America have a right to applaud themselves for having given to mankind examples of an enlarged and liberal policy—a policy worthy of imitation. All possess alike liberty of conscience and immunities of citizenship.

It is now no more that toleration is spoken of as if it were the indulgence of one class of people that another enjoyed the exercise of their inherent natural rights, for, happily, the Government of the United States, which gives to bigotry no sanction, to persecution no assistance, requires only that they who live under its protection should demean themselves as good citizens in giving it on all occasions their effectual support. . . .

May the children of the stock of Abraham who dwell in this land continue to merit and enjoy the good will of the other inhabitants—while every one shall sit in safety under his own vine and fig tree and there shall be none to make him afraid. . . .

On December 13, 1790, Manuel Josephson of Philadelphia visited the President in his New York office and presented him with a joint letter of congratulations from the "Hebrew Congregations in Philadelphia, New York, Richmond, and Charleston."

Washington sent a response to the four congregations, expressing his gratitude:

Gentlemen:
The liberality of sentiment toward each other, which marks every political and religious denomination of men in this country, stands unparalleled in the history of nations. . . .

The power and goodness of the Almighty, so strongly manifested in the events of our late glorious revolution, and His kind interposition in our behalf, have been no less visible in the establishment of our present equal government. In war He directed the sword, and in peace He has ruled in our councils. . . .

In this manner did all six of the Jewish congregations in the United States in 1790 express their high regard for their and our first President; and President George Washington, "first in war, first in peace, and first in the hearts of his fellow-countrymen," responded in words that will be long remembered and often repeated, avowing his deep understanding and great respect for "the temporal and spiritual blessings of that people whose God is Jehovah."

"WHATEVER YE WOULD THAT MEN SHOULD DO UNTO YOU—"
(1809)

Freedom of religion and religious equality are not synonymous terms. Far from it. The constitution and Bill of Rights adopted by the

State of North Carolina in 1776 made this quite clear. The Bill of Rights declared that "all men have a natural and unalienable right to worship Almighty God according to the dictates of their own conscience." But the Constitution provided that no place of public trust could be occupied by anyone who denied the truth of the Protestant religion and the divine authority of the New Testament. On the first of these counts, Roman Catholics were excluded and, on both counts, the Jews.

As happens so often with a bad law, those charged with its implementation ignored it. In 1781 North Carolina had a Roman Catholic governor; and occasionally a Roman Catholic served as a member of the state legislature.

Then in 1808 a Jew named Jacob Henry came into the legislature as the representative from Cartaret County, an area in the southeastern part of the state on the Atlantic Ocean near Cape Lookout. No one raised any objection to Henry's Jewishness. In 1809 he was elected to a second one-year term. This time someone invoked the restrictive provision in the state constitution and objected to Henry being seated. The result was that Henry made a speech to the North Carolina legislature which is a classic in American Jewish historical folklore.

Before we sit in on the speech, let us learn what there is to learn about Jacob Henry.

An aura of mystery hangs about Jacob Henry in that much which is believed about him is based on coincidence rather than on authentic documented data. It is like trying to put together a jigsaw puzzle when one is not absolutely sure that all the pieces were meant to fit into one pattern. Extracting a little bit of this and a little bit of that from a heap made up of facts, surmises, and possibilities brings us to an account that goes something like this:

Jacob Henry was born in Furth, which is near Nuremberg in Bavaria, Germany, about 1746. His father Joel was a brother of the mother of Bernard and Michael Gratz of Philadelphia fame. After coming to America prior to the Revolutionary War, Joel became involved in trade with the West Indies and Jacob worked in Philadelphia.

Toward the end of 1777 Jacob enlisted in the Pulaski Legion and served in the campaigns in South Carolina and Georgia. After Count Pulaski was killed in the attack on Savannah in October 1779, the unit was commanded by German Baron Johann de Kalb. Henry served in the cavalry-infantry brigade commanded by Jewish Major Benjamin Nones of Philadelphia. There was a sizable number of Jews in the brigade. In the battle of Camden, South Carolina, in August 1780, the Americans were defeated, Baron de Kalb was mortally wounded and Jacob Henry was among those taken prisoner. He was confined in a British prison ship in Charleston harbor. After Washington defeated Cornwallis at Yorktown in October 1781, the prisoners were freed.

Henry decided to remain in Charleston and to go into business there. A number of years later he moved to Cartaret County in North Carolina. After he retired, he spent the rest of his life in Charleston. He was residing in Charleston in 1820. The exact year of his death is not known.

Now to the speech of Jacob Henry. We have it in its entirety because it was considered worthy of inclusion in a volume published shortly after it was delivered. The volume is titled *The American Orator* and was used as a public speaking textbook in American schools.

Mr. Speaker,
    Though I will not conceal the surprise I felt that the gentleman should have thought proper yesterday to have moved my expulsion from this House, on the alleged grounds that I "disbelieve in the Divine authority of the New Testament," without considering himself bound by those rules of politeness, which, according to my sense of propriety, should have led him to give me some previous intimation of his design, yet since I am brought to the discussion, I feel prepared to meet the object of his resolution.
    I certainly, Mr. Speaker, know not the design of the Declaration of Rights made by the people of this State in the year'76, if it was not to consecrate certain great and fundamental Rights and Principles, which even the Constitution cannot impair; for the 44th Section of the latter instrument declares that the Declaration of Rights ought never to be violated on any pretence whatever;—if there is any apparent difference between the two instruments, they ought, if possible, to be reconciled. But if there is a final repugnance between them, the Declaration of Rights must be considered paramount. For I believe it is to the Constitution as the Constitution is to a law,—it controls and directs it, absolutely and conclusively.
    If, then, a belief in the Protestant religion is required by the Constitution to qualify a man for a seat in this House, and such qualification is dispensed with by the Declaration of Rights, the provision of the Constitution must be altogether inoperative, as the language of the Bill of Rights is "that all men have a natural and unalienable right to worship Almighty God according to the dictates of their own conscience." It is undoubtedly a natural right, and when it is declared to be an unalienable one, by the people in their sovereign and original capacity, any attempt to alienate it, either by the Constitution or by law, must be vain and fruitless. It is difficult to conceive how such a provision crept into the Constitution, unless it was from the difficulty the human mind feels in suddenly emancipating itself from the fetters by which it has long been enchained.
    If a man should hold religious principles incompatible with the freedom and safety of the State, I do not hesitate to pronounce that he should be excluded from the public councils of the same; and I trust, if I know myself, no one would be more ready to aid and assist than myself. But I should really be at a loss to specify any known religious principles which are thus dangerous. It is surely a question between a man and his Maker, and requires more than human attributes to pronounce which of the numerous sects prevailing in the world is most acceptable to the Deity. If a man fulfils the duties

of that religion which his education or his conscience has pointed out to him as the true one, no person, I hold, in this our land of liberty has the right to arraign him at the bar of any inquisition. And the day, I trust, is long past when principles merely speculative were propagated by force, when the sincere and pious were made victims, and the light-minded bribed into hypocrites.

The proud monuments of liberty knew that the purest homage man could render to the Almighty was in the sacrifice of his passions, and in the performance of his duties; that the Ruler of the universe would receive with equal benignity the various offerings of man's adoration, if they proceeded from an humble spirit and sincere mind; that intolerance in matters of faith had been from the earliest ages of the world the severest torments by which man could be afflicted; and that governments were only concerned about the actions and conduct of man, and not his speculative notions.

Who among us feels himself so exalted about his fellows as to have a right to dictate to them his mode of belief? Shall this free country set an example of persecution which even the returning reason of enslaved Europe would not submit to? Will you bind the Conscience in chains, and fasten conviction upon the mind, in spite of the conclusions of reason, and of those ties and habitudes which are blended with every pulsation of the heart? Are you prepared to plunge at once from the sublime heights of moral legislation into the dark and gloomy caverns of superstitious ignorance? Will you drive from your shores and from the shelter of your Constitution all who do not lay their oblations on the same altar, observe the same ritual, and subscribe to the same dogmas? If so, which among the various sects into which we are divided shall be the favored one?

I should insult the understanding of this House to suppose it possible that they could ever assent to such absurdities. For all know that persecution in all its shapes and modifications is contrary to the genius of our Government and the spirit of our laws; and that it can never produce any other effect than to render men hypocrites or martyrs. When Charles the Fifth, Emperor of Germany, tired of the cares of government, resigned his crown to his son, he retired to a monastery, where he amused the evening of his life in regulating the movements of watches, endeavoring to make a number keep the same time; but not being able to make any two go exactly alike, he was led to reflect upon the folly and crimes he had committed in attempting the impossibility of making men think alike!

Nothing is more easily demonstrated than that conduct alone is the subject of human laws, and that man ought to suffer civil disqualification for what he *does,* and not for what he *thinks.* The mind can receive laws only from Him of whose divine essence it is a portion; He alone can punish disobedience, for who else can know its movements, or estimate their merits?

The religion I profess inculcates every duty which man owes to his fellowmen; it enjoins upon its votaries the practice of every virtue, and the detestation of every vice; it teaches them to'hope for the favor of Heaven exactly in proportion as their lives are directed by just, honorable maxims.—This, then, gentlemen, is my creed; it was impressed upon my infant mind, it has been the director of my youth, the monitor of my manhood, and will, I trust, be the consolation of my old age. At any rate, Mr. Speaker, I am sure that you cannot see anything in this religion to deprive me of my seat in this House. So far as relates to my life and conduct, the examination of these I submit with cheerfulness to your candid and liberal construction.

What may be the religion of him who made this objection against me, or whether he has any religion or not, I am unable to say. I have never considered it my duty to pry into the belief of other members of this House, if their actions are upright and their conduct just; the rest is for their own consideration—not for mine. I do not seek to make converts to my faith, nor do I exclude any man from my esteem or friendship because he and I differ in that respect. The same charity, therefore, it is not unreasonable to expect will be extended to myself, because in all things that relate to the State and to the duties of civil life, I am bound by the same obligations as my fellow-citizens; nor does any man subscribe more sincerely than myself to the maxim.

"Whatever ye would that men should do unto you, do ye so even unto them, for such is the Law and the Prophets."

Henry's speech made a powerful impression upon the North Carolina legislators. They got out of their embarrassing predicament not by repealing the offensive section in their constitution but by interpreting its dictate in a very farfetched manner. They decided that the Constitution prohibited non-Protestants from holding state appointive, i.e., civil service, jobs but did not prohibit them from holding state elective, i.e., legislative, positions! Jews did not obtain full political equality in North Carolina until 1868, when a constitutional assembly which included thirteen blacks finally removed the bigoted clause from the North Carolina constitution.

In 1818 H. M. Brackinridge of the Maryland legislature, one of a committee of three appointed to study the advisability of giving Jews full civic equality in the state of Maryland, speaking in the legislative debate on this so-called Jew Bill, declared:

In the state of North Carolina there is a memorable instance on record of an attempt to expel Mr. Henry, a Jew, from its legislative body, of which he had been elected a member. The speech which Mr. Henry delivered on that occasion I hold in my hand. It is published in a collection called *The American Orator*, a book given to your children at school and containing those republican truths you wish to see earliest implanted in their minds. Mr. Henry prevailed; and it has become part of our education as Americans to love and cherish the sentiments uttered by him on that occasion.

Despite Mr. Brackinridge's noble efforts, the bill he was advocating was defeated. Jews did not achieve full civic equality in Maryland until 1826.

THE ROPE-SKIPPING "JEWISH INDIAN"
(1817)

Edward Kantor the "Jewish Indian" was born in Germany in 1798. He ran away from home in 1815, came to America as a stowaway on a French vessel, jumped ship in Charleston, took to peddling, and then clerked in a drugstore.

Many years later he was to become the proprietor of a general store in Detroit, Michigan, and a favorite of the neighboring Indian tribes—so much so that one of them adopted him and gave him the name "Bosh-bish-gay-bish-gon-sen," the Indian word for "firecracker" and a name that Edward Kantor laughingly described as sounding more Jewish than his own.

This "Jewish Indian" was born in Germany in 1798. He ran away from home in 1815, came to America as a stowaway on a French vessel, jumped ship in Charleston, took to peddling, and then clerked in a drug store.

By March 1817 Eddie had gone back to horse-and-wagon peddling in the Deep South. He pulled into Fort Deposit, Alabama, a frontier town 25 miles southwest of Montgomery. Fort Deposit had been founded by General Andrew Jackson as a military outpost during his 1814 war with the Creek Indians. Eddie's horse had gone lame, but the traveling young merchant had been able to trade some of his goods to an Indian for another horse.

Before the sun had set the Fort Deposit sheriff arrested Eddie for horse-stealing, a capital offense. The horse had been stolen by the Indian, who disappeared into the forest as soon as he got hold of Eddie's merchandise.

Northern peddlers were not popular in the South, especially one with a heavy accent. At the trial justice was dispensed by a hostile judge and jury. The jury heard the evidence, closeted themselves in the local saloon for their deliberations and, within an hour, returned with a verdict of guilty. During the same hour the judge retired to his private chambers where he finished off a quart of prime rye whiskey. When he came back to the bench to hear the expected verdict and pronounce sentence, he was weaving gracefully. Focusing his eyes with some difficulty upon the convicted peddler, he belched out the order, "Prisoner, stand up." The prisoner stood up.

"Edward Kantor," declaimed His Honor, "in but a few short weeks it will be spring. The snows of winter will flee away, the ice will vanish, and the air will become soft and balmy. In short, Edward Kantor, the miracle of the year's awakening will come to pass. The rivulets will come to life. The first timid flowers will put forth their tender shoots. The glorious valleys of this blessed region will blossom as the rose. From every treetop some wildwood songster will carol his mating song. Butterflies will sport in the sunshine and the busy bee will hum happily as it pursues its accustomed vocation. All of nature, Edward Kantor, will be glad. But you—you miserable, horse-thievin', foreign son of a bitch—you won't be around to enjoy it, because you are going to be hanged four weeks from this coming Friday."

For the next four weeks Eddie languished in the town jail, visited only by the judge's young and well-proportioned daughter Geraldine, who brought him his grub. Through a tiny, barred window he witnessed the construction of the scaffold. . . . Now all was ready. Today was the day. The circuit hangman had arrived. The sheriff had polished his boots. The townspeople had gotten dressed in their festive Sunday-go-to-meetin' clothes. The judge had prepared another speech for the gala occasion. . . . The fateful hour came. The sheriff entered the jailhouse to fetch the condemned. . . . Lo and behold—his cell was empty!

On the cot was a note addressed to His Honor: "My dear Judge Murchison, Before the rising of the new moon in all its silvery glory, the Shenandoah Valley of Virginia will be fragrant with the scent of apple blossoms. The song of the meadow lark will bring joy to the hearts of young lovers as they listen to nature's own music. Graceful swans will make silhouettes against the soft blue skies, and the setting sun will cast its amber glow upon that far-off area, bathing it in celestial beauty. And I shall be there to enjoy it, Your Honor, together with your lovely Geraldine, who so sweetly helped me to borrow your horse for my wagon. While Geraldine and I are finding pleasure in the fragrance of the flowers, basking in the golden Virginia sun and bathing in the rippling streams, we shall do our very utmost to forget that you exist, you pompous bastard.

(signed) Edward Kantor.

N.B. As my father-in-law-to-be, you may, if you so wish, whenever you refer to me, call me Eddie."

The Organ That Was "Erected in the Synagogue"
(1840)

What was the basic issue that in 1840 caused the Reform Jews and the Traditionalist Jews affiliated with Congregation Beth Elohim of Charleston, South Carolina, to part company? Was it observance or non-observance of the dietary laws? No. Observance or non-observance of the Sabbath? No. Belief or disbelief in the coming of the Messiah, the resurrection of the dead, or any other theological matter? No. What was it? The break came because of a heated dispute over a subject on which the Halacha, traditional Jewish law, takes no solid position. The issue was: Is a synagogue permitted to have an organ? The Reform-minded Jews of Congregation Beth Elohim said, "Yes." The Tradition-minded Jews of Congregation Beth Elohim said, "No."

Gustavus Poznanski, spiritual leader of the congregation, born in Poland in 1805 and educated for the rabbinate in Hungary, had been strongly influenced in his youth by the Reform group in Hamburg, Germany. After ordination he came to the United States and was on the staff of Sephardic Congregation Shearith Israel of New York City. Recommended by Rabbi Isaac Leeser of Philadelphia and other Traditionalist leaders, Poznanski was chosen in January 1837 as chazan or minister of technically Sephardic Congregation Beth Elohim of Charleston. The term "technically Sephardic" is employed because a large proportion of the synagogue members were West European Ashkenazim. The congregation was so pleased with Poznanski that, after a year, it elected him chazan for life.

In April 1838 the Charleston synagogue burned down. A new synagogue was constructed on the same site. This lovely edifice of Greek Revival design is still the congregation's place of worship. It is second only to Newport's synagogue in age and, in terms of length of uninterrupted use, is first among all American synagogues.

As the new building neared completion, many former members of the Reformed Society of Israelites, estranged from Beth Elohim for many years, began to return to the fold. The Reformed Society of Israelites was a group of 44 families, including that of Phillip Benjamin, father of Judah P. Benjamin, which broke away from Beth Elohim in 1825 and organized its own congregation, the first Reform congregation in the United States. The Society lasted until 1833. When it disbanded, a few of

---

This article is based on the definitive paper, "The Charleston Organ Case," by Rabbi Allan Tarshish, presented at the 62nd Annual Meeting of the American Jewish Historical Society, March 1964, Charleston, South Carolina.

its members returned immediately to Beth Elohim, but many others did not go back until 1840.

On July 14, 1840, 38 members of Beth Elohim requested the Board of Trustees to call a congregational meeting to consider having an organ in the new synagogue. The Board agreed to call such a meeting but expressed its own opposition to the organ proposal by a vote of four to one.

The special congregational meeting was held on July 26. Ninety members attended. By a vote of 56 to 31, Chazan Poznanski, who had decided not to attend, was invited to the meeting to express himself on the issue. Poznanski came and stated that he favored having an organ, cited a number of authorities to show that this was not in conflict with the Halacha, answered a number of questions, said he did not want the ensuing deliberations to be influenced by his presence and left.

A resolution was then introduced:

> Whereas, instrumental music, the universal language of the soul ... has been felt and cultivated by all nations..., be it resolved as the determination of this congregation that, as early as possible, an Organ shall be procured and erected in the new Synagogue, to be purchased by voluntary contributions and not drawn from congregational funds.

The Traditionalist presiding officer declared the resolution out of order. There was an appeal from the decision of the chair. The appeal was upheld, 47 to 40. Then the resolution was passed by a vote of 46 to 40.

The sizable minority felt that its synagogue constitutional rights had been violated. The constitution required that the worship of the congregation be according to Minhag Sephard which, the complainants maintained, forbade the use of the organ. A change in the constitution required a 75 percent affirmative vote. The majority insisted this was not a constitutional question because many Sephardic synagogues outside the United States had organs.

Rabbi Leeser suggested that the Traditionalists take out a civil injunction against the Beth Elohim majority to prevent it from purchasing an organ. Instead of heeding Leeser's advice, most of the minority withdrew and organized their own congregation, Shearith Israel. They put up a synagogue a few blocks from Beth Elohim.

On February 21, 1841, the Board of Beth Elohim officially accepted the organ as a gift to the congregation from a group of its members. The organ was played for the first time about a month later at the dedication of the new edifice.

This sequence of events caused deep bitterness between the two groups. The Traditionalists felt that Chazan Poznanski had betrayed them. Their feeling reached an unseemly pitch when some of the

Traditionalists spread a report that Beth Elohim's spiritual leader was, literally as well as figuratively, a bastard. There was not much that Beth Elohim could do to negate the figurative aspect of the charge; but it could and did take effective action on the literal accusation. It secured an affidavit from the synagogue in the town in Poland where Poznanski was born, an affidavit signed by the synagogue president and the rabbi, testifying that Gustavus Poznanski was of legitimate birth, the son of Joseph Poznanski, "a highly respectable gentleman and a pious Israelite," and his wife Sarah who, at the time of her marriage, was "a virtuous Jewish virgin" and that their marriage "took place according to the Jewish laws and with the usual ceremonies."

An irate Congregation Beth Elohim then retaliated by placing a new final article in its constitution:

> The organ, erected in the Synagogue, may be used on all occasions of Divine Service, and it shall not be in the power of any Parnass or President, or any other presiding officers, nor in that of the Board of Trustees, or any administration whatever, either to stop or suspend the use of said organ on any occasion whatever, unless sanctioned by three-fourths of the members living within one mile of the city.

A legal tug of war ensued between the Reformers of Beth Elohim on one side and the Traditionalists, consisting of the members of Shearith Israel and a minority of Beth Elohimites, on the other. The matter landed in the Court of Common Pleas of Charleston at the Spring term in 1844 when 45 members of the Reform group charged 41 members of the Traditionalist group with having "intruded themselves into the enjoyment of the liberties, privileges, and franchise of the members of a body corporate called the Charleston Jewish Congregation of Beth Elohim or House of God."

The Traditionalist defendants maintained that, by playing the organ on the Sabbath and by teaching concepts that contravened ancient Jewish traditions, the Reform accusers had forfeited their right to control Beth Elohim. The judge ruled that a civil court is without competence to deal with matters of religious belief and practice, but he added his personal opinion that the Traditionalists had intruded into the affairs of Congregation Beth Elohim to an extent that was obviously illegal.

The Traditionalists appealed this decision to the South Carolina Court of Appeals. The appeal was heard in that court in January 1845 and was ordered kept under study for one year. In January 1846 Judge A. P. Butler delivered the decision of the court majority, a lengthy opinion sustaining the lower court. The opinion stated that use of the organ did not constitute a basic change in the synagogal ritual, but was merely a change in the manner in which the ritual was conducted. Judge Butler uttered these ponderous words:

The granite promontory in the deep may stand firm and un-
changed amidst the waves and storms that beat upon it, but human
institutions cannot withstand the agitations of free, active, and
progressive opinion. Whilst laws are stationary, things are progressive. Any system of laws that should be made without the principle
of expansibility, that would, in some measure, accommodate them
to the progression of events, would have within it the seeds of
mischief and violence.

This ended the legal struggle, with the Reform group in complete
control of Beth Elohim and its organ and with the Traditionalist minority
of Beth Elohim becoming members of Shearith Israel.

A third congregation, Orthodox, was organized in Charleston in
1855, with a German and Polish membership and following the Ashkenazic mode of worship. The unhappy situation of having two technically Sephardic congregations in a community big enough for only one
came to an end at the close of the Civil War. During the shelling of
Charleston by the Union forces, both Sephardic synagogues were
damaged, Shearith Israel worse than Beth Elohim. The war caused a
number of Charleston's Jewish "first families" to leave the city and many
of those who remained were in financial distress. As the years had gone
by the new generation at Shearith Israel had become much more liberal
religiously than were their fathers. Many of them had concluded that the
quarrel over the organ was rather foolish.

So in 1866 Congregation Shearith Israel was merged into Congregation Beth Elohim. The Shearith Israel synagogue was sold. It is still
standing and now houses a Roman Catholic church with a predominantly
black membership. The reunited congregation repaired the Beth Elohim
structure—and at every service ever since organ music has accompanied
the singing and the praying.

The 1841 synagogue building endures but the 1841 organ wore out
long ago. The organ now in use at Beth Elohim is organ #3, installed in
1912.

YOULI TO LEVY TO YULEE

(1845)

David Levy Yulee, the first Jew to serve in the United States Senate,
was Senator from Florida from 1845 to 1851 and again from 1855 to 1861.
There are those, including his son and his biographer in the *Dictionary of
American Biography,* who assert that he left Judaism and became a
Presbyterian; but there is no firm evidence that this is so and there are

indications that his son and his *Dictionary* biographer were trying to tone down the fact that Yulee was of Jewish extraction.

❖   ❖   ❖   ❖   ❖

Here is the story.

David Levy Yulee's grandfather was a Muslim named Jacoub ibn Youli, a functionary in the court of Sidi Muhammed ibn Abdallah, Sultan of Morocco from 1757 to 1790. During his long reign Sidi Muhammed improved the conditions in his country somewhat, but that is not saying very much. From the sixteenth to the nineteenth centuries the nation of Morocco cut itself off almost completely from the rest of the world and continued to live as it had lived for a thousand years, despite the great changes taking place elsewhere, especially in Europe and North America. Sidi Muhammed maintained some contacts with the outside; but oceanic piracy, holding European prisoners for ransom and the enslavement of the unransomed continued throughout his reign. He was one of the first heads of state to recognize the infant United States of America and for this he received a letter of thanks from President Washington. When he died in 1790, a bloody power struggle began within his court. For two years the country was in absolute chaos until Sultan Suleiman ascended the throne and restored a semblance of order.

Rachel Levy, daughter of an English Jewish physician, was captured by Moroccan pirates while en route to the British West Indies. She was taken to the slave market at Fez, sold to Jacoub ibn Youli, and added to his harem. Youli lived at Mogador, which was probably Sidi Abdullah's summer capital. Here a son was born to Rachel. Ibn Youli was probably killed during the 1790-92 power struggle. Rachel, again pregnant, and her son managed to escape to Gibraltar. In Gibraltar Rachel gave birth to a daughter. From there Rachel and her children went to England. In England Rachel resumed her maiden name. Her son was given the name Moses Elias Levy.

In 1800 Moses Elias Levy, now grown to manhood, migrated with his mother and sister to St. Thomas, Virgin Islands, where he went into the lumber business and married a Sephardi, Hannah Abendanone. David Levy was born in St. Thomas on June 2, 1810. By that time his father had become a wealthy lumberman.

In 1815 the British gave the island to Denmark. This may have had something to do with Moses Levy's quitting St. Thomas in 1816 for Havana, Cuba, where he served as a contractor for the Spanish government. Levy now became interested in land speculation in Florida and dreamed a beautiful dream. He would go to Florida, buy a large tract of land, and establish a refuge for the oppressed Jews of Europe. According to a contemporary Floridian, Prince Achille Murat, son of the late King of

Naples and nephew of Napoleon, Levy was "a Hebrew visionary who desired to establish in Florida a colony for Israelites, provided that he be permitted to substitute Deuteronomy for the common law and the Prophets for statute law."

In 1818 Levy came to Florida and acquired 89,000 acres of land in Alachua and Marion counties, ten miles south of Gainesville in the area now surrounding the town of Micanopy and adjacent to Levy Lake. Here he established a plantation which, according to some, he called Pilgrimage, symbolic of a refugee's journey from spiritual bondage to spiritual freedom, and, according to others, he named Parthenope, in tribute to the short-lived and ill-fated republic of that name in Naples, Italy, in 1799. This alleged honoring of a brief experiment in European democracy plus Levy's deep-seated hatred of the institution of slavery caused him to be labeled a "religious socialist" by David Levy Yulee's *Dictionary* biographer.

In 1819 Levy placed his sons Elias and David in the private boarding school of a Protestant clergyman in Norfolk, Virginia. In 1820 he left Philadelphia for Europe to recruit Jewish settlers for his Florida colony. He returned to Philadelphia in 1821 with five Jewish males, three Jewish wives, and fifteen indentured servants. This immigrant party reached St. Augustine shortly after Spain turned Florida over to the United States. Levy took his Europeans to Pilgrimage, helped them build homes and clear the land. He had a cargo of sugar roots and plant seeds brought in from Cuba. With these the colonists were to initiate the growing of sugar cane and tropical fruits. A road was cut through the forest to connect the colony with the St. Johns River and the town of St. Augustine.

At about this same time Levy wrote a letter to Congregation Shearith Israel in New York City proposing that a Jewish academy of higher learning be established in New York and stating he would help support such an academy. Presumably he was interested in having his sons study in a Jewish-oriented school. A committee was formed in New York to study the proposal but nothing came of it.

The same fate overtook Levy's Florida Jewish colony. After a brief experience of laboring to bring forth sugar cane and tropical fruits, the colonists decided that agricultural life was not for them. They departed for the North and went into various businesses in New York and Philadelphia.

Levy refused to admit defeat. He bought 50,000 additional acres in Volusia County on both sides of the St. Johns River, south of Lake George in the vicinity of the present village of Astor. On this land he built a beautiful home, named Hope Hill, indicative perhaps of his determination to make his dream come true. He went back to Europe a second time, tried to find more Jewish colonists, and found none. After this vain effort he abandoned his dream.

David and Elias studied in Norfolk until 1826 and then entered Harvard College. After about a year their father ordered them to return home. It seems that he had been informed that they had abandoned their religious heritage and were associating exclusively with Christians. He put his sons in charge of the plantation at Pilgrimage while he continued to reside at Hope Hill and manage the plantation there.

Moses Levy had now become an ardent crusader for the abolition of slavery. When he discovered to his great dismay that his sons shared neither his love of Judaism nor his abhorrence of slavery, he attempted to convince them that they were wrong. When this failed, he disowned them and ordered them to get out. The further activities of Elias are not recorded; but David's career is spelled out clearly on the pages of Florida's history.

David went to work in a law office in St. Augustine, studied hard and in 1832 was admitted to the Florida bar. He then became extremely active in territorial politics. A natural born leader, he was given important governmental assignments. First he was appointed Clerk of the territorial legislature. Soon thereafter he was elected a member of that body. He was a delegate to the Constitutional Convention at Tallahassee in 1840-41 and then was sent to the U.S. Congress as the representative of the Territory of Florida. Here he directed the strategy that won statehood for the territory. He is referred to by Florida's historians as "the key architect" in the achievement of this goal.

On March 3, 1845, Florida was admitted to the Union. One week later, in grateful recognition of Levy's efforts in the cause of statehood, the Florida legislature named a newly formed county on the west coast Levy County and suggested that its county seat be named Levyville. The suggestion was not heeded. The village of Bronson was chosen as the county seat.

The state legislature was empowered to select the state's first U.S. Senators, one for a six-year term and the other for four years. On July 1, 1845, by a vote of 41 to 16, David Levy was selected as Florida's first six-year Senator. Shortly thereafter, newly elected Senator Levy petitioned the state legislature to permit him to change his name to David Levy Yulee. Permission was granted.

Why did the Senator change his name? He was already well-known in Washington as David Levy. The reason is not clear. David had just become engaged to the beautiful daughter of Postmaster General Charles A. Wickliffe, former Governor of Kentucky. Miss Wickliffe was an ardent Christian. It has been said that the change was made to please Miss Wickliffe because she did not wish to go down in history as a Mrs. Levy. If this is so, it should have been easy for her to persuade David to drop the name Levy entirely, especially since he and his father, Moses Levy, were not on speaking terms. But David did not remove the Levy from his name. He simply added the name Yulee. Whatever the motive, David Levy had decided to take as his surname a reasonable facsimile of what he must have mistakenly thought was the family name of his Jewish father's Muslim father.

Yulee and his bride took up residence in Fernandina, a town on the Atlantic coast just south of the Georgia border. Some years later a village ten miles west of Fernandina was named Yulee in his honor.

Senator Yulee was a political conservative, a firm believer in State's rights and in the infallibility of the doctrine that blacks are an inferior race and fit only to be slaves. He became chairman of the Naval Affairs Committee in 1846 and, in this capacity, opposed strongly but unsuccessfully the 1849-50 efforts of Uriah P. Levy and Senator Hale to have flogging abolished in the United States Navy.

Yulee advocated the building of a railroad across northern Florida from the Atlantic Ocean to the Gulf of Mexico to make unnecessary the long journey of cargo vessels from the east to the west coast of Florida. This advocacy brought about his defeat for reelection to the Senate. The citizens of southern Florida feared that Yulee's proposed railroad would adversely affect their section's economic future.

This did not prevent the construction of the railroad. The Florida Railroad Company, later named the Atlantic, Gulf Coast, and West Indies Railroad Company, was chartered in 1853. Yulee was named president. The cross-state route chosen by the railroad company was, to say the least, a tribute to the Yulee influence. It began on the Atlantic coast at Fernandina, ran through Yulee to Callahan, then turned south to Gainesville. Here it veered southwest and traveled right through the heart of Levy County and ended at Cedar Key on the Gulf Coast. Work got underway in 1855. By 1858 the track had been constructed from Fernandina almost to Gainesville. The Civil War halted its completion. The railway was finally finished all the way to Cedar Key in 1867.

In 1854 Moses Elias Levy died. He showed his ill will toward Elias and David by leaving them only $100 each and bequeathing the bulk of his estate to his two daughters. The sons contested the will and broke it. The court decided that each of the four children should receive an equal share of the estate.

Yulee was again elected to the Senate in 1855. On January 10, 1861, Florida seceded from the Union. On January 21 Senator Yulee resigned from the Senate. He did not participate wholeheartedly in the War between the States. Although he had ardently defended slavery and State's rights, he was not enthusiastic about the splitting of the federal Union. This helps explain the action of the Governor of Florida on May 13, 1865. He appointed Yulee one of five commissioners to go to Washington to negotiate the readmittance of Florida to the Union. The governor must have felt that, because Yulee had abstained from complete involvement in the war, he would be among the state's political figures most acceptable to the federal government.

The governor's assumption was incorrect. When martial law was proclaimed in Florida in late May, Yulee was seized by federal troops and sent to the military prison at Fort Pulaski in Savannah. No formal charge was ever filed against him. Through the intercession of General Ulysses S. Grant he was released in the spring of 1866.

Yulee never again sought public office. He devoted himself to developing Florida's railroads. Having acquired much wealth, he retired in 1880 and moved to Washington, D.C. His wife died in 1884. He died in New York City on October 10, 1886. His funeral was held in the New York Avenue Presbyterian Church in Washington. He was buried in the Georgetown Cemetery.

Yulee showed no interest in Jewish affairs. His children were reared as Christians. Yet no evidence has thus far been forthcoming to prove that he ever formally converted to Christianity or that he was regarded by his political and business associates, before he changed his name and after, as being anything but Jewish. Perhaps the best proofs of this are found in the diary of Yulee's Congressional colleague, ex-President John Quincy Adams, and in a statement attributed to the U. S. Senator from Tennessee, later President, Andrew Johnson.

Under date of June 12, 1841, Adams wrote:

> David Levy's qualifications for American citizenship have been examined and found to be satisfactory. Levy is said to be a Jew, and what will be, if true, a far more formidable disqualification, is said to have a dash of African blood in him, which, sub rosa, is the case with more than one member of the House.

On May 16, 1842, the same source refers to Levy as "the Jew delegate from Florida," and, on May 25, 1842, "the alien Jew delegate from Florida." Like his father, John Quincy Adams was on the liberal side of most issues. Like his father, John Quincy Adams was an intellectual anti-Semite. John Adams and John Quincy Adams did not like Jews; but, à la Voltaire, they were ready to fight to the death to defend the rights of all human beings, even those they did not like.

Historian Charles Francis Adams, son of John Quincy Adams, reports that Senator Andrew Johnson once said to him:

> There is that Yulee, miserable little cuss! I remember him in the House—the contemptible little Jew standing there and begging us— Yes! begging us to let Florida in as a state. Well, we let her in, and took good care of her, and fought her Indians; and now that despicable little beggar stands up in the Senate and talks about *her* rights!

✿   ✿   ✿   ✿   ✿

Yulee was not the last of this variety of ethnic Jew to gain prominence in Florida politics. From 1932 to 1936 David Sholtz, reared as an Orthodox Jew in Brooklyn, New York, and a leading attorney of Daytona Beach, was the able "New Deal" governor of Florida. He, too, married a non-Jew. His children, too, were reared as Christians. He was listed in *Who's Who* as a Congregationalist.

Early in 1942 I was introduced to ex-governor Sholtz by a mutual Jewish friend, a Daytona Beach attorney, who had assured me that Sholtz definitely considered himself a Jew. After the introduction, I smiled and said to Sholtz, "Shalom aleychem." Without the slightest hesitation, Sholtz responded, "Aleychem shalom." "Bist a Yid? [Are you really Jewish?]" I asked. "Vu den? [What else?]" Sholtz replied. "So why are you listed in *Who's Who* as a Congregationalist?" I asked. Sholtz laughed. "Oh, that," he said. "Don't believe everything you read, rabbi. Politics, that's all it is, just politics. If you ever want to find out whether I'm really Jewish or not, have your wife fix some blintzes and gefilte fish and invite me to dinner and watch me eat!"

THE BEWITCHED BOAT
(c. 1850)

This is a bit of pre-Civil War Americana about a Southern Jewish slave dealer and a black slave who cast a spell upon his means of conveyance to keep him from separating the slave from her daughter. The story was told to Susan B. Morton of Haymarket, Virginia, in 1939 by Elizabeth Carter, who heard it from her grandfather, Josiah Conklin of Potts Creek, Virginia.

Rod Collins, who lived near Lynchburg, was a notorious gambler. Once, in a poker game with Dick Greer and some other fellows, he lost more money than he had, but he promised to pay them back later. Old Dick was hardhearted and ornery and Rod was afraid of him, so he knew he had to find the money to pay him soon.

Now this was back before the War between the States and Rod had a big farm which he worked with slaves. One of them was a wizened old crone who was reputed to be a witch, but she had the prettiest young daughter you ever saw. Her name was Betsy; and soon after Rod lost his money in the poker game, a slave buyer from Norfolk named Abe Goldstein came by and saw Betsy. He knew he could get a high price for

From *The Silver Bullet and Other American Witch Stories*, edited by Hubert J. Davis, Jonathan David Publishers, New York, 1975.

her, so he sounded Rod out about selling her. Rod had never thought about selling any of his slaves, but this seemed like too good a chance to get some ready cash to miss, especially as Dick Greer had told him he wanted his money soon or it would be too bad for Rod. So he sold Betsy to Abe for a good sum.

Abe took Betsy and the other slaves he'd bought down to the river and loaded them on his boat, put his supplies on board, cast off, and prepared to set off down the James to Norfolk. Well, sir, that boat wouldn't move an inch. They pushed it, they pulled it, they pried it, and they swore at it, but it just stuck there like it was frozen in an ice cake. They unloaded the supplies and tried again, but the boat wouldn't move. Then they unloaded some of the slaves, but again it didn't budge. Then they took off more slaves, Betsy among them, and the boat floated right away.

Of course, there was no doubt about it that that boat had been hagged. But Abe was hardheaded and stubborn, and didn't give up easy. So he reloaded the boat with everything and everybody except Betsy and sent it down the river. Then he bought him a buggy and two good horses and prepared to take her to Norfolk by land. He loaded his buggy, told Betsy to get in, climbed in himself, and told the horses to "giddup." The horses started to pull, but their feet began to slip and that buggy didn't move an inch. Abe got out and told Betsy to get out, too, and the buggy moved with no trouble 'tall. So Abe knew the buggy had been hagged also.

But Abe wasn't about to give up. He unhitched the horses, told Betsy to get up on one and he mounted the other. But when he said "giddup," his horse moved off, leaving Betsy's standing like a statue. So Abe switched horses with Betsy, but her horse still wouldn't move an inch.

This time Abe gave up in disgust, hitched the horses to the buggy and drove off, leaving Betsy to find her way back to Rod Collins' farm. He knew he'd been swindled and decided it must have been Betsy's mother who had bewitched the boat, the buggy, and the horses so he couldn't take her away.

General Grant's Order Number Eleven
(1862)

The first 40 years of the life of Hiram Ulysses Grant were neither happy nor successful. When he was sixteen he was a hard-working farmhand; and that was what he wanted to continue to be. His father had other ideas. He got his son an appointment to the United States Military

Academy, which Hiram Ulysses Grant entered very unwillingly. Through a clerical error his entrance papers listed him as Ulysses Simpson Grant; and Ulysses Simpson Grant he became for the rest of his life. This change in name resulted in his being nicknamed Uncle Sam while he was at West Point and in his being dubbed, after his victory at Fort Donelson in February 1862, "Unconditional Surrender" Grant.

Grant was graduated from the Academy in 1843, served with distinction in the Mexican War, did not like Army life because it separated him from his wife for long periods, resigned his commission in 1854, and returned to his earlier occupation, farming. He failed at running his own farm. He then failed as a real estate salesman. He then failed as a professional bill collector. He then went to work for his younger brothers as a salesman in their leather goods store. This is where he was when the Civil War broke out.

He immediately offered to return to active military duty. By the end of June 1861, he was a colonel; by the end of August, a brigadier general. Until his victory at Vicksburg, July 4, 1863, Grant's career as a commanding general had its ups and downs, more downs than ups. His generalship at Shiloh in April 1862 was so bad that he was relieved from command and given no combat assignment for five months. In September he returned to combat duty as commander of the Union forces in the campaign being waged in Tennessee and Mississippi. In October he tried unsuccessfully to capture Vicksburg. He came to believe that one of the contributing factors to the failure of this effort was that the movements of his troops were being hampered by cotton buyers who followed on the heels of his Army wherever it went. Many of the overly zealous businessmen were Jews.

These militarily undesirable individuals were described by Rabbi Simon Tuska of Memphis as "greedy birds of prey." They caused Grant, beset by many problems, to commit a grave blunder. Harried into imagining that all the Jews in his military area were a pack of troublemakers, he issued a series of orders for which, in later life, he tried diligently to disclaim major responsibility.

On November 9 he instructed his units to refuse all permits to traders, and especially Jewish traders, to work in the vicinity of the Mississippi battle zone. On November 10 he ordered the railroads in his area to discontinue selling tickets to any Jew desiring to travel southward. As if these biased actions were not sufficiently senseless, on December 11 he issued his odious Order Number Eleven, expelling all Jews from the territory under his control. In his dealings with Jewish military personnel and during his later eight years as President, Grant never displayed the slightest sign of anti-Jewish prejudice. This 1862 blot on an otherwise exemplary record of lack of religious bigotry must be regarded as the impulsive reaction of a distraught general to almost unendurable criticism resulting from a series of military reverses.

* * * * *

Cincinnati and Paducah became the storm centres of the Jewish reaction mainly by reason of their proximity to Grant's field of operations. The agitation eventually extended to the halls of Congress. Rabbi I. M. Wise in the *American Israelite* demanded the recall of the order on the ground that "the President had an oath registered in Heaven to enforce the laws," and he urged that justice should be demanded from the chief magistrate of the country. A Jewish captain serving in a New York regiment wrote the New York *Jewish Messenger* urging that the President compel General Grant to apologize or dismiss him from the service.

The Jews of Paducah transmitted the following appeal to President Lincoln:

Paducah, Kentucky, December 29, 1862.

Hon. Abraham Lincoln, President of the United States,
General Order No. 11 issued by General Grant at Oxford, Mississippi, December the 17th, commands all post commanders to expel all Jews without distinction within twenty-four hours from his entire Department. The undersigned good and loyal citizens of the United States and residents of this town, for many years engaged in legitimate business as merchants, feel greatly insulted and outraged by this inhuman order; the carrying out of which would be the grossest violation of the Constitution and our rights as good citizens under it, and would place us as outlaws before the world. We respectfully ask your immediate attention to this enormous outrage on all law and humanity and pray for your effectual and immediate interposition. We would especially refer you to the post commander and post adjutant as to our loyalty, and to all respectable citizens of this community as to our standing as citizens and merchants. We respectfully ask for immediate instructions to be sent to the Commander of this Post.

Cesar Kaskel, a prominent Jewish citizen of Paducah, was delegated to go to Washington to place the matter directly before the President. He arrived at the National Capital on the evening of January 3, 1863. Accompanied by Representative Gurley of Ohio, the two at once sought an audience with the President, reaching the White House at about dusk. Having announced their presence, with an apology for calling at such an

---

Part of this account is an abbreviated version of an article by Isaac Markens in Volume 17 (1909) of the Publications of the American Jewish Historical Society.

hour, the President sent word that he was "always glad to see his friends," and shortly made an appearance. On learning the object of their visit, he remarked, "And so the children of Israel were driven from the happy land of Canaan?" "Yes," replied Kaskel, "and that is why we have come unto Father Abraham's bosom, asking protection." "And this protection they shall have at once," said Lincoln. Seating himself at a table the President penned an order to General Halleck, Commanding General of all the Union forces, requesting his visitors to deliver it to General Halleck at once. Halleck refused to believe in the existence of Grant's order until Kaskel showed him an official copy. Halleck's instruction to Grant was delayed in transmission and so the latter's revocation of Order Number 11 did not appear until January 7. Two weeks later Halleck wrote to Grant:

> The President has no objection to your expelling traitors and Jew peddlers which I suppose was the object of your order, but, as it was expressed in terms proscribing an entire religious class, some of whom are fighting in our ranks, the President deemed it necessary to revoke it.

Before the result of Kaskel's mission became known, Rabbis Wise and Max Lilienthal of Cincinnati, accompanied by Edgar M. Johnson, a Cincinnati lawyer, Martin Bijur, a Louisville lawyer, and Abraham Goldsmith, a Paducah merchant, went to Washington. En route they learned of Kaskel's success. Nevertheless they decided to complete the journey to express their thanks to the President for his prompt action. Rabbi Wise wrote in the *Israelite:*

> We went to the White House in our traveling habiliments and spoke about half an hour to the President of the United States in an open and frank manner and were dismissed in the same simple style. Having expressed our thanks for his promptness and despatch in revoking Grant's order, the President gave utterance to his surprise that such an order should have been issued. "I don't like to see a class or nationality condemned on account of a few sinners," he said. The President fully convinced us that he knows of no distinction between Jews and Gentiles and that he feels no prejudice against any nationality and especially against the Israelites. We had little chance to say anything, the President being so splendidly eloquent on this occasion. He spoke like a simple, plain citizen and tried in various forms to convince us of the sincerity of his words on this matter.

Disregarding the revocation of the order, Senator Powell of Kentucky offered a resolution in the Senate on January 5 condemning Grant's order as "illegal, tyrannical, cruel and unjust"; but, considering the matter settled, the Senate tabled the resolution. During the discussion of his proposal, Senator Powell stated he had documents that would establish beyond the possibility of a doubt that some thirty Jewish gentlemen, residents of Paducah, were driven from their homes and their businesses by virtue of this order of General Grant. They had only the short notice of four and twenty hours. The Jewish women and children of the city were expelled under this order. Not a Jew, man, woman or child was left, except two women who were prostrate on beds of sickness. Powell continued:

> If we tamely submit to allow the military power thus to encroach on the rights of the citizens, we shall be setting a bad and most pernicious example to those in command of our Army. General Grant might just as well expel the Baptists or the Methodists or the Episcopalians or the Catholics as a class, as to expel the Jews. All are alike protected in the enjoyment of their religion by the Constitution of our country. They are inoffensive citizens and it is set forth in papers that I have before me that two of the Jews who were expelled had served three months in the Army of the United States in defence of the Union cause. It may be that some Jews in General Grant's department have been guilty of illegal traffic. If this be so, let those who have violated the law be expelled and punished.

Did Grant issue this obnoxious edict of his own volition or at the behest of higher authority? The Cincinnati *Commercial*, after the affair was over, published a communication intimating that Grant had acted on orders from Washington. The *Israelite* was of the opinion that such an order could have come only from Secretary of War Stanton or Secretary of the Treasury Chase, since the President and Halleck absolutely maintained that they knew nothing of it until seventeen days after it was issued.

In his *Personal Memoirs,* Grant makes no reference to Order Number 11. On December 8, 1907, his son, Frederick D. Grant, wrote to me [Markens] as follows:

> In reply to your letter of November 23, I write to say that when my father was writing his memoirs I asked if he would refer to the order No. 11 about which you enquire in your letter. He replied that that was a matter long past and best not referred to. Therefore, following his example, I shall have nothing to say about that order.

THE YOM KIPPUR MIRACLE
(1864)

This incident occurred during the American Civil War.

A battle was being fought on Yom Kippur in the state of Virginia. The conflict was being waged with great ferocity. The plight of the Northern soldiers was desperate. They were outnumbered but they fought bravely. One of these soldiers was a Jewish captain, Aaron Green. He was a German immigrant. Green loved the Jewish religion and faithfully observed the laws of the Torah. He was devoted to President Abraham Lincoln and the principles of human rights that Lincoln had enunciated. Furthermore Green knew that the Torah states that every human being has been created in the image of God. Therefore he believed that this war which was being carried on to bring freedom to the blacks of the South was, according to the teachings of the Torah, a righteous struggle.

On this Yom Kippur day Green fought with all his might. From the Eve of Yom Kippur he fought without eating any food or drinking any water. His effort was so strenuous that he became weak from lack of nourishment. Suddenly his knees buckled under him and he fell to the ground in a faint. His comrades raised him up and revived him. One attempted to give him a drink of water. Green said, "Thank you; but I must refuse. I am not permitted to drink. Today is my Day of Atonement, a holy fast day of the Jews; and I am forbidden to eat or to drink."

Later that day Captain Green was wounded and was taken to a field hospital. In the next bed to his was a soldier who was eating. Green recognized him. He was a Jewish soldier. Green said to him, "What are you doing? Have you forgotten that today is Yom Kippur and that we are not allowed to eat? How can you account yourself worthy to be a faithful follower of President Lincoln if you do not revere your God and observe His commandments?"

As soon as he could, Captain Green gathered together a minyan of ten Jews to form a congregation for prayer. As Green and his companions

---

This story appeared in 1894 in the High Holy Day issue of the Hebrew journal *Hatsefira*, published in Warsaw, Poland, under the editorship of the famed Zionist writer, Nachum Sokoloff. It was repeated, in September 1977, in the young people's Hebrew magazine, *Olam Hadash*, published in New York under the editorship of Asher Wolk. The story, written in simple Hebrew by A. R. Malachi for the youthful readers of *Olam Hadash*, has been translated for inclusion here. If the story is true, it could only have happened on Yom Kippur in 1864 in connection with one of the numerous infantry skirmishes during the siege of Petersburg, Virginia.

poured out their hearts before God, the sounds of battle could be heard clearly. Despite his pain, Green acted as leader of the worship service.

When the sun went down Green called out with all his strength the traditional words which bring the Yom Kippur prayers to a close. He called out seven times, "The Lord, He is God! The Lord, He is God!" As he finished reciting these words for the seventh time, a messenger came running from the battlefield with the news that the enemy ranks had just broken and the enemy soldiers were fleeing in seven different directions. The Jewish soldiers were overjoyed. Together they recited the first words which Jews say to each other at the end of this solemn day: "May we be privileged to celebrate next Yom Kippur in our holy city of Jerusalem!"

The inhabitants of the town near which the battle had been fought heard of the prayers of the Jewish soldiers. They believed that the prayers of Captain Green had gone straight up to Heaven and had been heard by God and that it had been God Himself Who smote the enemy. The following Sunday a Christian chaplain paraphrased at his church service the statement in the Book of Samuel about Saul and David:

> Our commanding general has vanquished thousands of our adversaries; but Captain Green has vanquished tens of thousands! Not since the days of the Hasmoneans has such a great and holy military miracle occurred as that which our hero, Aaron Green, has brought about in plain view of all of us!

THE BELOVED JEW
(1886)

For many years he was the only Jew in Boone County, Kentucky. He lived in a village of less than 300 inhabitants, a simple, kindly man who peddled household goods among the country families of the surrounding area. He never married. To his neighbors and friends he had about him almost a Messianic aura—he was wise; he was good; he was deeply religious; he was a mystic; to the very end of his life there was a sense of mystery about him. Yet withal, he was very human. He laughed often. He was pleasant company. He loved people.

What his name may have been originally is not known. He was born in eastern Europe in 1827. When he was a small boy, the Jews in his little town were accused of murdering a Christian child and using its blood in a Jewish ritual. The aroused peasants attacked the Jews, burned down their synagogue, killed many innocent people, including his parents and baby sister. He was saved by a great-aunt who took him to another town and put him in the care of his grandfather. After his Bar Mitzvah he left the ghetto, wandered about Europe and finally came to London where he lived for a number of years. In London he took the name of Felix Moses.

Then he traveled by ship to New Orleans. At New Orleans he boarded a steamboat that was going up the Mississippi and Ohio rivers. He got off the steamboat at Ghent, Kentucky, just before it reached Cincinnati. What prompted him to get off the boat at Ghent, no one knows. For a pious Jew, one accustomed to living among his own people, this was literally the middle of nowhere, a desolate, sparsely inhabited area, populated by well-meaning but illiterate and superstitious whites and blacks.

He trudged along the dirt road leading from Ghent toward Covington, trying to sell the items of merchandise carried in the pack strapped to his back. He had a number of narrow escapes from death because he did not understand the ways of the backwoodsmen and they did not comprehend either his broken English or his strange ways. The worst experience was when he came face to face with a fanatically religious giant of a man who had never seen a Jew but had sworn that, if he were ever to meet one, he would kill him because his preacher had said that the Jews killed his god. This would have been the end of Felix Moses if others who were present had not persuaded the fanatic that this particular Jew was not involved in the deicide.

After that, Moses decided it would be better if he found a permanent place of abode from which to conduct his peripatetic business. For this purpose he selected the Williams House, a tavern in the village of Florence, ten miles from Covington, on the mud road that ran from Covington to Lexington. That road is now covered by a broad band of concrete known as the Dixie Highway. By 1859 Moses owned a horse and wagon which made it much safer and easier for him to travel about to dispose of his merchandise.

In 1930 John Uri Lloyd, a native of Florence and a professor at the University of Cincinnati, published a book about Moses titled *Felix Moses, the Beloved Jew of Stringtown on the Pike*. The latter was the designation given by Lloyd to his hometown because, said he, Florence was just a bunch of little houses strung along a pike.

Lloyd wrote:

> In 1859 Felix Moses, who had made our village his home, came to be called "Old Mose," not because of his age, which was not known to us, nor was he what might be termed old, but rather as a familiar and endearing term, applied to a person loved by everyone. From a mere pack peddler he had now become the proprietor of a one-horse covered spring wagon, in the possession of which he took

great pride. To have carried the load of household items he purchased in the city for the accommodation of his customers or the
produce he picked up on a return trip would have been impossible
for a pack peddler. To him the whole county of Boone and adjacent
country had become familiar. With his covered wagon he passed
through the country, visiting alike the home of wealth and the forest
cabins where little could be purchased or offered in trade. Perhaps a
few coon skins were the sole assets of the cabin dweller.

His aim seemed to be to bring the pleasure of human fellowship
and good will to homes where a visitor seldom found his way, where
the cheer of his countenance lighted the day for the inmates. What
was needed by them he bought in the city and delivered, asking no
immediate payment. He kept no book accounts, accepting that
others would deal honestly with him as he did with them. He seemed
amply repaid by the welcome he received, the pleasure his coming
brought, especially to the children, who looked eagerly for the sight
of Old Mose on the day he might be expected. He took more pains, if
possible, to serve the poor than those in better circumstances.
Perhaps he considered that a family living in an out-of-the-way
place was his especial care.

In religion he remained a Jew, though, so far as the narrator
knows, he had no close Jewish companions outside those living in
Cincinnati and Covington. If he had any concern in the religious
debates or creeds of the village churches, he made no exhibition of
the fact. He attended alike the different churches, and to all he
contributed liberally when the contribution box was passed. With
politics he did not meddle. Even in the critical days of 1859 and 1860,
when men's souls were racked by conflicting interests and opinions,
Mose went on his way as huckster and peddler, welcome alike to the
homes of those who sympathized with the South and those who
believed in the cause of the North.

Later on Lloyd states that on the Jewish High Holydays Moses attended
services in one of the Cincinnati synagogues.

Even though Moses did not discuss the tense political situation
publicly, he was strongly attracted to the southern side. In April 1861, just
after Fort Sumter fell, Moses drove to Covington and then crossed over
to Cincinnati on the ferry. First he went to his good Jewish friend, Mr.
March, told him he was going to enlist in the Confederate Army and that,
if he was killed, he wanted Mr. March to have him buried in a Jewish
cemetery. Then he paid a visit to Rabbi Isaac M. Wise. To Rabbi Wise he
entrusted for safekeeping a valuable diamond given him by his grandfather when he left his ghetto home. If he did not return, Rabbi Wise was
to sell the diamond and give the proceeds to charity.

Because northern Kentucky was occupied by Union troops, Moses
had a difficult time getting to the Confederate forces. First he headed for
Lexington to try to enlist in the Lexington Rifles, organized in 1857 by
Captain John H. Morgan, later to become famous as the leader of
"Morgan's Raiders." When Moses was prevented from getting to Lex-

ington by the omnipresent Kentucky Home Guard, a Union outfit, he set out to join a Boone County rifle company that was part of General Buckner's force at Bowling Green. It was a long journey that was made even longer by the circuitous route Moses had to take to avoid detection. A fellow soldier, writing later to Professor Lloyd, describes what happened:

> Some time in December [1861] I was roused early one morning by loud cries and confusion. Everyone seemed happy. On investigating, I saw Mose walking into camp, hat in hand, covered with mud to his knees. He had traveled through southern Indiana and Illinois, passing himself off as a purchaser of sheep pelts and coon skins, finally reaching Bowling Green after many trials and difficulties. He joined the Company immediately and soon became a great favorite with all his comrades. He was a brave and gallant soldier. A better and truer friend no man ever had.

In the battle of Fort Donelson, fought in Tennessee about 100 miles southwest of Bowling Green, February 13-16, 1862, the Union forces of General U. S. Grant defeated the Confederates under General Buckner and compelled them to surrender unconditionally. Moses and his comrades were imprisoned on Johnson's Island, near Sandusky, Ohio.

Of these prison days it has been written,

> His island prison companions constantly spoke of Moses as having lightened their gloom by means of his inexhaustible stories and his wonderful satires on the Yankees, with whom, for this very droll freedom of tongue, he became a favorite. The guards came to love Old Mose, to exchange anecdotes with him, to enjoy his company, and for these reasons were led to lighten, when possible, the conditions of other prisoners.

In late 1862 Moses was released in an exchange of prisoners. He enlisted promptly in Company G, Ninth Kentucky Cavalry, part of Morgan's Raiders. The Raiders invaded Kentucky five times. On one of these occasions the daring cavalrymen occupied Frankfurt, the state capital, for a short time. The United States flag was flying from the front flagstaff of the Capitol building but the cupola flagstaff was empty. The Confederate troopers did not disturb the American flag; but Felix proposed that a Confederate flag be put on the empty flagstaff. One of the cavalrymen reported later:

> A rebel flag was procured. To climb the cupola was an arduous feat, but was at last accomplished by Felix and his companion. For the first and only time the rebel flag floated over the Capitol of Kentucky. Tired out but safe, the two men came down and rested on the grass of the lawn. Old Mose laughed aloud as he rolled over on the soft turf. "What are you laughing at?" he was asked. "It took us

fellers two hours to get dot flag up." "Well, what is so funny about that?" "I vas laughing at vat fools vee bees. It took us two hours to put dot flag up, but it won't take the Yankees ven dey comes two minutes to shoot it down." Just then came the sound of the bugle. Soon the raiders passed on toward Lexington. The prediction of Mose was soon verified.

In 1864 Moses was able to get back to Florence for a brief leave. At the conclusion of the furlough, as he was endeavoring to make his way back to the Raiders, he was captured by a Federal scouting party and became a prisoner of war a second time. He was confined in the military prison at Rock Island, Illinois, and there he stayed until the war ended. He returned to Florence in rags, half starved and penniless. The people of Florence, grateful that he had survived, fed and clothed him and bought him another horse and wagon. Old Mose was back in business.

In 1886 Moses told his friends he was going to Louisville for a week's vacation. He would go and return by steamboat. Outside of spending the High Holydays in Cincinnati, this was the first time since coming to America that he had allowed himself the luxury of a vacation. The week passed. Moses did not return. More weeks passed. One day the Cincinnati *Enquirer* reported that the body of an unidentified man had been washed ashore on the Ohio River near Rising Sun, Indiana. Fearing the worst, several men went from Florence to Rising Sun to look at the corpse. It was that of Felix Moses. There were no marks of violence. The contents of his purse were intact. The hands on his watch had stopped at 10:55, presumably the time of night when he fell, or possibly jumped, from the steamer. Whether his death was accidental or deliberate will never be known. Those who knew him best believed that Old Mose was not the kind of person who would commit suicide.

The people of Florence wanted their beloved Jew to rest among their own dead. As they were preparing for the funeral service and burial, Mr. March of Cincinnati appeared and informed them that their cherished friend had expressed a strong desire to be interred in a Jewish cemetery. At first the villagers demurred: "You cannot have Felix. He was one of us. Yes, he was a Jew, a noble Jew, the only Jew in our community. Ours must be the privilege of honoring one who was as dear as a brother to all of us." Then reason replaced emotion. They realized that their Felix had the right to be buried where he wanted to be buried. Tearfully, they placed his precious remains in a hearse and escorted the body to Cincinnati. Their friend was buried in the United Jewish Cemetery in Walnut Hills. There he rests beneath a monument which bears this inscription:

FELIX MOSES
A Confederate soldier
and
A true friend
1827-1886

A New York Yankee Marches Through Georgia
(1911)

A meshullach [a Jew who traveled about collecting money for a religious or charitable institution] got off the train in a little town in Georgia. Being a pious Chassid from New York City, he had the normal appearance that goes with being a pious Chassid from New York City: a full beard, curly earlocks hanging down from each side of his head, a black velvet hat, and a long black coat. As he walked down the main street of the little town, looking for a store with a Jewish name, a store in which he could make his first pitch for a contribution and also secure the names and addresses of the other Jews in the community, he attracted unto himself a crowd of curious little children. They had never before seen a person who looked like this and they were wondering just who and what this strange man was. At first the meshullach tried to ignore them; but they kept following him and looking at him and whispering to each other their theories with regard to this unusual person. Finally the meshullach lost his patience. He turned around, faced the children, shook his fist at them and cried out: "What's the matter with you, you rude boys and girls? Haven't you ever seen a Yankee before?"

The "New York Jew Niggerlover"
(1933)

Well over a century ago, Abraham Lincoln said, "As a nation we began by declaring that 'all men are created equal.' Now we read it, 'All men are created equal except Negroes.'"

In 1933 in Alabama almost everyone who was white from the governor on down to the most illiterate peasant in Jackson County did his utmost to prove that Lincoln's words were still true, even though there had been an amendment in the United States Constitution for 63 years declaring that a black is just as equal as a white. For the governor of the sovereign state of Alabama and most of its white citizens, the oath taken by every public official and every person in military service "to uphold, protect and defend the Constitution of the United States" was just words.

About noon, on March 25, 1931, Victoria Price and Ruby Bates, two dissolute, promiscuous, white female tramps got on a freight train at Chattanooga to bum their way back to their homes in Huntsville, Alabama. On the train with them were seven white and several black males. Shortly after the train rolled across the Alabama border into Jackson County, from 20 to 30 more blacks got aboard. The whites and the blacks got into a fight and the blacks threw all the white males except one from the train. The defeated whites phoned the sheriff, told him what had happened and asked him to arrest the blacks when the train stopped at Painted Rock, about 20 miles west of Scottsboro, the county seat.

The sheriff and his deputies halted the train at Painted Rock. Only nine blacks were still aboard. They were scattered along the whole length of the cars. One of the two white girls, who were so unfeminine in both dress and manner that at first the sheriff thought they were boys, asserted that she and her female companion had been raped by all nine blacks. Her story spread like wildfire. The blacks were locked up in the Scottsboro jail. As lynch fever began to inflame the community, they were hurriedly removed to a stronger jail in Gadsden, 60 miles south.

A week later the blacks were brought back to Scottsboro for trial. Two were thirteen years old, one sixteen, four seventeen, one nineteen, and one twentyone. One was so badly crippled by venereal disease that it was completely impossible for him to have sexual intercourse. Another was almost blind. Four were mentally retarded. Only three could read and write. After a series of brief trials, all were found guilty. One was let off with life imprisonment because he had just passed his thirteenth birthday. The other eight were sentenced to die in the electric chair.

The nine strongly proclaimed their innocence, saying they had not touched either of the girls and, had they done so, they most certainly would have jumped from the train before it reached Painted Rock. The verdicts were appealed to the Alabama Supreme Court by the Communist dominated International Labor Defense. That Court granted one of the thirteen-year-olds a new trial but affirmed the verdict on the rest. The I.L.D. then carried the case to the U. S. Supreme Court. That Supreme Court ruled the boys had not had fair trials and would have to be retried.

At this juncture, in January 1933, the I.L.D. asked Samuel Simon Leibowitz, a forty-year-old New York Jewish lawyer, to assume control of the defense of the "nine Scottsboro boys," as they were now known from one end of the world to the other as a result of the herculean efforts of the international Communist propaganda machine. Over a million dollars had been raised for their defense at Communist sponsored meetings in this country and abroad. Only $60,000 of this sum was used for this direct purpose. The Communists had a pat answer for those who accused them of having engineered a ripoff. It had been clearly announced, said the Communists, that these funds were being raised "for the defense of the Scottsboro boys and for mass protest against the ruling capital class." The Communists allotted 5 percent of the money to the Scottsboro defense and the remaining 95 percent to their mass protest media, for such purposes as buying a new and much larger printing press for their New York paper, the *Daily Worker,* and putting big propaganda ads in the capitalist urban dailies.

Samuel S. Leibowitz was born in Roumania and brought to this country at the age of four. His father's last name was originally Lebeau. When Mr. Lebeau took up residence on New York's East Side, a neighbor told him that Lebeau sounds too foreign; he should Americanize his surname. He did. He changed the family name to Leibowitz.

The Leibowitzes later moved to Brooklyn, where papa operated a store. Sam graduated from Cornell Law School in 1915, passed the New York bar in 1917 and opened his own law office in 1919. He specialized in criminal law. By 1929 he had such an unrivaled reputation as a defense attorney that the N. Y. *Times* described him as "one of the most successful criminal lawyers of all time." Of 140 clients charged with murder whom he defended, only one was executed. But Leibowitz was no Communist, God forbid. He was a loyal, faithful, regular party Democrat.

When Leibowitz read the record of the Scottsboro trials he was horrified. That this could happen in his beloved United States, the land of the free, the home of equal opportunity and truth and justice—at first this was to Sam Leibowitz incomprehensible, unbelievable. But his naïveté was dissipated when he made further inquiries. He soon learned that there were still many millions of white Americans who believed that blacks are subhuman, who were determined "to keep the nigger in his place," and who saw in the technique employed in Scottsboro an excellent example of the way periodically "us white folks has got to teach uppity niggers a lesson."

Leibowitz informed the International Labor Defense he would take the case. In order that it would be clearly understood he was not a Communist, had no sympathy with Communism, and would take no money for any nefarious Communist purpose, and that he was motivated only by a desire to obtain for these nine blacks equal handed justice with nine whites in a similar situation, Leibowitz told the I.L.D. he would take not one cent for his efforts in this case from them or anyone else. He would not even accept reimbursement for his expenses.

The second trial of one of the boys, Haywood Patterson, began on March 28, 1933. To avoid the poisoned atmosphere of Scottsboro, it was held in Decatur, a neighboring and equally unreconstructed county seat. Leibowitz began by challenging the validity of the court proceedings because no blacks had been included on the list of prospective jurors. Then he committed an even greater heresy. He demanded that the black males who would testify at the trial be addressed as "mister." That same evening five National Guardsmen were assigned to guard Leibowitz and his wife Belle to prevent their being murdered. Belle had insisted on accompanying Sam into this Alabaman lions' den. Many outraged Decatur whites made no secret of their intention to get rid of this "New York Jew niggerlover"one way or another.

At this second trial Leibowitz established that there was not the slightest medical evidence that either of the white girls had been raped, that Victoria Price had had intercourse for years with many men, white and black, and that she was a habitual liar. On the night after these facts were brought out, a pamphlet titled "Kill the Jew from New York" was sold on the streets of Decatur for 50 cents a copy. Then both Leslie Carter, the white boy who had been on the train, and Ruby Bates, Virginia's female companion, testified that their previous testimonies regarding the alleged mass rape was a complete fabrication. When the prosecution summed up, one of its counsel declared, "Ruby Bates didn't really understand what it was they told her to say because it was in Jew language." As for Carter, he said, "That's the prettiest Jew you ever saw—this Carterewsky who moved his hands this way and that way."

For appearances' sake, the jury stayed out 22 hours. They reentered the courtroom laughing and happy. They were going to show this New York Jew just how much good it does to go messing around in other people's business. Their verdict: Guilty. The penalty: Death. Leibowitz commented, "This verdict is the act of bigots spitting on the tomb of Abraham Lincoln."

Two months later the judge before whom the second trial had been held amazed the American legal profession and stunned the South by granting Leibowitz's motion to set aside the Patterson verdict because the evidence that had been presented did not justify the severity of the sentence. He ordered the defendant retried.

The third trial began in Decatur on November 27, 1933, before a different and much more prejudiced judge. Within a few days two of the boys had again been sentenced to death. Leibowitz asked that the trials of the rest of the defendants be postponed to give him time to appeal these verdicts. The request was granted. On October 5, 1934, the Alabama Supreme Court upheld both death sentences.

At this point the tactics of the Communists became so obnoxious that Leibowitz announced he was severing his relationship with the I.L.D. and would continue to defend the boys without further I.L.D. help. On April 1, 1935, the U. S. Supreme Court handed down a unanimous decision severely condemning the Alabama system of justice and ordering new trials for the convicted youths. It also ordered that, henceforth, in any jury trial involving a black defendant, a guilty verdict be set aside in any case where it could be shown that there was any attempt to exclude qualified blacks from the jury panel. The Commissioner of Agriculture of the State of Georgia reacted to this decision by declaring, "No question is ever settled until it is settled right. We still have the right to secede!"

On January 19, 1936, Patterson was placed on trial for his life for the fourth time. The names of 12 blacks had been put on the jury roll; but the prosecutor challenged all of them peremptorily and none got on the jury. The jury stayed out seven and a half hours. It brought in the expected verdict "Guilty!" but no death sentence. It recommended a prison term of 75 years.

Sympathy for the "Scottsboro boys" had now spread to all corners of the nation, including many parts of the South. The governor of Alabama went to New York City to arrange for a state loan. In the past this had been a cut-and-dried procedure. This time it was different. The New York bankers informed the governor that the bad publicity given his state by the Scottsboro case made it an undesirable investment risk. The governor returned home humiliated and depressed. Wheels began to turn. The state tried to make a deal with Leibowitz. If he would allow three or four of the defendants to plead guilty, the rest would be freed. Leibowitz refused.

On June 5, 1937, the Alabama Supreme Court affirmed Patterson's 75-year sentence. Leibowitz again took the case to the U. S. Supreme Court. On July 13, 1937, three more boys went on trial, one got the death sentence, the second 99 years, and the third 75 years. When these trials ended, the prosecution announced the rape charge against the remaining five would be dropped. One of the five had stabbed a sheriff in self-defense; for this he was sent to prison for 20 years. When Leibowitz returned to New York City with the four released blacks, a cheering crowd of 20,000 was waiting at Pennsylvania Station.

Over the years Alabama paroled four of the five who had been jailed. The fifth, Haywood Patterson, escaped. The police never found him. In 1976 Patterson voluntarily surrendered, returned to Alabama and received a full pardon from Governor George Wallace.

In 1949 Leibowitz's career as a successful defender of accused murderers and rapists came to an end. He was elected judge of the Kings County Criminal Court. Kings County is another name for Brooklyn. In 1961 Leibowitz was elevated to the New York State Supreme Court. After retiring from the bench, Judge Leibowitz lived quietly in Manhattan Beach in his beloved Brooklyn. He died, on January 11, 1978, at the age of eighty-four.

THE LADY TELLS HER AGE
(1940)

There are many old Jewish superstitions connected with numbers. One is that it is unlucky to actually count the number of persons present in a room. When one counts, he must pretend that the person being counted is not there. So how does one count? He counts by using the following numerical system: "Not one, not two, not three, etc." It is also considered bad luck to tell one's age. So, when a person is asked his age, he does not give it directly. He says, "I am going to be (whatever his age now is) bis hundert zwanzig, i.e., until I am one hundred twenty years old."

❀   ❀   ❀   ❀   ❀

So there was this little old lady, a refugee from Nazi persecution, whose only language was Yiddish and who was called upon to testify before a judge in Louisville, Kentucky, about a robbery that had occurred in her neighbor's house.

The court interpreter was not Jewish. He could understand some Yiddish from his knowledge of German; but he did not comprehend the traditional nuances in the answers some Jews give to certain questions. So the following colloquy took place in the courtroom in an assortment of languages:

Interpreter: What is your name?

Little old lady: Malke Schwartz.

Interpreter: How old are you?

L.o.l.: Seventy-seven until one hundred and twenty.

Interpreter to judge: She says she's seventy-seven until one hundred twenty.

Judge: I don't understand. Repeat the question.

Interpreter repeats question and gets same answer. Judge becomes annoyed.

Judge: Tell her that if she doesn't give a straight answer to the question she may be held in contempt of court.

At this point a spectator in the courtroom steps forward.

Spectator: If it please your honor, I am this woman's son. Allow me to ask her the question.

Judge: Go right ahead, my good man. Go right ahead.

Spectator: Teiere mama, bis hundert zwanzig, wie alt bist d'? i.e., mama darling, until a hundred and twenty years, how old are you?

Mama replies. Interpreter translates.

Interpreter: The lady says, "I am seventy-seven years old, what else?"

No Mistake
(1943)

During World War II, Mrs. Dixie Dee of Spartanburg, South Carolina, decided it would be the patriotic thing to do to have some soldiers at her table for Thanksgiving dinner. She called the office of the Third Regimental Chapel at Camp Croft and asked the chaplain to provide her with four dinner guests, which the chaplain said he would be happy to do. Before hanging up, Mrs. Dee said, "And, by the way, Chaplain, I would appreciate it if none of the soldiers was Jewish." "I understand," replied the chaplain. "That can be arranged."

The appointed day and hour arrived. Mrs. Dee's doorbell rang. She went to the door and opened it; and there stood four fine-looking black soldiers. Mrs. Dee was taken aback. "Surely," said she, "there must be some mistake." One of the blacks looked at her and smiled and said, "Oh, no, ma'am. Our regimental chaplain is Chaplain Goldberg and he is a very smart man. He doesn't make mistakes."

Not Quite a Blood Relative*
(1956)

Rabbi Charles Mantinband of Congregation Bnai Israel, Hattiesburg, Mississippi, was prevailed upon to submit an application for membership in the local Ministerial Association. He went to the next meeting and was warmly welcomed by all the clergymen except one. "It is nothing personal, Rabbi," this minister said. "It is just that you are not a Christian." When the matter was put to a vote, his was the only one in the negative. After the vote he felt in a facetious mood and rose to inquire, "Rabbi, how shall we address you? I call my Christian colleagues 'Brother Smith,' 'Brother Jones,' 'Brother Robinson,' etc. What should I call you?" The rabbi responded, "Just call me Brother-in-law." And so it was for all the years the rabbi belonged to the Association.

---

*Contributed by Rabbi Stanley R. Brav, St. Petersburg Beach, Florida.

Smart Is Sometimes Better Than Learned

(1960)

In February 1915 Sol Lowenfeld, a recent immigrant, was stranded in a town in Mississippi without a job. Learning that a shammus, a sexton, was needed at local Congregation Beth Israel, he sought out the store of the Temple president who immediately asked him, "Can you read and write English?" Sol replied in the negative. "Then I'm very sorry. We can't use you. In a big northern city like New York, you could probably get by with Yiddish, but in a southern town like this, if you can't read and write English, you're a dead duck."

Some days later Sol was fortunate enough to find a job helping a man on his early morning milk route. After saving a little money, Sol opened a little corner grocery, and then after a while, an even bigger grocery, and so it went until, after many years, he had supermarkets all over Mississippi. But he never learned to read or write English. He was too busy working. He found out that one can always hire someone to do his English reading and writing for him.

One day in 1960 Sol was in the biggest bank in the city negotiating a loan for a million dollars. When the deal was completed and the note was to be signed, Sol said to the banker, "I don't write English, so I'll put an 'X' on the line where I'm supposed to sign my name." The banker was amazed. "Mr. Lowenfeld," he said, "if you have made such a tremendous financial success without any formal American schooling, just imagine what you might have become if you had been able to read and write English!"

"I know exactly what I would have become," replied Sol laughingly. "I would have become the shammus of Temple Beth Israel!"

A Modern Jewish Troubadour

(1963)

From the twelfth through the fifteenth centuries itinerant minstrels wandered through Spain, southern France, and northern Italy, composing songs of love and valor and singing their songs, to lyre accompaniment, in princely courts before the assembled rulers and nobles, ladies

---

The Streets of Miami is printed here with the permission of its copyright owner, Curtain Call Productions, Inc., Los Angeles, California.

and gentlemen. These poet-singers were known as troubadours, an Old French word meaning "composers." They were greatly honored and well paid. Many were themselves patricians. And many were Marranos, crypto-Jews who sought to escape from the dread and drab world of the Inquisitor into the glitter and glamour of the world of the aristocrat.

During the 1960s a modern Jewish troubadour occupied center stage for a short time in the American entertainment world. Unlike the medieval troubadours who sang of love and chivalry to the delicate sound of the lyre, this poet-singer was a master of satire, Jewish satire, clever pokes at himself and his people, sung with tongue-in-cheek artlessness while plucking on the strings of a "big old geetar." He put it all together in 1963 in a smash-hit record, "My Son, the Folk Singer."

His name was Allan Sherman. He was a Chicago-born "country boy," fat, mild mannered, sharp as a tack. By day he was a TV writer and producer; by night a minstrel to the manor born, i.e., a man of the people, his people, the Jewish people. He exemplified in himself and his songs what may be the real secret for the survival of the Jew—the ability to laugh at oneself and one's foibles and one's surroundings. Allan had the uncanny knack of expressing his Yiddishkeit in a way that not only endeared him to his fellow-Jews but also won the appreciation and admiration of warm-hearted non-Jewish Judeophiles. When Allan sang, these gentiles did not laugh *at* the Jews; they laughed *with* them.

Allan Sherman worked and made his home in Hollywood, California; but he is being included in the South section of this book because the sample that will be given of his genius has, as its background, America's very own Tel Aviv, Miami Beach, Florida.

So here it is:

The Streets of Miami
(to be sung to the tune of the Western ballad *The Streets of Laredo*)

As I wandered out on the streets of Miami,
I said to myself, "This is some fancy town";
I called my partner and said, "Hello, Sammy,
Go pack up your satchel and mosey on down."

I got me a bunk in the old Roney Plaza,
With breakfast and dinner included, of course,
I caught forty winks on my private piazza;
Then I rented a pinto from Hertz-Rent-a-Horse.

My partner flew down on a non-scheduled airline;
You never did see such a pale looking man;
I recognized him from his receding hairline;
He recognized me from my beautiful tan.

'Twas then that I heard fighting words from my podner;
He said, "Marvin, the Roney is no place to stay.
I'm going to the Fontainbleu; podner, it's modner;
And I'll charge to the firm sixty dollars a day."

I said to him, "Paleface, you haker for trouble;
With the company checkbook, you quick on the draw";
He smiled and said, "Stranger, for me that goes double,
'Cause west of the Fontainbleu I am the law."

Next morning the whole Lincoln Road was deserted;
And somewhere a hi-fi was playing a tune;
'Cause everyone knew someone's gung be murdered
In a duel in the sun at the stroke of high noon.

I took careful aim with my trusty revolvah;
The clock in the Fontainbleu struck twelve o'clock;
I shot; and Sam crumbled just like a piece halvah;
And that's what they call a bad day at Black Rock.

They came with a posse and took my six-gun away;
The crowd was too angry to keep me in jail;
The sheriff said, "Outlaw, I'm gung let you run away
But don't ever be seen south of Fort Lauderdale."

So now I can never go back to Miami;
And New York is so cold that a person could die;
I'd be better off dead like my late partner Sammy
'Cause he's in that Big Fontainbleu in the sky.

"HALLELUJAH! PRAISE THE LORD!"

(1970)

During the 1970 Yom Kippur service at Temple Israel, Tallahassee, Florida, the mother of an active and noisy two-year-old doggedly ignored the glares of the congregation and the admonitions of the ushers.

Not wishing to embarrass the mother, Rabbi Stanley Garfein waited patiently for a long time for the childish disturbance to cease. Finally, he interrupted his reading of the prayers to ask the mother, as gently as he could, to remove the disruptive child from the sanctuary, which she did, much to the relief of the congregation.

When quiet was restored, the rabbi resumed his reading. To his

Contributed by Harold D. Mendelson, Tallahassee, Florida.

astonishment, he was immediately interrupted again—this time by a burst of spontaneous laughter from the congregation.

In continuing the service, the first words he had read were: "Hallelujah! Praise the Lord!"

PART FOUR

The Midwest

"Lincoln Country"

Introduction

As the tide of American history rolled westward, the ethnic composition of American Jewish life changed. While the number of Jews in colonial America was small, the quality of the early arrivals was such that their influence outweighed their number. As a group the Sephardim were well educated, cultured, sophisticated. The typical colonial Ashkenazi was not so high class. Usually he came from a German or Polish farm or manual labor background, with a social and religious outlook that was more parochial than that of the well-bred Sephardic immigrants from the West Indies, Holland, and England. It was not until the revolutionary upheavals of 1848 that a better educated and more polished kind of Ashkenazi began to appear in America. A goodly percentage of those who arrived from Germany, Austria, and Hungary in the 1850s were persons of learning with a progressive outlook. Many did not linger in the seaport cities but spread throughout the East, South, and Midwest. They avoided New England because, until less than a century ago, that section continued to be a breeding ground of the Puritan syndrome, the domain of naïve, self-righteous, bigoted rustics, an unsuitable environment for Jews.

These forward-looking Middle European immigrants of the 1850s were responsible for the rapid growth of American Reform Judaism, especially in the midwestern states—Illinois, Indiana, Iowa, Kansas, Michigan, Minnesota, Missouri, Nebraska, North Dakota, Ohio, South Dakota, and Wisconsin. Jews who did not journey into the hinterland but remained in the eastern port cities tended to be more conservative than their more adventurous brethren. Through them Orthodoxy was able to maintain a foothold on the American scene; but it did not exercise a dominant or even a modifying influence on the evolution of countrywide American Judaism during most of the nineteenth century. Because of the westward surge of progressive-minded pioneers, the center of Reform Judaism was established in Cincinnati, Ohio. During the latter half of the century the Jews of the Midwest achieved a more advanced civic, social, financial, and religious status than their coreligionists in the rest of the country.

With the arrival of many hundreds of thousands of East European Ashkenazim in the 1880s and thereafter, the situation changed. Conservative Judaism, an attempt to weave the traditional and the liberal into a consistent religious pattern, was born and rapidly became a powerful influence in American Jewish life. With a decline in the number of West European immigrants, twentieth-century Reform lost its position of dominance in the hinterland and had to contend for supremacy with the virile, strongly Zionist, mitzvot-centered Conservative movement. Orthodoxy gained control of the inner-city ghettos. Most of its devotees were and still are unwilling to go where their way of life will be difficult to practice. So, perforce, they turned the religious destiny of the American Jewish hinterland over to Reform and Conservative Judaism. Illustrating this in concrete fashion is the current synagogal situation in Illinois. Within the corporate limits of Chicago there are 92 synagogues: 60 Orthodox, 17 Conservative, 15 Reform. In the rest of the state there are 66 synagogues: 12 Orthodox, 30 Conservative, 24 Reform.

The midwestern Jew no longer occupies a more important position in the affairs of his city and state than do Jews in the rest of the nation. Nowadays the prominent Jew is most likely to be found in those communities which have the largest number of Jews, i.e., in those communities where Jews have political clout. These are not confined to any one section of the country. They are, preeminently, the ten city areas which collectively house 65 percent of the Jews of the United States: Baltimore, Boston, Chicago, Cleveland, Detroit, Los Angeles, Miami, New York, Philadelphia, and San Francisco, i.e., one in New England, three in the Middle Atlantic states, one in the Southeast, three in the Midwest, and two in the Far West.

Illinois

Illinois is a French word meaning "land of the Illini Indians." Illini is an Algonquin Indian word meaning "warriors." French fur traders and priests came down from Canada into what is now Illinois in 1673. The first settlements were established in the southwestern area of the state, along the Mississippi River at Fort Chartres and Fort Kaskaskia and farther north, opposite the present site of St. Louis, at Cahokia, about 1720. In 1763 France ceded the area to Great Britain. In 1778 American General George Rogers Clark took it from the British. In 1787 it was included in the newly formed Northwest Territory. It became a separate territory in 1809. Illinois entered the Union in 1818 as the 21st state.

In the early years the population of this area was concentrated in the southwest. The rest was wilderness. What is now Chicago was originally

Fort Dearborn. The community was incorporated and given its present name in 1837, a name based on the Indian word Checagou, meaning "strong smelling wild onions." The first non-Indian to settle within the city's present limits was a black who set up a trading post in 1777. The first white did not arrive until 1803. The city and state began to receive large increases in population in 1832 when the Indians were crushed in the Black Hawk War and again in 1850 when rail travel became available. For a long time Chicago was the nation's second largest city.

The first Jewish connection with what is now the State of Illinois dates from 1765, when Levy Andrew Levy of Fort Pitt, Pennsylvania, future father of first Jewish West Pointer, Simeon M. Levy, and then partner of and agent for Joseph Simon of Lancaster, Pennsylvania, sent Colonel George Groghan to the area to negotiate a business deal with the Indian tribes. On behalf of his Jewish employers the colonel bought from the Indians a huge tract of land along the entire length of the Illinois River, from the Mississippi to Lake Michigan. The American government declared this and similar land purchase agreements null and void when it created the Northwest Territory.

The first person living in the area who may have been Jewish was Dr. Isaac Levy, physician, merchant, and banker, a resident of Cahokia in 1782 and perhaps for quite some time before that. The first positively identified Jew is John Hays, 1770-1836, of the New York Hays family which won fame and glory in the American Revolution. He came to Cahokia in 1790 and made his living as an Indian trader. From 1798 to 1818 he served as county sheriff. After that he was for a number of years the government's Indian agent for the region. He married "a lady of excellent family" from Vincennes, Indiana, and, when he passed on, left his three daughters a handsome fortune.

The first Jew known to have settled somewhat further north was Abe Lincoln's good friend, Abe Jonas, who came to Quincy in 1838 from Williamstown, Kentucky. The first Jew to make his home in Chicago arrived in 1841. The first congregation in Illinois, Kehillat Anshe Maariv, Congregation of Men of the West, was established in Chicago in 1847. In the early 1850s Jews began coming into Illinois in sizeable numbers. These pioneers were Ashkenazim, predominantly German. Most started their Illinois business careers as pack peddlers, including Samuel Rosenwald, father of Julius Rosenwald, president of Sears, Roebuck, and Company, and Henry Horner, grandfather of Henry Horner, governor of Illinois. Other communities which had congregations at a comparatively early date were Springfield, 1855; Peoria, 1865; and Quincy, 1870.

Illinois has 269,000 Jews, 2.4 percent of the state's population. Ninety-four percent of them or 253,000 live in Chicago. The next largest Jewish community is Peoria with 2,000. Although in overall population

Chicago is now either the second or third largest city in the country, Jewishly it ranks fourth. New York, Los Angeles, and Philadelphia, in that order, have more Jews.

Indiana

In 1679 and again in 1681 the Frenchman, Rene Robert Cavalier, Sieur de La Salle, did a bit of exploring in the area where South Bend is now located. In 1731 the French built a trading post at Vincennes in the southwest of the present state on the east bank of the Wabash River. This was the first and only permanent settlement in Indiana prior to the Revolution. In 1763 the French ceded the region to Great Britain. In 1779 the Continentals under General Clark drove the British from Vincennes and Indiana, as they had already done in Illinois. In 1787 the area became part of the Northwest Territory. In 1800 the Indiana Territory was formed. In 1816 Indiana entered the Union as the 19th state with Corydon as its capital. The Indiana legislature voted to relocate the capital at the exact geographic center of the state and to name it Indianapolis. The transfer from Corydon to Indianapolis took place in 1825.

About 1825 a group of German Jewish settlers established the farming community of Rising Sun in Ohio County, Indiana, on the Ohio River 25 miles southwest of Cincinnati, the first agricultural settlement in American Jewish history. Rising Sun is presently a thriving rural town of 2,200 inhabitants. Not one of them is Jewish.

The first Jews arrived in Fort Wayne and Evansville in the 1830s, in Lafayette in 1840, and in Indianapolis about 1850. The first few Jewish settlers in Indianapolis were English Sephardim. Nearly all the other Jews in Indiana until the end of the nineteenth century were West European Ashkenazim. In 1842 Adam Gimbel opened the first Gimbel Brothers Department Store in Vincennes.

The first congregation was in Fort Wayne in 1848. It had an unusual name, The Society for Visiting the Sick and Burying the Dead. In 1861 the name was changed to Congregation Achdus Vesholom. Other congregations were organized in Lafayette, 1849, Indianapolis, 1856, and Evansville, 1857.

Indiana has 25,000 Jews, 0.5 percent of the state's population. The largest Jewish communities are Indianapolis, 11,000; Gary area, 5,200; South Bend, 2,800; Fort Wayne, 1,350; and Evansville, 1,200.

Iowa

In 1673 the explorers Marquette and Joliet claimed for France the area now occupied by the State of Iowa. The first white settler was Julien Dubuque, a Frenchman who came from Canada in 1788 to operate a lead mine at the site of the city which now bears his name. When he died in 1810 he was buried by the Indians with the honors accorded a chief. In 1803 the United States acquired the area through the Louisiana Purchase. In 1838 Iowa became an independent territory. In 1846 it entered the Union as the 29th state. In 1857 Des Moines became the capital.

The first settlements were along the west bank of the Mississippi River. A number of them began as military stockades to protect the surrounding farms from marauding Indians. The very earliest was Fort Clark in the extreme south, where Iowa, Missouri, and Illinois now abut. Built in 1820, it was incorporated in 1847 and renamed Keokuk in honor of a prominent Indian chief who had tried to live peaceably with the white man. Next came Fort Madison in 1832, 20 miles north of Fort Clark.

After the Indian menace was eliminated by the Black Hawk War of 1832, the number of white Iowans increased rapidly. In 1833 four more Mississippi River towns were born: Flint Hills (which in 1838 became Burlington), 25 miles north of Fort Madison; Bloomington (which in 1851 became Muscatine), 50 miles above Flint Hills; Dubuque, about 100 miles above Bloomington; and McGregor, 65 miles north of Dubuque.

The first Jew to live in Iowa, a French Sephardi, opened a store in Dubuque before the end of 1833 and lived there for 60 years as one of its most prominent citizens. Jewish peddlers were working out of Fort Madison as early as 1841. Between 1846 and 1856 about a hundred additional German Jewish peddlers arrived. Many of these settled in Davenport, which dates from 1835 and is also on the Mississippi. German Jews organized congregations in Dubuque, 1857, and Davenport, 1861. Both soon turned Reform. About the middle of the 1850s, Russian and Polish Jewish peddlers began to come into Iowa. They made their homes principally in Burlington and Keokuk, They organized congregations in Burlington, 1857, and Keokuk, 1863. Both were strictly Orthodox. By 1870 Keokuk was an important commercial center; but in a few years its business began to decline steadily and so did its Jewish population. About 1900 the Keokuk congregation ceased to exist.

Iowa now has approximately 7,000 Jews, 0.2 percent of the total population. The principal Jewish communities are Des Moines, 3,300; Sioux City, 1,100; Davenport, 1,000.

Kansas

Kansas lies almost precisely at the geographic center of the United States. It was traversed by Coronado's Spanish expedition in 1541. French explorers from Louisiana visited it in 1719. The United States acquired it from France in 1803. Leavenworth was established as a military post in 1827 and as a town in 1854. The Santa Fe and Oregon trails, which began at St. Louis, Missouri, and ended at Santa Fe, New Mexico, and the Columbia River Basin in Oregon, respectively, passed through Kansas.

Kansas Territory was created in 1854. At that time it had only 700 inhabitants. Its citizens were to decide whether they wanted slavery within their territory. This issue caused many ardent abolitionists and pro-slavery people to come to the new territory to fight for what each believed to be right. Within a year the Free Staters founded the towns of Lawrence, Topeka, and Ossawatomie; and the slavery advocates the towns of Leavenworth, Atkinson, and Lecompton. From the beginning the Free Staters were in the majority, but the other side was aided by the pro-slavery stand of Presidents Pierce and Buchanan and by the Border Ruffians, bands of armed and sympathetic Missourians who periodically raided the Free State settlements. On May 21, 1856, the Border Ruffians sacked Lawrence. Two days later Free Stater John Brown and his sons killed five slavery partisans at Pottawatami Creek. This sequence of events precipitated a miniature civil war that had to be stopped by the intervention of federal troops. In 1859 a state constitution prohibiting slavery was adopted by popular vote by a margin of two to one. In 1861 Kansas entered the Union as the 34th state.

Leavenworth had the state's first Jewish congregation, organized in 1859. The only other Kansas community to have a congregation prior to the twentieth century was Wichita, 1889. There were many years between 1859 and 1935 when there was no rabbi in the entire state. In these years the rabbis of Kansas City, Missouri, were summoned to minister as the needs arose.

There are now 11,000 Jews in Kansas, 0.5 percent of the population. The largest Jewish communities are Kansas City, 5,000 and Wichita, 1,200.

Michigan

The first known white men to visit this region were French fur traders and missionaries from Canada in 1616. In 1668 the French established the first settlement at Sault St. Marie. Antoine de la Mothe Cadillac built Fort Pontchartrain on the present site of Detroit in 1701. The English captured the fort during the French and Indian War. It was besieged unsuccessfully by Pontiac in 1763. It was held by the English until 1796 and then, under the terms of the Jay Treaty, turned over to the Americans. By that time it was known as Detroit and was a town of 2,500 inhabitants.

In 1805 Michigan became an independent territory with its capital at Detroit. After the completion of the Erie Canal in 1825 provided easier access, the population increased rapidly. There was an unusually long delay in granting statehood to Michigan because of a dispute with Ohio over their boundary. The dispute was settled in Ohio's favor. To compensate Michigan for its loss of southern territory to Ohio, the upper peninsula was taken from Wisconsin and given to Michigan. Michigan entered the Union in 1837 as the 26th state. In 1847 the capital was moved from Detroit to Lansing.

The French did not allow non-Catholics to live in or even visit New France, their name for Canada. So it was not until the English conquered New France in 1759 that Jews were allowed to enter this part of the world. Eager Jewish traders came into the Great Lakes region almost on the heels of the British soldiers. The story of how a number of these Jewish traders were captured by the Indians in the 1763 Pontiac War is told in this section.

The first Jewish congregation in Michigan was Temple Beth El of Detroit, established in 1850 as an Orthodox synagogue. Other Michigan congregations in existence more than a hundred years ago as either Orthodox or Reform institutions were: Temple Beth Israel, Jackson, Orthodox, 1859; Congregation Bene Israel, Kalamazoo, Reform, 1865; Au Sable, Orthodox, 1870-1911; Temple Emanuel, Grand Rapids, Reform, 1871; Congregation Anshe Chesed, Bay City, Reform, 1876.

Until 1883 the majority of Michigan's Jews were of German extraction. After 1883 Russian and Polish Jewish immigrants came in in such large numbers that they soon became a substantial majority. There are now about 95,000 Jews in Michigan, constituting one percent of the total population. The largest Jewish communities are Detroit, 80,000; Flint, 2,700; Grand Rapids, 1,500; Lansing, 1,500; Ann Arbor, 1,150.

Minnesota

French fur traders and missionaries from New France were in this region as early as 1659. Part of Minnesota was acquired by the United States as a result of the Revolutionary War and the remainder in 1803 through the Louisiana Purchase. In 1819 Fort St. Anthony, later called Fort Snelling, was built on the present site of Minneapolis. The village of St. Anthony, which grew around the fort, was the first permanent white settlement. In 1837 the United States acquired by purchase large tracts of Indian land. St. Paul was founded in 1841 and incorporated in 1847. In 1849 the Territory of Minnesota was created with St. Paul as the capital. Minneapolis, which developed first as a rival to its neighbor, St. Anthony, and then gradually absorbed its competitor, was incorporated in 1856. In 1858 Minnesota entered the Union as the 32nd state. In 1862 the Sioux Indians rebelled, were defeated and driven from Minnesota. During the 1870s many immigrants came in from the Scandinavian countries.

Many German Jews came to St. Paul and the surrounding area in the 1850s and went into business, mostly as traders with the Indians. The first Jewish congregation, Mount Zion Hebrew Association of St. Paul, was organized in 1857. Jews did not settle in Minneapolis until after the Civil

War. Congregation Shari Tov, now known as Temple Israel, in Minneapolis dates from 1878. The first Jew came to Duluth in 1870. Duluth's Temple Emanuel was established in 1891. In the 1880s large numbers of East European immigrants arrived and founded their own Orthodox synagogues.

There are now about 35,000 Jews in Minnesota, 0.9 percent of the state's population. The largest Jewish communities are: Minneapolis, 22,000; St. Paul, 9,500; Duluth, 1,000.

Missouri

The Spaniard Hernando de Soto passed through what is now Missouri in 1541, the year he discovered the Mississippi River. Marquette and Joliet went by in their journey down the same river in 1673. The French established the first settlement in the area about 1735 at Ste. Genevieve on the Mississippi, almost directly opposite Fort Kaskaskia, Illinois, built about fifteen years earlier. In 1764 the French set up a fur trading post at the present site of St. Louis. In 1803, through the Louisiana Purchase, the region became part of the United States. The French continued to dominate the fur trading business even though they no longer had political control. Kansas City began in 1821 as a French trading post. St. Louis did not become an incorporated community until 1808, Kansas City until 1850.

In 1808 steamboats began to travel up and down the Mississippi. As a result St. Louis became an important center of river commerce until the Civil War. After this war the railroad displaced the steamboat as the major carrier of passengers and freight; and St. Louis' commercial influence diminished somewhat. Many wagon trains of the 1840-70 era that followed the Santa Fe and Oregon trails to the West set out from Saint Louis and used Kansas City as a rest-stop to refresh the travelers and their animals and to replenish their supplies. This aided the growth and prosperity of both cities.

Missouri became an independent territory in 1812. It entered the Union in 1821 as the 24th state. Most of its early settlers came from the South and brought their slaves with them. The population in 1820 consisted of 59,000 freemen and 11,000 slaves. Missouri's third major city in the early years, St. Joseph, was founded in 1843 and incorporated in 1851. In the late 1840s a large number of Germans and Irish migrated into the state, bringing with them strong feelings about human freedom and equality. A bitter struggle developed between the pro- and antislavery elements. The conflict had a strong ethnic as well as ideological flavor. The later arrivals won, but it was not an easy victory. Missouri just barely managed to remain loyal to the Union in the Civil War: 109,000 of its men wore the Union blue, 50,000 the Confederate gray.

The first Jews came to St. Louis in 1808. The first St. Louis congregation, United Hebrew, was started in 1837. Its ritual was Orthodox and many of its members maintained kosher homes; but outside the home and the synagogue they were not very observant. A shechita code, written in 1844, states that animals are to be slaughtered in conformity with "the customs and laws of the German and Polish Jews." This indicates that there must have been a sizeable percentage of East European Jews in St. Louis in its growing years.

Jews arrived in St. Joseph about 1850 and organized Congregation Adath Joseph in 1857. Jews were in Kansas City as early as 1846 but not in sufficient numbers to form a congregation until Bnai Jehudah got under way in 1870. In the latter half of the nineteenth century there were years when Leavenworth, Kansas, had a rabbi and Kansas City, Missouri, did not, and vice versa. In such years one community would depend upon the other for rabbinic service. For most of these same years the German Jews controlled Missouri's Jewish life. By 1905 this had changed. By then the East European Jews outnumbered their West European brethren. Their influence grew with their numbers. The nineteenth-century German dominance is now only a historical memory in St. Louis and Kansas City.

There are presently about 85,000 Jews in Missouri, 1.8 percent of the state's population. Ninety-six percent live either in St. Louis, 60,000, or Kansas City, 22,000.

Nebraska

In 1540 Coronado passed by the southern border of what is now Nebraska. By 1700 the French traders who did business with the Indians in the area were so well acquainted with the terrain that they carried with them fairly accurate maps of the locations of the Indian villages and the river fords. In 1803 the region became American via the Louisiana Purchase. In 1807 an Indian trading post was established at Fort Calhoun, ten miles north of the present Omaha city limits. The first permanent settlement was at Bellevue, five miles south of present Omaha, in 1823. More trading posts were set up along the Missouri River at Omaha, 1825; Nebraska City, 1826; and Plattsmouth. All were situated at good river crossings, used from the early 1840s to the late 1860s by the covered wagons known as "prairie schooners" en route to the Oregon Trail to make the long journey to the Northwest. Consequently these towns developed into bustling trade marts.

In 1854 Nebraska was given territorial status. After much haggling Omaha was chosen as the territorial capital. In 1867 Nebraska entered the Union as the 37th state. That same year Omaha was incorporated. In 1869 the capital was transferred forty miles southwest to Lancaster, whose name was almost immediately changed to Lincoln in honor of the Great Emancipator. That same year the transcontinental railroad was completed. This, combined with the complete subjugation of Nebraska's Indians, the extermination of Nebraska's buffalo herds, and the weakening of the power of Nebraska's baronial cattle ranchers, made Nebraska a prosperous state by the end of the nineteenth century, a state of small farms and tall farmers dominated by an agrarian political philosophy which has projected onto the national scene some very genuinely liberal Nebraskans and some equally genuine Nebraskan crackpots.

Attracted to the various Missouri River towns and to the capital city by their excellent economic prospects, business and professional Jews, mostly West European, came to Nebraska in fair numbers in the latter half of the nineteenth century and homesteaded. The first Jewish congregation in the state, Temple Israel of Omaha, was organized in 1868; the second, Congregation Bnai Jeshurun of Lincoln, in 1882.

There are now about 8,500 Jews in Nebraska, 0.5 percent of the population. The principal Jewish communities are Omaha, 6,000, and Lincoln, 1,000.

North Dakota

French fur trappers and traders came into the area from Canada as early as 1738. After the English obtained control of Canada in 1763, there was great rivalry between French and English for the trapping and trading in this region. The United States acquired most of present-day North Dakota in 1803 through the Louisiana Purchase. The rest was obtained from Great Britain in 1818 by 'mutual agreement. The first permanent settlement was Pembina in the northeast corner on the Canadian border. It was founded in 1812 by French Canadians. In 1861 the Dakota Territory was formed. It included both of the present Dakotas, most of Montana, and parts of Idaho and Wyoming.

As the railroads which would intersect the territory approached completion, a new town came into being at the point on the Missouri River where the two lines would meet. The town was named Edmonton. Shortly afterward it was renamed Bismarck, after the famed Prussian chancellor, in the hope that the new name would help to interest German investors in the town's enterprises. The two railroads linked up in 1873. They brought thousands of homesteaders into Dakota Territory. North Dakota and South Dakota entered the Union simultaneously in 1889 as the 39th and 40th states. Bismarck became the capital of North Dakota.

One of the founders of Edmonton (Bismarck) was Abe Eppinger from Sioux City, Iowa. Some Jews were among the early homesteaders. A cemetery was established at Devil's Lake in 1889 by an Am Olam farming colony. Both colony and cemetery were soon abandoned. The first congregation was organized at Grand Forks in 1891. In the 1890s East European Jews came as homesteaders with the help of the Baron de Hirsch Fund. They established Orthodox synagogues in Grand Forks, 1900; Minot, 1905; Ashley, 1907; Regan, 1907; and Fargo, 1908. The Ashley and Regan congregations lasted less than ten years. In the early 1940s many Jewish families left the state because of bad economic conditions and also because they wished to rear their children in a better Jewish environment. There are now about 1,500 Jews in North Dakota, 0.2 percent of the population. The largest Jewish communities are Fargo, 700, and Grand Forks, 100. Some of the information in this paragraph was furnished by Toba Geller of Fargo, an authority on the history of the Jews of North Dakota.

Ohio

The French explorer La Salle visited this area in 1669. After that the French established good commercial relationships with the Erie Indian tribe which inhabited the region and exchanged their manufactured goods for the Indians' pelts. English fur traders came over the Allegheny Mountains in 1685 to barter with the Indians. The French and Indians combined forces to drive them back. In defiance, the English built a trading post in 1749 at the Indian village of Pickawillany on the Great Miami River. In 1752 the French destroyed this trading post.

The English acquired Ohio in 1759 by winning the French and Indian War. The Americans acquired it in 1783 by beating the British. The oldest existing town, Marietta, was built in 1788 by the Ohio Company, a corporation of Revolutionary War officer veterans. Cincinnati and North Bend date from 1789. Colonel David Salisbury Franks, prominent Jewish Revolutionary officer, in late 1790 led a group of immigrant French families westward to establish a settlement where Gallipolis now stands. Just before reaching the Ohio River, the newcomers and their guide were set upon by Indians and brutally slaughtered. The victory of General Anthony Wayne over the Indians at the battle of Fallen Timbers, August 20, 1794, fought near present-day Maumee, ended the warfare with the Indians in this region.

Cleveland and Chillicothe were settled in 1796. Ohio entered the Union as the 17th state in 1803. The capitals in the early years were Chillicothe, 1803-10, 1812-15, and Zanesville, 1810-12. Columbus was founded in 1812 for the purpose of serving as the state capital. It assumed this status in 1816.

The first Jew in Ohio, Joseph Jonas, watchmaker and silversmith, came to Cincinnati from England in 1817. When he told some Philadelphia friends where he was going, they tried to dissuade him. They warned, "In the wilds of America and entirely among the Gentiles, you will forget your religion and your God." In 1824 Jonas and about twenty other English Jewish immigrants organized Cincinnati's Bnai Israel congregation, the first west of the Alleghenies. They could not afford to engage a rabbi until 1855. In 1840 German Jews began to arrive in Cincinnati. Because their English co-religionists did not make them feel welcome, they organized their own synagogue, Bene Yeshurun, in 1841. By 1850 Cincinnati's German Jews outnumbered its English Jews. It was to the German congregation that Isaac Mayer Wise came as rabbi in 1854. Almost immediately he began to edit and publish the weekly *American Israelite*, oldest existing Anglo-Jewish periodical in the United States. In 1875 Wise founded and became president of the Hebrew Union College, oldest existing rabbinical seminary in the United States. Until the Union of American Hebrew Congregations moved from Cincinnati to New York City in the middle of the twentieth century, Cincinnati was the national headquarters of American Reform Judaism.

The earliest congregations in other Ohio communities: The Israelitish Society (later Congregation Anshe Chesed, now Fairmount Temple), Cleveland, 1839; Agudas Achim, Bellaire, and Bnai Yeshurun (now Temple Israel), Dayton, 1850; Bnai Jeshurun (now Temple Israel), Columbus, 1852; Children of Israel, Circleville, Anshe Emeth, Piqua, and Beneh Abraham, Portsmouth, 1858; Akron Hebrew Congregation (now Temple Israel), Akron, and Ohavey Zedakah, Springfield, 1865; Bnai Israel, Hamilton, and Bnai Israel, Toledo, 1866; Rodef Sholem, Youngstown, 1867.

Until the East European influx of the latter part of the nineteenth century, Ohio Jewry was overwhelmingly Reform. Now none of the Jewish denominations is in a dominant position in Ohio. The present affiliation of the state's congregations is Orthodox, 28; Conservative, 25; Reform, 24.

There are about 160,000 Jews in Ohio, 1.2 percent of the population. The principal Jewish communities are Cleveland, 80,000; Cincinnati, 30,000; Columbus, 13,000; Toledo, 7,500; Dayton, 6,000; and Youngstown, 5,400.

South Dakota

French explorers from Canada were in this area in 1742. In 1780 French fur traders began to arrive to do business with the Indians. They traveled south from Canada and north from St. Louis. The first permanent trading post was established near Pierre by a Frenchman in 1817. An agricultural settlement was set up near Sioux Falls in 1857 but had to be abandoned in 1863 because of Indian hostility. In 1861 the Dakota Territory was created with Yankton as its capital. In 1874 gold was discovered on the Sioux Reservation and prospectors rushed in to take advantage of the find. When the Indians resisted this encroachment, the government forced them to give up most of their land. In 1877 the "great Dakota Boom" began. So many homesteaders entered the territory that in five years the population tripled. In 1889 South and North Dakota entered the Union simultaneously. Pierre became the capital of South Dakota. The final Indian uprising in 1890 was crushed by the Wounded Knee massacre of Indians old and young, men, women, and children, by soldiers of the United States Army.

The first Jews in South Dakota were a group of the Am Olam, led by Herman Rosenthal, who founded the agricultural colony of Cremieux in Davison County in 1882. After bravely enduring all manner of obstacles, hazards, bugs, drought, prairie fire, and hailstorms for three years, the colonists called it quits and Cremieux ceased to be.

There was a small immigration of Jews into South Dakota in the first two decades of the twentieth century. At the peak of this development the state may have had as many as two thousand Jews. The first Jewish congregation, Sons of Israel of Sioux Falls, was organized in 1916. It was followed by another congregation in the same city and by congregations in Aberdeen and Rapid City. For the last 50 years the Jewish population of South Dakota has gone steadily downward. It now numbers about 500, less than one-tenth of one percent of the state's population.

Wisconsin

A French explorer entered Green Bay in 1634. In 1654 the first French fur trader arrived to exploit the natural resources and the Indians. In 1759 the British gained control of the area. In 1783 the United States became the technical owner but the British did not relinquish their hold until the conclusion of the War of 1812, when the United States asserted its authority by placing military garrisons at Green Bay and Prairie du Chien. Milwaukee was founded in 1818 by fur trapper Solomon Juneau. The Territory of Wisconsin was created in 1836 with Madison as its capital. Wisconsin entered the Union in 1848 as the 30th state. In this same year a large number of German immigrants began to move into the state.

Wisconsin's first Jew, Jacob Franks, arrived in Green Bay in 1792 from Canada as agent for a British fur company. In 1797 Franks went into business for himself at Fond du Lac. In 1804 he sent an agent into the Milwaukee area to buy deerskins from the Indians, 14 years before Juneau founded the city. In 1805 he built a gristmill and sawmill, the first of each in this part of the country, three miles east of De Pere. At the end of the War of 1812, Franks, loyal to Great Britain, abandoned his Indian family and returned to Canada. He left his business in charge of his nephew, who became a prominent citizen and joined the Episcopal Church.

In 1820 a "Jew peddler" was robbed and murdered by three Indians near Kaukauna. The first Jewish families came to Milwaukee in 1836. Wisconsin's first Jewish congregation was Emanuel of Milwaukee in 1847. This was not the present Reform congregation of the same name. The original Emanuel merged with another congregation in 1856 to form Bnai Jeshurun. The present Emanuel dates from 1869. In 1927 it absorbed Bnai Jeshurun.

In the early 1840s Bernard Schlesinger Weil became a farmer near Cedar Lake. For his time he was a very atypical rural Jew. He brought a Hebrew teacher by ox-team from Chicago for his four children, sent his two sons to Milwaukee for their Bar Mitzva ceremonies, presented a Torah to Congregation Bnai Jeshurun and, as a state legislator in the early 1850s, persuaded the state legislature to open one of its sessions with a prayer by the Milwaukee rabbi. The town of Schlesingerville was named in his honor; but, the name being rather difficult for non-Germans to pronounce, it was later shortened to Slinger. Weil died in 1893 at the age of ninety-one and is buried in Milwaukee. In 1843 Samuel (Dutch Doc) Snow was one of the founders of La Crosse and was twice its mayor.

Other early Wisconsin congregations were: Shaare Shomayim, Madison, 1856, ceased to exist in 1922; Anshe Cheset, La Crosse, 1857, which no longer exists; Congregation Zion, Appleton, 1874, whose first rabbi, 1874-83, was the father of the famous magician Harry Houdini, born as Ehrich Weiss. Between 1891 and 1901 a large Russian element was added to Wisconsin's Jewish population with the help of French Baron Moritz de Hirsch.

Wisconsin now has about 32,000 Jews, 0.7 percent of the population. The largest Jewish communities are Milwaukee, 24,000, and Madison, 3,000. The strong individualism that marks Wisconsin's political life is also found in its organized Jewish religious life. Appleton, 340 Jews, Kenosha, 250 Jews, and Sheboygan, 200 Jews, each has two synagogues, "the one I belong to and the other one I wouldn't be caught dead in."
—D.M.E.

Did the Inquisition Get as Far North as Indiana?
(1724)

The Inquisition, also known as the Sanctum Officium or Holy Office, an ecclesiastical court for seeking out and punishing heretics and infidels, was established by the papacy in the first half of the thirteenth century. Initially it had a twofold purpose: to suppress the Albigensian heresy in southern France and to prevent Jews who had converted to Roman Catholicism from reverting to Judaism. The management of these courts was given to two of the mendicant orders, the Dominicans and the Franciscans, because these friars, being the least worldly of all the monks, would be the most zealous in cleansing the Church of its impurities. The first backsliding Jews were burned at the stake in southern France in 1276. By the end of the century another type of individual was made subject to the inquisitorial court: the Jew who attempted to convert a non-Jew to Judaism.

The Inquisition sank to the most depraved depths of its five-century-long reign of terror in the last quarter of the fifteenth century, in Spain during the reign of Ferdinand and Isabella. They added a fourth type of victim to the roster: the Muslim who would try to convert a non-Muslim to Islam. In October 1483 the infamous Thomas de Torquemada was appointed inquisitor-general of Spain. During his 15-year blood orgy more than 8,000 Jews were burned to death.

All sorts of false accusations were leveled against the Jews, particularly the wealthy ones, both those who did not convert and those, designated New Christians, who did. This was done so that the unprincipled Spanish monarchs could get hold of Jewish properties by imprisoning and executing their owners or compelling them to flee. Large numbers of terror-stricken Jewish families converted outwardly but remained Jews secretly. The Spaniards called these Marranos, meaning "the accursed, the damned." In Hebrew they are known as *anusim*, "the compelled ones," those who converted under pressure.

The Inquisitorial kangaroo court put on a show known as an *auto da fe*, "an act of the faith," which included a so-called trial, the pronouncing

295

of the death sentence on the heretic by the religious authorities and the carrying out of the sentence in an elaborate ritual by the secular authorities. The last recorded Jew-burning in Europe was in Poland in 1749. The Inquisition was not officially abolished in Spain until 1834.

That Christopher Columbus was a Marrano has advanced from the rank of a historical possibility to a very real probability. His name was not Columbus. He was not an Italian born in Genoa. He was a Spanish Jew by the name of Juan Colon born in or near Pontevedra, a seagoing captain who had converted to Roman Catholicism. He beguiled the greedy Ferdinand and Isabella by telling them he was going to find a short route to the East Indies through which they would obtain untold wealth and power. In reality he was sailing for a New World, a continent he knew existed because of his thorough acquaintance with the findings of the earlier Viking explorers. His secret intention was to try to find a place of refuge for his hapless fellow Jews. His flagship, the *Santa Maria,* was named for a locale near the mouth of the Pontevedra River. Many of the names he gave the various regions he "discovered" were the names of towns near Pontevedra. He called San Domingo "Cap San Miguel" and Cuba "Cap San Nicholas." Both were names of sailors' societies in Pontevedra. There are many more facts—too many to mention here—which substantiate this thesis.

The Inquisition spread its tentacles into the New World with the help of the Spanish, Portuguese, and French. The first Marrano was burned in Mexico in 1574, in Peru and Colombia in 1581, in Portuguese Brazil in 1647. The last recorded Jew-burning in the Americas was at Lima, Peru, in 1776, a quarter of a century after the last recorded Jew-burning in Europe. In the two centuries from 1574 to 1776, hundreds of Jews were burned alive in Central and South America. Were there any such burnings in North America and, more particularly, in the United States?

One such instance has been reported. Its historicity has not been firmly established. The story was told in the *Inter-Ocean,* a Chicago newspaper, on October 1, 1899.

On April 23, 1615, Louis XIII of France decreed that no Jew would be permitted to reside in the French colonies in the New World. When the Spanish established settlements in Florida, they, too, excluded Jews. In most of British North America Jews were allowed to enter soon after the colonies were founded.

The French prohibition was not firmly enforced for more than a century. The number of Jewish traders in the French colony of Louisiana began to increase in the early years of the eighteenth century. In 1724 the Regency of Louis XV decided to enforce the edict of Louis XIII. Governor Bienville of Louisiana was instructed to order all Jews to leave his province in no more than three months. Some of his zealous underlings did not wait for the three months to elapse. They rounded up the Jewish traders in the Mississippi Valley, said to have numbered several hundred, confiscated their possessions and force-marched them north to Fort Chartres, a military post on the Illinois side of the Mississippi River, about 35 miles south of St. Louis. From there they had to make their way out of the French territory as best they could.

It was discovered that some of these Jews who were being deported were Marranos. At least three are reported to have been burned at the stake by the French—one in Mississippi near the present town of Yazoo and two in what is now Indiana, one on the northern bank of the Ohio River and the other 45 miles south of the present city of Vincennes. There may have been more whose burnings were not recorded.

THE SOUP WAS TOO HOT
(1763)

Soon after the British took Canada from the French, English settlers began to move into the Great Lakes and western Allegheny areas in sizable numbers. This development alarmed the indigenous inhabitants, the Algonquin Indians, who had been fighting on the side of the French to prevent such a happening. The Indians realized that, if the English kept on coming into their territory, they would in time lose their land. The French encouraged this fear and gave the Indians the impression that, if the Algonquin nation would continue to fight the English, it would receive massive support in men and materiel from the French.

Encouraged by this hope of French assistance, Pontiac, c. 1720-69, illustrious chief of the Ottawa tribe, persuaded the Algonquins to resist the English intruders. Simultaneous surprise attacks were launched early in 1763 against all fourteen forts the British had established in the Algonquin domain. Ten of the forts were quickly overrun and their defenders slaughtered. The two most important, Detroit and Fort Pitt, were not taken. Pontiac personally directed the year-long siege against Detroit. When he learned that the French and English had signed a treaty of peace, he knew that all hope of French help was gone and he lifted the siege. In August 1765 a formal peace treaty was concluded between the British and the Algonquin nation. Pontiac was murdered in 1769 in East

---

Part of this account is based on "The Startling Experience of a Jewish Trader during Pontiac's Siege of Detroit in 1763," an article by David E. Heineman in the Publications of the American Jewish Historical Society, No. 23 (1915), pp. 31-35.

St. Louis, Illinois, by a fellow Algonquin who is said to have been bribed by an English trader to commit this treacherous act.

✦   ✦   ✦   ✦   ✦

The French did not permit Jews to live in any of their North American territories. The English victory over the French gave Jews the opportunity to enter many parts of North America that had been inaccessible to them. A number of Jewish traders came into Michigan with its earliest English settlers. In 1763 when, without warning, Pontiac and his warriors attacked the English forts and towns along the Great Lakes, some Jewish traders who were traveling about in order to sell their goods were among those taken captive by the Indians.

Major Roberts, a member of the Detroit garrison, wrote in his diary on May 13, 1763, that the Huron tribe had captured six Englishmen, including three Jews, and were holding them for ransom:

> A message has been received from the Hurons that they had taken Chapman [a Jew] and his Merchandize, as also a Cannoe with five Englishmen coming from Sandusky yesterday, among whom were Mr. Smallman and two Jews, who must have fallen into worse hands if they had not taken them, as they had not killed any of them; they desired to know what opinion the Commandant had of them, that if he would make Peace with them they would give up their Prisoners and pay Chapman for Part of his Merchandize that fell to their Lot in the Division of them with the other Indians.

On July 11 the diary states that the Miami tribe had captured a Mr. Levy, who, in all probability, was Levy Andrew Levy, a fur trader from Fort Pitt who, in 1774 would become the father of Simeon Magruder Levy, West Point Military Academy's first Jewish graduate. The Indians captured Levy while he was on his way from Presque Isle, now Erie, Pennsylvania, to Fort Pitt. The captors came to Fort Detroit under a flag of truce to try to negotiate the ransoming of Mr. Levy. One may assume that the ransom was paid and that Levy was freed. However, what is known about the subsequent fate of Chapman would lead to the belief that all the captives were not released and that at least some were tortured to death.

The Reverend John Heckewelder of Bethlehem, Pennsylvania, a United Brethren missionary, heard of Chapman's dramatic escape from death from the lucky man's own lips. Here is the story as the minister later recounted it:

> At the commencement of the Indian war in 1763, a trading Jew named Chapman, who was going up the Detroit river with a batteau-load of goods which he had brought from Albany, was

taken by some Indians of the Chippeway nation, and destined to be put to death. A Frenchman, impelled by motives of friendship and humanity, found means to steal the prisoner, and kept him so concealed for some time that, although the most diligent search was made, the place of his confinement could not be discovered. At last, however, the unfortunate man was betrayed by some false friend, and again fell into the power of the Indians who took him across the river to be tortured and burned. Tied to the stake and the fire burning by his side, his thirst from the great heat became intolerable, and he begged that some drink might be given to him. It is a custom with the Indians, previous to a prisoner being put to death, to give him what they call his last meal; a bowl of pottage or broth was therefore brought to him for that purpose. Eager to quench his thirst, he put the bowl immediately to his lips, and the liquor being very hot, he was dreadfully scalded. Being a man of very quick temper, the moment he felt his mouth burned he threw the bowl with its contents full in the face of the man who handed it to him. "He is mad! He is mad!" resounded from all quarters. The bystanders considered his conduct as an act of insanity, and immediately untied the cords with which he was bound, and let him go where he pleased.

This fact was well known to all the inhabitants of Detroit from whom I first heard it, and it was afterwards confirmed to me by Mr. Chapman himself, who was established as a merchant at that place.

Other documents show that Mr. Chapman was still in business in Detroit in May 1796.

Who Is the Real Number One?
(1802)

After the Revolutionary War officially ended in 1783, the British continued to harass the newly independent United States in every way possible. One of their most successful techniques was bribing the Indians to attack, rob, and murder the settlers on the infant nation's western frontiers. This tactic was employed effectively along the perimeter of the Maumee River, which rises near what is now Fort Wayne, Indiana, meanders in a northeasterly direction and empties into Lake Erie near what is now Toledo, Ohio. The tribe which lived along the stream called both the river and itself the Miami. The colonial French pronounced Miami as though spelled Maumee. The French pronunciation finally became the American name for the river. The British built a fort near the "great rapids" on the northwest bank of the Maumee, close to what is now the city of Maumee, Ohio. They called it Fort Miami.

From Fort Miami a steady supply of guns and ammunition flowed to the Indians. With these the Algonquin nation, a strong tribal confederacy, harassed the border settlements. In 1790 President Washington decided to use military force to subdue the Algonquins. Troops commanded by General Harmar marched north from Cincinnati into the Indian country. The Indians cut General Harmar's brigade to pieces. The next year a second expedition commanded by General St. Clair was ignominiously routed by the Algonquin nation. The Algonquins were a brave and hardy lot, resolved to defend their territory against all intruders.

Washington was determined to end this menace to the westward expansion of the United States. In 1792 he requested the popular Revolutionary War hero, General "Mad Anthony" Wayne, 1745-96, then a farmer at Presque Isle, Pennsylvania, to organize, train, and lead a third military force against the Algonquins. Wayne agreed. He sent recruiting officers to a number of Middle Atlantic communities. About 200 easterners joined up. One of them was Simeon Magruder Levy, an eighteen-year-old Jewish lad of Hagerstown, Maryland. These volunteers were added to 500 Army regulars and 200 western recruits. General Wayne spent almost two years preparing his force of 900 for its difficult task. In August 1794 he marched his men to the vicinity of the Maumee rapids, a few miles from Fort Miami. By this time Levy had attained the rank of Sergeant in the Fourth Infantry company commanded by Lieutenant Lockwood.

About 2,000 Indians had assembled in the same region to prepare for battle. They were commanded by Chief Blue Jacket of the Shawnee tribe. Leading the Shawnee contingent was young Chief Tecumseh, c. 1768-1813, brilliant and implacable enemy of the white American and destined to die in battle as a British general in the War of 1812. Although the garrison of Fort Miami had armed the Indians, it did not participate in the battle preparations, lest this give General Wayne an excuse for attacking the fort. However, 70 Canadian rangers had been brought down from Detroit to teach the Indians how to use their new weapons. In the battle that ensued these rangers fought alongside their Indian comrades.

On August 18 Wayne held a powwow with the Indian chiefs in a last-ditch effort to conclude the matter peacefully by getting an Indian promise that the attacks on the border farms and villages would stop. When the powwow failed, both sides prepared for action. At about ten A.M. on August 20 Wayne led his 900 men against the 2,000 Indians plus the 70 Canadians at a spot three miles west of what is now Maumee, Ohio, a place known to the Indians as Fallen Timbers. Sometime before, a tornado had howled through this neighborhood, plowing a path through the forest and twisting the fallen trees into what seemed to be an ideal natural barrier for blocking the progress of oncoming troops.

Wayne's soldiers advanced along a two-mile front with fixed bayonets. It had been learned in former battles with the Indians that the bayonet charge was a tactic that terrified the Indians. The fallen timbers proved to be an ineffective obstacle. The battle lasted less than an hour. The Indians broke ranks and fled. In an earlier article, the abandonment of the Indians by the French in 1763 was mentioned. This time it was the English who betrayed the redskins. Having encouraged them to fight the Americans, having given them arms and ammunition for this purpose, having provided them with Canadian cadre-men, the British closed the doors of Fort Miami on the warriors fleeing from Wayne's bayonets and refused their duped allies all further help.

On August 3, 1795, Wayne signed a treaty with the Indians at Greene Ville in southwest Ohio near the Indiana border. The Algonquin nation agreed to let white settlers enter its land. Through this treaty what was then known as the Northwest Territory, embracing a very large area northwest of the Ohio River, north to Lake Erie, west to the Mississippi, was gradually taken over by the white man, acre by acre, mile by mile.

❂   ❂   ❂   ❂   ❂

Leib ben Reb Anshel was born in Oxford, England, in 1734. He was given the English name of Levy Andrew Levy. At the invitation of his mother's brother, Joseph Simon, first Jew to settle in Lancaster, Pennsylvania, he came to America in 1746 and was taken into Simon's household as a kind of adopted son. At first he was a clerk in Simon's store. Later he became his business partner.

In 1757 Simon opened a fur trading post at Fort Pitt and put Levy in charge. For the next 15 years Levy spent most of his time traveling through what are now the states of Ohio, West Virginia, and Pennsylvania, exchanging white man's merchandise for Indian fur skins. In 1761 he married a lady by whom he had eight children. It seems that for a while his wife and firstborn, a son, lived at Fort Pitt, because the child was not brought to Lancaster to be circumcised until he was two years old. After that it appears that Mrs. Levy remained in Lancaster. As told in a preceding article, Levy was taken captive by Miami Indians during the 1763 Pontiac war and was ransomed.

Shimon ben Reb Leib, third child, second son of Levy Andrew Levy, was born in Lancaster on January 18, 1774. He was given the English name of Simeon Magruder Levy. Why such an un-Jewish-sounding middle name? Christiana Magruder, 1732-1813, lived in the Levy home for much of her long life as, technically, a household servant. But she must have been much more than that because, when she died, she was buried in the Levy family plot in Baltimore. She was probably a close companion of Mrs. Levy and a nurse for the children, a person very much needed because of Mr. Levy's many and prolonged absences. Perhaps she acted as midwife at Simeon's birth. It was probably as a tribute to her goodness and helpfulness that the Levys gave to their third child her surname as his middle name.

Levy Andrew Levy is listed as having served in the Fort Pitt militia during the Indian wars and in the Lancaster militia during the Revolutionary War. Simon and Levy supplied both money and clothing to the Continentals. It appears that in 1785 the partners quarreled over money matters and dissolved partnership. The Levys moved to Hagerstown.

There at age eighteen Simeon Magruder Levy enlisted in the troops under General Wayne. Sometime before 1799 his parents moved to Baltimore, where they ran a boarding house. His mother died in Baltimore in 1807, the same year that Simeon's life came to an end in Georgia. His father died in 1829 at the age of ninety-five.

*   *   *   *   *

In the fall of 1794 President Washington decided to open a school at the military post at West Point, New York, to train deserving non-coms to become commissioned officers. He requested Anthony Wayne to recommend for the school non-coms who had demonstrated bravery and efficiency in the battle of Fallen Timbers. Among those recommended by Wayne was Levy "for his good conduct as Orderly Sergeant in the Battle of Maumee Rapids." In the *Memoirs* of Joseph Gardner Swift, General Swift states that his West Point classmate Levy was "formerly a sergeant in Captain Lockwood's company of infantry and was promoted to cadet for his merit and mathematic attainments." Before the end of 1794 Sergeant Levy reported to the military school at West Point.

The school was operated as one of the responsibilities of the West Point garrison. Its curriculum consisted entirely of courses in military science. In 1796 the school building burned down. Classes were suspended until 1801. On March 2 of that year the school resumed, with the addition of a course in mathematics. On this day the first large group of cadets began their studies, forty to be trained as artillery officers, the remaining ten as engineers. On March 16, 1802, by act of Congress, the United States Military Academy officially came into existence as an academic institution, located at West Point but completely separate from that post's military garrison. On October 12, 1802, West Point Military Academy held its first graduation. There were two cadets in the first graduating class. Listed in alphabetical order, they were Simeon Magruder Levy, 1774-1807, and Joseph Gardner Swift, 1783-1865.

Lieutenant Levy, at the time of his graduation, had been in the military service for ten years. He was a combat veteran. He was the first enlisted man in the history of the United States Army appointed to USMA and graduated therefrom as a commissioned officer. He came to West Point as an artilleryman but was graduated as a military engineer.

He was at the school from the time of its beginning in 1794 until its first graduation in 1802. He was graduated at the age of twenty-eight.

Lieutenant Levy remained at West Point for two more years. In 1804 he was assigned to Fort Wilkinson, Georgia, as assistant engineering officer. He resigned from the service because of serious illness on September 30, 1805. He died in Georgia in 1807. The nature of his illness, the exact date of his death, and his place of burial are not known.

What about Lieutenant Joseph Gardner Swift? What was his background? What was his previous military record?

Lieutenant Swift was born in Nantucket, Massachusetts, and educated at Bristol Academy, Taunton, Massachusetts. His family was one of the "first families" of Massachusetts. On his mother's side he was descended from a French Huguenot who came to Massachusetts in 1621 and on his father's side from a Puritan who was in Massachusetts before 1634. He was appointed to the Military Academy on May 12, 1800, at the age of seventeen, by President John Adams, resident of Quincy, Massachusetts. He was graduated from West Point two years and five months later at the age of nineteen, having attended the Academy for one year and eight months and having had, to this point, not a single day of extended active duty. The West Point tradition that Lieutenant Joseph Gardner Swift was the first graduate of USMA is probably based on the statement in his *Memoirs* that "Cadets J. G. Swift and S. M. Levy were the graduates and they were both commissioned *to rank in the order just named*." [Editorial underlining is for purpose of emphasis.]

Lieutenant Swift went on to an admirable career both as military officer and civilian. He advanced during the War of 1812 to the rank of Brigadier General. He resigned from the Army in 1818 and became an outstanding civil engineer.

* * * * *

Now consider this: It is graduation day, West Point Military Academy, October 12, 1802. Two fine young men are to be commissioned. One, twenty-eight years old, son of a Jewish immigrant, battle veteran with ten years of military service, a former Sergeant who has earned promotion to officer rank because of his "merit and mathematic attainments." The other, nineteen years old, scion of first-vintage colonial stock, his sole contact with the military one year and eight months at the Military Academy. Given the mood of the time and the place, which of these two will be granted the honor of receiving his diploma first? In October 1802 Jews had been granted full civil rights in only nine of the sixteen United States. So which one? The nineteen-year-old blue blood, of course. The feelings of Lieutenant Levy on that graduation day are not difficult to imagine.

Any doubt as to the manner in which Lieutenant Levy reacted to his role of rankly-discriminated-against military officer should be dispelled by sentiments expressed in letters written by Jonathan Williams to Joseph Swift on February 8 and August 26, 1805. Williams was Superintendent of West Point in 1802 when Levy and Swift were graduated.

On February 8 Williams wrote:

> Pray, do you know anything of Levy? If all be true that has been said, it would be desirable if he were to resign. Though I have no concern in the Corps at present, I cannot bear to hear that a certain disease called the Rum-itis should attack anyone belonging to it.

And on August 26 he wrote:

> Levy has resigned. I suppose your promotion over his head roused his benumbed spirit and induced him to do what, from a conscientious sense of his dependence on *artificial* spirits, he should have done long since.

In an age when love for the bottle was common among American military officers and almost unheard of among American Jews, behind those few sentences written by Williams may lie the story of a talented young officer who turned to drink in order to forget that he could not get ahead because he was a Jew.

Levy did not actually resign until more than a month after Williams wrote his August letter. The reason for his resignation is recorded as "because of serious illness." Two years later he was dead. There is a possibility that Levy died of cirrhosis of the liver brought on by excessive drinking. There would seem to be an even greater possibility that the cause of his early demise was a broken heart, induced by the poison of religioethnic prejudice.

Every history of the United States Military Academy which I have examined avers, without further explanation, that General Joseph Gardner Swift was the first graduate of the Academy. It would seem, in the given set of circumstances, that Academy historians would be on more equitable and impartial ground if they would simply state that the first two graduates of the United States Military Academy were Simeon Magruder Levy and Joseph Gardner Swift.

John Brown's Jewish Soldiers
(1856)

Was Abolitionist John Brown saint or sinner, martyr or madman? The answer depends on whose book one reads. Here is part of a description of John Brown's ability to influence others, written by a member of the band of Free Soil Kansans which, under Brown's command, drove back the "border ruffians," the pro-slavery terrorists who, in May 1856, invaded Kansas and pillaged and burned the town of Lawrence:

We were united as a band of brothers by the love and affection towards the man who with tender words and wise counsel, in the depth of the Kansas wilderness, prepared a handful of young men for the work of laying the foundation of a free commonwealth. He expressed himself to us that we should never allow ourselves to be tempted by any consideration to acknowledge laws and institutions to exist as of right if our conscience and reason condemned them. He admonished us not to care whether a majority, no matter how large, opposed our principles and opinions. The largest majorities were sometimes only organized mobs, whose howlings never changed black into white or night into day. A minority conscious of its rights, based on moral principles, would, under a republican government, sooner or later become the majority.

Regarding the curse and crimes of the institution of slavery, he declared that the outrages committed in Kansas to further its extension had directed the attention of all intelligent citizens of the United States and the world to the necessity of its abolishment, as a stumbling block in the path of nineteenth century civilization; that while it was true that the pro-slavery people and their aiders and abetters had the upper hand at present, and the free state organization had dwindled to a handful hid in the brush, nevertheless we ought to be of good cheer, and start the ball to rolling at the first opportunity, no matter whether its starting motion would even crush us to death. We were under the protection of a wise providence, which might use our feeble efforts.

Time and again Captain Brown entreated us never to follow the example of the border ruffians, who took a delight in destruction; never to burn houses or fences, so often done by the enemy. Repeatedly he admonished us not to take human life except when absolutely necessary. Before every meal the captain spoke the blessing aloud. He was an orthodox Christian; some of his sons were free thinkers, regarding which he remarked that he had tried to give

The source materials for this article were made available by the Kansas State Historical Society of Topeka, Kansas, and the Hebrew Union College Library and American Jewish Archives of Cincinnati, Ohio.

his children a good education, and now they were old enough to choose for themselves.

The further time removes this struggle of the distant past, the more thorough becomes the purity of John Brown's principles and intentions and heroic sacrifices. My old friend will appear to impartial history as equal to the most exalted characters produced by humanity, and will so go down to the end of time. Truly, in his behalf can we say with Hesiod: "His is the immortal reward of the labor of the great."

Thus, in 1884, did August Bondi, a foreign-born American Jew, write about John Brown, a descendant of New England Pilgrims, and his beloved leader in the Kansas "Wakarusa War" of 1856. [Wakarusa was the original name of Lawrence, Kansas.]

     ❖   ❖   ❖   ❖   ❖

Anshel Bondi was born in Vienna in 1833. His parents were originally from Prague. On May 15, 1848, Anshel, about to enter Vienna University, became the youngest member of Company Five of the Philosophy Battalion in the Academic Legion, composed of thousands of university students designed to be part of a civilian army which would overthrow the tyrannical government of Prince Metternich and establish a democratic regime. Before the bloody events of the following October ended the Metternich dictatorship, Bondi's parents decided to take him to a land of brighter promise, the United States. They arrived in New Orleans in November, took a Mississippi riverboat to St. Louis and settled there. Soon thereafter Anshel Bondi's name was Americanized to August Bondi.

In the summer of 1851 August joined an adventurous outfit designed to liberate Cuba from the Spaniards. The day before his company was to embark from St. Louis, word came that the first wave of the invasion had been overcome by the Spaniards and annihilated. In consequence, the St. Louis contingent abandoned the project.

In the fall of 1851 August traveled down to New Orleans to enroll in Commodore Matthew Perry's trade expedition to Japan. He arrived too late. The expedition's complement was already full. So he worked for five-and-a-half months as a bartender on a ship on the New Orleans-Galveston run. He returned to St. Louis in May 1852. In September 1854 Bondi became a clerk in the store of Jacob Benjamin, a roly-poly Bohemian Jewish immigrant, who was about the same age as Bondi.

On May 30, 1854, Kansas was designated a Territory and opened to white settlers. Almost at once it became the focal point of a bitter struggle between pro-slavery homesteaders from western Missouri and the South and antislavery homesteaders from the Middle West and the East. In

May 1855 Bondi and Benjamin decided to go to Kansas to homestead, to operate a general store as partners, and to participate in the fight to keep slavery out of.the Territory.

On May 25 they staked out a claim in Franklin County, on the Mosquito branch of Pottowatomie Creek, about four miles west of the present town of Lane. In July Benjamin went back to St. Louis to purchase goods. While he was gone Bondi became acquainted with the sons of John Brown, who had a farm and cattle ranch four-and-a-half miles away, just north of the site of Lane. Benjamin returned on August 1 with word that another Jewish partner had joined the business, Theodore Wiener, a thiry-seven-year-old immigrant from German Poland. Wiener had lived for a number of years in Texas and Louisiana. As a result of this southern exposure, he arrived in Kansas in November as a pro-slavery man. In February 1856 Wiener was insulted by a six-foot-three inch 300-pound pro-slavery, anti-Semitic bully. Five-foot-ten inch, 250-pound Wiener beat the tar out of his weightier and taller opponent. Thereafter he was numbered with the antislavery fighters, partly because he became convinced that most of the pro-slavery gang were professional hoodlums and partly because he had come under the spell of John Brown, who journeyed from Akron, Ohio, to his sons' Kansas ranch in October 1855 to join the antislavery crusade.

Benjamin left again for St. Louis in September 1855 to fetch more goods. While in St. Louis he became sick and had to remain there a while. Then Bondi became ill and in November he, too, went back to St. Louis for medical attention. That same month Benjamin married a St. Louis Jewish girl. In March 1856 Benjamin and his wife came to Kansas. In April Wiener journeyed to St. Louis to restock. In May Wiener and Bondi started back to Kansas. They arrived in Kansas City on May 17. Bondi remained in Kansas City to attend to some business and Wiener continued on.

Bondi returned to Pottawatomie Creek on the evening of May 21. Just moments after he arrived, news came that this same day a pro-slavery force from Missouri had raided the antislavery settlement of Lawrence, 50 miles to the north, and left it in ruins. Plans were made immediately to drive the raiders from the Territory. The business partners decided that Bondi and Wiener would join the free-soil militia. Benjamin and his now pregnant wife would stay with a friend who lived about sixteen miles to the northeast, three miles north of Osawatomie.

Under command of John Brown, armed men from Pottawatomie, Osawatomie, and the Palmyra-Prairie City (now Baldwin City) area assembled on May 22 near Palmyra and prepared to advance on Lawrence. That evening they received a request from the Lawrence settlers to advance no further, lest the people of Lawrence be subjected to more suffering.

On May 23 a messenger arrived from Pottawatomie Creek to report that, after the antislavery men had departed, a number of pro-slavery settlers in the area had gone from house to house and grossly insulted the free-soilers' wives and children. They had attempted to rape the twenty-three-year-old sister of one of the militiamen. Greatly incensed, Brown announced that he, his sons, his son-in-law, and Wiener would go back to Pottawatomie to put an end to these shameful doings. He instructed Bondi to proceed to the Brown farm to let the women there know where their menfolk were. Brown and the others mentioned then went to Pottawatomie Creek where six unarmed men, men who had threatened the antislavery households, were shot down in what has been termed "the Pottowatomie massacre." Wiener did not take part in the killings. He was assigned to guard the horses. The killings were strictly a Brown family affair. Bondi believed the action justified. In his *Autobiography* he wrote, "John Brown and his handful of men only executed upon those scoundrels a just sentence of death for the benefit of many unprotected families."

On May 26 ten men, including Bondi and Wiener, were gathered at the Brown farm. They received a plea from the settlers in the southern part of Douglas County to help them get rid of the marauders who had pillaged Lawrence. After sunset eleven men rode north on this rescue mission. Brown had a sabre and a revolver. His five sons each had a revolver, cutlass, and squirrel rifle. Another man was similarly armed. Another had a revolver; still another, an old musket. Wiener had a double-barreled shotgun. Bondi had an 1812 flintlock musket given him by John Brown. Thus equipped the "army" rode north to battle.

On the morning of the 28th an additional member of the "Pottawatomie Rifles" arrived. He reported that the "border ruffians" had burned Bondi's cabin, stolen his cattle, and plundered Wiener's storehouse. Bondi later wrote:

> All this had happened in the presence of U. S. troops. Their commanding officer, Captain Cook, Company F, 2d U. S. Dragoons, was asked by the settlers to interfere. He refused, saying he had no orders to that effect.

Brown and his small force caught up with the ruffians on June 2 on the old Santa Fe trail at Black Jack Spring, near Palmyra, and immediately attacked. In after years, Bondi recalled the action for the American Jewish Historical Society:

> We followed Captain Brown up the hill toward the Border Ruffians' camp, I next to Brown and in advance of Wiener. We walked with bent backs, nearly crawled that the tall dead grass of the year before might somewhat hide us from the Border Ruffian

marksmen. Yet the bullets kept whistling. Wiener was 37 and weighed 250 pounds. I was 22 and lithe. Wiener puffed like a steamboat, hurrying behind me. I called out to him, "Nu, was meinen Sie jetzt? [Well, what do you think of all this now?]" His answer was, "Was soll ich meinen? [What should I think]" [In a time like that, one Jew answers another Jew's foolish question with another foolish question. What else?] I quoted a Hebrew saying, "Sof adam maves [Everyone has to die sooner or later]." In spite of whistling bullets, I had to laugh when Wiener said, "Machen wir dem alten Mann sonst b'rogez [We'd better stop talking this Jewish lingo or else old man Brown will get angry]."

Although greatly outnumbered, Brown's brave little band won a complete victory. Twenty-four mercenaries surrendered, thirty ran away, seven seriously wounded were stretched on the ground. The free-soilers' casualties: one seriously wounded, one less seriously. The flint-lock musket used by Bondi in "the battle of Black Jack" is now on display in Topeka in the museum of the Kansas State Historical Society.

After Black Jack, Wiener went to Louisiana to attend to some old business. Bondi and Benjamin returned to their land at the end of June. But the conflict was not yet over. Bondi went with a company under Brown's command that moved out of Osawatomie on August 24 to deal with a large gang of Ruffians who were harassing the Free State settlers of Linn and Bourbon Counties, due south of Osawatomie on the Missouri border. When the Ruffians heard that Brown was on the way, they fled back to Missouri, although they outnumbered Brown's fighters better than five to one. Such was the fear which merely the mention of "old John Brown" inspired. So there was no battle.

Benjamin reached Brown on August 28 with the report that a large pro-slavery force had come over the border just south of Lawrence and was headed for Osawatomie. Brown and his men hurried north to Osawatomie and stationed pickets on the roads leading to Paola and Lawrence. Bondi and Benjamin were the pickets assigned to the Paola road from two to six A.M. on August 30. At about five A.M. they heard the sound of firing. Four hundred Missourians had attacked Osawatomie and driven Brown and his small troop from the town. Four antislavery men were killed, including one of Brown's sons. Osawatomie was looted and burned. The Free Staters retreated to Lawrence, regrouped and prepared to continue the struggle. On September 17, just as a battle was about to start near Lawrence between 2,500 Missourians and 500 Kansans, a truce was declared and the "Wakarusa War" came to an end. From that time on the Kansans became stronger and stronger and the number of raids from Missouri steadily decreased.

Benjamin returned to Possawatomie and took his wife, heavy with child, to Osawatomie because he wanted her to be near a doctor. Bondi went back to his land and rebuilt his cabin. There, toward the end of September, John Brown paid him a brief visit. Then Brown left to spend the winter in Iowa. That was the last time Bondi saw "the [fifty-six-year] old man." About the middle of October, Mrs. Benjamin died in childbirth; her infant son died a few hours later.

In December 1856 Benjamin, Bondi and Wiener were among the six founders of Greeley in Anderson County, seven miles southwest of Bondi's first homestead. Bondi was appointed postmaster. He and Benjamin opened a store in the new town. Bondi's parents, who had moved from St. Louis to Louisville, Kentucky, joined him in Greeley and lived with him for the rest of their lives. On December 1, 1857, Bondi was one of 45 Free Staters who drove a band of 250 marauding Missourians back over the border. The Missourians lost three dead and seven wounded. Not a single Kansan got so much as a scratch. But Bondi suffered a personal loss. He was removed from his job as postmaster because, during the December 1 engagement, he fired at a U. S. Marshal. The accusation was true. The marshal was a member of the invading gang. So strong was the political clout of the slavery advocates at that time that the federal government penalized Bondi for helping defend his Territory against an illegal invasion.

*   *   *   *   *

All three of John Brown's Jewish soldiers served in the Union Army during the Civil War.

Benjamin enlisted in Company E of the Eleventh Kansas and, according to Bondi, "was considered a D.B. in the service." *Webster's New International Dictionary* states that D.B. is the abbreviation for daybook. That meaning has no relevance in the Bondi context. Perhaps, as used, it stands for "deadbeat" or "drawback." These meanings would fit Bondi's final estimate of Benjamin. The two had a violent quarrel in July 1860 and, after that, spoke to each other no more. Benjamin died in late 1865 of injuries suffered when the team of horses he was driving ran away and threw him from his wagon.

Wiener never actually lived in Greeley. Shortly after the "Wakarusa War," he moved to Washington, Iowa. He died in 1906 and is buried in St. Louis.

Bondi enlisted in Company K of the 5th Kansas Cavalry on December 23, 1861. He was promoted to First Sergeant in November 1862. He was severely wounded in September 1864 and spent two months in the hospital. He was mustered out on December 2, 1864.

He moved to Salina, Kansas, in July 1866 and spent the rest of his life in that community. He served as probate judge, 1876-78; police judge, 1879-85; postmaster, 1894-97. He was admitted to the county bar in 1896 at the age of sixty-three. He died, September 30, 1907, while on a visit to St. Louis.

His funeral was held in Salina the following Thursday. The local newspaper reported:

> The funeral services of Judge August Bondi were held this afternoon at 2 o'clock at the Masonic Temple. The services were largely attended, the building being packed to standing room. Rabbi Harry H. Mayer of Kansas City performed the Jewish rites. The sermon he delivered was pronounced to be one of the best ever heard in Salina. His eulogy of the deceased was especially fine and went direct to the hearts of the friends present. In honor of Judge Bondi the county courthouse was closed during the funeral service.

DID THE TEN LOST TRIBES EVER FIND THEMSELVES IN OHIO?
(1860)

Over two thousand years ago an agricultural civilization developed in the Ohio River Valley and spread slowly down the entire Mississippi Valley, culminating in a great confederacy of tribes that reached from the Gulf of Mexico to the Canadian border and from the Atlantic coast to Kansas. These people built majestic mounds all over the eastern part of the United States.

Some of the mounds were used for ceremonial purposes but most of them were for burial. They represented a series of burials over a long period of time. Each new burial was on top of the earth that covered the previous ones. Each new grave was covered with its own little mound which, in time, grew to be one giant mound.

The archeologists call this mound civilization the Hopewell culture, the name of one of the sites excavated in southern Ohio. The Hopewell culture reached its peak from 400 B.C.E. to 400 C.E. Much is known about it because of the artifacts found in the graves. The mound builders used the pearls of fresh-water mussels, probably made into necklace beads, as their means of exchange. To enhance their own looks, they bored openings in their earlobes and inserted plugs made of copper, wood, shell, or stone. These ear plugs look like thick roundheaded carpet tacks. The women wore wraparound skirts and the men breechcloths. Their garments were dyed red, black, and yellow. They also made clothing and moccasins from fur, blankets and capes from feathers, necklaces

---

Much of this account has been taken from an article by Rabbi David Philipson in the Publications of the American Jewish Historical Society, No. 13, 1905.

from shells and silver. Their medicine men were attired in an antler headdress and the teeth and jawbones of humans and animals.

The culture died out about 500 C.E. By the time the white men arrived in the Ohio Valley in the seventeenth century, the area was almost completely depopulated. Southern Ohio was a no man's land, used primarily as a hunting ground and, in time of war, as a battlefield. Just why there was such a dramatic change in what had been a busy, thriving, many-towned area is not known.

The largest center of the Hopewell mound culture discovered thus far is on the western outskirts of Newark, Ohio. It was originally four square miles in size. In August 1881 workers digging out a building foundation in West Newark found a six-inch-long stone effigy of a seated man, evidently a shaman, dressed in the skin of a bear with the bear's head on top of his own. In the shaman's lap is a human head with round plugs in its earlobes. This is the most advanced piece of sculpture yet found from the period of the Hopewell culture.

✿   ✿   ✿   ✿   ✿

In June 1860 D. Wyrick, a Newark printer who was greatly interested in the mound builders, announced that, in a mound a mile southwest of Newark, he had found a wedge-shaped stone not quite six inches long and three inches wide at its widest part. On each of its four sides was a Hebrew inscription. Their translations were "King of the earth," "The Law of the Lord," "The Word of the Lord," and "Holy of holies."

The following November the printer asserted he had made an even more important find. He had unearthed a stone casket 18 inches long and 12 inches wide, containing a stone slab 6⅞ inches long, 1⅝ inches thick, and 2⅞ inches wide. On one side was carved a human figure, fierce and pugnacious looking, in turban and priestly robes. Above it was the Hebrew word, "MOSHEH," Moses. The Ten Commandments were written in Hebrew in abbreviated form all over the rest of the slab.

In 1865 Wyrick informed the community that he had dug up a third treasure in a mound about three miles east of Newark: two small human heads chiseled from sandstone. Each was about 1½ inches long and had some letters that looked like Hebrew carved on its forehead.

Wyrick claimed that this series of what he called "the Holy Stones of Newark" discoveries proved beyond the shadow of a doubt that the mound builders were the Ten Lost Tribes. Many pious Christians believed him. A few rabbis half believed him. Most did not. One of the Jewish disbelievers sent photos of the "Holy Stones" to the eminent German scholar, Rabbi Abraham Geiger. Geiger declared categorically that they were clumsy forgeries of recent manufacture, created by someone with a faulty knowledge of Hebrew.

Many continued to believe that the finds were genuine. Wyrick sold the stones to David M. Johnson of Coshocton, Ohio. A plaster cast of the "Commandment Stone" was placed in the Smithsonian Institution.

Years later Wyrick died. After his death bits of slate with Hebrew letters carved on them were found in his office, as well as a woodcut of Moses exactly like the one on the slab. It was obvious that Wyrick had made the "relics," hidden them in the mounds, and then had "found" them in the presence of witnesses.

As late as 1904 there were still some who believed that Wyrick's "discoveries" were genuine. An archeological magazine published in Ohio in 1904 stated that, in former days, one could discern on a cliff above the Licking River a large black hand. The rock on which it was engraved was known as Black Hand Rock. The writer continued:

This hand pointed to the mound that contained the remains of the last rabbi who had ministered at the tribal altar. Doubtless, when his work was done, his followers gave him a burial that went to show their love and esteem in the mound they raised over his remains and the tablet that was as a guide to their faith, and then they put the hand on the rock, pointing to the place of his burial.

LINCOLN AND THE JEWS
(1865)

There are many who regard Abraham Lincoln as not only the greatest American President but also the greatest of all Americans. The folklore that surrounds the relationship of Abraham Lincoln to the Jews is a fascinating intermixture of fact and fiction. Although more than a century has passed since Lincoln's time, no one can yet say with absolute certainty what is fact and what fiction.

✿　✿　✿　✿　✿

William H. Herndon, Lincoln's law partner from 1843 until Lincoln became President, wrote in 1888:

Beyond the fact that he was born on the twelfth day of February, 1809, in Hardin County, Kentucky, Mr. Lincoln usually had but little to say of himself, the lives of his parents, or the history of the family before their removal to Indiana. If he mentioned the subject at all, it was with great reluctance and significant reserve. There was something about his origin he never cared to dwell upon.

Among the earliest newspaper men to arrive in Springfield after the Chicago convention [of 1860 which nominated Lincoln] was the late J. L. Scripps of the Chicago *Tribune*, who proposed to prepare a history of his life. Mr. Lincoln deprecated the idea of writing even a campaign biography. . . . Soon after the death of Lincoln I received a letter from Scripps, in which, among other things, he recalled meeting with Lincoln, and the view he took of the biography matter.

"Lincoln seemed to be painfully impressed," he wrote, "with the extreme poverty of his early surroundings, and the utter absence of all romantic and heroic elements. He communicated some facts to me concerning his ancestry, which he did not wish to have published then, and which I have never spoken of or alluded to before." What the facts referred to by Mr. Scripps were we do not know; for he died several years ago without, so far as is known, revealing them to anyone.

On the subject of his ancestry and origin I only remember one time when Mr. Lincoln ever referred to it. It was about 1850, when he and I were driving in his one-horse buggy to court in Menard County, Illinois. The suit we were going to try was one in which we were likely, either directly or collaterally, to touch upon the subject of hereditary traits. During the ride he spoke, for the first time in my hearing, of his mother, dwelling on her characteristics, and mentioning and enumerating what qualities he inherited from her. He said, among other things, that she was the illegitimate daughter of Lucy Hanks and a well-bred Virginia farmer or planter; and he argued that from this last source came his power of analysis, his logic, his mental activity, his ambition, and all the qualities that distinguished him from the other members and descendants of the Hanks family. His theory in discussing the matter of hereditary traits had been that, for certain reasons, illegitimate children are oftentimes sturdier and brighter than those born in lawful wedlock; and, in his case, he believed that his better nature and finer qualities came from this broad-minded, unknown Virginian. The revelation—painful as it was—called up the recollection of his mother, and, as the buggy jolted over the road, he added ruefully, "God bless my mother; all that I am or ever hope to be I owe to her"; and immediately lapsed into silence. Our interchange of ideas ceased, and we rode on for some time without exchanging a word. He was sad and absorbed. Burying himself in thought, and musing no doubt over the disclosure he had just made, he drew around him a barrier which I feared to penetrate. His words and melancholy tone made a deep impression on me. It was an experience I can never forget.

Earlier in his book Herndon had written:

After Mr. Lincoln attained some prominence in the world, persons who knew both himself and his father were constantly pointing to the want of resemblance between the two. The old gentleman was not only devoid of energy, and shiftless, but dull, and these persons were unable to account for the source of his son's ambition and his intellectual superiority over other men. . . . Regarding the paternity of Lincoln a great many surmises and a still larger amount of unwritten or, at least, unpublished history have drifted into the currents of western lore and journalism.

In the Cincinnati *Commercial* of April 20, 1865, five days after Lincoln died, Rabbi Isaac M. Wise is quoted as follows:

> Abraham Lincoln believed himself to be bone of our bone and flesh of our flesh. He supposed himself to be of Hebrew parentage. He said so in my presence; and, indeed, he possessed the common features of the Hebrew race both in countenance and expression.

Many years later Lincoln's son Robert stated he had never heard his father state such a belief, which is hardly surprising. One would not be likely to tell his child that his father is, as one writer bluntly put it, "a bastard and the son of a bastard." From this has grown one of many legends regarding Lincoln's paternity. The "Hebrew" version is that Lincoln was sired by a Jewish peddler who serviced Nancy while Thomas was not at home.

This might be dismissed as baseless slander were it not for certain hard, incontrovertible facts: Abraham Lincoln was a deeply religious man. Whenever he quoted the Bible, which was frequently, he almost always quoted from the Old Testament. He rarely went to church. He was never formally affiliated with any religious denomination. Once, when asked to designate the thinker whose views on religion most nearly coincided with his own, he named Theodore Parker, 1810-60, a left-of-center Unitarian minister. Early in 1834, while Lincoln was considering running for the state legislature, he wrote a lengthy essay asserting that the Bible was not divinely revealed and that Jesus was not God. He showed it to the owner of the store in which he was employed. The merchant, after reading the essay, destroyed it, telling Lincoln that its publication would demolish the possibility of his being elected to public office.

Here are statements about Lincoln's religious beliefs from people who knew him intimately:

> Herndon: He was a fatalist. He did not believe, except in a very limited sense, in freedom of the will.
> Another friend: Mr. Lincoln believed in a Creator of all things, who had neither beginning nor end, possessing all power and wisdom, who established the principle in obedience to which worlds move and are upheld, and animal and vegetable life come into existence.
> Another friend: He did not believe in what are regarded as the orthodox or evangelical views of Christianity. His religious views were eminently practical, and are summed up in two phrases, the Fatherhood of God and the brotherhood of man.
> His wife: Mr. Lincoln had no faith and no hope in the usual acceptation of those words. He never joined a church; but still, as I believe, he was a religious man by nature. Religion was a kind of poetry in his nature. He was never a technical Christian.

*   *   *   *   *

Morris J. Raphall, a distinguished New York City rabbi, was an ardent supporter of the institution of slavery. He declared that the Bible approves of slavery and, therefore, it was divinely established, a theological point of view shared by Rabbis Isaac Leeser of Philadelphia and Isaac M. Wise of Cincinnati. He came to see Lincoln to ask him to help get his son Alfred promoted from Second to First Lieutenant. The visit coincided with a day on which Lincoln had asked that prayers be said in all houses of worship for the victory of the Union forces.

When Raphall came into Lincoln's office, the President said to him, "Rabbi, as God's minister, should you not be at home today praying with your people for the success of our arms?" Greatly embarrassed, Raphall stammered out, "My assistant is performing that duty." "Ah," said Lincoln, "that explains it." He then wrote a note to the Secretary of War, instructing him to promote Alfred. He handed the note to Rabbi Raphall, saying, "Take this to Secretary Stanton. Then, doctor, you will be able to go home and do your own praying."

❊   ❊   ❊   ❊   ❊

Late in 1861 lawyer Simon Wolf and Ohio Congressman Thomas Corwin went to see Lincoln to plead for the life of an Ohio Jewish soldier sentenced to be shot for desertion. Wolf describes what happened in his book *Presidents I Have Known:*

> It was two o'clock in the morning. The President walked up and down with his hands hanging by his side; his face wore that gravity of expression that has been so often described by his historians and biographers, and yet greeting us as if we were his boon companions. He listened with deep attention and, when Corwin had exhausted the subject, the President replied, "It is impossible for me to do anything. I have no influence in this administration." The twinkle in his eyes was indescribable. "Stanton [the Secretary of War] has put his foot down and insists on one of two things, either I stop interfering in his departmental affairs or he will quit." Corwin turned to me and said, "I told you, my dear friend, that it was hopeless"; and he was about to leave the room.
>
> I said, "Mr. President, you will pardon me for an additional moment. What would you have done under similar circumstances? If your dying mother had summoned you to her bedside to receive her last message before her soul would be summoned to its Maker, would you rather have been a deserter to her who gave you birth or a deserter in law but not in fact to the flag to which you had sworn allegiance?" Lincoln stopped walking. He touched a bell. His secretary, John Hay, who time and again spoke of that occurrence, came in. Lincoln ordered a telegram sent to halt the execution.
>
> That American citizen of Jewish faith subsequently led a doomed charge with the flag of his country in his hands at the battle of Cold Harbor [June 1-3, 1864] and was shot to death. When months

afterward I told the President what had become of that young soldier, he was visibly moved. With great emotion, he said, "I thank God for having done what I did."

＊　＊　＊　＊　＊

In September 1862 a young English Jewish chiropodist, Isachar Zacharie, began to take care of Lincoln's feet. Zacharie was a charmer. He was described by the New York *Herald* as "a wit, gourmet and eccentric, with a splendid Roman nose, fashionable whiskers and eloquent tongue, a dazzling diamond breast pin, with great skill in his profession and an ingratiating address." He and Lincoln became quite friendly. What is supposed to have happened after that is believed by most historians to be more fancy than fact.

General Benjamin Butler, "the Beast of New Orleans," military governor of that city, was accused in 1862 of mistreating southerners and being abusive to Jews. Zacharie volunteered to go to New Orleans to find out if the charges were true. Before Zacharie arrived, General Butler was succeeded as Commanding General by General Nathaniel P. Banks. Banks asked Zacharie to ascertain the attitude of the Jews and other citizens toward the Union forces. Zacharie tried to persuade Rabbi James K. Gutheim to take the oath of allegiance to the United States. Gutheim refused and was expelled from the city. Zacharie's efforts with other prominent citizens of New Orleans, Jewish and non-Jewish, were more successful, so much so that Zacharie came to believe that he could singlehandedly end the war.

He returned to Washington in July 1863 and persuaded Lincoln to send him through the lines to meet with Jefferson Davis in an effort to halt the conflict in a way that would "save the face" and satisfy the pride of the Confederacy. He was smuggled into Richmond by way of Harper's Ferry. He did not get to talk to Davis; but, so the story goes, he did confer with Secretary of State Judah P. Benjamin, Secretary of War James A. Seddon, Secretary of the Navy Stephen R. Mallory, and Provost Marshal General John H. Winder. The plan for ending the war presented by Zacharie, presumably on behalf of President Lincoln, was not acceptable to the leaders of the Confederacy.

What was this plan? The New York *Herald*, on October 21, 1863, "revealed" what it claimed was the proposal made by Zacharie to the rebels: The Federal government would finance a military expedition of the Confederate armed forces against Mexico. After Mexico was conquered, it would become a republic in which slavery would be permitted. Jefferson Davis would be its President. Those Confederates who so wished would develop their own way of life in Mexico. The southern states would return to the Union. It does not seem likely that such a weird scheme would have had Lincoln's approval.

When his proposal, whatever it may have been, was turned down, Zacharie returned to Washington. He continued to take care of Lincoln's feet and be his friend. Years later Zacharie returned to England. He died in 1897.

*   *   *   *   *

Lincoln's closest Jewish friend was Abraham Jonas, 1801-64, a politician and lawyer in Quincy, Illinois. Jonas and Lincoln first met in 1834, when Jonas was operating a store in Williamstown, Kentucky.

Jonas was born in England. He came to Cincinnati in 1819, two years later than his brother Joseph, the first Jew to settle in that city. In 1821 he helped purchase a small plot for use as a Jewish cemetery from Nicholas Longworth, great-grandfather of the Ohio Congressman of the same name who married Alice, daughter of President Theodore Roosevelt. He was a charter member of Cincinnati's first synagogue. He married twice. His first wife was the daughter of Rabbi Gershom Mendel Seixas of New York City. She died in 1825. He remarried in 1829.

In 1827 Jonas moved to Williamstown, county seat of Grant County, Kentucky, 35 miles south of Cincinnati. He served in the Kentucky legislature in 1828-30 and 1833. In 1838 he left Williamstown and settled in Quincy. Until this time he had been a merchant. Now, in his leisure hours, he studied law. He was elected to the Illinois legislature in 1842. Here he and fellow-legislator Lincoln strengthened their already existing friendship. He was admitted to the Illinois bar in 1843.

Lincoln and Jonas were founding members of the Republican party in Illinois. They campaigned together in 1856 for John Fremont. In 1860 Jonas worked hard for the election of his friend Abe. When Lincoln was charged during the campaign with having been a member of the Quincy branch of the American (Know Nothing) Party, an anti-Irish, anti-Catholic nativist political group that flourished briefly during the 1850s, it was to Jonas that Lincoln wrote on July 21, 1860, vigorously denying the charge.

Jonas served as postmaster of Quincy from 1849 to 1852. Lincoln appointed him to the same position in April 1861. Jonas occupied this post until he became seriously ill in the Spring of 1864.

Jonas had five sons. One, Edward, attained the rank of Major in the Union Army. The other four were in the Confederate Army—Benjamin (later became U. S. Senator from Louisiana), Charles, Julian, and Samuel, who wrote the poem "Written on the back of a Confederate note." Lincoln's affection for Jonas and his family did not change because the boys were fighting for the enemy. Whenever he met someone from New Orleans he would inquire after the welfare of Ben Jonas and his wife and children.

As Abraham Jonas lay dying in June 1864 his wife sent Lincoln a telegram asking for a parole for son Charles, a prisoner of war on Johnson's Island in Lake Erie, near Sandusky, Ohio, so that he might visit his dying father. Lincoln immediately issued an order granting Charles a three-week parole. Charles reached Quincy "on the day of my father's death, but in time to be recognized and welcomed by him." Afterward Lincoln appointed Mrs. Jonas postmistress of Quincy to fill the vacancy created by the death of her husband.

It Ain't Necessarily So
(1883)

There is a widely believed folktale that American Conservative Judaism was born in Cincinnati in the early summer of 1883. How and why? Rabbi Isaac M. Wise invited a number of traditionally minded rabbis, including Rabbi Sabato Morais of Philadelphia, to attend the first graduation exercises of the Hebrew Union College. It is alleged that, at the evening banquet celebrating this academic milestone, shrimp cocktails were served. The traditionalist rabbis present were shocked and offended. Rabbi Morais, so the story goes, returned to Philadelphia vowing he would create an American Jewish seminary and an American Jewish movement that would integrate Judaism and Americanism while preserving the appropriate amenities of both.

If such a strictly trefe dish was actually served, Rabbi Morais must have cooked his anger on a very slow burner because he continued his association with the Hebrew Union College until the end of 1885. While there are some who credit Rabbi Isaac Leeser, 1806-68, of Philadelphia, with being the founder of American Conservative Judaism, the actual break with Reform did not occur until 1886.

Morais joined with Leeser in establishing the first American Jewish college, Maimonides College, in Philadelphia in 1867. Maimonides College lasted six years. When the Hebrew Union College was founded in 1875, Morais gave it his approval and support. He was appointed official student examiner at the College and fulfilled this responsibility through the academic year of 1884-85. It was not the Hebrew Union College graduation banquet that triggered Morais' determination to found a new rabbinical seminary. It was the radical Pittsburgh Platform, adopted by a group of Reform rabbis in November 1885.

In January 1886 Morais sent out an appeal, signed by seven rabbis, urging that a strong effort be made "for the perpetuation of Judaism in America." He was determined "to form an institution in which Bible and

Talmud shall be studied to a religious purpose." The institution that was born as a result of this appeal, the Jewish Theological Seminary, opened in New York City on January 2, 1887. For the remaining ten years of his life Sabato Morais served as its president. From the concept of Catholic, i.e., universal, Judaism developed at JTS by Morais' eminent successor, Solomon Schechter, emerged the religioethnic philosophy and the powerful movement of American Conservative Judaism.

ARCTIC HERO

(1884)

August 1, 1882 to July 31, 1883 was designated by eleven nations as the First International Polar Year. During this year these nations cooperated in exploring previously unexplored Arctic areas. The United States was assigned the area accessible through Smith Sound and encompassing the northern ends of Greenland and Ellsmere Island, Grant Land, and Grinnell Land. Congress appropriated $25,000 for this project, the first time our government was the sole sponsor of an American polar venture. Three-fourths of the appropriated money was used to charter a sailing vessel to take the expedition north and bring it back.

Army Signal Corps Lieutenant Adolphus Washington Greely, 1844-1935, was in command. Greely had risen to the rank of brevet major in the Civil War before he was twenty-one. He was a keen student of meteorology. His party consisted of four Army officers, twenty enlisted men, and two Eskimos.

The expedition left St. John's, Newfoundland, in July 1881 and journeyed through Davis Strait, Baffin Bay, past the western bulge of Greenland (where Thule Air Force Base is now located), through Smith Sound, Kane Basin, Kennedy Channel, to Lady Franklin Bay at the northern end of Ellsmere Island. Here an exploration station was set up less than 500 miles from the North Pole. And here the party remained for two years carrying out its assigned missions. One of its sorties reached 83 degrees 24' N. latitude and 42 degrees 45' W. longitude, the closest point to the North Pole hitherto attained by man.

In the summer of 1882 the ship which was to bring fresh supplies did not appear. Neither did the ship which, in the summer of 1883, was to

---

The material for this story was furnished by Alexis A. Praus, Director of the Kalamazoo Public Museum. The primary source was an article by Alden L. Todd, "Edward Israel: Michigan's Arctic Pioneer," in the *Michigan Alumnus Quarterly Review*, Spring 1961, pp. 204-12.

return the expedition to civilization. The first ship was unable to get through the Arctic pack ice. The second ship was crushed by the ice and sank. On August 9, 1883, Greely, despairing of outside help, ordered the hazardous trip south in small boats to Smith Sound, the prearranged rendevous if the more northern channels became blocked with ice. On August 26, within sight of their goal, Cape Sabine on Smith Sound, their boats froze to the ice. In the middle of September all but one boat were abandoned. The men dragged their equipment over the ice floes to the land. In a message left in a cairn on Cape Sabine, they found the shattering news that they would have to spend the winter where they were with what little supplies they had left. Their relief ship had sunk seventeen days before they left Ellsmere Island. There was no chance of rescue until the following summer.

Their struggle for survival through that Arctic winter against overwhelming odds has been summed up in these words: "By the manner in which they fought for life and faced death, the Greely party at Cape Sabine proved themselves a band of heroes whom America should remember with pride." Of the twenty-six only six, including Greely, managed to survive. One died from exposure in a storm, one drowned while trying to catch and kill a seal, seventeen died of starvation. The individual unaccounted for in this listing was the only one who failed to measure up. He was detected stealing food which was meant to be shared by all. He was given a summary court-martial and shot.

A Navy rescue ship reached Cape Sabine on June 22, 1884. It returned to St. John's on July 17 with the six survivors and twelve of the bodies of the dead. It was only then that the world learned of this Arctic tragedy. The details were grim indeed. Later some members of the expedition were accused of having survived by eating their dead comrades' flesh, an accusation Greely stoutly denied. An intensive investigation indicated that none who survived had done this; but there was a possibility that a few of the dead may have hastened their demise by feeding on putrid, poisonous human meat.

Greely went on to become Chief Signal Officer of the Army, a major general and a highly respected authority on the Arctic.

✿   ✿   ✿   ✿   ✿

When the cannibalism charge was made in the aftermath of the ill-fated Lady Franklin Bay expedition, Sergeant Edward Israel was not among those accused of having eaten human flesh.

Edward Israel was born in Kalamazoo, Michigan, July 1, 1859. He was the son of Mannes Israel, born in Germany in 1819, a pioneer Kalamazoo merchant who came to the United States about 1841. Mannes Israel died in 1868, leaving a wife and five children.

Edward Israel entered the University of Michigan in 1877. He majored in astronomy. Greely wrote to a number of universities, stating that he was seeking a young man to join his expedition with the Army rank and pay of sergeant to do the astronomical and mathematical calculations required. A Princeton professor replied, "Two of my young men would answer your purpose very well, I think, but I don't suppose they would like to go to such an out of the way place." The University of Wisconsin's answer was that no one had been located with the needed capability. The Michigan response was prompt and affirmative. On April 11, 1881, Greely wrote to Professor Mark W. Harrington at the Astronomical Observatory at the University, Ann Arbor, Michigan. Three days later Harrington replied:

> I would nominate Mr. Edward Israel for the position referred to. He is an unusually bright man, a member of our senior class; has strong mathematical and scientific tastes and desires to make the pursuit of astronomy a specialty. He has already had sufficient practice with the sextant and transit to successfully undertake determinations of time latitude and longitude and has sufficient mechanical aptitude to readily pick up any class of observation which he might be required to make. I think he would do very creditable work and I should be glad to see him appointed. He has already signified his willingness to go if appointed.

Israel was so eager to join up that he said "yes" to Professor Harrington almost immediately, after making sure his mother would consent to his going.

A week later Greely informed Israel that he had been selected. On April 26 Israel wrote Greely he would arrive in Washington on May 1. On May 2 Israel was sworn into the Army as a Signal Corps sergeant. His pay: $100 a month. In June the university granted Israel his A.B. degree in absentia. With the exception of the Army surgeon, Israel was the only member of the expedition who was a college graduate. And he was its only Jew. While he had participated in college athletics, he was not as rugged as the carefully chosen professional soldiers in the Greely command. They were mostly from the infantry and cavalry and had been frontier Indian fighters.

For almost two years Israel was kept busy by his scientific duties on Ellsmere Island. On one occasion, in January 1882, he had to remain out of doors so long in 56 below zero temperature that one of his feet was temporarily frozen. With the possible exception of the photographer, George Rice, Israel was the most popular man in camp. He played chess with Greely and Dr. Pavy. He spent much of his time reading. He helped keep up the morale of the men by giving lectures on science and coaching them in math. He was cheerful and friendly, calm and brave in the most trying of circumstances. He was the youngest person in a group that became so closely knit that the men regarded each other as brothers. Lieutenant Greely nicknamed Israel "our Benjamin," à la the youngest of the twelve sons of the Biblical Jacob, because the soldiers felt toward Israel as they would toward their youngest brother.

On Cape Sabine, early in October 1883, Israel lost his temper the one and only time. He wrongly suspected First Sergeant (later General) David L. Brainard of distributing the food unfairly. Greely wrote in his journal: "I reprimanded Israel, pointing out how thoroughly he was in the wrong, and he seemed to regret his words. It is his first indiscretion since his service with me, and can be readily attributed to his nervous frame of mind, growing out of hard work, insufficient food, and severe exposure, which affects him, the youngest and weakest of the party, more than any other." The next day Greely wrote, "Israel today apologized to me in a manly, touching way, and in words which were very affecting, for his injustice to Brainard." On October 30 Greely noted, "Israel is suffering excessively from our unaccustomed privations, but he refrains from any utterances in the nature of complaints."

Although, as Greely recorded, Israel was "the youngest and weakest" of those enduring this dreadful ordeal, he clung tenaciously to life. One man died in January, six in April. The good fortune of shooting a bear on April 11 helped to prolong the lives of a number of men whose strength was slowly ebbing away. On April 18 the doctor listed Israel as one of seven who were "in a very bad way." Four of these died before Israel passed away.

Israel's final days were painfully recorded in the Greely journal:

> May 23—Ralston, Israel and I were sharing the same sleeping bag. Ralston died about 1 A.M. Israel left the bag before his death, but I remained until driven out about 5 A.M., chilled through by contact with the dead. . . . The weakest of the party moved up to the tent upon the hill this afternoon. . . . Israel was able to walk half way, but the strongest had to haul him the rest of the distance.
>
> May 24—The tent is much more comfortable. The temperature reached thirty-nine degrees inside it this morning. . . . Israel is exceedingly weak; he realizes that his end is near and is reconciled.
>
> May 26—Israel is now in an exceedingly weak condition, and unable even to sit up in his bag. I am compelled to raise him and feed him, which is a tremendous drain on my physical strength. He talks much of his home and younger days, and seems thoroughly reconciled to go. I gave him a spoonful of rum this morning; he begged for it so exceedingly hard. It was perhaps not fair to the rest to have given it to him, as it was evident it could not benefit him, as he was so near his end. However it was a great comfort and relief to him, and I did by him as I should like to have been done by in such a time. Nobody objected to my action openly, as Israel has always been a great favorite.
>
> May 27—. . . Israel died very easily about three o'clock this morning. I gave him yesterday the last food he ate. . . .

Sergeant Brainard, the man whom Israel had falsely accused, wrote in his private diary on May 27:

> Everyone was his friend. He had no enemies. His frankness, his honesty, and his noble generosity of nature had won the hearts of all his companions. His unswerving integrity during these months of agony has been a shining example; and, although his sacrifices were lost to a few, still the effect has produced good fruit. For lack of strength we could not bury him today.

When Greely later wrote a book about the expedition, this is what he wrote about Edward Israel:

> His death affected me seriously, as his cheerful and hopeful words during the long months he was my sleeping bag companion did much to hold up my hands and relieve my overtaxed brain. He had always endeared himself to all by his kindness, consideration, and unvarying equanimity, and was often called at Sabine our Benjamin. His services were very valuable in our scientific work, and, despite his weak physique, he sought field assignments. In reading his burial service I was mindful of him and his people, and omitted every portion which could be distasteful to his coreligionists.

One of the twelve bodies brought back was that of Edward Israel. Encased in a black iron coffin, Edward Israel returned home to Kalamazoo in the early afternoon of August 11, 1884. Three thousand people were waiting for him at the railway station, including the mayor and city council and an honor guard of eight of his University of Michigan classmates. The Kalamazoo *Free Press* stated:

> At 4 P.M. the funeral services were conducted by the Rev. Ignatz Mueller of Cincinnati according to the ritual of the Hebrew faith. Rev. Mueller delivered an address of rare pathos. The remains were then taken to Mountain Home Cemetery, followed by a large concourse, and buried in the Hebrew Society's lot. That the funeral was conducted so quietly and without any bands or music was in deference to the wishes of his mother who is loved by all classes of the community.

On May 27, 1972, the eighty-eighth anniversary of Edward Israel's death, the State of Michigan designated his grave a Michigan Historic Site and set up a bronze marker there. This was accomplished mainly through the efforts of Alexis A. Praus, Director of the Kalamazoo Public Museum.

THE LITTLE GIRL FROM APPLETON
(1912)

Edna Ferber, 1885-1968, is one of the very large number of modern Americans who have gone from the little town to the big city and made good. Her first novel and a number of her short stories were published before she took the big step in 1912. Soon after arriving in New York City she was interviewed by a reporter from the New York *Sun*. He asked her to what she ascribed the acclaim she had received at such an early age (she was twenty-seven). She thought a moment and then said, "Well, I think that what success I have had is due to the fact that I was born a Jew." Her reply shocked the reporter. "I couldn't put that in the story," he exclaimed. "Why not?" asked Miss Ferber. "I just couldn't," he stammered. In relating this incident in her autobiography, Miss Ferber comments, "It was as though I had said something obscene."*

Only a Jew, and perhaps a small-town Jew at that, could fully appreciate what Miss Ferber meant. Until fifty or so years ago, industrious, well-qualified Jews did not have an easy time getting ahead in the United States, particularly in the little places where a Jew was seldom seen and where the people had been taught that all Jews are Christ-killers and Shylocks. In order to make it in this hostile environment, small-town Jews had to be twice as good and to try twice as hard.

✻   ✻   ✻   ✻   ✻

While working on this article I decided to play myself a kind of game. I went through the *Universal Jewish Encyclopaedia* to try to find the ten prominent American Jews of the last hundred years who had gone to the big cities from the smallest towns. Here is the result of my research, listed by birthplace in descending order from little to tiniest. The population figures are from the 1930 census.

1. David Philipson, 1862-1949, scholarly dean of the Reform rabbinate, Wabash, Indiana, 8,915.

2. Ted Lewis, 1891-1971, dance band leader, Circleville, Ohio, 7,366.

3. Samuel L. (Roxy) Rothafel, 1882-1936, theater and radio impresario, Stillwater, Minnesota, 7,083.

---

*The passage from *A Peculiar Treasure* by Edna Ferber has been used with the permission of the Executrix of Miss Ferber's Estate and her literary trustee, Harriet F. Pilpel of New York City.

4. Cyrus Adler, 1863-1940, scholarly president of the Jewish The-ological Seminary, Van Buren, Arkansas, 5,182.

5. Bernard M. Baruch, 1870-1965, financier, Camden, South Carolina, 5,142.

6. Morris L. Ernst, 1888-1976, lawyer and author, Uniontown, Alabama, 1,428.

7. Carrie Obendorfer Simon, 1872-1961, founder of the National Federation of Temple Sisterhoods, Uniontown, Alabama. Yes, Uniontown, Alabama! One tiny community in western Alabama produced two of the ten!

8. Leo S. Rowe, 1871-1946, director general, Pan American Union, McGregor, Iowa, 1,040.

9. Julian Morgenstern, 1881-1976, scholarly president of the Hebrew Union College, St. Francisville, Illinois, 1,201.

10. Frederick B. Opper, 1857-1937, famed cartoonist, Madison, Ohio, population 926.

This list is impressive. Less than two percent of American Jews have lived or continue to live in towns of this size. And, almost inevitably, these small-town Jews intermarry and disappear. Yet look at the ten notable Jews these little places have produced—not only entertainers and businessmen but also Jewish leaders and scholars. Two factors are noteworthy: geographic location and individual longevity. None of the ten is from the East or the Far West. Six are from the Midwest; three from the South; one from the Southwest. All, with the exception of Roxy, who died at age fifty-four, lived exceptionally long lives. Even counting in Roxy, their average life span was eighty-two. This was also the length of the earthly life of Edna Ferber.

❖ ❖ ❖ ❖ ❖

Edna Ferber's parents came to Kalamazoo, Michigan, in 1881 from Chicago. They opened a dry goods' store known as "My Store—Ferber's Popular Bazaar." Father Jacob was a Hungarian immigrant. Their first child, Fannie, was born in 1882, their second and last, Edna, in 1885. Like Edna, Fannie did some story writing; but she was not nearly as successful or as famous as her younger sister. Her best known work was *Fannie Fox's Cook Book,* published in 1923.

Edna's parents had a hard time making a living. To try to better themselves, they moved back to Chicago in 1889 and then, in 1890, to Ottumwa, Iowa, a tough, unenlightened coal mining town with only a half dozen Jewish families. Here Edna learned the hard way that, when prejudice ensnares a Jew, it is accompanied by ignorance and cruelty. The experience is described in the first volume of her autobiography, from which comes the following excerpt.

❖ ❖ ❖ ❖ ❖

Through* the seven years during which we lived in Ottumwa, I know that I never went out on the street without being subjected to some form of devilment. It was a fine school for a certain sort of fortitude, but it gave me a strong dash of bitterness at an early age, together with a bewildered puzzlement at what was known as the Christian world. Certainly I wasn't wise enough or old enough at five, six, seven, eight, nine, ten, to philosophize about this. But these people seemed to me to be barbarians.

On Saturdays, and on unusually busy days when my father could not take the time to come home to the noon dinner, it became my duty to take his midday meal down to him, very carefully packed in a large basket; soup, meat, vegetables, dessert. This must be carried with the utmost care so as not to spill or slop. No one thought of having a sandwich and a cup of coffee in the middle of the day with a hot dinner to be eaten at leisure in the peace of the evening.

This little trip from the house on Wapello Street to the store on Main Street amounted to running the gantlet. I didn't so much mind the Morey girl. She sat in front of her house perched on a white gatepost, waiting, a child about my age, with long red curls, a freckled face, very light green eyes. She swung her long legs, to and fro. At sight of me her listlessness fled.

"Hello, sheeny!" Then variations of this. This, one learned to receive equably. Besides, the natural retort to her baiting was to shout, airily, "Red Head! Wets the bed!"

But as I approached the Main Street corner there sat a row of vultures perched on the iron railing at the side of Sargent's drugstore. These were not children, they were men. Perhaps to me, a small child, they seemed older than they were, but their ages must have ranged from eighteen to thirty. There they sat, perched on the black iron rail, their heels hooked behind the lower rung. They talked almost not at all. The semicircle of spit rings grew richer and richer on the sidewalk in front of them. Vacant-eyed, they stared and stared and sat humped and round-shouldered, doing nothing, thinking nothing, being nothing. Suddenly their lackluster eyes brightened, they shifted, they licked their lips a little and spat with more relish. From afar they had glimpsed their victim, a plump little girl, in clean starched gingham frock, her black curls confined by a ribbon bow.

Every fiber in me shrieked to run the other way. My eyes felt hot and wide. My face became scarlet. I must walk carefully so as not to spill the good hot dinner. Now then. Now.

"Sheeny! Has du gesak de Isaac! De Moses! De Levi! Heh, sheeny, what you got!" Good Old Testament names. They doubtless heard them in their Sunday worship, but did not make the connection, quite. They then brought their hands, palms up, above the level of their shoulders and wagged them back and forth. "Oy yoy, sheeny! Run! Go on, run!"

I didn't run. I glared. I walked by with as much elegance and aloofness as was compatible with a necessity to balance a basket of noodle soup, pot roast, potatoes, vegetable, and pudding.

Of course it was nothing more than a couple of thousand years of bigotry raising its hideous head to spit on a defenseless and shrinking morsel of humanity. Yet it all must have left a deep scar on a sensitive child. It was unreasoning and widespread in the town. My parents were subject to it. The four or five respectable Jewish families of the town knew it well. They were intelligent men and women, American born and bred, for the most part. It probably gave me a ghastly inferiority, and out of that inferiority doubtless was born inside me a fierce resolution, absurd and childish, such as "You wait! I'll show you! I'll be rich and famous and you'll wish you could speak to me."

Well, I did become rich and famous, and have lived to see entire nations behaving precisely like the idle frustrated bums perched on the drugstore railing. Of course Ottumwa wasn't a benighted town because it was cruel to its Jewish citizens. It was cruel to its Jewish citizens because it was a benighted town. Business was bad, the town was poor, its people were frightened, resentful and stupid. There was, for a place of its size and locality, an unusually large rough element. As naturally as could be these searched for a minority on whom to vent their dissatisfaction with the world. And there we were, and there I was, the scapegoat of the ages. Yet, though I had a tough time of it in Ottumwa and a fine time of it in New York, I am certain that those Ottumwa years were more enriching, more valuable than all the fun and luxury of the New York years.

There was no Jewish place of worship in Ottumwa. The five or six Jewish families certainly could not afford the upkeep of a temple. I knew practically nothing of the Jewish people, their history, religion. On the two important holy days of the year—Rosh Hashana, the Jewish New Year; and Yom Kippur, the Day of Atonement—they hired a public hall for services. Sometimes they were able to bring to town a student rabbi who had, as yet, no regular congregation. Usually one of the substantial elder men who knew something of the Hebrew language of the Bible, having been taught it in his youth, conducted the service. On Yom Kippur, a long day of fasting and prayer, it was an exhausting thing to stand from morning to sunset in the improvised pulpit. The amateur rabbi would be relieved for an hour by another member of the little improvised congregation. Mr. Emanuel Adler, a familiar figure to me as he sat in his comfortable home talking with my parents, a quaint long-stemmed pipe between his lips, a little black skullcap atop his baldish head as protection against drafts, now would don the rabbinical skullcap, a good deal like that of a Catholic priest. He would open on the high reading stand the Bible and the Book of Prayers containing the service for the Day of Yom Kippur; and suddenly he was transformed from a plump middle-aged German-born Jew with sad kindly eyes and a snuffy gray-brown mustache to a holy man from whose lips came words of wisdom and of comfort and of hope.

The store always was closed on Rosh Hashana and Yom Kippur. Mother put on her best dress. If there were any Jewish visitors in the town at that time they were invited to the services and to dinner at some hospitable house afterward. In our household the guests were likely to be a couple of traveling salesmen caught in the town on that holy day. Jewish families came from smaller near-by towns—Marshalltown, Albia, Keokuk.

I can't account for the fact that I didn't resent being a Jew. Perhaps it was because I liked the way my own family lived, talked, conducted its household and its business better than I did the lives of my friends. I admired immensely my grandparents, my parents, my uncles and aunt. Perhaps it was a vague something handed down to me from no one knows where. Perhaps it was something not very admirable—the actress in me. I think, truthfully, that I rather liked dramatizing myself, feeling myself different and set apart. I probably liked to think of myself as persecuted by enemies who were (in my opinion) my inferiors. This is a protective philosophy often employed. Mine never had been a religious family. The Chicago Neuman family sometimes went to the temple at Thirty-third Street and Indiana Avenue, but I don't remember that my parents ever went there while in Chicago. In our own household there was no celebration of the informal home ceremonies so often observed in Jewish families. The Passover, with its Seder service, was marked in our house only by the appearance of the matzos or unleavened bread, symbolic of the hardships of the Jews in the wilderness. I devoured pounds of the crisp crumbling matzos with hunks of fresh butter and streams of honey, leaving a trail of crumbs all over the house, and thought very little, I am afraid, of the tragic significance of the food I was eating or of that weary heartsick band led by Moses out of Egypt to escape the Hitler of that day, one Pharaoh; or of how they baked and ate their unsalted unleavened bread because it was all they had, there in the wilderness. I still have matzoth (matzos, we always called them) in my house during the Passover, and just as thoughtlessly. Now they come as delicious crisp circlets, but they seem to me much less delicious than the harder, tougher squares of my childhood munching.

❂   ❂   ❂   ❂   ❂

Business in Ottumwa got worse and worse. In 1897 the Ferbers moved to Appleton, Wisconsin, a more prosperous and friendly town. The forty Jewish families in Appleton had a Reform Temple. Edna sang in the choir. Father Jacob started to go blind. Mother Julia had to work in the store. Edna wanted to go on the stage; but her parents could not afford to give her a dramatic education. After graduating from high school, Edna got a job at age seventeen at $3.00 a week as a reporter for the Appleton *Daily Crescent*. One and a half years later she was fired by a new city editor who thought she had no talent. In 1906 she went to Milwaukee and was on the staff of the Milwaukee *Journal* for three and a half years. Then misfortune struck the family heavily. Father, who had gone blind, died. Mother had to run the business. Edna became seriously ill and had to return to Appleton. It was in this time of crisis that Edna turned to fiction writing to help alleviate her family's financial distress. She met with success almost immediately.

In 1910 mama closed the store. She and the girls went back to Chicago, where, for a year and a half, Edna was a reporter for the Chicago *Tribune*. Her first novel was published. Her short stories appeared in two of the leading periodicals of that day, *Everybody's Magazine* and *American Magazine*. Edna felt that the time had come for her to make the big move. In 1912 she left her job and migrated to New York City.

From then on she turned out a seemingly endless stream of successful short stories, novels, and plays. She became famous and she became wealthy. Beyond her determination, her dedication, and her writing skill, wherein lies the secret of her literary magic? A fellow writer, Charles Reznikoff, had this explanation:

> Miss Ferber selects her scenes and characters from the broad panorama of American life. They deal with plain people who may be passing on the street at any time, with people who work for a living in stores and shops, who keep house and work hard as people in America generally do; she has no use for idlers or social climbers. Her characters and their problems are so natural that they suggest sketches from life rather than works of fiction. Without preaching, she drives home moral lessons and champions the cause of those who have less than a fair share of life—the uncomplaining supporters of selfish wives or sisters, the women who are compelled to become bread-winners, the homely girl, the humble immigrant, the old father who is no longer able to work and who must live with his relations. *Fanny Herself*, as well as other references to Jewish characters in her writings, contain shrewd observations as to the position of the individual Jew in the American picture, indications of the obstacles he or she must face in a non-Jewish world, and suggestions on how to overcome them.

Edna Ferber never married. In 1939 her feeling of ethnic identity was sharply stirred by the Nazi anti-Jewish persecutions. While under the strong influence of this mood she wrote her autobiography *A Peculiar Treasure*. Deeply revealing is the Biblical source from which the title was taken, Deuteronomy 14:2, "You are the holy people of the Lord your God; the Lord has chosen you as His own peculiar treasure from among all the peoples upon the face of the earth."

Despite this profound recognition of the depths of her Jewish roots and of the spiritual power through which her genius was galvanized, Edna Ferber was not a practicing Jew. After she came to New York she never affiliated with a synagogue. She left word that, at her death, she wanted no religious service. Three good friends, writer Bennett Cerf, playwright Marc Connelly, magazine editor Herbert Mays, eulogized her at her funeral. She died as she had lived, as one who had been kept afloat on life's stream by her people and her religion; but who wanted to be remembered as one who thought and wrote and lived as a free spirit, an unfettered creature of the universe.

On her eightieth birthday, Edna Ferber was asked whether she was bothered by the thought that she was now an old woman. She replied by citing Maurice Chevalier: On his sixty-fifth birthday a female admirer said to the Frenchman, "Maurice, how can you bear to think of growing old?" Chevalier's eyes lit up and he smiled his most charming smile as he responded, "But, madam, consider the alternative."

THE WEDDING GUESTS

(1916)

In the chapel of a Midwest Catholic convent a group of nuns wearing wedding gowns were awaiting the ceremony in which they would profess the vows that would sanctify them for their religious careers. The archbishop who was to preside over the ceremony saw two bearded gentlemen wearing skullcaps sitting in the rear row. He walked up to them to bid them welcome to the rite which was about to take place. "We are delighted to have you with us," he said, "on this day when these young ladies are to become 'brides of Christ.' Would you care to introduce yourselves to the rest of us?" One of the two got up and replied, "This is my friend, Rabbi X, and my name is Rabbi Y. We are relatives of the groom!"

A True Champion

(1932)

Barnet David Rosofsky, Dov Ber David ben Yitschak ha-Cohen, known to his papa and mama as Beryl or Beryleh, was born on December 23, 1909, on the Lower East Side of New York City. His parents came from Russia in 1903. His father, a pious scholar, at first tried to make a living as a melamed, a Hebrew teacher; but in those days there were too many Hebrew teachers on the Lower East Side. Papa had to give up teaching and sell canned goods and vegetables from a sidewalk pushcart. In 1911 the family moved to Chicago and opened a little grocery store, Rosofsky's Dairy, in the heart of Chicago's West Side ghetto.

Beryl was an apt Hebrew student. Papa hoped that when Beryl was grown he would become a melamed or perhaps, who knows? even a rabbi. On the morning of December 13, 1924, papa was shot down by two thugs who tried to rob his store. Thirty-two hours later he died, leaving a widow and six children. The store was sold. Ma went to Connecticut to live with her blind mother-in-law. The oldest son, Ben, was married. His wife had just had a baby. Ben was not in a position to either house or support his younger brothers and sisters. Morrie and Beryl went to live with a cousin. Sammy, Georgie, and Ida were put in an orphanage, the Marx Nathan Home at Albany and Sixteenth Streets.

Beryl was angry at God for letting his father be murdered. He abandoned his Orthodox beliefs and practices. For several years he considered himself an apikoros, an unbeliever. He swore a solemn oath that no matter what it took, no matter what he had to do, he was going to find enough money to get his sister and brothers out of that orphan asylum.

Beryl was an asthmatic. He had arthritis in his left arm. He was a puny, skinny kid, but a very determined one. In his efforts to make money for his family he constantly got into trouble with the law. He became known as Beryl the trumbenik, the troublemaker. He conned customers into being fleeced in shadily operated West Side clothing stores; he ran illegal crap games in his neighborhood. Ma came back from Connecticut in September 1925. Morrie, Beryl, and Ma moved into a cold-water, walk-up flat at Tenth Street and Turner Avenue. To support Ma and themselves, Morrie and Beryl quit school and went to work. Beryl had finished two years of high school when his formal education ended.

He was unsuccessful as a delivery boy and as a shoe salesman. He then became, in a mild sort of way, a racketeer. He never mugged or killed anyone. But he was a runner for Al Capone, the notorious gang boss. One day Capone, who knew Beryl's family background, gave him a $20 bill and ordered him to go straight. Capone had a deep respect for religious people. "Your father was a pious man," Capone told the lad. "Live the kind of life he would want you to live."

Beryl got a job in the stockroom of Sears Roebuck. He was a good stock boy. Soon he was making $17 a week, the highest pay of any of the stock boys. That was enough to help take care of Ma but not enough to get Ida and the boys out of the orphanage. Beryl had to find something that paid better.

A fellow a few years older than Beryl, Jake Finkelstein, had overcome the same ghetto poverty by becoming a professional prizefighter. He was no longer known as Jake Finkelstein. Professionally he was now Jackie Fields. Skinny little Beryl decided to have a go at boxing. He was pretty good with his fists. If he made it he could bring the three kids back home. In keeping with the prevailing custom and, even more, to prevent his mother from learning that her Beryl had become a fighter, he boxed under the name of Barney Ross.

He did so well as an "amateur" fighter that soon he was able to quit his job at Sears. Bruises and cuts incurred in one of his bouts made Ma suspicious. He told her he had been jumped by a bunch of roughnecks on his way home from work. His mother refused to believe. "Zug nisht kayn ligen!" she shouted. "Don't lie to me!" She made Beryl tell her dus emess, the truth. She became hysterical. Beryl pleaded with her: He did not enjoy fighting; he would do his best not to get hurt; he only wanted to make enough money to get Sammy, Georgie, and Ida out of the orphanage. His mother finally relented. She would let him continue to fight provided that: a) After he made enough money to bring the kids home, he would quit the ring; b) if he ever got badly hurt, he would give up boxing immediately. Beryl promised.

He fought 250 fights as an amateur. He won a title in the Golden Gloves. On his eighteenth birthday he turned professional. Shortly thereafter he got the kids out of the orphanage. He rented an apartment on Independence Boulevard big enough for Ma and Morrie and Ida and Sammy and Georgie and himself. Ma became his most ardent fan. She attended every fight. On Friday nights she would go to shul and then walk to and from the boxing arena, sometimes a very long walk. "Because of Beryl," she said, "there are no more orphans in this family. Pa is looking down on Beryleh and is very proud of him."

On June 21, 1932, Barney fought Tony Canzoneri in Chicago for the world's lightweight and junior welterweight championships and won. His friends planned a big celebration at a downtown hotel. Barney was unable to attend. He had an important obligation to fulfill. After the top of his head was sewed up and a patch was placed over a cut on his face, Barney walked his mother home. It was a Friday night and it was five miles from the Stadium to their apartment. So, after a grueling fifteen-round fight for a world championship, two championships in fact, little Beryleh topped off the evening by hiking five miles to walk his Ma home.

A return match with Canzoneri was scheduled for September in New York City. Barney went up to Wisconsin to train for the match. Barney tells what happened:

> When I left for camp, I took along some of Pa's religious books. After I was through the day's training, I spent my time reading. When I finished with Pa's books, I went into the town library and got out more books on religion. I got out the New Testament and Catholic and Protestant and Christian Science books and pamphlets. I read up on Mohammedanism and Buddhism and Hinduism. As I read, I discovered for the first time the similarity in all religions. This was new to me—I had always assumed that the Jewish religion I'd been brought up in was nothing like any other religion in the world.
>
> I found the same message running through all the books and the holy passages: Live morally and justly; help your fellow man; love and honor your family; do good deeds in the name of the Lord. The more I read, the more I wanted to go back to my faith. I realized I needed faith; it was so much a part of me that I felt disturbed and restless without it. I came to understand that God has reasons—very good reasons—for the things He does or allows to happen. Man is only mortal—he must follow God on faith and his faith will show him ultimately that God always acts with righteousness and justice.
>
> One night in a dream I talked to Pa. He was happy, smiling. The next morning I woke up with a clear head, with a feeling of contentment and peace. Sure, maybe it was just a dream, I told myself, but somehow I knew that Pa was in Heaven, that he was happy, and that God had taken him because He needed good people there. Before I took off for my roadwork, I dug out the bag of tefillin which I hadn't touched for a couple of years, fastened the little black boxes around my arm and my head and said my morning prayers.

The first Saturday after he got back to Chicago Barney went to the morning service at his old synagogue on Maxwell Street. When the time came for the erste Aliyah, the honor of being the first to be called to the reading of the Torah, an honor traditionally accorded those of priestly descent, the rabbi intoned, "Ya-amod Dov Ber David ben Yitschak ha-Cohen," "Come forward, Barnet David, son of Isidore, member of the priestly tribe."

> I touched the Torah with my Talit, my prayer shawl, and then I kissed the Talit. I recited the proper berachot, the blessings. When I finished, the rabbi said, "Amen." There were tears in his eyes. We clasped hands and then he threw his arms around me. "Gott sei dank, Beryleh, God be praised," he said. "You've come back."

In September in New York Barney again beat Canzoneri. During the next year and a half Barney defended his titles five times. Then came his most publicized fights. They were with the welterweight champ, "Baby Face" Jimmy McClarnin, innocent looking, blue-eyed Irishman, with one of the deadliest rights in the business. The first time the two met was on May 30, 1934. Barney beat McClarnin and became welterweight champ. He is the only fighter in the history of boxing to hold three division titles at the same time. On September 17, in a rematch, McClarnin regained the title. They fought a third time in May 1935. Barney broke the thumb of his left hand in the sixth round but kept on fighting. He won the welterweight title a second time. After defending this title successfully for three years, he was defeated on May 31, 1938, by another superboxer, Henry Armstrong. Twenty-nine-year-old Barney then called it quits. He had fought 329 times, had lost only a handful of fights, had never been knocked out.

Shortly before his last fight Barney married a Jewish girl whose father had a clothing store in New York City. After he hung up his boxing gloves Barney went into partnership with his father-in-law. It did not work out. Barney had no knowledge of nor interest in the clothing business. Selling clothes was too tame. He tried acting. No go. He opened a cocktail lounge in Chicago. This was a success. His marriage was not. It ended a short time after he started operating the lounge.

He fell in love with Cathy Howlett, a non-Jewish showgirl. He wooed her while waiting for his divorce to become final. Then came Pearl Harbor. At age thirty-two Barney enlisted in the Marines. He went through boot training at San Diego. He married Cathy the day his San Diego training ended. Six weeks later Barney shipped out to the Pacific with the Second Marines. On November 4, 1942, they landed on Guadalcanal Island in the Solomons.

Two weeks later Barney was sent out on patrol with three other seasoldiers. They were ambushed. One was killed, two so badly wounded they could not continue fighting. Barney fought on alone for fourteen desperate hours with wounds in his side, leg, and arm. When Barney and his wounded comrades were finally rescued, there were twenty-two enemy dead in front of the small shell hole where Barney had taken cover. This terrible experience gained Barney the Silver Star but it also caused him to contract malaria and nearly lose his mind. During the hours in the shell hole his hair turned from jet black to gray.

It took a long while for Barney to recover. To ease his pain and to overcome the chronic dysentery brought on by the malaria, the Navy corpsmen gave him frequent injections of morphine. As a result a craving for this drug developed and Barney became addicted. He went downhill rapidly, mentally, physically, and morally. Cathy divorced him. In desperation Barney turned himself in to the Public Health Service narcotics rehab center at Lexington, Kentucky. Morphine users seldom are able to kick the habit. The strength of will required is possessed by very few. Barney was one of those few. He was pronounced cured at Lexington in 1947. He and Cathy remarried. Twenty years later cancer struck him down for the final count. During those twenty years Barney devoted himself untiringly to helping fight the dope racketeers and to trying to aid in the reconstruction of lives ruined by drug addiction.

In 1956 Barney was asked to testify before a Senate committee that was investigating the international drug traffic. While he was in the hearing room an outstanding medical authority on the subject told the committee, "One of our major problems is that the addicts we treat are never really cured. Sooner or later, they all go back on dope." Barney sprang to his feet and shouted, "That is not so. Here is one fellow who did not go back and who never will go back." The Senate hearing was disrupted. The doctor who was testifying leaned forward to see who it was that had caused the uproar. As a look of recognition came over his face, he smiled and said, "Oh, it's you, Barney. I wasn't talking about you. Your kind of man is not put on this earth very often. You are an exception."

Indeed he was. In the battle of life Barney was truly a champion. God rest your soul, Reb Dov Ber David ben Yitschak ha-Cohen.

DETROIT'S "BRONX BOMBER" DID NOT PLAY ON YOM KIPPUR
(1934)

The great American game of baseball has had comparatively few Jewish stars. One reason given for this is that to play baseball a large open area is required. Such areas are rare in the big cities, not too easily found in the suburbs, but abound in rural America. As a result big league ballplayers have been developed mostly on the farms and in small towns, less frequently on the "sand lots" of suburbia, and seldom, except for pitchers and catchers, in the confined surroundings of the inner cities. Since Jews in the United States, until recently, have been primarily an inner-city people, this has tended to keep down the number of top-notch Jewish ballplayers. Now that the Jews are leaving center-city for suburbia, one of the unlooked-for fringe benefits of this move may be that there will be more Jews in future big league lineups.

Jewish speaking, 1935 was about as good a baseball year as we have yet enjoyed. That year Dolly Stark was named the most popular umpire in the National League; Buddy Myer, second baseman of the Washington Senators, led the American League in batting; and Hank Greenberg, first baseman of the Detroit Tigers, was selected by the Baseball Writers

Association as the most valuable player in the American League. It is generally agreed that in baseball's first 100 years, 1839-1939, Greenberg was the most outstanding Jewish player.

✿   ✿   ✿   ✿   ✿

Henry (Hank) Greenberg was born in the Bronx in 1911 of Orthodox Jewish parents of Rumanian extraction. He grew up tall and strong, six feet four inches of superb athlete. He excelled in high school baseball. Detroit signed him up for $9,000. He got $3,000 immediately. The remaining $6,000 were to be given him when he got his bachelor's degree from New York University. But Hank decided not to wait that long. After one semester of college he quit to become a professional ballplayer. For three seasons he played for two Detroit farm clubs, Raleigh, North Carolina, and Beaumont, Texas. He was brought up to the big-time in 1933. In 1935 the "Bronx Bomber," as he was called because of his ability to hit the ball hard and far, tied with Jimmie Foxx for the season's home run record. He also led the league in number of runs batted in. In 1938 he hit 58 home runs, two short of tying Babe Ruth's record established in 1927. He was the highest paid player in baseball in 1940, 1941, and 1946. Before World War II began, the $60,000-a-year star entered the Army as a private and came out some months later as a sergeant. After Pearl Harbor Greenberg immediately went back into uniform. He ended up in the China-Burma-India theater of operations as a major in the Army Air Force. In the late summer of 1945 the thirty-four-year-old Greenberg returned to the Tigers. In the part of the season that was left Hank batted .344, hit 13 home runs, and led the team to the league championship. He was traded to the Pittsburgh Pirates in 1947. In 1948 he ended his career as an active player and became general manager of the Cleveland Indians.

✿   ✿   ✿   ✿   ✿

Baseball lore contains many legends about its heroes. Since Jewish baseball heroes are few in number, so, too, are the Jewish legends. One of these legends is associated with the baseball career of Hank Greenberg.

The year is 1934. The Detroit team is in the midst of a hotly contended pennant race. Manager Mickey Cochrane wants Greenberg to play on Yom Kippur. At first Greenberg refuses. He finally consents to play if Cochrane can find a rabbi who will say it is OK. The manager first approaches Greenberg's own rabbi, Abraham Hershman of Detroit's Conservative Congregation Shaarey Tsedek. Hershman says "No." Cochrane then goes to Reform Rabbi Leo M. Franklin of Temple Beth El. Franklin says "No." In desperation Cochrane appeals to an Orthodox rabbi. The Orthodox rabbi does not say "No." He says, "I'll study the matter. I'll see what our literature has to say about it." Later he contacts Cochrane and says it will be all right for Greenberg to play on Yom Kippur, provided that he fulfills certain conditions.

The Orthodox rabbi explains the Talmudic background and sets forth the conditions: The Mishna says that the boys of Jerusalem played ball in the streets on Yom Kippur day. If the Jewish boys of Jerusalem could play ball on Yom Kippur so could Greenberg, provided that, in every other way, he properly observed Yom Kippur. He must fast. He must attend synagogue services the evening before and the morning of Yom Kippur. He must walk to the ball park before the game and remain there until nightfall after the game. He must donate to charity the money he receives for playing in the game.

Greenberg observed these conditions faithfully. He stayed at a hotel between the synagogue and the ball park, fasted, walked to and from the synagogue, walked to the ball park and contributed the day's pay to charity. In the game that afternoon, he hit two home runs and won the game for Detroit.

That is the legend.

When I researched the matter I discovered quickly that it is truly legendary for a very substantial reason. In 1934 Yom Kippur fell on September 19. Greenberg's name is not in the Detroit lineup for that day's game.

I wrote to Mr. Greenberg to ask him to tell me how this legend got started. Mr. Greenberg replied as follows:

"Let me help you set the record straight:

1. I *never* played on Yom Kippur.
2. In 1934, because of the tight pennant race, the question arose as to whether or not I was going to be in the lineup during the holidays. The press was concerned only because it made a good story. They went to Rabbi Franklin, who was reported to have said, 'Rosh Hashana is a joyous holiday and so Greenberg could play that day; but he definitely should not play on Yom Kippur.' I played on Rosh Hashana, hit two home runs, and we won the game two to one. This is all documented in the Detroit *Free Press*.
3. No one contacted Manager Mickey Cochrane on this. He would have had no jurisdiction over whether or not I would play on the holidays.
4. The possibility of my playing on Yom Kippur did come up at the beginning of the 1935 World Series. Yom Kippur that year was on October 6. The series began on October 3. On October 4, in the second game, I broke my wrist, which ended the matter. I never played on Yom Kippur during my entire baseball career."

This is an excellent example of how, in a comparatively few years, a story can grow and grow and grow.

The Detroit *Free Press* reported, following the Yom Kippur game in

1934, in which Hank did *not* play, that the affection and respect of Detroit's fans for Hank Greenberg became even greater when they learned that he had not participated in the game because of his fidelity to his religious heritage. The popular poet, Edgar A. Guest, wrote a long poem praising the diamond star for his loyalty to his ancestral faith.

Fifty Wasted Years
(1936)

Henry Horner, 1878-1940, was Governor of Illinois from 1932 until he died. When he was eight years old his grandfather told him that, if he wanted to be invited to nice places, he must never crumple crackers in his soup. "So," declared Governor Horner, "I didn't, but I never had soup without wanting to—bad. Then came the day when President Roosevelt had six midwestern governors to luncheon at the White House, and there was the soup, and there were the crackers, which I ate one by one as my grandpa would have wished. Suddenly there came a sound that froze me—the sound of crumpling crackers, splashing lightly into soup. From the corner of my eye I saw the President of the United States, scion of the bluest blood in America, crackling crackers into his soup with aristocratic assurance. I dropped whatever conversation I was making, seized my crackers with both hands, snowed them into my soup, and damned my dear grandfather for fifty wasted years."

Israel's Midwife
(1948)

When the smoke of battle has cleared away completely and the conception and birth of the State of Israel may be viewed in accurate historical perspective, who are the non-Jews about whom the scholars will write, "They were the Jewish people's best friends"?

The conception of the State of Israel occurred on November 2, 1917, when His Britannic Majesty's government issued a declaration that "it views with favour the establishment in Palestine of a national home for the Jewish people, and will use their best endeavours to facilitate the achievement of this object." The parent of the idea was British Bible Christian Arthur James Balfour, British Foreign Secretary, ably abetted by Bible Christian Thomas Woodrow Wilson, 28th President of the

United States, nobly counseled by Louis Dembitz Brandeis and Rabbi Stephen Samuel Wise.

The birth pangs that culminated in the emergence of the State of Israel from the womb of history began at midnight on May 15, 1948. They lasted for eleven minutes. At 12:11 A.M. the government of the United States granted de facto recognition to the newly born infant. In that moment the natal process was completed. In that moment Israel became a nation. The political midwife who performed this modern miracle was Bible Christian Harry S. Truman, 1884-1972, 33rd President of the United States, nobly inspired by his Kansas City World War I buddy and haberdashery store partner, Eddie Jacobson, and the guiding genius of world Zionism, Polish-British Chaim Weizmann.

David K. Niles, staff advisor on religious matters to Presidents Roosevelt and Truman, later said, "I seriously doubt that Israel would have come into existence if Roosevelt had lived." On April 5, 1945, Roosevelt wrote to King ibn Saud of Saudi Arabia that the United States would not assist the Jews in their struggle with the Arabs. One week later Roosevelt died and Truman became President. Four years later Rabbi Isaac Herzog, Chief Ashkenazic Rabbi of the State of Israel, stood in the Oval Room of the White House and said to the President of the United States, "God put you in your mother's womb so that you would be the instrument of bringing about the rebirth of Israel after two thousand years." As the outwardly tough, inwardly humble, deeply emotional, devoutly religious man from Missouri heard these words, tears streamed down his cheeks.

The Bard of Avon wrote, "Some are born great; some achieve greatness; and some have greatness thrust upon them." Franklin D. Roosevelt came from a rich patrician family—he was born great; Thomas Woodrow Wilson, son of a Presbyterian minister, reared in an atmosphere of piety and learning, achieved greatness; Harry Truman, farm boy from Independence, Missouri, who never went to college and who in his wildest imaginings never dreamed of being President, had greatness thrust upon him. No Divine plan in the universe? To quote another poet: "Some call it Evolution; others call it God."

❋   ❋   ❋   ❋   ❋

In World War I Truman was CO first of Battery F and then of Battery C, 129th Field Artillery Regiment, 35th Infantry Division. Eddie Jacobson of Kansas City was an enlisted man in Battery F. When the outfit got to Fort Sill, Oklahoma, at the end of September 1917, Truman was named regimental canteen officer. He had no previous business experience. Eddie had been a traveling salesman for a shirt manufacturer. So Captain Truman selected Eddie Jacobson as his canteen manager. It was a wise choice. The canteen made much money for Uncle Sam.

After arduous combat duty in France the 129th was mustered out of service in May 1919. Harry, who had achieved the rank of Major, did not know exactly what he would do for a living; but two things he did know: He was not going back to farming and he was going to marry his childhood sweetheart, Bess Wallace, which he did, on June 28, 1919, after a romance of 28 years. Harry and Bess were never ones to act on impulse. He was thirty-five; she thirty-four. He was Baptist; she Presbyterian. They got married in an Episcopal church. Harry's best man was Ted Marks, a Jewish tailor, who had also served as CO of Battery C, 129th Field Artillery, 35th Division.

In July 1919, while visiting Kansas City, Harry met Eddie Jacobson by accident. Eddie did not want to go back on the road. Truman still did not want to be a farmer. Harry and Eddie decided to jointly operate a men's furnishing store. The emporium of "Truman and Jacobson" opened on November 29, 1919, directly across the street from the Muehlebach Hotel in Kansas City. At first all went well; but the Midwest farm panic of 1921 did them in. The store folded in the middle of 1922. The partners tried manfully to avoid bankruptcy by making a settlement with their creditors. Eddie went back on the road. Unable to endure the dunning of his creditors, he filed personal bankruptcy papers in 1925. Harry refused to take this way out, even though his lawyer advised him to do so. Over the years he paid off all his own debts and some of Eddie's as well. Truman estimated that his total losses from the haberdashery business amounted to about $30,000.

Harry then turned to politics. He became a county judge. In 1934 he was elected to the U. S. Senate. In 1944 he was elected Vice President. On April 12, 1945, FDR died and he became President. In 1948 he was elected to a full four-year term as President.

Through the years Harry and Eddie remained warm friends. During a visit the President made to Kansas City he and Eddie and some of their Army buddies spent an evening playing poker. Jacobson didn't win a single pot. Next day Truman walked into the men's store Eddie now operated and bought eighteen pairs of hose. "I thought you'd need the money after what we did to you last night," Harry said. Through his entire life, before, during, and after being President, Harry Truman was, in the finest sense of the term, a "regular guy." He once said, "Whenever everybody starts to praise me and I'm worried about getting a swelled head, I remember Luke 6:26 'When everyone speaks well of you, beware; for that is a sure sign that you are a false prophet.'"

In 1945 Truman proposed that 100,000 Jews from the concentration camps be admitted to Palestine; but the British refused to agree. Truman's pro-Jewish sympathies were sharply contested by James Forrestal, Secretary of the Navy, who was convinced that Arab oil was much more important to American security than a Jewish Palestine. Many of the State Department careerists were openly pro-Arab and anti-Zionist. Some of them were covertly anti-Jewish. A number of American Zionist leaders gave the President a hard time, claiming he was not exerting as strong pressure on the Arabs and the British as he should. Truman was strongly opposed to the tactics of the Irgun and the Stern gang. He felt they would turn world sympathy away from the Zionist cause.

In March 1948 Chaim Weizmann came to Washington to plead with Truman to increase his efforts for the Zionist cause. Truman, embittered by the abuse he was getting from all sides, refused to meet with Weizmann. At this juncture Eddie Jacobson came to the White House and, as always, was warmly received.

A detailed description of what happened next is contained in Volume Two of Truman's White House memoirs. Here, considerably abridged, is what the President tells:

> Eddie urged me to see Dr. Weizmann. Eddie had never been a Zionist. In all my years as Senator and President, he had never asked anything for himself. Eddie said he wanted to talk to me about Palestine. I said I would rather not discuss the subject with him; but he kept right on talking. He said, "Andrew Jackson has been your Number One hero all your life, hasn't he?" Not knowing what he was leading up to, I said, "Yes." Eddie continued, "I have never met the man who has been my hero all my life; but I have studied his deeds as you have studied those of Jackson. This man is the greatest Jew in the world. He is a statesman and a gentleman. He is an old man and a very sick man. He has traveled thousands of miles to talk to you and you are refusing to see him. Harry, this isn't like you."

That remark did it. Five days later Truman and Weizmann met and conversed for almost an hour. Truman assured Weizmann that he was completely in sympathy with the yearning of the Jews for the establishment of a Jewish state in Palestine and that he was doing what he could to try to help bring this about without bloodshed.

Then the British announced that, on May 14, 1948, their troops would withdraw from Palestine. Truman soon learned that, prior to the withdrawal, "perfidious Albion" would supply large quantities of arms and ammunition to the Arabs. That, too, did it. Truman felt that the British were welching on the promise made in their Balfour Declaration. He placed the prestige of the American government solidly behind the soon-to-be-born State of Israel. Eleven minutes after the State of Israel declared its existence and independence, Truman's press secretary announced the de facto recognition of Israel's provisional government. After Israel held its first elections in January 1949, the de facto recognition was changed to de jure.

After being elected first President of Israel, Chaim Weizmann came again to the White House to thank President Truman for the key role he had played in the birth of the new little country. He presented Truman with an Israeli Torah as a gift of appreciation from the Jewish nation. During the presentation ceremony, he smiled and said, "You may not be aware of this, Mr. President, but I am a more important President than you." Truman looked at him in mild astonishment. "I don't quite understand," said Harry. "Well, Mr. Truman, you are the President of one hundred seventy million people; but I am the President of a million presidents." The man from Missouri, remembering his difficulties with the highly volatile American Zionist leaders, roared with laughter.

THE RABBI BUSINESS
(1950)

Rabbi B. Benedict Glazer, known affectionately to his friends as "Babe," was the spiritual leader of Temple Beth El in Detroit. He was big and burly and looked more like a professional football player than a rabbi. While riding in a Pullman club car one day, he was seated next to an equally burly traveling salesman, a friendly guy who wanted to ease the monotony of the train ride by engaging in some professional chit-chat. Turning his chair toward the rabbi, he stuck out his hand and said, "I'm Schmidt of Milwaukee—hardware. What's your line?" An equally friendly rabbi grasped the outstretched hand and replied, "Pleased to meet you. I'm Glazer of Detroit—notions."

THE JEWS LIKED IKE
(1952)

Dwight David (Ike) Eisenhower, 1890-1969, 34th President of the United States, was a deeply religious man and a warm friend of the Jews. He was an able administrator, a shrewd appraiser of human beings, affable and intelligent. The picture his detractors painted of him— peasant mentality stemming from a peasant background, mechanical man disciplined by his military career to lean entirely on staff advice and to respect only the powerful and the rich, George ("Edgar Bergen") Marshall's "Charlie McCarthy," a fumbler and a bumbler—is inaccurate. Like much that passes for fact on the pages of history books, folklore began to obscure fact while this man was still very much alive.

Eisenhower was originally Eisenhauer, German for "ironcutter." His father David's folk were from the Pennsylvania Dutch country, from Elizabethville in Dauphin County "a little piece" above Harrisburg. They were "wonderful good" people, members of the River Brethren, a Mennonite offshoot. The River Brethren were so named because they baptized publicly in the Susquehanna River. They did not smoke, drink, play cards, bet. They were pacifists. The men wore beards, flat hats, collars but no ties. The women wore large black bonnets outdoors and white lace bonnets indoors. Ike's mother was Ida Stover, originally Stoever, a German Lutheran from Virginia. David and Ida met while they were students at a United Brethren college in Kansas.

David and Ida Eisenhower were well educated people of above average intelligence. For their kind and time, they were quite tolerant. David was a mechanical engineer, manager of the local gas company. After Dwight David was already at West Point, David and Ida came under the influence of the teachings of Pastor Charles T. Russell and joined his Bible Students Association. Despite the teachings of the River Brethren, David and Ida's six children, all boys, smoked, drank, played cards, bet, were not pacifists, and wore regular "store-bought" clothes. Four of the boys belonged to no church—the banker, the lawyer, and the engineer because they felt no need for organized religion, the army officer because he was turned off by the compulsory chapel attendance requirement at West Point. The other two boys, the university president and the druggist, became liberal Episcopalians. When Ike—all his friends at West Point and thereafter called him Ike—changed from General to President, he joined the Presbyterians because he felt that, as President, he should belong to a church. Why the Presbyterians? His wife was Presbyterian. As President he attended church more regularly than any other twentieth-century American President prior to "born again" Jimmy Carter. In the area of responsibility fulfillment, Ike was a very disciplined individual.

He was born in Denison, Texas. His father worked there for the railroad from 1887 to 1891. Except for these years, Ike's parents lived in Kansas all fifty-seven years of their married life; and all their children except Ike were born in Kansas. Ike lived in Texas less than a year. He was in temperament and outlook a midwesterner.

Ike graduated from West Point in 1915. In June 1928 Major Eisenhower, an outstanding battalion CO at Fort Benning, Georgia, was assigned the task of writing a battlefield guidebook for the European Battle Monuments Commission. He fulfilled this mission in Paris as a member of the staff of General of the Armies John J. Pershing. During the period of this assignment Colonel George C. Marshall became aware of Ike's capabilities. When Ike returned to the States in 1929 he was detailed to the staff of an Assistant Secretary of War as his expert on military management problems. In Washington he got to know Bernard M. Baruch and General Douglas MacArthur. When MacArthur became Army Chief of Staff in 1933, he selected Ike as one of his assistants. In 1935 MacArthur was sent to the Philippines as Military Advisor to President Manuel Quezon. He took Ike with him.

In Manila the Spanish community was pro-Franco, pro-Hitler, and anti-Jew. Some of this sentiment seeped into the Philippine American military. Eisenhower had many friends among the German Jewish refugees who had escaped from Hitler and managed to get to Manila. He became vigorously and outspokenly anti-Hitler. His reputation as a doer, an anti-Nazi, and a friend of the Jews combined to get him an offer from a Jewish relief agency of a five-year contract at $60,000 a year plus traveling expenses to find places of settlement for the victims of Nazism in eastern Asia and the islands of the Pacific. Ike was greatly tempted to accept; but feeling that, in the face of the approaching international storm, he should remain in the military, he declined the offer.

In those years MacArthur thought highly of Eisenhower. Eisenhower had great respect for MacArthur's capabilities as an intellectual and a leader but felt that his superior was too arrogant and too stubborn to be trusted with absolute authority. Eisenhower returned to the United States in 1939.

In August 1941 he was promoted to Brigadier General and made Chief of Staff, Third U. S. Army, Fort Houston, Texas. On December 12, five days after Pearl Harbor, Ike received a telephone call from Washington: "The Chief [Army Chief of Staff General George C. Marshall] says for you to hop a plane and get up here right away." Ike became Marshall's Chief of Operations, i.e., the boss' top assistant. During this time Ike got his second star.

> General Marshall asked me to prepare a directive for a Commanding General for our forces in Europe. I drafted one. When he asked for a recommendation for a Commander, I proposed Air Force General McNarney. Instead, General Marshall sent me [in July 1942] to command the European Theatre of Operations.

On D-day, June 6, 1944, the *Queen Mary* left New York harbor with 7,000 members of an armored division, 4,000 officer replacements for the Normandy beach casualties and one officer "tourist," Second Lieutenant John Doud Eisenhower—Ike's only child, fresh out of West Point, "instructed" by Ike to spend his thirty-day leave with papa at ETO HQ before reporting to Fort Benning for advanced infantry training. Eight Jewish chaplains, including myself, and six just-graduated West Pointers, including John, were assigned to the same suite aboard ship. En route, I asked Johnny, "What's so special about your dad that he got the Number One slot in Europe?" The tall, thin, likable young man replied, "Damned if I know. He's a wonderful father, a square shooter, a great guy, but Superman he ain't. What he had that the hundreds of other colonels I knew as an Army brat did not have I do not comprehend." In the years since, as I have learned more and more about Ike Eisenhower, nothing I have discovered has impressed me as much as this recollection of a great military leader who was so truly humble that his only child was genuinely unaware of his father's genuine greatness.

By the time World War II ended Ike had five stars. Then until 1948 he was Chairman of the Joint Chiefs of Staff. Then until 1950 he was President of Columbia University. Then until 1952 he was commander of NATO. Then until 1960 he was President of the United States. Both times he ran, in 1952 and in 1956, the majority of American Jews, who normally support the Democratic nominee, voted for Republican Ike, even though, in both elections, the Democratic candidate was Adlai E. Stevenson, whom American Jews greatly loved and admired.

After leaving the White House Ike went back to the Pennsylvania Dutch country from which his Kansas forebears had come. He bought a farm at Gettysburg, about fifty miles southwest of Elizabethville. He died on March 28, 1969, and is buried in Abilene, Kansas.

❁   ❁   ❁   ❁   ❁

What follows was written especially for this book by a rabbi who was very close to Dwight David Eisenhower during World War II, the distinguished spiritual leader of Park Avenue Synagogue in New York City, Rabbi Judah Nadich, who served with General Eisenhower in Europe as a member of his chaplaincy staff.

❁   ❁   ❁   ❁   ❁

The attitude of Dwight David Eisenhower toward the Jews was influenced by his upbringing. He once said, "I grew up believing that the Jews are the chosen people, that they have given us the high ethical and moral principles of our civilization."

On at least two occasions Eisenhower was himself labeled a Jew. In his book, *Crusade in Europe,* he describes the situation in Morocco and Tunisia that had been under pro-Nazi rule for several years:

> For years the uneducated population had been subjected to intensive Nazi propaganda calculated to fan their prejudices. The country was ridden, almost ruled by rumor. One rumor was to the effect that I was a Jew, sent into the country by the Jew Roosevelt to grind down the Arabs and to turn over North Africa to Jewish rule.

Almost a decade later, some who were seeking to block his selection by the Republican Party as its candidate for the Presidency tried to take unfair advantage of the jesting remark next to his name in the Yearbook of his West Point graduating class: "Dwight David Eisenhower, the terrible Swedish Jew."

Eisenhower's reaction to these efforts to "Judaize" him may be deduced from a story told by Quentin Reynolds. Reynolds was with Eisenhower in London when he received a letter from his brother Milton. He read it, snorted, and showed it to Reynolds. "I was at a cocktail party here in Washington," wrote Milton, "given by one of those real old dowagers. She said very nicely to me, 'You must come from a fine family, young man. You have an important job here and your brother is leading our troops and I understand another brother is a banker. What a pity it is that you Eisenhowers are Jewish.' I looked at her, sighed unhappily, and said, 'Ah, madame, what a pity it is that we are not!'"

When the conquest of Germany revealed the full extent of the Nazi horrors in the concentration camps, Rabbi Stephen S. Wise sent a message to General Eisenhower in August 1945 declaring "the urgent necessity of assigning a liaison officer to HQ G-5 for the purpose of coordinating activities regarding Jewish displaced persons." Two days later General Eisenhower turned down the suggestion saying, "This Headquarters does not agree that the assignment here of a liaison officer for Jewish displaced persons would materially assist such persons and regrets that it cannot accept the proposal."

As a result of the report on conditions in the DP camps made to President Truman by Dean Earl G. Harrison and a cable from Secretary of War Stimson to Eisenhower stating some of the findings, Eisenhower changed his mind. He cabled back to Secretary Stimson, "Only yesterday I declined to accept a recommendation of Rabbi Wise of New York City that I designate a Jewish chaplain to be special advisor on affairs dealing with Jewish displaced persons. I have now reconsidered this suggestion and am going to detail such an individual at once."

General Eisenhower appointed me as his first advisor on Jewish displaced persons affairs. He personally visited the assembly center at Stuttgart and the large displaced persons camp at Feldafing. His sudden and unannounced appearance at the Yom Kippur service at Feldafing, attended by several thousand people, electrified the congregation. The people gave him a stirring ovation. Eisenhower told them:

> I feel especially happy to be in a Jewish camp on this holiest day of your year. You are only here temporarily. You must be patient until the day comes—and it will come—when you leave here for the places you wish to go. The American Army is here to help you. The part you must play is to maintain good and friendly relations with your appointed authorities. I know how much you have suffered. I believe that a sunnier day will soon be yours.

He listened to the reading of a memorandum prepared by the Camp Committee describing the unsatisfactory conditions of DP camp life, asking for removal of all Nazis from German public life and appealing for the opening of the gates of Palestine and the creation of a Jewish state. The memorandum ended with these words: "Long live Field Marshal Eisenhower! Long live the United Nations! Long live the Jewish people!"

In one of my periodic reports to General Eisenhower on DP camp conditions, I told of the American armed guards stationed at the gates of the camps in the area commanded by General George Patton. The Jewish DPs had to apply for passes to leave the camps and only a limited number were issued. The psychological effect of this upon persons imprisoned by the Nazis for years may be imagined, especially as they could see the Germans, the erstwhile enemies of the Americans, coming and going as they pleased. General Eisenhower ordered the removal of the guards and the elimination of the pass system. After my next visit to this same area, I reported that the guards were gone but the pass system was still in effect. Eisenhower's Chief of Staff, Walter Bedell Smith, telephoned Patton in my presence to come to talk to Eisenhower. Later General Smith told me that when Eisenhower had Patton before him he asked, "George, why aren't you doing something for these Jewish displaced persons?" The answer he got was, "Why the hell should I?" To which General Eisenhower retorted, "Because I am ordering you to do so!"

In the course of Eisenhower's campaign for the Presidency in the fall of 1952 he visited Boston. While there he made an impromptu speech at a street corner in Roxbury in a section heavily populated by Jews. A large crowd gathered to see and hear him. Replying to false charges made against him that he was anti-Semitic, he pulled from his pocket the current issue of the *American Zionist*. "If you want to know how I feel about the Jewish people," he exclaimed, "read the article about me in this magazine by one of your own rabbis." The article to which he referred was written by me. I was then serving a congregation in the Brookline section of Boston. The article described the role of General Eisenhower in saving the lives of tens of thousands of Jewish refugees during and after World War II. "Appeals to prejudice and bigotry have no place in America," he said. "Those were the tactics of the Nazis and the Fascists. That was why the freedom-loving peoples of the world had to destroy them. Only the Communists still use these same tactics."

I visited General Eisenhower at Gettysburg in 1962 to present him with a copy of *Rabbis in Uniform*, a book edited by Chaplain Louis Barish and published on the occasion of the one-hundredth anniversary of the commissioning of the first American Jewish military chaplain. Eisenhower had written a message for the book. The former Commander-in-Chief asked that his best wishes be conveyed to all present and former Jewish chaplains from "an old comrade in the ETO."

A few years later the twentieth anniversary of the liberation of the first Nazi concentration camp by the American forces under General Eisenhower's command was observed at a Sabbath service in my present synagogue, the Park Avenue Synagogue in New York City. The former President attended as guest of honor. As he sat on the pulpit next to me, he joined the congregation in reciting all the traditional Jewish prayers that were said in English. He told me later that he was greatly moved by the anniversary service.

In the last letter I received from him, written from Indio, California, on April 11, 1967, he wrote:

> You and I had the high privilege of being associated with millions of comrades. representing many nations and many creeds, in a crusade against an evil power whose enthronement of racial hate menaced all our ideals and tightly held beliefs, beliefs that, whatever be our faith, may be summarized as an effort to achieve the brotherhood of man under the Fatherhood of God.

She Was Just a Sweet Little Housekeeper
(1956)

Nelson Glueck, renowned archeologist and President of Cincinnati's Hebrew Union College, had delivered a lecture to a Los Angeles audience on his scholarly volume, *The River Jordan*. Afterward he autographed copies of his book. A sweet looking, little, middle-aged lady brought hers to be autographed. As the tall, handsome scholar wrote his name in her book, she said to him, "I've also written a book, Dr. Glueck, and, if you will give me your office address, I would very much like to send you an autographed copy." Dr. Glueck gave her his card.

Several weeks later, while Dr. Glueck was out of town, the book arrived. It was *A House Is Not a Home* by retired brothel madam Polly Adler. The book passed from hand to hand among the secretaries in the office, but was not given to Dr. Glueck. The girls did not consider it suitable reading for their rabbinical boss.

A few months went by. One day Dr. Glueck said to his secretary, "You know, there was a nice little lady in Los Angeles who promised to send me a book she had written. I wonder why we haven't received it." With reddened faces, the girls in the office told their boss what they had done. With reddened face, Dr. Glueck confessed that he would never have connected that nice little lady with such a profession. Then; being the very human human being that he was, he took the book, read it, enjoyed it, and sent its author a thank-you letter containing an apology for not having acknowledged her kindness at an earlier date.

THE NEW JEWISH HOLIDAY
(1960)

A non-Jewish traveling salesman was visiting one of his Jewish accounts in Cincinnati in an effort to collect the money due for merchandise which his firm had delivered quite some time before. The hard pressed but quick thinking merchant explained that he could not pay the bill immediately because the day was a special Jewish holiday on which one was not permitted to pay any of his debts. The salesman, never having heard of such a Yom Tov, asked, "What holiday is it?" "Oh," replied the merchant, "this is Erev Mechulah [the Eve of Bankruptcy]." The salesman accepted the explanation and said he would return at another time to get the money.

The next day the salesman called on another Jewish account, this time in Columbus, Ohio, on a similar mission; and was told once again that the merchant could not pay him because the day was a special Jewish holiday. "Now don't tell me that you can't pay because today is Erev Mechulah," replied the exasperated salesman. The surprised merchant grasped the cue and said that "yes, today is Erev Mechulah, on which Jews are not permitted to repay debts."

At this the salesman's face lit up in triumph. He said, "You are not telling me the truth. You are trying to fool me. Yesterday I was told that yesterday was Erev Mechulah and today you are telling me that today is Erev Mechulah." "Who told you that yesterday was Erev Mechulah?" asked the merchant. "Your friend Kopfdreher in Cincinnati told me," said the salesman. "Oh, Kopfdreher," responded the Columbus merchant. "He's one of these Cincinnati Reform Jews who observes a holiday for only one day; but here in Columbus we keep it for two days!"

Told by the late Rabbi Charles E. Shulman of Riverdale Temple, Bronx, New York.

SOME OF OUR BEST SYNAGOGUES ARE CHURCHES
(1962)

Cantor Isaac Schoen of Cleveland tells about a man who took his friend, a European immigrant, for an auto tour of the old Cleveland neighborhood in which the long-time resident had grown up. Things had greatly changed. Most of the Jews had moved to the suburbs. Many synagogues had been converted into churches. As they moved along, the Clevelander pointed out many places of religious significance in his earlier years. "In that church," he said, "I became a Bar Mitzvah. . . . In that church I was married. . . . In that church, my son had his Bar Mitzvah." "Ah," said his friend, "now I understand why you and your family are such goyim!"

Contributed by Rabbi Stanley R. Brav.

PART FIVE

The Southwest

"Arroyos, Coyotes, and Injuns"

Introduction

The enormous influence of motion pictures and television upon the minds of America's "adolescents," who range in age from fifteen to eighty, has created the fiction that the American Southwest—Arizona, Arkansas, Louisiana, New Mexico, Oklahoma, Texas—is the major repository of American folklore. Day after day and night after night big movie screens and smaller TV screens all over the world promote the hoax that life in frontier America was primarily a struggle between the good guys and the bad guys: the brave cavalryman and the ignoble redskin; Robin Hoods like the James boys and dirty cowards like the one who "laid Jesse James in his grave"; gallant buffalo hunters and the stupid, ugly buffalo; noble homesteaders and lowdown sheep herders and cattlemen.

This is, indeed, folklore with a vengeance. It was the Indian who fought valiantly for his land and his rights and callous soldiers who robbed him of both. Frontier bandits were a bunch of tough, hardhearted rogues and those who rid their communities of these human vermin were the heroes. To engage in a buffalo hunt with a high powered rifle took little skill or courage. Those who took part in this cruel pastime laid waste one of America's most unique and useful animal resources. And the linsey-woolsey struggle reflects little credit on either the farmers or the herders. Many on both sides of this prairie war were equally greedy and equally unmindful of the privileges and needs of the other.

To spread the notion that life in the developing Southwest was more attractive and more adventuresome than pioneering in other parts of the country is to spread an untruth. Nowhere else in the continental United States was so large a proportion of the real estate harsh, uninviting, devoid of verdure, difficult to endure. All credit and glory to those who transformed these desolate areas into places of usefulness and beauty; but their lives were often far from glamorous. Their splendid achievements were the end products of years of backbreaking work and

355

monotony and boredom. Small wonder that so many Arizona and New Mexico early birds, after making their pile, took off for the love nests of California to spend the rest of their days in soft-feathered comfort and contentment. The Southwest has its fair share of interesting bits of Americana—that is the proper way to state it, its fair share, no more and no less.

Joseph Stocker of Phoenix, in his *Jewish Roots in Arizona*, puts the matter in appropriate perspective, both with regard to the Jews and the others who contributed to the upbuilding of the Southwest. He writes:

> The temptation is to assume, as has been assumed in the mythology of the American Southwest, that every Jew was a peddler. Our careless cataloguing of frontier types causes us to see, in our mind's eye, the Chinese cook, the bad Indian, the good sheriff, the pretty schoolteacher from the East—and the Jewish peddler. We envision him trudging with his cart into the primitive back country, bringing precious calico to sunburned ranchers' wives and selling eggbeaters to Indians who have no eggs.
>
> These are romantic stereotypes and make fine grist for the movies. But it wasn't necessarily so. All the Chinese were not cooks, nor were all Indians bad, all sheriffs good, or all schoolteachers pretty. Neither were all the Jews peddlers. They were, in point of fact, a little bit of everything, just as the others were. They came as miners of gold and silver and copper. One cropped mesquite off the harsh desert to use as fuel for the smelters. Another was a freighter. Still another built a railroad. And, to be sure, some were peddlers.

Arizona

In 1539 Marcos des Niza, a Spanish Franciscan friar, explored the southeastern portion of what is now the state of Arizona. He carried back to Mexico an Indian tale that somewhere in the area were seven Zuni pueblos, the "seven cities of Cibola," constructed from gold and laden with precious jewels. Spurred by a desire to get hold of this loot, Francisco Vasquez de Coronado, Spanish governor of a Mexican province, organized an expedition in 1540 that occupied Cibola, which was about forty miles south of what is now Gallup, New Mexico, and a few miles east of the present Arizona border. Alas, no gold or jewels were found. Still looking for treasure, Coronado sent members of his party in all directions, northwest as far as Tusayan and the Grand Canyon of the Colorado, east to the Rio Grande, northeast as far as what is now Kansas—to no avail. After three years of fruitless search, Coronado returned to Mexico with only a small fraction of the large force with which he had started out. In disgrace he was deprived of his governorship; but, on the basis of his journey, a vast area north of Mexico was claimed for the Spanish crown and remained under Spanish control until 1821.

Brave and dedicated monks established missions in many places in the new territory. Their conversionist efforts were stoutly resisted by the Indians. In most instances the bold missionaries were killed and their places of worship destroyed. In Arizona only two of the early missions survived, Tumacacori Mission, 1691, twenty miles north of Nogales, and San Xavier del Bac, 1700, in southwest Tucson. In 1752 the Spanish established a presidio or military post at Tubac, a few miles north of Tumacacori.

The first permanent white settlement was in 1775 on land now part of Tucson. North Americans began to arrive as traders, hunters, and a few as settlers in the first quarter of the nineteenth century. In 1821 Spain ceded Arizona to liberated Mexico. At the end of the Mexican War Mexico gave all the land north of the Gila River to the United States. The portion of Arizona south of the Gila was obtained from Mexico in 1853 through the Gadsden Purchase and was occupied by the North Americans in 1856.

Arizona became a territory in December 1863. Prescott, settled that same year, was named the capital. Phoenix, founded in 1870, became the state capital in 1889. In the post-Civil War years Arizona was plagued by Apache uprisings, which ended with the surrender of Chief Geronimo in 1886. Arizona was admitted to the Union as the 48th state on February 14, 1912.

For many years it was believed that the first Jew to enter Arizona was Herman Ehrenberg, who arrived in 1854. It has now been quite definitely established that Ehrenberg was not Jewish. Just who may have been Arizona's first Jew is not known. As early as 1860 B. Cohen was operating a store in the boom town of La Paz.

There were not enough Jews to support a congregation anywhere in Arizona until the twentieth century. The earliest synagogues in the state were: Congregation Sons of Israel, Douglas, 1907; Temple Emanuel, Tucson, 1909; Congregation Emanuel, Phoenix, 1918. There are currently 33,000 Jews in Arizona, 1.4 percent of the total population. Nearly all live in or near Phoenix, 25,000, and Tucson, 7,500.

Arkansas

In 1541-42 Spaniard Ferdinand de Soto spent the winter exploring the eastern part of Arkansas. In 1673 Frenchman Louis Joliet, traveling down the Mississippi, camped at the mouth of the Arkansas River. The first white settlement was established by Frenchman Henri de Tonti in 1686 at Arkansas Post on the Arkansas River, about fifteen miles west of the Mississippi. The settlement, the river and the state were named after the area's original inhabitants, the Arkansas Indians.

Little Rock was founded as an Indian trading post in 1722 by the

French, who called it Le Petit Roche. The area was French until 1762, Spanish to 1800, and then again French. Americans began to move in after 1790. In 1803, through the Louisiana Purchase, Arkansas became part of the United States.

Arkansas Territory was organized in 1819 with Arkansas Post as the capital. The next year the capital was moved to Little Rock. Arkansas was admitted to the Union on June 15, 1836, as the 25th state. It seceded in May 1861 and was readmitted in June 1868.

The first Jews known to have come to Arkansas arrived in Little Rock, 1838; Fort Smith, 1842; Pine Bluff, 1845; and Hot Springs, 1856. The oldest congregations in the state are Bnai Israel of Little Rock, 1866; Anshe Emeth of Pine Bluff, 1867; Beth El of Helena, 1868. . . . Jonas Levy was mayor of Little Rock from 1860 to 1865. Cyrus Adler, the Oriental scholar, was born in Van Buren in 1863. Jonathan Eichhorn, the rabbi, was born in Texarkana in 1936. . . . There are 3,300 Jews in Arkansas, two-tenths of one percent of the total population. Fourteen hundred live in Little Rock, 600 in Hot Springs, 300 in Pine Bluff.

Louisiana

The first white men to enter this region were Spaniards Cabeza de Vaca and Panfilo de Narvaez in 1530. In 1682 Rene Robert Cavalier, Sieur de La Salle explored the region, claimed it for France and named it Louisiana in honor of Louis XIV. In 1699 the explorer Iberville visited an Indian town named Istrouma, meaning in the Indian tongue "red stick." He liked Istrouma so well that he suggested the establishment of a white settlement there. A generation later his suggestion became a reality. The white town that supplanted Istrouma was named Baton Rouge, which in French means "red stick." In 1700 Iberville constructed a military post about fifty miles north of the Mississippi delta.

The first permanent white settlement was in 1717 at St. Jean Baptiste, now known as Nachitoches. New Orleans was founded in 1718 by Iberville's brother, Jean Baptiste Le Moyne, Sieur de Bienville. Bienville served as first colonial governor.

In 1762 the region was ceded to Spain but remained essentially French in population and character. In 1800 the French regained possession. In 1803 they sold it to the United States. In 1804 Congress gave it official status as the Territory of Orleans. On April 30, 1812, it was renamed Louisiana and admitted to the Union as the 18th state. In 1861 Louisiana seceded from the Union and was readmitted in 1868.

The following cities have served as the state capital: New Orleans, 1812-25; Donaldsville, 1825-31; New Orleans, 1831-49; Baton Rouge, 1849-64; New Orleans, 1864-82; Baton Rouge, since 1882.

There were Jews among the earliest New Orleans settlers. But they were not allowed to remain very long. In 1724 Governor Bienville issued a Code Noir which set up Roman Catholicism as the state religion and forbade Jews to live in the colony. Jews were not permitted to reside in Louisiana legally until after the United States assumed control. However, there were a number of Jews in New Orleans long before 1803, seemingly untroubled by the authorities. There was a Jewish merchant in the port city as early as the 1760s. When Judah Touro arrived in 1802 he learned that a son of Haym Salomon was a well-known and much respected citizen.

The state's first Jewish congregation, Congregation Shangari Chassed, was organized in New Orleans in 1828. Other early congregations were Bikur Cholim, Donaldsville, 1856; Har El, Shreveport, 1857; Hebrew Congregation, Baton Rouge, 1859; Gemilluth Chassodim, Alexandria, 1861; Bnai Israel, Monroe, 1868.

Louisiana has 16,000 Jews, four-tenths of one percent of the total population. Almost all live in the following cities: New Orleans, 11,000; Shreveport, 1,500; Baton Rouge, 1,100; Alexandria, 750; and Lafayette, 600.

New Mexico

The story of New Mexico, in its earliest years, parallels that of Arizona. It began to have its own history in 1609 when Santa Fe, first permanent white settlement in the entire Southwest, second oldest city in the United States, and oldest provincial and state capital in our country, was founded. Its Palace of the Governors, built that same year, is the oldest existing public building in the land. The Palace was used by the rulers of this area for 300 years.

In 1680 the Pueblo Indians, irked by the un-Christian behavior of their Spanish conquistadors, rebelled and drove the Spaniards from their country. Twelve years later Diego de Vargas reconquered the region. Albuquerque, named for the Duke of Albuquerque, viceroy of New Spain, came into existence in 1706.

In 1821 New Mexico became a province of the independent Republic of Mexico. That same year the Santa Fe Trail, an important artery between the North American frontier settlements and those of Spanish America, began to be used. At first the road was traveled by pack horses loaded with provisions, tools, and weapons. Later, caravans of covered wagons carried immigrants and merchandise from the Midwest to the Southwest.

The Trail began at Independence, Missouri. It moved west 150 miles to Council Groves, Kansas. Here the caravans were formed of about 100 wagons each. About 30 such caravans moved over the Trail annually. The road continued westward to Great Bend, Kansas, and then turned toward the southwest. It went on to Dodge City, Kansas, then down to and across northeast Oklahoma to Clayton, New Mexico. The distance from Independence to Clayton was about 565 miles.

At Clayton the men were separated from the boys. Hardy souls who were willing to face great danger to reach Santa Fe more quickly took the shorter route through 58 miles of waterless desert plus 150 miles of Comanche Indians. The more cautious followed the safer but 130-mile longer circuitous route from Clayton to Raton to Taos to Tres Piedras to Espanola to Santa Fe. Not until the Atchison, Topeka, and Santa Fe Railroad, after meandering through Kansas, southeast Colorado and New Mexico, reached Lamy, fifteen miles southeast of Santa Fe, in 1880, did the Santa Fe Trail lose its commercial value, its discomforts and dangers, and, finally, its existence.

The United States acquired New Mexico in 1848. It was given territorial status in 1850. It entered the Union in January 1912 as the 47th state. Santa Fe continued to be the capital, as it had been since 1609.

The first Jew in New Mexico may have been Eugene Leitsendorfer, a traveling merchant of German birth, who was in Santa Fe in 1830. He, together with his brother, Thomas, and another partner, Jacob Houghton, opened a store on the Plaza in 1844. The Leitsendorfers were the first of a long stream of Jewish merchants who contributed greatly to the commercial development of the state. Preeminent among these were the Spiegelberg, Seligman, Freudenthal, Lesinsky, and Ilfeld families.

The first New Mexican Jewish congregation was Congregation Montefiore of Las Vegas, 1886. Congregation Albert of Albuquerque dates from 1907. There are small congregations of more recent origin in Los Alamos, Santa Fe, and Las Cruces. New Mexico has about 9,000 Jews, eight-tenths of one percent of the total population. The largest Jewish communities are Albuquerque, 7,000; Santa Fe, 500; and Las Cruces, 200.

Oklahoma

Coronado visited Oklahoma in 1641. The first permanent white settlement was at Salina, 1796. The region was acquired by the United States in 1803 through the Louisiana Purchase. In 1834 Congress set aside a large area, including present-day Oklahoma, as the future home of the "Five Civilized Tribes," the Cherokee, Chickasaw, Choctaw, Creek, and Seminole Indians. This area was known as the Indian Territory. In 1866 the government reduced considerably the size of the original land grant. During the next seventeen years Indians from twenty other tribes were moved into the constricted Indian reservation area. In 1889 large tracts of uncultivated land in the Indian Territory were made available to white homesteaders. Tulsa was founded in 1882 and Oklahoma City in 1889.

Oklahoma Territory was created in 1890. Guthrie was chosen as the capital. Oklahoma was admitted to the Union in 1907 as the 46th state. In 1910 the capital was shifted to Oklahoma City. While farming and cattle raising were and are important elements in Oklahoma's economy, the production and refining of crude oil has become its most profitable enterprise.

Oklahoma Jewish folklore is practically non-existent because the state's Jewish community is less than a century old. Joseph Sondheimer came to Oklahoma in 1867, but there was only a handful of Jews in Indian Territory prior to 1889. Jews helped found Oklahoma City that year but did not settle in Tulsa until about 1900.

The first Jewish organization in the state was the Hebrew Cemetery Association of Oklahoma City, 1902. The oldest synagogues are Temple Bnai Israel (Reform), Oklahoma City, 1903; Congregation Emanuel (Orthodox), Oklahoma City, 1904; Temple Israel (Reform), Tulsa, 1914; Congregation Bnai Emuna (Orthodox) Tulsa, 1916. Oklahoma has 6,500 Jews, two-tenths of one percent of the total population. Tulsa has 2,600 Jews and Oklahoma City 1,500.

Texas

Coronado's search for Indian riches brought him into Texas in 1641. Ysleta, now a part of El Paso, was the first permanent Spanish settlement, 1682. Next came Nacogdoches, 1716, and San Antonio, 1718. The province of Texas was created in 1727.

When the Mexican republic took control in 1821 it encouraged only Roman Catholic immigration into Texas. Nevertheless, many non-Catholic Anglo-Americans ignored the Mexican bias. The first Anglo settlement was at Austin, 1821. By 1836 the Texas gringos far outnumbered the Mexicanos. A short but fierce war ensued in which Texas won its independence from Mexico. General Sam Houston was the first president of the Republic of Texas. The city of Houston, founded in 1836 and named for the first president, was the capital. Three years later Austin became the capital. In December 1845 Texas ceased to be a separate national entity and was admitted to the Union as the 28th state. It seceded in 1861 and was readmitted in 1870.

The founding dates of other important Texas cities: Galveston, 1836; Corpus Christi, 1839; Dallas, 1844; Fort Worth, 1849; El Paso, 1858; Amarillo, 1887; and Lubbock, 1891.

The first Jew to come to Texas, Samuel Isaacs, helped Stephen Austin found the town of Austin. A substantial number of Jews lived in Nacogdoches in the first half of the nineteenth century.

A Jewish cemetery was laid out in Houston in 1844. The oldest Texas congregations are Congregation Beth Israel, Houston, 1860; Beth Israel,

Austin, 1867; Bnai Israel, Galveston, 1868; Emanu-El, Dallas, 1874; Beth El, San Antonio, 1874; and Rodef Sholom, Waco, 1879.

There are 72,000 Jews in Texas, six-tenths of one percent of the total population. The largest Jewish communities are Houston, 26,000; Dallas, 20,000; San Antonio, 6,500; El Paso, 4,500; Fort Worth, 3,000; Austin, 2,000; and Corpus Christi, 1,100.

—D.M.E.

Corsaire—Oui; Pirate—Non
(1795)

The most authentic variety of folklore contains such a rich admixture of truth and fiction that it is almost impossible to separate one from the other. So understood, the story of Jean Lafitte, French-American freebooter, hero of the battle of New Orleans, is American folklore pure and choice. But that Lafitte could qualify for inclusion in a volume on American Jewish folklore did not become known until about 1950. Then, a memoir written in French by Lafitte, possessed by his great-grandson, John A. Lafitte of Kansas City, Missouri, and translated by Madeleine Fabiola Kent of Montreal, Canada, revealed that Lafitte's mother was Jewish, his first and dearly beloved wife, mother of three of his children, was Jewish, and that he himself was not formally identified with the Christian religion. Furthermore, the memoir contained the following statement by Lafitte with regard to his seafaring activities: "I am not nor have I ever been a pirate. I may have evaded the payment of dues at the custom house, but I have never ceased to be a good citizen."

✿　✿　✿　✿　✿

Jean Lafitte was born in French Port-au-Prince, St. Domingue, now Haiti, April 22, 1782. He was the youngest of eight children. His father was a French Huguenot and a leather worker. His mother died when he was a year old. He was reared by his mother's mother, a Marrano born in Bilbao, Spain. Her late husband, a member of the science faculty of the University of Zaragoza, had also been a Marrano. Publicly they were Catholic; secretly they practiced Judaism. Her husband was charged with heresy by the Spanish Inquisition, tortured and killed. She was accused of "Judaizing" and jailed. Before she was tried, her jailers were bribed, and she escaped and crossed the Pyrenees into France. She went

---

The primary source for this article is Madeleine Fabiola Kent's biographical novel, *The Corsair*, New York, 1955.

to Bayonne on the Atlantic seacoast in southwestern France. There, a short time later, she gave birth to Jean's mother. This family background explains why Lafitte was a lifelong implacable enemy of the Spanish.

In 1794 the blacks of St. Domingue, led by Toussaint l'Ouverture, gained control of the country. Toussaint remained loyal to France. He repelled a Spanish force which, taking advantage of St. Domingue's racial turmoil, invaded the western or French portion from the eastern or Spanish part of the island. In 1795 France and Spain made peace. Spain ceded her section of the island to France. Toussaint was named French governor general of all St. Domingue. Although slavery had been abolished in France, Napoleon attempted in 1801 to reestablish slavery on St. Domingue. This caused Toussaint to declare his country independent of France. France sent troops to restore its authority. Toussaint was seized, imprisoned in France and died there.

In 1795 Jean and brother Pierre were added to the privateering crew of their older brother Alexandre. Their ship brought foodstuffs to St. Domingue through the British blockade and captured and looted British and Spanish merchantmen. To the French their ship and they were known as "corsaires." Modern dictionaries treat the word "corsair," as it is spelled in English, as a synonym for "pirate." In Napoleonic times this was not so. A French corsaire was the equivalent of an English or American privateer. It was a privately owned ship authorized, in time of war, to help overcome the enemy by battling its naval vessels and confiscating its merchant fleet and cargoes.

After five hectic months of privateering, Jean and Pierre were sent to the island of Martinique for further schooling, because at that time there were no schools for white children on St. Domingue. Martinique fluctuated between French and British suzerainty. During the years that the boys studied there, 1795-98, Martinique was in the hands of the British. Their teachers, however, were French who did a good job of instilling in them a hatred of the British.

After returning to St. Domingue, Jean and Pierre again went to sea, this time on a merchant ship belonging to their grandmother's brother. They carried cargo first to New Orleans and then to Charlotte Amalie, St. Thomas, Virgin Islands. Here in January 1800 seventeen-year-old Jean rapidly courted and wed beautiful seventeen-year-old Rachel, daughter of merchant Thomas Levine, also of Jewish ancestry. He brought his lovely bride back to Port-au-Prince. Their first child, a son, was born in February 1801.

When Toussaint proclaimed the island an independent black nation Jean went to France and joined Napoleon's army. He returned in 1803 with the colonial expedition that defeated Toussaint and reestablished French rule. He learned that, in his absence, he had become the father of a second son and that, a month before, his grandmother had died. The

Napoleonic triumph was of short duration. Near the end of the year the British and the blacks combined to overcome the French. On January 1, 1804, the blacks again declared their independence and named their new country Haiti. This turn of events impelled the Lafittes to leave their native island and migrate to the United States.

They sailed on the great-uncle's ship to Louisiana, which had recently been sold by France to the United States. The inhabitants of Louisiana were predominantly French. Just before they reached the Louisiana coast Rachel died giving birth to her third child, a daughter. Grief-stricken Jean buried her on Grand Terre Island, at the entrance to Barataria Bay, about 55 miles south of New Orleans. Then the family moved on to New Orleans where for a few years Jean earned his living as a fencing master and Pierre labored as a master blacksmith.

The brothers became restless. The urge to sail the seas as rollicking collectors of booty was still strong within them. They got a letter of marque from the Republic of Cartagena, a city on the northwestern coast of New Grenada (now Colombia) which had freed itself from Spanish rule. They set up headquarters on Grand Terre Island and embarked on a successful career as privateers against the Spanish, with whom Cartagena was technically at war, and the British. France was at war with both Spain and England. Throughout his life Jean remained at heart a Frenchman and needed little excuse to fight the enemies of the French.

Technically Jean had a right to privateer against the Spanish but not against the British. To the Americans his anti-British activities made him, for the time being, a pirate, a charge which Jean stoutly denied. He could not and did not deny being a smuggler. The goods and slaves seized on Spanish and British ships were unloaded at Grand Terre Island, ferried through Barataria Bay, the bayous, and Lake Salvado, hauled a short distance overland, smuggled into New Orleans and sold. By 1810 Grand Terre Island was a thriving community of 300 persons. Business was so good that Jean bought a building in New Orleans on Royal Street, which he used both as warehouse and retail store, and a house on the same street for entertaining friends and business associates. Toward the end of 1810 he acquired a New Orleans mistress of French extraction. Their affair lasted until about the beginning of 1814.

On June 18, 1812, the United States declared war against Great Britain and the issuance of privateer commissions was authorized. Jean obtained one of these. This eliminated, immediately and completely, the stigma that his forays on British shipping had been and would be piratical. However, the anti-Lafitte sentiments of Louisiana's governor, William Claiborne, were not lessened by this change in status. He continued to regard Lafitte as a rascally smuggler, which legally he definitely was and continued to be. So Jean found himself waging a two-front war—against British shipping and against Governor Claiborne. The governor had to be very circumspect in his attempts to curb the smuggling operations because Lafitte had become a powerful figure in the political and business life of New Orleans and was an extremely popular man in its most elite social circles.

In the late summer of 1814 a fleet of British troopships left Bermuda, took on fresh supplies at Havana, and berthed at Pensacola in preparation for attacks on New Orleans and Mobile. A British officer came to Grand Terre on September 3 to attempt to persuade Jean to join the British in their attack on New Orleans. Jean was offered a commission in the Royal Navy and the future governorship of some British colony. Jean temporized. He said he would like to have time to consider. He sent a warning to Governor Claiborne of the imminence of the British assault. He volunteered himself and his men in defense of the city. Claiborne passed the information on to General Andrew Jackson, then at Mobile.

Both Claiborne and Jackson gave no credence to the report coming from one whom they considered little better than a pirate. Jackson termed Jean and his followers "hellish banditti." Claiborne did something far more drastic. On September 16, while Jean was away on a privateering enterprise, Louisiana militiamen attacked Grand Terre, took its male inhabitants prisoner, and set fire to its buildings and their contents. Two days later Jean's privateersmen returned to Grand Terre and retook it from the fifty militiamen left there to prevent such a happening.

Despite this hostile act Jean did not turn against the American cause. He continued his strenuous efforts to help resist the British. He made several trips to New Orleans to warn its citizens of the peril they faced. He had to move about in absolute secrecy because Claiborne had put a price on his head.

Finally, in the middle of November, enraged by the governor's obstinate refusal to face reality, Jean forced his way into Claiborne's presence and presented him with such indisputable evidence that the British would soon invade Louisiana that the governor did a very rapid volte-face. He sent a message to Jackson urging him to move his troops from Mobile to New Orleans without delay. He authorized Jean to assume a leading role in the preparations for defending the city. And, realizing at long last that he had misjudged the good there was in this maverick French-American, he wrote to President James Madison, requesting that Jean and his men be pardoned for their smuggling offenses.

Jackson arrived in New Orleans with his troops on December 1. The hot-tempered American general accepted Jean's cooperation reluctantly. In the next few days Jean turned over to the Army arms and ammunition from his bayou caches sufficient for 6,000 men. The experienced cannoneers among the Lafitte privateersmen were organized into a battery of field artillery. The rest of his fighters were ordered to join a Marine battalion.

On December 15 the British fleet appeared off the Louisiana coast and overwhelmed a small American naval force that bravely gave it battle. On December 23 the British soldiers made their presence known sooner and closer to New Orleans than was anticipated. They had struggled through five miles of what was considered impenetrable swampland and had taken up positions only eight miles south of New Orleans. General Jackson ordered the forces under his command to prepare to attack with all possible speed.

If ever there was a campaign that was fought and won by an American hodgepodge army, this was it. The American order of battle was composed of three battalions of Regular Army infantry; one battalion of U. S. Marines; one division of Louisiana militia; one division of Tennessee militia; one squadron of Mississippi Dragoons; one battalion of Creoles from Fort St. Jean; one battalion of "free men of color," i.e., blacks; 500 unorganized but very capable tomahawk-throwing and squirrel-rifle-shooting Tennessee backwoodsmen; Beale's Rifles—60 New Orleans lawyers, merchants, and other professional men smartly attired in high silk hats, ruffled shirts, and high starched collars; and 18 Choctaw Indians suitably painted for the occasion.

The Americans attacked at seven P.M. on December 23. By midnight the British had been forced to fall back. Other battles were fought on December 28 and January 1. On January 4 the Americans were greatly strengthened both in morale and numbers by the arrival of a division of Kentucky militia. The final and crucial battle was fought on January 8. The British were demoralized and routed. They lost 2,600 killed and wounded. The American casualties numbered 350.

In his after-action report General Jackson stated:

> Captains Dominique [Jean's brother Alexandre] and Beluche, lately commanding privateers at Barataria, with part of their former crews and many brave citizens of New Orleans, were stationed at Battery No. 3. The General cannot avoid giving warm approbation of the manner in which those gentlemen have uniformly conducted themselves while under his command, and of the gallantry with which they have redeemed the pledge they gave at the opening of the campaign, to defend the country. The brothers Lafitte [Jean and Pierre] have exhibited the same courage and fidelity and the General promises that the Government shall be apprised of their conduct.

On February 6, 1815, the President of the United States granted Jean Lafitte, his brothers, and his followers a full pardon for all past offenses. That spring Jean resumed his career as an anti-Spanish corsaire, acting under the authority of the Republic of Cartagena and the Mexican Revolutionary Congress. In 1817 Jean transferred his headquarters from

Grand Terre to Snake Island, now known as Galveston Island, Texas. He carefully confined his privateering operations to seizing Spanish vessels but some of his followers were less scrupulous. They began to capture and ransack vessels of other nationalities, including some American ships. Jean was in danger of being declared the pirate he had never been and had no wish to be. He decided the time had come to quit the privateering business; and he did. On May 7, 1820, he set fire to the buildings and stores on Snake Island and left. He went to Majores Island off the northeast coast of Yucatan and lived there for about a year. Then he caused a rumor to be spread that he had died. He assumed a new identity, that of John Lafflin, Yankee sea captain.

As John Lafflin he went to Charleston, South Carolina, and entered the import-export business. On June 7, 1832, he married Charlestonian Episcopalian Emma Mortimore. She was a pious woman who attended church regularly. Lafitte's memoir states that he seldom went to church with her and, when he went, he did so very unwillingly. In 1833 he moved to St. Louis and became a gunpowder manufacturer. He resided in Alton, Illinois, just across the Mississippi from St. Louis. He died there on May 5, 1854.

His children were, of course, aware of the true identity of John Lafflin. In later years his sons resumed the family name of Lafitte.

Aaron Wolf and Captain Charley
(1836)

Levy Meyers Harby was born in Georgetown, South Carolina, on September 21, 1793. He was one of five children of Solomon Harby who achieved prominence in the United States during the nineteenth century. The others: Isaac, journalist, author, dramatist, founder, and leader of the first American Reform Jewish congregation; Washington, educator and playwright; Henry, ardent States Righter; and Caroline, educator and poet.

As a youngster Levi acquired the nickname of Charley. In 1807 when he enlisted as a midshipman in the Navy Charley legitimated his nickname by enrolling as Levi Charles Harby, the name by which he was known for the rest of his life. Nowadays a midshipman is a Naval Academy cadet; but in 1807 the Naval Academy did not yet exist. Then a midshipman was a student naval officer who ranked above chief petty

---

The excerpt in this article from *Off the Capes of Delaware* is used with the permission of the book's publisher, the Union of American Hebrew Congregations.

officer and below warrant officer and learned his trade the hard way, i.e., at sea. Prior to the War of 1812 Charley served in the Mediterranean on convoy duty, protecting American merchantmen from the Barbary pirates.

In a sea battle with the British in the fall of 1813 Charley was taken prisoner and confined in Dartmoor Prison in southwest England together with thousands of other captured American naval personnel, including Uriah Phillips Levy. A peace treaty was signed on December 24, 1814. It provided for the release of all military prisoners, an agreement the British were slow in honoring. Charley learned the war had ended when an English Jewish friend baked a loaf of bread for him and placed inside the loaf a newspaper clipping stating that hostilities had ceased. This information, spread around the prison, created great dissatisfaction and culminated in a riot on April 6, 1815, in which 63 Americans were killed or wounded. This tragic event hastened the release of the prisoners. By the end of April all were on their way back to the States. One account of Charley's confinement in Dartmoor says he escaped "by swimming." This is very unlikely. The prison was located on a high plateau in a mountainous area and surrounded by dense forests.

Harby was given his first naval command, the U.S.S. *Beagle*, in December 1823. From then on he was known affectionately to his many friends and relatives as Captain Charley. His ship was with Commodore David Porter's squadron that wiped out piracy in the Caribbean in 1824-25. In December 1827 Harby resigned his commission and went to South America to support Simon Bolivar's effort to hold together the Republic of Gran Colombia, founded after the northwestern part of South America had been freed from Spanish tyranny. Bolivar's effort failed. After Bolivar died in 1830, Charley returned to the United States and reentered the Navy.

In the summer of 1835 Harby took a leave of absence from the Navy to join the revolutionary force that was being formed to fight for Texan independence from Mexico. When the Navy learned of Charley's intention it revoked his commission on the ground that Charley was planning to become a member of the armed forces of a foreign power.

✿   ✿   ✿   ✿   ✿

At this point we take temporary leave of the world of fact to narrate a fascinating bit of highly imaginative folklore from the story "Aaron Wolf, Young Hero of Texas" in Benjamin W. Blandford's *Off the Capes of Delaware*, published in 1940 by the Union of American Hebrew Congregations and described by the publisher as "fiction woven on the loom of fact."

Mr. Blandford relates that in the early fall of 1835 Captain Charley came to Savannah, Georgia, together with Texas Colonels James Bowie and David Crockett, to recruit volunteers for the army of Texas General Sam Houston. Here Charley succumbed to the charms of beautiful sixteen-year-old Leonara Rebecca de Lyon, daughter of Levi S. de Lyon, Judge of the Chatham County Court. For both it was love at first sight.

At that very same time there arrived from England a young Jew, Aaron Wolf, son of an old friend of the judge, who had promised Aaron a position in his law office. When Aaron, a sensitive artist and accomplished violinist, beheld the lovely Leonara Rebecca, he, too, was smitten by Cupid's dart. After learning that the girl was already deeply in love with Captain Charley, Aaron decided to go far away as quickly as possible. A number of Georgians, including Moses A. Levy, Savannah's most prominent physician, had already enlisted in Colonel Bowie's company of Texas volunteers. Aaron offered to accompany Dr. Levy as his medical assistant. The offer was promptly accepted.

Mr. Blandford's account continues:

"The next day the bugles sounded in Savannah's main street and, under Colonel Bowie's command, the little band of heroes who were to strike the first blow that added Texas to the United States, rode away.

"Day followed day, and soon the little company of four hundred Americans reached the outskirts of San Antonio, where General Cos, with fourteen hundred Mexicans and much artillery, was entrenched in the Alamo, a combination of fort and church. Led by the indomitable Bowie and the heroic Crockett, men whose names alone bred courage, the little company stormed the Alamo, and the captured Mexican general with his soldiers were sent away under guard. Dr. Moses Levy went with them to tend the many wounded prisoners. Aaron remained behind.

"Like some savage wounded beast, Santa Anna, 'the Napoleon of the West,' as he called himself, with his pride stung by the defeat, suddenly appeared before the battered Alamo with five thousand men, the flower of the Mexican army, and began a siege that has had no rival in history. For nearly two weeks the Mexican artillery pounded the Alamo with shot and shell, while their infantry, raking it with rifle fire, charged again and again. Still the Lone Star flag waved defiantly in the breeze, as one hundred and eighty-three heroes stood their ground.

"At daybreak on the morning of March the sixth, 1836, the little group of powder-grimed, bandaged heroes within the battered adobe walls of the Alamo heard in the distance the shrill deguello, 'no quarter,' bugle calls of the Mexicans. Immediately the defiant melody of *La Marseillaise*, sounding strangely inappropriate even on a violin, rang out in reply. This was followed by America's defiant war songs, hoarsely roared by manly voices.

"Then, as the long-drawn-out lines of little brown, Indian-like Mexicans in their dirty-white slovenly uniforms, led by Spanish officers in blue and gold, advanced over the yellow sands of the alkali desert, the last American cheer went up from the Alamo's battered walls, for the powder kegs were empty; and now it was every man for himself to do and die for Texas. On came the Mexican infantry, prodded to action by lively cavalry in their rear. Over the walls they came. From room to room the slaughter raged until, climbing back from over their heaps of dead, the breathless Mexicans sullenly withdrew. Death and Santa Anna ruled the Alamo; not one American remained alive.

"Among the few trophies gathered in front of the cruel Santa Anna was a smashed violin that never would play again; a tiny Lone Star flag taken from the body of a young Jew, who smiled at approaching death, an officer reported; and a little hand-painted cameo portrait of a smiling young Jewess, on the back of which was written 'Sweet Rebecca, the fairest flower of all the South!'

"Suddenly Sam Houston's little army, swooping down from the north to the cry of 'Remember the Alamo!' trapped the Dictator's forces in the bend of the river and 'Captain Charley,' Adolphus Sterne, Dr. Moses Levy, and other Jews, with their gentile comrades-in-arms, avenged the death of Aaron Wolf and the Alamo heroes! Santa Anna himself was led captive to the tree under which the wounded Sam Houston lay. There he surrendered Texas to its new settlers. The revolution was over. Texas was a republic in fact, as well as in name.

"The cameo portrait was given Captain Harby by one of the Texans who had found it on the body of a dead Mexican. As he read the words and gazed into the beautiful face of his young wife, painted by the skilled, artistic hand of one who had loved so hopelessly, Captain Charley wept so freely that even his comrades who knew and admired his courage were puzzled by his weakness; but, when he told the story of Aaron Wolf, there was not a dry eye in the company."

A touching tale; but, alas, not a true one. Bowie played only a minor role in the capture of the Alamo from the Mexicans on December 9, 1835. Crockett was not there. He did not arrive in Texas from his native Tennessee until almost a month later. Neither Bowie nor Crockett was ever in Savannah on a Texas recruiting mission. Dr. Moses A. Levy was from Richmond, not Savannah. He came to Texas as a surgeon with the New Orleans Grays. Captain Charley did not wed his lovely lady until 1838. And there does not seem to have been an Aaron Wolf. The A. Wolff whose name is on the list of Alamo dead on the memorial column in the State Capitol at Austin is generally believed by Texas historians to have been Englishman Antony Wolfe, artillery gunner, who, together with his two little sons, was slaughtered by the Mexicans when they stormed the Alamo. The whereabouts and fate of his wife are not recorded.

There is a possibility that another of the Alamo dead, Henry Courtman, a recent German immigrant, was Jewish. There is no doubt whatsoever that a number of Jews participated in the Texas war for independence. Adolphus J. Sterne, German immigrant, went into business in Nacogdoches in 1824. He contributed guns and ammunition sufficient for fifty men to aid the Texan assault on the Alamo. In the fighting at San Jacinto, fifteen miles east of present-day Houston, the crucial battle of April 21, 1836, at which Texan independence was won, at least eight Jews, including Captain Charley and Dr. Moses Levy, participated.

✿ ✿ ✿ ✿ ✿

Soon after Captain Charley got married in 1838 he obtained a commission in the Georgia militia and went away to fight in the war against Osceola and the Florida Seminole Indians. When Texas was admitted to the Union at the end of 1845, the Navy restored Captain Charley to its roster, since one who had fought for the freedom of Texas could no longer be regarded as having been in the military service of a "foreign power." Charley served in the Navy throughout the rest of the Mexican War. When that war ended, Charley and Leonara settled in Galveston. He became a captain in the Revenue Marine Service, now known as the U. S. Coast Guard, and commanded a cutter stationed in the Port of Galveston.

When the Civil War broke out Charley, aged sixty-seven, resigned from the Revenue Marine Service and became captain of an infantry company in the Confederate Army. In October 1862 Federal troops captured and occupied Galveston. Captain Charley and his company played an important role in the action on New Year's morning, 1863, when the Confederates destroyed the Union vessels in Galveston harbor and drove the Yankees from the city. In the naval encounter at Sabine Pass, about 90 miles east of Galveston, on September 6, 1863, Captain Charley commanded one of the gunboats that repulsed the fleet of the redoubtable Admiral David Farragut. From then until the end of his working days Charley was harbor master of the Port of Galveston.

He and his wife were active members of the Galveston Jewish community. Leonara helped found the Ladies' Hebrew Benevolent Society. She taught in the first Jewish Sunday School in Texas, established in Galveston in 1862. The Harbys had three children. Son John married Isaac Harby's granddaughter Leah. Leah, a well-known author, composed the words for the official Flag Song of the State of Texas.

Captain Charley died in Galveston on December 3, 1870.

THE SELF-ORDAINED "CHIEF RABBI"
(1839)

Albert J. Marks was an English Ashkenazi trained for the stage. The exact dates of his birth and death are not known. What is known about Albert makes him out to have been a quite good character actor, in addition to which he was quite a character.

Albert was described by a fellow actor as "a short, fat, round faced, good natured little Jew, and somewhat of a favorite with the public." Another acquaintance said of him: "He is a little below middle size, measuring in his stockings about four feet and some inches. A gleam of good humor is always beaming on his countenance, except when he experiences twinges of gout, which is unfortunately rather often; but he is one of the best natured fellows in existence." Albert was known to his friends and admirers as Roly, some say because of his roly poly appearance and others because of his ability to play in a superb manner the role of Rowley in Sheridan's *The School for Scandal.* He was particularly adept at playing funny old men and, like Zero Mostel of our day, was noted for his highly individualistic mannerisms on stage.

He gave his first performance in New Orleans in 1826. For a while after that he traveled about the South with theatrical stock companies. Then he came back to the city to live there full time. Since it was not possible for him to act often enough in New Orleans to provide sufficient sustenance for his family and himself, his acting became a part-time activity. He made a living by taking on a variety of other part-time jobs: part-time fireman, part-time building inspector, part-time secretary for various organizations. He also produced and directed amateur theatricals.

In 1828 New Orleans' Sephardim and Ashkenazim combined to organize their first congregation, Shangari Chassed, also known as Congregation Gates of Mercy. They had no rabbi. They had a learned layman, Manis Jacobs, who served as spiritual leader. In 1834 Roly acquired one more part-time position. He began to serve as part-time secretary of Congregation Gates of Mercy. Normally there would be nothing unusual in a Jew's assuming the task of part-time secretary of a synagogue; but, in Roly's case, there was a set of circumstances which made his selection something apart from the ordinary.

In the first place, he was a professional actor. Nu—so he's a professional actor. As long as he performs his duties satisfactorily, so what? But there were other complications. Roly was married to a Catholic; he did not keep kosher; he ate bread on Passover; he had not had any of his sons circumcised. He and his wife had the misfortune to lose one of their children. His wife wanted to put a cross over the child's grave. This far Roly refused to go.

Would all this disqualify Roly from being the secretary of a synagogue on a part-time basis? Normally one might be inclined to answer "Yes," but the Jewish situation in New Orleans in 1834 was not a normal situation. According to a contemporary German Jewish journal, only two New Orleans Jewish families at that time rested on Shabbat, only four observed kashrut, and more than two-thirds of the members of Congregation Gates of Mercy had not had their sons circumcised! So, in such a community and with such a congregation, perhaps Roly fitted in as secretary better than a bona fide religious Jew would have. But this is not all. Now comes the really amazing part.

In 1838 Manis Jacobs died. Whom then did Congregation Gates of Mercy choose as its new religious leader? Roly! Roly officiated at religious services, married, buried, and performed all the other functions normally associated with the duties of a Jewish spiritual leader. And, whenever the occasion required that a religious document be filled out and signed, Roly signed it "Albert J. Marks, rabbi."

At one Purim service, when the time came to read the Megilla, the President informed the congregation that, regrettably, there would be no Hebrew reading of the Book of Esther that year because the only person with sufficient Hebrew knowledge to read it, i.e., "the rabbi," had been called away by another of his part-time obligations to be with his fire company to help it extinguish a conflagration. The situation became a community joke. New Orleaners began to refer to Roly as the city's "chief rabbi." A fellow actor, in later years, spoke of him as "an unusual character, one who had been for many years high priest of the Jews of New Orleans."

Finally, in 1842, this became too much for one of the members of Congregation Gates of Mercy. He got up at the Rosh Hashana service and said that it was a disgrace for the Jewish community to have a person like Roly as its religious functionary. This aroused Roly's ire. Banging his fists on the pulpit, he shouted, "By Jesus Christ, I have as much right to pray as anybody here!" This may have been a logical statement; but it ended Roly's career as spiritual leader. Sometime after that Roly went back to full-time acting, a vocation he was still following in November 1849, the latest date of reference to Roly that has thus far been found.

In his *The Early Jews of New Orleans,* Dr. Bertram W. Korn says of Roly:

Marks never pretended to be other than what he was—part-time actor, part-time fireman, part-time religious functionary, part-time paid secretary for a number of organizations. He had a good reputation as a family man. Objection did arise to his being a religious functionary because he was also a stage actor—and a comic at that, not a leading man or tragedian.

So that's the way it was in New Orleans in Congregation Gates of Mercy from 1839 to 1842. It had a stage comic as its "rabbi," just as, conversely, there have been congregations with bona fide rabbis who have imagined themselves to be Hamlets or Rowleys. Those who were dissatisfied with the modus operandi of Congregation Gates of Mercy organized another congregation in 1846, the Dispersed of Judah. In 1881 Gates of Mercy and Dispersed of Judah merged and took a new name, the Touro Synagogue. Under this honored name the merged congregations still exist.

"THE NAKED LADY"
(1861)

Genesis 4:19 says, "Lemech had two wives. The name of one was Adah and the name of the other Tsila." "Adah" means "she who is bedecked with jewels." What an appropriate name for Adah Isaacs Menken.

She was born on June 15, 1835, in Milneburg, Louisiana, a small town immediately northwest of New Orleans. As the city expanded it swallowed Milneburg, so today her birthplace lies well within the present boundaries of New Orleans. She was named Adah Bertha Theodore. Her father was Jewish. That her mother was Jewish is not certain. Whether or not her mother was technically Jewish, Adah was reared as a Jew and considered herself a Jew. There is no proof for the oft-repeated story that she converted to Judaism when she married her first and only Jewish husband. Her father died when she was two. Her mother then married another Jew named Josephs, who died in 1853.

Adah was an attractive, precocious child. Her remarkable intellectual and physical talents were recognized when she was very young. She was given a thorough classical and religious education. She knew French, German, Spanish, and Hebrew. She could ride, sing, and dance excellently. As a grownup she was well-learned and brilliant, especially in matters of theology and philosophy. She wrote many poems, including some on Jewish religious themes marked by deep insight and spiritual fervor. During her years on the stage she never performed on Yom Kippur. She faithfully lit Sabbath candles every Friday night. Although a committed Jew, she was greatly interested in Spiritualism.

Adah was beautiful, brainy, and unconventional. She was not the greatest actress of her time but she was the highest paid, the most widely known, and the most gossiped about. She was subject to fits of sudden anger and of brooding melancholy. She was very generous, lived in high style, spent freely, gave to all who asked, especially actors in need. She chain-smoked cigarettes, sometimes smoked long cigars, drank several glasses of brandy a day. She wrote in free verse. Her poetic style was strongly influenced by the writings of her friend Walt Whitman.

Early on Adah yearned for the theatrical spotlight. In 1853 she and her sister performed a dance routine in the New Orleans French Opera House as The Sisters Theodore. That same year her stepfather died and Adah had to go to work to help support her widowed mother. For the next three years she was a language teacher in a girls' finishing school.

On April 3, 1856, she eloped with Alexander Isaac Menken and married him in Livingston, Texas, a small town 60 miles northeast of Houston. Menken was a handsome musician, son of a wealthy Cincinnati merchant. After their honeymoon the couple returned to New Orleans. Adah started acting in Southern theaters with Alexander serving as her business manager. At this time she adopted Adah Isaacs Menken as her stage and pen names. She used this name almost exclusively for the rest of her life. It is the name inscribed on her tombstone. She also began to write poetry. For a number of years her poems with Jewish motifs were published in the Cincinnati *American Israelite*.

The panic of 1857 caused a severe decrease in theatrical bookings. To tide themselves through this economic crisis, Alexander and Adah went to Cincinnati to stay with Alexander's parents. Adah soon became discontented with the sedate life of Cincinnati's German Jewish community. Her discontent was increased by Alexander's decision to give up the gypsy life of a performer and to settle in Galveston, Texas, as a music teacher. The prospect of being a housewife in a Texas hick town was not to Adah's liking. She left her husband and returned to her mother's home in New Orleans. Alexander got a rabbinical divorce from Adah; but he did not, at that time, divorce her civilly. Adah did not know this. She thought that Alexander had divorced her both religiously and civilly. This misunderstanding caused her some difficulty a few years later. In May 1858 Adah resumed her stage career. Her efforts were well received in a number of cities.

Early in 1859 Adah went to New York City to further her acting career. There in March she became the girlfriend of a popular Irish pugilist, John Carmel Heenan. They got married during the summer, which Adah thought perfectly proper since she believed herself legally divorced from her first husband. Her happiness with Heenan was short-lived. He was crude and boorish, gambled, drank, and ran around with other women. At the end of the year he sailed for England to prepare to fight for the world heavyweight championship. With his departure the association of Adah and her Irish brute came to an end.

On April 12, 1860, Alexander Menken informed the press that he had never gotten a civil divorce from Adah but now intended to do so. The New York newspapers had a field day, accusing the young actress of gross immorality. Meanwhile Adah was carrying Heenan's child. She gave birth in August to a boy who lived only briefly. During this same troublesome period her mother died. The sensitive young woman felt she had been abandoned by God and man. She became very ill. For a number of months she was unable to appear on the stage. During her convalescence she went often to Pfaff's, a Broadway café that was a gathering place for actors, drama critics, and journalists. Here she came to know and admire Walt Whitman.

She had no idea that she was standing on the threshold of international theatrical fame. Her leap to stardom was generated by an offer from Captain John B. Smith, a theatrical producer, to play the main role in a three-act drama, *Mazeppa*, based on Lord George Byron's romance with a lady of that name. The highlight of the performance would be when Mazeppa, i.e., Adah, clad in skin-colored tights from neck to ankle, but appearing to be nude, and tied to a horse, would be carried by the horse up a papier-mâché mountain. The scene was to be enacted in such a way that it would take fifteen minutes for the horse to climb the mountain, so that the audience, and most particularly the "male element," could feast their eyes for a long time on Adah's luscious figure.

At first Adah refused. She was afraid of the possible consequences of the daring of the costume and the danger of the ride. She finally gave in. Smith describes the early rehearsals:

> She was nervous and anxious. Full of trepidation she dressed, or rather undressed. I assured her that there was no danger, and that she had only to hold on like grim death, and the mare, "Belle Beauty," would do the rest.

The initial public performance was at the Green Street Theatre in Albany, New York, June 7, 1861. Adah was a sensational success. She was now destined to ride a horse up a papier-mâché mountain before adoring crowds in New York, Vienna, London, Paris. To the puritanically minded she was a vile hussy. From the more enlightened and appreciative her art and daring won her the designation of "The Naked Lady," a title by which she is still remembered in the annals of the theater.

Heenan, having fought English world champion Tom Sayers to a draw, returned to America in August 1860. He repudiated his marriage with Adah, claiming that, by reason of the Alexander Menken revelation, the union was fraudulent and, therefore, null and void. Adah was furious. She claimed that Menken had deceived her and that she had entered into the Heenan marriage in good faith. A judge agreed with her and granted her a legal divorce from Heenan in April 1862.

During the last week of September 1862 she married her third husband, newspaper editor and political satirist, Robert H. Newell, better known by his pen name, Orpheus C. Kerr, which was a play on the words "office seeker." The marriage, like the two which preceded and the one which followed, was foredoomed. Adah was just not the marrying kind. From time to time she tried very hard to follow society's rules, but her attempts always petered out.

In November, while playing in Baltimore, she expressed her sympathy for the southern cause publicly and emphatically. As a result she was jailed for a brief time and then let out on parole on condition that she refrain from further public outbursts. In 1863 she went to the Far West and continued her climbs up the paper mountain in California and Nevada, to the great delight of the pioneers in such places as San Francisco and Virginia City. In San Francisco she was the darling of a group of budding literati, which included such famous persons as novelist Bret Harte, poet Joaquin Miller, and humorist Artemus Ward. For a 60-day stay in San Francisco she was paid $500 a performance, the highest pay ever received by any stage performer anywhere up to that time. In Virginia City the miners presented her with a solid silver brick and made her an honorary member of the local fire brigade.

Adah's pronounced Confederate sympathies caused her popularity to decline in some sections of the North. She decided to go to England where there was strong support for the South and where she would probably be regarded as a martyr, one who had left her native land because of its harsh reaction to her loyalty to her Louisiana heritage. It worked out that way with many Englishmen but not with all. Criticism and hostility came to her in England in an unanticipated manner. She arrived at a time when Benjamin Disraeli was becoming increasingly powerful in British politics and when he was being denounced by his opponents for asserting that, although he had been baptized at birth, he regarded himself, ethnically and intellectually, to be a Jew. The anti-Jewish political poison this generated spilled over onto Adah. She was vilified as a Jewish wanton, a Jewish profligate, which she was not. Unconventional—yes; unfettered in thought—yes; but indiscriminately promiscuous—no; drunken, lewd, licentious, depraved—no.

Adah got to England in the early summer of 1864 and opened in *Mazeppa* at Astley's Theatre in London on October 3. Among her earliest and closest English friends and devotees were novelists Charles Dickens and Charles Reade. When the Civil War ended she returned to the United States just long enough to allow Newell to divorce her. She sailed into

New York harbor at the end of August 1865 and steamed out again on September 16. In October she opened in London in a new play, which was a flop.

In February 1866 she came back to the United States and went on a midwestern tour with *Mazeppa*. She became speedily enamored of a Wall Street broker, Captain James Paul Barkley, who just as speedily impregnated her. After her stomach swelling had become quite discernible, she and Barkley got married on August 19. That this was a "shotgun" and not a true-love marriage was clearly evident. On her "honeymoon night," Adah tried unsuccessfully to commit suicide by taking poison. Two days later she sailed for Europe alone. She went to Paris where, in November, her child was born. He was named Louis Dudevant Victor Emanuel Barkley. The New York Public Library has a photograph of the approximately one-month-old baby being held by its mother. What happened to this child is not known. It does not seem to have remained with Adah during the less than two years of life she had left.

By February 1867 it became public knowledge that Adah was having an affair with sixty-five-year-old, portly, one-fourth-black [a Haitian grandmother] novelist Alexander Dumas, père. The liaison was widely advertised. Photographs were sold showing Adah sitting on Dumas' huge lap less comfortably than she had ridden Belle Beauty sidesaddle. The whole episode may have been no more than a platonic arrangement designed to gain valuable publicity for both parties involved. The arrangement did not last very long. Adah worked in Vienna in June and July, in Paris in August, and in London in September.

In London a similar situation developed between Adah and the young poet Algernon Charles Swinburne. Adah asked Swinburne to do some editorial work on a volume of poems she was preparing for publication. Swinburne complied willingly. Although, in writing to an acquaintance during this time, Swinburne referred to Adah as "my friend and my mistress," it seems likely that, except for his writing ability, she took him neither seriously nor into her bed. In later years Swinburne downgraded Adah by saying her poetry was of poor quality and she was no great intellect. This put-down is contradicted by the opinions of many outstanding literary figures of that generation. When Adah's poems were ready for the press, she asked Charles Dickens to permit her to dedicate the volume to him. He replied, "I shall have great pleasure in accepting your dedication." When the book appeared about a year after Adah's death, Swinburne sent a copy to a friend with the inscription, "Lo, this is she who was the world's delight." A much older Swinburne, wishing perhaps to punish Adah posthumously because in life she had denied him the pleasurable use of her body, wrote about the dead woman with the mind and in the language of a cad. This accords with historians' evaluation of Swinburne's character.

In May 1868 Adah went to Paris to rehearse for a play that was to open in a few months. She took a garret apartment near the theater where she was to perform. Even before leaving London she had not felt well. At the beginning of July she became seriously ill. A cancerous tumor was discovered. She was told she did not have long to live. She endured great pain with stoical resignation and courage. Her constant and only truly faithful companions were her maid and her little dog. Hardly any of the great ones she had known, entertained, and charmed came to see her. Among the exceptions were the poets Henry Wadsworth Longfellow and Thomas Buchanan Reade, the dramatist H. B. Farnie, and Edwin James. Adah had first known Edwin James as a newspaper reporter and editor in New York City and later in London and Paris as a boxing promoter. She turned to him often for advice, consolation, and help when she was in trouble. She referred to him frequently verbally and in writing as "my brother."

Her condition grew worse rapidly. During the first week of August it was apparent that she had only a few more days to live. She asked that a rabbi be summoned. He came and together they recited "Viddui," the confession of the dying. She passed away during the afternoon of August 10, 1868. When she died only her maid and her dog were with her. A Hebrew prayerbook was under her pillow. It was given to Edwin James. She died almost penniless. The rabbi officiated at her funeral. Fifteen people attendèd the service.

James had her interred under a wooden marker in a temporary grave in the Jewish section of Père la Chaise. He raised enough money from friends to buy a permanent plot in the Jewish section of the Montparnasse Cemetery. Adah's remains were transferred there in April 1869. A beautiful little monument was placed over the grave. It bears a significant two-word epitaph selected by Adah: "Thou knowest." It has been said that the monument was paid for by one who thought highly of Adah, Baron Lionel de Rothschild, leader of the British Jewish community. This is not likely. The monument was probably purchased with the money from the same fund used to buy the grave.

The London *Morning Standard*'s obituary columnist wrote:

> Few women have been more maligned; few are among us of so noble a heart and so generous a nature. She was known well but by few; but those few will always retain a pleasant remembrance of her, and ever have a tender thought and a kind word for the memory of Adah Isaacs Menken.

Perhaps the most discerning description of the personality of this unique, fascinating woman is that of Edgar Lee Masters in his poem about her in his *Doomsday Book:*

My body and my soul are in a scramble and do not fit each other.

Big Mike, Uncle Morris, and Barry
(1863)

Hirsch Goldwasser was an innkeeper in Konin in the province of Posen, Prussian Poland. He had twenty-two children, one of whom was Michel, born in 1822. Life in Posen under Prussian rule was comparatively tolerable until 1848 when, as a result of the revolutionary uprisings of that year, rigorous restraints were imposed upon the inhabitants. In consequence Michel migrated to London, Anglicized his name to Michael Goldwater and, in 1850, married Sarah Nathan. "Big Mike," six feet three, straight as a ramrod, robust, tough, was joined in 1851 by his brother, "Little Joe," much shorter, much rounder and with a drooping left eyelid that gave him a rather sinister appearance. Despite the difference in height "Little Joe" was just as tough as "Big Mike."

The Goldwater brothers worked in a men's cap factory. Mike's oldest son, Morris, was born in 1852. Inspired by stories of fortunes being made in California's gold rush, Mike and Joe traveled to California in 1854. Sarah was left behind with two children, one boy, one girl. (There would eventually be eight—five boys, three girls.) They would follow when Mike had the money to pay their passage.

By 1856 Mike and Joe had saved enough to bring over Sarah and the kids and to start their own business. They went 125 miles east to the gold mining town of Sonora, intending to have a general store. When they got to Sonora they found so many general stores already there that they switched from dry goods to wet goods. They opened a saloon on the ground floor of a whorehouse. When Sarah arrived, she did not like the setup. She did not want to rear her children in such an environment. So several months later she took the children to San Francisco. Mike and Joe stayed on in Sonora.

Not wanting to be separated from the rest of the family, Mike and Joe left Sonora in 1860 and started a bar and billiard room in Los Angeles, directly across the street from where the City Hall is now located. This time there were no girls on the second floor; and Sarah rejoined Mike. In L.A., in 1861, Mike became an American citizen and, in 1866, his youngest son, Baron, was born. Mike, who preferred the out-of-doors, made extra dough by loading up a horse-and-wagon with whiskey, tobacco, dry goods, boots, hats, and many other items of wearing apparel and household goods, and going on peddling trips into what is now western Arizona.

In 1863 a depression hit the West California coast and the liquor business dried up. Mike decided to try his luck in the goldfields along the Colorado River. Once more Sarah and the children were left behind. Joe decided to look for work in San Francisco. Mike got a job in the general store of B. Cohen in the boom town of La Paz, Arizona, on the Colorado River, six miles north of present main highway I-10. In late 1866 Sarah and the children arrived in La Paz. Sarah augmented the family income by taking in sewing. The family lived in a crowded little apartment on the ground floor. And in the apartment just over their heads was—you guessed it?—another bordello!

In 1867 Mike and Joe bought out B. Cohen and the store became that of "J. Goldwater and Brother," so Joe must have put up most of the money. The brothers also went into the hazardous business of hauling supplies for the military. Joe tended the store. Mike handled the hauling of the freight. Once again Sarah balked at the inconveniences and improprieties of boom town living. She departed for San Francisco with the children in 1868 and there she stayed.

The Colorado River was a very fickle lady. Sometimes she followed one channel and sometimes another. The freight came up the river from the Gulf of California by side-wheeler. It was delivered at La Paz to Mike, who would load the cargo on wagons drawn by strings of mules or horses, depending on how urgently the items were needed at their destination. The terrain and the vagaries of the river were such that Mike usually had to put the merchandise on small carts and tote the stuff as much as a mile before he could load it on his wagon train.

This got to be such a nuisance that Mike decided to find a better place along the Colorado for unloading the steamboats. He found such a spot right where I-10 now crosses the river. The water flowed between steep banks and was deep enough for the steamer to come directly to a wharf where the goods could be transferred directly to the big wagons. Mike had the land surveyed and founded a town at the landing site. He named it Ehrenberg in honor of his good friend, Herman Ehrenberg, Arizona pioneer murdered a few years before. The Goldwaters moved their store from La Paz to Ehrenberg. The store doubled as a town hall and post office. Joe was the first postmaster.

In June 1872 Mike and Joe were driving in separate buggies from Prescott to Ehrenberg, a dangerous 150-mile trip. A few miles out of Prescott, they were attacked by a band of thirty Apache-Mohave Indians. For four miles they careened down a narrow defile, hotly pursued by the redskins who kept taking potshots at them all the way. They were saved by a wagon coming from the other direction and containing three Wyatt Earp-type country boys who fired at the Indians with such deadly accuracy that those who were able to do so fled in terror. Mike discovered that his hat had a bullet hole right through the top of the crown. Joe was less fortunate. He had two bullets in his back. Joe was rushed to a small army hospital a dozen miles away and put on the operating table. The bullets were extracted. Joe recovered. He wore the two rifle balls on his watch fob for the rest of his life.

In that same year a store was opened in Phoenix. Twenty-year-old Morris, who had come from San Francisco to work for his pop, was given charge. The venture was unsuccessful. In 1875 the Phoenix store was closed. Shortly before that, Joe sold Mike his share of the business. Joe went into partnership with a Yuma Mexican named Castenada. They opened stores in Benson, Tombstone, and Bisbee and made a fortune. Later they dissolved partnership. Joe moved to California where he became a member of the firm of Cohn-Goldwater, manufacturers of overalls. Joe and his son Lem were among the founders of the Los Angeles Cedars of Lebanon Hospital.

As previously mentioned, Mike had five sons. Ben was a professional gambler in the Northwest, and Sam was a tobacco salesman in San Francisco. Both died of T.B. at an early age. Morris came to Mike in the early 1870s. Henry also arrived in the late 1870s but did not remain. He was by nature a wanderer. Every now and then a letter came from him in later years from Central America or somewhere else asking for money. He finally settled down in Los Angeles and died there in the 1930s. Baron joined his father and brothers in Arizona in 1882.

Mike left Ehrenberg in 1876 and opened a store in Prescott. The store was a success. In 1885 Mike was elected mayor of Prescott. Shortly after that he decided to retire. He sold the business to Morris and Henry, went to live with Sarah in San Francisco, and died there in 1903. Soon after Mike retired, Henry sold his share of the business to Morris and left Arizona. In 1894 Morris made Baron a full partner in the business known then and since as "Goldwater's."

Arizona had achieved territorial status in 1863. Prescott was named the state capital. Phoenix was growing rapidly, more rapidly than Prescott. Baron was convinced that Phoenix would ultimately become Arizona's capital and principal commercial center. Morris disagreed. He thought Prescott would remain the state's chief city. Baron wanted to make a second try at setting up a Goldwater's in Phoenix. Being good sports and inveterate gamblers, the brothers decided to settle the argument with a game of casino. Baron won. In 1888 the Phoenix store became operational. Baron was right. In 1889 Phoenix became the state capital. Both the capital and Goldwater's have been in Phoenix ever since.

Morris would continue to manage the Prescott store. Baron would handle the Phoenix establishment after Morris helped his kid brother get started. The Army was stringing a telegraph line from Maricopa, south of Phoenix, to Fort McDowell, north of Phoenix. The line was routed to bypass Phoenix. Morris offered to give the Army a set of telegraph instruments he owned if the Army would run the line through Phoenix. He volunteered to serve as temporary Phoenix operator, claiming a greater acquaintance with the Morse code than he actually possessed. His offer was accepted. The line was installed and was about to begin transmitting messages. Morris began to doodle with the Phoenix key. This resulted in an irate Army operator sending the first telegraphic message to Phoenix, which was "Get the hell off the wire!" Morris did as requested. After that only duly trained, qualified, and authorized Signal Corps personnel handled the Phoenix key.

Morris became Prescott's leading citizen. He served three times as mayor for a grand total of 23 years. In between his mayoralty stints, he was on the city council, in the state legislature and senate, for a time as chief clerk of the legislature, for a time as president of the senate, and also was vice president of the state constitutional convention. He was vice president of the Prescott National Bank, treasurer of the Arizona Bankers Association, and the first Arizona Jew to become a 33rd degree Mason. He contributed generously to Jewish philanthropic and religious causes. He died in Prescott in 1939, childless.

On New Year's Day, 1907, forty-year-old Baron married Josephine Williams, Episcopalian. Two years later to the day, New Year's Day, 1909, Josephine gave birth to son Barry. Afterward there were two more children, brother Bob and sister Carolyn. Barry graduated from Staunton Military Academy and, in 1928, entered the University of Arizona. In 1929 Baron died. Barry left the university to become a full-time employee in the Phoenix store. Bob, one and a half years younger than Barry, finished college. Then he, too, went to work for Goldwater's. For a number of years Barry and Bob were under the business tutelage of wise Uncle Morris. Barry says, "I was raised more by my Uncle Morris than by my father." It was Uncle Morris who interested Barry in politics. When Uncle Morris died Barry and Bob became the executive heads of Goldwater's.

Had Uncle Morris been able to live another twenty-five years, he would have been even prouder of nephew Barry than he always was. In World War II Barry attained the rank of colonel in the Army Air Force. He is now a retired Major General in the Air Force Reserve. Barry's rise in the world of politics was super-spectacular. He held his first elective office in 1949 as a Phoenix city councilman. In 1952 he was elected to the U. S. Senate. In 1964 he ran against Lyndon B. Johnson for the Presidency of the United States. He was beaten badly, outclassed and outmaneuvered by a master politician. But he was a good loser. He retained his sense of humor, which he has always had in abundance. And whether one agrees or disagrees with "Mr. Conservative"'s views on foreign affairs, labor or national defense, one cannot but admire this charming, smiling, irrepressible, swashbuckling Westerner, successful businessman, athlete, flyer, sportsman, Senator, ham radio operator, expert photographer, explorer, author of three books on Arizona natural history, authority on and great friend and "bull snake" member of Arizona's Indian tribes, in whose languages he is known as "Curly Head," "Barry Sunset," and

"Barry One Salt." Barry says, "My love for the out-of-doors comes partly from my mother and partly from the blood of Big Mike that flows through my veins."

Baron's children were reared by their mother as Episcopalians. What does Barry Goldwater think of that part of him which is Jewish? "I'm proud of my Jewish father and grandfather. I've inherited some of the characteristics of the Jewish people and that has been a great advantage to me. They are warmhearted, understanding people who make friends easily. And I've never been discriminated against because I am part Jewish."

What do the Jews of Arizona think of the "Jewishness" of Barry Goldwater? That was stated loud and clear in 1954 when Arizona Jewry celebrated its centennial. The centennial committee drew up an honor roll of 22 living *Jewish* Arizonians whose forebears were among the state's pioneers. Barry Goldwater's name is on that list.

For years an apocryphal story about Barry has been making the rounds. Some sources say the story originated with Barry's brother Bob:

Barry is preparing to tee off on the golf course at a swanky country club when the golf pro comes up to him and very apologetically informs him that, because he is Jewish, he cannot play on the 18-hole course. Goldwater glares at the pro and replies, "Well, it so happens, sir, that I am only half-Jewish, so I suppose it would be O.K. for me, under your rules, to just play nine holes." He then adds a few unprintable and quite uncomplimentary remarks; picks up his clubs, gets in his car, and drives away.

"Wanted!—$50,000 Reward!"

(1865)

In 1808 Philip Benjamin and his bride of a few months, the former Rebecca de Mendes, both of Portuguese Marrano ancestry, migrated from London to the Virgin Islands. Their second child and only son, Judah Philip Benjamin, was born in St. Thomas on August 6, 1811. They did not do well in the Virgin Islands. So about 1815 they moved to Wilmington, North Carolina. In 1818 Judah was sent to Mr. Stewart's school in Fayetteville, 60 miles northwest, to begin his formal schooling. Sometime after that the Benjamins moved to Charleston, South Carolina. They were very poor. In Charleston Philip made a meager living operating a fruit store. In February 1825 he was a charter member of Charleston's Reformed Society of Israelites.

Judah showed signs of intellectual promise at an early age. He became the protégé of a wealthy Charleston merchant, Moses Lopez, who lightened the Benjamin family burden (there were six Benjamin daughters) by placing Judah in the Charleston Hebrew Orphan Home, paying for his upkeep and secondary school education. At age fourteen the boy, probably with additional help from Lopez, entered Yale College. He was an above average and popular student. In 1827 the Benjamin finances were in such a sad state that the family moved again, this time to New Orleans. Judah had to leave Yale to help support his parents and sisters. He found employment as clerk in the office of a New Orleans notary and supplemented his salary by tutoring the children of the well-to-do. At night he studied law. In 1831 all the Benjamins except Judah went back to Charleston.

In December 1832 Judah was admitted to the Louisiana bar. He achieved success rapidly. Within ten years he had an annual income of about $100,000. In March 1833 he married a girl he had tutored, Natalie St. Martin, a devout Roman Catholic, daughter of a wealthy French Creole sugar planter. They were married in church. There was a Jewish congregation in New Orleans at this time, but no synagogue or rabbi. Even if there had been, it is doubtful if Judah would have wanted a Jewish ceremony. When he entered Yale, he brought a Hebrew prayerbook with him. This is the last clear evidence of any association on his part with the Jewish religion. He never denied his Jewish origin, but he tried in later years to hide the fact that he had lived for a time in a Jewish orphan home.

Judah was witty, well read, urbane. He lived luxuriously, had a flair for the dramatic. In 1842 he started up the political ladder by being elected to the Louisiana House of Representatives. In 1843 eye trouble forced him to abandon his law practice temporarily. In 1844 he purchased Bellechasse, a sugar plantation south of New Orleans. At Bellechasse Benjamin experimented successfully with new methods of producing lump sugar. His wife was very dissatisfied with plantation life. She lived at Bellechasse briefly and then departed for Paris with the couple's only child, five-year-old Ninette. Mother and daughter lived in France for the rest of their lives. But the marriage did not dissolve. Whenever he could, Judah went to Paris to spend the summer with his family. The relationship seems to have been what the French call an "arrangement," a mutual understanding to keep the marriage in being legally but not actually—the persons involved live separate lives socially and romantically; they remain good friends but are no longer lovers.

In 1846 or thereabouts, Judah's father died. Judah remodeled Bellechasse to make it a suitable home for his widowed mother and sisters. He brought them there from Charleston early in 1847, by which time his eyesight had improved and he was able to resume the practice of law. In 1852 he was elected to the Louisiana Senate and then was chosen by that body to serve in the United States Senate. He is said to have been the best liked and most respected United States Senator of his time. He was a staunch States Righter but, on almost every other issue, a moderate liberal.

The story is told that, in Benjamin's early days in the Senate, a Kentucky Senator referred to him in debate as "that Jew from Louisiana." Benjamin replied, on a point of personal privilege, "It is true that I am a Jew. It is also true that while my ancestors were receiving the Ten Commandments from the immediate hand of the Deity, amidst the thunderings and lightnings of Mount Sinai, the ancestors of the honorable Senator were herding swine in the forests of Great Britain." An almost identical story is attributed to Benjamin Disraeli in a similar situation in the House of Commons in the late 1830s. If Benjamin did make the rejoinder attributed to him, it is more likely that he quoted Disraeli, now a prominent Tory leader, than that he tried to take original credit for the *bon mot*.

A number of years later, Senator Jefferson Davis of Mississippi also made a sneering reference to Benjamin's Jewishness, coupled with an inference that Jews are by nature timid. Benjamin promptly challenged him to a duel. Deeply embarrassed and regretful, Davis apologized publicly for his unkind remarks. The two men not only shook hands immediately but later developed an extremely close friendship. During the Civil War Judah Benjamin was the intimate confidant and chief advisor of Jeff Davis. Benjamin has often been called "the brains of the Confederacy."

Senator Benjamin tried desperately to keep the peace between North and South. He pleaded that slavery was necessary in the current phase of the South's economic development, but when circumstances permitted, it would be abolished. Most Northern Senators did not believe him. Senator Wade of Ohio angrily labeled him "an Israelite with Egyptian principles." Louisiana left the Union on January 26, 1861, and Benjamin resigned from the Senate nine days later.

Benjamin became successively the Confederacy's Attorney General, Secretary of War and, on February 22, 1862, its Secretary of State. He held the latter position for the rest of the war. An English correspondent described Secretary of State Benjamin as "short, stout, olive-colored, brilliant, the most open, frank and cordial of all the Confederates I met." Judah lived in Richmond in grand style. To the very end of the conflict he served his many guests the finest French wines and Havana "seegars."

He never lost his cool. In April 1865, on his way to a cabinet meeting at which he knew Davis would announce that Lee's army had collapsed and Richmond must be abandoned, Benjamin is said to have walked down the street with "his usual pleasant smile, his mild Havana, and the very twirl of his slender, goldheaded cane contributing to give to the casual observer an expression of casual confidence."

Davis and his cabinet left Richmond with the intention of re-establishing the rebel capital in Texas. A rapid series of irreparable reverses not only negated this hope but turned the retreat of the South's officialdom into a flight of fugitives from federal justice. The Union government offered big rewards for the capture of the principal Confederate leaders. The price put on the head of Judah P. Benjamin was $50,000.

On May 3 Benjamin left Davis at Vienna, Georgia, about 40 miles northeast of Albany. The still hopeful Davis instructed the ever optimistic Benjamin to seek fresh support for the doomed cause in Cuba and the Bahamas and then to rejoin him in Texas. Benjamin started for Florida in a two-man gig, disguised by a heavy beard and goggles and pretending to be a Frenchman named Bonfals who knew no English. He was accompanied by Colonel Leavy of New Orleans, who acted as his "interpreter." A week after leaving Vienna, Benjamin and Leavy learned that Davis had been captured. They separated, each to try to find his way to personal freedom.

Benjamin crossed into Florida in an altered disguise. He was now a South Carolina farmer planning to purchase property in Florida. He rode a mule and wore homespun clothing. He avoided big towns and main roads. For several weeks he hid in the swamps of western Florida along the Manatee River near the present town of Bradenton. One morning he discovered a parrot sitting in a tree and loudly squawking "Hi for Jeff!" Sure that the bird must belong to a Confederate sympathizer, Benjamin threw stones at the bird in the hope that it would fly toward the home of its owner. The stratagem worked. It brought Benjamin to the residence of a Mr. Gamble, who sheltered him and helped him on his way. This home, now known as the Gamble Mansion, located five miles northeast of Bradenton, is maintained by the State of Florida as a shrine honoring Judah P. Benjamin.

Gamble outfitted Benjamin in blue denims and got him a boat in which he went down the inland waterway to the south end of Sarasota Bay. Here he hid out with another friendly family for a few weeks. On June 23 he and two companions set out in a yawl on the long trip down the Florida coast. For two weeks they ate mostly turtle eggs and fish and drank coconut milk. Twice they were sighted and chased by federal gunboats searching for rebel escapees. The first time they eluded their pursuer. The second time they were boarded. Benjamin disguised himself as the yawl's cook, putting on an apron and smearing soot and grease on his face. One of the Yankee sailors remarked that this was the first time he had seen or heard of a Jew performing such a menial task. Fortunately for Benjamin this particular sailor, to twist biological nomenclature a bit, recognized the genus but not the family.

On July 7 the three reached Knight's Key at the southern tip of the Florida peninsula. Here they got a bigger ship and set sail for Bimini

Island, 125 miles to the east. The night before reaching Bimini they narrowly escaped being overturned by a waterspout. They landed at Bimini on July 10. Benjamin's companions remained on Bimini, but Benjamin bought passage on a small sloop loaded with sponges destined for Nassau. Thirty-five miles out of Bimini the sponges expanded, the sloop capsized, and all aboard were drowned except Benjamin and three blacks. These four managed to get into a skiff that the sloop had in tow and to get clear before the sloop sank. The skiff had only one oar. Benjamin and his black boatmates were having a hard time of it when, fortunately, they were sighted and picked up by a British warship which took them back to Bimini.

Benjamin's second boat trip from Bimini to Nassau was uneventful. From Nassau he went to Havana. He left Havana for Europe about August 6. Near St. Thomas his ship caught fire and escaped destruction only because of the valiant efforts of its crew and passengers. It reached St. Thomas with seven feet of water in its hold and its main deck almost burned through. Benjamin left St. Thomas two days later on another ship and he arrived in England on August 30 with no further misadventures. However, he had some serious personal problems: he had diabetes, a weak heart, and no money.

Benjamin's days of glory had not ended. He was admitted to the British bar after studying for only six months instead of the normally required three years. In 1868 he wrote a legal classic, *Benjamin on Sales*, which established his reputation in Great Britain as an outstanding and scholarly lawyer. In a few years his income was averaging about 40,000 pounds annually, the equivalent of $200,000 a year in American currency.

In 1880 he was severely bruised when he jumped from a Paris tramcar while it was in motion. He never recovered completely from this mishap. In December 1882 he retired from his English law firm and went to Paris to spend the remainder of his days with his wife, his daughter, now married to a French army officer, and his grandchildren. He died in Paris on May 6, 1884, and was buried in the Catholic section of Père la Chaise. It was rumored that he converted to Roman Catholicism before his death, but there is no proof of this. It may be that, while he was lying in a coma in his final hours, his wife summoned a priest to administer the Church's last rites so that in death she and he would not be separated.

In writing about Judah Philip Benjamin after his death, Rabbi Isaac M. Wise declared that he was "undoubtedly the most distinguished American Jewish statesman of the nineteenth century."

"Neither he nor any other Jew took part"
(1873)

The *Deutsche Zeitung* of Baton Rouge, Louisiana, reports:

Last week we reported that a German peddler had been murdered and robbed by some negroes at the ferry dock in West Baton Rouge. The slain man was a Jew and was given a decent burial by the Jewish Charity Organization in Baton Rouge. The culprits were unable to enjoy their booty for long; already the next morning four negroes were seized on suspicion; after a brief examination one of them was set at liberty; but the other three, still in possession of their booty, were hanged on the nearest tree without loss of time by the outraged citizens. Such a procedure, to be sure, goes far beyond the limits of the law, but, if one ponders that convicted murderers get off with one day in the penitentiary, a bit of lynch procedure like this is always to be preferred in the interest of personal security.

To this we add that the murdered man's name was Jacob Kriss and that he was supposed to have emigrated from Germany to New Orleans three months ago. Through the efforts of Mr. A. Kowalski it was possible to give the murdered man a decent burial in the local Jewish cemetery, but no further particulars about the unfortunate man could be learned. Mr. Kowalski is the elder of the local Jewish congregation and was very active in the matter; but in the execution of the negroes neither he nor any other Jew took part.

From Cincinnati *Die Deborah*, Volume XX (1873), No. 21. Translated by Rudolph Glanz and published in his "Source Material on Jewish Immigration," in *Yivo Annual of Jewish Social Science*, Volume VI, 1951, Section 86. Reprinted here with the permission of Dr. Glanz and the editor of the *Yivo Annual of Jewish Social Science*.

KING SOLOMON OF SOLOMONVILLE
(1876)

The rich copper development of eastern Arizona—a salient factor in Arizona's economy to the present day—owes much of its beginning to three Jewish families—the Freudenthals, Lesinskys, and Solomons. Of the three, the Solomons left the deepest imprint upon the history of Arizona. Isador Elkan Solomon not only helped to pioneer the earliest copper works of eastern Arizona but he founded a town, took part in the inauguration of the state's largest bank, and planted a family tree which is still alive and well.

I. E. Solomon was born in Germany in 1841 and migrated to this country in 1859. An uncle in Towanda, Pennsylvania, gave his nephew a job in his store at $50 a year plus room and board. After a few years Solomon left his uncle's store and bought and operated a livery stable. He prospered sufficiently to make a trip back to Germany to visit his parents. There he met and married Anna Freudenthal. They returned to Towanda. There the first three of their six children were born. Pennsylvania failed to provide them with the income needed to support their growing family. So they headed west, by railroad and stagecoach, to Las Cruces, New Mexico, where Anna's brothers were living.

After exploring the Las Cruces potentialities, Solomon found no field of activity that appealed to him. Leaving his family in Las Cruces, he journeyed further west to Clifton in southeastern Arizona, a copper mining town that already had a few Jewish merchants. The copper smelter at Clifton was badly in need of a regular supply of charcoal. Solomon discovered that the mesquite growing densely in the nearby Gila River valley made excellent charcoal. He secured permission from the Mormons who were farming the land to harvest and burn their mesquite. Having turned the mesquite into charcoal, Solomon sold it to the smelter for $30 a ton.

At first he lived in a brush shack in the desert, cutting trees from dawn to dark, then burning his charcoal at night, always on the alert for Indians. Before long he was able to build a small adobe dwelling and to bring his family from Las Cruces. The tiny settlement in which they lived was then called Pueblo Viejo. Its only other inhabitants were Mexicans and an itinerant peddler named Munson who had built a small store there. Solomon bought Munson's little building for $75 and he parlayed

This is an abridgement of an article with the same title by Joseph Stocker of Phoenix, Arizona, in his monograph *Jewish Roots in Arizona*, published in 1954. It is included here with the permission of Mr. Stocker.

this purchase into a major trading post serving the entire surrounding area.

This was only the beginning of what became an empire in miniature. Forming a partnership with a young Quaker, Solomon acquired a 1,300-acre sheep ranch. As more settlers came, the little adobe town grew and grew. Soon it got a postoffice and a new name. The name, suggested by another pioneer, was Solomonville.

I. E. decided the town needed a hotel. So he built one, a two-story adobe edifice. Anna ran the hotel. The Solomons raised the fruits, vegetables, and meats consumed by their guests.

In 1883 Graham County was organized with Solomonville as its county seat and I. E. as county treasurer. Economically, Solomonville became the most important community in the long stretch from El Paso to Tucson. It was not much to look at. It was a town made almost entirely from mud and had the brown, drab look of the desert. Its main street was scarcely more than a city block long. Not until 1893 did Solomonville acquire its first brick building, a new store that I. E. built.

The little frontier town was a pocket-sized kingdom with Solomon as its reigning monarch. He was a benevolent monarch. He supplied most of the credit required by local farmers and ranchers, making loans without asking for a single note or signature. I. E.'s faith in the people was reciprocated. Lacking a bank, they deposited their money with him for safekeeping and never asked for a receipt.

Difficult though it was in the Arizona waste, the Solomons tried to live a Jewish life. They insisted that their children marry within the faith and, miracle of miracles, all did. They did not keep kosher but Anna's father, who lived with them for a few years, attempted to do so. All the time he was in Arizona Mr. Freudenthal ate no meat. One day he could stand the deprivation no longer. He determined to go out to the barnyard, kill a chicken, and cook it. Just at that moment bandits burst into the store. They hurled rocks at Freudenthal and knocked him to the ground. Freudenthal considered this a message from on high chastising him for being about to go astray. Suitably warned, he sadly abandoned the idea of enjoying a non-kosher chicken.

In 1899, with Solomonville a sturdy, prosperous town, I. E. decided the time had come to launch the community's first bank. So on December 15 of that year the Gila Valley Bank came into being. It was the direct forebear of what is now the largest financial institution in the Rocky Mountain area, the Valley National Bank. I. E.'s Quaker partner was president. I. E. was vice president. His son Charlie was assistant cashier. The original stockholders included a number of other Jews.

It was a strangely gauche little institution, that pioneer cowtown bank. Its offices, such as they were, reposed in a corner of the Solomon store. Business was conducted with frontier informality. As soon as a deposit was made everybody in town knew about it. Life in the little town was close-knit and friendly. As one depositor observed good-naturedly, "I put in all I had but four bits, saved that for drinks, and by the time I got across the street the bartender told me how much I'd salted away!" Right next to the bank window was the store's credit window. If a customer who owed money to the store tried to make a deposit in the bank, someone was sure to sing out, "You're at the wrong window! Pay your store bill first!"

Banks in those precarious territorial days were sitting ducks for errant bad men who preferred not to work for a living. So the Solomons installed a holdup alarm. It was simply a pushbutton on the floor wired to a bell in the sheriff's office down the street. Nobody ever robbed the bank, but one or another of its functionaries was forever stepping on the button by mistake, bringing the sheriff on the double with his six-shooter drawn. After a time the sheriff learned to translate the signals. One short ring would mean that somebody had stepped on the button inadver-tently. A long, continuous ring meant that the cashier had caught the button under the leg of his high stool. What kind of ring the sheriff would have interpreted to mean a real, honest-to-goodness holdup, nobody knows. Eventually the Gila Valley Bank became a branch of the Valley National Bank and then vanished from the Arizona scene.

I. E. and Anna lived in Solomonville until all their children had married and left. You might like to know, incidentally, where the six young Solomons found their Jewish wives and husbands. Here's the list: Globe, Holbrook, Phoenix, Safford, Tucson—all in Arizona, and Denver, Colorado. Craving closer contacts with their Jewish brethren, papa and mama moved to California. I. E. passed away there in 1930 and Anna in 1933.

Even before every Solomon had left Solomonville the town had begun to fade in importance. The commercial focus of the region gradually shifted to Safford, five miles to the west. By 1930 there were 1,050 people living in Solomonville and 1,706 in Safford. Sometime between 1930 and 1970 the county seat moved from Solomonville to Safford. By 1970 Solomonville's name had been shortened to Solomon and its population had shrunk to 300. Safford's population had grown to 5,947. Today the gaunt ruin of a brick building in Solomon stands as a ghostly reminder of the combination general store and bank that was once the capitol of the little kingdom of King I. E. Solomon.

TEXARKANA'S FATHER GOLDBERG
(1876)

Texarkana has the distinction of being the largest city in the United States with no state postal designation. All outgoing mail is stamped "Texarkana U.S.A." because Texarkana is partly in Arkansas and partly in Texas. The border between the states is the main street and is appropriately named State Line. The postoffice straddles State Line at its northern end and occupies space in both states. Politically the city is divided into two separate municipalities, each with its own mayor and city council; but for all non-governmental activities Texarkana is one city. There is only one other community like it in our country, Bristol, U.S.A., similarly constituted and organized on the border of Virginia and Tennessee.

Texarkana was founded in 1873 by an arrangement between two railroads. The Texas Pacific Railroad controlled the right-of-way to the Arkansas border. The Missouri Pacific Railroad was allowed to run its tracks only to the Texas border. So the two companies created a railroad junction at the Texas-Arkansas line. The town of Texarkana emerged as a result. The city is now the principal commercial center on the 325-mile stretch between Little Rock and Dallas.

Visitors like to send their friends an earthy postcard which typifies the frontier spirit that still characterizes Texarkana. The card shows a man trying to pull a balky donkey across the middle of State Line. The caption beneath reads: "This man is in Arkansas but his ass is in Texas." Normally the people on both sides of State Line get along well with each other. But there was one occasion many years ago when the two municipal councils had a falling out. At that time the water was in Arkansas and the whiskey was in Texas. This was literally true. The waterworks for the whole city was on the Arkansas side. Hard-liquor-wise, Texas was wet and Arkansas was dry. The Texarkana, Arkansas, city council started the fireworks by cutting off the water supply of Texarkana, Texas. The Texarkana, Texas, city council retaliated by forbidding the liquor stores in its part of the community to sell whiskey to anyone from Texarkana, Arkansas. Faced by the indignant outcries of bereft citizens of both states, both the Texas whiskey-drinkers who were being deprived of their water and the Arkansas water-drinkers who were of the breed that "votes dry and drinks wet," the councils hastily reconvened and rescinded their harsh decrees and made peace with each other.

✿   ✿   ✿   ✿   ✿

Charles Goldberg was born in 1820 in Fraustadt, Poland, the youngest of a rabbi's seventeen children. A few years later the family moved to Warsaw. Charles was sent to an uncle in Germany to receive both a secular and religious education designed to prepare him for the rabbinate. After some years of study he left Germany to escape military service and came to America.

Like so many Jews who arrived during the 1840s for the same reason, Goldberg became an itinerant peddler in the Midwest. While traveling through Missouri he became very ill. He was nursed back to health in the home of a family of Cumberland Presbyterians, a sect established in Kentucky in the early nineteenth century. While he was recuperating the pastor of his benefactors convinced him that Christianity was the true religion and converted him.

In 1846 Goldberg married a non-Jewish woman. In 1847 he became an ordained Cumberland Presbyterian clergyman. He began his ministerial career in or near Galveston but soon moved to Clarksville in northeastern Texas. Here, in 1849, after bearing three children, his wife died. In 1859 Goldberg remarried. These facts about Goldberg's early life were furnished by a daughter of Goldberg and his second wife, the late Mattie Goldberg Wallace of Ozan, Arkansas.

When the Civil War began Goldberg was professor of languages at Daingerfield College, Daingerfield, Texas. He enlisted in the Confederate Army as a chaplain and served in that capacity throughout the war. After the war he served again as minister in Clarksville and then in churches in Columbus and Washington, Arkansas. In 1874 Goldberg moved to Texarkana to be pastor for the Presbyterians in the pioneer community. He also taught in its first public school.

There were Jews in Texarkana almost from the day it was founded. By 1876 a sufficient number was in the community and surrounding area to warrant the holding of High Holyday services. The Jews invited Father Goldberg, as he was affectionately known in the town, to conduct the services. The Texarkana *Democrat* printed the following account of this unusual event:

> Our Jewish fellow citizens, in celebrating their New Year, the first day of the month Tishri, on Tuesday and Wednesday last, had the opportunity of forming a synagogue for the first time in this place and of holding public prayers. They requested Reverend Charles Goldberg, a Christian minister and a convert from their faith, to deliver a discourse to them on the import of the day and the duties that devolve upon them as Israelites, which the reverend gentleman did, both in Hebrew and English, to the entire satisfaction of all hearers, both Jews and Gentiles. We hear the sermon spoken of in the highest terms by all.

In the October 8 issue of the Cincinnati *American Israelite*, Isaac M. Wise reprinted this news item with the comment, "There appears to be a mistake somewhere." There was no mistake.

Later the Southern and Cumberland Presbyterians in Texarkana separated into two congregations. The Southern Presbyterians invited Goldberg to be their pastor but he elected to remain with the Cumberland group which in 1888 built a beautiful edifice, the Pine Street Presbyterian Church. Goldberg was greatly loved and respected. He never attempted to convert any Texarkana Jew to Christianity. He prepared a number of Jewish boys for Bar Mitzvah.

In the fall of 1890 Texarkana's Mount Sinai Congregation engaged its first full time rabbi. Shortly thereafter Goldberg became critically ill. According to an account given me in 1937 by two elderly brothers whose father had been congregational president in 1890, Goldberg summoned the rabbi and the president to his bedside, recited Viddui, the confessional prayer of the Jewish dying, and asked to be buried in the Jewish congregational cemetery. A special meeting of the congregation's board was convened to consider the matter. The board decided, with the greatest regret, that, although Father Goldberg was held in the highest esteem by all, he could not be buried in the synagogue cemetery because he was not a bona fide Jew.

An account written for me by Goldberg's daughter told a different story. Mrs. Wallace stated that, at her father's funeral, the officiating minister declared that Goldberg's last words were, "I know in Whom I have believed, that He is able to keep me against that day." Her letter continued, "As many Jews were at the funeral, and as they had told my father, when he talked of Christianity to them, that at the last he would say the words in the Jewish phylacteries, those last words were a great relief to me."

Goldberg died on November 3, 1890. He was buried in Texarkana's Rose Hill Cemetery, which is non-sectarian. It is not possible to determine with finality which of the conflicting accounts is correct. But, if Mrs. Wallace's story is true, why was her father buried in a non-sectarian cemetery and not in the cemetery of the Christian denomination which he had served so faithfully for sixteen years?

NAVAJO SAM AND BILLY THE KID
(1878)

Samuel A. Dittenhoffer was born in New York City, in 1840, according to one account, or, according to another, in 1848. He went west, according to the first account, as early as 1860, or, according to the second, in 1868. He got a job in Santa Fe as clerk in the store of Spiegelberg Brothers. He acquired a knowledge of the Navajo language and was often used as an interpreter. Because of this proficiency he was nicknamed Navajo Sam.

In 1878 a group of merchants from Juarez, Mexico, came to Santa Fe and bought 100,000 Mexican pesos ($50,000) worth of merchandise from the store. The merchants carted the goods back to Juarez in their own wagon caravan; but they had brought no pesos with them to Santa Fe because of their fear of the bandit Billy the Kid. In order to be paid, Spiegelberg Brothers would have to pick up the pesos in Juarez.

Henry McCarty alias William Antrim alias Kid Antrim alias William H. Bonney alias Billy the Kid, 1859-81, was a famous New Mexican evildoer whom the movies and TV have tried to transform into a gentlemanly Robin Hood. He started out as a cowboy and ended as a cattle rustler and highway robber. After a bold and lucrative four-year criminal career, during which he committed several murders, he was apprehended and jailed. While trying to escape he was shot and killed by Sheriff Pat Garrett.

Navajo Sam volunteered to go to Juarez and bring back the Spiegelberg money. He and Billy had been good friends before Billy turned outlaw; and he felt sure Billy would not harm him.

Sam made the long trip to the Mexican border on horseback. In Juarez he had two large flour barrels made with double tops and bottoms. The tops and bottoms were filled with flour. The large, heavy silver pesos, wrapped tightly in paper and then in muslin to prevent them from rattling, were stuffed between the false tops and bottoms of the barrels. The barrels were marked "Extra fine Chihuahua flour for Spiegelberg Brothers, Santa Fe, New Mexico."

Sam put the barrels on a Mexican carreta, a small wagon, harnessed a mule to the wagon and began the return journey. On the second day, as he was driving through a narrow canyon in the Las Cruces area, a

---

Based in large part on the article, "Billy the Kid, the Cowboy Outlaw: An Incident Recalled by Flora Spiegelberg," edited by Rabbi Floyd S. Fierman and Dr. John O. West, faculty members of the University of Texas at El Paso. The article is in the American Jewish Historical Quarterly, Vol. LV, No. 1, 1965, pp. 98-106.

horseman came riding at him, standing upright in the saddle and shouting loudly, "Halt! Halt!" It was Billy the Kid. As he came close he recognized Sam. Jumping from his horse he came up to the wagon, shook hands and said, "Hi, Sam. What in hell are you doing in this rig so far from Santa Fe?" Sam explained he was taking some fine Chihuahua flour back to Santa Fe for the Spiegelberg women.

Billy tied his horse to the rear of the wagon. Then he tapped one of the barrels with his gun and said, "I've a good mind to open one of the barrels and take myself a few pounds of flour. I haven't had any real good baked biscuits for a long time." Sam replied, "Ah, Billy, you wouldn't want to break open a whole barrel of the ladies' flour for just a few pounds, would you?" Billy responded, "OK, old boy. We'll do it your way this time."

He jumped up on the front seat beside Sam and they rode on together. As they journeyed they exchanged flasks, as was the prevailing Western custom among friends, and drank to each other's health. The whiskey loosened Billy's tongue. He regaled Sam with stories of his latest exploits, including a tale of having recently robbed a northbound stage-coach:

> I opened the door of the stagecoach. Four men and an old woman were looking at me, trembling with fear. I said calmly, "Friends, although I have a very bad reputation, I promise to do you no bodily harm. Just fork over all your cash and jewelry." They quickly turned their pockets inside out and opened their valises for inspection. The old lady, fumbling about in her purse, took out a five dollar gold piece. Crying, she offered it to me, saying it was all she had. She reminded me of my own dear mother, not long dead. I refused the gold piece, saying, "Good lady, keep it for a rainy day. You need it more than do I and, besides, you remind me of my own beloved mother." My sombrero was already filled with the gold, watches, and rings of the four men. I told the stagecoach driver to drive on and to disappear as fast as his horses could trot.
>
> A week later I read in the Silver City newspaper how the mother of a prominent local merchant had fooled Billy the Kid, the notori-ous outlaw. He had refused to take a five-dollar gold piece from her when she pleaded that it was all the money she had. She neglected to mention to Billy that she had three hundred dollars in banknotes hidden in her stockings.

Billy and Sam both thought this a great joke and laughed up-roariously. After a few more miles of riding, drinking and story-telling, Billy jumped from the wagon, untied his horse, said "Adios, amigo," and galloped off. He left behind $50,000 hidden in two barrels of flour and a greatly relieved Sam, who "benshed geymel," i.e., recited the Hebrew prayer for deliverance from danger, completed the trip to Santa Fe, and delivered the money to the Spiegelbergs without having picked up any more unwanted companions.

A JEWISH INDIAN CHIEF
(1885)

The Bibos added much to the history of the old Southwest. Members of this family were engaged in trading, mining, and ranching, surviving the hardships that abounded in the Southwest of the latter half of the nineteenth century. The section was rich in Hispanic culture, in sun, sand, and cactus, and in bands of marauding Indians. The Bibos were drawn to this area, as were many before and after them, by the search for El Dorado.

Solomon Bibo came across the Atlantic to join his brothers in this quest. Solomon Bibo stands apart from the thousands of other pioneers of his time because he was a Jewish immigrant who became an Indian chief in the Territory of New Mexico.

He was born on August 23, 1853, in Brakel, Westphalia, Prussia, the sixth of eleven children of Isak and Blumchen Bibo. His father was a cantor-teacher. Solomon came to the United States in 1869. He left his native land to avoid military conscription, to seek greater religious freedom, and to look for broader business opportunities.

The Bibo brothers were not the first of their family to undertake this quest. More than fifty years earlier, their maternal grandfather, Lukas Rosenstein, had come to America. He left Prussia in 1812, amid the turmoil of the Napoleonic period, also in order to avoid military service. He spent eight years in the United States. In 1820 he returned to Prussia to marry his childhood sweetheart, intending to bring her to his new country. But the young bride refused to leave her family and friends to make the long, dangerous journey to a strange, distant continent. So the Lukas Rosensteins remained in Prussia. In 1822 they had their first child, Blumchen, the future mother of Solomon Bibo.

In 1843 Blumchen married Isak Bibo. The early years of the older Bibo children were strongly influenced by their grandfather's tales of America. Through his reminiscences Lukas Rosenstein passed on to his grandchildren his great love for America. Another powerful influence was the news of many Prussian Jewish families who had found opportunity and success in the new world. Among these was the Spiegelberg family, personal friends of the Bibos, and now in business in and around Santa Fe, New Mexico.

In 1866 Nathan and Simon, the two oldest Bibo children, journeyed to the southwestern frontier country. At first they were employed by the

This is a condensation of an article "Jewish Indian Chief" by Sandra Lee Rollins in the *Western States Jewish Historical Quarterly*, July 1969, Vol. I, pp. 151-63. It is used with the permission of the WSJHQ.

Spiegelbergs but they soon went into business for themselves. By 1869 or 1870 they owned a trading post in Cebolleta among the Navajos, northwest of Albuquerque. This was the place to which Solomon came to work for his brothers.

Solomon soon became deeply involved in the affairs of the local Indians. He became well acquainted and closely associated with Acoma Pueblo, about 55 miles southwest of Albuquerque, and with the governor or chief of this pueblo, Martin Valle. In 1875 Solomon became an American citizen but he never completely mastered the English language. He spoke Spanish quite well and was fluent in the Queres language of Acoma, a feat achieved by few white men.

For many years the Acomans had been trying to regain land taken from them by the Spaniards. This land question was one of many Indian problems inherited by the United States through its 1848 treaty with Mexico. The Acomans did not trust the white man, an attitude which was theirs since 1599, when their ancestors were slaughtered by the soldiers of Juan de Onate, leader of New Mexico's earliest conquistadors. Solomon Bibo was, indeed, a very special kind of white man because he succeeded in winning the friendship and the confidence of Acoma Pueblo.

In 1882 or 1883 Solomon was granted a license to open his own trading post in Acoma village. He had asked several times for this license but the Department of the Interior was slow in granting it because Solomon Bibo was already pleading the cause of the Acomans and the whites looked upon him as a potential troublemaker.

Government surveys in 1876 and 1877 had given the Acomans a reservation of about 95,000 acres. The Acomans were not satisfied. With Bibo's help, the Acomans petitioned for and obtained in 1881 a governmental investigation of their grievance.

The authorities asked the Indians to use a government map to delineate their territory. This was difficult for two reasons. First, because of the language. All conversations had to be translated from Queres to Spanish to English and vice versa. Second, the difficulty of making the white man understand the Indian method of determining tribal boundaries. The Indians knew the exact limits of what they considered their tribal area. This information was not on any map nor was it indicated by any physical boundary markers. It was part of the tribal knowledge passed on orally from generation to generation. To try to put this on a white man's map was completely beyond the Indian's comprehension and capacity. The Acomans did not know how to deal with distances in terms of the white man's measuring tables. They had their own tribal ways of expressing distances. Had the government men been willing to ride the circumference of the land with the Indians, the Acomans could easily have pointed out their land boundaries. But the government men would not do this. They ended the investigation by saying that the Acomans must be satisfied with their 95,000-acre tract.

Solomon Bibo's determined efforts to get justice for the Acomans only succeeded in increasing the feeling of the whites that he was a muddleheaded, meddling, no-good Jew.

In April 1884 Bibo signed a 30-year grazing lease with the Acoma Pueblo. Martin Valle entered into this contract with the presumed consent of the entire pueblo. The pueblo was to receive an annual fee of about $400 for the grazing privilege. All squatters, cattle rustlers, and stray cattle were to be kept off the leased land. The lessor would be responsible for the well-being of all Acoma cattle. The lessor was also granted coal mining rights and would pay the tribe ten cents a ton for all coal mined. A final important condition was that Bibo could at any time sell the lease to someone else.

Almost immediately after the agreement was signed, Solomon sold the lease to the Acoma Land and Cattle Company, a Missouri corporation. The Department of the Interior accused Bibo of having planned this sale before he obtained the lease. This was considered a violation of Bibo's trading license and therefore illegal. The Department took steps to have Solomon's license revoked. On July 21, 1884, it received a petition from the pueblo asking that Bibo be allowed to continue as its trader.

Solomon was allowed to keep his license but the government sued him on behalf of the pueblo. He had to appear in court in November 1884. The government accused Bibo of having gotten the contract without the common consent of the pueblo. An affidavit from Governor Valle was produced stating that he understood the contract to be for only three years and not thirty. The principal members of the pueblo were alleged to have declared they had not given their assent to the lease. The government charged that the lease was a complete fraud.

It was four years before a federal judge finally settled the matter. His findings completely demolished the government's case. He ruled that the government had no right to sue Bibo on behalf of the Acoma Indians. If such a suit were to be instituted, it would have to be done directly by the tribe. The tribe declared it had no such wish or intention. Thus Bibo was completely cleared of the accusation of having defrauded the Indians for personal profit.

The Acoma Land and Cattle Company used the land for seven or eight years and then went bankrupt. The lease reverted to Bibo, who held it until its termination.

On May 1, 1885, Solomon married Juana Valle, granddaughter of Martin Valle. By this marriage Bibo and his heirs became members of the pueblo. The May 1 ceremony was an Indian ceremony. It was followed, on August 30, 1885, by a civil ceremony. Before the end of 1885 the Acoma tribe named Solomon Bibo its governor or chief. This became completely official on October 9, 1888, when W. C. Williams, "by virtue of the authority vested in me, as Indian Agent, by the United States," and "having confidence in the ability, integrity, and fidelity of Solomon

Bibo," "hereby appoint Solomon Bibo Governor of the Pueblo of Acoma."

Exactly how long Bibo held this office is not clear. In August 1898 the editor of *The Land of Sunshine,* a Los Angeles publication, stated in his magazine that he had visited Acoma Pueblo and spent some time with "my friend Solomon Bibo, who married into the tribe, has been six times its governor, speaks the Queres language better than any white man ever did, and has done more for his pueblo than all of the Indian Agents in a lump."

In the fall of 1885 Solomon moved his trading post to the Hispanic village of Cubero, just outside the northern boundary of the Acoma reservation. Here four of his six children were born. In late 1898 he moved to San Francisco to provide a better education for his children. He was a partner in a San Francisco grocery store, but continued to travel back to New Mexico to care for his business interests there. In 1904 he sold his Cubero store to his brother Emil. About 1906 he opened a store in San Rafael, a few miles southwest of Acoma. For the rest of his life he maintained businesses in both New Mexico and California.

Juana learned to speak English and was an excellent wife and mother. She had good business sense and was her husband's able assistant in his commercial ventures. Solomon died in San Francisco on May 4, 1934, and Juana in March 1941. Both were cremated. Their ashes are interred at the Home of Peace Mausoleum, Colma, California.

Although there is no record that Juana ever converted formally to Judaism, the Solomon Bibos reared their children as Jews. The oldest son, LeRoy, who now [1969] lives in Charter Oak, California, celebrated his Bar Mitzvah at Ohabai Shalome (Bush Street) Synagogue, San Francisco, in 1912. Carl, the youngest son [there were four daughters], who now [1969] lives in Santa Fe, New Mexico, attended religious school in Temple Emanuel, San Francisco. When Solomon died, LeRoy and Carl recited Kaddish for their father at Temple Israel, San Francisco.

FLORA AND THE ARCHBISHOP

(1886)

Solomon Jacob Spiegelberg, born in Natzungen, Prussia, in 1827, came to the United States in 1844. After his arrival in this country he was known simply as Jacob Spiegelberg. He was employed as a traveling salesman by a St. Louis firm. When the Mexican War broke out he accompanied the Missouri Volunteers to New Mexico as their commercial agent. After his outfit captured Santa Fe in 1846 Jacob, strongly moved by the beauty of the New Mexico mountains, got permission from his commanding officer to remain. He opened a small grocery and dry goods store in Santa Fe which prospered from the very beginning. In 1848 his brother Levi joined him. The business was expanded and the name of the firm was changed to "The House of the Spiegelberg Brothers." In 1849 a third brother, Elias, was added to the firm.

In 1852, while making a trip along the Santa Fe Trail, Levi was stricken with such a severe attack of dysentery that he was unable to continue his journey. A French priest found him lying helplessly by the side of the road. The priest picked him up, put him on a horse, and brought him back to Santa Fe. In this manner began a long and close friendship between the priest and the Spiegelbergs. The priest's name was Jean Baptiste Lamy.

*   *   *   *   *

Jean Baptiste Lamy was born in Blempdes, France, in 1814. He was ordained in 1838. He was sent to do missionary work in southern Ohio and northern Kentucky. He labored so diligently and effectively that in 1850 he was named vicar apostolic of the newly created Territory of New Mexico, which included all of present New Mexico plus most of Arizona and part of Colorado. Father Lamy arrived in Santa Fe in August 1851. He was not welcomed warmly by his Mexican fellow priests. They did not relish having a non-Mexican ecclesiastical superior. Despite the splendid results which attended his religious labors, Lamy never succeeded in winning the complete favor of his Spanish-speaking colleagues nor did he ever fully accommodate himself to their thinking or way of life. To the end of his days he remained a cultured European who did not approve of the somewhat primitive beliefs and customs of his Southwestern padres and parishioners.

It soon became evident that the assignment given Father Lamy was beyond the capacity of one individual, even such a dedicated priest as this Frenchman. In July 1853 he was consecrated Bishop of Santa Fe. This reduced the area under his ecclesiastical jurisdiction to approximately two-thirds of what is now New Mexico, including its largest towns, Santa Fe and Albuquerque. The population of the diocese was overwhelmingly Roman Catholic; but this Roman Catholicism was strongly tinged with paganism and marred by widespread illiteracy and poverty. Bishop Lamy vigorously attacked these problems by bringing in better qualified clergy and nuns and, with their help, he established many new churches and schools. In appreciation of his valiant struggle in an extremely difficult situation, in 1875 the bishop was elevated to the rank of archbishop.

*   *   *   *   *

Over the years the "House of the Spiegelberg Brothers" grew steadily in size, wealth, and influence as the boys moved into and out of Santa Fe. In 1853 Emanuel arrived. In 1854 Jacob returned to Germany. In 1855 Elias was killed when an adobe building collapsed and crushed him. In 1857 Lehman arrived. In 1861 the youngest brother, Willi, age sixteen, arrived. Later in the 1860s Levi and Emanuel moved to New York City. This left Lehman and Willi in charge of the Santa Fe business.

Willi was the most handsome and gifted of the brothers. The Mexicans nicknamed him "Don Julian el Bonito," "the dapper emperor." He was dignified and imposing, daring and adventurous. During the Civil War he served for a time as a scout with the Union Army. He was a friend of Kit Carson and Chief Manuelito of the Navajo. While on an Eastern business trip he delivered to President Lincoln personally a gift from the Navajo, a beautifully woven blanket. This gained him the lasting gratitude of Chief Manuelito, who had been previously somewhat vexed with Willi for having declined the chief's offer to marry one of his daughters. By 1875 Willi was making about $50,000 a year. He decided to take a vacation. He went back to Germany to visit his family.

❖   ❖   ❖   ❖   ❖

Flora Langermann was born in New York City in 1857. After her father died in 1869, her mother took her to Nuremberg, Germany, to be educated. There in 1875 eighteen-year-old Flora met thirty-year-old Willi. In her memoirs, written in 1937, Flora states, "I was young and he was handsome and I soon became Mrs. Willi Spiegelberg." Theirs was the first wedding in Nuremberg's new Reform Temple. (It was destroyed by the Nazis on Krystallnacht in November 1938.)

❖   ❖   ❖   ❖   ❖

The newlyweds traveled from New York City to Las Animas, Colorado, by train. From there to Santa Fe was a 300-mile, five-day trip by stagecoach. Although Flora had been reared in an atmosphere of refinement and delicacy, she stood the arduous, dust-laden journey well and arrived tired but in excellent spirits. At Glorieta Pass, some eleven miles southeast of Santa Fe, the stagecoach was met by a party of horsemen, relatives and friends of the groom, and was escorted into town with many a whoop and holler in typical exuberant frontier style. At the city limits the couple received an official and colorful welcome from the commander of the state militia and then was paraded down the main street, preceded by a military band playing the Lohengrin wedding march. The pair went to live in a comfortable adobe house close to the Plaza, the historic square where the office and residence of the territorial governor were located.

Flora, beautiful and gracious, won the admiration of all who met her. Like her husband, she had the air of a born aristocrat, well-bred, poised, charm personified. She soon became one of Santa Fe's best known and best liked hostesses. Willi and Flora entertained frequently and lavishly. Flora was an accomplished pianist and a born actress. She gave concerts and took leading roles in amateur theatricals.

From the moment of her arrival, she and Father Lamy fell in love with each other in perfectly proper fashion. The sixty-one-year-old priest and the eighteen-year-old bride came from the same background of European culture. Flora spoke French fluently and so was able to converse with the bishop in his native tongue. They also shared a common love for beauty, art and music and flowers, especially flowers. They would confer often about the care and development of their respective gardens.

Soon after Flora arrived in Santa Fe, Lamy was elevated to archbishop. In celebration the community tendered a public banquet to its honored spiritual leader. Lamy asked the arrangements committee to have Flora plan the banquet and to have Willi act as toastmaster. The fine speech that Willi gave on that occasion was afterward printed and distributed.

In 1879 Flora helped organize the Santa Fe Academy, the city's first non-sectarian school. Its original enrollment was twelve students, all Protestant or Jewish. Then many Catholic parents also began to send their children to the school so that, two years later, it was necessary to erect a three-story school building. Flora taught courses in gardening, nature study, needlework, and sewing.

In 1882 she started a Jewish sabbath school with eight students. One of the eight, Arthur Seligman, was Governor of New Mexico from 1930 until he died in 1933. On the High Holydays and Passover, Jews would come to Santa Fe from all over New Mexico to attend services and Sedarim arranged and conducted by Willi and Flora. At these high points of the Jewish religious year, Archbishop Lamy brought gifts of wine, fruit, and flowers. This was his gracious way of saying "thank you" to the Spiegelbergs for the many times he was a dinner guest in their home.

In the early 1880s Willi and Flora moved into a spacious new home with lovely grounds. Archbishop Lamy planted willow trees from his garden on both sides of the home's main gate and took part in the Chanukat ha-Bayit ceremony asking God's blessing on the new domicile. In appreciation Flora presented him with an olivewood rosary she had purchased at Gethsemane, a rosary blessed by both the Bishop of Jerusalem and the Pope.

Among the prominent people entertained by the Willi Spiegelbergs in their home or in the local Jewish club, the Germania, were President and Mrs. Rutherford B. Hayes, Generals William T. Sherman, Philip H. Sheridan, Lew Wallace, and famed agnostic Colonel Robert Ingersoll. In

1880 Willi was elected Mayor of Santa Fe. In 1884 he was appointed County Probate Judge. In 1885 he declined an offer from President Cleveland to become Territorial Governor.

When Lamy became bishop in 1853 his diocesan headquarters was a modest adobe structure, St. Francis Catholic Church. His greatest desire was to build a stone cathedral like those in his native France, one worthy of being the see of a prince of the Church. As archbishop, working for the completion of this structure became his major activity. Worn out by his labors, he retired as archbishop in 1885. The following year he had the great joy of presiding over the majestic ceremonies attending the dedication and consecration of Santa Fe's attractive stone St. Francis Cathedral.

The Jews of Santa Fe, especially Willi and Flora, contributed generously to the cost of building the cathedral. Sometime prior to its completion the archbishop took Flora on a tour of inspection. Proudly he pointed out to her that in the keystone of the arch above the main entrance was a triangle in the middle of which was inscribed in bright black Hebrew letters the word "Adonai." Greatly pleased, Flora said to him, "Father, here has been carved in stone that which you have exemplified every day of your life, the Fatherhood of God and the brotherhood of humanity, with no distinction between race, creed or color."

Similar triangles containing the Hebrew word for God are found on and in many European churches as a representation of the Christian doctrine of the Trinity. But to Flora and to the Jews of Santa Fe from that day to this, that sign above the door stands as an everpresent reminder of the harmony and love in the relationship of Archbishop Jean Baptiste Lamy and the Jewish community of Santa Fe.

Archbishop Lamy died on February 13, 1888 at the age of seventy-three at his country home near Santa Fe. His death is described in graphic detail by the Catholic novelist Willa S. Cather in her *Death Comes for the Archbishop,* published in 1927. Miss Cather's book is filled with stirring descriptions of Father Lamy's wondrous works among the Catholics of New Mexico. But it contains not a single word about the affection he had for the Jews of Santa Fe, particularly Flora and Willi, and the love they had for him. This is regrettable. When one knows the real story and then reads *Death Comes for the Archbishop,* the reader is left with the feeling that Miss Cather was more interested in extolling her Church than in honoring the man and painting a word portrait of him that was true to life.

❋ ❋ ❋ ❋ ❋

In 1891 Willi and Lehman Spiegelberg sold their valuable New Mexico enterprises and moved their families to New York City because they wanted their children to mature in a strongly Jewish environment.

For the next fifty years Flora Spiegelberg was one of New York City's most brilliant and devoted Jewish communal leaders, working for Reform Judaism, philanthropy, and many worthy civic causes. She also became a well-known writer of children's stories, featured regularly on the radio network of the Columbia Broadcasting System.

Willi died in 1929 at the age of eighty-five. Flora died in 1943 at the age of eighty-seven. They had outlived their beloved friend, the archbishop, by forty-one and fifty-five years respectively; but, finally, as it must to all, death also came for them.

THE CARDINAL'S WEDDING
(1890)

In the state of Texas Henry Cohen of Galveston, 1863-1952, revered and saintly rabbi, is already a legendary figure. Many stories are told about him. Here are a few of those stories.

In 1890 a great Catholic scholar, Cardinal Satolli, paid a visit to Galveston. A banquet was given in his honor. Young Rabbi Cohen was asked to give the invocation. He did so in flawless Latin. At the end of the banquet the cardinal responded to the rabbi's beau geste by giving the benediction in equally flawless Hebrew.

During the banquet the cardinal and the rabbi were seated next to each other. They had a lively conversation, in the course of which the cardinal asked the rabbi, "Rabbi, is there any life situation in which you think you could be tempted to eat ham?" Without a moment's hesitation, Rabbi Cohen replied, "There certainly is, reverend sir—at your wedding!"

Later another Jew who was present congratulated the rabbi on his clever response. "Oh, I can't take any credit for that," responded Rabbi Cohen. "That's a very ancient *bon mot*. There is one in the same category that is even more ancient. It's the story about the Jew who went into a non-Jewish restaurant for breakfast on a balmy spring morning. When he emerged forty-five minutes later, it was raining cats and dogs. The Jew looked upwards and said, 'Dear God, isn't this a hell of a lot of fuss to be making over a couple little slices of bacon?' "

Some years later Rabbi Cohen took his wife and children on a vacation trip to Mexico City. They explored the city from end to end. On its outskirts they found a lovely Catholic shrine which they desired to enter. The rabbi pulled the bell at the locked entrance gate. A bent old man appeared and opened the gate part way. He told them in Spanish that no one was allowed to come in to the sacred precincts. "No one?" asked Rabbi Cohen, also in Spanish. "No one except priests." "But I am a priest," said Rabbi Cohen, meaning, of course, a Jewish priest, which Cohens are in Jewish tradition. "How can I tell?" "Look at my tonsure," replied Rabbi Cohen. Leaning forward he showed the old man the round bald spot on the top of his head. Convinced that he was in the presence of a genuine representative of the Holy One, blessed be they, the Mexican opened the gate. "And may my sister and her children accompany me?" "Of course," said the Mexican. And so it was that the Jewish priest and his relatives gained access to the little shrine and beheld with reverence the holy objects it contained.

In 1910 a Russian stowaway was caught on a ship in Galveston harbor and was to be deported. He had been a revolutionary in his native country. If he was returned he would be executed. Rabbi Cohen made a special trip to Washington to try to prevent the man's deportation. The Justice Department said it was a clear case of illegal entry and refused to act. The rabbi asked his congressman to take him to see the President, William Howard Taft, "on a matter of life and death."

What happened is described in the biography of Rabbi Cohen written by his son and daughter-in-law and titled *The Man Who Stayed in Texas:*

President Taft was friendly and kind. He told Rabbi Cohen that it was too bad he had made this long journey to no avail, but this was clearly a case for the Justice Department, and they had given their decision. The rabbi saw that he was beaten. He stood up to leave, and thanked the President for seeing him ahead of other appointments; he was sick at heart, and it showed on his tired, haggard face.

"I'm sorry this had to happen to you, Rabbi Cohen," President Taft said. "Allow me to say that I certainly admire the way you Jews help each other out—traveling all the way up here from Galveston, Texas, when a member of your faith is in trouble."

"Member of my faith? This man is not a Jew," Rabbi Cohen said. "He is a Russian Catholic."

President Taft's usually placid expression changed to one of surprise. "You mean to say you traveled all the way up here at your own expense to help out a Russian Catholic?"

"He's in trouble; they're going to deport him on the next ship, and he'll face a firing squad when he gets back to Russia. He's a human being, Mr. President; a human life is at stake. That's the way I see it."

"Sit down, Rabbi Cohen," said the President. "Wait just a minute." He rang for a secretary. He was silent until the man came in. "Take a telegram," he said. "It goes to the Chief Inspector of Immigration at Galveston. Say 'Hold Lemchuk in Galveston and release him in the custody of Rabbi Cohen.' Say they'll hear direct from the Department," said the President of the United States.

In 1938 when Galveston celebrated the fiftieth anniversary of its

rabbi's coming to Texas, *Reader's Digest* did a feature article on Henry
Cohen. The writer of the article told a final "Catholic" story:

In the recent mayoralty election in Galveston, the two chief candi-
dates were a Catholic and a Jew. The Catholic came to his padre seeking
his support. "My son," said the padre. "I'm going to vote for Adrian Levy.
Levy has been a good mayor and I think we ought to keep him on the
job." The priest told me that hundreds of his parishioners voted as he did.
Levy was elected, though the Jews form less than two percent of the
population. The priest said to me: "Why is it we judge a man in this town
not for his race or his creed, but for what he is himself? The answer is—
Rabbi Henry Cohen."

Is It Worth It?
(1896)

Sister Anne and a nice Jewish married lady who kept kosher were
teachers in the same fancy private academy in New Orleans. They were
both very outgoing and soon became fast friends. Finally they reached a
point where they could talk without embarrassment about anything—
well, almost anything. One day Sister Anne said to Rebecca, "Tell me,
Becky, have you ever tasted ham?" Rebecca replied, "Yes, I have. Just
once, while I was in college. I was curious to know what ham tasted
like—so I took just one bite." There was a moment's silence—and then
Rebecca said to Sister Anne, "Now you tell me, Annie—have you ever
made love to a man? You know what I mean—really made love—all the
way?" Sister Anne blushed and replied, "Yes I did—once—long before I
took my vows." There was another moment's silence. Then Rebecca said
to Sister Anne, "Better than ham, wasn't it?"

The Simpson Gun
(1929)

The Simpson Gun, a German 105 mm. artillery piece captured
during World War I and permanently emplaced at the summit of Signal

Taken from the recently published *American Jewish Landmarks*, Volume II, (The
South and Southwest) by Bernard Postal and Lionel Koppman, Fleet Press, New York,
1979. Used with the permission of the authors.

Mountain in the western corner of Fort Sill, the Army's Field Artillery headquarters at Lawton, Oklahoma, is a joint memorial to Fort Sill's World War I dead and Morris S. Simpson, pioneer Jewish settler. Affixed to the monumental stone in front of the gun is a bronze plaque with the inscription: "This gun was emplaced at the suggestion of Morris S. Simpson, an original settler of Lawton and a staunch friend of the Army."

Simpson, born in Russia in 1863, came to the United States at the age of twenty and settled with his brother-in-law, Morris Israelson, first in Marshall and then in Dallas, Texas. In 1901 they drove a covered wagon loaded with dry goods and house furnishings from Dallas to the present site of Lawton. Here on August 3, three days before the opening of the three-million-acre Kiowa-Comanche reservation to white settlement, they set up a tent and started Lawton's first store. From this modest beginning grew the Lawton Mercantile Company, one of the largest stores in the Southwest, known to all as "Simpson's." Before long Simpson's house and store became "a home away from home" for young and homesick officers who found the Simpsons friendly and sympathetic hosts.

Simpson's scrupulous honesty and friendship in dealing with the Indians made him their idol. They found the Jewish trader's fair dealing and aid in time of need a unique experience. Quanah Parker, last chief of the Comanches, who lived on the outskirts of Lawton for many years, named one of his sons for Simpson, "in honor of my good white friend." Lawton's development into a major cotton market was also one of Simpson's main concerns.

The Simpsons had no children of their own, so they adopted and reared a number of orphans. One such youngster, born as an Episcopalian, was given a Christian rearing by the ardently Jewish Simpsons. For many years their home was a makeshift synagogue for Jews from Lawton and the surrounding towns. The Torah Simpson brought with him to Lawton, said to have been the first in the Territory of Oklahoma, is now a prized possession of the Fort Sill Chapel.

From Simpson came the proposal that a memorial to Fort Sill's World War I dead should be set up on the post. Out of his idea grew the project of embedding the German gun on Signal Mountain. When the memorial was dedicated in 1929, two years before Simpson died, the Commanding General of Fort Sill declared that it would be known as "the Simpson Gun" in honor of the Jewish pioneer who had done so much for Fort Sill and for Lawton.

Stanley Stein, Né Sidney Maurice Levyson
(1931)

On the memorial tablet on the wall of the Liberal Synagogue in Baton Rouge, Louisiana, one of the plaques bears the name SIDNEY S. S. LEVYSON, who passed away in 1967. His parents had given him the name of Sidney Maurice Levyson. In 1931, when he entered U. S. Public Health Service Hospital #66, Carville, Louisiana, he was cogently advised by the hospital staff to change his name. He chose the name of Stanley Stein. His mother's maiden name was Stein. At that time, Carville patients were requested to hide their identity, lest members of their families be penalized or ostracized by society for having a blood relative who was a victim of the dread disease called leprosy. Many years had to pass before Stanley dared to call himself Sidney again.

It was my privilege to be his chaplain during the last eighteen years of his life. I first met him at the hospital in the late fall of 1949. The Commission on Jewish Chaplaincy of the National Jewish Welfare Board had asked me to serve as Jewish chaplain at the institution. To visit the only leprosarium in the continental United States evoked in me an initial reaction of fear.

My first visit brought the realization that the fear was based on ignorance and banished it from my mind. It also introduced me to Sidney. He was already totally blind. He could not employ Braille because he had lost the tactile touch in his fingers. Yet he had gathered valuable press equipment through friends, officials, and organizations, and had assembled a patient staff and was editor of a monthly magazine called *The Star*, dedicated to the elimination of baseless phobias about this ancient disease. This periodical continues today as a constant source of inspiration and scientific knowledge and as a constant reminder of Sidney. The number of its subscribers has increased steadily. They now number about 60,000. From 1949 on Sidney was for me a never-ending source of radiant spirituality. Beneath his soft spoken gentleness there was a fiery spirit, refined and sharpened by mental and physical degradation and suffering.

Born in Gonzales, Texas, Sidney was an only child. His father was a pharmacist who hoped his son would succeed him in the business. Sidney became a pharmacist chiefly to please his father, but his abiding loves were journalism, Little Theatre in all its aspects, and a lively appreciation of the pleasures, delights, and hopes of youth. His devoted mother,

---

Written by the late Rabbi Marvin M. Reznikoff, rabbi emeritus of Liberal Synagogue, Baton Rouge, Louisiana.

German born, was a lady of great sensitivity who wrote to Sidney almost daily as long as she was able to do so. During our meetings Sidney frequently used the word "mensch," a German-Jewish word learned from his mother and meaning a person of quality or character. That is what "Stanley Stein" was—a mensch. Much of the inner agony he carried with him he did not reveal to me. I never really knew the innermost "Stanley" until I read his excellent autobiography *Alone No Longer*, written in collaboration with his friend Lawrence G. Blochman.

It is no exaggeration to assert that, as Stanley Stein, he played the preeminent part in helping to change U.S.P.H.S. Hospital #66 from a kind of penal colony, embraced by a fence of barbed wire, into a community where patients are given abundant hope and guidance to carry on both within the hospital and after they leave it, as many now do. He fought to fashion an atmosphere of normalcy, where patients could vote as respected citizens, telephone loved ones openly and travel on hospital-granted leaves in public carriers without fear of being jailed or returned to be punished.

With the aid of wise government officials, humane medical officers, friendly organizations, and kindly sister-nurses and chaplains, the Hospital is presently a place where patients are given a wise freedom to enter and depart. Visitors find a relaxed atmosphere. Groups are invited to tour the facility to learn more about the true nature of leprosy. The exemplary institutional atmosphere achieved at Carville has paved the way for the improvement of the treatment of similar patients in hospitals and leper colonies all over the world. *The Star* has shone brightly on their darkness. The magazine is no longer required to be sterilized before it is mailed.

Many scientific and religious scholars have noted the fact that the Hebrew Biblical word for leprosy, "tsora-at," is a generic term for a skin malady that has little or no relationship to the disease presently called leprosy. The authors of the Septuagint, who translated our Bible from Hebrew to Greek in the third pre-Christian century, were hard put to translate the word accurately. Out of the welter of translations emerged the Latin "lepra," the French "lepros," the English "leprosy," regarded for centuries as a scourge from God inflicted on the sinful. What is presently known as leprosy is feebly communicable. Even cohabitation does not result in a transmission of the bacillus.

As founder and editor of *The Star* Sidney labored to change the nomenclature of the disease from leprosy to Hansen's Disease. Hansen was a Norwegian scientist who first isolated the bacillus. A trained pharmacist, a lover of both the written and the oral word, a crusader imbued with a passion for justice and truth that would overcome the cruelty of fate and circumstance, Sidney was eminently qualified to pursue his role. It was, above all, his heartfelt compassion for human beings, regardless of race, creed, or color, a compassion refined by intense suffering of body and soul, that characterized him most completely. The Hebrew word for "mercy," "rachamim," is related to a noun meaning "womb." The truly merciful, the truly compassionate, should have the concern for all of humanity that a loving mother has for the fruit of her body. In Sidney justice and truth, compassion and mercy were blended magnificently.

After reading mail addressed to Sidney from many lands, I would sit in amazement and wonder how this dark-spectacled, mildly spoken, little man, wasted away by illness, could be the repository of such an abundance of the Divine Spirit, which he perhaps would not have labeled as such. Had sulfones and their derivatives been discovered as arresting agents of the disease three years earlier, Sidney might well have saved the sight of at least one eye. It almost seems as if Fate allowed him to exchange physical sight for penetrating insight. Refusing to wallow in a mire of self-pity, he chose, in the noblest tradition of his people, to turn adversity into prosperity of spirit for the enhancement of human dignity and for the soothing of the pain of others, a pain he himself sharply experienced. His unshakeable resolve was free of the kind of fanaticism that sometimes destroys the innocent in the name of a noble cause. Sidney was usually among the first to offer himself as a guinea pig whenever the medical staff of the Hospital decided to experiment with a new drug. Often, after a short prayer service on a Saturday afternoon, we would talk. He would hope for more and more laboratory facilities at Carville. Were he living now he would rejoice over the progress that has been made in the last ten years. But he would continue to insist that much, much more must yet be done before educated scientific guesses become positive remedies, before the disease and the hideous stigma attached to it vanish from the body and mind of man. As his physical strength weakened with the passage of time, his crusading spirit seemed to quicken. He realized more and more that, while neither he nor his generation could complete the task, he had a responsibility to continue to do his bit until his final hour.

Ritually Sidney was not a meticulous observer of Judaism, but he believed strongly in the concept of *Mitzvot*, Good Deeds. This dedication earned him unbounded respect and love, whether he was helping an unemployed fellow patient or engaging in a dialogue with a government scientist or a distinguished physician, addressing a convention or dictating a letter or an editorial. Sidney became perhaps the world's most knowledgeable layman on the nature of Hansen's Disease. Talking records helped him also keep exceedingly well informed about world events and current literature, especially modern drama.

More than thirty years elapsed before Sidney broke down his inner walls of anxiety and entered a synagogue, the Liberal Synagogue of

Baton Rouge. He had been made an honorary member long before. He also had arranged to have the names of his departed loved ones placed on the memorial tablet of the synagogue. His first visit took place late one Saturday evening when no person, young or old, was about. A few of his friends in the congregation had finally persuaded him, with the help and encouragement of the Hospital staff, to travel the twenty-five miles from Carville to Baton Rouge. This visit, I believe, helped him to break down a long held feeling of lack of self-assurance. With the status of "improved patient," he began to travel with greater confidence about the country, visiting his beloved kin and friends from whom he had cut himself off in anonymity for so many years. Thereafter he attended High Holyday services at Liberal Synagogue. During his last years Sidney Maurice Levyson began to replace Stanley Stein as a person, though Stanley Stein remained the name of the crusading editor and speaker and the unfailing friend of the afflicted. In his modest will he left a goodly sum for the establishment of a Levyson Religious School Education Fund in the synagogue.

The last time we were together was in the infirmary of the Hospital the day before he died. Wracked with arthritic pain, blind, virtually deaf, lying on his mattress grave, he cried out to me in utter despair, "I'm becoming a breathing tomb." For the moment I was stunned, and then I shouted as loudly as I could into his left and better hearing ear, "Sidney, haven't you said time and again that it is not what one loses during a lifetime that matters most, but what one chooses to do with what one has left?" "That is right," he replied, very slowly. "I must try to live as I have told others to live. We preachers have to watch that." There was a slight smile on his face. Soon after, I said good bye. I was told that the next morning he tried to dictate letters and to discuss matters of *The Star* with a member of the editorial staff. In the afternoon he was gathered to his fathers. An ecumenical service was held in the Protestant chapel. As Sidney wanted, he was buried beside his elders in the cemetery of Congregation Beth El in San Antonio, where he had been a prominent member of the Temple Theatre Group in his youth before Fate launched him on a bizarre journey.

The influence of a person very great in spirit often becomes greater after his departure from this life. Sidney Stanley Stein Levyson remains in retrospect a giant of the spirit whose Maccabean courage continues to give renewed hope to those who grope to turn inner darkness into creative light. He would certainly have preferred a lifetime free from the hideous stigma of the disease that cruelly prevented him from taking root in his native Texas, denied him the joys of marriage and rearing a family. Yet had that been his destiny, he would never have gained the insight and the opportunity to serve others as a crusading journalist and, even more, as an ever-living example of courage and compassion. Example is still the most powerful form of persuasion.

Sidney, your Star shines on and on. Rest in peace, departed friend.

JUDGE JOSEPHS DOES THE IMPOSSIBLE
(1937)

In 1936, while I was serving as rabbi of Sinai Temple, Texarkana, U.S.A., I helped organize a school of adult education at the Texarkana Junior College. As part of the school's program, I gave courses on a number of subjects over the local radio station, which was owned by the *Texarkana Gazette* and located directly above the newspaper office.

One Sunday afternoon in 1937 I was delivering a lecture over the radio on Greek philosophy. As I was about to conclude, I noticed Henry Humphrey, editor of the *Gazette,* pacing nervously back and forth outside the broadcast booth. No sooner had I finished than Mr. Humphrey entered the booth and said, "Rabbi, something terrible has just happened. A Negro has shot and killed Bryce Williams [a prominent local real estate agent]. There will surely be a lynching unless preventive measures are taken immediately."

A few days before, I had been told by Dr. Leonce J. Kosminsky, immediate past president of my congregation, first Jew born in Texarkana [1877], and a very prominent Legionnaire [he would be in 1941-42 national commander of the Forty and Eight], that he had organized a group of members of the American Legion to handle just such an emergency. I called "Doc" Kosminsky. In a very short time the Legion group assembled at the local jail, were sworn in as deputy sheriffs, issued shotguns, and prepared to repel any lynch mob that might assemble. No such mob appeared that day.

Two nights later a cavalcade of about a dozen automobiles and trucks filled with armed peasants from the surrounding area came into Texarkana and attempted to storm the jail. By that time the prisoner had been removed to a jail in a distant city.

The next Friday night I preached a sermon in the synagogue which commended the people of Texarkana for their restraint and condemned the mob which came in from "the sticks" to lynch the black. Portions of my sermon were printed in next day's *Gazette.*

Sometime after that, when the case came to trial, I went to court to observe the workings of Arkansas "white man's" justice. The courtroom was jammed to capacity with hundreds of blacks and whites. The blacks, according to prevailing local custom, were seated in the rear rows. Because of my well-known interest in the case, I was given a seat in the very front row.

To my surprise and delight I learned that the black man would be defended by the president of my congregation, Louis Josephs, an attorney who had been a municipal judge for many years and was known to one and all as Judge Josephs. Although born in East Prussia, Josephs spoke with a thick Irish brogue, the result of having spent his boyhood and youth in Dublin, Ireland. Josephs had undertaken the defense of the accused without promise or hope of receiving any sort of financial recompense.

Before the trial began Josephs asked me if I would be willing to assist him with the defense. I readily consented. I was taken before the judge, sworn in as an amicus curiae, "friend of the court," and permitted to sit with Judge Josephs at the counsel table. I was not permitted to address the court or the witnesses directly; but, throughout the trial, I acted as an advisor to Judge Josephs, suggesting questions to be asked the witnesses, giving him my opinion of the effect his line of questioning seemed to be having on the jury, and so forth.

The facts in the case were clear and were authenticated by a number of eyewitnesses:

Bryce Williams, a white male about six feet tall and weighing about 200 pounds, had gone early on Sunday afternoon to a local bank where the black defendant, whose name I do not recall, was working as a janitor. The black was about five feet five inches and weighed about 140 pounds. Williams asked the janitor for the week's rent which was due. The janitor refused to give him the money because Williams had not fulfilled his promise to have a leaking roof in the janitor's home repaired. Williams became irate, pulled a revolver from his pocket, pointed it at the janitor and said, "You black s.o.b., give me that money or I'll kill you." The frightened janitor lunged for the gun. The gun went off, wounding the janitor in the side. The wounded janitor then wrestled Williams to the floor. Williams' head hit the tiled floor of the bank. The impact knocked him unconscious. The gun flew out of his hand. The janitor grabbed the revolver and shot and killed Bryce Williams. The janitor then got up, walked to the street, hailed a cab and went to the local Negro hospital, where his wound was treated. He then got back in the cab, rode to the local police station, turned himself in, and was locked up.

The case was clearly one of self-defense. Had it not been black vs. white, the prisoner would probably have been freed without the formality of a trial. The prosecution was handled by the county district attorney and also an attorney engaged by the deceased man's family. The district attorney was quite fair and objective in his handling of the case. But the family attorney was a venomous racist. He pounded the table and gesticulated and ranted like a lunatic. "If this criminal's life is spared, it will be unsafe for any white woman to walk the streets of Texarkana," he shouted and much more such rabble rousing nonsense. He demanded that the black be condemned to the electric chair.

Judge Josephs, much more dignified and self-controlled, was magnificently eloquent. He quoted profusely and cogently from both the Jewish and Christian Bibles to show that it was not the defendant who was really on trial but the people of Texarkana. No ancient prophet could have pleaded more fervently than did Judge Josephs for genuine justice and mercy and racial understanding. How proud I was to be there by the side of this wonderful man and to know that, through Louis Josephs, a Jew who was to be "little noted nor long remembered," our religion and our tradition were appealing to the consciences of twelve Christian citizens of Texarkana to do the decent and proper thing.

The case went to the jury about 3:30 P.M. on the second day. An hour later the jury sent word to the judge that it would not be ready with its verdict until the next morning.

That night Judge Josephs and I spent a number of hours discussing possible future legal strategy. We were certain that the black would be found guilty. We felt that the best to be hoped for was a verdict of "guilty of manslaughter" or of "murder in the second degree." I told Josephs that, if the verdict was death, we ought to enlist the aid of the American Civil Liberties Union. Judge Josephs had never heard of the ACLU, but he agreed to seek its help if that became necessary.

Next morning at 9:00 A.M., in a crowded and tense courtroom, the foreman of the jury delivered the verdict: NOT GUILTY! Twelve good men and true had not been poisoned by the racist venom but, moved by the spiritual eloquence of Louis Josephs, they had done that which was decent and right.

Judge Josephs was so stunned by the verdict that he fainted. The acquitted black was so fearful for his life that he did not return home. He took the first freight out of town and disappeared. The Texarkana black community looked upon Judge Josephs as a miracle worker. From that day on, any Texarkana black who became involved in any sort of legal entanglement with a white wanted Judge Josephs as his lawyer. He was a man who had done the impossible. For the first time, in the entire history of the State of Arkansas, a black who killed a white was acquitted!

A few weeks later I received a ticket for overtime parking. Like all Texarkana clergymen, I went to the police station to have the ticket annulled. The community's police had such respect for members of the cloth that they always did this for preachers who violated traffic regulations. After dutifully canceling the charge against me, the desk sergeant said, "It was you who helped get off that nigger who killed Bryce Williams, wasn't it?" I replied that it was. "What you did was wrong," the sergeant said. "They should have hanged that little black s.o.b. to the nearest lamp post." As calmly as possible I asked the sergeant for his name and badge number. "Whatever for?" asked the sergeant. I answered, "I am going to report you and your remark to the mayor and the *Gazette*. The people of our city have the right to know and to judge the thoughts of the men who are charged with protecting the lives and property of our citizens." The sergeant turned pale. "Oh, come on now, rabbi," he said, "you know I was only kidding."

A ROSE BY ANY OTHER NAME
(1946)

In less than three months forty-five-year-old Henry Frankfurter went to court in Reno, Nevada, three times—the first time to get a divorce, the second time to get married, and the third time to change his name.

"Why do you want to do this?" asked the judge. "Frankfurter sounds like a nice name to me."

"It is my new wife's idea, your honor. You know how these young girls are. They want their names to sound real American. So, to please her, I've decided to change it."

"And what do you want to call yourself now?"

"Wiener," said Frankfurter.

HURRAY FOR OUR SIDE
(1949)

In New Orleans a Jew whose son was a rabbi and a Catholic whose son was a priest were debating the question of which of their sons held the more important position.

After the Jew had spoken at length about the respected status of the rabbi in the Jewish community, the Catholic said, "That may be so, but Catholics look up to the priest much more than Jews do to their rabbi. And, furthermore, a priest has a great advantage which rabbis have not. Exceptional priests may advance in hierarchal rank and position—to monsignor, bishop, archbishop, and cardinal—and, if the priest is one in a million, he may even get to be Pope."

"Oh," said the Jew, "being Pope is not all that great. A Pope is a mere mortal, just like everyone else."

This remark made the Catholic angry. "Well," he cried out, "now just who is it you think a priest should try to become—Jesus Christ?"

To which the Jew proudly replied, "Why not? One of our boys made it."

HORSERADISH SPECIAL

(1952)

About a week before Passover in 1952, while serving as a chaplain at an Air Force HQ in Texas, I received an SOS via MARS radio. The operator said there was an emergency high priority message for me from Ramey Air Force Base in Puerto Rico, but he was unable to decipher it. "Spell it out for me and maybe I'll be able to help," I said. Letter by letter he spelled: "PESACH SEDER SUPPLIES—NO CHRAIN FOR GEFILTA."

Determined to prevent a serious violation of gefilta fish etiquette, I dropped everything and hastened to Shreveport, Louisiana, where I purchased three large gallon jars of horseradish. I packed them carefully, almost reverently, and marked the cartons "Religious Articles—Very Holy and Very Important."

Back at my base I contacted Flight Operations and found a courier plane going to MacDill AFB in Tampa, Florida. From there another courier could bring the precious cargo to Ramey in time for Passover. I went out to speak to the commander of the plane personally and asked him to deliver the cartons to the Base Chaplain at MacDill. Then I got on the direct wire to MacDill and told the Base Chaplain how urgent it was to deliver the "Passover supplies."

The day before Passover I received another call from the MARS radio operator: "Chaplain, it's another one of those classified and unpronounceable messages." "Spell it out," I said.

This time he delivered to me the following cryptic and hallowed communication from one American Jewish military chaplain to another: "CHRAIN ARRIVED B'SHOLOM. CHAG SAMEACH AND A KOSHER PESACH."

Written by Chaplain Michell D. Geller, USAF Reserve and rabbi of Congregation Brothers of Joseph, Norwich, Connecticut, for *Rabbis in Uniform*, Jonathan David Publishers, New York, 1962.

YES, SIR, ISRAEL IS JUST LIKE TEXAS
(1956)

A Texas Jew, while making his once-in-a-lifetime pilgrimage to Israel, bragged to an Israeli that one could travel across the state of Texas for days in a train and not reach the state border. The Israeli replied that there was no reason for the Texan to feel shame because of this situation. "Here in Israel," he said, "the trains also always run very slowly."

NOT ALL THAT BAD
(1966)

Among the handful of Jewish families in Flagstaff, Arizona, were the Greenbergs. The nearest large Jewish community was Phoenix, 150 miles away. Sally, seventeen years old and their only child, was very attractive, the most popular girl in the senior class. But the parents were very worried. None of Sally's boyfriends was Jewish. They wanted a Jewish son-in-law.

After much soul searching they arrived at a solution. They would send Sally to Jerusalem's Hebrew University. But Sally refused to go. "All my friends are here!" she cried. Finally a compromise was reached. She would go for one year. They would make no fuss if she wanted to come back to the States when the year was up.

At the end of August the Greenbergs flew to New York and put Sally on an El Al plane. Sally did not write home very often; but, when she did write, the tone was pleasant.

As the first year was drawing to a close, the Greenbergs got the following letter from Sally:

Dear Mom and Dad,

I'm sorry that I haven't been writing as frequently as I should; but, what with classes and exams and everything else, I haven't had much time. I hope you haven't worried. Everything here is OK—except for one thing. I just got my grades and haven't done very well. I flunked Math and Biology and Hebrew. I got a D in History and Social Studies and a C in Music Appreciation. I hope this won't upset you too much. I'll try to do better in my college work next year. I promise.

I haven't told you this before, but I have met a darling, handsome boy in one of my classes; and we are planning to get married. I know you will like him. He is really good looking and rather dark skinned, but not as dark as most Arabs. I have met his parents; and they are very nice. You'll like them. They are not Moslems like most other Arabs. They are Christians.

Mr. Greenberg had been reading the letter aloud to Mrs. Greenberg. At this point his breath was coming out in short pants and Mrs. Greenberg was on the verge of fainting. The letter continued:

You'll find more news on the other side of the page.

"What does she say there?" murmured Mrs. Greenberg. Mr. Greenberg turned the page and read:

What I just wrote on the other side of the page about the dark, handsome boy isn't true. I've only been going out with nice Jewish boys. What is true is that I failed Math and Biology and Hebrew; and I did get a D in History and Social Sciences and a C in Musical Appreciation. I just wanted you to realize that, although this is bad, things could have happened here that would have been even worse. As I said, I hope to do better next year—at the University of Arizona.

Your loving daughter,

Sally.

IT'S NOT WHO YOU ARE BUT WHAT YOU'VE GOT
(1968)

For many years hundreds of thousands of people have been coming to Hot Springs, Arkansas, to take advantage of the forty-seven therapeutic springs in and about that city. The waters of these springs are extremely hot. As they emerge from the ground they vary in temperature from 102 to 147 degrees Fahrenheit. They are said to contain more than twenty chemical substances which, singly or in combination, are effective for the alleviation and even cure of certain illnesses.

Three old friends, Manny, Moe, and Jack, came separately to take the baths at Hot Springs. As Fate would have it, they stayed at the same hotel and met in its steam room. Naturally, they quizzed each other about the status of their respective wives and children.

"My son Michael," said Manny, "is vice president of a resident buying office in New York City. He is making every year a quarter of a million dollars."

"My son Jerry," said Moe, "is a sales rep in Florida. He is making some weeks two thousand dollars and some weeks as much as five thousand dollars."

"My son Jonathan," said Jack, "is a rabbi in Kingston-on-the-Hudson. His congregation is paying him a salary of thirty-five thousand dollars a year."

Manny and Moe looked at Jack. Together they chorused, "A rabbi? That's a business for a Jewish boy?!"

The Way It Was
(1970)

When the Texas Jewish youngster came home from religious school, his mother asked him, "And what did you learn in Hebrew school today, Scott?" Scott replied, "Our teacher told us the story about the Israelites crossing the Red Sea."

"Oh, that must have been very interesting. Tell me what she told you."

"Well," said Scott, "it was like this. There were all these Israelites camped for the night by the Red Sea, worn out after their long truck ride from Egypt; and, just as they were about to fall asleep, one of their scouting planes landed and reported that the Pharaoh had left Egypt with three infantry and two armored divisions and that he would catch up with them about daybreak. And Moses told the people not to worry, that everything would be all right, because they had a Military Genius giving them tactical guidance and He would take care of every menacing situation they faced. Early next morning, when the commanders looked through their field glasses, they saw a big cloud of dust approaching from the west. Then the Genius told Moses to have his Chemical Warfare section lay down a smoke screen between themselves and the Egyptians and to have the Engineers build a pontoon bridge across the Red Sea. After the bridge was finished, all the Israelites got across safely just as the Pharaoh and his troops arrived. The Pharaoh immediately ordered his forces to cross the bridge. When they were strung out all along the bridge, the Genius told Moses to send up the Israeli Air Force to plant strings of bombs right on top of the Egyptians. The bridge was destroyed; the Egyptians were all drowned; and in this way Moses, with the guidance of his Military Genius, saved the Israelites from being overcome by the Egyptians."

Mama looked at Scott long and hard. "Are you sure this is really the way your teacher told you that story?"

"No, ma," the boy replied, "but, if I told it to you the way the teacher told it to us, you would never believe it."

The Dog? No, the Yarmelkes!
(1972)

This is a true American Jewish folktale. To conceal the identity of all involved, the year and locale have been changed, and no names will be mentioned.

❊   ❊   ❊   ❊   ❊

A recently ordained Assistant Rabbi in a large Southwestern Reform congregation was called upon to officiate at his first wedding.

The bride was the daughter of a member of the congregation whose community standing was very high. Among the 450 guests present were many socially prominent Jews and non-Jews. The groom, who was from another city, had been reared in traditional fashion and requested that he and his best man, who was also his father, be permitted to wear yarmelkes, a request which was agreeable to the officiating rabbi.

The time arrived in the ceremony for the exchange of rings. The rabbi turned to the best man and asked for the bride's ring. At that precise moment the groom turned, put his fingers in his mouth, and whistled. The rear doors of the sanctuary flew open and in came the family canine, a large Irish setter, with the wedding rings tied around his neck. He bounded down the aisle and up onto the altar, where the groom proceeded to remove the rings from his neck. The dog was then retrieved by a friend and taken to a corner of the sanctuary.

The Assistant Rabbi, with no foreknowledge of this proceeding, was thoroughly amazed. Some say he blanched; others, that his mouth formed the words "What the . . . !" Be that as it may, he continued the ceremony to its conclusion without having to endure any further unanticipated innovations.

Sometime after the wedding, which became the talk of the community, two further incidents were reported to the rabbi:

A member of the congregation who was present at the wedding,

Contributed by the Assistant Rabbi, who shall remain unnamed.

when asked whether such a custom was the norm at Jewish weddings, smiled and replied, "No, but sometimes we use pigeons."

The rabbi's wife went to the hairdresser where she happened to meet another member of the congregation. The congregant, after the usual pleasantries, remarked to the rebbitzin, "Wasn't that terrible about the wedding?" To which the rebbitzin responded, "Yes, it certainly was." "Imagine," said the congregant, "YARMELKES in *our* sanctuary!"

PART SIX

The Far West

"The Blessed Land of Room Enough"

Introduction

The first thing to note about the area we call the Far West—Alaska, California, Colorado, Hawaii, Idaho, Montana, Nevada, Oregon, Utah, Washington, Wyoming—is its size. It is huge, principally because of Alaska, which is two and one-half times larger than Texas. The Far West is big enough to enclose twenty-three New Englands or ten Middle Atlantics or four Souths or the entire Midwest and Southwest combined.

The second noteworthy factor is the lack of geographic cohesion. All other sections form a solid land mass. Not so the Far West. Alaska is separated from its nearest Far Western neighbor by Canada's British Columbia. Hawaii is out in the Pacific Ocean, 2,400 miles from the coast of California. There may be some who will argue that Alaska and Hawaii should not be considered part of the Far West, that each should be regarded as a completely separate entity. Perhaps so. The cartographers do not agree. They include Alaska and Hawaii among the Far Western states.

Just as there is no geographic contiguity there is also no common cultural pattern. The New England Yankee is a cultural type. So are the New Yorker (New York City, that is), the Mideasterner (the occidental variety, of course), the Southerner, the Midwesterner, and the Southwesterner. But the Far Westerner cannot be typed. Not even within the same state. A San Franciscan is in no way like a Los Angeleno. Sometimes not even within the same city. The Las Vegasite who works on the Strip and the Las Vegasite who never goes near the Strip are two entirely different Las Vegasites. How much the more difficult it would be to try to squeeze into the same cultural mold the Alaskan, Hawaiian, Nevadan, Oregonian, and Utahan. Each is unique, both as individual and as socius. The only commonly shared characteristic is that all are American Far Westerners.

California is, Jewishly speaking, a key state. Only New York has more Jews. If the present move away from New York continues, there may well come a day when California will be Number One American

427

Jewish state. In four of the Far Western states (Alaska, Idaho, Montana, and Wyoming), the number of Jews is minuscule. In the remaining six, the Jews are concentrated in a single urban community—Colorado, Denver; Hawaii, Honolulu; Nevada, Las Vegas; Oregon, Portland; Utah, Salt Lake City; Washington, Seattle.

Generally as well as Jewishly, the Far West urban centers are full of muscle, hustle, and bustle; but the section has not yet developed its own discernible temperament. Latest of all sections in terms of expansion and development, it is still experiencing growing pains. Most youthful part of our country, it is in some ways the most innovative and progressive and may in time become the most important.

Alaska

When one thinks of Alaska one must think big. It has more miles of seacoast than the entire eastern United States. Of the 35 active North American volcanoes, 28 are in Alaska. It has the highest mountain in North America, third highest in the world—Mount McKinley, 20,320 feet. The per capita income is the highest in the United States. Tempering this attractive fact is the additional fact that the cost of living in Alaska is also the highest in the United States.

The first white men in Alaska were the Russians, 1741. Their first permanent settlements were on Kodiak Island, 1784, and Sitka Island, 1804. Sitka was named capital of Russian America in 1805. In 1867 the United States bought Russian America for $7,200,000, less than two cents an acre, and renamed it Alaska. It became an American Territory in 1884. Juneau, founded in 1880, succeeded Sitka as territorial capital in 1906. The famous gold rush of 1896 temporarily attracted thousands of fortune hunters but, to use gold mining terminology, the event was a flash in the pan. In 1867 there were about 500 whites and 50,000 Eskimos and Indians in Alaska. Fairbanks was incorporated in 1906 and Anchorage in 1915. As late as 1940 the non-white population was about the same and there were only approximately 15,000 whites.

During and after World War II Alaska experienced a rapid increase in population, industry, and importance. It was admitted to the Union on January 3, 1959, as the 49th state. By 1960 its population had grown to 226,000; by 1970 to 302,000; and by 1976 to 375,000. Anchorage now has a population of about 200,000 or more than half the people in the state. About one-sixth of Alaskans are Eskimos and Indians. The Indians, members of the Athapascan tribe, are racially related to the Navajo and Apache. Eskimos and Indians own their tribal lands and control their tribal affairs.

There may have been a few Jews in Alaska prior to 1867. Jews did not begin to arrive in perceptible numbers until after 1867. The first and only Jewish congregation in Alaska is Temple Beth Sholom of Anchorage, founded in 1958. For twenty years Jewish Air Force chaplains stationed in Alaska served Temple Beth Sholom in addition to their military duties. In July 1978 the congregation's first full-time civilian rabbi was welcomed.

Alaska is estimated to have about 650 Jews, two-tenths of one percent of the population. Four hundred twenty are in Anchorage, 210 in Fairbanks.

California

California, first in human population and third in size among the 50 states, also has the most dogs and cats, about fifty million. It has the highest and lowest points in the contiguous 48 states—Mount Whitney, 14,494 feet above sea level, and Death Valley, 282 feet below sea level. It has the world's tallest tree, a redwood 362 feet high and 44 feet around, on Route 101 south of Eureka. It got its name from an imaginary earthly paradise featured in a novel written in 1510 by a Spaniard.

The area was visited in 1542-43 by Portuguese Jean Cabrillo and in 1579 by English Sir Francis Drake. In 1602-03 Spaniard Sebastian Vizcaino explored San Diego and Monterey bays. The first settlement, a Franciscan mission, San Diego de Alcala, was established by Spanish friar Junipero Serra in 1769, six miles east of present San Diego. In 1770 Monterey became the site of the headquarters of eighteen Spanish military posts strung along the coast. Missions and/or military posts were constructed at the present sites of California urban communities as follows: Los Angeles and Pasadena, 1771; San Francisco, 1776; San José, 1777; Santa Barbara, 1782. On September 4, 1781, "El Pueblo de Nuestra Senora la Reina de Los Angeles," "The Town of Our Lady, Queen of the Angels," now known simply as Los Angeles, was founded by Felipe de Neve, Spanish colonial governor.

In 1821 California became part of the Republic of Mexico. Anglo-American fur trappers began plying their trade in California in 1826. The pueblos of Yerba Buena and Sacramento date from 1834 and 1839 respectively.

California was seized by the Anglo-Americans during the Mexican War. Los Angeles, Mexican territorial capital, was occupied on August 13, 1846. Two days later California was declared a U. S. possession. On January 3, 1847, Navy Lieutenant George Washington Bartlett, military alcalde of Yerba Buena and said to have had a Jewish mother, changed the name of the pueblo to San Francisco. By the treaty of 1848 California was ceded to the United States.

Before the war ended gold was discovered, on January 24, 1848, at Sutter's Mill, Coloma, about 35 miles northeast of Sacramento. Eighteen hundred forty-nine, the year of the great California gold rush, brought tens of thousands of American and foreign fortune seekers to the discovery area. This same year San Jose was set up as the territorial capital. California was admitted into the Union as its 31st state on September 9, 1850. In 1854 Sacramento became the state capital. An attempt to create an independent Pacific republic, in which slavery would have been permitted, was foiled. In the Civil War the state remained loyal to the Union.

While California's attitude toward black slavery was commendable, the same cannot be said for its manner of handling Mexicans, Chinese, and Japanese. California's Mexicans felt they had been conquered by an alien aggressor. They waged guerrilla warfare against the hated gringo until nearly the end of the 1870s. The Anglos regarded these Mexican patriots as bandits and treated them accordingly. The Chinese, imported in large numbers during and after the gold rush to provide cheap labor for the consruction of towns and railroads, were regarded as untouchables and dealt with inhumanely. The confinement of loyal Japanese issei and nisei in concentration camps in World War II and the heartless confiscation of much of their property were acts of racial bigotry and stupidity.

The first California immigrant positively identified as Jewish is Jacob Frankfort, a tailor, who came to Los Angeles in 1841. The first absolutely authentic San Francisco Jews arrived on February 26, 1849, aboard the first Pacific Mail steamer. The first semblance of organized Jewish life was the holding of Yom Kippur services in San Francisco in 1849. Shortly thereafter two San Francisco congregations came into being, Shearith Israel (East European nusach) and Emanuel (West European nusach). At almost the same time a congregation was born at Coloma. High Holyday services were held in 1851 in San Diego. The San Francisco congregations completed their first synagogue buildings almost simultaneously in 1854.

Many California mining camps and communities had Jewish congregations and cemeteries and Hebrew Benevolent Societies. Few managed to survive beyond 1870. Early congregations still in existence are: 1852, Bnai Israel, Sacramento; 1855, Re'im Ahuvim (Temple Israel), Stockton; 1857, Bnai Brith, Marysville; 1862, Congregation Bnai Berith (Wilshire Boulevard Temple), Los Angeles.

There are now approximately 700,000 Jews in California, 3.1 percent of the total population. The principal Jewish communities are: Greater Los Angeles, 455,000; San Francisco, 75,000; Orange County, 35,000; Alameda and Contra Costa Counties, 28,000; San Diego, 21,000; Long Beach, 16,000; San José, 13,000; Santa Monica, 8,000.

Colorado

Colorado is the most mountainous of all the United States. The average altitude is 6,800 feet. It has fifteen hundred mountains more than 10,000 feet high. Mount Elbert, 14,433, Mount Massive, 14,421, and Mount Harvard, 14,420, are the second, third, and fourth highest mountains in the continental United States.

The first Europeans in this region were Spaniards from Mexico desiring gold and silver or wishing to convert the Indian natives to Christianity. The first was probably Francisco Coronado in 1540. In 1776 friars Escalante and Dominguez traveled through the southern section seeking a route to California through the mountains. In 1803 the northeastern half was acquired by the United States through the Louisiana Purchase. In 1806 Army Captain Zebulun M. Pike, while mapping the area, discovered the mountain that bears his name. From 1842 to 1845, John C. Fremont, guided by Kit Carson, explored much of the region. The southwestern half became Anglo-American in 1848 at the end of the Mexican War.

The area was sparsely settled until 1858, when gold was discovered near Pike's Peak. This led to an east-to-west human stampede which rapidly increased Colorado's population. Denver was settled that year and became the supply center for the mining camps. The gold veins were soon exhausted and many disappointed prospectors went elsewhere. The largest camp, Oro City, was almost completely deserted by 1868. Central City, founded west of Denver in 1859, was long a ghost town before being revived as a tourist attraction and a summer cultural center.

In 1861 Colorado became a territory with its capital at Colorado City, twenty-five miles south of Pueblo trading post. The next year the capital was moved to Golden, fifteen miles west of Denver. In 1868 the capital made its third and final move to Denver. On August 1, 1876, Colorado was admitted into the Union as the 38th state.

In 1874 came a second big rush to the mines, this time because of large silver and lead deposits found in the central and southwestern sections of the state. The largest camp was at Leadville, a few miles northwest of ghostly Oro City. Leadville was incorporated in 1878 and, for the next fifteen years, was an important and wealthy community. At its peak it had more than 15,000 people. It is still a mining center with a present population of about 4,000. Trinidad, hub of a large ranching industry, was incorporated in 1876, and Aspen, another mining community, in 1880.

Colorado's third and final taste of mining glory came in 1890 with the uncovering of a rich gold vein twenty miles west of Pike's Peak. This brought into being the mining towns of Cripple Creek and Victor, whose size and prosperity dwindled rapidly after 1905. Touring the ghost town of Cripple Creek is now one of Colorado's tourist attractions.

In the spring of 1859 the three Salomon brothers opened a general store in Denver. By autumn the town had more than a minyan of young, ambitious Jews and High Holyday services were held. The first Denver congregation, Temple Emanuel (Reform) was established in 1873 and built its first synagogue in 1876. Temple Israel (Reform) of Leadville was born in 1879 and erected a synagogue in 1884 on land donated by millionaire philanthropist Horace A. Tabor. Congregation Aaron (Reform) of Trinidad was organized in 1883 and built its synagogue in 1889. Keneseth Israel (Orthodox) of Leadville purchased an old Presbyterian church in 1892 and, with the financial assistance of millionaire Tabor, turned it into a synagogue. Other early Colorado congregations were: 1895, Bnai Jacob (Orthodox) but now United Hebrew Center (Conservative), Pueblo; 1897, Beth Hamedrash Hagadol (Conservative), Denver; 1899, Congregation Emanuel (Reform), Pueblo.

Colorado's Jews numbered about 32,000 in 1978 and are 1.2 percent of the total population. The largest Jewish communities are Denver, 30,000; Colorado Springs, 650; and Pueblo, 375.

Hawaii

Hawaii, an archipelago of 132 islands (seven inhabited), chiefly volcanic in origin, is located in the mid-Pacific, 2,400 miles west of the American mainland. Its climate is perpetually that of mild summer. The highest recorded temperature is 88, the lowest 56, the mean 74.6. Its chief industries, listed in order of importance, are: tourism, the military, sugar, pineapple. The 1970 census indicated that the racial origins of its present population are: Caucasian, 39.2 percent; Japanese, 28.3 percent; Hawaiian, Chinese, Filipino, Korean, and mixed, 32.5 percent.

Hawaii is believed to have been settled by Polynesians about 700 c.e. The first white man to visit was Captain James Cook in 1778. He named the archipelago the Sandwich Islands. The natives called the islands Owhyhee, meaning "homeland," from which the modern name is appropriately derived.

Until 1790 each major island was governed by its own native ruler, but in 1790 King Kamehameha established his rule over the entire archipelago. American missionaries arrived in 1820 and American businessmen in 1835. In 1893 a rebellion fomented by American commercial interests ended the Kamehameha dynasty by removing Queen Liliukalani from the throne. On July 4, 1894, the Republic of Hawaii was proclaimed, with Anglo-Hawaiian Sanford B. Dole as President. In 1898 the United States annexed the islands and set up the Territory of Hawaii with Sanford B. Dole as governor. On August 21, 1959, Hawaii was admitted to the Union as the 50th state.

In 1976 there were 887,000 persons residing in Hawaii. Eighty-one percent lived in Greater Honolulu.

It is said that there have been Jewish merchants living in Honolulu since about 1856. There is no indication of any organized Jewish life until 1930, when a Bnai Brith lodge was organized. Temple Emanuel (Reform) of Honolulu dates from 1935. In 1939 it bought a church for use as its synagogue. There is also in Honolulu a Jewish military congregation which worships in the Aloha Jewish Chapel and a Conservative congregation, Congregation Sof Ma'ariv.

Hawaii's 1,500 civilian Jews form two-tenths of one percent of the total civilian population. Almost every Hawaiian Jew lives in Honolulu.

Idaho

Idaho was part of the "Oregon country," whose ownership was originally claimed by Spain, Russia, Great Britain, and the United States. Spain relinquished its claim in 1819, Russia in 1824, and Great Britain in 1846.

The region was explored by Lewis and Clark in 1805. The first trading post within Idaho's present borders was built by the British in 1809. The first permanent settlement was that of the Mormons in 1860 at Franklin, just over the Utah border. In 1863 Boise was founded and the Territory of Idaho was established, with its capital at Lewiston. In 1865 the capital was moved to Boise.

The Nez Perce, a well organized and highly intelligent Indian tribe, controlled much of northwest Idaho and hindered white development in that area. In 1877 the tribe was forced to give up most of its land. It is now limited to a reservation in western Idaho that abuts the borders of Oregon and Washington. In 1884 the discovery of silver near Coeur d'Alene in northern Idaho brought many new settlers into that area. Ever since, Idaho has led all the states in the annual production of silver. Idaho was admitted into the Union on July 3, 1890, as the nation's 43rd state.

David Falk and Joseph Alexander, the first Jews to settle in Idaho, opened a store in Boise in 1865.

In 1895 Congregation Beth Israel (Reform) was organized in Boise at a meeting in the home of Moses Alexander, a German-born Jew who had come to the city in 1891 and was not related to Joseph Alexander. David Falk was elected congregational president and Moses Alexander vice president. In 1895 Beth Israel completed and dedicated its synagogue. Moses Alexander served as mayor of Boise, 1897-99 and 1901-03. A second congregation was formed in Boise in 1912, Ahavas Israel, originally Orthodox and now Conservative. Moses Alexander was Governor of

Idaho from 1915 to 1919, the first American foreign-born Jew to be so honored. In 1949 Ahavas Israel built a synagogue. By 1967 there were so few Reform Jews in Boise that services were being held only on the High Holydays. Since then there has been a slight increase in the Reform Jewish group and services are now held at Temple Beth Israel once a month. Conservative Congregation Ahavas Israel has a full-time rabbi and a regular schedule of services. There is also a small Conservative congregation in Pocatello.

Idaho has about 650 Jews, one-tenth of one per cent of the total population. Two hundred Jews live in Boise.

Montana

The part of Montana lying east of the Continental Divide was acquired by the United States in 1803 through the Louisiana Purchase. The part lying west of the Divide was gotten in 1846 through an agreement with Great Britain.

While there may have been French fur trappers in the area in earlier years, the first definitely known whites to explore the region was the Lewis and Clark expedition in 1805. A trading post was set up in 1807 by a fur trader from St. Louis at the junction of the Yellowstone and Big Horn rivers, about sixty miles east of present-day Billings. The first permanent settlement, 1847, was Fort Benton, fifty miles northeast of present-day Great Falls.

The discovery of gold in southwestern Montana in 1858 brought a surge of immigrants into the region. The Territory of Montana was set up in 1864. Its first capital was the mining town of Bannack and later the mining town of Virginia City. In 1876 the capital was moved north to Helena. The years of settlement of Montana's leading communities were: Helena and Missoula, 1864; Butte, 1866; Great Falls, 1884. On November 8, 1889, Montana was admitted into the Union as the 41st state.

The history of the Jewish community of Montana is a history of steady decline in numbers and importance.

There was a high percentage of Jews among those who came into the Montana gold fields in the 1860s. Jews were with the vigilantes who suppressed outlawry in Virginia City in the early days. Two of Butte's first three mayors were Jews. Charles M. Russell, famed Western artist, worked as a cowboy for a Jewish rancher. As the years went on, the state's Jewish population shrunk. In 1917 there were still 2,500 Jews in Montana; in 1940, 1,800; in 1977, 550. The Jews constitute one-tenth of one percent of the total population.

Temple Emanuel of Helena was founded in 1887. Its synagogue was built in 1891. The first rabbi was Samuel Schulman—later the rabbi of another Temple Emanuel, the one on Fifth Avenue in New York City.

The Jewish population of Helena declined to a point where the synagogue was no longer used and so the remaining Jews gave it to the state of Montana. In 1897 Bnai Israel of Butte was organized as a Reform congregation. It is now Conservative. At a much later date Reform Congregation Beth Aaron of Billings came into being. It has the state's only rabbi. He is now seventy-nine years old. He is likely to be the last rabbi to serve a Montana congregation for some time to come.

Nevada

A few Mexican priests and Canadian trappers penetrated the outskirts of what is now Nevada in the late eighteenth and early nineteenth centuries. The first white man to cross the entire area from east to west was American Jedidiah Smith in 1826. The first to explore the region systematically was John C. Fremont, 1843-45. Awarded to the United States at the end of the Mexican War, the area became in 1850 part of the Territory of Utah.

The first settlement, near Lake Tahoe by Mormons in 1849, was known initially as Mormon Station and later as Genoa. That same year gold was discovered a few miles from Mormon Station. This caused a large influx into the neighborhood and the rapid growth and development of Virginia City and Carson City. Las Vegas was also, in its beginning, a Mormon farming community. Thirty families settled it in 1855; but it did not become an incorporated community until 1905. Reno dates from 1868.

In 1859 the discovery of the Comstock Lode, an exceedingly large deposit of gold and silver ore in the bowels of Mount Davidson, greatly increased the size and importance of both Virginia City and Carson City. Virginia City was located on the very top of the mountain and Carson City near the base of its southern slope. For almost thirty-five years Virginia City was one of the richest and most glamorous boom towns in the West, providing all the luxuries and types of entertainment relished by lusty he-men and the kind of women whose pleasure and/or business it is to cater to such men.

In 1861 Nevada achieved separate territorial status, with its capital at Carson City. On October 31, 1864, Nevada was admitted into the Union as the 36th state.

By 1893 the quality of the ore being taken from the Comstock Lode had deteriorated considerably. In that year the passage of the Sherman Silver Act depressed the price of silver and bankrupted the silver mining industry. Virginia City rapidly became a ghost town. In recent years it has made a strong comeback as a tourist attraction. Today the sound of the slot machine is loudly heard in its resurrected buildings.

In the twentieth century Nevada has attained international notoriety by becoming an oasis of voluptuousness in a nation that still contains a high percentage of "squares." It is the most wide-open state in the United States. Its biggest attractions are legalized prostitution and gambling and "quickie" marriages and divorces. Because of these goodies, tourism is Nevada's chief industry. Forty-five percent of the state's revenue comes from gambling taxes. Its chief centers of commercialized gaiety are Las Vegas, Reno, and Lake Tahoe.

Nevada's population in 1978 was 610,000. Its largest cities are: Las Vegas, 360,000; Reno, 94,000; Carson City, 22,500.

The first Jews arrived in Nevada in 1859 shortly after the discovery of the Comstock Lode. By 1862 there were 200 in the mining towns. Few were miners. Most were storekeepers and artisans. Also most were of German origin and ethnic rather than religious Jews. In May 1862 a Bnai Brith lodge was formed in Virginia City; in November 1862 a cemetery was purchased, which is again being used by the revived Virginia City community. But Virginia City had no synagogue and no rabbi. A high percentage of these German Jewish frontiersmen intermarried, assimilated, and disappeared. In 1875 a small group of East European Jews formed an Orthodox congregation in Virginia City, a congregation which their German brethren scorned and refused to join. It is estimated that in 1880 Nevada had 800 Jews among its 62,000 total. When the silver bubble burst in 1893, most of the Jews left. In 1897 there were only 250 Jews in a state population of 45,000.

The first Nevada synagogue was Temple Emanuel in Reno in 1921, originally Orthodox and now Conservative. Since then a Reform congregation has been established. Las Vegas has two comparatively recent congregations, Conservative and Reform. There are 12,000 Jews in Nevada, two percent of the total population. Eleven thousand are in Las Vegas and 400 in Reno.

Oregon

The first sea captain who recorded landing on the coast of what is now Oregon was the Spaniard Bruno Heceta in 1775. He claimed the area for Spain. In 1792 Captain Robert Gray, a Boston fur trader, discovered and named the Columbia River. On the slim basis of the latter bit of history, the United States put in a bid for ownership of all the land drained by the river. In 1805-06 Lewis and Clark explored the Columbia's entire length.

The first permanent settlement was in 1811 by agents of John Jacob Astor's American Fur Company at Astoria at the mouth of the Columbia. During the War of 1812 the British occupied "the Oregon country." Afterward it was jointly settled and used by British and Americans. In

1846 a treaty was signed in which Great Britain acknowledged United States sovereignty over the region. In 1849 the Territory of Oregon was formed. It included all of present-day Oregon, Washington, Idaho, and western Montana.

Salem was founded in 1840 by missionary Jason Lee. The first large wave of immigrants came in from the East and Midwest in 1843 over the Oregon Trail. Portland was settled in 1851 and Eugene in 1854. On February 14, 1859, Oregon was admitted into the Union as the 33rd state, with its capital at Salem.

As early as 1849 a few Jews came into Oregon and worked as countryside peddlers. By 1857 a number had established thriving businesses in Portland. Oregon's first Jewish congregation, Portland's Beth Israel, dates from 1858. It started out Orthodox but soon became Reform. This led to a congregational split in 1866 and the formation of Congregation Ohawei Sholom, which began Orthodox and became Conservative. Beth Israel was known as the "Deutsche Schul" and Ohawei Sholom as the "Polishe Schul." In 1889 another Orthodox synagogue, Neveh Zedeck, was founded. It was referred to as the "Russische Schul." It, too, became Conservative. In 1962 Ohawei Sholom and Neveh Zedeck merged into one Conservative synagogue named Congregation Neveh Shalom. In 1905 a fourth Orthodox congregation, Shaarei Torah, was formed. It has managed to remain Orthodox.

The Jewish population of Oregon which, from the beginning, has been located almost entirely in Portland, increased until World War II and then, for a reason not readily apparent, began to decline. There were 6,000 Jews in Oregon in 1901, one percent of the total population; 12,000 in 1940, 1.1 percent of the total. In 1978 the number of Jews was down to 9,000, only four tenths of one percent of the state's population. The principle Jewish communities are Portland, 7,800; Eugene, 360; Salem, 200.

Utah

Parts of Utah were explored in 1776 by Franciscan friars Escalante and Dominguez. In 1825 James Bridger, an American fur trapper, reported finding the Great Salt Lake, which, it was later learned, has a salt density exceeded by only two other bodies of water in the world, Turkey's Lake Van and Israel's Dead Sea. In 1826 Jedidiah Smith studied the area west of the lake. In 1843-45 John C. Fremont conducted mapping expeditions through the area east of the lake.

All this time Utah was technically part of Mexico. In July 1847, while the Mexican War was in progress, the first Mormon colony was established at the present site of Salt Lake City. At the conclusion of the war

Utah became United States territory. The Mormons set up the State of Deseret and asked to be admitted to the Union. Their request was refused six times because of their religious advocacy of plural marriages.

In 1850 the Territory of Utah was formed. It also included present-day Nevada. Brigham Young, prominent Mormon leader, was named first governor. In 1890 the Mormon Church officially abandoned the practice of polygamy. On January 4, 1896, Utah was admitted into the Union as the 45th state.

In 1978 72 percent of Utah's population was Mormon.

The Mormon religion teaches that there are two categories of believers, Mormons and non-Mormons. Non-Mormons are subdivided further into Jews and Gentiles. Jews are known as "our brother Jews." They are considered God's Chosen and are looked upon with high and affectionate regard. Mormons are warmly attached to the Land of Israel and strong supporters of the State of Israel. From the Mormon religious position a Jew is less of an unbeliever than a Gentile. The relationship between Mormons and Jews in Utah has always been exceptionally good.

The first Jews to settle in Salt Lake City were Julius and Fanny Brooks. They came from Galena, Illinois, in 1853 in a prairie schooner and opened a millinery and a bakery. The Jewish community did not grow quickly. The first High Holyday services were held in 1864. The first synagogue, Congregation Bnai Israel, was organized in 1881. It switched from Orthodox to Reform in 1884. This caused a split. The families who withdrew conducted Orthodox services but did not formally incorporate as Congregation Montefiore until 1899. Congregation Montefiore is now Conservative. The only other synagogue in Utah prior to the twentieth century was Congregation Ohab Sholem (Orthodox), Ogden, 1890. Its membership is presently very small. It has not had a rabbi since 1935. And it has changed its name from Ohab Sholem to Brith Sholem.

The Utah Jewish community has never been large nor has its growth kept pace with that of the general community. In 1902 there were 1,000 Jews in a total population of 297,000 or 0.3 percent; in 1943, 1,900 of 586,000 or again 0.3 percent; in 1978, 2,160 of 1,228,000 or 0.2 percent. The principle Jewish communities are in Salt Lake City, 1,950, and Ogden, 100.

Simon Bamberger, 1847-1926, one of the founders of Salt Lake City's Congregation Bnai Israel, was the first non-Mormon governor of Utah, 1917-21.

Washington

Until 1853 Washington was part of "the Oregon country." In 1853 Washington was designated a separate territory, with its capital at

Olympia. Its present boundaries were not fixed until the Territory of Idaho was split away from it in 1863. Washington was admitted to the Union on November 11, 1889, as the 42nd state.

The first permanent settlement was at Tumwater in 1845. Two years later and two miles from Tumwater, another town started that eventually became Olympia and the state's capital. The birth-years of other important Washington cities are 1851, Seattle; 1868, Tacoma; 1872, Spokane.

The first Jew known to have settled in the Territory of Washington was Sigmund Schwabacher who opened a grocery in Walla Walla in 1862. Seven years later he moved to Seattle and established a wholesale grocery firm, Schwabacher Brothers and Company, which became one of the state's leading wholesale firms.

The first congregation, Ohabath Sholom of Seattle, dates from 1887. In 1899 it was reorganized as Reform Temple de Hirsch. In 1890 Congregation Emanuel was started in Spokane. It became Reform in 1935. Some years later it ceased to exist. Orthodox Chevra Bikur Cholum, Seattle, organized in 1892, is now the synagogue of Seattle's large Sephardic community. Reform Congregation Beth Israel, now Beth El, of Tacoma was also founded in 1892.

The trend mentioned in connection with Oregon is also true of Washington. There was a steady increase in Washington's Jewish population until World War II. Since then there has been a steady decrease. In 1978 Washington had 16,000 Jews or four-tenths of one percent of the total population. Seattle had 13,000 Jews, Spokane 800, Tacoma 700.

Wyoming

John Coulter, a member of the Lewis and Clark expedition, traversed the Yellowstone area in 1807. In 1824 white traders began to do business with the Indians in this region. The first white settlement was Fort Laramie, 1834. For fifteen years it was the center of the fur trade in eastern Wyoming. In 1843 Fort Bridger was built in the southwestern corner of the area. A chain of military posts was set up between Forts Laramie and Bridger to protect Oregon Trail travelers from the Indians. The Mormons, the California gold seekers, the Pony Express and, finally, the Union Pacific Railroad crossed Wyoming under the watchful eyes of these garrisons. Advance agents of the U.P.R.R. founded Cheyenne in the southeastern corner, just north of Colorado, in 1868.

In 1868 the Territory of Wyoming was created. In 1869 the legislature gave Wyoming women the right to vote in territorial elections, the first such legislative action in the United States. In 1872 the first national park, Yellowstone, was established in Wyoming. Wyoming was admitted into the Union on July 10, 1890, as the 44th state, with its capital at Cheyenne.

A few months after Cheyenne was born, German Jewish immigrant

Henry Altman went there to work as an itinerant peddler among the gangs that were constructing the Union Pacific tracks. In 1875 Altman went into the cattle raising business with partner Joseph Wasserman and became one of Wyoming's best known and most successful ranchers.

In 1880 it was estimated that there were forty Jews in Wyoming; in 1897, 1,000; in 1927, 1,320. Since the 1930s, Wyoming's Jewish population has steadily gotten smaller. In 1940 there were 1,000 out of a total population of 247,000; in 1978, 345 in a total population of 390,000. Two hundred eighty Jews live in Cheyenne. The only synagogue in the state is Mount Sinai Congregation of Cheyenne, Orthodox, organized in 1915.

The four American states having the tiniest percentages of Jews, listed from lonely low to lonelier lowest are: Wyoming, one Jew for every 1,130 non-Jews; Idaho, one Jew for every 1,132 non-Jews; Montana, one Jew for every 1,139 non-Jews; and South Dakota, one Jew for every 1,141 non-Jews.

—D.M.E.

Norton I, Emperor of the United States
(1859)

Joshua Abraham Norton was born in London in 1819. When he was about a year old, his father, John, emigrated to Cape Colony, South Africa, with his wife Sarah and two sons. They were among 4,000 Britishers who were brought in by the English government that year to colonize the eastern province of the colony. There are said to have been about a hundred Jews among these new colonists. The Norton family settled on farming land near Algoa Bay. In 1837 John Norton gave up farming and opened a store in Grahamstown. Joshua and his brother clerked in their father's establishment.

John Norton was a faithful Jew. In 1841 he helped organize Congregation Tikvath Israel of Capetown, the first Jewish congregation in South Africa. He attended its services mostly on the major holy days. To go to Capetown from Grahamstown was a 500-mile round trip, not the kind of journey one could take very often in those pioneer years.

Beginning in 1844, one misfortune after another struck the Norton household. First the Grahamstown store went bankrupt. In the next four years, Joshua's mother, then his brother, then his father died. By 1848 Joshua, who never married, was completely alone. He was tall, muscular, handsome, very popular, but not, like his father, religiously inclined. So far as is known he never affiliated with a synagogue in his entire lifetime. He decided to go to California and begin life anew.

Norton arrived in San Francisco on November 5, 1849, aboard the sailing vessel *Franziska* out of Hamburg. It carried him from South Africa to California via Rio and Valparaiso. Two months later he opened a mercantile shop that rapidly prospered. Success went to the young man's head. He speculated heavily in the commodity market and lost.

This article is based on (1) Louis Herman's "The Fantastic Career of Joshua Abraham Norton" in *Essays in Honor of Rabbi J. H. Hertz*, London, 1943, pp. 227-38; and (2) Theodore Kirchhoff's "Norton the First" in the *California Pioneers Quarterly*, Volume V, 1928, pp. 205-12.

Then his store suffered a devastating fire. In 1856 he went into bank-ruptcy, hopelessly insolvent. Ten years of continuous ups and downs, with the downs far outweighing the ups, were just too much, and Norton had a nervous breakdown. He emerged from the ordeal a changed person. In fact it would be accurate to say that, as a result of his misfortunes, he became an entirely new being.

❄   ❄   ❄   ❄

Toward the end of 1859 Joshua Abraham Norton issued a proclama-tion to the people of the State of California. On February 1, 1860, a new order and a new government would be inaugurated in the United States of America. The head of this new order and new government would be himself, Emperor Norton the First. From that time on, until he died twenty years later, Joshua Abraham Norton walked, talked, and acted like the monarch he professed to be.

He claimed he was the natural son of George IV of England and, consequently, the first cousin of Queen Victoria. He had placards printed and distributed around San Francisco stating that his entitlement to nobility and his right to ascend the American throne had been validated by the California state legislature. Shortly thereafter, His Royal Highness assumed another title, that of "Protector of Mexico." Duly awed and impressed, the City Council declared him the city's first and only "free citizen." The citizens of San Francisco were officially requested to give Norton the First anything he desired without charge. In consequence he exacted cigars as tribute from cigar stores, meals from restaurants, wearing apparel from clothing stores, drinks in saloons, and he rode without paying on the trolley cars. On one occasion, when he was greatly in need of a new uniform, the city fathers voted to provide him with such through a grant from the municipal treasury.

He extracted "taxes" from willing and amused San Franciscans in amounts normally ranging from two to ten dollars. Small contributions were acknowledged with a word of thanks. Larger ones were honored by a written receipt, signed "Norton I, Emperor of the United States of America," and bearing the imperial golden seal. He did not live in regal style. His life pattern was modest. The money he requisitioned was spent on room rent, laundry, and other personal necessities. He was very generous. A sizable proportion of his take was distributed among those whose lack he believed was greater than his.

He attended every important public gathering and major theatrical presentation. On all such occasions he appeared in uniform, was never asked to pay, and was ushered to the best seat available. His regular attire consisted of a blue-green coat with long tails, bright blue trousers with red side-stripes, gold epaulettes, and headgear of either a high hat with red cockade and long aigrette or a general's cap with a heron's plume. On very special occasions he wore a massive sword. On ordinary days he carried a heavy walking stick or a red cotton umbrella. He always had a red rose in his coat lapel and a brightly colored silk kerchief in his breast pocket. Since he was afflicted with corns, his shoes were cut out in front to relieve his discomfort. Despite this affliction he was a tireless walker.

Whenever the California Senate was in session Emperor Norton traveled to Sacramento to attend its deliberations. A special chair, large and comfortable, was reserved for his use. He listened attentively to the discussions and debates. He took voluminous notes in a big black book. Only once in all his years of attendance did he attempt to interfere with the legislative process. When Ulysses S. Grant sought to be nominated for a third term as U. S. President, the Emperor ordered the California Senate to protest. When it did not obey his command, he sent a telegram to Grant instructing him to cease attempting to get the nomination.

He belonged to no church or synagogue but attended religious services of every major denomination, including the Roman Catholic, even though he was an ardent Mason. He referred to God in all his proclamations but never mentioned Jesus Christ. He read and studied the Bible often and devoutly.

Part of the Norton legend is that in the early years, wherever he went, he was accompanied by two beautiful collies, Bummer and Lazarus. Lazarus is said to have died in 1868 and Bummer in 1870. They were given public funerals attended by large numbers of people and were buried in graves on a cliff overlooking San Francisco Bay. Norton missed them greatly. They were the only creatures he ever truly loved.... According to Rabbi William Kramer, eminent California Jewish historian, this canine tale is pure fiction.

A cartoonist once drew a caricature of the Emperor and his dogs, showing Norton having a free lunch and the dogs eating the scraps he was throwing to them. The cartoon was displayed in a downtown store window. Upon learning of this public evidence of lese majesty, Norton went to the storefront, viewed the cartoon, roared "This is an outrageous insult to the dignity of an Emperor," smashed through the window with his heavy cane and destroyed the cartoon. This is the only known instance during his entire reign when the Emperor committed what some might consider an illegal act. He was by nature very kind and courteous and seldom lost his temper.

From time to time Norton I issued proclamations of considerable national significance. In 1862 he published a decree abolishing the offices of President and Vice President of the United States. In March of 1864 he commanded Abraham Lincoln and Jefferson Davis to appear before him so that he might make known to them a procedure for bringing the Civil War to a speedy conclusion. During a nationwide economic depression in the fall of 1870, he issued elaborate one-dollar Norton treasury certificates, bearing seven percent interest and maturing in 1880. He sold them all. For many years the certificates were on display in many San Francisco offices and homes as treasured souvenirs of a beloved eccentric. As a Briton of noble birth he hated everything French. He despised Napoleon I and loathed Napoleon III. When Prussia defeated France in 1871 the Emperor declared a week of national thanksgiving.

Emperor Norton the First [and the Last] died on January 8, 1880. His death was mourned sincerely. The Pacific Union Club of San Francisco paid for his funeral, which was attended by more than 10,000 people. A choir of 200 children sang his favorite hymns. He was buried in the Masonic Cemetery.

Later he was commemorated in a poem written by Dr. George Chismore:

> No more through the crowded streets he goes,
> With his shambling gait and shabby clothes,
> And his furtive glance and whiskered nose—
>   Immersed in cares of state.
> The serpent twisted upon his staff
> Is not less careful of idle chaff,
> The mocking speech or the scornful laugh,
>   Than he who bore it late.
>
> His nerveless grasp has released the helm,
> But ere the Lethean flood shall whelm
> The last faint trace of his fancied realm,
>   Let us contrast his fate
> With other rulers and other reigns
> Of royal birth or scheming brains,
> And see if his crazy life contains
>   So much to deprecate.
>
> No traitorous friends or vigilant foes
> Rippled the stream of his calm repose;
> No fear of exile before him rose,
>   Whose empire was his pate;
> No soldiers died to uphold his fame;
> He found no pleasure in woman's shame;
> For wasted wealth no well-earned blame
>   Turned subjects' love to hate.
>
> No long and weary struggle with pain;
> One sudden throe in his clouded brain
> Closed forever his bloodless reign.
>   With every man his friend

For death alone did he abdicate.
What Emperor, Prince, or potentate
Can long avoid a similar fate
    Or win a better end?

In 1934 a committee of prominent San Franciscans raised a fund which was used to erect a redstone monument over the grave of their never-to-be-forgotten royal sovereign. The stone bears the following inscription:

NORTON I
Emperor
of the United States
and
Protector of Mexico

———

Joshua A. Norton
1819-1880

Chanukah and Christmas
(1866)

While the Jews lived in the medieval ghettos and during the early years of Emancipation, no self-respecting Jew would have given the slightest thought to celebrating Christmas in any way whatsoever. But, as the Jew moved away from the periphery and toward the center of the non-Jewish scheme of things, he became engulfed during the entire month of December by the trappings of Christmas. Attracted by the tinsel and the singing and the tree and the gift-giving and Santa Klaus and the empty talk about peace and good will, Jews, especially the children, began to mistake the shadow for the substance and to think that Christmas is a holiday well worth celebrating and that it's just too bad that God has deprived the Jews of taking part in such a meaningful and beautiful experience.

From about the middle of the nineteenth century this became a serious problem for the Jews of the United States. In self-defense they took the most minor of Jewish holidays, Chanukah, the only one that is

---

The material about Rabbi Julius Eckman has been taken, with permission, from an article written by Rabbi Stanley F. Chyet of Los Angeles, California, "Chanukah and Christmas" in the *Jewish Frontier*, December 1963, pp. 29-31.

post-Biblical but also the only one that occurs during the month of December, and made of it a major holiday in a valiant effort to combat the Christmas spirit. The result has been only moderately successful. Too many Jewish parents are unable to convince themselves that Chanukah is as important to the Jew as Christmas is to both Christian and Jew. Being themselves unconvinced, they have done a good job of conveying their ambivalence to their children.

Evidence of this uncomfortable situation began to appear in Jewish periodicals more than a century ago.

✻   ✻   ✻   ✻   ✻

San Francisco supplies a typical instance of a nineteenth-century traditional rabbi criticizing Jews for denying their Jewish identity through Christmas celebrations.

In February 1867 *The Occident,* a leading Jewish periodical of Philadelphia, printed an article entitled "Hannucah and Christmas" by Dr. Julius Eckman of San Francisco. German-born Dr. Eckman may not have been one of the best known Jewish leaders in America but he was surely among the most energetic. After officiating in a number of southern congregations he came to San Francisco in 1854 as Temple Emanu-El's first rabbi. There, in the frenetic gold rush atmosphere, he also founded a religious school and a newspaper, the *Weekly Gleaner.* In 1860 Eckman went off to China on a "missionary" venture to help restore the old Jewish congregation in the province of Honan.

By 1866 Eckman was back from China. In December 1866 he reproved San Francisco Jews among whom "their own festival" of Chanukah was "scarce noticed" while Christmas was "celebrated with presents to their children and illumination in their parlors." The rabbi resented "such a forgetfulness of what concerns us immediately, and such an injudicious celebration of what concerns us but distantly." Jews guilty of "such a want of taste," he said, came rarely from "families of education and refinement"; usually, they were "ignorant fathers" and "mothers whom nature intended to fill positions as honorable house-wives in the kitchen, but whom fortune, by her freaks, has misplaced into the parlor." Only those "who know little of Judaism and less of Christianity" would "betray their littleness of mind and their misplacement by fortune by playing such a ridiculous part as for a Jew to be aping Christmas."

Though Eckman thought it "quite improper" and "perverse" for Jews "to ignore their holy days and celebrate those of Christians," he disclaimed on his part any intention of disparaging Christianity or of denying "the great benefit Christianity has proved to the gentile world." It was simply that a Jew who admitted Christmas trees and Christmas presents into his home was committing "an act of denial of identity—an attempt to appear to be what he is not." Such a Jew was playing "the pigmy while he ought to prove himself a giant," and "self-negation" of this sort "must meet with the condemnation of the sincere Jew and the contempt of the intelligent Christian." It would also render its perpetrator "contemptible in the eyes of his children, who, one day, will find out the imbecility of their parents and will judge them accordingly."

Eckman made no mention in his article of Temple Emanu-El, where he had been rabbi, but one wonders whether he had in mind members of that congregation. Since his departure from Emanu-El's pulpit, Reform Judaism had made its appearance there in the person of Dr. Elkan Cohn, a German intellectual who came to America in 1854 and to Emanu-El in 1860. Dr. Cohn had not been in San Francisco very long when, according to a report in *The Occident*, he made short shrift of Chanukah. "On the Sabbath before Hannucah," reported *The Occident*, "Dr. Cohn explained the meaning of the festival, and why our ancestors lit lamps in order to celebrate it; but that now we required only the light of religion in our hearts. In consequence of this edict ex cathedra no lamps were lighted as usual in the Synagogue." Might not the careful reader of Dr. Eckman's feuilleton have recalled Dr. Cohn's "edict" and asked himself how Dr. Cohn viewed Christmas? Indeed, how Reform Judaism viewed Christmas?

Today, however, the picture is quite different. The radical Reform of an Elkan Cohn has succumbed to the exigencies of the twentieth century—to the rise of an American Jewry overwhelmingly East European in ancestry, to the ferment of Zionism and the trauma of anti-Semitism. Whatever Dr. Cohn's view of Christmas was, and whatever Reform Judaism may have thought of Christmas and Chanukah observance in the 1860s, in our own day there is no doubt about Reform's adherence to Chanukah and rejection of Christmas as a holiday for Jews. Chukkot ha-goyim [un-Jewish customs] remains a problem in Jewish life, but today that problem meets as much resistance from the Reform rabbinate as it does from the theological heirs of Julius Eckman.

✿ ✿ ✿ ✿ ✿

More than a century after Rabbi Eckman expressed his dissatisfaction with religiously wayward Jews, Susan Kastner wrote in the New York *Post:*

Some sociologists suggest that, if you are Jewish, Christmas can be an unhappy time, whether or not you have resolved the question of having a Christmas tree in the house. You could decide to have a tree, and try to allay guilt feelings by topping it with a Star of David or calling it a Chanukah bush. You could decide not to have a tree, and then suffer over your child's woebegone mien while you try to explain to him why Jews don't celebrate Christmas.

One father tried unsuccessfully to distract his son's attention from Christmas by spearheading a drive to "put the CH back in Chanukah" and teaching his four-year-old to love the Chanukah story. He was gratified to see the little fellow develop an engrossing interest in the Festival of Lights, insisting on lighting one candle of the menorah on each of the eight nights. On the last night, his heart overflowing, the father drew the child to him and explained that now there would be no more Chanukah candles to light until next year. "There are no more candles, daddy?" "No, son," the father answered gently. "You mean Chanukah is all over?" The father said it was. "Oh boy," said his son, "now comes Christmas, right, daddy?"

* * * * *

In December 1977 the following item appeared in the national Jewish press:

Rabbi Marc H. Wilson of Congregation Shearith Israel in Atlanta, Georgia, was contacted by a local civic organization to participate in an interfaith winter holiday fellowship celebration. It was suggested that he make a few remarks and then help decorate "the tree" with some Chanukah symbols. Taken aback, he stated that such a procedure would be in very poor taste. The obviously sincere non-Jewish lady on the other end of the line responded almost in disbelief, "Why, rabbi, I just don't understand. This suggestion came from one of our Jewish members."

ALASKA
(1867)

Leib Gerstle was born in Ichenhausen, Bavaria, in 1824. His father was a storekeeper and very Orthodox. His oldest brother came to the United States about 1835 and settled in Louisville, Kentucky. In 1845 Leib came to live with his brother. His brother was no longer Orthodox. Leib soon Americanized his first name to Lewis. His first job was as a peddler in the Kentucky countryside. Later other members of the family made the westward Atlantic journey. The American Gerstles either joined Reform temples or had no synagogal affiliation.

* * * * *

Louis Schloss was born in Untereisenheim, Bavaria, in 1823. He also migrated to Louisville in 1845. There he and Lewis Gerstle became good friends. Louis Americanized his last name to Sloss. In 1849 Sloss went to California. He worked in Sacramento as an auctioneer. In 1850 he and Simon Gruenwald opened a grocery store. Simon later Americanized his last name to Greenwald.

❖   ❖   ❖   ❖   ❖

In 1849 Lewis Gerstle was also smitten by the wandering itch. First he went to New Orleans. After working there for a while, he took a boat to Panama, traversed the isthmus on horseback, and boarded another boat for Frisco. He worked in that city as a fruit peddler and then labored unsuccessfully in Placerville as a gold miner. In 1853 he met his Louisville friend Louis Sloss. In 1854 he joined the Sacramento grocery firm of Sloss and Greenwald. From then to the end of their lives, Gerstle and Sloss were business partners.

In 1862 the Sacramento River overflowed, flooded downtown Sacramento and ruined the Sloss-Greenwald-Gerstle grocery business. The three moved to San Francisco and opened a brokerage office dealing in mining stocks. As they became more prosperous, they expanded into other lines—hides, fur, wool, intercoastal shipping.

❖   ❖   ❖   ❖   ❖

Danish sea captain Vitus Jonassen Behring, in the employ of Russian Empresses Anna and Elizabeth, discovered Russian America, now known as Alaska, in 1741. In 1799 the Russian American Company was formed to develop the seal fur industry in Russian America. In 1805 Sitka became the headquarters of this company. The Russians made half-hearted efforts to extend their domain southward. For a few years they had a toehold on the coast of California. In 1812 they built a military post, Fort Ross, about 80 miles north of present-day San Francisco. Spanish military countermeasures forced the Russians to abandon Fort Ross and to retreat to their Arctic islands.

By 1865 operation of the Russian American Company had ceased to be profitable. Russian America was remote from the motherland. England's powerful Hudson's Bay Company was casting a greedy eye at the area. The United States and Russia were on very friendly terms. Russia was the only major European power that supported the Northern side during the just concluded Civil War. If Russian America was to become the property of another nation, the Russians greatly preferred that nation to be the United States. The Russian governmental agreement with the Russian American Company would expire in June 1867. The government decided to protect the northwest land mass from British encroachment either by making a new sealing agreement with an American owned-and-operated company or by selling Russian America to the United States.

* * * * *

During a visit to Sitka this situation became known to a young, energetic American Jew then residing in Victoria, British Columbia. His name is usually given as Louis Goldstone; but in various documents he is also referred to as Jack Goldstein, Louis Goldstein, and Jack Goldstone. It has not been possible to determine which of these was his correct name. In this narrative he will be called Louis Goldstone.

In late 1865 Louis Goldstone came to San Francisco and persuaded a number of well-to-do citizens of that city to organize the California Fur Company for the specific purpose of securing from the Russian government the right to operate and control Russian America's seal fur industry. The company had nine stockholders, five Jews and four non-Jews. The Jews were Gerstle, Sloss, Greenwald, and two others named Wasserman and Barcowitz. Curious, indeed, is the fact that Goldstone was not a stockholder. The reason for this is not known. After being instrumental in the organization of the California Fur Company, Goldstone disappears from the scene.

The money behind the California Fur Company was almost all Jewish. The non-Jews were window dressing. They were included and named principle officers of the corporation to conceal from the Russians, who were notoriously anti-Jewish, that the California Fur Company was Jewishly financed. General John F. Miller, Collector of the Port of San Francisco and later U. S. Senator, was named President. The company was capitalized at five million dollars. Cornelius Cole, a San Francisco lawyer who had just begun a six-year term as U. S. Senator, was retained as legal counsel and given the assignment of obtaining the Alaska fur concession by negotiating through the Russian ambassador in Washington.

Senator Cole pursued this task avidly through 1866 with the Russian ambassador, Baron Edouard de Stoeckel. In October Baron de Stoeckel was summoned to St. Petersburg to discuss the matter with his government. There he learned that the Hudson's Bay Company was making such an all-out effort to obtain the desired privilege that it would be extremely hazardous for the Russian government to give the franchise to a newly organized American company. Faced with this dilemma, the Russian government had decided the best way out would be to sell Russian America to the United States. Ambassador de Stoeckel returned to the United States in February 1867 with instructions to sell.

Negotiations between de Stoeckel and William H. Seward, American Secretary of State, concluded at 4 A.M. on March 30, 1867, with the signing of an agreement by Seward and de Stoeckel that Russia would sell Russian America to the United States for $7,200,000. The agreement was ratified by the U. S. Senate on April 9 by a vote of 27 to 12, with 6 voting "absent." Since a two-thirds vote of Senators "present" was needed to ratify, this means that the treaty squeaked through the Senate with only one more vote than was needed. The United States took possession of Russian America on October 18 and immediately renamed it Alaska, which is what its Aleut inhabitants called it. Their exact term was "alakshak," the Aleut word for "peninsula." The money to pay for Alaska had to be appropriated by the House of Representatives. The necessary bill was passed by that body on July 14, 1868, by a vote of 113 to 43, with 44 abstentions. The purchase did not become completely legal until this bill was signed by President Andrew Johnson on July 27, 1868. In his memoirs, written in 1908, Cornelius Cole stated that the information about Russian America furnished him by Louis Goldstone and transmitted by Cole to Secretary of State Seward strongly influenced the decision of the American government to buy Alaska.

American military garrisoning of Sitka in October 1868 was followed almost immediately by the arrival of a number of Jews who established a variety of businesses in and around the settlement. A non-Jew who was in Sitka at this time wrote the following:

> On Friday evening before going to bed, I attended a curious ceremony. Our sleeping quarters, which were built only of planks, abutted on another hut which was used as a warehouse by Jewish traders. Up to then I had never heard a sound there in the evening, but on that night my curiosity was aroused by a murmur of several voices in the adjoining room. Looking through the crevice I saw quite an assembly of some twenty men, all of the Jewish persuasion, who were holding their Sabbath services and reading their prayers under the leadership of the oldest man present who took the place of a Rabbi. It was a memorable thing to see this religious gathering in so strange a setting and it said a great deal for the persistence with which the Jews everywhere, even in the most remote countries, practice their emotional exercises. I myself should scarcely have expected it in Sitka among a community which was engaged in such disreputable occupations.

The writer's closing statement is explained by a previous passage in his account:

> The [Sitka] traders, keepers of the billiard saloons and dealers in spirits, were mostly of the Jewish race and carried on a more or less illicit trade with the soldiers and Indians, evaded customs and excise duties, and were liable to prosecution at any moment had the administration of the law not been so lax.

That there were others who shared these unkind sentiments is indicated in a·book written by an Alaskan in 1870:

> The wandering Jews are not unknown here. They appear to have degenerated from the ancient stock and have a sharp eye for business, buying from the greasy Turks [i.e., the Eskimos, who were believed to be of Asiatic origin] their stores of whalebone, oil and walrus tusks, and making them happy with tobacco, powder and ball, guns, knives, kettles and the vilest of alcoholic concoctions.

With the American acquisition of Alaska, the California Fur Company disappeared and sometime later was reincarnated by the same group of stockholders under a new name, the Alaska Commercial Company. Thirteen companies bid for the twenty-year sealing contract offered by the United States government. The Alaska Commercial Company was the *lowest* bidder and yet it got the contract! How this was accomplished is indicated on page 67 of Ernest Gruening's *The State of Alaska:*

> When the bids were opened in Washington, July 20, 1870, the lowest of the thirteen bids proved to be that of the Alaska Commercial Company. However, the lease was awarded to it, but on the terms offered by another bidder. Just how this result was achieved was not explained at the time. It has been plausibly conjectured that the influence of Senator Cornelius Cole, former attorney of the principal stockholders, may have had something to do with it.

For the privilege of killing 100,000 seals per annum on the Pribilof Islands, the Alaska Commercial Company was to pay the United States $55,000 a year "rent," plus $2.62½ for each sealskin plus 55¢ a gallon for the seal oil extracted. By the time the twenty-year contract expired in 1890, the Alaska Commercial Company had slaughtered a yearly average of 92,811 seals and yielded a net profit to its stockholders of $18,000,000. It had decimated the Alaska seal population to the point where sealing in Alaska would no longer be profitable.

The same group of individuals who controlled the Alaska Commercial Company now formed a new corporation, the Alaska Packers Association, and proceeded to monopolize the market for catching and packing Alaska salmon. At a Congressional hearing held in 1916, James Wickersham, non-voting Delegate to the Congress from the Territory of Alaska, stated:

> [The Alaska Packers Association] became the first great Alaska Salmon Trust. They have been engaged in that business [since 1890] and they have made enormous fortunes out of it.

The manner in which these two commercial enterprises profited from and squandered two of Alaska's most precious natural resources is a sad and shameful story. A completely documented and detailed account is in the definitive volume, *The State of Alaska*, written in 1954 by Alaska's outstanding Governor and Senator, Ernest Gruening, a very great Jewish American.

❊   ❊   ❊   ❊   ❊

For a number of years Louis Sloss served as Treasurer of the University of California. When he died he was succeeded in that post by Lewis Gerstle. Both are said to have been liberal contributors to Jewish and general religious and philanthropic institutions.

BEECHER'S ISLAND:
"THE LITTLE JEW WAS THERE!"
(1868)

Sigmund Schlesinger was born in Hungary in 1848. He came to the United States during the Civil War. For a time he clerked in a store in Leavenworth, Kansas. Then, wanting to learn more about what was happening in the ever-widening West, he got odd jobs of one kind and another in the labor camps that were constructing the Kansas Pacific Railroad across Kansas from the Missouri to the Colorado borders. Toward the end of August 1868 he had reached Fort Hayes in central Kansas but was unable to find work. Almost out of money, he was living on coffee and hardtack given him by a kindhearted Army mess sergeant.

This sergeant told him that an Army major was recruiting a party of fifty civilians to act as scouts to follow the movements of hostile Indian bands. Schlesinger, who by now had Americanized his first name to Samuel and was called Sammy by his friends, knew little about the hazards of scouting and, badly in need of employment, decided to apply.

He went to see the Army major, George A. Forsyth. Forsyth had already enlisted forty-nine of the fifty frontiersmen he required. He later described Sammy's appearance as follows: "He was short, stout, rather awkward and boyish, with cherry cheeks, and verdant in some ways—in every outward respect unfit to be a soldier and entirely new to campaigning." But there was something about Sammy that appealed to Forsyth and so he accepted Sammy as his fiftieth recruit. Thus, on August 28 did Sammy find employment. That day he wrote in his diary: "I put my name down for Scouting. Drawed a horse."

❊   ❊   ❊   ❊   ❊

Roman Nose was one of the great military leaders of the Plains Indians. He was an imposing looking man; six feet three, a muscular 230 pounds, with a broad, handsome face and a very prominent hooked nose. The Indians called him "The Bat." Because of his outstanding proboscis, the whites dubbed him "Roman Nose." They did not do so in jest. Dealing with Roman Nose was no laughing matter. He was intelligent, bold, and brave. In battle he wore a sacred war bonnet with a long train of black and red eagle feathers. He and the Indians believed that this bonnet was a magic talisman, protecting him against arrow and bullet. He participated in many battles and was never harmed. He belonged to the Northern Cheyenne who, at this time, were cooperating with the Sioux and the Northern Arapaho in resisting the continual encroachment of the whites upon their ancestral lands.

In 1866 the Kansas Pacific Railroad began to penetrate Cheyenne territory. The Indians protested. At a powwow with the whites at Fort Ellsworth, Roman Nose declared that the trains and the homesteaders they carried would destroy the buffalo herds and, by so doing, the Plains Indians' way of life. These Indians depended on buffalo meat for their food, on buffalo hides for their clothing and tents, on buffalo ribs and bones for their tools.

Roman Nose's protestation was ignored. The trains continued moving ever farther westward. Railroad passengers shot at the buffalo just for the sport of it as their trains passed through the herds. Hunters wantonly slaughtered the buffalo, cut out their tongues and left the rest of the huge carcasses to rot. Thousands of animal skeletons were stretched along the Kansas Pacific right-of-way. The railroad organized roundtrip excursions from Leavenworth to western Kansas so that "civilized" whites might enjoy the exhilarating "sport" of shooting down helpless buffalo.

The Plains Indians were outraged. In August 1868 Roman Nose and his braves went on the warpath against all whites living along the route of the Kansas Pacific. Homes and settlements were attacked and burned. Women were raped, then scalped and killed. Their husbands and children were likewise shown no mercy.

*   *   *   *   *

Civil War cavalry hero Philip H. Sheridan was Commanding General of the Military Division of the Missouri, with headquarters at Fort Leavenworth. Major Forsyth was his Inspector General. Sheridan had only 2,600 soldiers with whom to maintain control of a vast territory west of the Mississippi. His men were employed either to garrison the large number of posts in the area or as guards on railroad trains in danger of Indian attack. He had no soldiers to use for tracking the warring Indians' movements. Forsyth suggested that civilian frontiersmen be used for this purpose. Sheridan assented and ordered Forsyth to recruit, organize, and command "fifty hardy frontiersmen, to be used as scouts against the hostile Indians." Lieutenant Frederick H. Beecher of the 3rd U. S. Infantry, nephew of famed Congregationalist minister, Henry Ward Beecher, was to be second in command. Lieutenant Beecher walked with a limp because of a leg wound received at Gettysburg.

The scouts were recruited at Forts Hayes and Harker in central Kansas from August 26 to 28. About one-third had served in the Union or Confederate armies. Most were drifters who were wandering from place to place looking for an easy buck. One, William H. McCall, had commanded a Pennsylvania regiment in the Civil War and had held the rank of brevet brigadier general. He was named Acting First Sergeant.

From September 7 to 13 the party scouted from Fort Hays to Fort Wallace in western Kansas without finding any hostile Indians. When they reached Fort Wallace they were informed that a band of Indians had attacked a settlement a few miles to the east. They immediately went in pursuit of this band. For the next two and a half days they followed them northwestward through Kansas and into Colorado. On September 16 they found a broad Indian trail with the marks of many travois poles, indicating that the marauders had joined a large band of traveling Indians, who must be encamped close by. At this point the experienced frontiersmen among the scouts urged Forsyth to turn back. They reminded him that his mission was to scout and not to fight. He should return to Fort Wallace and report the presence of this encampment. The road marks indicated that the Indians greatly outnumbered the scouts and, if battle were joined, the whites would probably be annihilated. Forsyth bullheadedly refused to heed these knowledgeable men and insisted that the scouts remain in the area until they had more definite information. In the meantime the Indians, through their own scouts, had become aware of the white men's presence and were preparing to attack them.

The place Forsyth chose to bed down for the night was on the north bank of the Arikaree branch of the Republican River in northeast Colorado, one and a half miles northeast of the present village of Beecher's Island. His men had not left Fort Wallace with sufficient materiel for an extended campaign. They had been given only seven days' rations. No tents. They traveled light so that they could move at a fast pace and maintain close pursuit. Each was armed with a repeating rifle with 140 rounds of ammo and a revolver with 30 rounds of ammo. Four mules accompanied the party carrying medical supplies and an additional 4,000 rounds of rifle ammo. These were the grossly inadequate arms with which Forsyth's folly forced his scouts to fight a band of Indian warriors who outnumbered them by about fourteen to one.

The Indians attacked at daybreak on September 17. Forsyth ordered his men to take up a position on a sandbar in the middle of the Arikaree stream. The riverbed was 140 yards wide at this point; but the summer heat had dried up its waters considerably, so that an oval-shaped sandbar had formed, about 200 feet long and from 40 to 60 feet wide. The sandbar was almost totally devoid of vegetation. The soldiers had no entrenching tools. They dug in as best they could with their hands, pocket knives, tin plates, forks, and spoons.

The number of Indian braves involved was about 700. The adult warriors had rifles, the youths bows and arrows. Those with bows stayed at a distance and sent a constant stream of arrows toward their foes. Those with rifles attacked in two major cavalry charges and a number of minor ones. The women and children were on the surrounding hills, encouraging their fighters with loud screams and wild dances.

About 300 Indians participated in the first charge at daybreak. In addition to shooting at the whites, they also directed their fire toward the horses and mules to make sure these would no longer be available to the scouts. As the first Indian charge thundered toward the sandbar, one scout cried out, "Let's not stay here and be shot down like dogs." He started to run. Forsyth drew his revolver and ordered the man to come back or he would kill him. The man returned. That was the only instance of this kind during the encounter.

Every Army horse and mule was killed early in the action. As the last horse went down, someone in the Indian ranks yelled out in fluent English, "There goes their last damned horse." Also at times bugle calls were heard when the Indians assembled and dispersed. It is believed, therefore, that among the Indians were one or more white sympathizers.

Roman Nose did not take part in the first charge. The sacredness of his talisman had been defiled and its magic power had been lost. How was it defiled? The war bonnet's special medicine became useless if, after Roman Nose's food was cooked, the food was touched by anything made of iron. On the evening before the battle Roman Nose ate in the lodge of a Sioux chief. The chief's squaw lifted the food from the cooking pot with an iron knife. Roman Nose was not made aware of this until after he had eaten. There was not sufficient time for him to go through the prescribed rites of purification before the battle. He was sure that if he joined in the fight he would be killed.

The first charge was not effective. The whites suffered only a few casualties. Roman Nose was prevailed upon to lead the second charge. He only consented after an Indian named White Contrary had accused him of cowardice.

The second charge of 500 warriors led by Roman Nose came at nine A.M. At Forsyth's command the scouts withheld their fire until the Indians were within thirty yards of them. The very first volley shot Roman Nose from his horse. He was carried back to the Sioux encampment, about ten to twelve miles away. As the sun was setting, he died. The news of his death unnerved the Indian warriors and destroyed their will to fight the scouts.

This was something the beleagured whites did not know. That second charge had been very costly to them. Lieutenant Beecher and their surgeon had been killed, together with three others. Forsyth's left leg was shattered. He received additional wounds on his scalp and right leg. Eighteen more were wounded, of whom two later died. Fort Wallace was about a hundred miles away. That night two scouts sneaked out to try to get help. For a long time they walked backward and barefooted so that, if their tracks were discovered, the enemy would think they were Indian tracks.

There were two minor cavalry charges the next day but, as it later developed, these were primarily for the purpose of recovering the bodies of the Indian dead that were still lying near the stream. If the Indians had continued to fight in earnest, they would easily have over-come the whites, whose food and ammo were about gone and whose strength was drained. The death of Roman Nose saved the lives of those marooned on the sandbar.

On the fourth and fifth days the Indian encampment moved away.

On the sixth day the two men who had gone for help reached Cheyenne Wells, 70 miles south of the Arikaree. From here they jour-neyed by stagecoach 65 miles east to Fort Wallace and arrived there on the evening of the next day. Two squadrons of the Tenth Cavalry—officers, white; enlisted men, black—were dispatched immediately to rescue the scouts. The Army, at this time, had two such black cavalry regiments fighting the Indians. The Indians called these black cavalry-men "buffalo soldiers," because they thought the kinky hair of the blacks resembled the kinky fur of the buffalo.

On the eighth day the men on the sandbar, without food or drinking water, were in a state of delirium and complete exhaustion.

On the ninth day the Tenth Cavalry arrived after two days and nights of hard riding. They were greatly moved by the plight of the living and the stench of the dead. They buried the dead men, horses, and mules and conducted the living back to Fort Wallace for medical treatment. It took Major Forsyth two years to recover from his wounds.

❖　❖　❖　❖　❖

This episode is known in American military annals as the battle of Beecher's Island, out of respect to the memory of Lieutenant Beecher. There never was such an island. There was only a sandbar in the middle of a stream, a sandbar which disintegrated speedily when the spring rains refilled the riverbed. The village which subsequently developed near the battle site was named Beecher's Island. Near its postoffice stands an appropriate monument, the only visible reminder in the area of the occurrence.

The incident added no luster to the military record of Major Forsyth. His superiors believed he had disobeyed his instructions which, indeed, had been to avoid close combat with the Indians. The experiment with civilian scouts was considered a failure and no further effort was made to organize similar units.

The Beecher Island affair was mild compared to what happened twenty-two years later, again as a result of Forsyth's incompetence and stupidity. As Colonel Forsyth, he commanded the 7th U. S. Cavalry when that famed outfit massacred 160 unarmed Sioux Indians, on December 29, 1890, at Wounded Knee, South Dakota—89 men, old and young, 49 women, 22 children—one of the most barbaric episodes in our country's long record of mistreatment of America's indigenous inhabitants, a chapter in our history that reflects little credit upon either our nation or its armed forces.

✸   ✸   ✸   ✸   ✸

How did Sammy Schlesinger, the "short, stout, very awkward and boyish" Jew, conduct himself during the battle of Beecher's Island?

In a letter written by Forsyth to Rabbi Henry Cohen of Galveston, Texas, December 27, 1897, Forsyth stated:

> Throughout the whole engagement, which was one of the hardest, if not the very hardest, ever fought on the Western plains, Schlesinger behaved with great courage, cool persistence, and a dogged determination that won my unstinted admiration, as well as that of his comrades. I can accord him no higher praise than that he was the equal in manly courage, steady and persistent devotion to duty and unswerving and tenacious pluck of any man in my command.

In his autobiography Forsyth writes that, after first being apprehensive about Schlesinger's ability to measure up, he "soon noticed his good care of his horse, his strict obedience to orders, and his evident anxiety to learn his duty and to do it." After writing in stinging language of the scout who tried to desert at the beginning of the battle, Forsyth continues:

> . . . while as for that little Jew! Well, the Indian that from dawn to dark was incautious enough to expose himself within range of his rifle had no cause to complain of want of marked attention on the part of that brave and active young Israelite. In fact he most worthily proved himself a gallant soldier among brave men.

In a poem about the battle, titled "The Island of Death," by General James B. Fry in the *Army and Navy Magazine*, August 26, 1893, the following verses are included:

> When the foe charged on the breastworks,
> With the madness of despair,
> And the bravest souls were tested,
> The little Jew was there.

> When the weary dozed on duty,
> Or the wounded needed care,
> When another shot was called for,
> The little Jew was there.

> With the festering dead around them,
> Shedding poison in the air,
> No matter what the crippled chieftain ordered,
> The little Jew was there!

In letters written later by Schlesinger describing the battle, there is no indication whatsoever that Schlesinger considered himself any special kind of hero. He speaks of himself and his comrades as human beings who found themselves in a desperate situation and were very lucky to emerge alive from their terrible ordeal.

When Forsyth's group of scouts disbanded, Schlesinger's brief military career ended. One such experience was enough. Schlesinger did not want to push his luck any further. He headed back east, settled in Cleveland, Ohio, and spent the rest of his life in that city as the proprietor of a clothing store.

THE MORMONS AND THE JEWS
(1869)

In the correspondence printed in the *Jewish Record* [at this time weeklies with this name were being published in both New York City and London] there is a letter from a fellow Israelite living in Utah. From it, it seems that up to the year 1864 only three Jews lived there. In the year

---

This document, labeled "a free translation" of an article in *Ha-Maggid*, Hebrew weekly of Lyck, Galicia, Austria, August 4, 1869, was found among the papers of the late Dr. Leon L. Watters, son of Salt Lake City pioneers Ichel and Augusta Watters. It is quoted in *History of the Jews in Utah and Idaho*, by Juanita Brooks, 1973, pp. 54-55.

1864 the number increased to approximately fifty, most of them without wives. They bestirred themselves to pray publicly on the days of New Year and the Day of Atonement.

They sent individuals to the prophet of the Mormons to request him to rent them one of the Temples of the city to offer prayer in it publicly. The prophet granted them their request willingly and permitted them without payment to assemble in one of the most beautiful temples of the city to pray in it to the Lord their God. And so it was. Then the Jews prayed to God according to their custom in a Utah city—something that had never occurred there from the time it had been established.

After the holidays had passed, our fellow Israelites established in their midst a society "Gemilluth Chasadim," which still exists and it has performed much good in the midst of the community. Likewise they also now have a place of burial set aside for themselves surrounded by a beautiful fence. The portion of land for this purpose was presented to them gratis by the officials of the city at the order of Brigham Young, who at all times shows his love for the people of Israel more than to all the rest of the members of other religions. And his saying always is, "that in the end, finally, all the peoples will accept the faith of the Jews."

All the Jews there are wealthy, through their trade, and they work faithfully, and the Mormons honor them very much and trust them in their words, and their number will increase from year to year, as they come there from the four corners of the earth, and everyone finds there his sustenance plenteously either through trade or tilling the soil, for the earth is fertile and blessed like the garden of Eden, and they dwell there securely with none to make them afraid, and the Mormons do not allow any members of any other religious group to dwell amongst them except the Jews whom they respect very much . . . and in their midst is not found even one of the sect of the Reformer.

Two Jews Meet Tiburcio Vasquez
(1870)

When California became part of the United States as a result of the war with Mexico, many California Mexicans felt they had been taken over by a foreign aggressor and that it was their patriotic duty to adopt whatever tactics were necessary to drive the intruders from their country. A number of brave Chicanos took to the California hills and, for the next thirty years, harassed the Anglos by stealing their cattle and horses, holding up their stagecoaches, and attacking and robbing their settlements. To the Anglos, these men were desperados, outlaws, bandits. To the Mexicans, they were heroes. And in Mexican annals they continue to be heroes.

The most famous of these outlaw-rebels was Joaquin Murietta, "the Robin Hood of El Dorado," whose reign of terror lasted for two years, 1851-53, before he was killed. The second best known was Tiburcio Vasquez.

Tiburcio Vasquez was born in Monterey, California, in August 1835 of mixed blood, Spanish and Indian. He became an outlaw in 1852 after killing a constable in his home town. In July 1857 he was caught stealing horses in Los Angeles County and spent the next six years in San Quentin. After his release he continued to steal horses and cattle, and in 1867 he was again jailed. When he got out in June 1870 he, too, began a reign of terror which caused the governor of California to offer $8,000 for his capture.

Vasquez was five feet five inches tall and weighed about 145 pounds. He was handsome and intelligent. His complexion was much lighter than that of the average Mexican. He was educated, had a beautiful handwriting, and spoke English well. He dressed immaculately—well-fitting coat, trousers, tie, polished boots, well-kept moustache and beard. He was quite a ladies' man. He fathered at least one child but never married. He regarded himself as the avenger of wronged Mexico. He was adored passionately by those for whom he fought. Mexican Californians still speak of Vasquez in the same ambivalent way that most northerners speak of John Brown—he was an idealist who committed evil deeds in the name of righteousness.

❈   ❈   ❈   ❈   ❈

Herman W. Hellman, 1844-1908, was born in Rickendorf, Bavaria. He came to this country in 1859 with his brother Isaiah, who was one year older. The two made the long sea voyage around Cape Horn to Los Angeles. They settled there in 1860. Isaiah got a job as a store clerk; but Herman, of a more adventurous nature, found employment at ten dollars a month as a hauler of freight from L.A. to its seaport, located near Long Beach and then known as Wilmington.

Some years later Herman became a driver for the Wells Fargo Express on the stagecoach route between Los Angeles and San Francisco. This was a very hazardous job. The life of a driver occupying the high seat on top of the coach was one of continual danger, both from runaway horses and highway robbers. It took a special kind of intestinal fortitude to be on that seat.

On a dark night in the early 1870s, Vasquez and his men ambushed Hellman's stagecoach in Cahuenga Pass, a narrow defile nine miles north of Los Angeles. The attackers planned to kill the driver and to seize the $5,000 in gold bullion they knew the coach was carrying. Hellman lashed his horses into a furious gallop. Then, guiding them with one hand, he used the other to engage in a gun duel with the bandits. He got away and delivered intact the bullion, the mail sacks, and the lone passenger that were in the coach. The Anglo community applauded his bravery.

This harrowing experience convinced Herman it was time for him to seek a less precarious and more financially rewarding career. He went into the banking business with his brother. They organized the Hellman Commercial Trust and Savings Bank, which later developed into the Farmers and Merchants National Bank of Los Angeles, one of California's leading banks. Hellman and his sons, Marco and Irving, contributed greatly to the development and improvement of Los Angeles.

* * * * *

On August 26, 1873, the Vasquez band raided the village of Tres Pinos, northeast of Salinas, and murdered three people. Later in the same year they attacked Kingsburg, south of Fresno. These exploits triggered an intensive but unsuccessful manhunt for Vasquez. His whereabouts were often known to his fellow-Mexicans; but they guarded this secret with a loyalty that was beyond the reach of bribe or threat.

Like Samson of old, Vasquez was finally done in because of a woman.

In the spring of 1874 Tiburcio, as was his wont, took certain liberties with a married woman which traditionally are reserved for the husband. Deeply disturbed by this improper use of what was his, the aggrieved spouse informed the Los Angeles police that Tiburcio was holed up on Greek George's ranch about ten miles due west of L.A. Greek George's real name was George Allen.

L.A. County Sheriff Rowland, a friend of Greek George, invited him to dinner and an evening of card playing. After the last hand was dealt, the sheriff arrested George, charged him with harboring a fugitive, and locked him up to make sure he would not be able to inform Vasquez that he was about to be ensnared. That was on the night of May 13, 1874.

At 1:30 A.M. on May 14 a posse of eight policemen left L.A. to capture Vasquez. One of the eight was L.A. detective Emil Harris. Harris, Prussian-born Jew, thirty-four years of age, had lived in the city for five years and been on the police force for three and a half years. A contemporary pamphlet published by the Los Angeles *Star* stated: "Officer Harris has detective qualities second to no man in the state, is brave, cool, and energetic, and just the man to have been associated with such a hazardous undertaking."

The posse arrived at the ranch at daybreak, about four A.M., and was able, because of a dense fog, to reach the ranchhouse unnoticed. Harris led the charge into the house. Vasquez ran from his bedroom into the kitchen, followed by Harris. "With the agility of a cat, [Vasquez] jumped through a narrow slit in the side of the adobe house, which served as a window." Harris fired at him with a shotgun. Pellets hit him in the left side from head to toe. Vasquez tried to reach his horse but his wounds felled him. As the policemen approached, "he threw up his hands and said, with a cool, passionate smile wreathing his thin lips, 'Boys, you have done well. I have been a damned fool. [My capture] is my own fault.' Despite his pain, he displayed great courage and politeness."

The wounded outlaw asked Harris for a drink of water. Harris brought it to him. Vasquez looked at the glass with suspicion, as though the water had been poisoned. He asked Harris to take a drink from the glass. Harris complied. Vasquez said, "You are a brave man. I like to drink to brave men," and he did.

Vasquez was taken to San José, imprisoned, tried for murder, and condemned to death. Like the legendary heroes of the I.R.A., the Mexican pleaded for the privilege of facing a firing squad. "Shoot me like a soldier; don't hang me like a dog." The plea was denied. Vasquez was hanged at San José on March 19, 1875. According to all accounts, he died like the martyr in a just cause he believed himself to be, calmly and without any sign of fear.

Vasquez' knife and rifle, owned by Harris, were exhibited in 1915 at the San Francisco International Exposition. Harris served for a time as Los Angeles Chief of Police. He was for many years an active member of Congregation Bnai Brith (Wilshire Boulevard Temple). He died in Los Angeles on April 28, 1921, and is buried in his synagogue's cemetery.

A LESSON IN MINDING ONE'S OWN BUSINESS
(1872)

The Nez Perce Indians of northwest Idaho had great difficulty in understanding the story of the Crucifixion and the Jewish involvement in it. They had had business dealings with a number of Jewish traders and had found them to be good, kind people, much better and kinder than many who called themselves Christians. A Presbyterian missionary, after preaching a sermon on the subject mentioned, had the following conversation with one of his listeners.

Indian: Mr. Preacher, was that man whom you say was nailed to the tree and killed, was he a Boston man [i.e., a white man]?

Missionary: Yes, he was a Boston man.

Contributed by Rabbi Stanley R. Brav.

Indian: Were those Jews who killed him from around here?

Missionary: No, they were Jews who live very far from here.

Indian: Were those bad Jews Boston men?

Missionary: Yes, they were Boston men.

Indian: Did this happen to the tribe to which you belong?

Missionary: No, it happened in a tribe that lived away beyond the salt creek [i.e., the ocean].

Indian: Well, then, Mr. Preacher, why are you trying to drag us Indians into a controversy which is no concern of yours or of ours?

Jake Sandelowsky and Baby Doe
(1877)

One of the most picturesque episodes in American history began in the summer of 1858 when gold was discovered near Pike's Peak, about 10,000 feet above sea level, in the rugged Rocky Mountain country of Colorado. Before the end of September thousands of enthusiastic adventurers were following all roads leading to the West, eager to dig a fortune out of the cold, hard earth. On the canvas-covered wagons was painted "PIKE'S PEAK OR BUST!" Most failed to find the fortune they sought. Bitterly disappointed, wagoners crossed out the exuberant slogan on their canvas, painted below it another phrase, "BUSTED, BY GOD!" and headed back East.

Many did not give up as easily. A few lucky ones struck it rich. In 1859 Auroria and Denver were founded on Cherry Creek, as was Central City, about forty-five miles west, on Clear Creek. By the mid-sixties so little gold was being mined that there was a general exodus from the region.

In 1874 the Colorado mountains again got into the news. A geologist announced that the hard-to-get-at gold was embedded in rich veins of precious silver and lead. This started a human stampede larger and more theatrical than the first. It brought into being the Wild West excitingly described in song and story, a gay and gory world of shantytowns, saloons, sporting houses, dance halls, shootings, vigilantes, and lynchings.

Central City's prosperity was renewed by the 1874 boom. It was a thriving town until about 1900 and then went downhill rapidly.

The largest bonanza of the 1874 resurgence was in an area adjacent

---

Some of the facts about modern Leadville were supplied by J. Leroy Wingenbach of the Leadville *Herald Democrat*.

to the Continental Divide north of the site of Oro City. Oro City was one of the major camps during the 1859 gold rush. When the gold played out, Oro City's official existence ended in 1867. A new community, nourished by the discovery of much silver and lead, sprang up a few miles northwest of Oro City. In 1878 it was given the appropriate name of Leadville and incorporated. By 1880 Leadville had 15,000 inhabitants and had already produced $150,000,000 worth of silver and lead.

Two hundred of the 15,000 were Jews. A Reform congregation, Temple Israel, and a Bnai Brith lodge were organized in 1879. A Jewish cemetery was bought in 1882. In 1883 there were 75 Jewish families with a religious school of 40 children. A synagogue, still standing, was built in 1884. In 1892 an Orthodox shul, Keneseth Israel, was founded. A building which had been a Presbyterian church, one block from Temple Israel, was purchased by the Orthodox group. At this time Temple Israel had 100 members, Keneseth Israel 30.

David May, born in 1848 in Kaiserslautern, Rhineland, Germany, arrived in Leadville in September 1877 and opened a modest department store. In 1889 he moved to Denver and began to operate the May Shoe and Clothing Company, which in the course of time expanded into the May Company, the well-known department store chain.

Meyer Guggenheim, born in Switzerland in 1828, came to Philadelphia in 1847. He started out as a peddler and then amassed a small fortune manufacturing lye. As his family increased, he also went into the imported Swiss embroidery business and made still more money. He had seven sons, all in his employ. Meyer set himself a lofty financial goal. He determined to help each of his sons become a millionaire. With this in mind, he came to Leadville in 1881 and purchased and operated the A. Y. and Minnie mines. He was not active in the Jewish religious life of the community; but he did spend many nights with Jewish cronies playing pinochle. From this Leadville beginning, Guggenheim and his sons went into mining businesses all over the world. By the time Meyer died in St. Augustine, Florida, in 1905, all his sons had become millionaires many times over.

In 1893 a financial panic swept through the United States, partially precipitated by the rapidly declining price of silver. Colorado was hit worst of all. The silver mines were closed. Thousands of miners lost their jobs. The population of Leadville shrank by two-thirds. Most of its Jews went elsewhere. After 1900 services were no longer held in either synagogue except on the High Holydays or when someone had to say Kaddish. By 1900 Temple Israel's membership was down to twenty-five and Keneseth Israel's to ten. The town recovered somewhat between 1900 and 1915 because of the demand for zinc; but the Jews did not return. By World War I Jewish community life had ended.

In 1934 the Orthodox synagogue was torn down to make way for an

Elks lodge. In 1937 the Reform synagogue became a boardinghouse and later the Episcopal rectory. It is now a two-family dwelling. One side of the building still has the large ornamental six-pointed star that was there when it was a synagogue. By 1951 there was only one Jew in Leadville, Miss Minette Miller. The latest population figure for Leadville is 4,314. There is still only one Jew in town, Miss Minette Miller. She has retired as head of the town's welfare department and is compiling a history of the Jews of Leadville and is also making sure that the Jewish cemetery is properly maintained.

The mining community of Aspen was established in 1880, mostly through the enterprise of a Jew, David Hyman. In his honor Aspen's main street is named Hyman Avenue. By 1892 Aspen had 11,000 inhabitants, six newspapers and an annual horse racing season. The 1893 panic brought its mining days to an end. It has come back to life in recent years as a cultural center in the summer and a skiing resort in the winter.

In 1890 a rich vein of gold was uncovered at Cripple Creek, twenty miles west of Pike's Peak. By 1892 there were 5,000 people in Cripple Creek plus another 5,000 in Victor and other nearby camps. The town described itself as "the world's greatest gold camp." By 1900 there were 150 Jews in Cripple Creek and Victor. They had a Bnai Brith lodge and held High Holyday services. After 1905 the town declined. The Bnai Brith lodge disappeared in 1912. Cripple Creek is now a summer tourist attraction.

❖   ❖   ❖   ❖   ❖

Of all the folklore created by Colorado's Wild West period, the most famous tale is that of a gal who began life in Oshkosh, Wisconsin, in 1855 as Elizabeth "Baby" McCourt, was married on June 27, 1877, to William Harvey Doe, Jr., became the mistress first of Jacob Sandelowsky and then of Horace Austin Warner Tabor, was married to Tabor on March 1, 1883, died from cold and starvation in March 1935 in a wooden shack near Leadville, and whose memory is now being perpetuated as the heroine of an American folk opera, *The Ballad of Baby Doe,* first performed in July 1956 at the Central City Opera House.

The legendary "golden haired, sloe eyed" beauty, of Irish Catholic extraction, was the daughter of a well-to-do clothier. Her first husband was the son of a Protestant father who made a fortune as a gold miner in Central City and then returned to his native Oshkosh to become a successful lumber merchant and politician. The wedding, in Oshkosh's St. Peter's R. C. Church was "the" social event of the year. W. H. Doe, Sr., gave the couple as a wedding present a principle interest in his Central City Fourth of July mine.

In July 1877 the young Does arrived in Central City to work their mine, which turned out to be worthless. Baby Doe, undismayed, put on miner's garb and, with the help of others, started to dig a second shaft. This created a furious argument between herself and her in-laws, who had decided to make their home permanently in Colorado. To get away from the senior Does, the juniors moved in October into some furnished rooms in Black Hawk, three miles east of Central City. The shaft started by Baby began to show signs of doing well. Harvey, Jr., labored at the mine. Baby, in order to keep peace with her in-laws, remained in Black Hawk, inactive and bored. Four doors up the street from the Doe's furnished rooms was the clothing store of Jake Sandelowsky.

* * * * *

Jacob Sandelowsky was born in Poland in 1851. His father brought him to the United States in 1866. Father opened a clothing store in Utica, New York. In 1867 Jake came to Central City to work in Abe Rachofsky's New York store. In 1874 Central City had a disastrous fire in which the entire business district, including Rachofsky's store, was destroyed. While Central City was recuperating and rebuilding, Jake and another young bachelor, Sam Pelton, started their own clothing business, Sandelowsky, Pelton and Company, in Black Hawk in 1876.

Jake was handsome. He was very popular. He loved to gamble, dance, and wench.

* * * * *

Baby Doe's beauty attracted Jake. At first everything was on the up-and-up. Harvey, Baby, Jake, and Sam Shelton became good friends, dined, danced, played cards, went to shows together. In June 1878 the second shaft at the Fourth of July petered out. At almost the same time Jake opened a new store in Central City. Baby, who was acquainted with the clothing business through her father, agreed to become a saleslady in the ladies' department of Jake's new establishment. The junior Does moved back to Central City. The senior Does now lived in Idaho Springs, five miles south of Central City. In September Jake and Baby became lovers. Their rendezvous were held in a small cabin between Central City and Black Hawk. The trysts were preplanned during business hours. Jake would hand his favorite saleslady a small envelope containing a little sheet with the significant words, "Meet me, my darling, at ten." In November Doe, Sr., got Doe, Jr., a job as an apprentice millhand in a stamp mill.

In December Baby Doe learned she was pregnant. When Baby told her husband the good news, he went out and got drunk. Then he came back and accused his wife of letting Jake enjoy what rightly belonged to

Harvey alone. An infuriated Baby hit Harvey with a chunk of ore. Bleeding profusely, Harvey reeled out of the house, borrowed $30 from a friend and took the train to Denver. A couple days later Baby went back to Oshkosh and mama. Doe, Sr., finally effected a reconciliation in June 1879, a month before the baby was due. Harvey swore off hard liquor. Baby came back. On July 13 Baby gave birth to a stillborn infant, a boy with big blue eyes and dark, curly hair, just like Jake Sandelowsky had. Again the Does separated. Again Harvey took to drink. Again he went to Denver.

While this was happening, Jake was in New York City buying merchandise for the store he would open in Leadville in November. After he returned, he wrote from Leadville inviting the Does to move to Leadville at his expense. He would help Harvey find a job. Harvey refused to leave Denver. So Baby went to Leadville alone. There Jake persuaded Baby to seek out Harvey and ask for a divorce.

On January 2, 1880, Baby went to Denver and told Harvey she wanted a divorce. Harvey pleaded with her to give him another chance. Baby remained in Denver with Harvey. On March 2 she saw him stagger into a house in the city's "red light" district. Accompanied by a policeman, she entered the house and found drunken Harvey cavorting in the nude with one of the girls, also nude. On March 19 Baby was awarded a divorce from Harvey for adultery and nonsupport. The next morning Baby boarded a train for Leadville.

¤   ¤   ¤   ¤   ¤

Horace Austin Warner Tabor, born in Holland, Vermont, November 26, 1830, worked as a stonemason. In 1855 he became engaged to his boss' daughter, Augusta, a plain looking, hard working, solidly built woman. In 1856 he left his sweetheart to homestead in Kansas. He did not do well as a farmer but found profitable employment as a stonecutter. Early in 1857 he returned to Vermont, married Augusta and brought her back to Kansas. There, late in the same year, Augusta had a son.

In February 1859 Tabor was smitten by the gold bug and took his wife and infant on the arduous trek to the Pike's Peak country. They arrived at Denver in June and proceeded west to Idaho Springs on Clear Creek. Augusta was the first white woman in the area. She helped her husband by serving meals to the miners while he worked on his claim. In 1860 Tabor was deprived of his promising diggings by the machinations of a seemingly friendly mountaineer. The Tabors moved southwest seventy-five miles to the gold camp of Oro City. Again Augusta was the first female in the camp. She set up a boardinghouse and Tabor prospected. In the fall Tabor opened a general store, the first Oro City structure to have real glass windows. Augusta became the town postmistress and gold weigher.

By 1867 the gold around Oro City was exhausted and the place became deserted. But the Tabors did not leave. Their store continued to furnish them a very meager living. In the middle of 1877 the Tabors moved their store to the new silver and lead mining camp that was booming just a few miles northwest of Oro. On January 14, 1878 the boom camp became the town of Leadville. Tabor was its first mayor, treasurer, and postmaster. His store served as city hall and post office. In April he got a one-third interest in a claim by grubstaking two prospectors with seventeen dollars' worth of his store's goods. Thirty days later and thirty feet down, the prospectors found a vein of high-grade silver and lead ore. Within a month the mine was yielding $8,000 a week. This success induced Tabor to buy up every available silver claim in Leadville. This was the beginning of the process that resulted in his becoming "the silver king" of Colorado, the richest and most powerful person in the state.

Blessed with seemingly boundless wealth, the fifty-year-old Tabor went in big for booze and women. The more gregarious he got, the more withdrawn and despondent Augusta became. Tabor determined that Leadville, through his money and knowhow, was to be one of the showplaces of the nation. He built the three-story Tabor Opera House, seating 5,000 people. He organized the Tabor Volunteer Fire Company, with the latest horse-drawn fire equipment and resplendent uniforms for the firemen. He outfitted Tabor's Light Cavalry and Tabor's Highland Guards, two splendid companies of local militia. He organized a telephone service through which one could make calls as far as Denver, 150 miles distant. He developed a horse-drawn streetcar operation that carried people from one end of Leadville to the other. He was truly monarch of all he surveyed. The only person he could not please or control was Augusta. In the spring of 1880 he exiled his wife and son to Denver. He bought a $60,000 Italian-style villa in that city and put them in it.

❈   ❈   ❈   ❈   ❈

On March 22, 1880, twenty-four-year-old Baby Doe arrived in Leadville. Jake met her at the railroad station. His store was on the ground floor of the Tabor Opera House. It was known as Sands, Pelton and Company. Jacob Sandelowsky had changed his name to Jake Sands. Jake and Baby soon became known as one of the swingingest pairs in town.

In May Baby met the "king." For both it seems to have been really and truly love at first sight. Within a few days Baby had become Tabor's mistress. He discarded his current girlfriend, an Indian club juggler in a local nightclub, and put Baby in the best suite in Leadville's best hotel. Jake, a realist, gave up Baby without a struggle. To requite him for his many kindnesses to Baby Doe, Tabor, through her, presented Jake with a diamond ring worth $5,000. In the good years that followed, Tabor and Baby and Jake remained the best of friends.

Before the end of the year Tabor moved his main headquarters and his Baby to Denver. In 1881 he built another Tabor Opera House in Denver. In April 1882 he obtained a secret divorce from Augusta in Durango, Mexico. In October he was secretly married to Baby in St. Louis by a justice of the peace. In January 1883 a Denver judge invalidated both the secret divorce and the secret marriage. The judge granted Augusta a valid divorce with a large financial settlement. On March 1, 1883, Tabor and Baby went through another marriage ceremony, this time by a Catholic priest in the Willard Hotel in Washington, D.C. One of the wedding guests was Chester A. Arthur, President of the United States. The priest did not know he was officiating at the marriage of two divorcees. When he found out he returned the marriage fee and publicly proclaimed that he had been deliberately deceived, a charge which the Tabors vigorously denied. "He didn't ask us; so we didn't tell him," they said.

The Tabors bought a $50,000 house in Denver, staffed by five gardeners, six horses, two coachmen, two footmen, and a substantial number of household servants. Daughter Elizabeth Pearl arrived in 1884. Daughter Rose Mary Silver Dollar was born in 1889.

In November 1893, when the Sherman Silver Purchase Act was repealed by Congress, the price of silver went down to almost nothing and Tabor and the silver-studded barons of Colorado were completely ruined. It is estimated that from 1878 to 1893 Tabor had squandered $42,000,000 and had saved not a penny for a rainy day. All he had left was Baby, two daughters, and the worthless Matchless mine in Leadville. The family left its fancy mansion for a small cottage in west Denver. In 1895 Tabor got a job hauling slag in a smelter for three dollars a day. In 1898 he was rescued from poverty by two prominent citizens who persuaded President McKinley to appoint him postmaster of Denver at an annual salary of $3,500. On April 10, 1899, Tabor died of peritonitis. His last words to Baby were, "Don't sell the Matchless. Some day it will make you rich." The city and state mourned his death. Official flags throughout Colorado were flown at half mast. His body lay in state in the capitol in Denver.

After her husband was buried, the forty-four-year-old widow moved back to Leadville to watch and wait for the Matchless to come back to life. It never happened. She was still beautiful, but she never remarried. She mourned for her one true love the rest of her days. Elizabeth, the older daughter, "cold, sullen," hated Leadville. She went to Chicago to live with an uncle. Silver Dollar, the younger daughter, "warm, witty, and exquisite," stayed with her mother until she was a grown young lady. Then she lived in Denver and Chicago, worked as a reporter, tried to write a novel. She did not succeed and became very discouraged. Her mother told friends she had become a nun.

About 1910 the once glamorous, wealthy Baby Doe Tabor could no longer afford the niceties of civilized living. According to Phyllis F. Dorset in *The New Eldorado:*

> To conserve what little money she had, the widow of H. A. W. Tabor moved out to the drafty shack adjacent the hoist house of the moribund Matchless. Here, with her feet clad in rags and old miner's boots, a shapeless rough wool dress covering her once fulsome body, and her hair, still pathetically lustrous, hidden in an oversized laborer's cap, Baby Doe lived out her lonely days cadging food from wherever she could find it, seeing no one except Sue Bonnie, a neighbor, and endlessly reading her favorite book, *The Lives of the Saints.*

In 1925 an inebriated Silver Dollar Tabor, using the alias of Ruth Norman, scalded herself to death in a sleazy boardinghouse on Chicago's South Side. She had come to the end of her life as a chronic alcoholic, a drug addict, and a prostitute.

In March 1935 Baby Joe Tabor, nearly eighty years of age, was found dead in her little wooden shack, frozen, starved, penniless. She was spared a pauper's grave by the good people of Leadville, who gave the money to have her interred beside Horace in Denver's Mount Olivet Cemetery. She had a Catholic funeral.

Among Leadville's current attractions are the Tabor House, where Horace and Augusta lived in the early days of their prosperity, the Matchless mine and the little wooden shack in which this strange, beautiful woman lived the last twenty-five miserable years of her long and hectic life.

❋   ❋   ❋   ❋   ❋

And what of Jacob Sandelowsky—pardon me—Jake Sands?

In 1885 Jake sold his Leadville store, leased two silver mines belonging to Tabor near Aspen, and opened a glamorous men's clothing emporium in Aspen. Shortly thereafter he married, lived in an elegant brick house (now an Aspen tourist attraction), and became one of Aspen's leading citizens.

In 1893 Jake was among the many who went "mechulla." He lost his mine leases, his store, his house, his $5,000 diamond ring. He left Colorado. He ended his days in Globe, Arizona, as the proprietor of a small tailor shop, pressing clothes, shortening pants and, once in a while, making a suit to measure.

Sutro's Tunnel
(1879)

Almost all the books and articles about Adolph Sutro refer to him as a mining engineer. He was not. He invested in mining stocks. For a few years he owned a small mine. He never worked in a mine in any professional capacity. He had no formal engineering training. At no time did he work as a mining engineer or any other kind of engineer. He made his living, successively, as a clothing merchant, the owner of a small chain of cigar stores, the operator of a stamp mill, the builder of a tunnel, and a buyer and seller of real estate.

As prime mover and entrepreneur, he devoted nineteen years of his life to a project that was a monumental engineering feat and a financial bust. It was a losing proposition for those who operated it after its completion. But not for its promoter. The tunnel made him rich. Mentally, he was a genius. Physically, he was strong as an ox. Although a number of times, while building his tunnel, he was on the brink of bankruptcy, he had the touch of Midas.

His enemies labeled him "Assyrian carpetbagger," "crazy Jew-crook," and other uncomplimentary appelatives. His admirers knew him to be irascible, stubborn, honest, and imbued with a sense of destiny. San Francisco, the city he helped bring to greatness, remembers him as an ideal citizen who gave it a library, an aquarium, a beautiful public park, fountains, statues and, for the two years that he was mayor, a taste of incorruptible municipal government.

Adolph Heinrich Joseph Sutro was born on April 29, 1830, in Aachen, Rhenish Prussia, in an upper middle class Jewish family that owned a woolen cloth factory. In December 1847 his father died. In 1849 unstable political conditions brought on a depression that forced the factory to close. In August 1850 his mother sailed for the United States with five of her sons and four daughters. One son was already in America. Another was left behind in Germany to continue his musical studies. After landing in New York, all but Adolph settled in Baltimore. Adolph, a brilliant and adventurous young man, impressed by the throngs of easterners who had headed westward to look for the pot of gold at the end of the California rainbow, went to San Francisco. He left New York on October 12 and steamed through the Golden Gate on November 21.

Sutro began his California career by going into partnership with a cousin in the clothing business in Stockton, fifty miles east of San Francisco. The store did well; but life in Stockton was too quiet for Adolph. In less than a year he returned to San Francisco and opened a cigar store on Long Wharf. By 1854 he had two stores and, by 1855, three.

In 1856 Adolph was married by Rabbi Julius Eckman to Leah Harris, of English Orthodox extraction. It was not a good match. Leah was a simple, good-hearted, traditional Jewish woman, whose idea of happiness was a life devoted to husband, children, the synagogue, and Jewish charities. Her husband was much more complicated than that. He was Jewish, to be sure, but only ethnically, not religiously. His parents were "freidenker," freethinkers. They had never belonged to a synagogue. They did not give their children a religious education or rearing. Adolph's knowledge of Judaism was minimal and his interest in organized religion even less. Spiritually and intellectually, the Adolph-Leah "union" was a mixing of oil and water. On the surface everything seemed to be going smoothly; underneath were feelings of intense dissatisfaction.

Adolph was handsome and brilliant and he knew it. He had a marked German accent. Height: Five feet ten inches. Weight: 225 pounds. Strong face. Black, curly hair. "The mind of a scholar and the temperament of a warrior." Despite their differences in life-style and outlook, the Sutros produced six children, two sons and four daughters.

In 1859 the famous Comstock Lode, $350,000,000 worth of gold and silver deposits, was unearthed in western Nevada. Adolph's fortune-seeking appetite was whetted. After making two exploratory trips to the site of the find, Adolph and a German chemist set up a small laboratory on Market Street in San Francisco and secretly developed a new process for getting metal ore out of quartz rock cheaply and efficiently. By April 1861 they were confident of the workability of their discovery. Adolph sold his cigar stores, left Leah and the children in San Francisco (where Leah supplemented the family income by operating two elegantly furnished lodginghouses), and departed with his partner for Dayton, Nevada, on the outskirts of newly founded Carson City and about five miles south of Virginia City. They began operating a stamping mill which, by 1863, was yielding a profit of almost $10,000 a month.

Twenty mines dug into the Comstock Lode were producing rich dividends, but they were plagued by serious health hazards. The heat in the mines, which at times reached 110 degrees, made work very difficult. Even more dangerous were the frequently encountered pockets of noxious gas. In addition, the dynamite blasts that loosened the ore-bearing rock also released pent-up water in the underground chambers and caused floods that constantly menaced the miners and the mining operations.

As early as 1860 Adolph figured out a way to solve all these problems. A tunnel should be bored into Mount Davidson, the mountain that contained the Comstock Lode. Dayton was at the foot of this mountain; Virginia City sat on top of it. The tunnel would provide a ventilating shaft for the mines. It would decrease the heat and the humidity and disperse the noxious gases. It would drain off the underground flood waters. The creation of this tunnel became Sutro's obsession. He estimated that the tunnel would have to be about four miles long and would cost about six and a half million dollars. His estimates proved to be very accurate.

The first legislature of the State of Nevada granted Sutro the right to construct the tunnel on February 4, 1865. He was required to begin the project within one year and to complete it within eight years. Despite Sutro's prodigious efforts, he was unable to meet these deadlines. They had to be extended.

In the beginning the Bank of California, headed by politically powerful William Chapman Ralston, gave the enterprise full financial support. But, when the banker learned that the mine companies had agreed to pay Sutro a fee of two dollars a ton for the ore removed from the mines through his tunnel, Ralston and his prestigious institution turned against Sutro and endeavored to get control of the project. First they tried to undermine Sutro's efforts by ridiculing his scheme. They said it was chimerical, impractical. And, they continued, Sutro should not be trusted. He is a scoundrel. He intends to collect large sums of money from naïve investors and then disappear.

Undaunted, Sutro made many trips throughout the United States and abroad to raise money for his venture. He traveled to Austria, Bavaria, Belgium, England, France, Holland, Hungary, Ireland, Poland, Prussia, and Switzerland. Europe's greatest scientists gave him strong letters of endorsement.

In February 1868 a special committee appointed by Congress recommended that the United States loan Sutro five million dollars to help build the tunnel; but the bill introduced to make this possible never came to a vote. Congress was too involved with impeachment proceedings against President Andrew Johnson to bother with a matter of miner importance.

On April 7, 1869, a tragedy occurred that put an end to the effort to stop the building of the tunnel. There was a terrible explosion and fire in one of the Comstock mines. Forty-five miners were killed. If a tunnel had been available, these lives could have been saved. The miners held the California bankers directly responsible for the deaths of their fellow workers. A mass meeting of protest was held in Virginia City on September 20. Sutro delivered an impassioned speech. The miners responded by raising among themselves the additional money needed to start the tunnel's construction. On October 19 the work was begun.

A village named Sutro came into being at the mouth of the tunnel, two miles east of Dayton. Sutro built a fine house there and brought his wife and children from San Francisco to live in the town named for him. Upon learning that they could no longer delay the work on the tunnel,

"Ralston's Ring," as Ralston and his financial gangsters were now known, tried to circumvent Sutro by organizing the Virginia and Truckee Railroad, whose tracks would run from Virginia City down Mount Davidson to the Carson River valley. This railroad would carry the ore from the mines to the smelters and would collect the $2-per-ton fee that had been promised to Sutro. Sutro sneeringly referred to the Virginia and Truckee as "the crookedest road in the world," which it just about was, physically, financially, and ideologically.

In 1875 Ralston's financial machinations in the Sutro and other matters led to his personal downfall and to a run on the Bank of California that almost ruined it. While crowds surged around the bank building demanding the return of their deposits, Ralston went for a swim in San Francisco Bay and drowned, some say accidentally, others deliberately. The bank went through a complete reorganization and thus averted collapse.

In the spring of 1879 Leah was told that her husband had acquired a girlfriend, a cutie named Mrs. George Allen who lived in Virginia City's International Hotel and whose neck, hands, and arms were so loaded with sparkling jewels that she was known as the "$90,000 diamond widow." One evening the quiet of the International Hotel was broken by the voice of a woman screaming for help. The voice was that of Mrs. Allen. Leah had stormed into Mrs. Allen's sitting room and hit her over the head with a champagne bottle. For the rest of his days Adolph insisted that his friendship with Mrs. Allen was a perfectly innocent affair. He was unable to convince Leah. In November 1879 she and the children left Sutro for San Francisco. Although the Sutros never divorced, they maintained separate residences from then on.

The Sutro Tunnel was completed in July 1879. It was constructed 1,600 feet below the surface of Mount Davidson. It was twelve feet wide and ten feet high. Tracks were laid throughout the tunnel over which men and materials were transported in mule-drawn cars.

In little more than a year Sutro became dissatisfied with the manner in which his associates were operating the tunnel. It is also likely, now that the tunnel was a reality, that Sutro's restless nature impelled him to look for a new world to conquer. He sold his 35 percent interest in the tunnel's ownership for about $900,000 and returned to San Francisco. There were exaggerated reports that Sutro had received as much as five million dollars for his tunnel holdings.

As an engineering feat, the Sutro Tunnel was an admirable accomplishment. As a business venture, it did not succeed. The Virginia and Truckee Railroad, operational in January 1870, hauled away most of the ore that Sutro had expected to transport through his tunnel. The tunnel, in use for about fifty years, did everything Sutro claimed it would do. It reduced the heat and humidity. It dissipated the poisonous gases and the pent-up waters. Unfortunately, as the miners dug more deeply into Mount Davidson, the quality of the ore began to deteriorate until finally mining the Comstock Lode ceased to be profitable. By 1889 the tunnel stock had become worthless. That year the tunnel was sold for $800,000 to a syndicate styled the Comstock Tunnel Company and headed by Adolph's youngest brother Theodore, a wealthy New York lawyer. The stock of the Comstock Tunnel Company also eventually was worth no more than the paper on which its shares were printed.

In San Francisco Adolph lived at first in the Baldwin Hotel and later in a lovely cottage he built in a hilly section known as Sutro Heights. He provided well for his wife and children. Leah was active in Jewish religious and philanthropic organizations. Shortly before she died in 1893, she and her husband began to appear in public together, even though they continued to live apart.

With strong faith in San Francisco's future, Adolph, in a time of economic depression, invested heavily in city real estate. It is estimated that, at the summit of his acquisitions, he owned about one-twelfth of the total area of the city. He was an avid collector of books and manuscripts and a great lover of art. He was very charitable and public-spirited. He served as mayor of San Francisco from 1895 to 1897 and then, because of ill health, retired from political and public life. He died on August 8, 1898. His funeral was conducted by Rabbi Jacob Nieto. His remains were cremated.

He left a library of over 200,000 volumes, including 135 rare Hebrew manuscripts and a large collection of early Americana. Some of the Hebrew works, sold to Sutro as original manuscripts written by Moses Maimonides, proved to be forgeries. These pseudo-Maimonean documents are now in the library of the Jewish Theological Seminary. Most of the Sutro books were destroyed in the fire that followed the 1906 San Francisco earthquake. About 70,000 volumes were saved. Since 1968 these volumes have been housed in the Sutro Branch of the California State Library.

On December 22, 1979, the Associated Press office in San Francisco sent out the following report:

> For 81 years no one knew where they buried the ashes of old Adolph Sutro, the man who made a mint on the Comstock Lode and came to San Francisco to spend it. Now, on a windswept hill which bears his name, Adolph Sutro has probably been found, in a weatherbeaten urn cemented into a rock. "We are 98 percent sure that it is Sutro," says James Delgado, a historian with the Golden Gate National Recreation Area.
> The area where Sutro built his mansion, a huge section called Sutro Heights, overlooking the famed Seal Rocks and the Pacific Ocean, is now mostly park land. "Bury me where I can watch the ocean and Seal Rocks," Sutro's will directed. "Bury me at Sutro Heights."

A man was exploring the cliff's face when he found the alabaster urn. He reported his find to Delgado and a park crew who were nearby excavating the ruins of Sutro's mansion as part of a park project.

THE PISTOL-PACKING RABBI
(1880)

In the early days of Jewish settlement in the Pacific Northwest, rabbis came and went in rapid succession. Synagogue members liked meetings sparked by debates, charges, and countercharges. The rabbi was usually one of the chief topics of the arguments as well as the scapegoat, no matter which side won the dispute.

In 1872 Congregation Beth Israel of Portland, Oregon, advertised for a chazan and teacher. Twenty-two applications were received. Mr. Moses May was elected. A small group devoted to the previous incumbent, Rev. Dr. Isaac Schwab, split away and formed a new congregation, Ahavai Shalom, more traditional in practice.

The atmosphere within Congregation Beth Israel became more explosive than ever with the engagement of its new, controversial minister. He came, a youthful, good-looking man, holding strong convictions and eager to put them into practice. He introduced a new prayerbook, *Minhag America,* written and published by Isaac M. Wise, founder of American Reform Judaism. In making his recommendation to stop using the Orthodox Hebrew-German prayerbook with which the congregational services were being conducted, Mr. May exercised neither tact nor patience toward those who disagreed with him.

The battle of reform versus tradition swayed back and forth. As Rabbi May described the situation, Beth Israel developed its own Minhag Portland, a kind of indecisive religious worship and practice designed by the congregation's Board of Directors exclusively for the use of its membership. The battle between rabbi and elected officers continued unrelentingly. In 1876 the congregation advertised for a new minister. But Rabbi May managed to stay on. In 1878 the congregation again advertised for a "moderate reform rabbi." Rabbi May was not to be gotten rid of so easily. He mustered his friends and fought to be retained. This was a fight with no holds barred.

On January 26, 1879, the walls of the synagogue fairly burst with the release of pent-up emotions. A member was fined one dollar for not

Written by Rabbi Julius J. Nodel of Temple Emanu-El, Honolulu, Hawaii, and former rabbi of Congregation Beth Israel of Portland, Oregon.

coming to order as requested by the President. After said member responded by using improper language toward the presiding officer, a further fine of five dollars was entered against him. The following excerpt from the minutes of the meeting indicates a quite hectic parliamentary situation: "Mr. Wasserman having accepted the amendment as well as the amendment to the amendment, the question upon the adoption of the resolution as amended was then put and carried by a large majority." The resolution thus passed was a decision to summon all parties making slanderous charges against Reverend May to a public hearing, so that these charges might be thoroughly investigated.

In addition to some matters preposterous and unprintable, the group opposed to the rabbi accused him of "conduct unbecoming a gentleman and more especially one holding a position such as Mr. May is enjoying at present"; to wit, referring to the married women of the congregation as ladies of easy virtue; casting aspersions upon his own wife in public and thereby receiving "the condemnation of Jew, Gentile and heathen"; outrageously slandering and blackmailing several members of the congregation; condemning himself, by his own actions, as an immoral man and disbeliever in the doctrines of Holy Writ; acting as a libertine and rake during a visit to San Francisco; calling the officers and members of the congregation outlandish names; threatening to join the Unitarian Church in the event that Mr. Philip Selling were reelected President; opening mail belonging to others for the purpose of slandering the authors of the letters; and, when called a liar, blackguard, scoundrel, and villain, "he offered no word for his defense but walked away and therefore gave rise to the belief that he felt himself guilty of these charges." A complaint was also made that "the Reverend May, when asked why, being such a libertine and of such worldly turn of mind, he attended the synagogue service in San Francisco when visiting that city, he answered: In order to satisfy his congregation when asked on his return whether he had visited the synagogue in San Francisco."

In the less cloudy light of one hundred years' removal from the time and place of these scandalous events, one is inclined to view the bitter diatribe against Reverend May as a ruthless attempt to rid the community of a religious revolutionary. Sometime during 1880 Reverend May was absolved of all accusations against him. The pages of the synagogue minute book charging him with these various derelictions were, by resolution of the Board, covered over.

The lively altercation between minister and congregation, gleefully aired in the local press, reached its climax on October 1, 1880. The preacher and a lay leader engaged in a stiff fist fight on a downtown street corner in plain sight of all who passed by. When the ecclesiastic felt he was coming out second best, he whipped a pistol out from under his frockcoat and fired twice at his opponent. Since he was a better verbal marksman than pistol shot, the bullets went wide of their mark. The police ended the fracas before any further damage was done.

The following account appeared in the *Daily Oregonian*, October 2:

A SHOOTING AFFAIR

Yesterday forenoon, about 10 o'clock, an affray occurred on Front Street opposite the store of Hexter & May, which attracted much attention at the time and has been the subject of a great deal of public comment since. The actors in the affair are Rev. Dr. M. May, the well-known Jewish rabbi, and Mr. A. Waldman, of the firm of Beck & Waldman. Some misunderstanding of a personal nature arose between these parties a few days ago, when it is alleged some hot words were indulged in. Waldman and May met yesterday on the street, when hostilities were renewed. Mr. Waldman struck Dr. May twice in the face, when the latter drew a pistol and fired twice at him. Fortunately, neither shot took effect. Parties interfered and separated the belligerents. Subsequently both Waldman and May were arrested by Constable Sprague.

The *American Israelite* of Cincinnati, in its October 22 issue, commented on the shocking incident:

A VERKEHRTE WELT [A TOPSY-TURVY WORLD]

Rev. Mr. May, of Portland, Oregon, took offense at Mr. Waldman, member of his congregation, for having reported him incorrectly, and upon meeting him in the public street—right under the window of the hotel where President Hayes was staying—fired two shots at his alleged traducer. Mr. Waldman was not hurt, but the rabbi was soundly thrashed for being such a poor marksman. But then Mr. May is not to blame, as it is not to be supposed that either he or his father ever fired a shot—but then did you ever hear of a rabbi carrying a pistol?

Mr. Waldman is a very respectable citizen of Portland, and Mr. May, though not recognized as a rabbi but merely tolerated, on account of relationship, as a Shatz Matz [Hebrew abbreviation for Jewish religious factotum], has ever been well spoken of, and we can not understand how a man of a family can take his life in his own hands, especially when he knows as little how to pull a trigger as he knows of the Shulchan Aruch [the standard Jewish code of religious laws]. There is, of course, a vacancy in the Portland congregation and poor May will either have to go to peddling or join the shooting Baptists. It is a pity that Israel should have produced a shooting clergyman, and still more a pity that the Christians in Portland believe that May is a high priest in the synagogue. From the accounts in the Portland papers, we would judge that, although not justified in shooting, Mr. May acted as he did under very great provocation. Is it not about time that the doctors, the rabbis, and reverends should be graded?

Soon afterward the Reverend Mr. Moses May disappeared from the Portland scene. His election was declared illegal and his office vacant. The minutes containing the charges against him were again uncovered and made available to anyone who wished to read them.

ASTROLOGER TO THE KING
(1887)

When Reb Elias Abraham Rosenberg died in San Francisco, California, on July 10, 1887, with his last breath he whispered the name of Hawaiian King David Kalakaua.

Was he invoking with reverence the name of the monarch who, during the previous six months, had befriended him in the island kingdom? Was he calling upon his royal pal to help him? Or was it, perhaps, a last desperate effort to indicate that the king had some things which belonged to him—some personal possessions he had intended to bequeath to his eldest son Adolph, as stated in his will: "For Adolph, the five books of Moses written on parchment and a certain silver pointer."

Adolph never got them—because they were more than 2,000 miles away, in Honolulu at the Iolani Palace of King David Kalakaua, next to last royal ruler of Hawaii.

Rosenberg first met King Kalakaua on January 19, 1887. Outside of his chief asset, an excessive amount of *chutspah*, the seventy-six-year-old "self-styled rabbi," in his first audience at the royal palace, did not appear as a man of great means. But he did bring with him a magnificent Scroll of the Law and a solid silver, filigreed, handcrafted Torah pointer ["yad" in Hebrew] studded with semiprecious stones.

His traditional way of chanting the Torah seemed to the king incredibly similar to the ancient chants of his Polynesian forebears. The king was mesmerized by this strange visitor who, like the Biblical Moses, came bearing the original text of the Word of God, the Torah, in his arms and the finger of God, the yad, in his hands. Rosenberg convinced the king that he possessed occult powers and soon became the king's influential "Kahuna-Kilokilo," a kind of astrologer and soothsayer.

As he ingratiated himself ever more closely to the monarch, Rosenberg was attacked and ridiculed in the Hawaiian press and, naturally, by some of Kalakaua's former key advisors. He was maliciously dubbed "Holy Moses"; but he was not dismayed. He was teaching the king Hebrew and was a power behind the throne. His horoscope readings had

Written by Rabbi Julius J. Nodel of Temple Emanu-El, Honolulu, Hawaii.

an important influence upon the king's actions and decisions. Given a soft job as Appraiser of Customs, he had no major worries for the time being. The king fixed up a room for "Holy Moses" where he could read the stars, make magic, and chant his Hebrew prayers. Since the king was sympatico with anyone who, like himself, took frequent nips from the bottle, he kept Rosenberg's room well stocked with liquor.

The royal magician's glory was short-lived. These were troublous times for King Kalakaua. A strong group of reformers publicly charged the regime with corruption and with substituting personal rule for law. It was not difficult for Rosenberg to "read in the stars" what was about to happen. At the end of June 1887, a revolution broke out which cost the king much of his power. A few weeks earlier soothsayer Rosenberg had the foresight and good sense to depart for San Francisco.

Before Rosenberg left Hawaii, the king gave him a silver cup and a gold medal, both suitably inscribed. He also received $260 from the king's chamberlain. He left the Torah and the pointer with King Kalakaua, possibly as security for the loan which enabled him to make his hasty exit. He sailed for California aboard the steamer *Australia*, in steerage class, on June 7, 1887. Little more than a month later he died and was buried in the Hills of Eternity Cemetery of San Francisco's Congregation Sherith Israel.

The few references to Reb Elias Abraham Rosenberg in Hawaiian and American Jewish sources are mysterious as well as frequently sarcastic. He began his Hawaiian adventure at an age when ordinary men would have long been retired. Information about most of his career lies hidden in obscurity.

He was born in 1810 somewhere in Russia and had a daughter who married a Russian soldier. He had three children by a second marriage. He seems to have lived in England and Australia. He claimed to have lost a document inscribed by Queen Victoria. He is reported to have sold "ausgeblosene" [blown out] emu eggs which he gathered down under. It is alleged that he was a peddler in San Francisco and went to Hawaii to avoid a stay in San Quentin for selling lottery tickets. He had a third marriage at the age of seventy-five. A year later, without benefit of civil divorce, he was granted a religious divorce in San Francisco by Rabbi Falk Vidaver.

Press descriptions of Rosenberg and his bizarre adventures in San Francisco and Honolulu were not delicately phrased. He was referred to as a "curio," "charlatan," "scalawag," "der gefarbter lamdan [the learned man with the painted beard]," "scraggy looking 'malihini [newcomer to Hawaii],'" "Rosy," and "self-styled rabbi." When the news of his death reached Honolulu, it got only brief and derisive mention: "Abraham Rosenberg, better known as 'Holy Moses,' has turned his toes to the daisies."

The terms of his will were as unique as his brief sojourn in Hawaii.

Beside the request that his body be prepared according to Jewish traditional custom, he directed that it be placed in a perforated zinc coffin with unslaked lime. Water was to be poured over it until the flesh was eaten away; and the skeleton was then to be buried in an Orthodox Jewish cemetery. His estate, reported as between $1,000 and $6,000 in cash, was left to his children and to charity. His half-divorced wife was cut off with one dollar.

What happened to the Torah scroll and the silver pointer left behind when he fled Hawaii? That's another story—as fascinating as quixotic "Holy Moses" himself. This writer, who discovered the Torah after it had been lost for almost fifty years, will be glad to tell you that story when you come to Temple Emanu-El in Honolulu, where the Torah, now damaged beyond proper fitness for ritual use, and the yad are on display in a special cabinet in the sanctuary of the synagogue.

If Rosenberg's dying words had anything to do with his unretrieved sacred articles, perhaps now that the Scroll and pointer are once more in Jewish care after a long and strange interlude, his soul is resting in peace.

Joe Fights the Greatest
(1889)

Ever hear of Joe Choynski? Probably not. Joe Choynski was born in 1868 and died in 1943. He was a prizefighter. He might very well have become the first Jewish heavyweight champion of the world; but he could not because no reigning champ would give him a crack at the title. In the years that Joe fought professionally, 1888-1904, such an opportunity was not given to two kinds of fighters, blacks and Jews.

Here is Joe's story.

Joseph Choynski's father had a store in San Francisco where he sold Jewish religious books and articles. A few blocks away was the undertaking establishment of the father of James John Corbett, a boy two years older than Joe. His father wanted Jim to be a priest; but Jim had other ideas. He went to work in a bank. In their early teens Joe and Jim developed into excellent boxers. Each had a brother working at City Hall. The brothers got into an argument about whether Jim or Joe was the best fighter. There was only one way to settle the argument. Sixteen-year-old Joe and eighteen-year-old Jim were matched against each other. The books do not tell how this first fight ended; but they do tell that the boys fought each other a number of times before either turned pro and were so skillful and evenly matched that their fights were the talk of San Francisco's sporting gentry.

Joe turned pro at eighteen. Jim continued to work at the bank. Each disliked the other because each felt he was the other's superior in the "manly art." (Twenty years later, after both had retired from the ring, they became very close friends.)

In 1889 a fight to the finish was arranged between the two, wearing five-ounce gloves and adhering to the recently enacted Marquis of Queensbury rules. Fighting with bare fists was on the way out. Fights "to the finish" were illegal in California. The bout took place in a barn loft in Sausalito, just northwest of San Francisco. The winner would receive $2,000. After five fast-moving rounds a sheriff apologetically stopped the fight, saying he was doing not his own will but that of the city fathers.

After several unsuccessful attempts to resume the fracas, the fight was finally completed a week later on a huge wheat barge moored in San Francisco Bay. Choynski's second chief was an outstanding boxer, the Nonpareil, the original Jack Dempsey, whose ring name was later used by his fond admirer, heavyweight champion William Harrison "Jack" Dempsey. While Choynski and his attendants were being rowed out to the barge, Dempsey quietly attached a weight to Joe's boxing gloves and dropped them overboard. The Nonpareil wanted the fight to go on with bare fists. Corbett refused to fight without gloves. He kept on his five-ounce mitts. Joe used a pair of driving gloves borrowed from a ringside spectator.

The fight began at noon under an intense sun that kept getting hotter and hotter. In the Sausalito encounter Jim had dislocated his right thumb. Fortunately for Jim, Joe did not know this. In the third round of the barge fight Jim broke two bones in his left hand, his best punching hand. During the rest of the struggle Jim used as his major means of attack a punishing left hook, delivered with the side of the hand and the first knuckle. Corbett claimed in later years that he invented this blow that day and that without it he would not have survived. What ensued was the most grueling fight in Corbett's career. In his memoirs Corbett states he was hurt more by Choynski in that fight than by any other boxer he ever faced. In the fourteenth round Joe had Jim on the verge of a knockout. Jim recovered and managed to knock out Joe in the twenty-seventh round. Both men were completely exhausted. Jim was so dazed he did not know he had knocked out Choynski until his trainer jumped into the ring and told him he had won.

It was after this fight that Corbett decided to turn professional. "Gentleman Jim" is considered by many boxing experts to be the most skillful, the most graceful, the most scientific, the most outstanding boxer of all time. Which tells us something about Joe Choynski, who came within an ace of knocking out this boxing genius at the very threshold of his career. If Joe had won, there is a good possibility that Jim would never have become a pro. Corbett went on to gain the world title by knocking out John L. Sullivan in the twenty-first round. He was champion from 1892 to 1897.

In 1894 Joe fought Bob Fitzsimmons in Boston. They agreed to fight a six-round exhibition match and not inflict excessive damage on each other. In the third round Joe saw an irresistible opening and he floored Fitz with a right to the jaw. An enraged Fitzsimmons went after Joe with such fury that he probably would have knocked Joe out if the police had not stopped the bout in the fifth round. The fight was declared a draw. Fitzsimmons gained the heavyweight title by knocking out Corbett in the fourteenth round. He was champ from 1897 to 1899.

In 1897 Joe fought Jim Jeffries ten rounds to a draw. In the tenth round he broke Jeffries' nose. Jeffries floored Joe three times but could not knock him out. He said years later that Joe was the hardest puncher he ever encountered. Jeffries won the heavyweight title by knocking out Fitzsimmons in the eleventh round. He was champion from 1899 to 1905.

In 1901 Joe went to Galveston, Texas, to fight a local black stevedore named Jack Johnson. He knocked out Johnson in the third round, one of the two times that the future champ was knocked out in his entire career. After Jack hit the deck, he and Joe were arrested because of a Texas law that forbade prizefighting. The sheriff who made the arrest watched the whole fight with great enjoyment before making his move. Bail for each man was set at $5,000. From his jail cell Joe appealed for help to Galveston's famed Rabbi Henry Cohen. Rabbi Cohen made a deal with the county authorities. "You know they can't make that bail," he said. "It's a shame for them to be cooped up like this. How about letting them go about their business in the daytime and return at night to sleep in the jail? I'll see that they get in on time." And so it was arranged. They were allowed to be out all day but had to be back by eight P.M. Local sports fans brought boxing equipment to the prison. Each evening they watched Joe give Jack Johnson lessons in the finer points of boxing. When the trial was held a week later, the jurors speedily declared the fighters "not guilty." By this time they were local heroes. The community rejoiced with them but regretted the ending of the evening sparring exhibitions in the county jail. On their last evening in the jail, the sheriff was their host at a big Texas-style whoop-de-do. Choynski, feeling that Jack Johnson had the makings of a really good fighter, took Jack with him to Chicago.

Almost immediately Jack began to pile up one of the most impressive records in the history of boxing. But, because he was black, a chance at the title was denied him for seven years. Jeffries retired in 1905 undefeated. In 1906 Tommy Burns was declared champ. No American promoter was willing to arrange a match between Burns and Johnson. Burns, a Canadian, agreed to fight Johnson in Sydney, Australia. The police stopped the bout in the fourteenth round with Burns on the verge of being knocked out. Jack Johnson thus became the world's first black heavyweight boxing champion.

In 1915 Jess Willard became world champion by knocking out Johnson in Havana, Cuba, in the twenty-sixth round. The difference between the Willard knockout and the Choynski knockout was as follows: Willard floored a worn-out thirty-seven-year-old Johnson in the twenty-sixth round. Choynski knocked out a much less experienced but much stronger twenty-three-year-old Johnson in the third round. Most boxing authorities would probably agree that Choynski's KO deserves the top billing.

Joe Choynski quit the ring in 1904 with a record of fifty victories, ten draws or "no decisions," and seven defeats. Few champs have that good a record. This box score achieves even greater respect after one learns that Joe was only five feet seven and never weighed more than 170 pounds. Corbett was six feet one and weighed 178. Fitzsimmons was six years older than Joe and weighed even less. Little wonder that Fitz has been described as "a physical freak and a fistic phenomenon." Jeffries was six feet two-and-a-half and weighed over 200 pounds. Johnson was six feet one and weighed 210. Joe was not scared of "nothing or nobody." The old boxing adage, "the bigger they are, the harder they fall," was the tag line on most of Joe's fights.

Yes, sir, if Joe Choynski had been born about forty years later, he might very well have gone into the history books as the first Jewish world heavyweight boxing champion.

The Truth at Last

(1920)

Four Jews occupied a private suite on a Pullman car all the way from Chicago to Los Angeles. Every hour on the hour they called on the Pullman porter for some kind of service—towels, soap, playing cards, soda water, etc., etc., etc. And not once did they tip him even a dime. When they arrived in L.A., the porter took their luggage, piled it outside the car, and stood by waiting for the tip he felt would now surely come. Instead, each of the four walked from the car, picked up his suitcase and, without a word to the porter, walked off. The porter stood there amazed, disappointed, and angry—in a frame of mind that, with a change in pigmentation, might have made him eligible for membership in the Ku Klux Klan.

Contributed by Rabbi Stanley R. Brav.

Five minutes later, just as he was about to get back on the car, one of the four rushed up and said, "Porter, please forgive us—you have been so kind to us—our minds have been so occupied with the business deal we hope to work out here that we temporarily forgot we had not rewarded your kindness properly." With that he put two $20 bills into the porter's hand. The porter was dumbfounded. This was the biggest tip he had ever received. He was sorry for the way he had misjudged the four Jews. He wanted to make amends. "Mister," he said, "Mister, now I know that that story about you Jews crucifying our Lord isn't true. You Jews didn't crucify him. You just worried him to death!"

KNOW THYSELF
(1926)

Georgie Jessel of Hollywood, California, who found fame and fortune playing the cantor's son in the original stage version of *The Jazz Singer,* has been keeping busy ever since as after-dinner speaker, eulogist, and squire of shapely young damsels. One of his favorite pastimes has been holding imaginary conversations with his mother. Some of these conversations on the phone or in person are truly hilarious. For example:

One day Georgie realized that, to be in the social swim, he must own a yacht. This is not only a sign of wealth but also of culture and urbanity. So Georgie bought a yacht and a very fancy yacht captain's uniform. Then he invited his mamma to go for a cruise. He welcomed her aboard dressed in his brand new outfit.

"Look at me, mamma," he cried. "Don't I look spiffy? Did you ever in your wildest imaginations expect your Georgie to afford a boat like this, and to be dressed up in a uniform like this? Imagine, mamma, I'm a captain, a real captain?" His mother smiled at him very indulgently and said, "That's nice, Georgie, that's very nice." "But, mamma," said Georgie, a little disappointed, "you don't sound very enthusiastic. You don't sound like you are really impressed." "Well, Georgie, I'll tell you," replied mamma. "It's all really very nice, but let's face it. By you you're a captain, by me you're a captain; but, by real captains, you're no captain."

SOMETIMES VINEGAR IS BETTER THAN HONEY
(1932)

Dorothy Rothschild Parker, 1893-1967, celebrated writer and caustic wit, gave a great boost to the yet unborn contact lens industry when she wrote the couplet:

Men never make passes
At girls who wear glasses.

Miss Parker was brought to Hollywood in 1932 by Metro-Goldwyn-Mayer to work on movie scripts. She was assigned a little cubicle in the studio. She was not given enough to do. No one seemed to be paying any attention to her. She felt forsaken. Her morale was very low. Reflecting one day upon her social isolation, she had a brilliant idea. She removed from her cubicle door the card saying "DOROTHY PARKER" and replaced it with one bearing the words "GENTS' ROOM." In a matter of hours her problem had been resolved beautifully. She then took down the "PAUSE THAT REFRESHES" sign and put back the original one.

"WAIT FIFTEEN MINUTES!"*
(1944)

During World War II my husband officiated at many weddings of servicemen stationed in the military installations near Fresno, California. One took place on an early Sunday afternoon between Becky and Joe (fictitious names). Becky, who had almost missed the matrimonial boat, was in her late thirties.

At 11:45 P.M. on the day of the wedding, many hours after the ceremony, our phone rang and I answered. It was Becky asking for the rabbi. My husband went to the phone with trepidation in his heart, fearing that for some reason Joe had walked out on his bride. "What is it, Becky?" he asked. Her reply was, "Rabbi, I'm reading the wedding certificate you gave us and I see that you dated it June 5th. But today is only June 4th. What should I do?" My husband's reply was, "Becky, just wait fifteen more minutes and then go ahead!" Becky seemed quite satisfied with the rabbinical solution of her problem.

---

*Contributed by Mrs. David L. (Estelle) Greenberg, Fresno, California.

My husband says that, when he finds time to write his memoirs about his forty-five years in Fresno, he is going to call the book *Wait Fifteen Minutes!*

WHOM ARE YOU TRYING TO KID?*

(1946)

Screenwriter Ben Hecht approached movie producer David Selznick for a contribution to help buy arms for Palestine's Jewish guerrilla fighters, the Irgun. Selznick, like many other Hollywood Jews, was not very deeply concerned about Jewish affairs. "I am an American," said Selznick, "why should I be interested in Jewish guerrillas?" "American Shmerican," responded Hecht, "everyone around here thinks of you as a Jew." "You must be kidding," said Selznick. Hecht made him a sporting proposition. Hecht would ask the next three people who came to his office a simple question, "Hey, what is Selznick?" He would report their answers honestly to Selznick. If the answers were what he thought they would be, Selznick would write a check for a contribution of $10,000. Selznick agreed to the sporting proposition. The first one asked said, "Jewish, of course." The second said, "Jewish. Didn't you know?" The third said, "He's as Jewish as they come. Why? Is he trying to deny it?" Selznick wrote a check for $20,000.

SUPERCOLOSSAL PIETY

(1956)

Michael Silverstone, the Hollywood movie mogul, wanted to have a Bar Mitzvah for his son that would outdo all other Bar Mitzvahs from the beginning of time. So he called in his ace director and instructed him as follows: "You are to stage for me a Bar Mitzvah production like unto which there ain't never been!" The director bowed, said, "Yes, Sir Boss!" and withdrew from the royal presence walking backward.

The director arranged for a safari to Tanganyika in Darkest Africa. Six C-47s would fly the guests to Mombasa in Kenya. From there the party would proceed westward to Mount Kilimanjaro, the highest moun-

---

* Told by Samuel Schreig in the *Bnai Brith Messenger* of Los Angeles, California.

tain in all Africa. In Tanganyika, at the foot of this majestic mountain, the Bar Mitzvah would be held.

At the appointed time the planes flew to Mombasa. The local tourist agency provided an English-speaking guide, 72 elephants, 200 native elephant keepers and pack-bearers, a chef trained at the Waldorf Astoria, and a rabbi. The long caravan journeyed many days to reach the mountain.

Finally, travel weary, tired of sitting on top of plodding elephants, the celebrants approached their final destination. The English-speaking guide informed them that, after another mile, they would break out of the jungle and into the clearing at the foot of the mountain.

Just as they were about to enter the clearing, they heard ahead of them the sound of a strange chant. The guide could not make it out. It was not in any of the native tongues with which he was familiar. Perhaps it was some hostile tribe from somewhere else. He asked them to halt. He would go forward to attempt to assess the situation.

Fifteen minutes later he returned, grinning from ear to ear. "There is no cause for alarm, Mr. Silverstone," he reported. "It's just that there is another Bar Mitzvah ceremony presently being held at the foot of the mountain. In about an hour we shall be able to proceed."

JEWISH BLACK IS SUPERBEAUTIFUL

(1961)

During the 1940s, '50s, and '60s, a number of prominent stage personalities converted to Judaism for a variety of reasons, primarily matrimonial. The three whose conversions received the greatest amount of publicity were Sammy Davis, Jr., 1925-   , Marilyn Monroe, 1926-62, and Elizabeth Taylor, 1932-

Why did these three convert?

Marilyn's first two marriage ceremonies had been performed by a judge. She wanted her third marriage to be solemnized by a clergyman. Her husband-to-be, playwright Arthur Miller, was Jewish, her closest friends were Jewish, intellectually she was a rationalist and traditional Christianity held no appeal for her. Arthur Miller was not a synagogue-identified Jew. Whether she converted or not was for him a matter of no importance. To become a Jew and to be married by a rabbi were decisions Marilyn made completely on her own. The rabbi who converted her and officiated at her wedding, Robert E. Goldburg of New Haven, Connecticut, put it this way:

Marilyn, in earlier days, did not have the feeling of belonging to a real family, of having real roots. She felt that, through associating with Jews, she had acquired a family, she had acquired roots. She wanted to formalize a mental and spiritual identification which was already very much part of her life.

Elizabeth Taylor's second husband was show and movie producer Michael Todd, 1909-58. Theirs was a supremely happy marriage. Elizabeth wanted to convert but Todd, an affirmative but also a non-synagogued Jew, dissuaded her. He told her he loved her just as she was. After Mike was killed in an aeroplane crash, she grieved deeply. She determined to convert because she wanted to be part of Mike's kind of people as completely as was humanly possible. Although she was converted religiously by Rabbi Max Nussbaum of Hollywood, hers was an ethnic rather than a religious conversion. She was and is an ardent Zionist and has generously contributed both her money and her talent to Erets Yisrael. Although now married to an Episcopalian, she still considers herself Jewish.

Sammy Davis? Well, here is his Jewish story.

*   *   *   *   *

Sammy Davis, Junior, although very dark of countenance, is technically a mulatto. His father, Sammy Davis, Senior, was a Baptist black. His mother, Elvita Sanchez Davis, was a Catholic Puerto Rican. Sammy's parents, vaudeville troupers, lived in Harlem, in a tenement at 140th Street and Eighth Avenue. Sammy was born in Harlem on December 8, 1925.

His parents separated when he was two-and-a-half. Sammy went to live with his papa's mama, Rosa Davis. Six months later papa began to take Sammy along on the road. By the time Sammy was four, he was part of the vaudeville act of Will Mastin and Company. Will was Sammy's "adopted uncle." The other two members of the company were Sammy, Sr., and Sammy, Jr. By the time Sammy, Jr., was six he had already been featured in two motion pictures. Sammy never attended a regular academic institution for even one day, except for the day in 1973 when he received an L.H.D. degree from Wilberforce University. He learned to write English at the age of eighteen as an Army private in a class sponsored by Uncle Sam. From earliest childhood he was a fabulously talented and intelligent person. Veteran trouper George Burns recently said of him: "Sammy Davis is the greatest performer who has ever appeared on the American stage."

In 1943 Sammy was drafted. He spent two years in the Army. After basic training he was assigned to Special Services and went from camp to camp entertaining the troops, all five feet six inches and 120 pounds of him. He was then and continues to be in perpetual motion, a complex human dynamo, whose supply of energy seems to be inexhaustible.

In 1951 Will Mastin and Company began to make it big, the finest night clubs in L.A. and Vegas and all that. Will and Sam, Sr., were great; but the shining star was "the kid in the middle," Sammy, Jr., musician, singer, and dancer, who could do it all. He and Eddie Cantor became close friends. Once he admired a mezuza Cantor was wearing. Cantor gave it to him. Sammy looked upon the mezuza as his good luck charm. He wore it wherever he went.

In November 1954 Sammy was appearing in the New Frontier in Vegas. He had to drive to Los Angeles to prepare part of the soundtrack for his first movie as an adult. Unintentionally, he left the mezuza lying on his dressing room table at the nightclub. Near San Bernardino another car crashed into his. When Sammy came to, he was in San Bernardino's Community Hospital. He had undergone surgery. His left eye had been removed. Just before he was taken to the operating room, his friends, Tony Curtis and Janet Leigh, rushed into the hospital. Into the hand of the semiconscious Sammy, Janet pressed a medal with a raised Star of David on one side and an image of St. Christopher on the other. She said, "Hold onto this as tightly as you can and everything will be all right." Sammy has Janet's word for this. He doesn't remember. All he knows is that when he regained consciousness in his hospital room the outline of the Star of David was deeply etched in the palm of his hand.

Sammy recalls: "I was lying on the hospital bed, feeling sorry for myself, believing my professional career had ended. In walks a fellow who looks like a pug, flat nose and big ears. He says, 'Are you Sammy Davis?' 'Yes,' say I. 'What's it to you?' 'What's it to me?' he says. 'I'll tell you. I see before me a young man who owns a talented voice and talented legs and who is feeling sorry for himself because he has lost an eye. You don't sing and dance with your eye, do you? You still got your pipes. You still got your legs. So, dammit, stop feeling sorry for yourself and start acting like a man.' With that, he turns and walks out of the room. I rang for the nurse. I asked her who that guy was that just left my room. 'Oh, him,' she says, 'he's our rabbi.' I was thunderstruck. The image I had of a rabbi was of an old man with a beard and a beanie on his head. I had no religion and I felt I needed one; and what that guy said to me made a lot of sense. I decided that, when I got out of the hospital, I would look into this Jewish religion thing to find out what it was all about."

Who was the wonder-working rabbi who entered Sammy's room that day? There was at that time only one rabbi in San Bernadino, Norman Feldheym, and Sammy's description fits him well. But Rabbi Feldheym has steadfastly maintained that he does not remember visiting Sammy while Sammy was a patient in the San Bernardino hospital. As a well-known king of Siam once said, "It's a puzzlement."

Sammy recovered fully and, minus his eye, reentered show business and was as sensational as before. About that decision to study Judaism? It was something Sammy kept in the back of his mind to do when he found the time.

In 1955, while appearing at the nightclub in the Fairmount Hotel in San Francisco, he participated in a benefit for San Francisco's pioneer Temple Emanu-El. He was sitting at a table having a drink with the temple's cantor, Reuben Rinder. He told Rinder the story of his rabbinical visitor in the hospital. He said that someday he was going to look up a rabbi and discuss Judaism with him. Rinder responded, "How would you like to meet our rabbi?" Sammy said he would like that very much. Rinder said, "Just stay right here and I'll go get him." Sammy said, "You mean he's here, in a nightclub?" Rinder smiled and answered, "Of course." Sammy later wrote that Rinder returned with a handsome young man who "looked like a fellow right out of an Arrow collar ad." Not only handsome but charming and smart. Rabbi Alvin Fine.

Rabbi Fine invited Sammy to come to his Temple for a chat. Sammy went, chatted, was taken for a tour of the Temple and was given a list of books on Judaism to read. Sammy got them, read them, then came back to Rabbi Fine and inquired, "What else do I have to do to become Jewish?" Rabbi Fine tried to discourage him. He told Sammy that were he to convert the action would be interpreted widely as a publicity stunt. Sammy vigorously disagreed. He said the publicity would probably do him more harm than good. He said there was another way to look at the situation. If the rabbi refused to convert him, people, and especially blacks, might say that it was not because Sammy was an entertainer but because he was black. This rejoinder greatly disturbed Rabbi Fine. Sammy was living in Hollywood; so Fine suggested that he continue his Jewish dialogue with Rabbi Max Nussbaum of Hollywood's Temple Israel. Sammy agreed to do so.

Sammy continued to work with Will Mastin and Company until 1957. After that he was completely on his own. He dropped the Junior from his name and was billed simply as Sammy Davis.

In 1959 he stated on Barry Gray's New York City radio talk show that, for some time, he had considered himself to be a Jew. Barry's rejoinder was, "Welcome, landsmann." On Erev Yom Kippur that year, Sammy was on location in northern California, making the movie *Porgy and Bess*. Sammy describes what happened: "When we quit that afternoon I notified the director that I would not work the next day. He turned pale and called Sam Goldwyn in Hollywood. Goldwyn called me right back and said, 'What's this I hear, Sammy, you won't be on the set tomorrow?' I told him that I was following the tenets of Judaism and would not work on Yom Kippur. There was a pause at the other end of the line; then I heard Goldwyn mumble, 'Bless you,' and he hung up.

Either there was somebody on his end of the line who had sneezed, or else he was saying it to me. Whichever it was, the production was held up for one day at a cost of $30,000."

That year also, Sammy proposed to a black chorus girl while he was drunk and married her. The marriage lasted three months.

In 1961 Sammy fell in love with actress Mai Britt, Swedish and white. They decided to wed. They wanted to get married in Temple Israel with Rabbi Nussbaum officiating and both wanted to be married as Jews. Sam was playing a lengthy engagement in Las Vegas. He was instructed and converted by Rabbi Harry Sherer of that city. Rabbi Sherer says he was tougher on Sammy than on any other person he ever instructed for conversion. Sammy studied with him every day for months. Rabbi Sherer says, "Sam is one of the finest men I have ever known. He came into Judaism with a 'kavana,' a dedication, that was for me a soul-stirring experience. He wanted me to be at his wedding and to share in the ceremony; but I came down with the flu and couldn't make it." At the same time Mai completed her instruction and was converted by Rabbi Nussbaum.

When it became known that Sammy and Mai were to be married in Temple Israel by Rabbi Nussbaum all hell broke loose. The Temple office was bombarded by obscene and threatening phone calls. The Temple trustees became frightened. They were afraid that, if the wedding took place in the synagogue, it would cause a race riot. They asked Rabbi Nussbaum not to have the wedding in the Temple and not to officiate. The rabbi was on the horns of a dilemma. He did not want to offend Sammy and Mai and he did not want to go against the wishes of his trustees.

He explained to Sammy the situation with regard to having the ceremony in the synagogue. Sammy understood and decided to get married in his own home. Rabbi Nussbaum did not tell Sammy that his "machirs" had asked him not to officiate. Instead, he told Sammy a "white lie." He told him he would have to be out of town on the day of the wedding because of an unanticipated but important speaking engagement and that his assistant, Rabbi William Kramer, would perform the wedding. Again Sammy was graciously understanding. He said Mai and he would be happy to have Rabbi Kramer marry them, and Rabbi Kramer did.

The wedding took place on November 13, 1961. It was a dramatic affair, full of emotion. Someone said to Sammy, "You are half black and half Spanish. Mai is white. What color do you expect your children to be?" Quick as a flash, Sammy responded, "Polka dot." Someone asked Mai, "Do you believe that the people of Sweden will resent your marrying Sammy Davis?" Quick as a flash, the Nordic beauty responded, "The people of Sweden are not anti-Semitic." A brilliant and true response. A noble people, the Swedes; not only not anti-Jewish, they are also color-blind. Rabbi Kramer believes that this wedding ceremony was a first—the first Jewish interracial marriage in which both bride and groom were converts.

A daughter was born to Mai. She was named Tracy Hillevi. Two boys were adopted. They were named Mark Sidney and Jeff. The marriage lasted eight years. Sammy and Mai both say that the difference in skin-color had absolutely nothing to do with their divorce. It was just that Sam was still too volatile, too temperamental, too edgy to live for a very long time with any one female. In the mass he loved everybody all the time; but, when the mass broke down into individuals, he could only stand being with one person for just so long. In these circumstances, Mai lasted a long time—eight years. Sammy refers to Mai as ".a wonderful human being." Sam and Mai are good friends.

In 1970 Sammy married Altovise Gore, a black dancer from Brooklyn. They were married civilly. So far as is known, Altovise has not converted to Judaism, but she has broken Mai's record. She has held on to Sammy for nine years. Maybe by now, at age fifty-four, Sammy is beginning to settle down a bit.

In 1975 Sammy and Mai jointly shared the joy of their son Mark's Bar Mitzvah. To prepare for the Bar Mitzvah, Mai, over a period of months, drove Mark three times a week to the synagogue nearest to where she now lives, a roundtrip of eighty miles, for his Hebrew instruction.

✿   ✿   ✿   ✿   ✿

In 1964 I was preparing for publication a book titled *Conversion to Judaism*. One section of the book would be "The Converts Speak for Themselves." I asked Sammy to permit me to include in this section an article he had written for *Ebony Magazine*. Sammy sent me a handwritten note, saying he would be honored to have the article in the book. A week later I got a letter from Sammy's lawyers stating that, in view of the impending appearance of Sammy's autobiography, they were rescinding Sammy's authorization. They explained that, if Sammy's article was in my book, the appearance of Sammy's book and my book almost simultaneously might hurt the sale of Sammy's book! I was annoyed, amused, and flattered.

A short time thereafter I was visited by a charming couple, Jane and Burt Boyar, the writers of Sammy's "autobiography" *Yes I Can*. We spent an evening together discussing Sammy's Jewishness. A copy of *Yes I Can* was sent me by Burt Boyar with a grateful inscription that includes the statement, "We hope you will find in these pages some things which will make you feel the time you spent with us was not wasted." Indeed, it wasn't. It is a great book.

And now, at long last, Sammy is in one of my books. I have had long conversations with the rabbis who influenced Sammy's Jewish thinking, Alvin Fine, Max Nussbaum, may he rest in peace, Harry Sherer, and William Kramer. All told me the same thing: "Sammy Davis is one of the finest Jews and the warmest human beings I have ever known."

I hope you get to read this, Sammy. Your love of Judaism and your loyalty to it has been a source of pride and of inspiration for many of your fellow-Jews.

THE TWINS EAT SANDY'S MATZA BALLS
(1965)

The year is 1965 and the month is October. Battling in the World Series are the Los Angeles Dodgers of the National League and the Minnesota Twins of the American League. The teams are well matched. The series lasts the full seven games. The first two games are played in Minneapolis, October 6-7; the next three in Los Angeles, October 9-11; the final two in Minneapolis, October 13-14.

The ace pitcher of the Dodgers is Sandy Koufax. Normally the ace pitcher takes the mound in the opening game of a World Series. But Sandy Koufax does not pitch that opening game. Why? Because Sandy Koufax is a Jew and the opening game's date coincides with the tenth of Tishri, 5726, which, as every good Jew knows, is Yom Kippur. And Sandy Koufax would never play ball on Yom Kippur. On that opening day Sandy is not at the ball park. He is in a shul in Minneapolis, fasting and praying, as is the way of the devout Jew.

The opening day assignment is given to Don Drysdale, another very capable Dodger hurler. The Los Angeles team has been through a rough campaign and has won the National League pennant by a hair. It is not up for these first games of the World Series. The Dodger players have not had enough rest since winning their league's pennant. The opening game is lost, 8-2.

Sandy is scheduled to pitch the second game. The morning of that game the St. Paul *Pioneer Press* carries a sports column titled "An Open Letter to Sandy Koufax." It contains a number of veiled uncomplimentary references to Sandy's ethnic and religious background. "Hey, Sandy," the columnist chortles, "can you beat the biggest threat outside a mortgage foreclosure? Can you back guys away from the plate who see T-bones on the dish? . . . Can you win with two runs? I don't believe so." The column concludes with these words: "The Twins love matza balls on Thursdays [the game was being played on a Thursday]." Sandy commented later, "I couldn't believe it. I thought that kind of thing went out with dialect comics." Sandy pitches the second game and loses, 5-1. Now that columnist must be chirping cheerfully.

The teams play their three games in Los Angeles. The Dodgers win all of them. Sandy shuts out the Twins in the fifth game, 7-0.

The teams return to Minneapolis to finish out the Series. The Twins win the sixth game, 5-1. With only two days' rest, Sandy pitches the seventh and deciding game. The Dodgers win the game and the World Series, 2-0.

What does Sandy do then about that columnist? "I clipped the column so that I could send it back to him after we defeated the Twins with a friendly little notation that I hoped his words were as easy to eat as my matza balls. I didn't, of course. We were winners. Two runs had, it seemed, been ample. The winners laughed, drank champagne, and gave the losers the benefit of all doubts."

❄ ❄ ❄ ❄ ❄

Sandy was born in the Borough Park section of Brooklyn on December 30, 1935, the son of Jack and Evelyn (Lichtenstein) Braun. He was named Sanford Braun. When he was three years old his parents divorced. For a number of years after that Evelyn and her son lived with her parents. Her father, Max Lichtenstein, was a plumber, a shrewd business man, a lover of good music, the movies, and the theater, especially the Yiddish theater. Evelyn worked as an accountant in Manhattan. Very early in his life everyone started to call Sanford "Sandy." Sandy spent most of his leisure hours with his grandparents. He and his granddad were pals. On weekends his granddad took him to concerts and movies and plays.

Sometimes Sandy's mother and her parents went out for the evening and left Sandy at home. A girl next door was employed as babysitter. The girl had a brother known as Butch, about five years older than Sandy. Butch was the bad boy of the block. He was always playing practical jokes on someone. He was always trying to be funny. He was always clowning. Sandy's grandma called him "the meshugena." His meshugass has really paid off. Today he is known as Buddy Hackett, one of the most successful comedians of this generation.

When Sandy was nine years old his mother remarried. Her second husband was lawyer Irving Koufax. Of his stepfather Sandy has written, "When I speak of my father I speak of Irving Koufax, for he has been to me everything a father could be."

Sandy entered Brooklyn's Lafayette High School in the fall of 1949. He had developed a great fondness for the game of basketball. He ran and jumped well; he was tall, six two, and could throw the ball far and fast. His first team· experience was playing in a league at the Jewish Community House on Bay Parkway. The best league players, Sandy included, were selected to represent the JCH in a tournament sponsored by the National Jewish Welfare Board for the "national Jewish basketball championship." The JCH team won the tournament.

That JCH team became, almost to a man, the varsity basketball team of Lafayette High. It was quite a team. One night a benefit game was staged for the Police Athletic League in the Lafayette High gym between its basketball team and, believe it or not, the professional New York Knicks! That night Sandy put on quite a show for these seasoned players, covering the court, rebounding and scoring. After the game one of the Knick stars, Harry Gallatin, came over to Sandy, asked him for his name and address and said, "I'm going to be looking for you in the years ahead."

Word of Sandy's basketball ability got about. When he graduated from high school he was approached by a number of colleges. He accepted an offer of a basketball scholarship from the University of Cincinnati. He played on the freshman basketball team in the 1953-54 season. Then in the spring of 1954, while still a freshman, he became a pitcher on U.C.'s varsity baseball team. How did that happen? By pure dumb luck.

Sandy had played some sandlot baseball in Brooklyn. He did some pitching but mostly he played first base. The reason was that, although he could throw a baseball umpteen miles an hour, as a pitcher he was very wild. He walked almost as many players as he struck out.

The coach of the U.C. freshman basketball team was also the coach of the varsity baseball team. Freshmen were allowed to play on the varsity baseball team in non-Conference games. One day, while kibitzing in the coach's office, Sandy heard the coach say that the baseball and tennis teams were going to take a trip to New Orleans to play Tulane and en route they would play some other college teams. Eager to go on the trip, Sandy told the coach that, in addition to playing basketball, he also pitched. The coach tried him out. Sandy describes the tryout: "I reported to the gym. I whistled a couple of fast balls past the ear of the catcher, who was the fullback on the football team. He turned to the coach, handed him the catcher's mitt and said, 'Get another catcher. I don't want any part of this guy.'"

Sandy was put on the varsity roster. He pitched and won one game on the road trip and kept pitching for the rest of the varsity season. He pitched a four-hitter against Wayne University, striking out sixteen. On his next start, against the University of Louisville, he pitched a three-hitter and struck out eighteen, a new U.C. record. His last effort, against

Cincinnati's Xavier University, was not nearly as impressive. In true early-Koufax style, he walked six, struck out seven, was taken out in the seventh, and was the losing pitcher.

His strikeout ability came to the attention of big league scouts. The scouts of the Cincinnati ball team regarded him as a flash in the pan, but scouts from Milwaukee, Pittsburgh, and Brooklyn offered him big league tryouts. He signed a Brooklyn contract in December 1954.

At the end of the first semester of his sophomore year, Sandy left the University of Cincinnati and, on March 1, reported to the Dodger camp at Vero Beach, Florida, for spring training. His first big league chance came on June 24, 1955, in Milwaukee. He went in as a relief hurler in the fifth inning, pitched two innings, loaded the bases in both innings but managed to avoid being scored on.

In 1958 the Dodgers moved from Brooklyn to Los Angeles. By that time Koufax had been with them three years and had been used mostly in relief. His reputation as a fast pitcher who lacked control was well established. He had started 28 games and finished only 4. He had a record of 9 wins and 8 losses, hardly a spectacular performance.

In the 1958 season Sandy began to get his ball under better control and was used oftener as a starting pitcher. Season record: 11 wins, 11 losses. On August 24, 1959, against Philadelphia, he struck out 13. On his next start, August 31, against San Francisco, he struck out 18, which tied the major league record for strikeouts in one game and set a new record for strikeouts in two successive games. On his next start, September 6, against Chicago, he struck out 10, setting a new major league record for strikeouts in three successive games. Despite this impressive statistic, Sandy's 1959 overall record was unimpressive: won, 8; lost, 6. He started 23 games but finished only six. His 1960 record was even less heartening: won, 8; lost, 13. He started 26 games and completed only 7.

By now Sandy liked L.A. so well that he decided to make it his permanent home. He bought a house and went into business. He and a partner opened up an office as sales reps for several lines of electrical equipment. In a few months Sandy learned that one cannot concentrate on two careers at the same time. He had to choose between staying in business or in baseball. He chose baseball and sold his share of the business to his partner.

His concentration on baseball paid off. He was already famous as the hardest and fastest throwing pitcher in the big leagues. Now, by dint of extraordinary effort and superconcentration, he gained that which is the quintessence of the successful pitcher, that which he had hitherto lacked, i.e., control. The 1962 story: 18 wins; 13 losses. His 269 strikeouts set a new National League record, breaking Christy Mathewson's record of 267, made in 1903.

Of these strikeouts, 262 were hurled prior to July 17, a phenomenal performance. Had Sandy continued at this rate for the entire season, he would have established a record that might have endured for centuries. But it was not to be. Toward the middle of May a numbness began to develop in the index finger of his pitching hand. It did not prevent him from pitching his first no-hitter against the New York Mets on June 30. In July the finger began to turn blue. On July 17, with a season record of 14-5, Sandy had to stop pitching. The finger required an operation. Gangrene had already begun to set in. Fortunately the condition was arrested and the finger was saved. But Sandy did not pitch again until September 21 and, when he did, he no longer had good control. He was used in four games, did not finish any of them, was knocked out twice and finished the season with a record of 14-7.

1963 was Sandy's second best year: won, 25; lost, 5. On May 11, Sandy pitched his second no-hitter, against San Francisco. He bettered his own National League record for season strikeouts, 306. On the night of September 17 he beat St. Louis in their own ballpark, 4-0, having made the fewest pitches of any game in his entire career, 87. Then he left the team and flew back to Los Angeles, where Irving and Evelyn also now lived, to be in shul with his parents on Rosh Hashana. In the World Series, the Dodgers beat the Yankees four straight. Sandy won the first and fourth games. He was named the National League's Most Valuable Player and won the Cy Young Award as best pitcher of the year.

In 1964 Sandy developed rheumatoid arthritis, an incurable ailment, in his pitching arm. The arm got so bad that, on August 16, Sandy had to quit pitching for the rest of the season. Up to that time he was again on the way to a superseason: won, 19; lost, 5. On June 4, he had pitched his third no-hitter, against the Phillies.

The condition of Sandy's arm would have meant the end of the professional road for almost any ballplayer. But not for Sandy. The tall, black-haired, handsome, modest, quiet man was not made of ordinary stuff. He was determined to keep on pitching as long as he possibly could.

The 1965 season was a nightmare. Sandy was in constant pain. His arthritic arm had to be packed in ice for a half hour after every game he pitched. But pitch he did. And how he pitched!

1965 was Sandy's year of years. He won 26 and lost 8 in the regular season. On September 14 he set a big league record that is likely to be there for a long, long time. He pitched his fourth no-hitter, against Chicago. It was a perfect game. Not a single Chicago player reached first base. No walks; no errors. That year he beat his own strikeout record. His new record for major league strikeouts: 382. For the second time he was named the National League M.V.P. and again he won the Cy Young

Award. In the World Series the Dodgers beat the Minnesota Twins, four games to three. Sandy's share in that triumph has been described at the beginning of this article.

In 1966 Sandy received the highest salary paid a baseball player up to that time, $135,000. He had another great year: won, 27; lost, 9. The Dodgers won the league pennant but were walloped by Baltimore in the World Series in four straight. For the fifth consecutive year Sandy had the lowest earned run average of any major league pitcher. He won the Cy Young Award for an unprecedented third time.

But Sandy had decided to call it quits. At age twenty-nine, at the height of his career, earning more money than any other player in the game, he walked off the mound and the diamond for good. "I've had it," he said. "I don't want to wind up with an arm I won't be able to use for the rest of my life."

There are some who argue that Sandy Koufax is the greatest pitcher in the history of baseball. A good case could be presented in support of that contention. But whether or not it is true, one thing is certain: Sandy Koufax was the greatest pitcher of his time. And he was not only a great athlete. He was and is a courageous, likeable, gentle human being who represents professional athletics in its most attractive form and sportsmanship at its very best.

What's in a Name
(1970)

In September 1970, when Dorothy H. Rochmis was drama editor for the *California Jewish Voice*, she wrote a column which clearly indicated much burning of the midnight schmaltz. It's a game the talented lady enjoys playing—a sort of Revelation you won't find in the New Testament in which she offers some unfamiliar names and then reveals their true identities. See if you can beat her to the punch.

✿   ✿   ✿   ✿   ✿

Suppose I were writing my usual bits of news about the big and little stars in our town and I told you that while I lunched at the [Hollywood] Brown Derby, I saw Benjamin Kubelsky kibitzing with Nathan Birnbaum, Emanuel Goldenberg, and Melvin Allen Israel. The talk was about

David Gruen, with a little bit of Mavis Fluck thrown in, because, after all, the big stars aren't going to spend their lunchtime talking only politics. Actually, what they were doing was comparing Mavis with Helen Gould Beck, about whom everyone insists there is not and never was anything but friendship for Arthur Teichman.

It was a friendly, quiet lunch when suddenly the three noticed a flock of autograph hounds around Isaiah Edwin Leopold. "Well," scoffed Kubelsky, "just look at that old codger. You sure have to give him credit not only for longevity and versatility, but for being one of the busiest stars in Hollywood. Not only that, but his son is busy—and now his grandson is a comer." "Not that I want to change the subject," grumbled Birnbaum, "but you remember when Mrs. Poetry-Reciter who claims she's Shakespeare's third cousin eleven times removed, used to be just plain Mrs. Aaron Goldbogen, may he rest in peace?"

Just at that moment who should walk in but David Kominski with Issur Danielovitch, Julius Mark, and Aaron Chwatt. And right behind them none other than Simone Kaminker—unescorted. They all called out to each other and for a while the Brown Derby was buzzing with hellos and darlings and kissing and hugging. But when they resumed talking, the conversation was not unified. One group talked about that "golden boy" Julius Garfinkle. Another talked about their friend Jacob Pinkus Perelmuth's son who had just produced his first film about one potato, two potatoes; maybe he'll make a bushelful. Another group talked about that movie, *To Russia, With Love,* and the part that Karoline Blaumauer had in it. [And what is a luncheon without mention of talented writer-director Norman Corwin?]

*   *   *   *   *

Now how many luminaries in my little game have you been able to identify? Kubelsky, Birnbaum, Goldenberg and Israel are Jack Benny, George Burns, Edward G. Robinson and Mel Allen. David Gruen is, of course, the late David ben Gurion. Mavis Fluck is Diana Dors. Helen Gould Beck, none other than Sally Rand. And Arthur Teichman is that master-teacher of the dance, Arthur Murray.

Isaiah Edwin Leopold is the late Ed Wynn. Aaron Goldbogen, the late Michael Todd, so, of course, the wife they referred to as "Mrs. Poetry-Reciter" is Elizabeth Taylor. David Kominsky and Issur Danielovitch are, as you probably know, Danny Kaye and Kirk Douglas. The lady behind them, Miss Kaminker, Simone Signoret.

Julius Garfinkle is the late John Garfield, and Jacob Pinkus Perelmuth is Jan Peerce, whose son made the movie, *One Potato, Two Potato.* Karoline Blaumauer is Lotte Lenya; [and Norman Corwin?— surely you know Norman Corwin *is* Norman Corwin].

Index

tally Retarded. *See* Institution for Feeble-minded Males.
Worcester, MA, 24, 27, 47
World, New York, NY, 116
World Jewish Congress, 143
World War I, 35, 36, 106, 158-159, 173, 174, 340-341, 409, 410
World War II, 42-47, 84, 106, 155-156, 184-187, 193, 196, 274, 335, 337, 345-346, 430, 487
Wouk, Herman, 202
Wounded Knee, SD, 293, 458
Wren, Christopher, 16
Wright, Orville, 150, 151
Wright, Wilbur, 151
Wu Pei-fu, 173
Wynn, Ed, 501
Wyoming, 290, 427, 428, 439-440
Wyrick, D., 312, 313

Xavier University, Cincinnati, OH, 498

Yale College. *See* Yale University.
Yale University, 25, 386
Yankton, SD, 292
Yazoo, MS, 297
Yerba Buena, CA. *See* San Francisco, CA.
Yes I Can!, 494
"Yid," 109
Yiddish, 39, 47, 58, 75, 94, 105, 108-109, 118, 121, 122-126, 128, 133, 137-140, 142, 146-150, 151, 152-153, 160, 165, 169, 170, 176, 183, 203, 204, 206, 207, 211-212, 228, 273, 275, 333, 412, 476
Yiddish-Deitsch. *See* Yiddish.

Yiddishe Gazetten, Woodbine, NJ, 113
Yivo Annual of Jewish Social Science, 28, 390
Yoelson, Asa. *See* Jolson, Al.
Yoelson, Etta, 153
Yoelson, Gertrude, 153
Yoelson, Hirsh. *See* Jolson, Harry.
Yoelson, Ida, 153
Yoelson, Moses, 153, 154, 155, 156, 185
Yoelson, Naomi, 153
Yoelson, Rose, 153
Yonkers, NY, 57
York, PA, 58, 59, 154, 185
Yorktown, VA, 24, 241
Yorkville, NY, 168
Youli. *See* Jacoub ibn Youli.
Young, Brigham, 438, 460
Young, Daisy C., 32
Youngstown, OH, 292
Ysleta, TX. *See* El Paso, TX.
Yulee, FL, 254
Yulee, David Levy, 250-256
Yuma, AZ, 383

Zacharie, Isachar, 317-318
Zafren, Herbert C., ix
Zafrulla Kahn, Muhammad, 77
Zaid, Judith and Ronald, x
Zanesville, OH, 291
Zangwill, Israel, 36
Zelser, Fannie, 99
"Zhlob," 206
Zion Congregation, Appleton, WI, 294
Zion Mule Corps, 160
Zionists and Zionism, 34-39, 86, 88, 97-98, 124, 143, 144, 145, 150, 160-163, 196, 197, 282, 340, 342-343, 447, 490
Zuni Indians, 356